Burgess-Carpenter Library
40.. B tler
Col mbia University
New York, N. Y, 10027

W9-ATS-912

CULTURES AROUND THE WORLD II: FOUR CASES

THE GURURUMBA / THE WASHO
TEPOZTLÁN / BUNYORO

edited by GEORGE AND LOUISE SPINDLER

BURGESS-CARPENTER LIBRARY

CULTURES AROUND THE WORLD II: FOUR CASES

THE GURURUMBA / THE WASHO TEPOZTLÁN / BUNYORO

edited by GEORGE AND LOUISE SPINDLER

Stanford University

WITHDRAWN

HOLT, RINEHART AND WINSTON   New York   Chicago   San Francisco   Dallas
Montreal   Toronto   London   Sydney

Berg —

GN
378
.C84
vol. 2
copy 1

Library of Congress Cataloging in Publication Data

Main entry under title:

Cultures around the world.

(Case studies in cultural anthropology)
Bibliography: v. 1., p. 499; v. 2. p. 436
Includes indexes.
CONTENTS: v. 1. Five cases: the Tiwi, the Ulithi, the Swazi, the Navajo, the Vice lords.—v. 2. the Gururumba, the Washo, Tepoztlán, Bunyoro.
1. Ethnology. I. Spindler, George Dearborn.
II. Spindler, Louise S. III. Series.
GN378.C84   301.2   76-20447
ISBN 0–03–039726–X

Knowing the Gururumba by Philip L. Newman
Copyright © 1965 by Holt, Rinehart and Winston, Inc.

*The Two Worlds of the Washo: An Indian Tribe of California
and Nevada* by James F. Downs
Copyright © 1966 by Holt, Rinehart and Winston, Inc.

Tepoztlán: Village in Mexico by Oscar Lewis
Copyright © 1960 by Holt, Rinehart and Winston, Inc.

Bunyoro: An African Kingdom by John Beattie
Copyright © 1960 by Holt, Rinehart and Winston, Inc.

Copyright © 1978 by Holt, Rinehart and Winston
All rights reserved
Printed in the United States of America
8 9 0 1   090   9 8 7 6 5 4 3 2 1

CONTENTS

JUL 12 1978

Introduction

SINCE 1960 several million students of anthropology have learned about diversities and commonalities in human culture from the Case Studies in Cultural Anthropology Series. Until 1977 they were available only in single copy editions. For the convenience of students and teachers of anthropology we brought several together in one volume in that year. The enthusiastic reception of the first volume has encouraged us to assemble another—*Cultures around the World II*. The culture cases included have been carefully selected to represent major culture areas. They also represent major subsistence types and different levels of sociopolitical complexity. And they have been selected for their readability and for the ethnographic competence their authors have displayed in these and other works. These are time-tested studies and are among the most widely used in the series. Any student reading these four studies will have acquired a background in world ethnography that will help him or her to understand better what human cultures are, how they work, and how anthropologists interpret them. As fellow anthropologists and teachers of anthropology this background seems to us to be an essential starting point for the ordering of anthropological thought, and for its communication.

With these purposes in mind, we have focused upon intact cultures, recognizable on their own terms though their adaptations to the modern world are considered as well. The ways of life described were never unchanging, or uninfluenced by the outside world. Virtually no culture described by anthropologists is free of influence from the post-Renaissance world of exploration and exploitation, and none are static, unchanging entities, existing in a social, political, economic, and relational vacuum. It is a matter of emphasis.

The essence of the anthropological position is the cross-cultural perspective. This perspective is involved, explicitly or implicitly, in nearly every statement made by an anthropologist talking or writing about human behavior. This volume gives concrete meaning to this perspective.

Using This Book

We suggest that you read these case studies, the first time, as though you were reading a novel. You should get a feel for the way of life without getting bogged down in details. The second time you can go over the studies for a better understanding of the ways in which each of the cultures works as a system. You may find it useful to do some systematic comparing among the four cases, or between pairs of them. Keith Otterbein's text, *Comparative Cultural Analysis* could be very helpful. It lays out quite explicitly just how a comparison can be made.

The case studies really come to life when you have an understanding of what it was like to work and live in the place, and with the people, described. We suggest, therefore, that reading a few chapters in *Being An Anthropologist, Understanding an African Kingdom, Return to Laughter*, or other books listed under *Fieldwork in Anthropology* at the end of this book would be very helpful.

There are also textbooks in introductory anthropology that use case materials, many of them from the Case Studies in Cultural Anthropology. Reading them will help you to interpret the case studies in *Cultures Around the World* and will put them into the broader perspective of anthropological concerns. Those most directly related to the case studies series are Ernest Schusky's *The Study of Cultural Anthropology* and Alan Beals' *Culture in Process*. The various books mentioned in this introduction and others are listed under *Further Reading* at the end of this volume.

There are many excellent textbooks in cultural and social anthropology with which this volume can be combined. The text should provide a conceptual ordering that can be applied to the interpretation of culture cases. Though not all parts of culture and society are represented equally in the four case studies included in this volume, for they were not written according to blueprint, there is scarcely any aspect of society or culture that is not represented in one or more of them. Questions formulated on the basis of textbook and lectures can be pursued through *Cultures Around the World II*, treating the cases as primary sources. In this way the meaning of concepts and theory can be discovered and extended.

Many students will want to increase their knowledge of the cultures in this book. To this purpose we have included a brief list of further readings at the end of each case study and a list of other case studies on cultures in the geographic areas at the end of this volume. Of course other anthropologists might well select quite different readings, but these will help one get into interesting territory.

We have also provided an index to all four of the case studies. It should prove especially useful because entries will indicate the individual case studies for which page references are provided. This will facilitate the use of *Cultures Around the World* for comparative exercises and problems, preparation of reports, discussions, and term papers.

The Four Cases

Knowing the Gururumba by Philip L. Newman

The Gururumba live in six large villages in the upper Asaro Valley, New Guinea, at about 5500 feet elevation, bounded by towering mountains, some rising to 15,000 feet. They have only very recently come into contact with Western culture.

The author tells us not only about the pattern of Gururumba life, but also of the way the ethnographer discovers what the patterns are, and how he sorts them into analytic categories and forms connections among them. We see the Gururumba in their natural setting, and then how their behavior is patterned and arranged in social groups and roles. But the treatment goes beyond the analysis of social structure to give us a dramatic picture of the values and meaning of life.

The author gives us a most useful analysis of the symbolic value of specific behaviors in ritual situations. So we come to an understanding of why the sounding of the flutes at the pig festival makes the Gururumba feel that others hearing them will "know we are strong and wonder at us"; why a girl reaching sexual maturity crawls through a sugar cane hoop to make her attractive to suitors; why men purify themselves by pushing small bundles of sharp-edged grass in and out of their nostrils to make their noses bleed; how eating half-decayed flesh symbolizes the presocial era of human life as the Gururumba conceptualize it.

Not content to leave us with only the rules for behavior in this culture, the author ends with episodes from his observations of specific persons to show how one knows the Gururumba individually and sees them operating within the cultural patterns described. He shows how this culture creates certain strains and does not resolve them, and how individuals are never simple replicas of cultural norms in their personal behavior.

The Two Worlds of the Washo by James F. Downs

This case study of the Washo Indians of western Nevada and the eastern Sierra slopes of California is one of those rare events in the vast professional literature on the American Indian where a picture of a single tribal culture as a whole is presented. Though Washo culture in its traditional form has virtually ceased to exist at all, its disappearance was gradual enough and its relatively full appearance recent enough so that Professor Downs has been able to put the memories of the older Washo together with known history and knowledge of the culture area to form a coherent and dynamic reconstruction of the traditional Washo way of life. But he never forgets history. There is a sense of time in the book, which is so often lacking in attempts to reconstruct traditional cultures. Even as the traditional patterns of subsistence techniques, of rituals and religion, of kinship and social organization are described, the reader anticipates the dramatic changes in the Washo world to be wrought by the coming of the white man. Each stage of readjustment brought about by this event is analyzed. The Washo are not seen in isolation, but as part of the development of the region and its economy. They interact with and are interdependent with whites in the earlier stages of contact. But then the needs of the white man's economy change and there is no longer any place for most of the Washo. The Washo adapt to this circumstance, as they have adapted to previous conditions. In doing so they exhibit some continuities with the past and their traditional culture and at the same time adopt new patterns of behavior. This is not a happy world for the Washo. For some of them poverty and uselessness sap their vitality and destroy motivation, but the Washo identity is retained, and the Washo continue to cope with life as it is.

Tepoztlán: Village in Mexico by Oscar Lewis

There is probably no small community in the world that is, anthropologically speaking, better known than Tepoztlán. This village was first described in detail in a classic ethnography by Robert Redfield in 1930 based on fieldwork done in 1926-1927. Oscar Lewis restudied the village seventeen years later and published *Life in a Mexican Village: Tepoztlán Restudied* in 1951, and this, too, soon became an anthropological classic. The case study included in this collection was first published in 1960 and has been one of the most widely used studies in the series. It includes one chapter summarizing changes that Dr. Lewis found had occurred in the village between his first visit in 1943 and his re-visit in 1956-1957. Today still more changes have taken place but they are mostly in the directions described in the concluding chapter of this case study. The emphasis in the study, as it is presented here in this collection, is upon the traditional way of life. This way of life is representative of the Mexican peasant culture as it was lived, and still is, in a large part of Mexico. Economics, intrafamily relationships, and the life cycle are described. The community is placed on a time line that extends from the tenth century A.D. and the Toltec Empire to the present, and from legendary history to contemporary anthropological observation.

Bunyoro: An African Kingdom by John Beattie

This case study is many things. It is a study of a feudal East African kingdom, with parallels to the England of William the Conqueror. It tells us of the

GENERAL BOOKBINDING CO.

79   326NY3   4   318   3   BB   3462

QUALITY CONTROL MARK

conflict between feudal and bureaucratic administration and of that between European and traditional Nyoro standards of behavior. History can be important not only for the great civilizations, but also for the smaller-scale societies; this book amply demonstrates that this is true of the Nyoro. In their history, myth is transitional to fact, starting eighteen royal generations ago and continuing through 1862, when the grandfather of the present king was on the throne and the explorers Speke and Grant arrived on the scene, to the present, where the consequences of this history are seen in the circumstances of the Nyoro people. But most importantly, this book is a case study of contemporary social relations within a complex and changing East African society. The social behavior of the Nyoro is analyzed in various significant dimensions—at the level of political action and legal control, in relationships between neighbors and between men and the supernatural, and within the system of reciprocal kinship obligations. Dr. Beattie has provided us with a useful combination of historical perspective and functional analysis of a social system.

This case study was published only a few years before Uganda, including the "kingdom" of Bunyoro, achieved independence in 1963. The relations with Europeans and of course particularly the British as described in this case study have been decisively affected by this change. The relations between the Bunyoro and the British are representative of a most significant time period and sociopolitical arrangement. We are left with a largely unanswerable question, given the difficulties of fieldwork or even of acquiring reliable information in the present political situation of Uganda: how have the Bunyoro fared under the dictatorship of President Ibi Amin? The British followed a policy of indirect rule, thus supporting native systems of government, where they existed, within the limitations of colonial rule. The kingdom of Bunyoro could thus continue to exist in some recognizable form. Distatorships do not usually permit competing power structures to flourish.

The editors
George and Louise Spindler
Stanford University

KNOWING
THE GURURUMBA

Philip L. Newman

*University of California,
Los Angeles*

Philip L. Newman is professor of anthropology at the University of California, Los Angeles. His graduate training in Anthropology was received at the University of Washington from 1955 to 1959. The field study reported on here was undertaken in 1959 and 1960 under grants from the Fulbright Commission and the Bollingen Foundation. The field materials were written up as a doctoral dissertation while he was an Ogden Mills Fellow at the American Museum of Natural History in New York, the Ph.D. being awarded in 1962. He has also carried out less extended periods of field work among the Aleut, the Nootka, and the Skokomish.

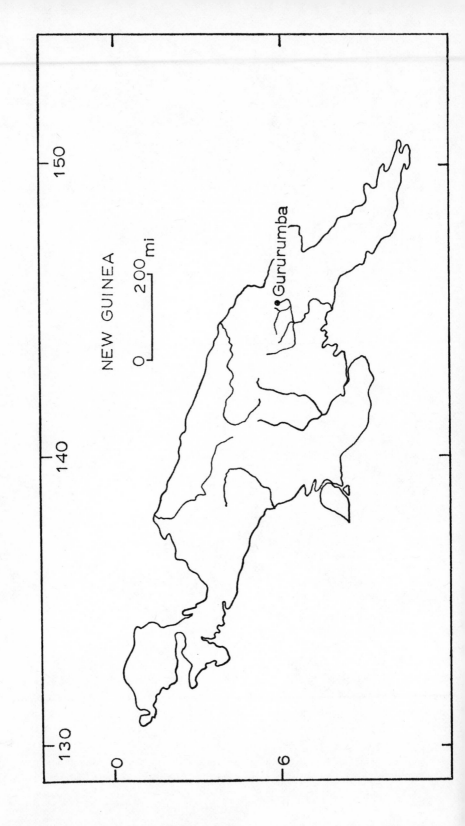

NEW GUINEA

Gururumba

0 200 mi

Contents

ght) Preparing a food offering for a
esticated nature spirit. The dome-
ed structure in front of the minia-
earth oven is the spirit house.
nter) Filling an earth oven with
r from bamboo tubes. (Bottom)
agers from Miruma arriving as
rners at a funeral in another village.

(Right) A newly planted sweet potato garden. Branches have been removed from the trees in the garden to reduce shade. (Center) Men carrying away gifts from a food distribution. The man in the foreground is carrying peanuts, a crop introduced by Australians. (Bottom) The entrance to the village of Miruma. The men's house is in the foreground.

Introduction

LL OF US at some time or another have been in the position of a stranger, not knowing what actions others expected of us nor what actions we could expect of others. However, the degree of strangeness in a situation can vary a great deal. A man brought up in Los Angeles who moves to New York city will find most of his expectations about people's behavior fulfilled. With only minor adjustments he will be able to operate in the new situation and interact with the people there. If, however, he moves into a community of forest-dwelling people in the Amazon basin, he will find his habitual system of expectations so unreliable that unless the host community has special techniques designed to care for strangers, he may not survive. Such differences, whether small or large scale, are cultural differences, and their description and explanation is an important part of the anthropological enterprise. The anthropologist interested in analyzing a culture other than his own is a stranger; his first task, therefore, is to learn the expectations and understandings the members of that alien group assume as a basis for interacting. He is a special kind of a stranger, however, because he attempts to be as conscious as possible of the way he gains this knowledge, and because he must make it explicit and formulate it in categories that will allow comparison with what is discovered about other cultures. While a stranger who is not an anthropologist may gain knowledge of an alien culture sufficient to operate effectively in it, he is not likely to know how he gained it or be able to reproduce it systematically.

The task of systematically discovering and describing cultural difference is called ethnography, and the task of analyzing it with reference to some limited problem is called ethnology. Each task complements the other, and understanding the process of coming to know another culture is as important as understanding what comes to be known about it. This is the case because the ethnologist's methods of analysis, theoretical commitment, choice of problem, and even his personality affect the range of facts he will attend and his understanding of them.

The range of data-gathering techniques, substantive foci, and methods of analysis available to the ethnologist is a respectably wide one. The techniques stress procedures that put him in intimate contact with the people he is studying, much like the stranger who discovers the properties of an alien situation by operating in it. Within this procedural limit, however, individual ethnog-

11

raphers mix participation in the daily affairs of the group with informal conversation, structured interviews, systematic observation, administration of tests, and the noting of events as they happen, in varying proportions. The selection of substantive foci also varies, for if the problem chosen requires a broad knowledge of many facets of the culture an attempt will be made to provide approximately equal coverage of a number of categories while in another problem coverage may be restricted to one or a few categories. Such categories as technology, economics, individual life cycle, religion, kinship, politics, and art, are frequently used, but these do not form a systematically interrelated set; others can be used as effectively. The concepts available to analyze data brought together in these categories include culture area, social structure, social function, ethos, basic personality, and ecology, among others. Each analytical concept cuts across the categories using data from all or postulating relationships among them. Each also implies a theory about the events, forms, or systems defined by the categories.

Each of the above techniques and concepts produces data of a distinctive kind and views it in a distinctive way. It is therefore important in assessing what an ethnologist communicates about a culture to understand the techniques and methods he uses to gather the data as well as to understand the results of their use. This case study is concerned with learning about a human group in both these senses. It will reveal something about the patterns of an alien culture and something about the process of discovering those patterns.

Implied, therefore, is that this case study begins with the life history of the author, for if the results of ethnography are in part the product of the investigator's personality, then his findings cannot be judged accurately unless his personality is known. Indeed, there was a period when it was suggested that ethnographers be psychoanalyzed before undertaking field work to use knowledge about the limitations and biases arising from the investigator's personality as a corrective. Not many took this extreme suggestion, preferring to rely on the objectivity built into their descriptive techniques and analytic constructs, and the self-awareness inculcated through training. It cannot be denied, however, that the way an ethnographer reacts to a new cultural setting and the behavior he is observing, what he experiences as deprivation and how he handles this experience, his awareness of how others are reacting to him, the kind of role he adopts, and many other responses derive in large part from his personality. These factors not only affect the way the people he is observing act in his presence, but also influence his very perception of what they are doing. Some of these problems will be discussed in various parts of the text, but my main concern will be with the techniques and concepts used to observe and describe an alien culture rather than with what is sometimes called "the personal equation."

The choice of New Guinea as an area of study was in part made on a subjective basis. During both undergraduate and graduate study, I had been fascinated by the published accounts of New Guinea peoples to the point of naïve romanticism. Fortunately New Guinea, especially the highland area, was an important area ethnographically. Its people had not experienced extensive contact with Westerners, and there were few reports on the cultures existing there. Not only could useful descriptive work be done, but the existing accounts indicated these cultures might be especially suitable for the investigation of a particular problem: the way individuals use, manipulate, and experience their religion. This was focused on the kind of intracultural variability one can find in a small-scale, relatively homogeneous society. The published accounts indicated that the people had a rich ceremonial life but not a society overly complicated by internal differentiation of a political or economic kind. They also appeared to value "individualism," and this combined with the fact that they lived in small groups easily managed by a single worker made them seem suitable for investigation of the problem.

Selecting the Gururumba as the particular group for study accommodated both research and personal needs. I learned from another anthropologist who had worked there that the upper Asaro valley, where the Gururumba live, contained peoples who had not yet been studied but who adjoined culturally different peoples on four sides who had been studied. Knowledge about the Gururumba would thus contribute to the accumulating information concerning the regional variability of highland groups. The degree of contact with Western culture in the upper Asaro valley had apparently not produced massive change but was extensive enough so that the groups no longer practiced warfare and some of the young men knew how to speak Neo-Melanesian, a pidgin language that could be used as a mode of communication. I also learned there was a road into the upper Asaro valley from the Australian governmental center of Goroka some twenty miles away and that an Australian coffee planter as well as a missionary were not far away. These facts were important since my wife and two small children were accompanying me. They meant that medical aid and food supplies would be available without excessive delay or complication, and that our safety would be reasonably certain. In New Guinea these are not inconsequential considerations. Of the several tribes living in the valley the Gururumba were chosen because they were near the end of the road and centrally located with respect to other groups.

These particular details should not be taken as representative of those considered by all ethnologists deciding on a field site. For some the decision is more closely related to considerations of problem, which may involve a particular constellation of variables found only in a severely limited number of cases and so dictate their choice of site. Others may specialize in a given area but work there on a variety of problems. Or the choice may be less systematic when circumstances bring some to a place that suggests certain lines of investigation. Several of the classic monographs in anthropology have come about in just this way. What should be clear, however, is that the ethnologist's basic research tool in the field is himself. Consequently what he does, how he does it, and even where he does it is partially a product of the kind of person he is as well as the kind of problem he has in mind. The actual field situation rather than the carefully constructed laboratory situation is still the primary source of the ethnologist's data, and the main recording instrument is still the human observer rather than the machine. Observation, therefore, is affected by many kinds of factors extraneous to the act of observation because ethnology is a science that has not yet separated the instrument of observation from the instrument of analysis.

1

The People, The Setting, The Beginning

"How long will you stay, red man?"

Preparing the Way

A TRAINED ETHNOLOGIST is not a stranger to an alien culture in the same way a non-ethnologist is. His background includes extensive reading in the accumulated literature on cultures of many types and from many areas of the world. This literature begins with the earliest records and although not all of equal quality, it provides enough knowledge about the variability of culture so that we no longer expect to find human groups whose general way of life falls outside the reported range. Ethnography still reveals cultural differences, and will continue to reveal them, but the magnitude of these discovered differences is not as great as it once was, at least with respect to the cultural features ethnologists habitually consider. In fact, enough is known so that if an ethnologist hears of a newly discovered group characterized by horticulture, root crops, stone tools, and an upland environment, his knowledge of the range of human culture will allow him to make accurate judgments about several other aspects of the culture of the group as well.

In addition to this general background the ethnologist attempts to prepare himself for the specific area he plans to work in by reading whatever material is already available on it or similar areas. There are several general reasons for this. First, it will probably be the case that the people he wants to investigate speak a language he does not know. Since language is the first key to understanding another culture he must learn it. If he can gain some command of the language from published accounts before going to the field it will save him a great deal of time once he gets there. If there are no published accounts he may have to learn a related language or a pidgin language which can be used with an interpreter until he masters the local language in the field. In some cases neither can be done in advance and he must rely on his ability and training to learn the language on the spot. Second, some research problems require prior knowledge of an area because they are focused on certain variables or phenomena having a limited areal distribution. Third, the ethnologist, if possible, wants to be cognizant of behaviors that may be expected of him as a newcomer to a group or of attitudes the people hold toward members of his race. If he can know these things in advance he can adjust his behavior accordingly and reduce the possibility of creating tensions during the initial period of his stay. He will inevitably make mistakes and create tensions anyhow, but minimizing them initially will help create attitudes toward him conducive to achieving a solution. Finally, many practical matters need to be planned. Some knowledge of the climate, health problems, modes of transportation, type of available shelter, availability of food, and the like, can usually be obtained in advance. This helps the ethnologist plan for various exigencies of self-maintenance, without which the field project might fail.

Fortunately for us, some important information was available on the peoples in the upper Asaro valley: They spoke a language closely related to that spoken in the lower Asaro valley, and they were in close contact with peoples in the Chimbu valley to the west who spoke quite a different language. Neither of these languages had been analyzed in the published literature so it was impossible to learn them in advance. Effective control by the Australian government had been established in the area for about ten years, and some of the younger men who had worked for the government or as laborers under a government-controlled labor program could speak Neo-Melanesian, a pidgin language utilizing a mixed vocabulary from European and Melanesian languages but with its distinctive syntax. I learned the rudiments of this language in advance from published sources and used it to establish communication immediately in the field.

From knowledge about highland New Guinea peoples in general, I could expect that those in the upper Asaro valley would live in villages rather than scattered homesteads, would be horticulturalists raising several varieties of sweet potato as their staple crop and keeping pigs, dogs, and chickens as domesticated animals, and their physical environment would be mountainous, cool, and damp. The technology would feature gardening techniques based on a system of rotating plots rather than soil replenishment through fertilization, watering by rainfall rather than irrigation, and the use of simple hand tools rather than animal drawn implements. Items such as digging sticks, axes, knives, arrows, or spears would be made of wood and ground stone, except as metal objects of European origin had replaced them, and there would be some pottery of a simple type imported from other groups. Social organization would reveal broadly defined units, such as dialect groups, divided into relatively small, politically autonomous territorial units and further divided into smaller groupings based on some combination of organizational principles centering around kinship and identification with a locality. The division of labor would be simple, based primarily on age and sex, and leadership would derive from personal qualities rather than from occupancy of a titled position.

There was no published information on the upper Asaro peoples specifically but there were accounts of the closely related Gahuku-Gama and Siane to the south and the southwest, and the more distantly related Chimbu and Gende to the west and northeast. Certain cultural similarities were discernable among these groups, making it probable that they would also be found in the upper Asaro valley. For example, such patterns as patrilineal descent, patri-virilocal residence, bride price, polygyny, ceremonialized economic exchange, and the men's club house were found throughout the area.[1] Belief in ghosts, demonic nature spirits, witches, and sorcerers also appeared to be prevalent. Some idea of the "character" of the people could also be found in the published materials as various authors noted that they were "flamboyant," "forceful," "materialistic," or that the culture was "male dominated."

Something was learned of the living conditions from conversations with other people who had been in the general vicinity. The area was said to be relatively healthy for persons coming from the United States. Unlike the hot humid coastal areas of New Guinea, the highlands are cool and fresh, and respiratory infections or dysentery would be more serious health problems than malaria or fungus infestations. We would be able to provide ourselves with vegetables from the native peoples, but would have to rely on tinned goods for meat and most fruits. We would probably be greeted with a mixture of curiosity and suspicion, since racially and culturally we were still something of a novelty and our motives would be difficult to comprehend, but hostility was not expected.

All these items of information, and others as well, served to build up a set of expectations concerning the nature of the cultural patterns we would find and what it would be like to live in that situation for a year. It might seem that if an ethnologist were attempting to be objective about his research, these expectations would hamper him and measures should be taken to limit their prior formation. In order to understand why this is not as harmful as it might seem, think again about the ethnologist and the untrained stranger. When the stranger encounters an alien group he attempts to operate in the new situation by identifying, connecting, and explaining events produced by an unknown culture pattern in terms of the classificatory schemes and explanatory principles of his own culture. If the magnitude of cultural difference is great he will find this a largely inadequate procedure producing behavioral "mistakes" because he cannot properly identify what kind of action he is viewing, does not know what actions properly follow one another, and cannot explain why the sequences of actions he does see should follow one another. His knowledge of culture patterns in the new setting will be distorted because he tries to make the behaviors he observes meaningful in terms of culture patterns from which they did not derive. The ethnologist, on the other hand, knows that much of his foreknowledge will be inadequate or even erroneous, but having this knowledge provides a series of reference points designed for cross-

[1] See Glossary for explanation of technical terms.

cultural use and hence less subject to distortion than those provided by his own nonanthropological culture. He does not expect what he sees to be meaningful in terms of the culture patterns useful at home in everyday affairs, but expects to use another set of patterns, constituting part of the culture of anthropology, to order what he sees so that meaning will be discovered. For example, to know that the people in the upper Asaro valley reckon descent patrilineally is also to know that they do not classify kinsmen in the same way contemporary Americans do. Furthermore, to use the language of our own system of kin terms could not possibly uncover the principles involved in their system of classification. The ethnologist in this situation knows he must begin by describing the designata of alien terms in a language calculated to be culturally neutral.

Arriving on the Scene

Only so much can be done in advance and the day arrives when the ethnologist must inject himself into the situation he wishes to study and begin discovering just what makes him a stranger to a particular group. As might be imagined the experience is not an easy one, and as my family and I traveled up the road toward the head of the Asaro valley in a rented Land Rover laden with supplies we wondered how the explanation of our presence and purpose would be received, how we would locate the appropriate person to explain ourselves to, what kind of impression we would create, and many other things. We knew there would be shelter available, for our destination was the government rest house near the native village of Miruma. Rest houses, usually made of poles and thatch, are established at central locations throughout the highlands where patrol officers can stay in the course of traveling about on affairs of native administration. It would be available to us until such time as we could construct our own house.

We turned off the main road and bumped along the ridge top leading to Miruma. As we neared the rest house people began swarming around our vehicle until it was halted by the impenetrability of their mass. We had expected a few people to greet us because our progress up the valley had been shouted far ahead as we passed by villages and gardens located near the road, but not the three or four hundred there. This gathering was not primarily due to our coming, however, but a result of two other events. We became aware of the first as an Australian official came out of the rest house and introduced himself as a government doctor on medical patrol. He had been at Miruma for several days performing various minor therapeutic tasks and gathering data on the health of the natives. Many were there because the doctor had called them in from surrounding villages for medical examination; others were there voluntarily, seeking relief from their ailments.

Thus it was that the first person we explained ourselves to was the doctor. The doctor, in turn, called in the *luluai* and *tultul* from the native village situated along the ridge directly behind the rest house. *Luluais* and *tultuls* are government-appointed native officials. The *luluai* is responsible for maintaining order in the community under his jurisdiction, carrying out any directives given him by the government, bringing matters of dispute that cannot be settled in the community before a patrol officer or district commissioner, and keeping possession of the village book. This book, kept current by patrol officers, contains census information, a record of patrols into the area, and notes concerning local incidents relevant to the administration of justice. The *tultul*, in theory, is a kind of assistant to the *luluai*. Both men arrived quickly, and after pushing their way through the surrounding crowd, stood before us at attention giving both my wife and myself the hand salute accorded government officials. The doctor took some pains to explain, through an interpreter, that we were neither government officials nor missionaries, but that we were in the area to learn the people's "fashion." He charged the *luluai* with looking after our welfare and seeing that our needs were met. After another salute the two men left and shouted their newly gained information to the people gathered around us as they proceeded back to the village. The doctor, assuring us that everything would now be taken care of, went back to giving innoculations and pulling teeth, and we moved our supplies into one of the small huts near the rest house designed to accommodate the contingent of native police that accompany most patrols.

We spent the next few hours establishing ourselves in the hut that was to be our home until the medical patrol left, while the native people gave us an initial scrutiny. In some instances the examination clearly put us in the category of objects. Older people, especially women, felt our bodies, pinched our flesh, and fingered our hair. One man, apparently sensing a golden opportunity to relieve a long-standing curiosity about footgear, removed my boots and socks so he could examine them, and my feet, in detail. Some young boys concentrated on imitating my stride and elements of my stance and posture. In other instances our objects rather than ourselves were the point of curiosity. Cameras, watches, mirrors, air mattresses, stoves, pans, items of clothing were familiar to them, but they discovered we put few restrictions on their handling and examining these things—a practice not followed by most nonnatives they had encountered. It led almost immediately to unexpected results, some of which we were aware of and some not. We were aware that people began demanding we relinquish various items that caught their fancy, not by sale, barter, or gift exchange, but uncommitted transfer. It became irritating, and we soon had to give up our pretense of openness in order to retain our possessions. It was some time before we understood some of the reasons for their behavior and I am not sure they ever understood the reasons for ours. For one thing, it was incomprehensible that two adults and two children could need, consume, or own the large amount of "stuff" we unloaded. Not being able to discern any reasonable need on our part for all these things, the freedom of access allowed to them was taken by some as an invitation to claim whatever they wanted. We were not aware, however, of more subtle attempts to claim part of this unprecedented bounty. Small bundles of native-grown food were presented to us or simply left at our doorstep. If the giver appeared in person, he would say that no "pay" or "return" was expected since the *luluai* had instructed everyone to bring us food. We accepted them naively, not suspecting that with each presentation the giver publicly announced to his fellows he was thereby claiming the right to enter into future negotiations with us for some specific item in our possession. Days, and even weeks, after arriving I would occasionally be put in the position of making someone angry because I would not enter into negotiations for the immediate transfer of my coat, my wife's hat, or some other item claimed on that first day.

It was somewhat puzzling that except for the brief meeting with the *luluai* and *tultul* arranged by the doctor no one had appeared to ask questions concerning our presence, so after the Land Rover had been emptied and started back down the road I walked into the village of Miruma. It was crowded and, judging from the piles of food and the arrangement of people, it seemed obvious an event of some public importance was in progress. This, then, was the second reason for the large number of people we encountered. My entry caused no stir whatsoever and several attempts to elicit the reason for the gathering only produced the answer that it was "nothing." Someone finally said it was a betrothal, which prompted me to begin taking notes, but nothing was recorded except what could be seen because most questions about the details of what I saw were answered by saying I was seeing "nothing."

As the afternoon passed, it became increasingly difficult to see any pattern in the response being given us. On the one hand we were the objects of intense curiosity and on the other we were being politely ignored. It was only in the evening, after the guests at the betrothal left the village, that I began to understand what was happening. At that time I returned to the village and sat down in front of the door to the men's house. The men inside stopped their conversation to inquire what I wanted, and when they found I wanted to come in were quite pleased to steer me through the low doorway and arrange a place for me in the crowded dwelling. Not knowing exactly what to say or do after getting inside, I resorted to the time-consuming process of lighting my pipe while waiting for them to question me. The lulai asked, "How long will you stay, red man?" I answered "a year" and added that my family would remain with me. This precipitated a long discussion punctuated by expressions of surprise between the older men and the young man who had been translating in Neo-Melanesian. It developed that although Neo-Melanesian counts time by "moons" there was no corresponding system of time-reckoning in the native language making it difficult to effect a translation. More important, it had not previously occurred to anyone that we were intending to stay for an extended period of time as a family unit. Nonnatives who were neither government officials nor missionaries had come to the village before, but had not stayed for long periods, contenting themselves with walking in the forest for a few days collecting plants and animals or with watching a single, short ceremony. Our arrival on the day of a betrothal put us in this latter class, and it had been as-

umed that if we did not leave with the doctor we would soon after. No one
bothered about our presence because it had been perceived as inconsequential
except for curiosity value or the prospect of gaining access to our supplies. In
other words, after a day in the community we had not yet arrived.

What happened that first day in Miruma is an example of the difficulties
the ethnologist can encounter in attempting to connect himself meaningfully to
an alien community. In this case it could be said the difficulty was of communi-
ation, that because of preoccupation with the betrothal ceremony no one took
the time fully to attend the implications of the information they received about
us. However, since that first day's experience was repeated, it cannot be fully
explained by the occasion. It can be partially explained as the difficulty in bringing people to comprehend a totally unfamiliar social role for which their cul-
ure provides few analogies. There was no precedent in this culture for a per-
on whose only purpose in a community was to examine its "fashion." It is true
that native people sometimes went to alien places specifically to observe dances
r rituals different from their own, and that they received both natives and
nonnatives into their community for the same reason. But such occasions were
of short span and focused observation on a limited range of activity. Furthermore, prior to the cessation of warfare under Australian control, such journeys
by natives were limited to those communities with which a person had already
established other kinds of ties and purposes so that his activity as an observer
of alien ways was part of a larger action context. When the people gathered in
the men's house learned our stay would be long, they began to realize I was a
different kind of person than they had yet encountered and, although they
never fully understood my purposes, the process of taking me into account had
begun.

Settling In

During the next ten days no attempt was made to carry out my systematic
ethnography. The time was given over to establishing a household and to building a basis for interaction with the community. The latter task is not one the
ethnographer can execute according to a plan as easily as he can the former be-
ause its form and impetus must come partly from the community itself. Since
this is the case, the form it takes is itself indicative of the culture patterns the
ethnologist is attempting to discover.

Both the form and the impetus came with unexpected formality and dis-
patch on the second day. I had planned to have a house built near the village
of Miruma because it was convenient both to water and the road, appeared to
be centrally located with respect to several native villages, and had a command-
ing view of the Asaro valley. The announcement of this plan was anticipated
by a delegation of men from Miruma headed by the *luluai* and *tultul* who came
before me and proclaimed that henceforth I was to be considered by all as
"their red man." They pointed out that another group living down-river "had

a red man," a coffee planter, and that a second group living up-river had one, a missionary. They further suggested that although they too occasionally possessed such a person when the rest house was occupied, it would be highly desirable to have a permanent resident. I had only to indicate my choice of plot and a house would be built. My "acceptance" of their "offer," if one can apply those terms to what was essentially acquiescence to a demand, involved much more than anticipated, but for that reason established the first important link connecting me to life of the village.

The link was primarily an economic one calculated to produce both direct and indirect gains. They counted on selling me the ground on which to build a house and were already figuring the price of construction. They supposed I would hire people to work in the house after the manner of other red men they knew. It was reasoned that all red men had a "business," and although mine was not altogether clear, it was certain to mean income. (Despite efforts to explain myself on the previous day, consensus was that I would open a trade store featuring very low prices.) The indirect benefits, if not precisely formulated, were grand in scope. At that time and place in highlands New Guinea it was prestigeful to "have a red man." The reasons for this are complex, but they are involved with the native attitude that the presence of a red man presages an improvement in the general state of affairs, especially an increase in the ability to control wealth and material things. I did not fully understand it at the time but this was what people were expressing when they came up after it became known we would settle in Miruma and made such statements as, "It is all right now." "Everything will occur now." "The past is finished." Or, "You have come, now everyone (other native groups) will eat our pigs." The last statement hopefully connected our coming with increased prestige of the community through exchange activity traditionally accompanied by the eating of cooked pork. The outcome of such exchange activities is calculated in terms of gains in prestige, but already established prestige is a factor in achieving a gain. In other words, to be known as a person from the village where a red man dwells is to have an advantage over persons from other villages because of the potential wealth and power he represents.

Having a red man in your midst can be a disillusioning experience, however. Natives living in the lower Asaro valley where red men are relatively plentiful no longer have high expectations of great material benefit flowing from their presence. Given the fact that the people of Miruma have frequent contact with these groups, the fact that some of the young men had worked for red men in Goroka and other places, and the fact that both the missionary and the planter were close at hand, raises the question of why they maintained these expectations. Subsequent investigation revealed they did not maintain them at a very high level, but my coming had increased the level considerably. The reason was simple. In efforts to explain myself, I had used the device of contrast of stressing the differences between myself and the other kinds of red men they knew. The effect of this was not an understanding of what it meant to live with a people in order to study their "fashion," but only the understand

ng that I was different from other red men. In their minds, the stress placed
on differences indicated I was the red man they hoped for rather than the red
man they knew.

One other factor enters into this situation—the mystic quality of red
men. In the initial contact between Australians and natives of this area, the
Australians were frequently perceived as ghosts. It did not take the natives long
to discover they were not ghosts, but some of the attitudes held toward ghosts
still carry over to these intruders on the native scene. The native term for them,
"red men," indicates the existence of these attitudes, for ghosts are thought to
be red. Various authors writing on these attitudes and their effects in other areas
of New Guinea point out that one of the most persistently puzzling things
about red men is their ability to generate and control vast amounts of material
goods. Since production processes are not seen by native peoples, red man's ability
to command resources derives from an unknown basis. It is, for many, a mystic
process controlled by mystic means producing miraculous results. This helps account for the high level of expectation characteristic of links established with
red men and the fact that the people of Miruma expected both very specific and
very general benefits to flow from my presence.

At the time of arrival in Miruma I was not aware of the extent to which
these factors were operative or, in some cases, that they existed. I only knew
people seemed to be pleased we were there and acted in a way that fit well with
my plans. Arrangements to build a house were easily made, a site for it selected,
and two young men agreed to work for us as cook and gardener. The cook had
worked for red men before and knew how to light a primus stove, the necessity
for boiling water, and the preparation of simple meals. He therefore seemed
acceptable. The gardener was an adolescent boy who, because most plant tending is done by women in his culture, did not know much about gardening at
all, but seemed to know more than we did. A third young man was hired at a
later date to act as guide and interpreter. All these seemingly smoothly executed
acts had unforeseen consequences deriving from the people's attitude toward me
as a red man. Some of them will be discussed in subsequent chapters.

Discovering the "Look" of Things

In the initial phases of field work there is a great deal going on around
the ethnographer that completely eludes him. During the settling in period I
was beginning to realize the importance attached to economic affairs simply
from the number of times such affairs came up, but only in a very limited way.
For the most part, the idiom of social action constituting the culture of these
people was unknown to me, and frequently all I "saw" when looking at people,
even when they seemed to be interacting, were human figures against a natural
background. There were, of course, many times when these scenes appeared
meaningful, but training induced me to be cautious in attributing a meaning
to them until greater access was gained through systematic observation to the

idiom in which they were conducted. There was, in my case, an interesting con
sequence of this: a heightened awareness of differences amenable to observa
tion in terms of physical properties.

For example, I found that everyone else was shorter than I, that roof
were not meant to be stood up under, that doorways were too small, or that th
rutted foot paths and mountain side toeholds made for bare feet would not ac
commodate my booted foot. I could not use any of the steel-headed axes owne
by natives because they had taken out the European style handles and put i
round handles of small diameter tapering to a point at the end. Attempting t
chop with one of these usually resulted in the implement's flying out of m
hand.

Noting the way people hold and move their bodies became a kind of pre
occupation. When going down hill, women habitually walk with their fee
angled sharply in to prevent slipping. Men usually trot when negotiating
slope. People of the same sex may hold hands or lock arms while walking, bu
not people of opposite sex. Men walk in front of women. A common stanc
consists of arms crossed over the chest, the hands inserted in the arm pits, an
one leg wound around the other. Squatting with feet flat on the ground, or sit
ting with legs extended fully to the front without a back rest is common. If fin
gers are used in counting, enumeration starts with the little finger and the en
numerated fingers are held together in a bundle rather than ticked off. Point
ing is as often done with the chin as with the extended arm. Body contact i
sought rather than avoided by people sitting or standing in groups. Kissing o
the mouth or face is never seen between persons of any age or sex, but adult
frequently kiss the genitals of infants. Greeting another person involves exten
sive rubbing of the arms, back, and legs, or pressing together by grasping th
buttocks. Feet and toes are used in amazing conjunction with hands and finger
for a variety of tasks.

Continually stimulated awareness of differences in the physical type an
dress soon began to dissolve my initial impression of sameness. All eyes re
mained "brown" and all hair "dark." No one's skin was darker than "darl
brown," but many revealed areas of skin protected from the sun that were n
darker than my own arms and legs. Faces looked "rugged" because of heav
brow ridge, prominent cheek bones, and widely flaring nostrils. Lips wer
"narrow" and mouths very "wide." Only old people were "thin" and only ado
lescent girls were "fat." Bulging abdomens were common, probably because o
parasitic infestation and other disease syndromes. All these characteristics be
came a kind of type useful as background for identifying the variations tha
were individual people.

With respect to dress, people at first seemed essentially bare. This was i
spite of the fact that all men and women wear some kind of pubic covering
Women wear two sets of string aprons suspended from a rope belt, a wide on
in front not quite reaching the knees, and a narrow one in back reaching to th
calves. Men dress in a variety of styles. Most men prefer a belt holding a fre
hanging length of cloth or netting in front and a bundle of leaves or grass i

back. This costume is borrowed from the culturally different Chimbu living to the northwest. A few men wear the tightly fitting G-string made of bark cloth identified with Asaro valley people, and some of the young men wear shorts in the fashion of red men. Little boys go naked, but little girls never do. In addition to these larger and more obvious garments the people also cover themselves in ways that are initially less obvious. One only begins to realize the degree they detract from bareness when people are seen without them. Men commonly wear wickerwork crescents in their hair studded with small shells; a head piece of fern leaves or a knit cap; ear pendants of small shells or the bodies of iridescent green beetles; a band of small shells around the forehead; nose decorations of shell wood, or bird quills; one or more large pieces of shell around neck; a small net bag hanging under one arm; bracelets made of vines; wrist cuffs, arm bands, leg bands, and ankle cuffs made in several styles and materials. Women always have a large netted carrying bag suspended from their head, even when it is empty, that covers their back. They occasionally wear nose ornaments of wood, and frequently wear several large shells around the neck. Knit caps, arm bands, and leg bands are common for women. All women have their faces tattooed and most men have a tattoo on the back or chest. Both men and women tie large numbers of short ropes in their hair producing a "mop" effect with different styles for the two sexes. This everyday wear is replaced by more spectacular adornment, especially for men, on ceremonial occasions.

Sizes and shapes, attitudes of the body, physical type, and dress or ornamentation are only some of the more obvious areas defining the "look of things." In situations where communication is at a minimum because of language differences they become points of concentration since they are readily accessible to observation and amenable to an ordering revealing a range of variation. The primacy of these areas in exploring the dimensions of strangeness is indicated when it is remembered that the people of Miruma as well as the ethnographer made them a focus of initial curiosity.

2

The Strategy of Counting

"Put my name in your book."

ERTAIN INITIAL observations the ethnographer assumes will yield a large amount of material on several aspects of culture and prove useful in solving a wide range of problems. These are relatively simple to make and require only limited knowledge of the culture under investigation to ascertain their reliability. They are frequently made at the beginning of a field study not only to provide necessary background information, but also because they do not interfere too directly in the lives of the people. This is part of the strategy of counting, and devices such as a map of the area, a census, and genealogies are such starting points. The classic ethnographic monograph commonly begins with chapters on physical environment or settlement pattern elaborated from information gathered by such devices. These topics appear in the first chapter of the comprehensive description of a culture probably not so much because they are logically prior as because they are amenable to quantitative statement and description in terms of objective properties. This is not to say that other topics are necessarily unsuited to such statement, only that an efficient and useful way has not yet been found to deal with all of them in that way. They also probably represent what an ethnographer comes to know first about a culture and are just a systematic step beyond discovering the "look" of things.

The Lay of the Land

A printed map taken from aerial photographs showing the Asaro river and its tributaries, and several days of tramping about the countryside provided a basic orientation to the land. The Asaro runs approximately northwest and southeast. The northern and eastern walls of the valley are formed by the Bismarck mountains, a massive range with one peak of over 15,000 feet elevation. The western wall is formed by a subsidiary range separating the Asaro and Chimbu river systems with elevations to 11,000 feet. Steep-sided ridges extend from

26

these bounding walls into the Asaro basin cutting it into a series of V-shaped valleys near the head of the basin and broader bays further down. In the lower part of the basin the walls are at some distance from one another thus opening the basin into a broad plain. The floor of the upper basin has an elevation of approximately 5500 to 5700 feet and runs for fifteen to twenty miles before broadening out into the lower basin. The people we are concerned with live in the smaller valleys and bays of the upper basin.

The mountains are young, geologically, giving them an abrupt, bulky appearance relieved only slightly by the fine engraving of narrow, swiftly running streams pouring down their sides. Little bare rock is visible, except for occasional limestone outcroppings, and the sharp contours of the larger ridges are softened by a thick covering of vegetation. The soil is dark and friable near the basin floor, but tends to be red and hardened with clay away from the river. The bays mentioned above are defined by limestone ridges extending almost to the river and separated from one another by varying distances ranging up to four miles. In between, the hills and spurs have a gentler, more rounded form.

Passageways through this land are not waterways, for they are too swift and shallow. Indeed, the people have no knowledge of rafts, canoes, or other forms of water transportation. Rather, there are paths extending along ridge lines or plunging directly down the precipitous slopes: the switchback trail is unknown. The government road, which runs about half way into the upper basin, is a dirt track maintained by native labor recruited through the institution of the work day. On this day, which comes once a week, all people living along the road turn out to make whatever improvements are needed on it under the supervision of *luluais* and *tultuls*. More complex tasks, such as building bridges or rerouting the road, are supervised by a government officer.

Map and compass provided an orientation for me, but these organize the landscape in quite a different way than the frame of reference employed by the people who live in it. For them, mountains and ridges are not part of the geomorphology, but part of the social universe. A ridge does not have meaning as part of a more massive earth formation, but as the boundary between human groups. Trails do not run along ridges, they go to named places. Directions are not in terms of the sun or the earth's poles, but have the more limited referents of uphill, downhill, upstream, downstream, toward or away from a place. A system like this works on the basis of a large number of invariant reference points that are local in nature. These are provided by named tribal areas, villages, plots of ground, and landmarks. The importance of knowing their names and relative locations is illustrated by the fact that their learning is not left to chance. At some point in a young boy's life he is taken to a high point on the Asaro-Chimbu divide from where almost all the upper Asaro valley can be seen. The major bays and other physical features are strikingly clear from there and the total relationship of one named part to another becomes obvious. A small ceremony is held during which he is told the names of groups occupying the various parts as well as which of them harbor friends and which enemies.

Although efforts at mapping the area produced only a rather crude chart by cartographic standards, its usefulness in revealing aspects of the culture must also be counted in assessing the utility of the operation. My seemingly random wanderings and very real difficulty in comprehending directions given by natives finally led them to put me through the little ceremony called "showing the land" given to young boys. Through it, information was gathered on the system of directions characteristic of this culture, one of the regular events in the life cycle of a male, and the names of distinguishable social groups. This last bit of information was an important prelude to analyzing the bases of social grouping.

People on the Land

A map of the land showing the way people are distributed over it is an unanalyzed description of settlement pattern. Analyzing this description produces an understanding of some of the factors people take into account when they organize themselves spatially.

The village of Miruma, along with several other villages, is located in one of the larger bays on the western wall of the Asaro valley. Since most of the villages formed two named groups counting one another as friends rather than enemies, this bay was taken as a unit of analysis on the assumption that its geographical discreetness identified some kind of social entity as well. An enlarged base map of this bay was prepared and details of settlement pattern filled in.

Putting on the base map every man-made structure found within the bay revealed the following: some structures occur singly and some in clusters; the clusters have different shapes and sizes; some clusters are far from the river and some near it; some clusters have different types of structures in them than others; and some are on the backs of ridges while others are not. At the outset it was not known how many of these variations were significant or what the reasons for them were, but they served as starting points for investigation.

The difference between houses occurring singly and in clusters is related to the fact that the people of Miruma are horticulturalists keeping small domesticated animals. Most single houses are referred to as "garden houses" or "pig houses," dwellings erected within the fenced enclosure of a garden. Gardens are not always located near villages, and these houses save a person the trouble of walking back and forth between village and garden during periods of intense gardening activity. They are also the place where a man's pigs are kept most of the time. The fact that people may reside in either the village or the garden serves other ends as well; these will be discussed below.

Two types of cluster can be distinguished on the basis of their use, shape and the presence or absence of structures that are not dwellings. One can be called a living village and the other a ceremonial center. Villages usually consist of twenty-five or thirty houses arranged lineally. The number of houses varies from as few as ten to as many as seventy, but there are special reasons for these extremes. The houses are circular in plan featuring a conical roof topped with a long, upright pole. There are no openings except the door which faces out onto a broad path running the length of the village. The house walls consist of a row of parallel stakes stuffed with dried grass held in place by long horizontal strips of tree bark. There is no division of the interior into rooms, but a low partition may separate the front half containing a hearth from the back half containing headrests used in sleeping. The linear arrangement of houses conforms to the rather narrow ridge backs where most living villages are located, but it is usually broken by one or two larger houses standing on the opposite side of the village path from the other buildings. These are men's houses. The adult males of a village live together in men's houses while each woman has her own house.

In ceremonial centers the houses are arranged in a rectangle rather than a line. At least one side of such a center is formed by a long, shedlike, noncompartmentalized structure with many hearths in it, and the remaining sides by circular houses. The long structure is used to house guests attending certain kinds of ceremonies that require their presence in the village for several days. All the buildings face the inside of the rectangle which becomes the center for activity during a ceremony. These centers also contain a fenced enclosure, not found in living villages, having religious significance. Ceremonial centers always have fewer inhabitants than villages except on ceremonial occasions when people occupying several villages band together as hosts and move into the ceremonial center. Both types of settlement are defined by a surrounding fence, and villages may be divided at several points by transverse fences.

By taking certain features of size and location as relevant characteristics two other types of villages can be distinguished. These may be called old villages and new villages. Old villages seldom contain more than twelve to fourteen houses and are located on ridges far back from the river near the edge of the forest. New villages are three to six times larger and are located on less abrupt prominences some distance from the forest or on flat land near the river. The new villages have come into being in the last ten years and reflect changes wrought by red man's law. Before the red man came warfare was common, and the flat, open grassland along the river was a dangerous place to live because it offered no natural defensive positions. People ventured into this grassland at their peril, and it was more often exploited as a battle ground than as a subsistence area. Villages were built away from the river for defensive reasons including the proximity of the forest as a refuge in case of attack. With the cessation of warfare people began to move down from their mountain perches to take advantage of the better soil at lower elevations and also because the government urged them to settle in more accessible areas. Accessibility, which made control easier, was also a matter of consolidation and so they were urged to erect larger villages. Old villages are not entirely abandoned and new villages are not always full, but the two now exist where only one existed before.

There is one village differing from all the others in the style of its buildings. These are oval or round-ended in plan rather than circular and are divided into rooms which sometimes open onto a central passageway. It is occupied by Chimbu-speaking people, and more will be said of it below.

The information gathered in the process of filling in the map produced material of important kinds. First, there was a large amount of quantitative data pertaining to the physical arrangement of people, buildings, and villages. The bay contained seven new living villages and three ceremonial villages. The exact number of old villages was uncertain because it was difficult to locate them, but nineteen had been found. A crude estimate of population size by counting houses in new villages produced the figure 1121. Figures on houses per village, distances between villages, distances and directions of garden houses from villages, number of men's houses per village, number of transverse fences per village, and the like were recorded and stored for possible future use. Three villages, including the village of Miruma, were investigated more intensively than others in that the owner and current occupants of each house were recorded. This produced an accurate but limited census.

Second, knowledge was beginning to accumulate on the way people fit into the pattern of buildings erected on the land. This might be called the social dimension of settlement pattern because it reveals those factors separating and combining people at given times and places. The form taken initially by this knowledge provides an illustration of an ethnographer's preconceptions at work and so has interest beyond its content. In the process of going from one village to another counting houses and recording positions, it frequently seemed that the villages were "empty." There was always someone there, but it would usually turn out to be a few children playing, an old person resting, or an adult passing through to somewhere else. In the late afternoon people would begin to come into a village, but more men than women appeared, and then never all the men who had a right to be there. After some time in the field it became apparent that villages were never fully occupied except when some matter of general importance occurred. The arrival of a patrol officer, a visitor from another area with affairs to discuss, marriages, funerals, court cases, planned fights, and ceremonialized food exchanges were events of an order sufficient to fill a village for a few days. I was surprised there were not more people in a village more of the time, for to me the existence of villages implied a center of group life in the sense that people do everything habitual there except what can only be done elsewhere. These villages, however, are centers of group life in the sense that people come to them mainly to do what must be done in some larger group than the family.

Adult men come into a village for three major reasons: (1) to stay in the men's house, (2) to attend public events, and (3) because their gardens are nearby. The men's house is an information center, a decision-making center, a ritual center, and a dwelling. Men who have not slept there the previous night, frequently gather at the men's house in the morning to discuss plans for the day. They meet there, away from the hearing of outsiders and the distraction of women and children, to decide on matters of importance or to perform ecret rituals. Men work in the men's house preparing costumes or practicing for ceremonial occasions and sleep there when they are in progress. A man may stay in a village because the garden plot he is currently working is nearby, but since every man has more than one plot, and they are scattered, his stay is dependent on the time spent working that plot. This, incidently, partially explains the continued use of old villages, for they are located near gardens still in use. It also explains the use of ceremonial villages during periods of ritual inactivity, for the central plaza may be converted to a garden. Adult women stay less frequently in a village than men. Young, unmarried adults commonly stay in a village. Girls are largely divorced from subsistence activities from the time of puberty to betrothal and a group of them may occupy a woman's house in a village where they receive suitors in formalized, evening courting sessions. Their agemates of opposite sex stay in the men's house which becomes a kind of dormitory for them.

Another aspect of the social dimension of settlement pattern can be seen if instead of asking what generally brings people into a village, we ask what brings the particular constellation of people together that is characteristically present in any given village. This question cannot be fully answered with the data presented to this point, but enough is known to suggest what kind of data will answer it. For example, new villages are divided into segments by transverse fences, and each segment has its own men's house. The women's houses in each segment shelter the wives of men who frequent the men's house of that segment. Each segment of a new village tends to contain the same people making up the personnel of one of the old villages. Many of the adult males in a segment claim to be descended from brothers or from a common father. All this suggests that the segments of a village may be based on a rule of patrilineal descent, and that villages themselves may be larger units built upon this base. Genealogies provide some of the data necessary to answer this question.

Before any genealogies were collected it became apparent there was one factor unrelated to the calculation of kinship operating to bring certain people together in some villages. This was the factor of conservatism. As mentioned above, new villages are located in the grassland away from the forest. Attitudes about the dangers of living in the grassland, deriving from the fact that it presents the problem of exposure to enemy attack as well as from certain supernatural beliefs, made living in these villages uncongenial to some people. They preferred to stay in the old villages and did not even build a token dwelling in the new villages. This further explains the persistence of old villages and indicates that although kinship may be a factor in organizing the personnel of a village there are other factors operating as well.

The third category of material accumulated through mapping is related to the problem of subsistence patterns and land use. Gardens and vegetation zones were put on the map as well as villages and buildings, and they form the data relevant to this category. The first obvious pattern seen in this data is a change in land use correlated with elevation. This pattern can be described in terms of use-zones. The first zone extends from the valley floor to an elevation of about 6000 feet. This zone becomes progressively narrower toward the head of the Asaro valley, but in the bay under consideration it is two or three miles wide. The natural vegetation in this zone consists primarily of a tall, reedy grass known as *pitpit* in Neo-Melanesian. It grows in clumps reaching eight or ten feet in height. The stalks and leaves of this plant are used for such things as roofing material, fences, and arrow shafts. Small animals and birds abound here and are frequently hunted for food. This was formerly a no-man's-land and is only beginning to come under cultivation.

The second zone extends from 6000 to 7500 feet. It is the zone of most intensive cultivation and all the new villages fall within it. Naturally occurring vegetation has been largely supplanted in this zone by domesticated plants, although there are remnants of an old forest cover dominated by oak trees to be seen in some of the small uncultivated gullies or along the banks of streams. It does not have the open appearance of the first zone, however, because of the remnant forest and large stands of casuarina trees planted in areas not under active cultivation or around villages. Bamboo, banana, and other tall plants are also abundant. Gardens cover the area, their fences, boundary markers of colored plants, and symmetrically arranged drainage ditches imposing a regularity on the land that marks the constant presence of man.

The third zone, ranging from 7500 to 8200 feet, is transitional between the zone of intensive cultivation and the forest. Prior to the cessation of warfare this area was under more intensive cultivation than it is now, but since then many of the more steeply inclined garden sites have been abandoned in favor of sites in the second zone. As a result, much of the area is reverting to a second growth of bushy plants, young forest trees, and giant tree ferns. Gardens are still maintained here, and pigs are allowed to root in the brush, but at the higher levels some important plants, such as sugar cane and taro, will not grow. Even the hardy sweet potato does not flourish above 8000 feet. On the other hand, some food plants do better here than at lower elevations. Pandanus trees, which yield an annual crop of highly prized nuts, are such a plant, and many kinds of wild plants found only in this zone are gathered for food or other purposes. It is interesting that people seem to prefer this zone to any of the others. They will, for example, comment that the lower zones are too hot or too dangerous because proximity to the road brings with it the possibility of sorcery attack from enemies who wander freely over it. They feel that pigs prefer the food found in this zone and that children should frequent the area for their health.

The fourth zone, which can be called the forest zone for the sake of convenience, reaches to the top of the dividing range. It is a complex of plant communities superficially divisible into an upper and lower forest. The lower forest is relatively dry and dominated by tall stands of antarctic beech, while the upper forest is damp and peaty with great accumulations of moss covering the mass of lower growing vegetation. No one lives in this zone but it is exploited for its timber, birds, marsupials, and various kinds of exotic plants including orchid vines which yield a bright yellow fibre used for decorative motifs in weaving.

The second pattern seen in this data relates to the positioning and arrangement of gardens. Gardens were not measured or examined in detail at this point in the study, but some of their general characteristics were noted in the course of locating them on the map. The positioning of gardens is largely determined by ideas the people hold concerning what kinds of plants grow best in which areas. Land ownership is also important, but land does not seem to be in short supply so that any given man usually has available to him, land of all the preferred types.

The slope of the land has little to do with whether or not it is used as a garden site. Slopes of over 45° off the horizontal are occasionally used as long as there is sufficient soil to maintain the crops. Terracing is not practiced, but long poles are staked down in rows against the slope at regular intervals on the steeper sites in an effort to check soil slippage. Irrigation or a water source is no problem because rainfall exceeds 100 inches a year. Rather, it is drainage that is one of the most serious problems, and gardens are usually oriented to facilitate maximum water run-off. Small gardens, or patches in gardens, given over principally to growing taro are the exception to this. This plant thrives in moist soil and is planted at the lower edge of gardens or in gullies or other low-lying places. Sugar cane is said to grow best at lower elevations and large portions of gardens in the first and second zones are given over to its propagation. Sweet potatoes and yams are the main crops; each comes in many varieties differing noticeably in color, texture, and taste. The people have definite notions about the need to plant certain varieties in certain kinds of soil and position their gardens accordingly.

The internal arrangement of a garden is ordered by several factors. First, what we have been calling a garden is a cultivated area defined by a fence. More than one nuclear family may have plots inside this fence, and these are separated from one another by rows of decorative plants. This gives one kind of arrangement to the garden. Second, a system of crop rotation and staggered planting is followed inside a garden as well as between gardens. Inside a garden this means some parts of it will contain mature plants, some young plants, and some will be in fallow. Third, certain combinations of plants are separated from other combinations in discreet areas of the garden. For example, sugar cane and an asparaguslike plant are commonly planted together, as are yams and a kind of native bean. Finally, drainage ditches divide the whole into a series of rectangular planting beds.

Examining the factors involved in the positioning and arrangement of gardens, besides contributing to knowledge of subsistence pattern, indicates why each man has more than one garden plot. He uses different soils and ecological zones for different crops, and he has several gardens in varying states of maturity to assure him a fairly constant food supply.

Counting Kin

In societies like the Gururumba it is assumed that social relationships based on kinship will be operative in some degree at almost all levels of social organization. Kin terms will name many roles in the society and kinship will be a principle of recruitment in various kinds of social groups. The most efficient way yet devised to begin systematically collecting data that will reveal the system of kin terms, kin ties, and the use made of kinship in forming social groups is through the collection of genealogies.

In collecting genealogies the ethnographer interviews all the adults comprising some easily identifiable unit, such as a village. He asks each person to list, in birth order if possible, all his own biological offspring, all those of his parents, the offspring of his parents' siblings, and the children of all of these. He may stop at this point or continue to the limits of the informants' knowledge, attempting to get the progeny of grandparents, the siblings of grandparents, and their children. At the same time that the names of all these people are being collected, the ethnographer also asks which of them are living, where they are living, and what kin term the informant applies to each one. In some areas of the world the ethnographer will find his informants continuing beyond the questions asked and extending the genealogy to ancestors living many generations in the past or even to supernatural figures such as creator gods. In the village of Miruma, however, it was difficult for adult informants to recall the names of ancestors removed by only two generations.

Once a mass of material of this sort has been collected it can be used in a variety of ways, but one of the initial problems the ethnographer may set himself is discovering the referent of the terms he has collected. At one level of analysis this is a simple task involving the listing of types of kinsmen referred to by a given term in the genealogies. Restricting ourselves to some kinds of consanguineal kin and assuming an adult male informant, the following list can be compiled from the genealogies collected in Miruma:

ahono	Fa, FaElBr, FaFa, MoFa.
iJEno	Mo, MoMo, FaMo, FaElSi, MoElSi.
omono	MoBr.
noho	SiCh, FaSiCh, MoBrCh.
uBono	ElBr, FaYrBr, FaFlBrSon, MoElSiSo.
naku'nE	YrBr, FaYrBrSo, MoYrSiSo, ElBrSo.
atEno	ElSi, FaYrSi, FaElBrDa, MoYrSi, MoElSiDa.
aru'nE	YrSi, FaYrBrDa, MoYrSiDa.
gipE'nE	So, FaBrSoSo, MoSiSoSo.
arunE	Da, FaBrSoDa, BrDa, MoSiDaDa.
gwo'mo	FaSiChCh, MoBrChCh, SiChCh.
na'BO	SoSo, DaDa.

This simple listing is not, in itself, very informative but there are several ways in which a more generalized statement can be made concerning the referents of these terms. They can, for example, be considered in terms of contrastive groups. Consider first the three terms *ahono, i]Eno,* and *omono.* In contrast to all other terms they indicate only kinsmen of senior generation to ego. *Ahono* and *omono* contrast with *i]Eno* in that the first two indicate male kinsmen in this group while the latter indicates female kinsmen. *Omono* contrasts with *ahono* in separating mother's male siblings from father's male siblings.

The next contrastive group is much more complex. It contrasts with the first group in that the terms designate only kinsmen of ego's own generation or a generation junior to ego's. On one side is the single term *noho.* It refers to kinsmen to whom ego traces a relationship through a sibling of opposite sex or a pair of siblings of opposite sex to each other. Assuming a male ego, a *noho* could be a sister's child or a father's sister's child. For the sake of convenience we will say these are kinsmen joined to ego by asymmetrical links. On the other side is a group of four terms contrasting with *noho* because they refer to kinsmen related to ego through a pair of siblings of the same sex or to ego's own siblings. These four terms contrast with one another on the basis of sex and relative age. Thus, *atEno* refers to a female in this group older than ego, and *aru'nE* to a female younger than ego. Similarly, *uBono* refers to a male older than ego, and *naku'nE* to a male younger than ego. We will refer to these kinsmen as joined to ego by symmetrical links.

The final group contrasts with the others because it only refers to kinsmen of generations junior to ego's. The terms *gipE'nE* and *arunE* designate ego's own children plus the children of anyone related to ego through symmetrical links with the first term applied to males and the second to females. These two terms apply to kinsmen one generation below ego, while the term *na'Bo* applies to kinsmen linked in the same way but removed from ego by two descending generations. These three terms contrast with the term *gwo'mo* because it refers to the children of anyone related to ego through asymmetrical links one or more generations below ego.

There are other, more complex ways of discovering what characteristics of the genealogical relationship between ego and alter are being taken into account in the various classes of kinsmen designated by the kin terms. Even this relatively simple analysis, however, indicates the importance of certain principles such as distinguishing between generational levels, symmetrical as opposed to asymmetrical links, sex, and relative age. Once these characteristics are discovered they can be used as clues in further research. For example, the separation of cross cousins from parallel cousins and the identification of mother's brother by a special term suggest the existence of social groups in which unilineal descent is an organizational principle. Further, the development of a terminology to distinguish between ego's own siblings and the children of ego's parents' siblings on the basis of relative age alerts us to the possibility that authority in kin-based groups may depend on differences in age among kinsmen of the same generational level as well as between generational levels.

The genealogies can be put to a number of other uses as well. Some basic demographic data can be tabulated from them, such as the range and average number of children born to a married couple, the number of infant deaths, and the population pyramid for a given community. They also provide clues concerning various aspects of the marriage pattern. From the Miruma genealogies it is evident that about 10 percent of the marriages are polygynous; the levirate is practiced, but rare; there are no spinsters, but about 4 percent of the men are bachelors; and more wives come from inside the tribe than from outside it. There are also indications in the genealogies that marriage is a difficult adjustment for girls. The first wife of 63 percent of the males in Miruma and the second wife of 40 percent ran away from her husband or was sent away by him because of her recalcitrance.

One of the more interesting classes of material evident in the Miruma genealogies relates to causes of death. No systematic attempt was made in this instance to collect statements concerning the cause of death of all those reported on the genealogies as deceased, but informants frequently volunteered the information. As the material accumulated it became evident that young married women frequently committed suicide at the death of their husbands, and that a large proportion of nonsuicidal deaths were described to the malevolent attacks of sorcerers and ghosts. Neither of these facts is meaningful by itself, but they suggest lines of further investigation.

The genealogies in combination with the census of a village provide initial insight into the composition of this residential unit. One can trace the precise kin links between the various families in the village, one can detect what kinds of kinsmen tend to stay in the village, what kinds tend to move out, and by identifying those individuals or families living in the village that are not kinsmen of some kind, one can ascertain what factors operate to bring nonkinsmen into the village. Some of the results of this investigation will be presented in the next chapter.

3

Focusing on Groups

"They are the ones that sit down together."

STRANGER soon discovers that while living with a particular household
or village he is expected to participate in certain kinds of activ:ties
with others of the same unit, he may be excluded from participating
in similar activities when they are carried out in another unit of the same order.
So too, the ethnographer finds the world divided by "we" and "they" and,
further, that the referent of "we" varies from one situation to another. He tries
to find out how people organize themselves for tasks and events, and how they
decide who is an "insider" and who an "outsider" in various circumstances.
The ethnographer focuses his attention on social groups early in the field study,
especially those that maintain their identity over a long period of time, control
some kind of property, or exhibit other characteristics of corporateness.

Identifying Groups

Discovering the social groups that make up a society can begin with a
map and census for these show significant concentrations of people and one can
usually safely assume that such concentrations represent relatively stable groups
of some kind. The map of the upper Asaro valley shows a series of bays and
narrower valleys with villages clustered in them. Each of these areas is separated from its neighbor by large, unoccupied ridges or stretches of open grassland, and each area tends to be treated as a unit in that a single name, or a pair
of names, is given to the people living in it. Thus, people from the village of
Miruma will point to the valley north of them and say, "There are Mandu-
Amoso," or to the valley south of them and say, "There are Kofena-Ka'nasa."
Similarly, people living in either of these areas will point to the bay containing
the village of Miruma and say, "There are Gururumba-FikEsE." In the Gururumba-FikEsE area people are seldom heard to refer to themselves by either of
these names, but if they do, it is usually by one or the other rather than both.

37

Furthermore, whole villages are either Gururumba or FikEsE, and a line can be drawn on an enlarged map of this bay separating all villages referred to by one of these names from all referred to by the other. This use of names presumably indicates some kind of territorial grouping. Collecting the names used by the people of each bay to refer to all the others produces a consistent list of names revealing fourteen such groups in the upper Asaro valley. In five instances the names are paired while in four they are not.

Miruma is a Gururumba village, but when people there talk of "we" or "us" in some large sense they do not usually mean Miruma and all other Gururumba villages. Asking them the rather ambiguous question, "What large group do you belong to?" most frequently elicits the answer, "Wa'muJuhu." The referent of this name is also a grouping with a territorial base, for in addition to Miruma it includes the two new villages on either side of it and the surrounding land where almost all the gardens of these villages are located. Similarly, the names AsErE'Juhu and KafindE'Juhu group the remaining Gururumba villages into two additional units having territorial identity. The common ending *Juhu* on these names is interesting and also occurs in the names Gwonambu'- Juhu, GulifE'Juhu, and LonohoNgu'Juhu for groups of neighboring FikEsE villages. *Juhu* means "dried seed." Its connotation is not that of potential growth or of inability to grow, but of established growth. Thus, the names ending in *Juhu* appear to indicate territorially discreet subdivisions of larger territorial units that have achieved some identity through time as well as on the ground.

Indication of another kind of unit with territorial identity is given on maps of villages. As mentioned above, the large, new villages are divided by transverse fences with a men's house in each segment. These segments can be referred to by the name of the plot of ground where they are located, or by the phrases "the uphills" and "the downhills" depending on their relative position on the ridge.

Map and census cannot by themselves tell us much more about the social groups characterizing this society. An additional bit of negative information is the lack of a name for all the people living in the upper Asaro as distinct from all those of the lower Asaro except the phrases "the uphills" and "the downhills." Whether or not the "uphills" form a social unit, and what identifies other named groups in addition to their territoriality, are questions that must be answered with material beyond that already considered. Groups must be identified as they are revealed in concrete assemblies of people. Observations must therefore await the occurrence of events and situations that generate such assemblies.

In an alien situation one learns that it is not always possible to tell when concrete assemblies of people are acting as members of groups or when they are a heterogeneous set of persons brought together by circumstance. In order to proceed with the business of gathering data the ethnographer makes certain assumptions that he hopes will guide him to those assemblies of people that manifest group identity. This is a justifiable procedure as long as he realizes the assumptions he is making. For example, I regularly assumed I was really seeing a group acting whenever visitors to Miruma stopped outside the village and arranged themselves into a compact formation before entering the village. I assumed that entering the village en masse was a deliberate act accentuating group identity. This assumption proved to be a reliable one, but I also assumed the interaction of groups whenever I saw a fight involving several people taking place in the presence of an audience that seemed to be arranged in "sides." This assumption proved to be unreliable in the sense that sometimes it was correct and sometimes it was not. The most reliable and consistently used assumption was that group identities were involved whenever food was publicly distributed in the context of an assembly divided into givers and recipients.

The purpose of identifying those assemblies of people that seem to represent social groups are to observe their activities in order to learn what kinds of affairs are managed by groups and to observe their personnel to learn what criteria of membership are employed. The village of Miruma became a kind of sociological benchmark in gathering data of this kind. All the people having houses there or regularly coming into one of the men's houses were known to me. For the whole period of the field study records were kept of the way these people divided themselves or joined together in various kinds of activities. Because it was physically impossible to watch all of them all the time, the records represent only a sample, but an attempt was made to check this validity by hiring several young boys to report daily on the activities of four or five adult males. This provided a complete picture of the way the men of this village arranged themselves for the more routine affairs of daily life. In addition to looking for data relevant to the internal divisions of Miruma, data was also sought on the way Miruma joined other villages to form larger groupings. For example, its common participation with villages designated Wa'muJuhu as guests of host villages called GulifE'Juhu became part of this data.

It may happen, of course, that one never sees certain social groups as concrete entities. Some kinds of groups only manifest themselves through representatives; others never assemble because the rights and obligations entailed in group membership do not involve it; still others find no occasion for assemblies during the observer's stay. Therefore, some groups are only "seen" as analytic constructs or through the descriptive accounts of informants, and identification of them may not occur until after the ethnographer returns from the field.

Identifying groups by seeing them in concrete assembly attests to their existence but does not identify their membership criteria. To discover these criteria the ethnographer attempts to find some features common to all the people participating in the activities of named social units or the assemblies he thinks may be social groups. Here again assumptions are made in order to start data collection. For example, my first assumption was that kinship would be an important criterion and viewed every assembly of people or named unit as bounded in some way by kinship. Discovering when this assumption was not warranted was my first step in discovering other membership criteria.

Over a period of time a body of knowledge is accumulated about groups by locating named entities on the ground, observing concrete assemblies, and finding the membership criteria of assumed social groups. There is a final area of information that may also help in the discovery process, although the degree of its usefulness varies a great deal from one culture to another. This is the understanding people themselves have of the system of groups into which they are organized. They may have terms for different kinds of groups, as in the terms "family," "state," "nation," "club," or "corporation" from our own culture. They may have explanations of group structure or accounts of how the current arrangement of groups came to be. Not much of this kind of information was available, for the people did not seem to have speculated much about the inner workings of their own society. What they did say will be reported in the following sections.

Who Are the Gururumba?

The name "Gururumba" appears in the title of this book and has been mentioned in a previous section. What kind of group is this? How does it articulate with similar groups or differ from others? The Gururumba will be the immediate referent for the rest of the book because most of the observations on which it is based were made among them rather than similarly constituted groups in the area.

The question "who are the Gururumba" can be answered as if one were describing the physical properties of an object. The name designates 1121 people living in six large villages in the northern half of a large bay on the west side of the upper Asaro valley. It designates a territorially distinct unit of approximately thirty square miles in the sense that none of these six villages, nor any of the gardens belonging to people living in the villages, are outside this territory. The people living inside this territory see themselves as a unified entity indicating a more complex group than one characterized solely by territorial discreetness. The name not only designates an "it" but also a "who," and in the minds of non-Gururumba it designates "those people standing opposed to us" and not simply "people of that place."

The people called Gururumba apply this name to themselves and, in addition, point up their existence as a unified entity by explaining how they came to be. There is a story telling of a time when the upper Asaro valley was largely uninhabited. People from the lower valley made excursions into it to hunt and gather, but they did not live there. Those who used it most frequently lived in a large village (the name of which has been forgotten) on the edge of this region which was at that time covered with forest. One day a fight broke out in this village because a man killed a pregnant woman for stealing some mushrooms he had been saving for his supper. The fight divided the village into several warring factions each of which moved off into a part of the upper valley as a defensive measure. They remained there, planted gardens, flourished, and became part of the present population. The Gururumba were one of these groups. This story may not provide us much actual history, but it does tell us that the Gururumba think of themselves as a social unit in existence over a long period of time.

Other aspects of this story inform us about the internal structure of this group. To the ethnographer schooled in working with societies where kinship is an important structural feature, it is interesting that this story does not depict the factionalization of the village along descent group lines. It was not brother against brother or the descendants of one man against the descendants of another who formed the factions generated by the killing. As the story depicts them, these factions were those residents in a village who took common cause in a dispute, and although they may have been kinsmen the story makes the point irrelevant by exclusion. This detail of the story mirrors the fact that although the Gururumba consider themselves to be the descendants of a common set of ancestors, these ancestors are not specifically known nor do they form a descent group among themselves. The ancestors are simply the original group to occupy this territory and defend it against outsiders. Similarly, the Gururumba are the present day descendants of this heterogeneous group who remain committed to common defense of the territory.

The cohesiveness of this group, which we will call a phratry, derives primarily from occupying a common territory, acting in common defense, and feeling a continuity with the past. The authority structure in the phratry may be regarded as a secondary source of cohesion, for none of the three primary sources is utilized by the Gururumba to devise rules specifying positions of central authority. There is no phratry head picked generation after generation from the occupants of one village, the ranks of hereditary war leaders, or some particular descent line. In fact, one seldom finds a single, dominant leader of an Asaro phratry. As we will see below, becoming a leader means becoming a man of renown, and this is a complex process requiring men of certain temperament and skill. The extent of a man's influence is dependent on his renown, and the phratry can be regarded as the largest unit within which a man of renown can influence others on matters of policy. Thus, strong central authority in the phratry depends on the existence in it of a man with greater renown than all others. Since this does not usually occur, authority comes to be shared among several men.

The authority structure itself is not so much a source of cohesion as is the fact that the phratry is considered a field of action for reaching a settlement in matters under dispute. This is exemplified in the notion of two kinds of warfare. One is called roBo, warring with deadly weapons such as spears, axes, and arrows. The other is called nande, fighting with sticks, stones, and hands. In addition, roBo connotes fighting with the intent to decimate the enemy, while nande connotes fighting that can be halted short of extensive killing or property destruction and, further, that a settlement of the dispute giving rise to the fight can be reached by nonviolent means. It is said that people of different phratries war (roBo) with one another, while people of the same phratry only fight (*nande*). The phratry, then, is not the group in which one finds the authority to which disputes can be referred for final adjudication, it is simply the group within which people are willing to admit the possibility of an amicable settlement of a dispute.

Just as the group has not used the sources of cohesion of the phratry, which we have broadly defined, to build a separable authority structure within it, neither has it utilized them to rigidify the boundaries between "insiders" and "outsiders." Whole groups may be incorporated into the phratry by moving onto its territory and agreeing to defend it. For example, one of the Gururumba villages is made up entirely of people from the Chimbu valley who speak a different language, wear different costume, and are culturally different in other ways. They were invited by the Gururumba to come as a unit and settle there with the understanding they would help defend it, and although they have not been in the area long enough to lose their identity they are in the process of doing so. In other words, "continuity with the past" is not based on the notion of the past as a specifically defined segment of time but as something being continually created, and "occupying a common territory" does not imply a boundary that never changes.

To this point, the phratry has been considered as an entity appearing on the ground, as a field of political action, and as a unit in warfare. It also appears as a unit within which certain kinds of activities carried out by its constituent parts are coordinated, and as a unit in a religious ritual. The two main activities coordinated within the phratry are the pig festival and grass-burning for hunting purposes. The pig festival is a large-scale ceremony occurring at intervals of five or more years and involving many hundreds of people. If a phratry is large, like the Gururumba, the festival is organized and implemented by the parts of the phratry we will come to know as sibs rather than by the phratry itself. In such a case there is agreement that the various sibs should hold their ceremonies seriatim over a brief period of time rather than all at the same time or at irregular intervals. Therefore, the complex arrangements entailed in the ceremony have to be coordinated among the sibs. When the sequence will begin and what the order of precedence will be must be decided on the phratry level; this is done by agreement and mutual consent rather than by dictation or traditional rule. The grass-burning is no longer done on a large scale because the lowland grass area is now being used for gardens, but in former times the grass was frequently fired in order to drive the rodents and other small animals living there into the open where they could be caught in large numbers. Coordination was utilized here to control the fire and maximize the catch.

In addition to these coordinated activities the phratry appears as a unit in a religious ritual called the *jaBirisi*. This takes place around a fenced enclosure located near the center of the phratry territory and occurs during times of crisis. Representatives from each village of the phratry are the main actors in this ritual, but they act as a unit in directing the ritual to the ancestral group which gave rise to the phratry.

The Larger Picture

The Gururumba are part of two larger kinds of units. The first of these will be called a tribe and designates named units like the two phratries Gururumba-FikEsE. This tribe occupies the land of a single bay, numbers approximately 2300 people, and is distributed among ten new villages. Warfare (*roBo*) may break out within the tribe but the two phratries do not regard one another as traditional enemies. Furthermore, neither one will combine with an outside group to attack the other. They may not aid the other in defense against such an attack, but neither will they contribute to the efforts of the enemy. The story concerning the origin of the Gururumba mentioned in the preceding section states that the FikEsE were living in the area before the Gururumba entered it. The two phratries are thus depicted as deriving from different ancestral groups. It will be recalled that ten of the fourteen phratries in the upper Asaro valley are linked in named pairs of this nature. In each case, one of the members of the pair is said to have come from the original dispersion mentioned in the story and the other from some other background. The Ka'nasa of KofEna-Ka'-nasa are said to have come from the Siane area to the southwest; the Mandu of Mandu-Amoso from Chimbu; the AnaNgu of KErEmu-AnaNgu from over the mountains to the northeast; and the LunEmbe of LunEmbe-Gifukoni from another part of the lower Asaro. Some of these groups are said to have been in the area at the time of the dispersion and some to have come after it. All this evidence indicates that the unit we are calling a tribe is a political alliance of long standing between two phratries occupying what they consider to be a common territory. This distinguishes the tribe as a unit from short-term alliances formed between phratries outside these territorial blocks. Thus, the Gururumba now consider the KErEmu their allies, but the KErEmu are outside the Gururumba-FikEsE territorial block; they were enemies as a result of the incident related in the origin story; it is expected the alliance will not continue for long; the alliance is recent; and a common name is never applied to the two groups.

This analysis implies either that the phratries that do not occur in pairs are coterminous with a tribe, and there are fourteen tribes in the valley, or that a tribe represents a degree of political integration not achieved by all phratries, thus making five tribes and four phratries in the valley. The latter interpretation seems preferable since although tribes do not perform any activities that phratries do not also perform, they are a more complex grouping.

The Gururumba are part of a second kind of unit defined primarily on cultural grounds consisting of all the people in the upper Asaro valley. No name is applied to this unit, but the recognition of its existence is embodied in the statement that all these people are "of one leaf." This statement has a double connotation, for it indicates they all eat the same kind of food and also that they all use the same kinds of plants in various magical manipulations. Linguistic differences are also recognized in a relative as well as an absolute sense, so that dialectical differences between upper Asaro and lower Asaro are not equated with the greater degree of difference between Asaro speakers and Siane speakers. Chimbu speakers, with a remotely related language, are put in another class. Other cultural features they see as distinctive to themselves include items of dress, the use of a sacred object called a geruna board, and certain songs and dances. If the actual distribution of any of these traits were plotted on a map one would see that while they are not distinctive to the upper Asaro valley, their particular constellation is.

The unit defined by this constellation of cultural traits and by the geographical boundaries of the upper valley is the world the people living there know most intimately. It is the territory they most frequently walk over, it contains the groups they most frequently fight with, most mates are found within it, all myths and tales refer to happenings within its boundaries, and the lines of economic exchange focus in on it. We regard it as a unit, then, because it is the effective center of the social world for any person in it, and is so recognized by the people themselves.

The Smaller Picture

The Gururumba are made up of smaller units. The first of these is apparent to the outsider because it is geographically distinct and because it is named in a peculiar way, adding *Juhu* as a suffix to its name. Every phratry examined has at least two of these as constituent parts, and the Gururumba have three. The term "sib" will be used to refer to these groups. There is no native term for this kind of group, but in attempting to explain its character to the ethnographer people will frequently say, "They are the ones who sit down together," or, "They are like brothers." The first statement refers to the fact that when this group acts as a unit vis-à-vis other units, as in a food distribution, they sit together during the proceedings. The phratry and the tribe never manifest themselves in this way. The second statement refers to the fact that all members of a sib think of themselves as a descent group. In one case the group is explained in terms of visibility and in the other in terms of membership criterion.

The sib appears as a unit in a much larger number of activities than the phratry or tribe. It arranges and executes the pig festival mentioned above. If food is particularly plentiful in a given year it will hold a food distribution very similar to the pig festival in its intent and structure except that sugar cane, taro, and yams are the foods involved; it is somewhat smaller in scale, and it does not have the religious overtones of the pig festival. The sib also appears as guest group at these occasions to perform spectacular dances and little dramas full of subtle humor or surprising effects. Its members may appear as mourners or the bereaved in funeral ceremonies, but this is partially dependent on other factors. The sib was the basic unit in warfare before the Australian influence and larger war parties were made up of several sibs individually agreeing to participate with the instigating sib in the action. Ceremonial labor, as when the first garden plot is cleared for a newly married couple, is carried out by the sib as a unit, and the new government-imposed work on the roads is organized by sibs.

In addition to appearing as a unit, the sib becomes visible through its members' exercise of obligations and rights that produce actions outside the context of an assembled group. Thus, a man may recruit aides from among his sib mates to avenge a close kinsman's death by killing some member of the killer's sib. Any man from one sib may call any man from another sib by the kin term *niJimo* (affine) if any man in the one is married to any woman of the other. If a man kills a member of another sib, whatever the circumstances he can expect that his own sib mates will not regard it as a punishable act, in most instances defending him against attempts of the other sib to punish him. If he kills a member of his own sib, however, he must defend himself. The sib is also the widest exogamous unit since mates can be found in any sib except one's own.

The term "sib" designates social groups whose membership is defined by descent, although the actual genealogical links between all the members cannot be traced. This is the case, for example, with the Gururumba sib named Wa'mu-Juhu. The Wa'muJuhu say they are descended from a pair of brothers, but the names of the brothers are not known, and no one knows who is descended from the elder brother and who from the younger. Common descent is implied rather than actual. The imputation of common descent means that all one's sib mates are, in a general way, regarded as consanguineal kinsmen. This is evident in the fact that terms used to refer to consanguineals can be extended to sib mates as terms of address; this is rarely done for members of other sibs in the phratry. The appropriate term is selected on the basis of the sex and age of the referent rather than a calculated consanguineal link. Thus, any very old man or woman in ego's sib may be addressed by the terms "father" or "mother," any slightly older man or woman as "elder brother" or "elder sister," and so on. The rule of descent in the sib is patrilineal as indicated by the facts that the ancestors of the sib are always depicted as males, and the extended families comprising the sib are linked together in patrilineages.

The patrilineages comprising a sib are not spread evenly over the sib territory; they occur in the clumps recognizable as villages. These villages are not simply genealogical subdivisions of the sib, however, for if they were, one would expect that all the lineages in the village would see themselves as descended from some ancestor who was in turn descended from the sib ancestor by some known link. Looking at the genealogies from any Gururumba village shows this is simply not the case. Villages may contain from six to fifteen lineages and even in small villages no common ancestor is cited except the remote and unknown sib ancestor. It is significant in this connection that the members of different patrilineages living together in the same village do not usually use kin terms to refer to or address one another. Personal names and teknonomy are used instead. This indicates the village is not the same kind of unit as the sib, differing perhaps only in scale. This is further supported by the fact that the village includes people who would be excluded if it were based on the same principle as the patrisib. In a patrilineal descent group all descendents of the female members of the group and all persons who are not connected to it through consanguineal links are systematically excluded but in a Gururumba village one finds people, of precisely these types living there and participating in its affairs. For example, the wives of all the men claiming descent from the sib ancestor are persons not connected to the sib through consanguineal links for the sib is exogamous and wives usually leave their natal sib at marriage to live with their husband in a village of his sib. Asking wives of Miruma men if they are Wa'muJuhu usually elicits a negative response accompanied by the naming of their natal sib, and observing their behavior indicates they have not given up membership in their own sib for they may move back to it and activate their property rights at any time. In addition to wives, the village contains other people not members of the sib. These include affines more distant than wives, matrilineally related kinsmen, and men from other tribes. The first two types have some kin link to at least one lineage in the village, but the last is there by agreement only or because they are married to lineage women and reside with their wives' lineage rather than their own. Virilocal residence is the most frequently occurring form of residence, but uxorilocal residence also occurs and it is not viewed as deviant or unusual. Of the fifty-three married couples with children in the village of Miruma, fifteen, or 28 percent fall into these three categories.

If the village were only a collecting point for people, there would be no problem in specifying the relationship of village to sib. The wives and others would be nonsib members residing with sib members. A problem arises, however, because the village is itself a social unit in that it has an internal structure, a sense of identity indicated by the use of a village name, and activities not performed by other units. The inhabitants of a village frequently act as a unit in court cases; they move into the forest during a certain time of the year to gather pandanus nuts; they perform a ritual to insure the future growth of pandanus nuts; they may act as guest or host in a food distribution; and they are a unit in one form of ceremonial courtship. Funerals are usually a function of the sib, but if a person dies while living in a village not part of his or her own sib, the village organizes the funeral. The village is also the most important unit in negotiating bride price and all subsequent exchanges between the bride's group and the groom's group. All village residents are potential contributors to the price for in-marrying women and are all potential recipients of the price given for out-marrying women. The internal structure of the village consists of a division into wards each of which centers around a different men's house.

The village, then, can be thought of as a unit recruiting some of its members on the basis of patrilineal descent, which makes it a localized segment of a sib, and on the basis of several other criteria as well. Since the most frequently employed of these other criteria is a rule of residence operating to move most wives into their husbands villages, the village will be classified as a clan or compromise kin group as defined by Murdock.[1] It can then be said that the relationship between sib and clan is such that sib membership depends on birth and

---

[1] George Peter Murdock, *Social Structure,* New York, The Macmillan Company, 1949.

cannot be changed while clan membership may depend on either birth or residence and changes whenever residence changes. Lineages are composed of sib
mates recognizing a known, common ancestor, and wards are all those extended
families in a clan whose adult males belong to the same men's house. In this
conceptualization, lineages are subdivisions of sibs, and wards are subdivisions
of clans.

Some further observations help demonstrate the relationship between sib
and clan. In any village most of the men are members of the same sib and most
of the women are of various other sibs. There are a few women, however, who
are of the same sib as most of the men. These are sib sisters whose husbands
have taken up uxorilocal rather than virilocal residence. There is an observable
difference in the degree to which these two classes of women are allowed to
voice their opinion concerning public affairs. In the village of Miruma those
few women who are Wa'muJuhu are occasionally allowed to stand in court cases
or other public gatherings where issues are being decided and speak in an attempt to influence decisions. The majority of women, who are clan mates but
not sib mates, are usually enjoined to remain silent or speak only on points of
information. Also, these Wa'mu Juhu women are residing with their natal lineage, and when they become old they may be allowed to become guardians of
a sacred object identified with the lineage and with the men's secret cult. The
other women are not allowed to do this and, supposedly, do not even know the
object exists. Again, Wa'muJuhu women residing with a clan of their natal sib
more frequently become leaders of women's activities than do other women.
One final observation concerning the relationship between sib and clan focuses
on the descendents of those men who are members of a clan but not the sib of
which it is a localized segment. If a man resides most of his life in a clan not
of his own sib, his descendents become members of the clan sib rather than his
natal sib. This can happen in one generation although it usually takes at least
two. Putting this observation alongside the fact that the sib is a group where
kinship is imputed rather than actual leads one to the supposition that a sib
grows through the incorporation of ousiders as well as the expansion and division of the lineages within it.

Other Kinds of Groups

The groups discussed so far have been defined by culture traits, political
alliance, territoriality, descent, and residence. They form a series of greater in-
clusiveness based on combinations of these criteria. There are other kinds of
groups that do not fit this series and two of them will be mentioned here. The
first was identified through discovering the meaning of the word *ambo*. Men
were observed calling one another *ambo* and referring to one another as "my
ambo" or "his *ambo*." The term did not appear to be a kin term because it was
never elicited while collecting a genealogy. The first meaning offered for it was

"men born on the same day." This did not seem true because it was used between men of different ages. Subsequent investigation revealed that it designated all men initiated at the same time into the men's cult. This initiation takes place at irregular intervals and may include boys as young as ten or eleven and as old as fifteen or sixteen years, thus accounting for the discrepancy in age. The reference to birth is intended to indicate sociological rather than biological birth, for the initiation moves a boy from the status of child to the status of unmarried adult. We will translate the term as "age mate" because the relationship between one group of *ambo* and another is thought of by the people as similar to the relationship between an older and a younger group of siblings. Because the initiation is sometimes performed by the sib and sometimes by the clan, a man may or may not have age mates in other clans. If he does he is regarded as fortunate, since age mates are as friends and quite responsive to one another's needs. They support one another in arguments, help in subsistence activities, and stand together in dance groups. To have someone in another clan who will do these things "spontaneously" is regarded as an advantage. Age mates appear most conspicuously as a unit during the initiation itself and the long period of Spartan living following it. In later years they do not appear as an assembled unit, but can be seen analytically as constituting a field of friendship.

The second kind of grouping uses sex as the criterion of membership and produces the two groups "men" and "women." It is debatable whether or not these divisions can be called social groups in the strictest sense of the term, but it is at least interesting to think of them in this way. Men are organized into a secret cult from which women are excluded. The women have no comparable cult, but they stand, as a unit, in opposition to men in various contexts. For example, men own pigs, but women carry out the day-to-day tending of them. A woman is spoken of as the "mother" of the pigs she tends, and when they are killed she mourns them. If large numbers of pigs are killed for exchange purposes, there may be an organized stickfight between all the women and the men who have become "killers" of their "children." The men's cult is organized around the playing of sacred flutes kept secret from women, but myths relate that these flutes once belonged to women who revealed them to men. Women carry out some rituals associated with first menstruation, betrothal, and birth, from which men are excluded. There is residential segregation by sex after puberty. This grouping by sex does not crosscut all other groups, so that men do not stand as a unit against women on the tribe, phratry, or sib level. It does crosscut the clan and ward, however.

4

Focusing on Roles

". . . so Elder Sister carried Younger Brother away."

ISCOVERING HOW PEOPLE organize themselves for certain tasks and events as "insiders" and "outsiders" locates points of reference for the stranger. A particular set of rights, duties, and attitudes becomes associated with a particular set of membership criteria. Other sets of rights, duties, and attitudes are associated with kinds of persons rather than kinds of groups. When the ethnologist begins to think about a human group in this way he tries to see it as a set of relationships between socially defined persons who behave toward one another in expected ways. He applies the concept of role to bring the situation into focus. Information contributing to the discovery of these patterns comes from a wide variety of sources: observing consistencies in behavior, eliciting statements concerning how certain categories of persons ought to act toward others, attending disputes arising from unfulfilled expectations, and even examining myths and tales that recount the deeds of people standing in particular relationships to one another.

Before the ethnographer can begin systematically collecting information from any of these sources, however, he must identify the various kinds of social persons recognized by the people he is studying. In an alien culture this process of recognition proceeds rather slowly for although the ethnographer can comfortably assume that some roles will be organized around differences essentially similar to those he knows from his own culture, he must also assume that there are recognized differences that will not appear familiar to him. In all known cultures distinctive patterns of behavior are built around the sexual dichotomy and around differences in age. These differences are relatively easy to observe visually and provide a convenient starting point for the ethnographer. All known cultures also have distinctive patterns of behavior built around differences in degrees of kinship, but these differences are not so easy to observe visually. A mother's brother does not look any different than a father's brother; hence the ethnographer must rely on his knowledge of the distinctions inherent in the system of kinship terminology to tell him whether or not such a pair is regarded as one social person or two.

The ethnographer may also easily assume that there will be recognized differences in prestige or in task specialization, but recognizing these differences entails difficulties because the visual cues marking them are unknown to him initially, and because, in a society like the Gururumba, these cues are not usually elaborately developed. There are, for example, prestigeful men in Gururumba society, but their dress and style of life is almost indistinguishable from that of their less prestigeful fellows. Similarly, there is some task specialization beyond that organized around differences in sex and age, but these specialists wear no distinctive uniform nor are they so occupied with their specialty that their activity pattern stands conspicuously apart from the activity pattern of others.

In this chapter I will examine some of the roles characteristic of Gururumba society and some of the ways the ethnographer becomes aware of them.

Men and Women

The Gururumba have two words, *EvEnE* and *vEnE,* that correspond closely in meaning to our words, *man* and *woman*. They designate a pair of roles contrasting with one another in terms of sex but linked with one another through the shared characteristic of adulthood. Casual observation is sufficient to reveal some of the rights and duties defining these roles. This is most obvious with respect to duties that have a tasklike quality. Certain tasks are allocated to men, others to women; this can be discovered by watching the daily routine around the village and in the gardens. In the garden, for example, men plant and tend sugar cane, bananas, taro, and yams, while women are responsible for sweet potatoes (the staple crop) and a wide variety of green vegetables. Men break the soil in a new garden, build the fence, and dig the drainage ditches, while women prepare the initially broken soil and do almost all the weeding. In house building men perform all phases of planning and construction except the cutting and carrying of thatch, which is left to the women. Both men and women prepare food for daily consumption, but only men engineer the preparation and cooking of large amounts of food in earth ovens for festive occasions. Men kill, castrate, loan, give, and trade pigs, while women tend to their daily care and feeding. Men cut and carry wood, while women dig and carry sweet potatoes. There are some tasks that men and women alike perform, such as tending the fire or boiling food, but for the most part the work activities of the two sexes are complementary rather than parallel.

Some kinds of rights characteristic of these roles are also fairly easy to observe. Attending court cases and minor disputes makes it clear that men and women have different kinds of rights over various classes of property. Men exercise ultimate control over land and the usable products on it. For example, a woman planted a pandanus nut tree on her husband's land when she first married him and tried to claim the nuts from the tree after she divorced him. She lost the case because, although she had planted and tended the tree for many years, it was on his land. Women sometimes argue with their husbands over pandanus nuts because the wife wants to send nuts to her consanguineal relatives while the husband wants to allocate them in another way. The woman invariably loses if the issue is decided in terms of legalistic rights. In fact, there is very little property over which a woman can exercise final control except her implements, clothing, ornaments, and a few spells or charms associated with garden magic. She has rights of usufruct over land, dwellings, or patches of forest containing usable plants that are contingent upon her marriage or family affiliation, but she has no rights of alienation over any of these things for that right rests with men—either individually or in groups.

The enumeration of rights and duties could be continued, but doing so would ignore the fact that in Gururumba culture the roles $EvEnE$ and $vEnE$ are more than a bundle of rights and duties associated with limited areal activity. In some degree they pattern almost all sectors of an individual's life, and the relationship between them is one of the most important recognized by the Gururumba. For example, examination of the inventory of roles reveals that the majority of roles are appropriate to one sex or the other but not both. Almost all the recognized categories of kinsmen are appropriate to only one sex, so that the kinds of kinsman a person can be are fundamentally different for men and for women. Furthermore, the kinds of roles an individual can play beyond the kinship system are quite different for men and for women. The difference lies primarily in the fact that men can play a wider variety of roles than women. A man can become a warrior, a person of renown and influence, or a curer. Women can become none of these things nor is there a parallel set of roles to which they have access. It is clear, then, that the roles $EvEnE$ and $vEnE$ are very general roles; that being one or the other largely determines a person's total life pattern in so far as it is structured by roles.

It is in the area of ritual and supernaturalism that the importance of the relationship between these two roles is most striking. It is also the area where the ethnographer acquires knowledge slowly and, occasionally, in unexpected ways. Early in the field study it became apparent that Gururumba men were puzzled by certain aspects of the relationship between my wife and myself. Specifically, they expressed concern over the fact that night after night I slept in the same house with my wife and, indeed, in the same room. It developed that their concern was for my general health and physical well-being. The connection between these two things was not apparent to me and direct questioning on the subject elicited only vague answers to the effect that prolonged cohabitation with a woman should be avoided because it would leave one physically weak or susceptible to illness. While this information was not in itself particularly enlightening, it did set me to compiling a list of prohibitions and avoidances relating to contact between men and women in the hope that it might shed some light on the problem. I found, for example, that a woman should not touch a man's bow, a man should not accept food from the hand of a menstruating woman, a woman should not touch the drinking tube of a man while menstruating, a man should not have sexual relations the day before undertaking a difficult task, a woman should destroy all traces of menstrual blood lest a man come in contact with it, and a young man should avoid any contact with his wife-to-be until he has a fully grown beard. Failure to practice these avoidances and others like them was said to result in illness, weakness or, in some cases, death. Observation of Gururumba behavior demonstrated that these avoidances were in fact followed very closely in daily life.

Other facts discovered from time to time seemed relevant to this general pattern. On certain ceremonial occasions the men played pairs of bamboo flutes in the gardens and forests around the village. Since they believe these flutes embody the power of growth and fertility, playing them induced growth. Women do not take part in this activity and, in fact, are debarred from seeing the flutes. Moreover, women are encouraged to believe that the sound produced by the flutes is the cry of a mystic bird. However, a seeming paradox is found in a myth explaining the origin of these flutes. The myth relates that the flutes and their power were revealed to a young man by a woman who eventually changed into a small animal, thus leaving the secret of the flutes with men rather than women. In another ritual, that of male initiation, boys are made to vomit and sweat in order to remove contaminating substances from their bodies accumulated through contact with their mothers. Also, blood is made to flow from their noses, an act said to be equivalent to menstruation. These things are done in the initiation, it is said, in order to make the young boys grow and develop physically. Further, the Gururumba believe that childbirth, or anything associated with it, is dangerous to men. Thus, there is a ceremony soon after childbirth designed to indicate whether or not the father's physical strength has been impaired by the birth. There is a prohibition against a man eating any of the food prepared for the feast announcing the first pregnancy of his wife because this feast is associated with childbirth. This proscription even extends to all a man's age mates if they are not themselves fathers.

These various items of ritual and belief indicate the roles *EvEnE* and *vEnE* constitute a relationship thought to have a far-reaching and fundamental influence on human affairs. This influence appears to stem from the difference in sexual functioning between men and women, but the Gururumba see its effects in more generalized terms than are inherent in the biological distinction. Controlling the relationship between men and women is equated with controlling physical well-being and growth in the broadest terms. These roles, then, are not only connected with the organization of tasks or the definition of rights, they are also connected with ideas concerning the basic causative forces in the world. What these forces are and how they operate will be described at greater length in succeeding sections.

Leaders

In describing our arrival in the village of Miruma I mentioned that the government medical officer charged two men in authority with looking after our welfare. These were the *luluai* and *tultul*, government-appointed native officials. These roles are important, but they will not be considered at this point because they are a product of the contact situation and not a part of the aboriginal role system. Even the names of these roles, which come from Neo-Melanesian, are not native names. The role to be discussed here is designated by the term *EvEnE nambo*, "big man." It was not difficult to identify the men who play this role because they were pointed out to me almost casually during the first few weeks of the field study. At gatherings where important matters were being discussed or while walking with a group of people from one place to another someone would simply indicate one of the assembled group and say, "Luiso is a big man," or "Those two are big men." Men's houses were consistently referred to as the house of a particular individual, followed by the comment that the person in question was a "big man." In the context of group discussions the men so designated were observed to open and close discussions and to make longer, somewhat more involved speeches than other men. It seemed clear that this term designated some kind of leadership role, and therefore those men referred to in this way were observed over a long period of time in various contexts to determine the nature of the role.

In the course of daily affairs "big men" are not particularly noticeable. They tend to be in their late thirties or forties but not much older. Their dress is not distinctive except on ceremonial occasions when they appear in less resplendent costume than other men. They wear no badge of office, do not carry any symbol of authority, nor is their place of residence distinctive. The contexts in which they become noticeable are the settlement of disputes, food exchanges, certain kinds of ritual, and discussions concerning matters affecting the group as a whole. If disputes become so involved that they are seen as between lineages, villages, sibs, or phratries, the "big men" of the units concerned will attempt to arrange a meeting at which most of the members of both groups are present. They do not "conduct" these meetings in any formal sense nor do they sit as arbiters or judges. Rather, they tend to stay in the background while the disputants in the case speak to the points involved; occasionally they will step forward to emphasize a point, clarify an issue, or voice a strong stance. If the issue seems to be reaching an impasse, they frequently resort to long, rambling speeches full of historical illusions, generalities about their own or their group's past achievements, and references to the strength of their group. They are also the men who speak for the group, expressing a consensus informally derived, in instances where the forceful statement of a position rather than appeal to precedent or rule often wins an argument.

The Gururumba engage in food and wealth exchanges at various levels of complexity, but if anything more than an exchange between two individuals is involved, "big men" can be seen playing important parts in various phases of the exchange. In large exchanges, as between tribes, phratries, or sibs, they are often the ones who are instrumental in initiating and organizing the exchange, while in smaller exchanges they oversee the distribution and make set speeches on behalf of the group they represent. The part they play in rituals is much the same. They are not ritual specialists nor are they important figures in all the various types of ritual, but in certain types involving the general well-being of the lineage, village, or sib, they act as organizers and initiators. Finally, in such matters as whether or not the village should be moved, where it should be moved, or whether or not a raid should be carried out against an enemy group, the "big men" are instrumental in formulating opinion and planning action.

It seems inappropriate to describe the role of "big man" in terms of rights and duties. The role is not associated with an office or administrative position, and it is clear that a "big man" is not simply fulfilling obligations when he makes speeches or initiates rituals. Furthermore, the role is not one primarily defined in terms of its relationship to some other role, as in the case of the pair *EvEnE* and *vEnE*, indicating that its content is much more diffuse and general than in roles patterning a specific relationship. The nature of the role becomes clearer if the way people are recruited to it is considered. "Big men" are men of prestige and renown; men whose "names are known," as the Gururumba put it. The characteristics essential to becoming a prestigeful person include physical strength, demonstrated ability as a warrior, heading a lineage, oratorical skill, success in manipulating a rather complex system of economic exchange, an ability to determine and express group consensus, and a forcefulness or assertiveness of character exceeding that of most men. Men with these characteristics, and especially men who actively engage in establishing relationships outside the sib that involve them in economic exchange, gain prestige and become known as *EvEnE nambo*. The power concentrated in this role derives from their ability to attract followers outside the circle of their own immediate kinsmen and the general respect accorded them on the basis of their abilities. Related to this is the fact that the role is not peculiar to any one level of social integration. Rather, the sphere of a "big man's" influence is dependent on the degree of his prestige and it may be limited to his own lineage, his own village, or spread over several villages. It should be emphasized, however, that the sphere of one man's influence is never very large in Gururumba society because there are no institutionalized means for extending it much beyond the sib.

Curers

Certain Gururumba men are referred to as *EvEnE lusuBe*. *Lusu* denotes a body of magical techniques and practices used for curing illness, predicting the future, attracting lovers, controlling the weather, and ensuring a safe journey. Every adult knows and uses some of these techniques, but some men know especially effective ones and are thought to be more adept at their execution. Although the term *lusuBe* may be applied to a person with special skill in any of these areas, it is most frequently applied to men who cure illnesses.

Once one knows this role exists, it is not difficult to detect men performing it. Curers are always older men in their late forties or fifties. Only a small number of men in the whole upper Asaro valley are regularly asked to act in this capacity and as a result, whenever a curer is called to a village he usually stays two or three days dealing with a number of cases in addition to the one that initially brought him, since it may be some time before he returns to that area. Furthermore, if the illness is at all serious, the cure will involve a number of people in addition to the patient so that it is a highly visible performance.

In very general terms the role of curer involves discovering the cause of illness through divination plus examination of the patient's life history for clues as to potential causes, and carrying out a cure directed at the cause. Determining the nature of the illness is not nearly so important as discovering the cause because the cure is directed at counteracting the cause, which is usually a supernatural agent, rather than symptom relief. Techniques used in diagnosis and cure include divination by smoke, causing the return of body substances extracted by a sorcerer, casting pain out of the body, sucking objects out of the body that have been magically shot into it, and administering various kinds of magical poultice. These techniques are part of the role in the same sense that planting and hunting techniques are part of the male role. The interesting thing from the observer's point of view is that the cures could not possibly be brought about by the techniques themselves. Also, the incidence of actual cures is very small and many of the techniques involve fakery. Sleight-of-hand is frequently used, as when it is made to seem that a magically induced object is sucked from the body. Since a man becomes known as a curer primarily because it is believed that he is highly successful in effecting cures, the ethnographer must also attempt to discover how it is that anyone comes to be seen as successful in a role with failure built into it.

Some of the reasons are not hard to see. First, the Gururumba believe in the effectiveness of the techniques the curer uses. When he finishes working with a patient, the patient is highly disposed to believe he is cured regardless of whether or not there is any manifest change in his condition. Second, this very strong belief may make people feel somewhat better, at least temporarily, after the *lusuBe* has visited them. If malaise returns, it is not usually seen as a failure of the curer but as a new illness. Third, if the curer is confronted with a failure he may explain it as the fault of the patient for not giving him enough information to expose the "real" cause of his trouble. Finally, some of the things the curer deals with are not physical ailments and it is easy to find confirmation for the belief that the *lusuBe* has been successful if one is disposed to do so. For example, a man may feel things are going badly for him; that there is too much in his life of a negative or frustrating sort. He may come to see the untoward events of his life, both important and trivial, as a pattern resulting from malevolent influence of some kind. What the *lusuBe* does for such a person will not alter the circumstances of his life, but it can alter the person's attitude toward future events that will impinge upon him.

There are other factors at work that are not so easily seen because they involve the way a man plays this role so as to make others confident of his abilities. Not all men have the capacity to do this skillfully; consequently, few men are successful in establishing themselves as *lusuBe,* although many try. The factors indicated here are what have been called the techniques of impression management. For example, it is observable that successful *lusuBe* are very careful to reveal to others only those things about themselves tending to substantiate their claim of continued success in curing. They seldom have casual conversations with other people and if they do they limit the topics to a particular case, or long, vivid descriptions of dramatic cures they have effected in the past. They do not speak of their failures nor are they willing to talk casually about the details of their lives not directly related to curing activities. It is interesting in this connection that the well-known curers do not practice in their natal communities and tend to participate less than other men in the regular affairs of their village or kin group. It is also observable that the successful *lusuBe* tend to be selective in the cases they treat. They do not claim to be capable of handling every case and appear to avoid those cases in which the patient is in such poor condition that death seems near: the risk to their reputation is much less in refusing a patient than in failing a patient. Observing these men operate also indicates they have something like a "bedside manner" which instills confidence and trust in others. They are firm, but quietly so. They have a confidently reserved manner contrasting sharply with the flamboyantly assertive manner of "big men." They sympathize with the patient, and people typically go away from their presence expressing admiration for them. Finally, administering a cure is not simply a job done proficiently but has some of the aspects of a performance. They are not spectacles by any means, but they seem carefully staged for dramatic effect. Thus, in the cure where stolen bodily substances are made to return from the sorcerer holding them, the packet in which they eventually appear is conspicuously never touched or even approached by the curer himself. He directs the kinsmen of the patient in its construction and handling, which eliminates any suspicion that the return of the material could have been a plant and contributes to the mystery of its eventual appearance.

To what degree these things are done consciously is beside the point here. The fact is that only those men who have the capacity to manage the situation in these ways become successful curers; therefore observation of these techniques should be included in a description of the role.

Kinsmen

The Gururumba exemplify the kind of society in which many of the named relationships between people are kinship relationships. A large number of Gururumba role names are kin terms and the mere fact of an individual's birth establishes an important series of relationships for him. In Chapter II a set of kin terms was given and an attempt made to identify the dimensions discriminating among them. This section will outline the content of some kinship roles with particular emphasis on that part of the content that structures relationships within the lineage. Using the notion of role in this way helps the ethnographer see identified groups as systems with parts having different functions rather than as a collection of people expressing an identity.

The Gururumba lineage is a patrilineal descent group controlling marriage and certain kinds of property including land. It has an authority structure based partially on age and partially on position in the lineage such that the lineage head is a senior male in the oldest group of lineage siblings still active in public affairs. When the lineage head is superannuated or dies, his younger sibling assumes the headship. Or his eldest son assumes it depending on the age and capabilities of his younger sibling, or if all his siblings have retired from active public life. Looking at the kin terms in this context, we can see that a certain group of them differentiate roles based on differences in sex and seniority within the lineage.

Three pairs of seniority relationships among males within the lineage can be identified: *Ahono-gipE'nE* (father-son), *uBono-naku'nE* (elder brother-younger brother), and *wan ahono-na'Bo* (grandfather-grandson). *Ahono* designates ego's own father and his father's eldest brother, and these men call ego *gipEn'E*. The relationship of both these men to ego is similar in that they make decisions concerning whom ego will marry, what plots of land he will till, and what contributions ego will make to various tasks and events sponsored by the lineage. The relationship is not one-sided since they keep the welfare of ego in mind and contribute food, protection, and valuables to him. *UBono* designates ego's elder brother, father's younger brother, and father's elder brother's son, and these men call ego *naku'nE*. This produces a situation in which each person, even if he is himself an elder brother, has someone whom he calls *uBono* and who calls him *naku'nE*. This is important because the role of *uBono* is one of supportive responsibility toward *naku'nE*. *UBono* organizes the wealth for *naku'nE's* bride price, helps him in the preparation of his first garden, speaks for him in disputes, and contributes heavily to expensive curing ceremonies if *naku'nE* becomes seriously ill. In addition, the *uBono* who is the eldest brother of the most senior group of active siblings is lineage head. His role as lineage head is similar to that of elder brother except that he also acts in the capacity of a group representative. He receives and cares for lineage guests, makes presentations of food and valuables on behalf of the lineage, receives and distributes presentations from outside sources, and is the final authority in the allocation of lineage land. *Wan ahono* (old father) designates father's father, and his male siblings. They call ego *na'Bo* regardless of ego's sex. Life expectancy among the Gururumba is not long and it is rare that ego has personal contact with *wan ahono* beyond his childhood. If the role is activated it is characterized by feeding, friendliness, and even a certain amount of frivolity: *wan ahono* has the authority of age but exercises very little control over *na'Bo* in economic or other terms.

Thinking back to the earlier attempt to formulate the major dimensions that produce the various categories of kinship, we can see that terms that appeared to differentiate kinsmen on the basis of relative age or generation are better understood now as differentiating them on the basis of seniority within the lineage. The men called *ahono* are ego's own father and the head of ego's patrilineage; those called *uBono* are ego's elder brother and men who are immediately potential successors to lineage headship; those called *naku'nE* are ego's younger brother and men who would succeed to lineage headship only after ego; those called *gipE'nE* and *na'Bo* are ego's son and grandson plus the descendents of other lineage mates too young to consider as bearers of authority. This interpretation can be supported by pointing out that the lineage is the unit within which these terms are most consistently used, even to the exclusion of personal names. If this interpretation is accepted, the further implication is that the use of these terms to address a person outside the lineage is an extension of the term in the sense that the person so addressed does not habitually play the full role designated by the term but is being asked to enact a part of it temporarily. Thus, as noted in Chapter III, sib mates who are not also lineage mates may be addressed by these terms, and observation indicates this is usually done either as a matter of respect for advanced age or as a prelude to asking a favor of some kind. Such extended usage emphasizes the role's nurtural and helpful rather than authoritarian aspect—a point neatly exemplified when an old man will approach a young sib mate, call him father, and ask for tobacco, food, or a small favor.

Another set of roles in some respects parallels those between male members of a lineage but is not related so directly to the lineage structure. This comprises the roles of *iJEno, atEno aru'nE,* and *arunE.* The persons to whom these terms are primarily applied are ego's mother, the wives of ego's lineage mates, ego's female siblings, ego's daughters, and the daughters of ego's lineage mates. In other words, some terms applied to females are connected to the lineage both consanguineally and affinally. Furthermore, because most women leave their natal lineage at marriage, some terms refer to some women resident both in ego's lineage and in other lineages. It is therefore understandable that although these roles structure authority with reference to ego according to relative age, it is authority derived from greater age alone rather than from the combination of greater age and seniority in the lineage.

IJEno and *atEno* are persons ego can look to for protection, food, and hospitality. The content of these roles varies importantly according to the exact genealogical link between ego and alter, ego's age, and ego's sex. For the sake of simplicity and consistency in this brief discussion, a male ego will be assumed throughout. *IJEno* includes ego's own mother, mother's elder sister, father's elder sister, and the wives of senior lineage mates. When ego is an infant and young child, his own mother behaves toward him in a nurtural, protective, and supportive manner. The Gururumba do not see the role as "disciplinarian" or "trainer," and mothers seldom attempt to impose any kind of strict regimen or physical punishment on ego. From about the age of seven or eight, boys begin to associate more and more with other boys of approximately their own age. It is at this point that individuals other than ego's own mother begin playing the role of *iʃEno* in an important degree. As ego grows older, *iʃEno* becomes a term applied to several women beyond his immediate family who have approximately the same capacity to effect his life.

AtEno includes ego's own elder sister and the sisters and wives of lineage mates junior to ego. *AtEno,* especially as elder sister, is a very important figure to ego, and interesting because of the "warmth" characterizing the role. Elder sister cares for younger brother as a child, carrying him on her back, playing with him, and sharing food with him. Close emotional attachments are frequent between individuals so related, and when elder sister is sent away in marriage it frequently produces trauma for younger brother. In fact, the situation has become institutionalized in the form of a stick fight that takes place just before the girl is handed over to her husband's lineage between all the young people in a village and all the adults led by the girl's younger brother. He attempts to keep his sister from being sent away, but after vigorous effort is always defeated. The character of the relationship is also depicted in stories involving elder sister and younger brother as the main characters. These stories are quite poignant, as they are in the form of tragedies showing one of the pair vainly trying to protect the other against harm. For example, one tells of an elder sister who discovers her father has eaten her mother while the two of them were out gathering vines. She knows he will eat younger brother and herself next, so in the night she carries younger brother away, setting fire to the house as she leaves to prevent father from following by burning him to death. All seems well as she searches for a new home, but she falls into the clutches of a two-headed witch and must stand by helplessly as the witch eats younger brother finger by finger, arm by arm, and leg by leg. Her own escape is only accomplished by promising to marry a sorcerer who destroys the witch through his superior powers.

Ego's relationship to *aru'nE* and *arunE* is somewhat different. The first term refers to his own younger sister and the daughters of lineage mates junior to him, the second term to his own daughters. He is, respectively, "elder brother" and "father" to them and as such exercises control over them particularly concerning their marriage. A man's younger sister is less under his control in this respect than his own daughter and again it is interesting that tales depict a relationship of greater affective attachment between the sibling pair than between the filial pair. In tales featuring this sibling pair, for example, elder brother is frequently depicted as leading younger sister through all the ceremonies of marriage, and while he protects her from danger during this time there comes a point at which he must abandon her to the care of her spouse's lineage. At this juncture disaster overwhelms her in such forms as cannibalistic in-laws or demonic nature spirits. After marriage both *aru'nE* and *arunE* provide important links between ego and the natal members of alien villages, and they are expected to extend hospitality and food to ego should he come to the village where they are resident. There will also be women in these villages ego calls *atEno*, but since ego had no hand in arranging the marriages of these women his closes contact with the natal members of an alien village will be through *aru'nE* and *arunE*.

Each of the roles discussed has many contexts of action outside the lineage itself and a more comprehensive description would characterize the patterned actions appropriate to those contexts. By focusing on the single context of the lineage, and its authority structure, a number of roles can be compared with one another against a common background.

5

The Flow of Objects

"Give Me!" "Take!"

IN THE TWO preceding chapters we have tried to see order in Gururumba life by examining the way behavior is patterned in social groups and social roles. The human scene thus is seen as a system of parts standing in ordered relationships to one another. Beyond the question of what the parts are, this particular point of view suggests many others, such as how the parts maintain their identity and how the system achieves integration. Such highly abstract questions are major analytic rather than empirical objectives, but they are approached at the empirical or ethnographic level by observation of various aspects of the interaction between individuals playing certain roles and representing certain groups. For example, the ethnographer may observe interaction in an attempt to see how the learning of values or norms takes place, how power is wielded, or how groups maintain their boundaries. In this chapter the focus will be on a series of observations of the flow of objects between individuals and groups and an attempt to discern the social functions of this flow.

Gift Exchange in the Gururumba Setting

Cultures vary considerably in the emphasis placed on the accumulation and exchange of food, utilitarian objects, or items of value. Only a little acquaintance with the Gururumba shows they are very much concerned with these matters. A few weeks living with them convinces the outsider they are "thing-oriented," that they have an overriding concern with material objects. As recounted in Chapter I, on our arrival in the village of Miruma it became apparent that the people were not so much interested in us as in our possessions, and when their interest did turn to us it was initially because we might provide links to the "red man's" world of material goods.

Other observations tend to substantiate this impression. In the first instance, Gururumba are noticeably fond of "taking inventory." Men will fre-

61

quently sit down with their stocks of shells, feathers, decorative armbands, necklaces, and pieces of Australian money to count and fondle them. This is sometimes done as a genuine stocktaking prior to payment of a debt or making a loan, but it is also done simply for the pleasure it gives. They do not have an elaborate counting system as do other peoples in New Guinea (indeed it becomes cumbersome above ten and almost impossible above twenty), but they do keep track of numbers of items by bundling sticks together, each stick representing one item and each bundle a class of items. Next, the most frequent topic of conversation among the adult men in a village concerns the number and size of pigs, taro patches, banana plantations, sugar cane stands, and yam patches. How many piglets of each sex in a new litter, how fat a man's sow, how many pigs are owed a man, how tall his sugar cane, how numerous his bunches of bananas, how gigantic his yams, and how abundant his gardens are matters the Gururumba never tire or hearing or talking about. Men carry little sticks with them marked so as to demonstrate the thickness of fat on their sows or the length of tusk on their boars, and every man's house has a rack outside for displaying the jaws of all pigs given the members of that house for many years past.

Finally, the impression of concern with objects comes from what might be called the tenor of daily life. There is a great deal of banter between people, both young and old, centered around such small favors as giving another a bite of sweet potato, letting someone have a puff on your cigarette, giving someone a small piece of dried banana leaf in which to roll a cigarette, breaking off a section of sugar cane for another person, or lending another your digging stick or shovel. Two things impress the outsider about this behavior: its frequency and the manner in which it occurs. Sit with a small group of Gururumba for half an hour and you will hear dozens of such requests made; watch a group of children and you will see they amuse themselves by "pestering" one another for bits of rubbish or other inconsequential objects in a child's version of the adult pattern. To call these actions "requests" is a misnomer for they are made in the form of demands. Thus, when one man asks another for tobacco he will probably do so by using a verbal form best translated into English as "Give me!" If the potential giver refuses or claims he has no tobacco, the person making the demand will frequently accuse him of lying and may go so far as to search his person in an attempt to ferret out the supposedly hidden item. If the giver relinquishes the item in question, it is usually done with a shouted, "Take!" It must be emphasized that this is usual behavior not only between persons in a superordinate-subordinate relationship, but among village mates; it is the most common mode of social intercourse. This demandlike behavior is not the only mode in which things are solicited from other people. An older person may take on the demeanor of a child, or a young man that of an *EvEnE nambo* as a prelude to asking for something; the multiplicity of the forms contributes to the impression that the Gururumba are "thing-oriented."

The Gururumba might more accurately be characterized as "exchange-oriented," however, for they appear more concerned with controlling the flow of objects than with the objects themselves. There are three sets of observations barring on this statement. First, it is observable that public, formalized gift exchange occurs frequently. These occasions involve from as few as two to as many as a thousand or more people, the participants being divided into a host group and a guest group. In very general terms, one side is obligated to the other in some way, and the point of the exchange is to discharge the obligation through presentation of food and wealth objects. Exchange by barter or purchase is another type and the Gururumba themselves refer to it by a different term. Accurate records were kept on the exchange activities in the village of Miruma for a period of fifty weeks. In that period there were 110 occasions in which the forty-five or so adult males of the village were involved in exchanges of this type, averaging more than two per week.

Second, there is a noticeable elaboration and institutionalization of instances when obligation can be incurred and discharged through gift exchange. Many of these are built around points in the individual's life history and involve exchanges among ego's father's kinsmen and ego's mother's kinsmen, among people related affinely through ego, or among ego's parents and other members of the lineage and ward. Some of these occasions are birth, naming, walking, the assumption of hair ornaments by prepubescent girls, nose-piercing for boys, a boy's first productive hunt, the onset of menstruation, male initiation, the rejection of a girl's marriage offer to a boy of her choice, betrothal, the passage of a betrothed girl's first month in her new village, the planting of a betrothed girl's first garden, the presentation of first food by a wife to her husband, any pregnancy, the first crop from any new garden, the successful conduct of a trading expedition, preparation for death, and death itself.

Most of these occasions do not simply provide the basis for a single exchange between the parties concerned, but involve a whole complex of exchanges. Male initiation, for example, consists of a series of rituals and taboo periods, each marked by an exchange, occurring over a ten- to twelve-month period. In addition to exchanges of this type others are related to the pattern of reciprocity between villagers and lineage mates. People within these groups are expected to aid in a variety of tasks such as house building, carrying out an exchange, clearing land for a garden, or cutting and carrying long poles from the forest to prop up sugar cane. The Gururumba say no compensation is expected for this kind of help and that helping others ensures help for yourself when needed. However, help of this kind is always followed by an exchange in which the person receiving help feeds the helpers and presents them with small gifts such as salt or sugar cane. In other words, instances of reciprocity are made into occasions for exchange.

Finally, there are exchanges involving groups of large size such as the village, the sib, and the phratry. Some of these repay another group for helping in warfare against an enemy. Others repay a group for providing protection and shelter for a vanquished people who have been driven from their land by an enemy. Some are exchanges based on the reestablishment of peace between two groups who have seriously disputed with one another. The largest exchanges in terms of numbers of people involved and amount of goods distributed have no single reason for their occurrence but are built around the specific obligation existing between a large number of individuals. These are held at fairly regular intervals between groups on good terms with one another whenever one group considers its resources are sufficient to the task. In all these instances the main exchange is followed by a smaller exchange given by the guest group in recognition of their host's efforts.

Third, it is clear from the form that these exchanges take and the speeches made during their course that it is the activity of exchange itself that is important to the Gururumba rather than a materialistic interest in things. The exchanges vary somewhat in form, depending on the ocassion and the number of people involved, but an element common to all of them is the food and wealth display. Whatever is being presented in an exchange, no matter how large or small the amount, is always displayed prior to presentation in a symmetrically arranged pile. In a small exchange such a pile might consist of a base made by arranging bundles of cut pieces of sugar cane arranged in a hollow square, a filling for the square consisting of several layers of different kinds of sweet potatoes and yams, and on top a bunch of bananas decorated with multicolored leaves. The whole pile might only measure three or four feet along each side and be intended for half a dozen recipients. At the other extreme are displays made by erecting a large square tower some ten to fifteen feet along the sides of the base and rising twenty-five or more feet into the air. This tower provides a framework for a huge pile of food and wealth objects, such as shells or pieces of cloth, whose combined weight would be several tons. Such a display would be distributed among three to four hundred people. It takes a great deal of planning, work, and coordination of effort to erect one of these displays, even a small one, and the men who put them together are proud of their accomplishment. The displays are not simply of accumulated riches; they are displays of the capacity to be productive and energetic. This is explicitly recognized in the speeches made at the time the displays are presented. Speakers for the host group extol the strength and vitality of the group or individual acting as host, and speakers for the guest group also recognize their proficiency.

These observations all indicate that gift exchange is an elaborately developed institution among the Gururumba and functions as an important medium for the expression of social relations.

Gift Exchange and the Ordering of Daily Affairs

From the information in the preceding section it is clear that participation in exchange activities is a focal point of Gururumba life. Observation also indicates that daily affairs, especially for adult males, are importantly patterned by anticipated involvement in gift exchanges. This is true with respect to both food-producing and social activities.

Gururumba food-producing technology is such that every able-bodied adult works in the direct production of food. However, pig raising, gardening, and land management are geared to more than producing the necessities of daily subsistence. This can be most easily seen in the utilization and raising of pigs. Pigs are never killed only to provide meat for daily consumption. A gift of pork, or of a live pig, is the most important item a person can give in a food presentation, and pigs are saved for such occasions. Thus, although a pig may sometimes be killed because it has become sick or is about to die, its meat is not simply eaten by the owners; some reason is found for turning the untimely death into a food presentation. This feeling that pork is too valuable to waste on daily consumption is so strong that it effects the pattern of protein consumption. Pork is the major source of animal protein for the Gururumba, who either get only a few ounces of meat per week or get so much in a short time that they can hardly consume it. More than this, however, the manner in which a man tends his pigs clearly shows that he is not thinking of them as a food resource but as an exchange resource. The pig herds are not kept at an approximately constant size by regular slaughtering to provide a supply of meat, but vary cyclically with the demands of exchange activity. In the short run the size of a herd fluctuates with the small-scale and frequent demands associated with life-cycle events or the meeting of other interpersonal obligations. In the long run the size of a herd increases steadily through a five- to seven-year period. At that time almost all pigs will be killed for a very large exchange called the *idzi namo,* or pig festival, leaving only enough to reseed the herd. Also, there is an interesting pattern of farming out mature pigs. Each man has some pigs that other men keep for him. They receive a portion of each litter for their efforts, and the owner, who keeps the matter secret, is protected from excessive demands being made on him because the exact number of his pigs is not known. It is also a convenient way for a man to keep more pigs than his land can support.

Gardening activities follow much the same pattern. It was mentioned earlier that although both men and women work in the gardens, they tend different crops. The crops tended by the men, such as bananas, sugar cane, or taro, are raised primarily for use in exchange activities, while the crops raised by women are the staples of daily fare. The Gururumba recognize this distinction by applying different names to these two classes of food. The prestige foods, as we will refer to the crops raised by men, are occasionally eaten as part of the regular diet. This is especially true of sugar cane, which is plentiful, but except for this the eating of prestige crops is much like the eating of a sick pig—it is done to avoid waste and may itself be the impetus for a small-scale exchange. It is also observable that the planting, tending, and harvesting of prestige crops is attended by more concern and ceremony than is evident for ordinary crops. For example, sugar cane is allowed to grow fifteen to twenty feet tall, but because of its great weight and slender stalk, cane this tall would fall over unless supported by a prop. The production of these props has been elaborated into a ceremonial occasion by the Gururumba. Instead of using bamboo poles or young saplings for the props, both of which are readily available, groups of men who have promised someone they will make his props for him go into the forest and cut down large trees several feet in diameter from which they laboriously split off slabs twenty feet or more in length. These are eventually cut down to the appropriate shape, decorated, and presented as a group to the man being helped who then uses the occasion for a food presentation. It might also be noted that there is more magic associated with the growing of these crops than with others.

Land management includes two kinds of activity. One consists of the actions a man takes to utilize the land he has for his particular needs, and the other the actions he takes to safeguard or expand his claim to land. Participation in exchange affects both these kinds of activity. When a Gururumba is deciding what to plant, where and when, he keeps in mind that his gardens must supply both his daily needs and his exchange needs. As a result he has several gardens planted with everyday crops, each in a different stage of growth and he also has a series of plots, each with one or two kinds of prestige crops. The first kind of garden tends to be large and in areas with greatly differing soil conditions. The second is smaller and in areas where conditions are best for growing the particular crop to which it is devoted. It is frequently at the side or edge of a garden of the first type. A third kind of garden is much like the first in that it has a variety of crops within it, but it is smaller in size and is planted to provide for a particular anticipated exchange rather than for daily use. A man knows that his daughter's marriage, his son's initiation, or the pig festival will be coming and in preparation he may plant a garden a year or more in advance. Such a garden will be largely stripped when the event is at hand and allowed to return to fallow more quickly than usual. Given the system of crop rotation used by the Gururumba and the special needs created by the exchange system, it is incumbent on a man that he keep careful track of what state his various gardens are in so he can plan his land needs. This is especially true for prestige crops requiring special growing conditions. The Gururumba seem to have enough land to meet their basic needs, but there is not always enough land just right for taro or just right for bananas. Because of this a man must be careful that others do not usurp his claim to these special plots, and at the same time he must actively seek to establish claim to additional plots of this sort if he wishes to expand his exchange activities. Most court cases concerning land are disputes over these special plots associated most directly with exchange activity.

The manner in which concern with exchange activities structures daily affairs can also be seen in social activities on either an individual or group level. This is most evident when considering relations between individuals from different villages, sibs, or phratries, because the planning and execution of exchanges is the major basis on which individuals outside the village come together and interact. A Gururumba village is a relatively closed unit; one does not see people in it who are strangers or whose links with the village are unknown to most of its members. Furthermore, people do not simply go into a village other than their own, even if they are known there, unless they have been invited or unless they have come to discuss a particular matter: sight-seeing and casual visiting are patterns only now becoming known to the Gururumba through the changes wrought by European contact. Individuals from different villages come together in the first instance because they want to arrange, carry out, or argue about exchanges. The relationships between ego and those kinsmen living outside his own village, for example, are ordered in large part by the obligations existing between them concerning exchanges. Some of these relationships are very specific with respect to the occasions when participation in exchange activity is expected, but others are more diffuse so that it is primarily a matter of individual choice how deeply the kinsmen become involved. Thus, the kinsman called *omono* (mother's brother) is expected to be the chief mourner outside the nuclear family if ego dies while a child. On hearing of ego's death, *omono* appears in the village with a group of his own lineage mates, wails loudly, and attacks the deceased person's lineage for not watching after his sister's son more closely. He is calmed, presented with food and wealth in recognition of his grief, and in turn presents a live pig to the deceased's family as an expression of sympathy for the bereaved. This is only one of the many specific obligations that exist between *omono* and ego's kinsmen bringing them together from time to time. An example of a relationship with more diffuse exchange obligations is that between ego and his brother-in-law. Men so related have the right to ask one another for aid in arranging exchanges, particularly as this might involve loaning pigs, shells, feather pieces of Australian money, or work in preparing a garden. Some men so related become indebted to one another or freely give of their time and effort to arrange a food presentation, but others do not. Whether or not this happens is related to factors quite outside the nature of the relationship itself, such as age differences, spatial contiguity, and personal liking. The point is that if the relationship is activated at all, it will find its most meaningful expression in exchange-related activities.

Interpersonal relations outside the village are so much structured by exchange activities that the Gururumba tend to think of them primarily in terms of exchange potential. This is especially true of men who are or who are trying to become "big men." Thus, there are several young girls to whom a man applies the term "daughter." Some are his real daughters and some are classificatory daughters. A "big man" will actively become involved in arranging the marriages of these girls and will attempt to find husbands for them in a wide variety of sibs rather than marrying them all into a single sib. The reasoning behind this is that a marriage is the starting point for a whole series of kin ties between the members of the bride's sib and the groom's sib, and each of these ties is the focal point for exchange activity. By marrying daughters into several sibs, the potential number of exchanges one can engage in is increased. There are a variety of reasons for this, but one of the most important is that it creates ties with a larger number of individuals of any particular kin class and therefore avoids reduplication of exchange activity. The Gururumba also point out that if all one's daughters are married into a single sib and relations with that sib break down, the number of exchange relationships a man has will be drastically instead of minimally reduced, as they would be if his affinal ties were scattered among several sibs.

The structuring of affairs through exchange is also apparent at the group level. Participating as a unit in some kind of exchange is part of what all Gururumba social groups do. The nuclear family gardens together and lives together—at least some of the time; it also comprises a unit in one kind of exchange relationship unique to the nuclear family. This relationship exists between the family and a nature spirit. The spirit dwells in a miniature house built in one of the family's gardens, and in return for food presented by the family as a unit, it helps tend the gardens or watches after the pigs. The lineage acts as a unit in the complex of exchanges centering around first menstruation and around the harvesting of the first crop from the new garden of one of its members. The village becomes a unit in funeral ceremonies especially when an important man has died: it receives, feeds, and presents gifts to guest mourners. The sib is the main unit in the pig festival, the most complex exchange activity of all. Phratries and tribes seldom act as hosts in an exchange activity, but they occasionally appear as units in the role of guest. All the tribes in the upper Asaro valley never act together as a cohesive unit, but analytically they can be seen as a unit because any tribe within the area carries on more exchanges with tribes in the same area than with tribes outside the area.

The observations listed in this section provide a kind of documentation for the point that much of what goes on in daily affairs among the Gururumba is ordered and arranged in terms of exchange activities. In addition to noting that gift exchange is something the Gururumba do, the ethnologist can also see gift exchange as "doing something" for Gururumba society: i.e., it can be viewed analytically in terms of its social functions.

Gift Exchange and Gururumba Society

Preceding discussions of the various levels of social integration among the Gururumba have shown that social groups above the level of the patrilineage represent something more than patrilineal descent groups. The sib, for example, does not use patrilineal descent as the only principle of recruitment nor is authority within the sib structured by the descent relationships of its members. Furthermore, the relationship between lineage, ward, village, sib, phratry, and tribe does not correspond to a series of increasingly inclusive descent groups. To understand the internal integration of any one of these groups, or the integration of all of them into a single system, it is therefore necessary to go beyond descent to locate integrative mechanisms; gift exchange can be viewed as one such mechanism.

In looking for the sources of integration of the ward, for example, it is noted that a ward consists of all the lineages in a village whose initiated males are identified with a single men's house. It is true that most of the lineages in a ward claim dimly known patrilineal links with one another, but some lineages trace connection to the ward through affinal ties while others have no known kin ties or only very remote and tangential matrilineal ties. Furthermore, the members of a ward think of themselves as a group held together not so much by one kind of genealogical tie as by ties of reciprocity among themselves and allegiance to a "big man." The focal point of a ward is not an ancestral figure located in the past, but a prestigeful figure located in the present, and the sources of integration are much more in the power structure than in the kinship structure. Power, it will be remembered, comes largely from renown gained in gift exchange.

The Uphill ward in the village of Miruma can be taken as a concrete example of what is meant here. This ward consists of five resident lineages. The composition of each lineage, described in terms of married "couples" without reference to polygamous unions, is as follows:

L 1—eight married couples including three in which the females are L 1 daughters, and one couple in which the male is a collateral relative of the husband of an L 1 daughter.

L 2—eight married couples including one couple in which the male is a lineal of an L 2 wife.

L 3—eleven married couples including one couple in which the male is a lineal relative of an L 3 daughter, and four couples in which the males are collateral relatives of L 3 wives.

L 4—one couple of immigrant Gende.

L 5—one couple of immigrant Chimbu.

It can be seen that twelve of the twenty-nine couples in this ward, or 41 percent of its couples, are connected to the ward by nonpatrilineal ties. In addition, the first three lineages, which all have a core of patrilineally related males, only suppose they are related to one another and cannot actually trace clear genealogical links. At the time of the field study, the most prominent man in the Uphill ward was LuBiso, the oldest male in L 1. The integration of this ward cannot be understood without understanding his position in it.

It is usually the case that the lineage of a "big man" like LuBiso is the largest in the ward, but as the preceding tabulation indicates, this is not true of L 1 and there is evidence that a shift in the locus of power was taking place in this ward at the time of the field study. However, LuBiso was still in fact the most prominent man in the ward. He had twelve wives during his life, four of whom were still with him, and the ties established with other groups through these unions and their offspring gave him a social field in which to operate of greater extent than anyone else in the ward. He was a warrior of note and when walking from one village to another frequently took the occasion to recount stories of fights he participated in at points along the route, a convenient technique for reminding others of his past achievements. His name was well known not only in the Asaro valley but in neighboring areas as well. In fact, the families from Gende and Chimbu settled in Miruma because of admiration and personal liking for LuBiso. The next village to the north of Miruma is inhabited entirely by Chimbu who originally came into the valley as battle allies of LuBiso's sib but were so impressed with him that they decided to leave the Chimbu valley and settle near his land.

LuBiso is thought of as having the good name and welfare of the whole group in mind when he acts and as being willing to make sacrifices for the group. A striking example of this attitude toward him can be seen in a story told by several people independently concerning the introduction of a new ritual item by LuBiso. The peoples to the west of the Gururumba in the Chimbu and Wahgi valleys wear a distinctive wig made by matting human hair in a small, rigid, curtain-shaped bamboo framework which is tied to the back of the head and hung to the shoulders. These wigs are worn during the pig festival and are thought to induce fertility and growth in pigs and gardens. LuBiso is said to have deliberately set out for Chimbu when a young man to learn the making and ritual manipulation of these wigs so that men of his sib could wear them in an upcoming pig festival. This was not only to create a sensation among those observing the dance, because of its novelty, but also to contribute magically to the strength of the group. The wigs are dangerous, however, if not handled correctly and he made himself quite sick several times before learning the proper means of manipulating them. Regardless of the facts of the actual introduction of this cultural item to the Gururumba, people believe the story and use it to illustrate the qualities they admire in LuBiso. LuBiso also has the kind of personality admired in a "big man," being somewhat more forceful and assertive than most men. On several occasions he dismissed minor claims made against him for damages by his pigs or dogs simply by announcing loudly that he did not have time to consider such trivial matters. There would be reaction against LuBiso if he became truly despotic, but in relatively unimportant matters of this sort his forcefulness is taken as the sign of a strong, vigorous personality.

All these factors combine to make LuBiso the kind of man who attracts followers. His extensive social contacts are avenues other men can utilize in establishing their own exchange relationships, and the vigor of his own exchange activity assures participation in many food distributions. Attracting followers is only part of what makes LuBiso the focal point of the ward, however. Examination of his activities shows that he binds people to him economically. His economic resources are greater than anyone else's in Miruma and he uses them to support the exchange activities of others. When one man repays the support given, LuBiso uses the income to support someone else or to expand his own resources so that an even wider group can become the recipients of his help. People are tied to him by debt, by dependence on him as a source of resources and as a source of contacts. It is as if LuBiso were making an investment of material wealth through his exchange activities in which the profit was prestige rather than more material wealth. Remembering that prestige is power and that the ward's power structure is based on prestige, one can begin to understand the importance of gift exchange in holding this group together.

Rather similar factors operate to hold the village and sib together. A village has more than one ward, but the ward of the most prominent man is the focal point of the village. Similarly, one of the villages in a sib will be considered as having within it a "big man" of greater prominence than other "big men" in the sib and greater control over exchange activities will be concentrated in that village than in others. As in the ward, the power structure in the sib corresponds to the prestige structure rather than the genealogical structure. The "big men" in a sib are heads of lineages, but their authority derives from their effectiveness in exchange activities rather than from an ethic of kinship.

Furthermore, the members of a sib see their interrelationship as coparticipants in exchange activity rather than as segments of a familistic unit. Sib mates are meaningful to one another because they jointly constitute a unit that can effectively prepare for and carry out the pig festival and other kinds of large-scale exchanges demonstrating the strength and vitality of the group to outsiders. Engaging in exchange is not only a matter of discharging obligations, it is also a means of expressing some of the most important values in Gururumba culture. These values concern the ability of a man or a group to be strong, to grow abundant crops, to raise a defense against attackers, to be assertive, and to produce healthy, vital children. One seeks many obligations to discharge as a means of demonstrating these abilities; it is in the grand manner. Far from being just a kind of interesting economic game for the Gururumba, engaging in exchange is a mode of self-expression on the individual level and a means of achieving identity on the group level.

Just as exchange can be seen as relating to the integration of social units within Gururumba society, it can also be seen as relating to the integration of the total social system. Several points might be discussed here, but only one will be mentioned. Every society has some institutionalized means for distributing food and resources among its members, and such a distributive network connects certain of the segments of a society with one another. In societies like the Gururumba where there is no market economy gift exchange constitutes the distributive network, and the boundaries of the society are largely defined by the limits of exchange activity. It is interesting to note that the Gururumba do not think of trade except in the context of social relationships involving exchange obligations. That is, trading partners barter with one another, but only rarely do people barter who are not already linked to one another through gift exchange. As the Gururumba put it, if a man wants to barter for the oil-bearing pandanus nuts found in the Gende area, he must first activate an affinal tie or a distant matrilineal tie by meeting the exchange obligations implied in these links to create a "road" leading to a trade partner. Incidentally, several kinds of quasi kin ties can be established for the same purpose if no direct links exist. Thus, the distributive network not only operates through exchange activities, but the existence of relationships involving exchange establishes further ties accomplishing the flow of resources in terms other than reciprocal gift exchange.

6

Ritual and Social Structure

"Women cannot see the flutes."

T HE GURURUMBA IDENTIFY a number of entities and forces in the world that we would label supernatural and have institutionalized means for dealing with them that we would call ritual. A stranger among the Gururumba can observe the rituals and learn of the entities without much difficulty. What he learns from observation and conversation concerns the form of the rituals and their immediate aim, or the names of entities and their major attributes. This knowledge may seem superficial, comprising a set of curious and disparate items, because the Gururumba are not given to talking about them as objects of contemplation nor, therefore, the assumptions on which such matters are based or in what way they constitute a system. The ethnologist attempts to consider these questions by arranging the items of ritual and belief he collects,to reveal their relationship to other institutionalized systems, their thematic connections with one another, or the view of man and nature they imply. In this chapter, and the next two, I will describe parts of Gururumba supernaturalism and ritual in these three kinds of arrangement. The present chapter aims at arranging a series of rituals according to the social groups characteristically carrying them out so as to suggest possible relationships between ritual and social structure.

Nature Spirits and the Family

When walking with the Gururumba outside their villages or gardens, or especially through unfamiliar territory, one notices that they are quite cautious. They seldom stray from the clearly marked paths and manifest little interest in exploring the countryside. This is partly because they still retain some fear of being ambushed, partly because they want to avoid straying onto someone else's property, and partly because they fear being attacked by nature spirits. There is no generic name for these spirits, but there are two varieties of them:

72

nokondisi, which live in the upland forest zone, and *gwomai,* which inhabit the clumps of tall reeds and riverbanks of the lowlands. Aside from this difference in location there seem to be no other differences between the two kinds of spirits. Neither of them is easily seen because they are said to be like smoke or mist, meaning they are physically present but transparent. There are quite definite notions concerning their physical characteristics, however. They are male, and occur in a number of fantastic semihuman forms such as half-men, bats with human heads, or with long hair covering their bodies. They may also change from one form to another even including the fully human form. Certain physical signs are taken as indicating their presence in an area, such as a certain kind of fecal material and pieces of half-eaten food with the marks of tiny teeth on them.

By looking over all the events whose cause has been attributed to nature spirits, a summative statement can be formulated concerning their behavioral characteristics. First, they have lusty sexual appetites, but since there are no female nature spirits they satisfy themselves with human females. The birth of twins, considered abnormal by the Gururumba, is attributed to such a relationship. Second, nature spirits have proprietary interests. Each spirit has its own dwelling place—a certain clump of reeds, a particular configuration of boulders along the river, or the exposed roots of some tree. Anyone wandering into one of these sanctuaries is attacked by the spirit which may cause him illness or even death. The Gururumba do not conceive such attacks as motivated by maliciousness but only by the spirit's desire to defend its property against invasion. Third, ritual contact with a nature spirit can bring about good health and can increase a person's strength and productivity. Finally, nature spirits are motivated by ideals of reciprocity. One can enter into a relationship with a nature spirit that resembles a contractual agreement. Every adult male with a family has a small fenced enclosure called a *ropo'ne* in one of his gardens. Inside the fence is a dome-shaped hut about two feet in diameter with an entryway and a miniature earth oven in front. This is the dwelling place of a nature spirit with which a man has entered into a reciprocal agreement. The man provides the spirit with a house, food from each of the gift exchanges he initiates, and information about his gardening activities and the disposition of his pig herd. In return the spirit takes a proprietary interest in the man's gardens and pigs. It protects the gardens against theft and rides herd on the pigs when they are not under human supervision. It may even "doctor" the pigs if they are ill or receive an injury.

The ritual itself is quite simple. Small amounts of food are prepared and placed in the earth oven. Meat is always presented: if a pig has recently been killed cooked pieces of its liver and heart will be offered, otherwise, rats and mice. As water is being poured over the hot stones in the bottom of the cooking hole to produce the steam that cooks the food, all the family members gather in close and speak to the spirit. After the food is cooked it is eaten by the family except for a very small portion placed in the spirit house. There are two reasons for performing the ritual, and what is said in the speeches depends on which reason is involved. Each time a man kills one of his pigs the ritual is per-formed to compensate the spirit for having watched after that pig and to as-suage the anger of the spirit at the killing of one of "his" pigs. The ritual may also be performed to cure illness caused either by the spirit or by some unknown agent. In the former case the cure consists of placating an angry spirit which is attacking a person and making him ill for some "breach of contract," and in the latter case the cure consists of putting an ill person in physical contact with the strong, vital, qualities of the spirit in order to restore those qualities to the patient. In fact, whenever a ritual is performed at the *ropo'ne,* for whatever reason, it is thought to increase the vital energies of those involved.

Presentation of food to a nature spirit is a ritual exclusive to the nuclear family. A man and his wife, or wives, plus their unmarried children are the only ones who participate, and a man will not allow even his own brother or father into the *ropo'ne* enclosure. Furthermore, it is the only ritual in which the fam-ily acts as a unit, and in which the unity of the family is stressed. One of the interesting things about the form of this ritual is the fact that men and women perform the same actions in it: both pour water into the earth oven, both help prepare the food, and both speak with the spirit. In all other rituals they either perform different actions or do not participate in the same rite thus emphasiz-ing their complementarity and separateness. The family, it will be remembered, is residentially segregated much of the time and the task patterns of its mem-bers are sharply differentiated by the sexual division of labor. Nonetheless, the family is the basic producing unit in Gururumba society, and the ritual at the *ropo'ne* brings the family together to augment and maintain their productive capacity.

Rituals of the Lineage

There is no single ritual characteristic of the lineage as there is of the family, and some of the rituals performed by the lineage may, on occasion, be performed in a broader social context. These extensions can justifiably be viewed as special circumstances, however, in the sense that rituals come to be occasions for gift exchange. With this proviso in mind, one class of rituals is usually performed by a lineage, namely, the life-crisis rites.

Life-crisis rites occur at points in an individual's life when some signifi-cant change is thought to be taking place in his social position. Among the Gururumba there are many such points, mostly concentrated in childhood and early adulthood, some of which were noted in the last chapter in connotation with various occasions for gift exchange. Male initiation, which occurs around the time of puberty, is the only one that is not primarily a lineage ritual. There is not space here to describe all these rituals even briefly, so only the series cen-tering around birth and a few other life-crisis rites will be discussed.

Actual birth is attended by only a few older women of the village who aid the mother in delivery. No males, including the father, may enter the house during birth because it would pollute them. The infant and its mother remain in the house for at least five days. Many visitors come and go during this period of isolation because birth is an exciting and eagerly awaited event, but no male may yet enter since it is thought that the fluids of birth, which have only been recently cleared away, might cause them illness or weaken their physical powers. Food and firewood are brought by lineage mates to the mother and father, for both of them suspend all gardening and collecting activities during this period. The mother is not yet able to return to her work after the ordeal of birth and the father abstains from labor for the sake of his child. It is felt that such actions as splitting wood, chopping trees, or pounding of any kind might break the bones of the child.

On the second or third day after birth, a naming ceremony is held. This is an affair of the lineage and requires the killing of at least one pig. The pig belongs to the father, but he does not kill it himself to avoid harming his child. All those attending the naming ceremony gather outside the house where the mother and child are secluded and begin filling an earth oven. It is an easy, pleasant occasion, but there is great concern for the fragile infant inside the house. People are cautioned not to talk loudly in order that the child may not be disturbed; wood for the fire is split at a distance from the house because of the noise; the pig is muzzled when it is killed to prevent its squeals from being heard in the house. All males must be cautious in their actions as they go about the business of building fires and preparing food lest they harm the child with the forcefulness of their actions. Even such a seemingly innocuous act as dropping nuts into a dish must be done with care.

If the mother is having difficulty with lactation, this is remedied by a little ritual performed by the older men of the lineage and their wives. Each person takes a length of sugar cane and sits down in front of the seclusion house. The cane is pounded with a stick until the fibers in it are loose, then twisted and sucked until the juice runs copiously as the command "Milk come quickly, milk come plentifully" is uttered. This is the same method of extracting juice from sugar cane used by old people whose teeth are no longer strong enough to chew it, but for this ritual everyone mashes the cane with a stick regardless of how he eats it on other occasions because of the magical efficacy adhering in the abundant flow of juice that can only be produced by this method.

When the food has been cooked and a name has been decided on, the name is sent in to the mother along with a large platter of food. If the child is a girl, a miniature digging stick or net bag is placed atop the food, and if it is a boy a miniature bow or some arrows are included. These symbolize the major activities the child will engage in as an adult and are placed near the child to give it skill in these endeavors.

After the name of the child has been fixed, another ritual is performed. Part of it releases the father from various taboos and restrictions he has been subject to during the months of his wife's pregnancy and does not concern us here. The other part relates to the well-being of the new born child and involves the sibling, if any, who precedes it in birth order. The older child is made to sit down next to his father while an elderly male holds out to them large pieces of belly fat from the pig that has been killed. This portion of the pig is considered to be a great delicacy eating which solemnizes many occasions. The older child is expected to take several bites of this delicacy, and then he is rubbed with liquified pig grease and perhaps given a new ornament to wear. The Gururumba are well aware of the frustrations that can arise from sibling rivalry. They point out that an older sibling may have "bad thoughts" concerning the newly arrived addition to the family, and that these may enter the body of the newborn child to cause it illness or even death. The extra attention and place of prominence given the older sibling are aimed at forestalling the "bad thoughts" and thus protecting the infant. There is particular concern in the case where the siblings are males.

The various parts of this little series of rites can be understood as making symbolic statements about the lineage as a social unit and the place of the newborn infant in it. First, the protection given the young by the old is expressed through the concern they exhibit for the physical well-being of the child. This same concern is also expressive of the notion that the lineage as a whole, and not just the parents, are responsible for the growth and physical development of the child. Indeed, an important element in many life-crisis rituals performed by the lineage is an attempt to contribute to the growth of the individual by magical means. Second, the continuity of the lineage over time is expressed in the naming ceremony, for someone in the lineage gives the child his own name. People with the same name in a lineage call each other by a special term meaning "namesake," and a person who has given his name to a child will address the child's parents as "father of my namesake" or "mother of my namesake" rather than by their names or the appropriate kin term. A lineage, especially a large one, has a characteristic stock of names used over and over from one generation to the next. Finally, the potential threat to the unity of the lineage that the individual poses through the possibility of quarrels with a sibling is recognized, and the value of lineage unity is upheld in the face of this threat by a rite designed to reduce the possibility of such antagonism.

All the life-crisis rites manifest the same concerns, and it is significant that the performance of these rites is concentrated in the lineage, the only unit in Gururumba society having continuity over time that reproduces itself primarily from within rather than by recruitment or illiances with outside groups. The emphasis in lineage rites on the protection and growth of its human material thus becomes understandable.

The Ward and the Men's Cult

In previous chapters we have seen that the ward is partly a lineage group assuming common ancestry and partly a group of men arranged around a power figure. The ward is also the localized segment of a male secret cult organized around the ritual manipulation of sacred flutes.

Once every few years, all the boys in the ward between the ages of ten and fifteen are brought into the men's house to live. This is the beginning of an initiation ritual lasting for several months. There are many facets to this initiation, but only those relating to the flutes and induction into the male cult will be discussed here. When the boys enter the house they are neophytes. They are subject to a certain amount of teasing and must serve the older men in the house in various small ways. For example, the older men may announce that they are going to repay the boys for all the help they have given their elders in the past by working in the gardens, carrying wood and water, and the like. This is facetious because young boys are notable for their intractability when asked to assist in minor chores. Nonetheless, the men go off in a group to gather sugar cane which they bring back in bundles weighing several pounds each. When the boys are called out to receive their "compensation" and extend their arms for the cane, one bundle after another is piled on them until they collapse under the weight amid adult laughter. The boys are teased in many ways, all directed at their lack of cooperation in the past, their physical weakness, and their lack of sexual prowess. They are also lectured at various points about adult male responsibilities and are told they must begin preparing themselves physically to accept these responsibilities.

After spending a few days in the men's house the boys are brought together one night and the men remind them of times in the past when they have heard a strange sound said to be the call of a mystic bird. It is revealed to them that this sound was really made by pairs of men playing side-blown bamboo flutes. They are told they must learn to play these flutes, for doing so will make them physically, sexually, and behaviorally strong. The flutes are called *namo*, the generic term for "bird," and the boys are cautioned never to allow a woman to look upon the flutes. If a woman saw them it is said she would have to be killed. In the weeks to follow the boys will spend a great deal of time in a special enclosure deep in the forest learning to play these instruments.

The tunes the boys learn are limited in number, for each ward has a group of tunes belonging to it alone. If an adult hears flutes being played he can usually identify the ward affiliation of the players because of the distinctiveness of the tunes. The tunes have no particular story behind them, and their names refer to characteristics of the tonal or rhythmic pattern rather than to subject matter. The throbbing rhythm of a tune is most important, for it is thought to stimulate a substance in the body I will call vital essence and, thereby, growth, fertility, and strength. In addition to the initiation, the flutes are also played during various phases of two other rituals to be discussed below, called the *idzi namo* and *jaBirisi*. They are also manipulated in other ways as when they are fed, greased, decorated, hidden in garden houses, or put in association with other ritual objects to achieve their effect.

After the secret of the flutes has been revealed to them, the boys undergo a series of purification rites and observe a number of taboos whose purpose is to make them grow and become strong. The general idea behind all of them is that women can exercise a contaminating influence on men making them weak and even causing them illness. The efficacy of these rites and taboos depends, there fore, on separating the individual from all things female so he may develop without hindrance. Even after a boy becomes a man he will observe some of these taboos and occasionally purify himself in order to maintain the strength and other capacities the Gururumba deem necessary to function as an adult. The fact that men live separately from women much of the time is a further applica tion of this idea.

The rituals of the men's cult embody two important principles: females can have a contaminating influence on males, and males can exercise ritual con trol over growth. The ward is the center of ritual activity relating to these prin ciples, and whatever political, economic, or genealogical ties bind the members of the ward together are supplemented by common participation in the male cult. It should be noted in this context that the boys initiated together form a group of age mates, and individuals will call each other by a special term desig nating this relationship in preference to using a kin term obtaining between them.

The Sib and the Pig Festival

The pig festival is called *idzi namo* or "pig flute," and is a large-scale gift exchange occurring on the sib level at intervals of five or more years. In the festival a sib acts as host to one or more sibs belonging to neighboring tribes plus guests from distantly removed tribes. The main item in the exchange is pork, and the ceremony involves killing and cooking hundreds of pigs. The exchange is economically complex because it is structured in terms of both group and individual commitments. It is also politically complex because the fulfill ment of these commitments in a grandiose, spectacular manner is an avenue to renown, and renown is one of the principles governing political action. Renown devolves on the organizers of the festival through its assertive display of strength in the piling up of vast amounts of food, vigorous discharge of obligations, and impressive pageantry. Finally, in addition to culminating a growth cycle by the killing of almost the total pig population and the depletion of gardens, it also starts a new growth cycle. Its ritual aspects can be seen as referring to both. In order to illustrate this, the use of flutes and gerua boards in the pig festival will be examined.

The *namo* flutes are blown and paraded during the preparations for the pig festival in ways that announce the achievement and strength of their own ers. Their music signifies that the elusive processes involved in achieving growth, as evidenced in accumulated food and wealth, have been mastered. They are first sounded after the decision has been made to hold the festival, a second time when formal invitations are presented to guest groups, and a third time in the village of each man who accepts an invitation.

The flutes are also manipulated in certain ways to ensure that the vital power they control will continue to operate and produce another cycle of growth.

Thus, the flutes are wrapped in a leaf representing pigs so that when the flutes are played, real pigs will be stimulated to copulate and thus reproduce themselves. From time to time the flutes are also "fed" by placing bits of food in them in order that their power will not diminish. Finally, the flutes are placed in association with a wooden pole erected in a house on the ceremonial ground containing dance paraphernalia and other festival objects. This pole take on the power inherent in the flutes and the power acquired by the other objects through association with the pig festival. After the festival is over the pole is buried at some propitious spot in the sib territory so that its stored potency can regenerate the strength of sib members dissipated in the festival.

Another phase of the pig festival involves the display of *iNgErEBe*, or gerua boards, as they are usually called in the literature. These are wooden planks varying in size from a few inches to several feet in height painted with polychrome geometrical designs. One class is anthropomorphic in shape, but they usually are rectangular, square, round, or crescent-shaped. They are made ostensibly to honor the ghosts of the long dead, or ancestors, but their designs symbolize growth and the products of human endeavor.

The boards are worn or carried around the dance ground prior to the killing of the pigs. Amid the hundreds of people gathered for the occasion, the large numbers of pigs, the great piles of food, the boards move about on the shining bodies of children and youths laden with wealth in the form of feathers and shells. This juxtaposition of the boards and the accumulated wealth of the group is a tacit recognition of the dependence between the ancestors and their progeny. "The ancestors see the *iNgErEBe* and they know we have not forgotten them. They look and their bellies are good." There are special gerua dances done in imitation of the ancestors feverishly going about the work of raising pigs and gardens. Young children wearing gerua are allowed to "kill" a pig symbolically for the ancestors by striking it on the head with a red flowered bush which is a vegetable substitute for gerua board itself. Honoring the ancestors in this way ensures their continued contribution to the growth and vitality of the sib.

The designs on the boards symbolize prosperity and well-being, growth and vitality—qualities manifest in the pig festival itself. The markings on the boards represent things associated with wealth, display activities, and food. One design, called *girifoi,* represents the long strands of grass used to make brilliant bustles worn at dances where large amounts of food are given away. *Mondo numbuno* depicts the wooden cask for steaming food, food that nourishes both one's family and one's pigs. Another is *idzi oku'ne,* "pig skin," representing the marks made on a cooked, dressed pig before it is cut up into parts for distribution.

When the display is over, the boards are placed among the branches or trees in the gerua enclosure, a fenced area near the dance ground used in the pig festival. At times of crisis the boards may be removed and cleaned to stave off the harmful decaying forces manifest in sickness, death, and misfortune that periodically attack the sib.

The sib is the largest unit in Gururumba society acting as a unit in ex
change affairs. The use of flutes and gerua boards in the pig festival is clearl*
aimed at maintaining the ability of the sib to engage successfully in exchang*
and, one might add, at maintaining a position of prominence in the wider scheme
of intergroup relations.

The Phratry and the *jaBirisi* Ceremony

JaBirisi is a ritual centering around the ancestors performed by the phratry
just prior to the pig festival or at times when it is judged that the phratry as *
whole is experiencing difficulties. These difficulties include epidemics in the pig
population; widespread illness among the people; difficulties with garden crops
and the general feeling that children are not growing rapidly enough. A factor
in judging the seriousness of a crisis is the condition of the wooden structure
around which the ceremony takes place. It is a circular fence fifteen to twenty
feet in diameter and made of long, irregularly shaped posts. If this structure is
dilapidated it is taken as a sign that the rite, which includes rebuilding and
cleaning the structure, should be performed.

The rite begins with men going into the forest for several days to hunt
for various small animals and birds. While the men are gone from the villages
taboos are placed on those remaining behind against doing "things the ancestors
did not do." It is believed that in the time of the ancestors, man lived in a
much simpler technological and social state than he does now so that there are
taboos against making new fire or working in the gardens because the ancestors
did not know how to do these things. When the men return from the forest,
the animals they have collected are allowed to decompose partially and then are
eaten in a village feast where the unsavory food is gobbled up in what the
Gururumba consider to be a crude and disgusting fashion.

After this the taboos are lifted and the older men from various villages
of the phratry gather at the *jaBirisi* structure to repair and clean it. When this
is finished, pigs, which have been washed and decorated, are brought from all
the villages of the phratry and killed at the structure, then cooked in earth ovens
dug around its perimeter. All the food is then exchanged, each village giving
some food to every other village. None of the food is sent outside the phratry
as is usually done when large amounts of food are involved. As water is poured
into the earth ovens, speeches are made calling on the ancestors to make things
grow and flourish as they did in times past.

Both the structure and the rite are called *jaBirisi,* a term referring to
plants characteristic of the forest as opposed to plants of the low-lands. Leaves
of such plants are symbols of growth and fecundity and are used to induce these
qualities in several kinds of rituals. Some of the *jaBirisi* structures are said to
have stones buried in them. These stones, called ancestors, are thought to have
been brought to their present location from the homeland of the phratry further down in the Asaro valley. The stones have a dual symbolism for they not

nly connect the present with the past, but they are in themselves symbols of ermanence and indestructibility: they are used in the lightning exorcism rit-al with expressly this meaning.

In addition to directly involving the ancestors and using symbols of rowth and permanence, the rite also uses ritual drama to gain efficacy. This s done in two ways: First, the whole series of events is an enactment of the ef-ect hoped for. It begins with the members of separate villages eating the rot-ing flesh of animals laboriously collected in the forest and ends with the con-umption of well-larded pork freely exchanged among the members of a tribe. Connecting the ends of the rite is a renewal ceremony in which the decompos-ng fence housing the symbols of indestructibility is refurbished. Second, there s an attempt to achieve the aims of the ritual by symbolically participating in he course of human development, which the Gururumba see in terms of gen-ral improvement. Thus, the rite begins by imposing taboos that in effect re-urn the community to its original unsophisticated state. The ritual as drama epicts the human group without the means of making fire, depending for sub-istence on hunting small animals, and in general acting like primal men by obbling half-rotten food. It ends with a bountiful spread of food, properly aised and cooked according to current methods. As one informant put it, "The nen of long ago had nothing. They were like dogs. If we do as they did, we will ncrease as they did."

The phratry derives much of its identity from a sense of continuity with he past. This is not the recently known and experienced past, but the distant ast of myth and the ancestors. When illness or misfortune strike the phratry nd threaten its future, its link with the past, in the form of the ancestors, be-omes a source of strength.

Groups and Rituals

Arranging a series of rituals according to the social level on which they ccur is a device the ethnologist employs in understanding and explaining the ituals he observes in their relationship to social structure. The fact that each evel of social grouping in Gururumba society has a ritual, or class of rituals, distinctive to it suggests to him the possibility of such an understanding. Fur-hermore, the symbolism of the rituals, and the aims they profess, manifest an 'appropriateness" to the social level on which they occur. It is therefore under-tandable that the family has no ritual relations with the ancestors because the ncestors are seen as remote, distant figures and the family has no great genea-ogical depth. Beyond this, the juxtaposition of ritual forms and social forms llows the ethnologist to examine various ways the rituals may serve to stress alues and ideals common to the group, or the way they bring the members of he group together in an activity of single, common purpose stressing their unity gainst factors that tend to divide them.

7

A Theme in Supernaturalism

"The Woman Showed Him the Flutes."

IN THE PRECEDING Chapter a set of rituals was arranged in such a way as to reveal relationships with social structure. In this chapter a set of rituals, beliefs, and taboos will be arranged so as to reveal their thematic interrelationships. Here I attempt to come closer to the meaning they have for the Gururumba.

The Concern with Growth and Strength

Just as it did not take long to formulate an impression that the Gururumba were "thing-oriented," so an impression of their great concern with growth and strength was formulated early in the field study. The Gururumba are horticulturalists and the growing of food is much on their minds. Casual conversation frequently turns around the state of one's garden or the health of one's pigs. Many of the songs they sing concern growth. These songs consist of very short stanzas, often simply one line, sung over and over in a variety of rhythmic and tonal patterns. Thus, the words of one song are, "The taro, its leaf unfolds." Another is, "Mothers, cut sweet potato vines, cut them!", and a third consists of "The bamboo shoot is growing." Similarly, some of the more elaborate string figures[1] depict plants or animals passing through phases in their growth cycle. A concern with physical strength is also manifest in everyday life, since a strong body is necessary for carrying out the tasks associated with gardening, hunting, and defending the group. It is a characteristic highly admired in both men and women, amounting to one of the major standards of beauty.

Concern with growth and strength is also evident in a number of small-scale rituals. For example, both men and women will rub themselves liberally

[1] These figures are made by manipulating string with the fingers to form patterns or designs recognizable as objects or animals. This "game" is very widely distributed throughout the world.

82

with stinging nettles or eat fresh ginger to stimulate strength before undertaking a difficult task. Men induce vomiting in themselves and bleed their noses for the same reason (these acts will be discussed more fully below). A man will spit into his son's mouth to make him grow rapidly, and a mother will put garlands of sweet potato vines around her daughter's head for the same purpose. Several kinds of rituals performed in connection with gardening manifest this concern, and a few examples will be presented to indicate their form.

First there are spells, in the form of commands, said over plants or over tools used in planting. They are quite simple, differing little from one another, but their secrets are jealously guarded. Some of these spells are "I am planting, I am planting!", "Grow taro, grow!", "You are the real climbing bean!", and "Sprout, sprout, out, out!." A few spells collected were said over the digging stick while it is being made. Except in one case where the spell was to prevent the maker of the digging stick from cutting himself while whittling the point of the tool—an event bringing misfortune to the garden—all were aimed at making the digging stick work quickly and efficiently.

Second, certain kinds of leaves and wood are placed in the ground to protect growing plants from insect pests or plant diseases and make plants mature rapidly. For example, a favorite method is to place a piece of dried betel nut shell in the earth piled up around each hillock of sweet potatoes. The Gururumba do not themselves chew betel as a rule, but their neighbors, the KErEmu, do, and it is from them that the nut husks are obtained. The Gururumba are aware of the slightly stimulating effect produced by chewing betel, and it is this quality that is drawn upon in planting the betel nut shells with sweet potatoes. Or, there is a kind of hardwood having a faintly unpleasant odor when freshly cut, large chunks of which are buried in the earth around the edges of a garden to keep the garden clear of insect pests: it is thought that the odor of the wood will keep them away. One might also include here the magic bundles tied to fence posts surrounding a garden for protection against thieves and marauding pigs. One such bundle consists of sweet-smelling grass twisted together into a short rope. Commands are "blown" into the grass where they are "held" by the odor. The commands, to bite and paralyze anyone coming over the fence who has no business in the garden, are thought to act of their own volition.

Finally are rituals performed after a garden has been planted to ensure its longevity. Stones are used for this purpose, drawing on their qualities of indestructibility and permanence as in the *jaBirisi* ritual. One method is to broadcast small stones around the garden while another is to bury a large stone near the center of the garden. In either case the object is to seed the garden with the quality of indestructibility and permanence.

The most complex ritual to promote the growth of plants is that for pandanus nuts. All the rites alluded to thus far can be performed by a single person, but the pandanus nut fertility ritual is performed by groups varying in size from the family to the sib. Furthermore, it does not have a series of variants which can be owned by individuals. Pandanus nuts are highly prized by the Gururumba, and during the nut-bearing season they largely abandon the nor-

mal routine of life in their lowland villages to move into the midmountain fo:
est where the pandanus groves are located. These nuts are the Gururumba's on!
food resource that can be stored for long periods of time after harvesting. Som
nuts are kept for three or four years after drying, and these are the most highl
prized of all. The Gururumba do not fully understand the pattern of nut-bea.
ing pecu'iar to the pandanus. They observe that in a particular grove in a pai
ticular season, some trees bear a nut head and others do not. Circumstances ma
be such that almost all the trees in a grove bear nuts or almost none bear then
They have noted this also. In an attempt to control this erratic growth patter!
they perform *mohin-gururu* in order to ensure that the trees that did not bea
nuts in the current season will bear them in the next.

Part of the pandanus ritual consists of preparing food in an earth ove
in honor of the ghosts of the recently dead. While the water is being poure
in, speeches are delivered to the ghosts entreating them to "get inside" the ba!
ren trees and make them grow next season. The rest of the rite consists in builc
ing a kind of box on the ground near a pandanus grove and filling it with nu
husks plus several kinds of leaves in an effort to stimulate the next season
growth. Two of these leaves are hot and peppery to the taste. They are "vita!
izers" acting on the trees in much the same way that rubbing stinging nettle
act on a person. Another of the leaves is thought to be particularly effective i
attracting and holding the ghosts of the recently dead, while a fourth has
pungent odor capable of "capturing" commands spoken into it. The command:
which direct the trees to grow, are thus kept near the grove and work of thei
own efficacy on the trees. Other kinds of leaves added to the pile come fror
plants characteristic of the high forest. The forest is regarded as a fertile place
these leaves, imbued with its quality, become symbols of fertility. Moreover, i
the context of the ritual they are thought to induce fertility.

Many other rituals aimed at inducing growth and strength can be recalle
here from previous chapters. The playing of the flutes makes boys grow int
men and causes pigs to reproduce. Gerua boards are cleaned in order to counter
act forces that impede growth. The wooden pole put in contact with the para
phernalia of the pig festival stimulates strength in the sib. One aim of th
jaBirisi is to restart the growth cycle brought to an end by the pig festival.

Growth and Strength: Productivity and Assertiveness

A concern with growth and strength is manifested directly and simpl
in rituals like those involved in garden magic, but familiarity with larger, mor
complex rituals, such as the pig festival or male initiation, reveals growth an.
strength to be imbedded in a broader, more inclusive context. Thus, while it i
true that the Gururumba are, in many instances, simply concerned that thei
gardens, pigs, and children should grow as a matter of survival, it is also tru
that achieving growth and showing strength have come to be values in thei

own right. The ability of an individual or group to be productive and assertive are among the most general values in Gururumba culture, and to produce
food, to grow children, and pigs, to protect the group, to seek out and discharge
obligations vigorously, is to demonstrate the presence of that ability. The rituals
of growth and strength, then, are not only of importance to the Gururumba because they add to their technical mastery of the physical world, but because they
relate to the mastery of affairs in the social world as well.

This statement about the meaning of rituals dealing with growth and
strength is an ethnological construction. The Gururumba do not speak so directly and analytically about their own culture, but they do provide the clues
recommending its plausibility. Some of these clues come from the simple
straightforward acts of garden magic itself. Growing gardens in the upper
Asaro valley is not particularly hazardous. In general there is a great deal of cer-
tainty that when a crop is planted most of it will survive and flourish. However, certain factors introduce an element of uncertainty into the situation.
When the crops of one garden plot are becoming depleted while the crops of
another are not yet mature, people may be short of food or have little variety
in their diet. A pig may break into a garden and do a surprising amount of damage in a short time. There is a slight but persistent problem with insect pests,
plant diseases, and theft. Thus, although the Gururumba do not live in an environment hostile to their horticultural practices, these are areas where magic
plays its role alongside technology. One other problem connected with gardening is dealt with by magic. People take pride in having a neat, abundantly productive garden. Moreover, to have such a garden is a sign that a man has the
capacities for coping with life as the Gururumba understand it, and a man can
gain or lose prestige according to the condition of his gardens. If a man's garden is near a main trail so that passers-by can easily see its quality, he may take
ritual precautions to ensure its quality for this reason alone.

Other clues are to be found in the pig festival. Recall the meaning that
the sounding of the flutes has in terms of announcing the strength and vitality
of the sib. In speaking of this, one informant said, "The pig festival is no
small matter, it is something of importance. The first time we sound the flutes,
everyone hears us. When they hear it, they really know what we are like. They
know we have watched after our pigs, our gardens, and have been active in trading. They know we are strong and wonder at us." The very form of the pig festival is calculated to have the same effect. The pigs to be given away are displayed in long rows after they have been cooked, and the length of these rows
will be remembered for years by the guests who use it as an index of group's
strength. The other food and wealth objects are piled in massive displays for
all to see, not simply brought forward at the moment of distribution. Sometimes
an attempt is made to hold male initiation throughout the sib at the same time
as the pig festival so that the newly initiated youths can be paraded before the
guests as a show of the future strength of the group. Songs are sung by groups
of dancing men, amounting to a public demonstration of the vital quality neces-

sary for growing crops and pigs. The songs deal with growing food plants and exchange, and the dance consists of a mass of men who run in place for two or three hours without stopping. The pig festival is more than an exchange: it is a display of the fundamentally important capacity to be productive and assertive.

Productivity, Assertiveness, and Sexual Energy

Productivity and assertiveness are not simply personality traits for the Gururumba; they are behavioral characteristics stemming from a vital essence in the body which they call *gwondefoJe*. In the broadest sense, this vital essence is the animating principle of the body, for death is the result of permanently losing it. Similarly, life is produced by combining substances that contain it. These two substances are semen and womb-blood, and they contain vital essence in slightly different forms: womb-blood in the form of amorphous life-principle, and semen in the form of vital material substance. Conception occurs when womb-blood is made solid and held in the body by semen, but menstruation occurs when it is not "solidified." In fact, menstrual blood becomes the antithesis of vital essence because it is regarded as dead womb-blood.

Vital essence is "hot," and as it courses through the body it causes affective states such as fear, anger, and sexual arousal. It also produces the physical strength of the body which allows men to grow food and protect the group, the behavioral assertiveness necessary for managing human affairs, and the capacity to reproduce the race.

In a very important sense, vital essence is identified with sexual energy. This can be seen by examining a list of bodily substances thought to contain it as opposed to those which do not. It is in semen and womb-blood, the two substances involved in conception, but is not in menstrual blood or in other genital secretions such as urine. It is in spittle and mother's milk. The viscous nature of the former is compared to semen by some informants, and the latter is a fluid only generated by the body in connection with childbearing. It is also in pubic hair and the beard hair of adult males, but not in other body hair. A full-grown beard is the sign of sexual maturity in males.

The connection between vital essence as the source of productivity and assertiveness and its identification with sexual energy is neatly exemplified by the fact that men are very much concerned about loss of semen and about being contaminated by menstrual blood. Semen loss occurs through excessive sexual activity or through having it stolen and transported to a sorcerer. Such a loss is of concern not only because it may eventuate in the loss of physical strength, manifested in general lassitude or illness, but also because it may impair one's ability to be assertive, as manifested by a decline in personal fortune. Thus, a man believes himself to be sorcerized not simply because he is ill—he believes it because his pigs are not growing, his wife has left him, and he finds he cannot meet exchange demands being made on him. The ultimate reason for all this is that he has lost semen, which means he has lost vital essence. Similarly, menstrual blood is contaminating because it is antithetical to vital essence, and women must be very careful to dispose of it lest a man, or a pig, come in contact with it. Such contact would produce illness, but the Gururumba do not see this as an attack on their bodies so much as on their capacity to function as human beings.

These connections can also be seen in the symbolism and ritual surrounding first menstruation. A relatively full account of this event will follow to demonstrate the connections. When a girl first menstruates she tells her mother, who calls the news out to the girl's father. It quickly becomes a matter of public knowledge, and it is important that it be so, for no male may enter the house where the girl must stay during the course of this first menstruation.

During the days the girl is secluded in the house, she is under certain restrictions. She must not go outside except at night, and then only briefly, because she is considered to be so dangerous that any male seeing her would become ill. Similarly, she must not touch herself or eat with her fingers because she can be dangerous even to herself. She is made to sit on a layer of leaves and moss so that the blood can be collected and carefully disposed of lest it come in contact with a male or a pig and cause illness. She must not drink water since it might "cool" the "hot" sexuality developing within her and rob her of procreative abilities.

During this time she is constantly attended and made aware of how carefully she must act in the future to guard the community against the contaminating influence of succeeding menstruations. She hears tales of misfortune befalling men and pigs because some woman did not properly dispose of her menstrual blood. She learns that she must never step over food because she may contaminate it, nor may she straddle a stream or hand food directly to anyone for the same reason. A day or two before it is expected she will emerge from seclusion to ensure the potency of her reproductive powers, her father prepares a ritual meal consisting of beetle grubs, roasted and sprayed with masticated *gimbi* (tree bark) and *gafu' gifiri* (a nut). Ingestion of the grubs and the tree bark ensures the growth of many children, and the nut, which has a peppery taste, is a vitalizer making her active after her confinement.

Soon after this the girl emerges from the house and a final rite is performed. As part of the preparation for this rite the path leading from the seclusion house to a nearby earth oven is thickly covered with leaves of several kinds: *afagule, akumaku, gwonumbu' gini,* and *morEnge.* The first three are species of *Cordyline* (tanket), and the last a variety of *Setaria palmiforlia* (edible pitpit). Tanket leaves are used in several ritual contexts as symbols of growth and productivity. This derives in part from their remarkable ability to take root from even apparently dry pieces of stalk, and in part from their association with gardens where they are used as boundary markers. *Afagule* with its red midrib and *akumaku* with its red edges are said to represent menstrual blood, but in this ritual they emphasize the positive rather than the negative side of menstruation.

Menstrual blood is itself dangerous, but menstruation is the sign that reproduc
tion is possible, that the vital energy that produces children and gardens exists.
Gwonombu' gini are such a deep shade of green as to appear black, and thus
representing pigs whose skins are black. *MorEnge* has a firm but pliable stalk
and is used to prepare a girl's vagina for sexual intercourse by repeated manipu
lations that enlarge the vaginal opening and break the hymen.

When the leafy path has been completed, and other things are in readiness, the girl is brought out of the house. Two men, each carrying one end of
a long piece of sugar cane approach the door of the house. They split the cane
for most of its length leaving only the ends intact. The ends are then pushed
together so that the two halves of the cane bulge apart forming a hoop. The
split cane is held in front of the door, and a third man crawls into the house.
Taking the girl by the hand he leads her out and through the hoop making sure
her body comes in contact with the juicy cane. This act is compared to the emergence of a butterfly from its cocoon, and it is also said that the sweet juices of
the cane will attract suitors from a great distance. The girl stands on the leaf-
strewn path holding the hands of her guardian and of her father's brother while
listening to a speech concerning marriage; then she is led down the path to
become the center of attraction at a food exchange.

These rites at once celebrate the onset of reproductive powers in a girl,
magically assist in its development, and symbolize the several modes of its expression in everyday life. The celebrative aspect is evident in the seclusion period as well as in the terminal feast. During seclusion the girl becomes the object of much attention as old women, age mates, and prepubescent girls gather
to give advice, instruction, or just to stare. The focus of their conversation is on
the new potency within her and how it is to be handled. The terminal feast is
in part a public announcement that a girl has reached sexual maturity and is now
capable of assuming adult status through marriage, and in part a celebration of
achievement by the community that grew her. The new power she has is not
simply left to its own course of development and expression, however: It has
to be made prolific by feeding the girl the bark of a coniferous tree notable for
its abundant display of seed cones; it has to be turned to developmental growth
by feeding her grubs notable for their ability to change from amorphous pupae
to intricate insects; its negative expression in menstruation has to be limited by
imposing taboos. Finally, the symbolism stresses the dual meaning of this power
in the narrow sense of sexuality and the wider sense of productivity. The seclusion period is a time for the open discussion of intercourse outside the circle
of a girl's age mates. Older women encourage her to prepare her vagina for it
and men spread *morEnge* on the path she trods after seclusion. There are, in
addition to the sugar cane hoop, several other magical devices to make the girl
attractive to males. But the path she trods also contains leaves symbolizing
growth, gardening, and pigs. These are the productive concerns to which she
must turn her vital energies in adult life. She observes similar restrictions in subsequent menstrual periods so that the health and well-being of the community
can be preserved.

Male and Female Sexuality

The rather puzzling notion that women can contaminate men has been mentioned several times in the preceding sections, and it may have occurred to the reader that this indicates a kind of institutionalized antagonism between the sexes. It would be a mistake to see the symbolism of the rituals we have been discussing in this light, however. Male–female represent complementary not antagonistic forces for the Gururumba, and the rituals deal with differing kinds of control over them rather than with their opposition. This can be seen by describing more fully the rituals of male initiation and comparing them with those just described concerning first menstruation.

After the secret of the flutes has been revealed to the boys, a second phase of male initiation occurs. In it the boys are introduced to further ritual techniques contributing to their growth and vitality by ridding their bodies of contaminating substances. Men have two such contaminating substances in their bodies: menstrual blood, which males inadvertently ingest while in their mother's womb, and the remnants of food given them by women in the period prior to moving into the men's house. This blood, which is contaminating because it is dead, is purged by bleeding the nose. This is accomplished by pushing small bundles of sharp-edged grass in and out the nostrils. The resultant bloody flow is said to be equivalent to menstruation, and informants explicitly refer to the act as "our (male) menstruation." Food, contaminating because it may have been touched by a menstruating woman, is purged by vomiting. This is induced by placing a piece of bent cane in the mouth, forcing it down the throat into the stomach, then working it up and down until vomiting occurs. The first time the cane is swallowed it is also said to break a tissue somewhere inside the body. The Gururumba consider that this tissue must be pierced before the penis will grow properly or semen will form. In later life males employ both these techniques to purify themselves after possible contamination or to strengthen themselves before undertaking difficult tasks.

There is a final phase of male initiation in which food taboos, behavioral restrictions, and a strict life regimen are imposed on the boys. Some of these last for about a year, some until marriage is consummated, and some until they are old men. During this final phase they cannot accept any food from the hand of a woman, any food grown by women, or any food distributed at ceremonies connected with pregnancy and birth. They should generally avoid contact with women; if one of the group of boys initiated together is betrothed during this period, they all must carefully avoid the bride-to-be as well as the betrothed boy. These restrictions last for about a year, except the one against accepting food at pregnancy or birth ceremonies, which lasts until the boy himself becomes a husband. They must also refrain from eating lizards, snakes, frogs, and salamanders for these creatures are said to feed on menstrual blood, a taboo that continues until old age. During the ensuing months the boys lead a Spartan life; each morning they purify themselves by vomiting in a nearby stream; they bathe in cold water; their noses are bled frequently and their bodies rubbed with stinging nettles; their diet is restricted to bananas, sugar cane, and greens from the forest (male food). Boys say of this time, "We eat nothing but the vomiting cane." All these things are done to make their bodies grow strong and vital. They also spend long hours practicing on the flutes in a specially built structure deep in the forest.

Male and female initiation are similar in that they both are importantly concerned with the sexual potency and growth of the body, but they differ in the way this concern is manifested. Female initiation celebrates the fact of growth and the onset of reproductive power and deals symbolically with the latter's nonsexual aspects. Control of this power is not a problem except as it may adversely effect others. In male initiation the principal aim is to induce growth and reproductive power, not celebrate its existence. Controls are for the good of the initiate rather than the good of others. The Gururumba point out that newly initiated boys are not equivalent to girls who have recently menstruated because the boys are not yet strong enough to cope with the vital sexuality of these girls. To have contact with them for sexuality, even in such an innocuous form as a pregnancy feast, would stop the boys' growth and impair the development of their own vital essence. Until they have developed a full growth of beard they must continue to strengthen themselves through ritual or protect themselves through avoidances; even after that they must continually guard against the contaminating and weakening influences of sexual activity. In initiation, then, males assume a ritual control over the same vital power that females assume a natural control over when they menstruate for the first time.

From all this material we can conclude that for the Gururumba there is a kind of fundamental disparity between the sexes because women are naturally endowed with reproductive capacity, which is the working of the vital essence in them. This disparity is overcome in the rituals of the male secret cult aimed at generating and maintaining the productive capacity, which is the working of the vital essence in man. In effect, men reproduce symbolically all the important elements given naturally to women: the flutes are reproductive power, nose bleeding is menstruation, and breaking the tissue during the first vomiting is breaking the hymen. It is interesting in this connection that the myth told in explanation of the origin of the flutes specifies that it was a woman who revealed their secrets to men.

This myth tells of a young boy forced by an old woman to accompany the men into the forest to collect animals for a *jaBirisi*. The boy, who is really too small for such a task, gathers up a ragged net bag, a small bow, a few reed arrows, and sets out for the forest. Deep in the woods he meets a woman. She recognizes his pitiable situation, throws away his inefficient implements, and invites him to come to her house. There she lives alone surrounded by a magnificent garden including all the plants traditionally grown by men. After giving him gifts, she shows him how to make traps and place them along animal trails. That night, while the boy sleeps, the woman fills the traps with animals she has caught herself, and repeats this on the second night. In succeeding days the two prepare other foods to be used in the *jaBirisi* including pigs which the woman pulls up out of the ground. On the day before returning to the village, she teaches him to play the flutes, and when they play together he is transformed into a young man. On their way to the village the woman tells the young man to make her a knife for peeling sweet potatoes, but cautions him to make it of dried rather than green bamboo. The young man forgets this interdiction, and the woman cuts her finger while using the knife. When the blood flows she disappears. The young man follows the bloody trail back into the forest because he plans to marry the woman, but finds she has turned into a tree kangaroo and will not change back because he disobeyed her command. He thus loses a wife but gains the flutes.

This myth is not only interesting because it identifies a woman as the original source of the flutes, which supports the notion that male rituals are the equivalent of natural female endowments, but also because of the kind of being she is. She is a total human: her knowledge of trapping, her tending of male plants, and her possession of the flutes are all male attributes, and yet she is female. It is also noteworthy that she is not an ogre or dangerous being, but is generally nurturant. These features can be taken as a symbolic statement concerning the fundamental complementarity of the sexes in achieving life-sustaining goals.

One more fact can be introduced at this point illustrating the complementarity of the sexes and the identification of vital essence with sexual energy. All the rituals and taboos relating to male control over female reproductive power and the possibility of female contamination do not obtain throughout life but only during the reproductive years. This is the only period when the natural potency of females may hold some danger for males. Thus we find that old men can once more eat frogs, lizards and snakes, and we also find that old women are sometimes made guardians of the flutes. It is careful control over reproductive power, the well-spring of human energy, that is emphasized in these rituals and beliefs rather than male-female antagonism.

Body and Cosmos

If an ethnologist observing contemporary Americans attempted to characterize the way they dealt with their physical environment, he would probably stress the point that the man-nature relationship is mediated primarily by technological means. The resources used to wrest from the environment the things deemed necessary are tools, technological knowledge, and nonhuman energy sources. For the Gururumba, on the other hand, the man–nature relationship is probably best characterized as mediated by man's own body. They make tools and possess a corpus of technological knowledge, but there is no nonhuman energy source known to them. Ultimate control over nature therefore rests on control over the energy source in their own bodies, and this, we have argued, is primarily sexual in nature.

Additional support for this characterization comes from an examinatio of Gururumba notions concerning nature. The immediate physical environmer is an object of interest for the Gururumba. The flora and fauna are well know to them, and they name, classify, and have a body of knowledge about lif forms which is quite impressive. Their interest is largely oriented to utilitaria ends and plant classification is in terms of use rather than morphology. Thi utilitarian orientation to nature is not the sole interest they display in it intel lectually, however, as indicated by the existence of such things as a large bo of knowledge concerning the life cycle and habits of insects which has littl uilitarian application.

The more remote objects of nature are of little interest to the Gururumba The sun, although referred to in a few myths and sometimes dep'cted on geru boards or war shields, is not an important figure in their system of supe nat ural entities. In myths, the sun is always a secondary character, if personifie at all, and none of the myths are specifically about the sun. The Gururumb know the sun gives warmth and contributes to plant growth, but they do not se it as an all-powerful force in nature, nor do they even care to speculate about it apparent movements. Much the same is true of the moon, stars, meteorites, th wind, rain, and other aspects of the cosmos. There is no world creator in Guru rumba myth.

What we think of as nature simply consists of the immediate physic environment for the Gururumba. It is not a vast machine understood mechan cally, nor is it an apparent reality understood in terms of hidden, mystic force It is a "thing" which man manipulates and contends with, using the vital force within himself. As the corpus of ritual discussed in this chapter reveals, co trolling man's body means controlling the rest of nature. The only myth her the Gururumba have is a male being who passed through the Asaro valle teaching men how to grow yams and taro, and whose body sprouted plant when he died. The important aspects of the cosmos are inside man's body, nc outside it.

8

A View of Man and Society

"We are like pigs."

IN ADDITION TO the rituals concerned with control of man's vital energies, the Gururumba also have a series of beliefs postulating the existence of entities and forces we would call supernatural. Some of these, nature spirits and ancestors, have already been mentioned, but there are others as well, and their characteristics will be presented below. The entities do not form any very obvious system, as in a hierarchy of gods for example, but they can be viewed as systematically related to the notion of vital essence. Furthermore, in combination with other material they can be used as clues to assumptions the Gururumba make about their own human nature.

It should be mentioned at this point that our use of the notion "supernatural" does not correspond to any Gururumba concept: they do not divide the world into natural and supernatural parts. Certain entities, forces, and processes must be controlled partially through *lusu*, a term denoting rituals relating to growth, curing, or the stimulation of strength, while others need only rarely be controlled in this way. Entities falling within this realm of control are here included in our "supernatural." However, *lusu* does not contrast with any term denoting a realm of control where the nature of the controls differ from *lusu*. Consequently *lusu* is simply part of all control techniques, and what it controls is simply part of all things requiring human control.

The Realm of *Lusu*

Rituals and taboos relating to the control, stimulation, or protection of vital essence are referred to as *lusu*. The notion of vital essence has already been discussed a length, and only a few aspects need be added here. Humans are not the only creatures animated by vital essence, for pigs and dogs are thought to have it as well. In fact, there is a ritual designed to capture the departing vital essence of a dying pig in order to introduce it into a living pig to make it grow

93

faster and larger. It consists of passing a sweet potato around the dead pig's body; the essence enters the potato which is then fed to another pig. Death may result from a variety of sorcery techniques acting on vital essence. The sorcery performed on semen has already been mentioned, but there are other techniques such as one that pulls vital essence out of the body. When a person is asleep his vital essence passes in and out of his relaxed body upon inhaling and exhaling. A clever sorcerer is able to hold a little noose in front of a sleeping person's nose, tighten it around his vital essence as it protrudes from the nose, and pull it out. Another technique "cools" the "hot" essence by magically shooting mud balls into a person's viscera. Cigarette smoke, which is "cool," is used with the same effect by blowing it on a person.

When a person dies his physical body ceases to function, but the vital essence that animated him continues to exist in the incorporeal form of a ghost (*foroso*). These ghosts remain in contact with the living members of the village and sib, but the general effect they have on the living is undesirable: serious lingering illnesses, accidents, trouble with pigs, the occurrence of rain storms at inappropriate times, madness, and death. The ghost of a person recently deceased has to be driven away from the community by shouting at it and exploding segments of green bamboo lest it remain in close and dangerous association with the living, but it does not go far and stays close by the place where its body is buried. The most frequent actions on the part of the living toward ghosts are ritual attempts to dissuade them from disruptive activity. Ghosts may also be helpful toward the living, but acts of this type are infrequent and have consequences of only minor importance. They appear in dreams, usually to predict death or misfortune, but occasionally to reveal new kinds of garden magic or new magic to cure illness in pigs. They may also halt impending rain and keep intruders out of gardens, but they cannot be depended on to do these things nor are they frequently enjoined to do them.

Examination of cases in which ghosts have caused illness, death, injury, or madness reveals some rationale in the seemingly capricious behavior of ghosts, although it may not be immediately apparent. Here, for example, is an instance of ghostly attack that seems to indicate that ghosts attack people for little or no reason at all, yet falls into a classifiable pattern as shown below.

A party of men from the village of Miruma had gone into the high mountain forest to search for wild pandanus nuts. While there, some of them decided to go hunting for tree-climbing kangaroos. They left the camp, but returned in a few hours without any kills, only BoNgire did not return. The men were beginning to wonder what had happened to him when suddenly he burst into camp. He was bleeding at the nose and his body was badly scratched. He rushed to the edge of the campfire where he stood for a moment without saying anything, then quite unexpectedly began shouting wildly and attacking anyone within reach. He was quite agitated and it took several men to restrain him. He was finally subdued and tied to a tree at the edge of the clearing. Judging from this behavior it was decided that he had been attacked by a ghost. At this point what had happened could not be ascertained for BoNgire continued to shout nd speak incoherently and no one could communicate with him. Accordingly, he fire was built up a bit, and then smothered with wet leaves to create smoke. BoNgire was then suspended from a pole, in much the same way as when a pig s carried from one place to another, and was held in the smoke until he began to hoke and vomit. Finally, after about five minutes of this treatment, he cried out n normal speech to be taken out of the smoke. This signalized that the danger- us contact with the ghost had been exorcised from him and that he was once more normal. A short time later, BoNgire was able to give his own account of what happened. He said, "I was in the forest looking for a tree-climbing kan- garoo. I looked up into a tree and saw a nest. I knew there would be a tree kan- garoo in it. I climbed the tree next to the tree with the nest. I went up. I kept on going up. When I got to the top I could see there was a tree kangaroo in the nest. I did not have my bow. I called to Usi [a man BoNgire had gone into the forest with and whom he thought was nearby] to come up the tree with his bow. I called Usi several times [Usi had gone back to camp]. I said his name, but he did not come. Then I saw Usi's namesake in the tree with me [the ghost of a departed village mate with the same name], and he was red. Usi's name- sake said, "Why do you keep calling my name? I do not like to have my name called.' Then he bit me. I fell out of the tree. He kept on biting me. I could not see, I could not hear."

In other cases ghosts attack because they want to have their bones cleaned, because their graves are being disturbed by soil slippage or dampness, because no one mentioned their name at the last pig festival, because they are lonely, or simply because they feel like it.

One fact is quite clear from the material on ghostly attack: ghosts do not attack because they are punitive or vengeful. Informants were asked specifically f ghosts would attack a person who had committed some act considered wrong, and the answers were consistently in the negative. In other words, ghosts are not moral agents punishing the living for acts of wrongdoing. Neither are they thought of as vengeful. Wrong between living individuals is not made right by ghostly attack when the wronged individual dies and becomes a ghost. In gen- eral terms, ghosts act because of affonts to their physical person, as in the case of wanting their bones cleaned; to their esteem, as in the case of not wanting to be forgotten; or to express some strong personal desire, as in the case of not wanting to have one's name spoken. There is no taboo against speaking the names of the dead, and when BoNgire was attacked it was because the ghost of Usi simply did not want his name called out. The Gururumba regard ghostly attack as stemming primarily from their overbearing self-assertiveness: that's just the way ghosts are.

Foroso are the ghosts of the recently dead, the dead whose names are known. Ancestors (*aBwaho*) are the ghosts of the long dead, whose names are no longer known or were never known. Ancestors have been mentioned previ- ously in connection with the *jaBirisi* ritual which is classed as *lusu*. To call these beings ancestors is slightly misleading since that term usually denotes the known dead to whom specific genealogical connections can be traced. *ABwaho,* on the other hand, are not known as individuals but only as a group. They are like "forefathers" or "founders of the race," and ritual contact is made with them only as a group. Unlike ghosts they are distant rather than near figures, they do not enter directly into the affairs of a person, nor are they "seen" as "ghosts frequently are.

The Gururumba think of the ancestors as having two quite distinct set of characteristics. As we have seen they regard the ancestors as sources of the vital energy necessary to grow food and children. They speak of them with admiration for having produced the present generations of men and depict them in songs and dances as busily engaged in growing food and children. At the same time they place their existence in a distant past when human society and culture was not as it is now. Men did not have domesticated plants and animal and did not live within the bounds of a society but as social isolates. They raped, murdered, and stole as whim directed them and ranged freely over the countryside without concern for boundaries. On the one hand, then, their vital energies are manifested in generally nurturant concerns, on the other, in strong assertive behavior that amounts to aggression.

The term *lusu* also applies to rituals curing illness caused by witches and to divinatory techniques for finding witches. Witches are called *gwumu*, this term also being applied to a substance inside them causing them to be witches. The term comes from the root verb meaning to steal. Witches can fly through the air, change shape, and get inside things, including the body of a human or pig. They usually attack by eating the liver, which is the main seat of vital essence, but they also eat the flesh of fresh corpses. They "mark" their victims by pushing small sticks into the ground near the intended target and project themselves into the victim by changing into insects or reptiles with mystic powers. They also have superpowerful garden magic at their command.

The outstanding characteristic of witches is their inordinate acquisitiveness and envy of others. Witches get inside packets of food given at gift exchanges and gobble it up before the recipient can get the bundle home. Witches grow superabundant gardens simply as a means of shaming others rather than to provide food for the family or the exchange group. Witches attack the pigs of others because the pigs belong to others rather than to themselves. They attack elaborately decorated dancers, good warriors, or handsome persons out of envy. They steal food from gardens and valuables from houses because they want them. The eating of corpses falls into this pattern also because the Gururumba explain it as a desire to acquire meat beyond any normal human needs. *Gwumu* is such a voracious force it may even destroy the body it inhibits.

There are two other important characteristics of witches. First, they are real in the sense that actual persons are occasionally accused of being witches. Second, witches are generally thought to be females, all the serious accusation of witchcraft being made against women. If a real witch is found, she may be killed or may commit suicide before any action can be taken. On the other hand she may admit guilt and be willing to pay compensation for damage done and

hus escape serious harm; or the witch may be "rehabilitated" through a rite of
exorcism which rids her body of the witch substance.

Accusations of witchcraft are frequently made in the heat of argument
and such accusations are made of men as well as women. Serious accusations involving a concerted attempt to find the witch are only made against women,
however. There is the belief that men may consort with witches but they do not
thereby become witches. They can gain certain benefits from such contact as indicated in the following statement:

A witch can turn into many things; birds, dogs, another person. If a man
sees a witch turning into something else he should go up to her afterwards
and tell her he knows she is a witch. She will offer to give him some valuable thing such as a shell if he lets her alone and does not tell anyone else.
He must refuse. Then she will say that he can fondle her breasts if he does
not tell. He must refuse. Then she will say that he can have sexual intercourse with her if he does not tell. A wise man will refuse this also and ask
for a piece of her hair or a piece of her string apron. He will take it and
hide it in a tree or under a stone so that others cannot find it. In the time
of warfare he could bring it out, wrap it around sugar cane and burn it.
Rubbing the ashes in his hair would make enemy arrows miss him. Now it
could be used in court cases. A head man can ask someone else to do this
for him if a court case is coming up.

Lusu is also used to cure illness caused by harmful thoughts. It may happen that the bad thoughts one person harbors about another leave his head and
enter the body of the other person where they cause illness or even death. An
individual cannot will his thoughts to do this, nor can he restrain them from
doing it; it just happens. Although the Gururumba do not comment on it, illness or death from this cause occurs exclusively between village mates or sib
mates who have had a serious argument without its erupting into physical violence. Blame is not placed on the person whose bad thoughts did the harm, for
it is felt that they were partially caused by the actions of the other person. The
cure for illness caused in this way brings together the two people involved so
that each may rub the other with water in which some valuable object has been
immersed.

Nature spirits are also within the realm of *lusu*, but they do not need to
be discussed further. The only remaining force of any consequence to the Gururumba that is dealt with by *lusu* is lightning. Lightning is not personified, but
when it strikes a tree owned by someone it is thought to remain in the tree as
a malignant force which can cause harm to the owner of the tree or some member of his immediate kin group. It is especially dangerous to "weak" men, men
who are ill or who are not close to the male ideal of assertiveness and
strength. Such a threat is met by a ritual exorcising the lightning and strengthening the persons potentially in danger. Like any kind of illness caused by agents
discussed in this chapter, a lightning strike is of concern because of its effect
on a person's vital energy, and thus his ability to be an effective person, which

explains the emphasis on strengthening in this rite although no one is actually ill.

These, then, are the major supernatural forces and entities postulated by the Gururumba. Although they differ in form, abode, and other features, the similarities in the way they enter into human affairs are of interest here. First, they are viewed as involved directly rather than remotely in human affairs. They are not of importance to the Gururumba because they created the world or significant parts of it, nor because they are the forces that run the natural order, nor because they are the guardians of the moral order. Rather, they are of importance because they affect an individual's capacity to cope effectively with the demands and opportunities he meets in daily existence. The fact that ghosts cause illness is not meaningful to the Gururumba because it explains illness or because it is a punishment for moral transgression; it is meaningful because it robs a woman of the strength necessary to carry out her daily tasks in the garden or deprives a man of the vigor needed in social intercourse. Second, insofar as these entities and forces exercise a benevolent influence on human affairs it is through the contribution they make to productive activity. This may occur, as with spirits, in the form of directly participating in some task or, as with vital essence, in the form of the forceful energy needed to carry out any enterprise. Conversely, these entities and forces are regarded as malevolent when they impede productive activity. It is significant in this regard that illness or death is always regarded as only one element in a general pattern of personal misfortune when one of these entities is thought to be the cause.

The realm of *lusu* can be seen as that in which positive control is exercised over entities and forces affecting man's capacity to be productive and assertive: it protects and nourishes. Its opposite is not the realm of the natural but of sorcery in which negative control is exercised: it attacks and destroys. There is no single term for sorcery, only a series of terms for classes of sorcery techniques. None of them are classed as *lusu,* nor are rituals for counteracting sorcery called *lusu.* Some parts of such a ritual, those dealing with symptoms but not with cause, may be referred to in this way; the specialist who performs the ritual is called *lusuBe.* Sorcery is not practiced against persons in one's own village or sib, nor are its techniques mysterious as are those of witchcraft. Some sorcery is known by almost every adult, and it can be purchased or sold like any object. *Lusu* relates to gardening and exchange partners, sorcery to warfare and enemies.

System in the Realm of *Lusu*

We have spoken above about the importance of productivity and assertiveness to the Gururumba. Much of the character of Gururumba life can be understood as if it were the result of striving to attain these ends. More particularly, it can be understood as if it were an attempt to achieve some balance between nurturant and destructive tendencies in man—an attempt to turn strength into nurturant channels. To a Westerner, daily life among the Gururumba appears to be carried on in a highly aggressive fashion: the constant banter about giving and taking, the frequency of fights and violent emotional eruptions, and the fact that many of the idioms in the language are built around "violent" verbs such as "hit," "strike," or "kill." "I hit him" can mean "I gave it to him," rather than the reverse as in our own language. In most contexts this kind of behavior is not aggression to the Gururumba; it is a display of the strength stemming from vital essence, the strength man draws upon to endure and flourish. Within that part of the social world defined by the sharing of food, assertiveness is not aggressiveness because it creates food and the social channels through which food flows. Furthermore, making a demand implies the obligation to be demanded of, and giving is not a means of overwhelming others because reciprocity will transform givers into takers. The possibility of gift exchange becoming a competitive spiral is thus held in check by striving for a balance between nurturance and strength.

There are several ethnographic facts illustrating this tendency toward balance and reciprocity. Repayment of a debt should be equivalent to the amount lent, no more nor less. Games, and certain kinds of warfare, should end in a tie rather than victory. The difficulty of achieving this when both sides strive to display strength accounts for the fact that games, such as a rough and tumble version of soccer introduced by Australians, may go on for several days. Finally, there is the interesting elaboration of the notion of compensation. Compensation can be demanded for injuries received while working for another, the damaging of tools or objects lent to another, or for damage done to gardens by another's pigs or children. In addition, compensation may be demanded for dancing too well at someone else's food distribution or for giving a food distribution of a more elaborate nature than expected by the guest. Thus, within a certain social context failure to achieve the proper balance has its cost, for a person 'injured" in this way will appear before the men's house weeping and crying loudly that he has been "killed" by the offenders and he must then be taken into the house, fed, greased, and presented with valuables.

If one accepts this as an accurate characterization, then the supernatural entities and forces postulated by the Gururumba can be seen as conjoined in a system expressing balances and imbalances of strength and nurturance.

We can start with the notion of vital essence and view it as an expression of the most perfect balance between nurturance and strength. The hot substances flowing in the body make a person physically, sexually, and behaviorally strong. Within the food-exchanging community this display of strength is not destructive. The assertion of physical strength protects the group from enemy onslaught by force of arms and enables men and women to carry out the heavy tasks associated with providing food and shelter. A man acts assertively in the sexual act by having intercourse repeatedly, but this is in order to bind firmly the substance that will develop into the child he is helping to grow. When his sexual energies are not helping to develop his child, they must be conserved and protected so they can contribute strength to the performance of other productive tasks including the forceful fulfillment of obligations that leads to renown for the individual and group.

The notions of ghost and harmful thought express a harmful imbalance between strength and nurturance created when strength is focused primarily on self-assertion. Ghosts act in an overbearing, "pushy" manner to make their own desires and needs known. They are not linked with one another or with the living in striving for common goals, nor is their assertiveness connected in any significant way with productive activity. They are "strong" without being nurturant and are harmful in that they display strength unmodulated by the limiting factors of reciprocity and obligation. A ghost is vital essence released from the social forces that directed it into nurturant channels and consequently turned to forcing others to recognize it as a self. Assertiveness, even within the context of reciprocity and obligation, can also lead to harm as indicated in the notion of harmful thoughts. People can harm one another in the course of everyday events simply because of the assertiveness normally inherent in their actions. Strength and nurturance may be balanced in each man, but when men interact the forcefulness characterizing their behavior can bring about unintentionally harmful consequences.

The notion of nature spirit expresses a harmful imbalance between strength and nurturance created when strength is focused on concern with objects and rights of ownership, or when sexual energy becomes lust. Nature spirits seek out opportunities to copulate with human females, but their interest in females is fornicative, not procreative. Similarly, they watch over pigs, gardens, and territory because they are "theirs" rather than because they are needed resources. Nurturance, insofar as it means an interest in growth and feeding, is separate from strength in nature spirits, but they can be made to work for the good of man if their proprietary interests are taken into account. Spirits are helpful or harmful largely to the extent that their proprietary interests are either taken into account or ignored. Having such interests is not harmful in itself, but ignoring such interests in others may lead to harm.

The characteristics attributed to ancestors are interesting in terms of our interpretation because they suggest a fundamental separation of nurturance from strength in human nature that is only resolved through the agency of society. When ancestors are spoken of as giving free reign to their impulses and living by their individual wits and strength, they are described as living in a presocial era. Informants typically say of this period that it lacked institutions of marriage and gift exchange, and point out that the ancestors did not live in villages. When ancestors are spoken of as busily engaged in producing food and growing children, however, it is always within a social context since the food is grown by the combined labor of men and women, and because it is depicted as used in exchange activities. The behavior of the presocial era the Gururumba call strong; we might refer to it popularly as motivated by "the baser instincts." The notion of ancestors can be seen as an institutionalized recognition that man has such "base instincts." To anticipate the next section somewhat, this interpretation is especially borne out by the fact that informants spontaneously suggested in a variety of contexts that they would be like ancestors of the presocial era if they did not have to live in the company of other men.

The notion of witchcraft expresses a separation of strength from nurturance that cannot be resolved within the food-producing unit. The outcome is aggression. Witches are similar to ghosts in certain respects, but ghosts can be placated while witches cannot. When a ghost attacks it is to make its desires known or its presence felt, and its attacks cease when these desires have been fulfilled or its presence recognized. Ghostly attacks can be seen as the means whereby ghosts maintain their self-esteem and identity through the display of strength in the form of self-assertion. The Gururumba do not view witches as being concerned with their self-esteem or identity. A witch makes no demands and gains a general satisfaction through the attack itself rather than a specific satisfaction from the results of the attack. Witches not only manifest strength without nurturance, they turn strength into aggression since their actions have no purpose, not even assertion of the self. Lightning is witchcraft's counterpart in nature. It is destructive to no particular end, striking at points of weakness like the trees of a sick man, rather than points of strength like a handsomely decorated dancer.

A correspondence between this characterization of witches and general attitudes concerning the position of women within the sib partially explains why women, rather than men, are regarded as witches. Men point out that women do not really care about planning and preparing lineage- or sib-sponsored food distributions. They would rather tend their gardens for their own use. They do not always like to have the pigs which they have tended and cared for taken away from them and killed for the benefit of their husbands' kin group. On occasion Gururumba wives are called to the nearest coffee plantation and offered temporary jobs as coffee pickers. The men object to this employment because the women neglect their gardens and pigs during the picking and are not at all eager to share their proceeds with their husbands. This runs counter to the ideal of male dominance in making economic decisions. Children are the future strength of the group, but after a woman has had a child or two she may complain that childbearing is painful and thwart the growth of the group by refusing to have any more children. Also, women are in a position to steal semen which they can send away to sorcerers, and they are a source of contamination through menstrual blood. In a variety of ways, then, women are thought to impede activities of the lineage and sib.

The women themselves are not unaware of this attitude toward them as is evident in the following speech made to a young girl about to be sent away from her village in betrothal. The speech is part of an evening of instruction given a girl by the women of her village in the seclusion of a woman's house away from male ears:

When you get to *gwota* (place name) there will be many things to do. You will be told to work in the garden, to weed, to plant, to bring firewood. You must look after the pigs and bring water when you are told. You will carry heavy loads, and if they are too heavy to carry you must make two trips. You cannot ask someone else to carry part of it for you. You will give food from your garden to your husband's father and his brothers when they call out for it. When you have pigs, you will give those also, even if you have suckled them at your breast. If you do all these things people will say, "Oh, those Miruma send us good wives." If you do not, they will call you "witch" and you will be sent home before it is time to sit down with your husband (consummate the marriage).

Women are both a productive and an obstructive force in the sib. They create and withhold creation, they produce and desire to retain the fruits of production, they take semen to generate both life and death. They are like the retentive, acquisitive witch who wants but does not give.

Of Pigs and Men

The systematization of beliefs in the preceding section serves in part to illustrate an analytic technique. It compares and contrasts a number of seemingly discrete cultural items as variables along a dimension, the dimension of balance between nurturance and strength in this case. Such an arrangement is meant to emphasize those features of a set of concepts that the people who hold them see as most important for giving meaning to some situation. The analysis also prefigures a few statements concerning the Gururumba's understanding of themselves and their relationship to society. It is argued here that part of the importance these concepts have for the Gururumba is the understanding they give them of themselves.

As mentioned above, the Gururumba compare themselves to ancestors of the presocial era. One male informant said, "That is what we are really like, we are really like that, but now we understand [now that we have advanced culture]. If there were no villages or no headmen we would be like that." Other informants, independently of one another, would comment after giving an account of some ghost's unsavory behavior, "I'm like him" or "I'm like that." Informants also compared themselves with pigs that must be watched lest they eat their own offspring. On one occasion some men captured a runaway pig and were holding it over a smoking fire to calm it down since it had been on a rampage, attacking people, breaking into gardens, and ignoring entreaties to return to the fold. In an effort to explain the pig's behavior its owner said, "Pigs are like us. They tire of the rope and the fence."

These statements the Gururumba make about themselves indicate certain understandings they have of their inner nature. First, man has selfish, destructive, and aggressive impulses in himself. Witches are real people, ghosts and ancestors once were. Death releases harmful tendencies that have always been in man. Ghosts are not harmful because they are attempting to punish man or subvert his basically good nature; they are harmful in the same way men are.

Second, these impulses are curbed by the forces of society. This understanding is present in the statement that men would be like ancestors of the presocial era if they did not live in society, and in statements drawing a parallel between men and unwatched pigs. It is also implied in the notion that the display of strength is good when applied to the attainment of institutionalized goals. The Gururumba never indicated any particular longing to be like the voracious pig or the presocial ancestor, but their statements indicate an understanding that they would be that way more often than they are if it were not for social constraints. It is important to realize that in some situations they are this way. Specifically, they are this way toward other men outside the food-producing and food-exchanging group, their enemies with whom relationships are not modified by reciprocity and obligation. These are the men one can sorcerize. Killing such men is the occasion for celebration, a celebration in which even women can join by building a huge fire on a ridge top visible to the stricken group and singing derisive songs which are hopefully audible to the relatives of the deceased. These are men one can take pleasure in brutalizing when they lie wounded on the battlefield or from whom one can steal with honor. But, these are precisely the men who are outside the boundaries of society as the Gururumba know it. Within the food-exchanging group such behavior is not allowed. Sorcery does not occur here and murder is punished.

Finally, society itself represses but does not eradicate impulses that cannot be allowed expression within its boundaries. This is clearly present in the notion of harmful thoughts and in the statement that pigs, like men, ". . . tire of the rope and the fence." It is also apparent in the attitude toward men who exhibit a behavior pattern people refer to as "being a wild pig." These men run amok, attacking people and stealing objects. There is no attempt to restrain such behavior beyond keeping a watchful eye on it to avoid serious injury and no recriminations are made when it is over. The reason is that the Gururumba see such a performance as caused by certain social demands that the individual can no longer bear. The proper stance for society, then, is to withdraw and let the individual have his outlet. The name given this behavior is instructive since there are no truly wild pigs in the upper Asaro valley, only pigs that have temporarily escaped their masters.

9

Patterns and People

"There are no lightning balls."

O THIS POINT IN the presentation the emphasis has been on pattern and form. A social morphology has been sketched out and the gross dimensions of certain concepts, beliefs, and values have been delimited. Knowing the Gururumba in this way is like knowing a region of the earth through studying a series of maps, some topographic, some climatic, and some demographic. Being in the landscape and looking at a map are two quite different experiences, however. For one thing, a map necessarily excludes some of the variety in the landscape. For another, looking at a map is not equivalent to using it. Similarly, human behavior is not fully analogous to the traveler moving through a landscape with map in hand: It is not simply a matter of following directions, for men can create new directions and new cultural landscapes. Remember, too, that one can become lost even with a map.

In this chapter our aim will be to know the Gururumba as one knows them individually and as one sees them operating within the cultural patterns I have described. Such a presentation could be systematic, but this one will present incidents and situations that have occurred in the life histories of individuals. It should be emphasized that none of the incidents described here represent deviant behavior as the Gururumba define it. The Gururumba do identify several kinds of deviant acts and persons, but these are not included here.

Gambiri

An important part of an adult man's life among the Gururumba consists of participation in exchange activities. As we have seen, one of the ways he can display himself as a fully functioning person is actively to seek out involvement in such affairs. However, not all men are as successful in these endeavors as others so that some men become leaders and others do not. Within the group who do not, there is quite a range of variation in the adaptation they make and

104

the attitudes of others toward them. There are men who because of low intelligence or mental abnormalities barely function at all. These are deviant by Gururumba standards. There are "outside men," men who never form an allegiance of significant duration to any group they may be affiliated with and wander from one group to another. These are also deviant. Occasionally one discovers men who live out their lives in semiseclusion away from the village of their kinsmen and age mates. These are not deviants to the Gururumba because they do remain attached to a local unit, but they participate in group affairs so infrequently that they are seldom taken into account when decisions are being made.

There is another kind of person who while not a deviant, does not find the same degree of satisfaction and pleasure in exchange affairs as do the majority of men. A person like this is placed in a difficult position. He is normal in all the ways that matter to the Gururumba, and other people assume he is motivated and satisfied in the same way they are. He does not see himself in this way, however, and wants to reduce his involvement in exchange affairs without withdrawing from some participation in them or other spheres of group activity.

Several factors create frustration in such an individual. His situation can be characterized as one in which the pressures and demands of the exchange system itself are sufficient to create frustration, but not deep feelings of alienation. Gambiri was such a man. He was in his midthirties, married, had one small child, and his wife was pregnant with a second. Miruma was not Gambiri's natal village but his wife's. It is not unusual for a man to take up residence in his wife's village, in fact it is usually a move calculated to be of some advantage. In Gambiri's case, however, it eventually created a series of difficulties in his life having major consequences for his own adjustment to the dominant patterns of adult male culture.

Soon after Gambiri became married he found himself in the rather difficult economic position of all young married men in this society. His kinsmen and village mates had provided the food and wealth necessary to make the brideprice payment at his betrothal and had also supplied food at the numerous small gift exchanges occurring between affinally related groups during the betrothal period. After the couple form a domestic unit, pressure to repay this aid is put on the young man in the form of direct requests for food and wealth, and indirectly in the form of obligations to contribute to the gift exchanges of kinsmen and village mates. It should be remembered that all exchange activity relates to the acquiring of renown, and the help that a young man, or anyone else receives, may be a calculated political ploy. Failure to repay or to contribute to someone else's exchange, then, is not simply a matter of failing to meet an obligation, it is a roadblock on someone's way to renown. The pressures to repay are therefore heavy, and if a young man is not sufficiently aggressive in his pig-tending and gardening, if he is not assertive enough to make others indebted to him, or if he sustains any drastic personal misfortunes, he may find himself in a seemingly inextricable situation. Gambiri's life history indicates he was in essentially this kind of position when he decided to leave his natal village. Also, his gardens were not doing well there because of poor soil, according to Gambiri, and he felt his father-in-law's land would yield a better crop.

Economic demands and pressure to become more deeply involved in exchange activities were too great for Gambiri in his own natal village, so he left. To him it appeared a good move. However, new sets of demands were made on him in Miruma as his new village mates began attempting to draw him into their affairs, the old debts were still there, and he had cut off one possible source of aid by leaving his own kinsmen. His wife's lineage was not willing to help Gambiri discharge any obligations incurred at his marriage and, besides, they considered it somewhat of a triumph to have their daughter return after having received bride-price for her. If Gambiri had waited until some of his debts had been discharged and his wife had been longer removed from her own natal group this probably would not have been the case.

Gambiri simply did not know how nor did he really care to cope with it. He was interested in his gardens and his child, and he liked to participate in some small way in the larger-scale exchanges, but the intricacies of exchange were oppressive demands rather than interesting challenges to him. The real problem for a person like Gambiri is to convince others of this fact without appearing to be deviant or without drastic loss of social support. A relatively young man like Gambiri does not want to announce withdrawal or weakness, and other people tend to attribute his failures to unfamiliarity with economic affairs. They tend not to see him as a different kind of person but just as someone who needs a bit more time to develop.

One day Gambiri began exhibiting the behavior the Gururumba describe as "being a wild pig." For three days he roamed about the village and its environs attacking people, bursting into houses and stealing things. His actions had all the classic signs of anxiety hysteria: his speech and hearing were partially blocked, he had lost full motor and respiratory control, he behaved irrationally, and when he did speak it was either in the form of commands or blatantly false statements. The onset of this attack was sudden and when it was over, he claimed no memory of it.

There are several features of this affair to be noted. First, Gambiri's actions were not so much concerned with people as they were with objects. He stole a large net bag, and at the end of the three days it was full of things taken from others. He destroyed all this material at the end of his attack. Second, people not only did not attempt to restrain him in any way, but they felt he should be allowed to take things. To be sure, they put valuable objects out of his reach if he were known to be near, but always conspicuously left something out for him to carry away. Third, after the attack was over no mention of it was made to Gambiri nor was he made to pay compensation for any of the damage done. Fourth, Gambiri left the village for several days after the attack and while he was gone people talked about him, about his attack and its meaning, and about his past. In these conversations there was explicit recognition of the economic pressures on him and his inability to cope with them. There have been other men like Gambiri in the past and this behavior syndrome has come to have this meaning for the Gururumba. In fact, they can predict how such a man will act once an attack starts as indicated by their secreting of valuables. Finally, in the months following Gambiri's return there was an observable reduction in the intensity with which people attempted to draw him into their exchange affairs or use him as an avenue to establish exchange relationships.

Gambiri was a man who saw himself as committed to the basic patterns of Gururumba life, and as gaining some satisfactions from conforming to them, if only he could be allowed to operate at something less than the expected level of intensity in exchange affairs. Others finally came to realize this when he presented himself as others appeared to him—as demanding and taking in an aggressive manner. This realization then opened the way for him to achieve a more personally satisfying adjustment to his society.

Tomu

After young girls have passed their first menstruation, their lives take on a new and distinctive pattern. Before, they spent most of their time with their mothers performing small tasks in the garden or playing in mixed groups of other children. There were points of pleasure and excitement during this period, for small girls are frequently decorated lavishly when the men dance and accompany them onto the dance ground where they are admired by the assembled audience. There were also life-cycle rituals when they received new names, new hair arrangements, or facial tatoos that made them the center of attention. It is the period between first menstruation and betrothal that remains unique in their lives, however, in terms of the freedom of action and personal expression allowed. It will not be until they are old women that a similar freedom will again be possible.

Tomu was about sixteen or seventeen at the time of the field study. Some of her age mates had already been betrothed and had left the village. Indeed, some were betrothed before they menstruated. For some time she and several other girls had occupied an old house in the village belonging to Tomu's father. They lounged there during the day and went about largely as whim directed them. Very little is expected of such girls in the way of helping in the tasks of daily routine, although they do not withdraw completely from productive tasks. Their physical activity is reduced enough however, so they tend to put on weight, but that is not altogether undesirable, since it is thought to contribute to their handsomeness. Tomu and the other girls lavished a great deal of attention on themselves in the form of face and body painting, decorative arm bands made with the brilliant yellow fibre from orchid vines, string aprons interwoven with soft tufts of fur from forest animals, and piles of shells and beads. They seemed always to be eating and frequently slept in the daytime.

Sleeping in the daytime was not unrelated to their total pattern of activity because the abiding concern of these girls was participation in evening courting sessions. These occur when a girl invites a boy to serenade her. The boy recruits his age mates as a chorus and they proceed to the girl's house after dark. The girl has her friends present, and as the boys arrange themselves in a circle with their backs to the fire, the girls form a circle around them with their backs to the wall of the house. The boys sing long, complicated love songs in fa'setto voices imitating the twittering of birds, each chorus being punctuated by a stylized sound intended to resemble a heart-rending sigh. The girls respond with songs extolling their own virtues. Various kinds of sexual play may occur during such a session as well. The girls are in control of this whole situation for they do the inviting and initiate the sexual play.

Girls who are not betrothed early may spend several years in this kind of activity. As they grow older, they spend more and more time primping and devote more and more energy to arranging serenades. It sometimes happens that these girls develop a feeling of independence and ability to control their own affairs that is not commensurate with reality. Such was the case with Tomu. She admired a boy very much and invited him many times to serenade her. He always came. She spoke to her parents about him, indicating to them she would like to marry him, but they were evasive and spoke of other possibilities. Finally, Tomu decided to take matters into her own hands. She went to the boy's village, sat down in front of the men's house, and announced to the men inside that she had come to present herself for betrothal to the young man she admired. The response of the men was graceful and even tender. They came outside, sat around Tomu, and explained the impossibility of her suggestion: No discussion of the matter had been carried on with her kinsmen, no one from her group had come to suggest a bride price, and other plans were being considered for the boy's betrothal. Tomu became quite upset and cried and beat the ground with her fists. By this time a crowd had gathered and Tomu was given over to the care of the women. They took her to a woman's house, the men began preparing an earth oven, and Tomu's parents were sent for. While food was being prepared, Tomu was calmed, and the women oiled her body and also dressed her in a new set of aprons including a special one made of bark strips rather than string. When Tomu's parents arrived they were presented with food as compensation for the embarrassment caused them, and Tomu was also fed to compensate for the rejection.

Tomu's action can be understood in cultural terms as the result of a conflict in norms. Arranging marriages is primarily a matter for adult decision in the cultural world of adults. But, in the youth culture of girls this cultural fact its only dimly realized and may be further obscured by the freedom they have in choosing their own courting partners. For girls like Tomu, the realization that they do not control the final selection of a mate may create a feeling of rebelliousness in them which manifests itself in marital instability during their early years.

Namo

Being married is the normal condition for Gururumba adults. No institutions demand celibacy, and no individuals feel remaining single would be of any particular value for them. Occasionally, very old men and women do not remarry after their mate dies, but if a person is productive at all, a new mate will be sought. For example, an old woman may marry into a polygynous family unit not as a sexual partner for the male but because she can contribute to gardening, pig-tending, and child care. No one seems occupied with how to remain single, but how to get married has perplexed some.

Arrangements for a man's first wife are made by the older males in his lineage. They carry out all the negotiations, assemble the bride price, and engineer the rituals and gift exchanges accompanying this procedure. As we have seen before, these older men are interested in widening the scope of their exchange activities or strengthening already existing ties so that the selection of a bride and the timing of betrothal is partly dependent on economic and political considerations. Ideally, the older men in a lineage begin thinking about arranging a betrothal for their unmarried sons sometime after the taboo period following initiation is over. A betrothal is arranged, the girl is brought to the village where she remains under the tutelage of her in-laws until her husband-to-be is deemed strong enough to enter the dangerous business of procreation. The husband-to-be will be in his middle or late twenties by this time. Also, ideally, all the young men who are age mates should become betrothed at about the same time.

A variety of circumstances can postpone betrothal, however, with the result that a young man finds himself in the position of being the only one of his age group who is not betrothed. This is what happened to Namo, a young man of about twenty-five. Namo's father, Bambu, was an old man who had been active in exchange affairs, but had never made a special name for himself. He only had one wife, but his marriage had been stable and he had two surviving children of whom Namo was the youngest. Namo's brother Luiso was about twenty-nine or thirty and had been married for two or three years. Namo's father's elder brother's sons were all married and had children, so that Namo was not only the only one in his age set who was not married, he was also the only eligible male in his lineage not married.

Namo had made it plain to his kinsmen that he wanted a wife, but he was told he would have to wait. The marriage of Namo's brother had severely taxed his father's resources, and Bambu and Luiso were still in the process of reciprocating the aid given in this marriage by Bambu's elder brother and his sons. Since Bambu had not been particularly energetic in exchange affairs there were few men outside his lineage willing to help in accumulating the bride price. Further, neither Bambu nor his brother had any daughters old enough to become betrothed, which cut off one possible source of wealth for the lineage. In addition to all this, Bambu's brother's eldest son was becoming quite active in exchange affairs in the context of the ward and exerted pressure on Bambu to contribute what resources he had to aid him. A betrothal would be arranged for Namo "soon," it was said, but he would have to be patient.

A promised betrothal was of little consolation to Namo. He expressed shame at being the only one of his group without a wife and anger at his kinsmen for not meeting a lineage obligation. Namo was simply caught and there was little he could do about it since he wielded no real economic or political power. Certain unusual actions Namo took can be viewed as reactions using existing cultural patterns to force a deeper realization of his plight on the members of his lineage in the hope of quicker action on his betrothal.

First, Namo had accumulated a small amount of cash by working for me as a guide. He treasured this as wealth to be used in his betrothal, keeping it locked in a wooden chest entrusted to me for safekeeping. At about the time the situation described above began to develop he took the box away. This in itself was odd because he was keeping his treasure secret to prevent its being siphoned off by lineage commitments. Shortly after this a dog belonging to someone in Namo's lineage killed a chicken belonging to a man in another lineage of the same ward. Heated words were exchanged, but as sometimes happens in a case like this, no demand for compensation was made. Without consulting anyone, Namo took his money and gave all of it, including the box it was in, to the man whose chicken had been killed. The amount of money was small, but it was far in excess of any compensation that might have been paid even if it had been demanded. His father and brother reprimanded him for doing a foolish thing, but he replied with some eloquence that he was only meeting a lineage obligation as any man should do. Such an exaggerated and uncalled for act was a calculated maneuver to impress others with their obligation to him.

Second, Namo also tried a more forceful maneuver involving a threat. Sometimes the boys of a village will congregate around the house where girls are being serenaded by youths from other villages and beat on the roof in a kind of mischievous prank. Namo organized such a prank, leading a group of boys much younger than himself, but carried it far beyond the limits of mischievousness. Instead of beating on the roof, he tore it apart, jumped into the house, scattered the hot coals of the fire about the room, and struck anyone coming under his hand in a wild display of ferocious behavior. It nearly burnt the house down and sent the serenaders scattering. He claimed the whole thing had only started out as a prank, but on arrival at the house a ghost bit him, which caused his wild behavior, and the ghost said it bit him because it did not like unmarried men. The implication of this being that the ghost might continue to bite him and cause similar disruptive behavior as long as he remained single.

Sekau

One would not describe the Gururumba as ridden with fear of witches, or accusations of witchcraft, but such accusations do occasionally occur. It is the rare individual indeed who might gain by allowing circumstances to develop that seemed clearly to lead to such an accusation. The problem is to manage other people's opinion in such a way that one's own behavior does not come to be seen as witchlike even when in fact it has been.

Sekau was an old woman, but amazingly active and strong for her advanced years. She was skinny and bent, but she still went to the gardens every day to weed, plant, and carry home net bags full of heavy sweet potatotes. Sekau was in a rather unique position among the women of Miruma because she was one of the oldest and certainly the most active of the old women, and because Miruma was her natal village. Her husband had come from Chimbu many years before to take up residence in his wife's village where he founded a lineage of some renown. Two of his sons were well on the way to becoming big men. In fact, they had even established their own men's house in the village, although it was still considered to be part of another ward and not a separate entity. Because of all these factors, Sekau exerted a great deal of influence in the village for a woman, even to having her opinion sought on matters of exchange. Consequently, she was in the habit of speaking her mind in public when affairs of the village were being discussed—a practice younger women or women of less prestige would not be able to carry off.

It happened that a dog belonging to Sekau's son died, and since dog meat is food for the Gururumba, it became the occasion for a small food distribution. Sekau's son divided the dog in such a fashion that almost all the meat went to his wife's father, the man who had given him the dog in the first place. Sekau got none of the meat, which angered her. In the midst of the food distribution, standing before the assembled guests, Sekau chastised her son for not giving her a share of the meat. She was told it was none of her business what her son did with his own dog, but she persisted in her complaints until several people were involved in trying to quiet her. No one supported her, and as tempers rose someone shouted in anger that she was acting like a witch. At that point Sekau stalked away and the situation returned to normal.

In talking with Sekau after this incident it became quite clear that the charge she was a witch worried her a great deal. It is true that accusations of this sort made in the heat of argument are not intended seriously, but Sekau realized she *had* been acting like a greedy, acquisitive witch and, furthermore, that her general position in the village might cause people to think of her in this way even more certainly. Sekau was wise enough to know that out of just such circumstances real accusations of witchcraft grow. She also knew there was no very obvious or direct course of action she could take to undo what had been done.

Several days later, while walking through some brush, a branch displaced by the person walking in front of Sekau snapped back unexpectedly hitting her in the face. It scratched her face and also made a scratch on her eyeball. It was very painful and in a few days the wound was infected to the point where her eye was swollen shut. An accident of this magnitude has supernatural causation for the Gururumba, and of all the possible causes to which it could have been attributed, Sekau chose to say it was the ghost of her husband punishing her for acting in such a nasty manner at her son's food distribution.

It will be remembered that in an earlier chapter ghosts were characterized as being unconcerned with punishment of the living for misdeeds they might have committed. This characterization emerged from asking people in what kinds of situation ghosts will attack, and from examining cases of ghostly attack.

There is less variation in the elicited accounts given of the nature of ghosts than in the case material representing the way the notion of ghost is actually used. Ghosts do have certain well-defined characteristics including capriciousness and unpredictability. Consequently within certain limits the notion of ghost can be applied to situations one would not ordinarily associate with it. A notion like ghost is meant to be used in situations, and to be useful it must have a certain flexibility. In Sekau's case, we see culture put to work: the map is used and modified to the user's need. Sekau was trying to avoid the accusation of witchcraft and the consequent punishment. Interpreting her eye injury as a ghost-caused punishment was a conscious or unconscious attempt to avoid punishment for the same fault by being "proved" a witch.

After Sekau announced the cause of her eye injury a small ritual was held to placate the ghost in order to heal the eye. It did not work, however, and Sekau became seriously ill as the infection spread through her body. The original diagnosis must have been wrong, therefore, and at this point Sekau announced she had had a dream in which a witch was revealed as the cause of the accident. By revealing this dream, Sekau made a serious accusation of witchcraft and a divination was subsequently held to discover who in the village was a witch. This second diagnosis was not unusual at all since Sekau was in a position of strength in the village and witches are prone to attack such people, but there were many other causes that she could have invoked. The fact that this cause rather than another was put forth is explicable, I feel, as a further means of dissociating herself from a possible witchcraft accusation because it made her the victim rather than the perpetrator of witchcraft.

LEnduwe

A great deal has been said about male dominance and assertiveness among the Gururumba, recognized as a desirable mode of behavior. We have also seen in the notion of harmful thoughts that this can create interpersonal hostility within the food-producing unit, with unfortunate consequences. If animosities between individuals reach a point of great intensity, open hostility may break out. In a sense, this is good because various social machineries then begin to operate to restore the relationship. If animosities remain hidden so that no drastic breach is created, this, too, can be dealt with in the ritual that assuages harmful thoughts. Another kind of situation, for which the culture offers no ready solution, is the sudden spiteful outburst that devastates another person, catches him off guard, and overwhelms him with shame. To be assertive a man must maintain self-confidence and must wield power in some form, but there are moments in a man's life when his self-confidence is undermined and power cannot be brought effectively into play.

LEnduwe was in his late thirties and had been married for several years to the same woman, but was without children. A man in this position would usually have sent his wife back to her kinsmen charging her with barrenness or would have taken a second wife. LEnduwe did neither of these things largely because of a deep personal attachment between them. Gururumba marriages are typically unstable in the early years, and although a couple may achieve a mutually satisfying adjustment after a time, it is unusual to find a man and woman with the kind of attachment that obtained between this pair. As sometimes happens with childless couples in our own culture, LEnduwe and his wife had a pet dog on which they lavished a degree of care and attention usually reserved for children. There was nothing special about the animal, it was just a scrawny, half-wild mongrel like other dogs in the village. The dog got fed a little more often than other dogs, but mostly it got petted, carried, and fondled while other dogs received little or nothing resembling affection from their masters.

One afternoon while LEnduwe was sitting with a group of people around a recently opened earth oven eating the food distributed at a naming ceremony, a woman strode into the village with a mangled chicken in her hands. She was wailing loudly so that her entrance onto the scene did not go unnoticed. She threw the bloody carcass into LEnduwe's lap and shouted, "Your child has killed my chicken," then launched into a long tirade against LEnduwe for pampering his "child" instead of training it properly. LEnduwe's dog was identified as the culprit beyond doubt as she described the animal she had seen kill her chicken, in terms that ridiculed LEnduwe's relationship to the dog.

Knowing the culture, and knowing LEnduwe to be a man in control of his position and resources, it would be predicted that such a display would have brought LEnduwe to his feet chastising the woman for making a public spectacle over such a small matter and offering compensation on the spot. He could have done this easily and done it in such a way as to make the woman look foolish. Instead he sat quite still and continued eating, responding in no visible way to the woman but concentrating all his attention on the food in front of him. His dog was sitting beside him and it appeared that LEnduwe had extended one hand toward the dog in a gesture of protection. It quickly became apparent, however, that he was attempting to choke the dog to death. Others became aware of this as the gasping and struggling of the dog increased in violence. All activity stopped as people watched with amazement. It was completely silent except for the slight sounds LEnduwe made as he ate and the noises of strangulation. Several minutes passed in stunned silence, but the dog did not die. Finally, someone took the dog away and in an awkward, bungling fashion tried to kill it by hitting it on the head with a sweet potato. People began to move once more and someone else tried a stick, but it was too small and broke. Another man stepped forward, arranged a noose, and hung the dog by the neck from a protruding house rafter which eventually brought an end to its life. Through all this LEnduwe continued to eat. The woman simply left.

LEnduwe's reaction to this situation was complex but relates primarily to his emotional involvement with the dog. No one, even jokingly, had ever referred to the dog as his "child" nor had there been any sentiment expressed to

him about his childless condition. He speculated with others about possible reasons for it but nothing more. Suddenly he was confronted with the possibility
that others thought him ridiculous because of this and, as he said later, "People
saw my mouth," an idiom expressing great shame. For that moment he lost his
ability to control the situation as it might have been controlled because he no
longer knew the basis on which others responded to him. It was only when
others completed the task he could not fully bring himself to do that the basis
was affirmed as unchanged and interaction allowed to proceed.

DaBore

For the purposes of certain kinds of research it is convenient to think of
societies like the Gururumba as relatively homogeneous. There is no class system, nor a complex division of labor, and many political and economic processes
are embedded in kin and local groups. One expects to find little ideological
variation in such a system, and the variation one does find is not of the same
magnitude as in a structurally complex society. The difficulty with this convenience is that it does not direct our thinking to the existing variability and may
thereby obscure the relationship between patterns as we describe them and human behavior as it occurs.

When lightning strikes a tree the electrical discharge sometimes appears
to roll down the trunk and disappear into the ground. The Gururumba have
seen this happen enough to believe that the ground near a tree struck by lightning will have a lightning ball in it somewhere. Such balls, if they can be found,
are prized as objects usable in garden magic. As a result, whenever lightning
strikes a tree men gather during the lightning exorcism ceremony to hunt for
these balls. They dig holes, sometimes fifteen or twenty feet deep near the tree
in this quest, and they frequently find things in the ground thought to be lightning balls. They are usually odd-looking pieces of decomposed stone, although
badly rotted wood and bone have also been identified in this way.

I was sitting on the edge of one of these holes one day when a man named
DaBore came along and sat down beside me. He asked the men in the hole what
they were doing, and after they explained, he turned to me and said, "There
are no lightning balls." He then got up and walked away. The men in the hole
laughed at my surprise and assured me that as long as they had known DaBore
he had never believed lightning balls could be found in the ground or that they
were good for anything even if they could be found. As far as could be discovered,
this was the only part of the supernatural belief system he did not believe in.
He had no rationale for his disbelief, nor did it stem from trying one out and
finding it did not work. Like other men he had a spirit house in his garden, and
attributed his various illnesses and misfortunes to ghosts, sorcerers, and witches.
There was nothing in his life history or his position in society that would help
explain it; he just did not believe in them.

One might speculate that variation of this order, equivalent to minor variations in dress or personal taste, identify a person's individuality and function psychologically to maintain the self—other boundary. In studies of culture, the inclusion of this kind of variation seems unnecessary, but it serves us here as a reminder that people see themselves apart from the patterns of their culture and to some extent mold those patterns to their own needs. DaBore's case and the others in this section, also, serve as a reminder that knowing a cultural description of the Gururumba is knowing them in a special sense, which goes only a little way toward knowing how to be a Gururumba.

Glossary

AFFINES. Kinsmen related by marriage.

ANTHROPOMORPHISM. The ascription of humanlike attributes to nonhuman phenomena.

CLAN. A social group recruited on the basis of common descent and common residence.

CONSANGUINEALS. Kinsmen related by descent.

ENDOGAMOUS. A social group is endogamous when members of the group feel that proper marriage partners come from inside the group.

EXOGAMOUS. A social group is exogamous when members of the group feel that proper marriage partners come from outside the group.

GENEALOGY. A systematic representation of the recognized kinsmen of a person.

LINEAGE. A corporate group in which recruitment is based primarily on a rule of unilinear descent. Resident lineage is used here to mean the lineage one is residing with as opposed the natal lineage, the lineage one was born into.

PATRILINEAGE. A lineage in which membership is defined on the basis of the genealogical linkage between fathers and their children.

PATRISIB. A sib in which the constituent units are patrilineages.

PHRATRY. A group of sibs occupying contiguous territory, committed to common defense, and recognizing a common origin.

POLYGAMOUS. A marriage pattern in which a man may legitimately have more than one wife simultaneously.

SIB. A loosely structured series of kin groups among which the genealogical relationships are vaguely defined.

TEKNONOMY. The practice of addressing an individual as the parent of his or her child. Instead of addressing a man by his name, for example, he is addressed as, "Father of ———— (name of the child)."

UXORILOCAL. A mode of residence in which the household of a married pair is established in the community under the sponsorship of the wife.

VIRILOCAL. A mode of residence in which the household of a married pair is established in the community under the sponsorship of the husband.

WARD. Political divisions of a village.

Recommended Reading

AUFENANGER, HEINRICH, The Kanggi Spirit in the Central Highlands of New Guinea. *Anthropos* 55:671–688, 1960.
A descriptive article concerned with the various forms of belief in demoniacal nature spirits found in highlands New Guinea.

BARNES, J. A., African Models in the New Guinea Highlands. *Man* 62: 5–9, 1962.
A discussion of differences between African and New Guinea lineage systems.

BERNDT, R. M., Excess and Restraint: Social Control Among A New Guinea Mountain People. Chicago: The University of Chicago Press, 1962.
An analysis of the way various aspects of culture and society impinge on the individual as socializing forces. Rich in case material.

BROWN, PAULA, Chimbu Tribes: Political Organization in the Eastern Highlands of New Guinea. *Southwestern Journal of Anthropology* 16:22–35, 1960.
An analysis of the organizational principles of Chimbu tribes.

LEAHY, MICHAEL AND M. CRAIN, The Land That Time Forgot: Adventures and Discoveries in New Guinea. New York: Funk and Wagnalls Company, 1937.
An autobiographical account of discovery and early exploration of the eastern highlands.

LUZBETAK, L. J., The Socio-religious Significance of a New Guinea Pig Festival. *Anthropological Quarterly* 27:102–128, 1954.
The symbolism and social function of the pig festival.

MEGGITT MERVYN, Growth and Decline of Agnatic Descent Groups Among the Mae Enga of the New Guinea Highlands. *Ethnology* 1:158–165, 1962.
Important because of the insight it gives into the nature of descent groups in the western highlands.

NILLES, JOHN, Natives of the Bismark Mountains, New Guinea. *Oceania* 14:104–123, 15: 1–18, 1943.
General ethnography of peoples in the upper Chimbu valley.

READ, K. E., Nama Cult of the Central Highlands, New Guinea. *Oceania* 23: 1–25, 1952.
A descriptive account and analysis of the symbolism of the men's secret cult among the Gahuku-Gama of the lower Asaro valley.
Cultures of the Central Highlands, New Guinea. *Southwestern Journal of Anthropology* 10: 1–43, 1954.
A general survey of cultural variation in the highlands.
Leadership and Consensus in a New Guinea Society. *American Anthropologist* 61:425–436, 1959.

A discussion of the personality type of men who rise to positions of leadership in Gahuku-Gama society.

REAY, MARIE, The Kuma: Freedom and Conformity in the New Guinea Highlands. Carlton: Melbourne University Press, 1959.

General ethnography of peoples living in the Wahgi valley.

SALISBURY, R. F., From Stone to Steel: Economic Consequences of a Technological Change in New Guinea. London and New York: Cambridge University Press, 1962.

An analysis of changes wrought in Siane society by the introduction of steel tools, money, and other elements of Western economy.

THE TWO WORLDS OF THE WASHO: AN INDIAN TRIBE OF CALIFORNIA AND NEVADA

James F. Downs

*University of Hawai,
Hilo Campus*

Before becoming an anthropologist the author served in the U.S. Navy during World War II and the Korean War, worked as a newsman, professional horseman, and farmer. After conducting field research among the Washo of California and Nevada and the Navajo of Arizona, he received his M.A. and Ph.D. in anthropology at the University of California at Berkeley. He has studied oriental languages and conducted research on Tibetan culture at the University of Washington and has taught at the University of Rochester, the University of Wyoming, and California State College at Los Angeles. He is now professor of anthropology at the University of Hawai, Hilo Campus. He has been a pioneer in conducting intercultural training programs for Navy and other personnel and has recently taken leave of absence from his position to return to active duty with the Navy for two years.

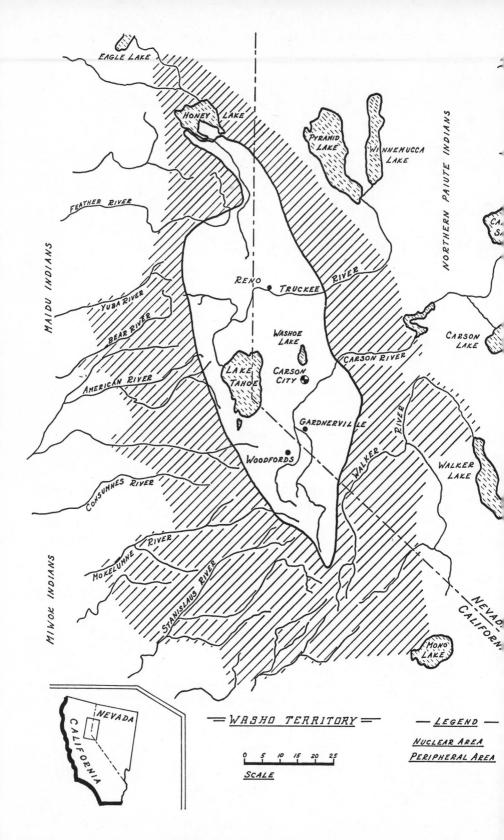

EAGLE LAKE

HONEY LAKE

PYRAMID LAKE

WINNEMUCCA LAKE

NORTHERN PAIUTE INDIANS

MAIDU INDIANS

FEATHER RIVER

YUBA RIVER

BEAR RIVER

AMERICAN RIVER

RENO

TRUCKEE RIVER

WASHOE LAKE

CARSON CITY

CARSON RIVER

CARSON LAKE

LAKE TAHOE

GARDNERVILLE

WALKER RIVER

WOODFORDS

WALKER LAKE

CONSUMNES RIVER

MOKELUMNE RIVER

STANISLAUS RIVER

MIWOK INDIANS

NEVADA
CALIFORNIA

MONO LAKE

NEVADA

CALIFORNIA

= WASHO TERRITORY =

— LEGEND —

NUCLEAR AREA

PERIPHERAL AREA

0   5   10 15 20 25

SCALE

Contents

A Washo family at the turn of the century. The man is erecting a gadu of branches and canvas while the woman dresses her daughter's hair. A tin bucket and iron frying pan have been added to the family's equipment but a woven cradleboard and small carrying basket are still in use. (Courtesy of The Southwest Museum, Los Angeles)

Two Washo women encamped near Lake Tahoe in the late 1890s. White style dress worn in this manner had come to be considered distinctly Washo. The cradleboard was in use as late as 1960. (Courtesy of The Southwest Museum, Los Angeles)

A storage basket made by the famous Washo basket weaver Dah-So-Lah-Lee. For many years she was subsidized by a Nevada physician so that she could devote herself to perfecting her art. Her baskets are among the best in the world and are prized by collectors and museums. (Courtesy of The Southwest Museum, Los Angeles)

1

The Two Worlds of the Washo

LAKE TAHOE LIES about 6000 feet above sea level in the eastern Sierra Nevada Mountains. The boundaries of the states of California and Nevada join in the center of the lake which has become a great monument to a modern affluent society in which hundreds of thousands of people can spend time and money on leisure activities.

On the southern shore in Nevada where gambling is legal, the view of the lake is blocked by elaborate casinos and night clubs vying with neon signs, fantastic architecture, and the nation's leading entertainers for the attention of the vacationers driving along the highway. Hotels, motels, restaurants, and curio shops crowd each other for space. On the slopes along the lake, real estate developers compete fiercely for land on which to build vacation homes. The California shore, less flamboyant but no less crowded, is lined with vacation homes, summer camps, and lodges. The lake is lashed by the wakes of motor boats and the beaches crowded with funseekers.

Lake Tahoe is the center of a mountain and desert world of recreation. From the tree line above Sacramento, the capital of California, to the glittering casinos of Reno and Carson City, Nevada, the area is devoted to camping, fishing, hunting, skiing, hiking, boating, gambling, and entertainment. To be sure, cattle graze in the mountain meadows and lumbermen work in the forests, but these activities are almost unnoticed in this world of leisure.

Lake Tahoe, however, is the center of another world. The lake was and is the center of a land inhabited by a small and virtually unknown people—the Washo Indians. To their descendants who live almost unnoticed and ignored in a number of "colonies" in the valleys of Nevada east of the lake and on small homesteads in the California mountains, the lake is still the center of the Washo world. These people view the lake as a precious and indeed a sacred spot. In the summer, Washo families frequently visit the lake, not for recreation, but to look at the blue waters and reflect on what they mean. They know that the lake contains the gigantic remains of the Ang, a monster bird which once terrorized their ancestors. They recall the incidents of their own history at each camp-ground, boat dock, and beach where once the Washo camped to fish in the summer. The great rock, towering over the public boat launching is the site of a sacred cave, sanctum of powerful shamans. Each creek flowing into the lake, each stand of trees or outcropping of rocks or lake in the high valleys is associated not only with the secular history of their people but with the sacred myth of the creation of the Washo world. At Emerald Bay, the mischievous companions, the long-tailed weasel and the short-tailed weasel, performed some miracle or committed some misdemeanor. The mysterious and malevolent Water Baby spirit lives in the Carson River, and a monster inhabits a sacred spring near there. In the heights beyond the lake, the dangerous wild men, half man and half demon, still roam. And in a cave above Double Springs the terrible one-legged giant Hanawuiwui lives. A remote meadow is remembered because there an offended shaman worked terrible vengeance against his enemies. In the eyes and hearts of the Washo this is the real world. The vacationers, the casinos, and the flashing speed boats are merely evidence of the latter day intrusions of powerful, numerous, and unknowing strangers. And yet, the Washo must live in this world created by the white man.

This book will describe how the Washo have managed to adjust to the dramatic changes that have occurred in their world in the past century and a half without losing their cultural identity or their contact with their own country. To understand this it will be necessary to examine something of Washo life before these changes occurred. With this understanding we can proceed to analyze the Washo response to the problem of the white man which they have shared with all American Indians.

Anthropologists who study the modern American Indian cannot boast of the romantic aloneness of the pioneering ethnographer reporting for the first time on the lives of some remote and previously unknown people. Instead, we stand on the shoulders of those who have gone before us and share our labors with our contemporaries. The many questions that have been asked of American Indian societies can seldom be answered by a single person. Several generations of anthropologists have studied the American Indian, first reporting the rapidly disappearing cultures of the prereservation times, then turning to documents of history to fill in the gaps in our understanding, and then returning to the modern Indian communities to study the effects of the intrusion of Euro-American culture on their land and their lives. This multifaceted interest in the American Indian has led to the development of specialists. Some students have concerned themselves only with linguistics or, in some cases, only with certain aspects of linguistics. Others have been interested in religion, personality, child-raising practices, economics or intercultural relationships. The list of specific interests is limited only by the imagination of science. One of the areas of widespread interest has been the question of change. How have the various American Indian tribes responded to the presence of another powerful and expansive culture? This study of change in its broadest form has come to be called acculturation. This study of the changes in the life of a small and relatively unknown people can draw then not only on the fieldwork of the author but on over a century of data collected by travelers, government officials, missionaries, and over six decades of specific research by anthropologists.

One of the earliest references to the Washo is to be found in a magazine article printed in 1873. A decade later the famous historian Hubert Howe Bancroft mentions the Washo and recounts a number of their myths, myths which are told today, sometimes in a somewhat altered form, but indesputably reminders of the heritage of the Washo. Since those early references to the Washo, such famous anthropologists as Alfred Kroeber, Samuel Barrett, Edward P. Gifford, and Robert Lowie have studied and reported on various aspects of Washo life. Among later generations of anthropologists such renowned names as Julian Steward, Omar Stewart, E. E. Siskin, and Robert Heizer have appeared in the Washo bibliography. In the past decade a number of younger anthropologists, including the author, have under the inspiration of Warren L. d'Azevedo continued research among these people. In addition to the professionals, a number of dedicated and expert amateurs have made major contributions to our understanding of the Washo. Of these Dr. S. L. Lee and Grace Dangberg are outstanding.

My own field experience among the Washo, a few months in 1959 and several shorter trips in the area in subsequent years, composes only a part of the total fund of knowledge that has been drawn upon to complete this book. A complete bibliography of Washo sources has been published recently and it covers some forty-five pages (d'Azevedo 1964). Many of the people who have contributed to our knowledge of the Washo Indians must of necessity go unmentioned in this book. It is only fair to them and to the reader to indicate the vast amount of labor on the part of many people from which I have been privileged to draw in an attempt to present the following discussion of the changes in the life of the Washo people over the past century.

The Washo inhabited the western edge of a vast area known as the Great Basin and display in a general way a special adjustment to the Basin environment that we can observe from the Sierra Nevada to the Great Salt Lake. Basic to an understanding of the Washo response to the appearance of the white man is an understanding of the adjustment these people had made to their environment. They were people without agriculture, domestic animals, metallurgy, or even a knowledge of pottery making. The tools available to them in exploiting their habitat were simple and few. They also, as we look at the whole history of mankind, were extremely old in a way perhaps representing very little more than the technical capacities of early man. From this base the Washo have been assaulted by the expansive, creative, and enormously technical culture of modern America as it spilled across the continent and at the same time developed and changed from a largely agricultural nation to the largest urban-industrial nation in the world. As the economic development of modern America has turned the sacred lake of the Washo into a gleaming, blinking, and glittering leisure world, so have other developments in American history created situations to which the always adaptable Washo have been forced to adjust. This book will examine the problem of how the Washo have managed to make these adjustments without losing their identity in the process.

2

The Washo

COMPARED TO their nearest neighbors, the Paiute and Shoshone peoples of the Great Basin, the Washo have never been a numerous people. Because their way of life was so generally similar to other Basin peoples, early explorers, when they met Washo bands in western Nevada, seem not to have differentiated them from the other pedestrian hunting and gathering peoples of the area. Even when it became clear that the Washo were not of the same stock as their neighbors, they were seldom encountered, for reasons we shall understand later, in groups larger than a family and, at the most, a few families. Moreover, the Washo often spent the summer months high in the Sierra Nevada, a practice which obscured the true numbers of the population. White observers tended to count only those Indians who were on hand, thus consistently underestimating the tribe. Nonetheless, researches among hunting and gathering peoples throughout the world, particularly groups in arid and semiarid regions, suggest that population density is very low and population seldom rises above the minimum capacity of the environment to support human life. Compared to much of the Great Basin, Washo country was provident and, we can assume, could have supported a larger population. In the middle of the nineteenth century perhaps as many as 3000 speakers of the Washo language lived along the eastern slope of the Sierra Nevada. Some authorities argue that the number was much lower but few would suggest that it was much greater. The Washo seldom, if ever, congregated in a single place. Washo speakers were distributed from the valley of the Walker River in the south to the southern edge of Honey Lake in the north. In general, the Washo remained in a series of valleys at the eastern foot of the Sierra Nevada, wandering both east and west as their search for food directed them but always returning to the gathering and hunting grounds in the lowlands. Each of these valley dwellers were in practice independent of one another, with their own food-taking cycle, their own leaders and their own network of social relations. A common relationship between all Washo speakers was recognized but it carried few obligations with it.

128

It is difficult to draw distinct boundaries when describing the distribution of primitive peoples because the concept of national territory, to be defended on principle because it lies on one side of an imaginary line, is most frequently absent. This is the case with the Washo, who viewed their territory as a series of layers. In the center was Lake Tahoe and the previously mentioned valleys where the Washo fished and hunted and regularly camped. This land was more or less vigorously defended from the intrusions of neighboring Paiute people from Nevada or the Maidu or Miwok to the west. However, even these invasions could be measured in degree. The Washo tended to fight most readily if the strangers sought to fish in "their" lake or hunt "their" large game, such as deer. On the other hand, the Washo seemed to feel the invasion was much less serious if the strangers had simply come to gather plant food. Beyond this central zone was a much wider area in which the Washo wandered on hunting and gathering trips during part of the year. This peripheral zone extended to Walker Lake in the southeast and almost to Pyramid Lake in the northeast. To the west, Washo informants all assert that gathering expeditions went almost to Sacramento, California. Washo hunters pushed into the foothills above the Sacramento Valley, but Washo fishermen were never safe if they attempted to fish in the westward flowing rivers of California. It is certain that if one were interviewing Paiute, Maidu, or Miwok informants the zones described as peripheral Washo would be described as peripheral Paiute or Miwok, and so on. Thus each of these peoples tended to occupy a central area which they defended as their own on certain occasions and returned to as to a home port. But between groups were vaguely defined "grey" zones which were often jointly exploited without undue hostility. It is clear that in the northern and southern extremes of the Washo area Washo bands lived on quite intimate terms with Paiutes in the same area. Such groups were often referred to as "half Paiute" by the Washo living in the central area around the present sites of Carson City, Minden, and Gardnerville, Nevada. To the west, Washo often married into Miwok groups without abandoning their Washo identity.

It should be emphasized that although we speak of Washo movements as "wandering" there was nothing casual or unplanned about these movements. The common view of simple hunting and gathering peoples, or even pastoral nomads, wandering aimlessly over the land in search of food is, as we shall see, quite far from the truth. The exploitation of even a relatively provident environment with such a simple technology required careful planning and a great deal of knowledge about the plants, animals, climate, and soils of the area. However vaguely the boundaries might be defined, it is possible to rather definitely locate the aboriginal Washo country as a lozenge shaped area with Lake Tahoe as a rough center, Honey Lake as the northern extreme, and the headwaters of the Stanislaus River as a southern extreme. Many Indian tribes in the United States have been moved to reservations far removed from their aboriginal grounds or encompassing only a small portion of their original range. The Washo have always lived and continue to live on their home grounds. This is important in understanding how, in spite of enormous changes in their lives, the Washo have remained stubbornly Washo.

Physical Description

The Washo clearly illustrate the fallacy of the still popular belief that there is some meaningful connection between the way of life of a people and the genetic makeup of that people. Beset by a century of dramatic changes, the Washo have remained an identifiable social and cultural unit despite the fact that they have mingled their "blood" with that of many races. The Washo population today carries in its inheritance legacies from all the races which have entered the West as well as that of many if not most of the Indian tribes of the United States. Almost since the earliest period of Indian-white contact, prostitution and common-law and formal marriage have contributed a regular flow of Caucasion genetic material into the population. In addition, Negro individuals frequently have married into the tribe, and many Washo have married or lived with Mexicans. Specific instances of possible oriental parentage have been pointed out by informants. In more recent times, Filipino and even Eskimo genes have entered the Washo genetic heritage. The increased association between Indian groups brought about by the automobile and the Native American Church has led to many intertribal marriages and the integration of schools in both California and Nevada has led to a number of Indian-white marriages. With this mixed genetic history it should be no surprise that there is no single Washo type. For the most part, those people who think of themselves as Washo and are so considered by others display the common features of almost all American Indians. Straight black hair, dark brown eyes, and brown skin are almost universal. Many Washo men and women share characteristics common among the tribes of central California, a kind of robust roundness. Some men may be well over 6 feet and weigh over 200 pounds, and a few women are also large in proportion to their sex. On the other hand, many Washo appear well below average height and some older informants, reportedly "full-blood," are scarcely above 5 feet. Many individuals would be considered to be either Chinese or Japanese were they encountered in the cities of the west coast and many others would pass as Mexicans if they were seen in California. Facial structure tends to a roundness more characteristic of the statuary of early Mexico than the high cheek bones and acquiline noses of the warriors of the Great Plains who serve as the popular model for Indians in this country. Despite the wide variations in physical type, white residents of the area and anthropologists, after a bit of practice, are seldom wrong in identifying the Washo from among the neighboring Paiutes. However, it is more than likely that such observers are responding to a series of subtle and unnoticed cultural clues rather than any distinguishing physical characteristic.

The Language

While genetics or "race" is not a unifying factor among the Washo, the language which they speak has been. Linguistically, the Washo constitute a unique group in the Great Basin. In that vast region, covering all of Nevada and parts of Idaho, Oregon, and Colorado, the languages spoken were all representatives of a language family or stock known as Uto-Aztecan. In this area there were two major divisions, Paiute and Shoshonean.

Shoshonean speakers occupied a broad band extending out of the Basin to the Pacific Ocean. Various dialects and languages of the Uto-Aztecan stock extended south from the Great Basin to the valley of Mexico where the civilized Aztecs spoke a language of this stock, Nahuatl. In the Great Basin the only language not related to Uto-Aztecan was that spoken by the Washo.

For many decades students of American Indian languages, beginning with Leslie Powell who first attempted to classify the languages of North America, listed Washo as a separate language stock with only this single representative in all the world. However, later linguists, continuing the investigations, have decided that Washo is a representative of a widely scattered language stock known as Hokan. Hokan languages are found in California and are spoken by the Esselen, Salinan, and Chumash of the central coast of California. To the north the Achomowi or Pitt-River people of northern California also speaks a Hokan language. These western representatives of the Hokan languages are not closely related to each other, suggesting that the separation into distinct languages occurred many thousands of years ago. There is one school of thought which holds that Hokan speakers are the oldest California population and that subsequent invasions of the west coast have submerged or dispersed the original settlers of the area, leaving only these scattered groups widely separated from each other, each language developing without contact with the other. Another enclave of Hokan languages, even more distantly related, is located in the extreme southern portion of California. Some linguists believe that even more distantly related languages are found far to the east. These people include the Creek, Cherokee, Choctaw, Chickasaw, and Seminole of the southeast and the famous Iroquois of the north. These tenuous relationships should not be considered evidence of anything more than very ancient common stock from which all of these languages must have sprung. Certainly there is no direct relationship between even the Hokan enclaves on the west coast, let alone the eastern representatives of this language family. As this book is being written, linguists are in the field working with Washo speakers attempting to describe the language fully and to further understand its history.

Today all Washo speak English from childhood. The older people speak an "English" that may be difficult for the untrained ear to understand. Perhaps a few younger people no longer understand their language, but the majority of the tribe still speak the language and use it in everyday life. Many of the words used to describe conditions of the past have slipped from their memories. Old people often argue for hours trying to decide for a linguist or an anthropologist whether a certain word means moose or buffalo or elk—all of these species have been extinct (if indeed they ever existed) in this area for well over a hundred years. On the other hand, the language has expanded and developed in order to deal with modern conditions. Washo can discuss such problems as the settlement of the tribe's land claim suit against the government or the problems dealing with white law with only an occasional need to use an English word for which there is no Washo equivalent.

3

The Land

A
S THE WASHO today live in two cultural worlds, so they have in the past
lived in two environmental worlds. The central zone of the Washo
homeland lay along the boundary between two life zones. In their quest
for food the Washo drew on the resources of three other life zones. The most
important area, the strings of valleys lying along the eastern edge of the Sierra
Nevada, is part of the region known as the Great Basin. This vast interior area
lies to the north of the Colorado River and between the Sierra Nevada on the
west and the Rockies to the east. Rivers which rise on the western slope of the
Rockies and on the eastern slopes of the Sierra do not drain into the sea but into
the center of the Basin. The Great Salt Lake is the largest consequence of this
phenomonon known today, but in the past even greater lakes existed in the
Basin.

Today the Basin is a high arid area lying in a life zone known to biolo-
gists as *Artemisian*. To anyone who has driven through the interior of the United
States, the artemisian zones can be recalled as the least inspiring scenery one is
apt to encounter. The stark waterless beauty of the true southern desert or the
vast almost oceanlike quality of the Great Plains or the spectacular vistas of the
mountains provide delights for the eye and the emotions of the traveler. The
artemisian zones, however, are remarkable for their unbroken sameness. Sagebrush is the most common plant, growing grey and dull over millions of acres
and giving way in the higher reaches of ground to the dull green of greasewood. Rising above these plains are the mountains which form ranges across the
entire Basin running generally from north to south. These mountains, rising
only a few thousand feet above the already high valleys, are as arid and as unin-
viting as the valleys. In the higher ranges the stunted, twisted piñon pine grows
in great profusion and, as we shall see, greatly affects the life of the Basin peoples. Rivers are few and pitiful in this area. Seldom does a river run year-round,
but in the few places where this does happen, an oasis of green marks the central valley floor. Watercourses are often dry for most of the year and then be-

come roaring torrents during the season of cloudbursts. They drain into sinks which remain swamps throughout the year or in the lesser sinks they slowly diminish until only a salt-rimmed plate of drying mud remains in midsummer. Springs are small and generally infrequent, and the water table is often extremely deep or in many areas seemingly nonexistent. Extremely detailed hydrographic surveys of recent years have revealed many more natural springs than we had previously suspected, but these are tiny, often dry and of little modern significance, although they may have been important to the Indians of the past.

Wagon train pioneers dreaded the Great Basin perhaps more than any other portion of the trip from east to west. Dry camps were frequent and grazing often sparse or unobtainable. The crossing of the Humboldt sink, some 85 miles of a waterless basin, was a graveyard of pioneer hopes and dreams. It was dotted with the carcasses of oxen, mules, and horses; the wrecks of abandoned wagons; and the treasures of eastern homes thrown away to lighten the load as the travelers struggled to reach water before they and their animals gave out completely. Much of the Great Basin offered little to the white man save for grazing cattle, often at a ratio of 80 or 100 acres per a single head. The stark mountains contain a great many metal and mineral deposits and therefore attracted the most interest in the area. The infrequent well-watered areas became the sites of the small towns of central Nevada; Winnamucca, Battle Mountain, and others.

Despite its formidable appearance, the Basin provided, for those who knew the land and how to exploit it, a surprising amount of food. While the sage and the greasewood provided little more than firewood, the dry earth regularly produced short-lived harvests of seed-bearing grasses of many kinds. Water-holding roots grew underground. The gopher, ground squirrel, and jack rabbit existed in amazing numbers. The pronghorned antelope, although not as numerous as on the Great Plains or in the verdant valleys of California, was common. In the mountains were the desert bighorn sheep. The mule deer was distributed, not thickly, but widely through the area. In addition, numerous edible insects existed, wild fowl came to the sinks and in the higher ranges, the piñon pine provided a singularly plentiful and important staple crop. While the Basin seldom could provide a living for large populations, a small group, energetic and alert to all the possibilities of the area, could survive surprisingly well.

The lowland valleys of the Washo country were perhaps the best of all the Basin environments. Compared to the waterless and frequently rainless steppes to the east they were well watered with rains falling in the winter and spring and occasionally in summer cloudbursts. The larger watercourses such as the Carson and Walker rivers flowed during the entire year. Each of these valleys repeated the general Great Basin pattern. Streams and rivers flowed east out of the Sierra Nevada into lakes and sinks in the low portion of each valley. Aside from the green belts along the rivers and the luxuriant growth of the sinks, the land was covered with the dull sagecovered plant life of the Basin steppes, giving way to greasewood and finally to the dark green of the piñon forests. Antelope and jack rabbit lived in the valleys. Deer were to be found in the foothills to the east and west. Waterfowl flocked to the sinks, and wild fowl such as sage hen were numerous. In addition, ground squirrels, gophers, and field mice were especially plentiful. As attractive as the land was, in comparison to the bone dry steppes to the east, the Washo country was not a benign habitat. Winters were cold with snowfall a regular occurrence. Freezing temperatures were common in the winter, and severe floods in the late winter and spring turned the valleys into quagmires. After the brief blooming of the spring, the valleys became dry very quickly, save along the margins of the watercourses. Summer heat was often intense, remaining in the 90s for long periods and frequently soaring well above 100° F. The more mobile game tended to drift out of the hot basins and into the higher country. As this occurred, many Washo turned to the other half of their physical world, the high mountains to the west. The Artemisian zone of the eastern valleys is at an altitude of from 3000 to almost 5000 feet. The transition to the *Sierran* zone is abrupt. The mountains rise directly out of the floor of the valleys without intervening foothills. The great eastern escarpment of the Sierra soars to 8000 and 10,000 feet above the valley floor. The sheer mountain sides are covered with pine and cedar, and are in many places virtually impossible to traverse. Entry into the mountain world from the valleys was by way of a number of passes. Many of these are the sites of today's modern highways as they were in the past the routes of immigrant wagons. Others, too high and tortuous for either wagon or automobile, are even today little more than trails. The major passes such as Carson, Ebbets, Donner, Monitor, Beckwith, and Walker have played important roles in the history of the modern west. In many cases the pass is linked to the lower valleys by the dramatic canyon of a large river such as the Carson or the Truckee.

Once over the eastern escarpment the mountains fall off into a series of high valleys from 6000 to 8000 feet above sea level. The largest of these valleys is the site of Lake Tahoe, some 30 miles long and 10 miles wide. In addition, there are dozens of other high mountain lakes and hundreds of streams watering this high country. Damp mountain meadows abound amid the pine-covered slopes. The mountain world provided an entirely different set of resources for the Washo. Although the lowland rivers provided some fishing, it was the high country to which the Washo turned for this all important food. Deer were common throughout the mountains, and mountain bighorns in the higher peaks. The woodchuck and a number of species of squirrel were numerous. Fur bearers such as the fox, lynx, bobcat, mink, beaver, and weasel were taken in the mountains. On the highest peaks eagles, prized for their magical feathers, nested. The damp mountain earth provided a wide variety of root and bulb plants and a number of greens and berries in the summer, and as the millions of vacationers have learned, the temperature is never uncomfortably high. There was always an adequate water supply and plenty of food. Firewood and shelter were easily obtainable. However, in the high country winter came early, with the first snows falling in October, and stayed late, with some of the valleys snowbound in May and early June. The winters were severe. The land was covered many feet deep with snow, and lakes and streams were frozen. Game animals either went into hibernation or drifted into the lowlands. In ancient times it is doubtful that any Washo remained in the mountains in the winter. The problem of survival in such an environment was quite beyond the capabilities of a people with such a simple technology.

Above the high valleys the mountains provided yet two more life zones from which the Washo could draw sustenance, although they seldom dwelt there. Above the lakes are the high *Alpine* plateaus where pine gives way to green and silver aspen groves set in wide grassy meadows. Deer often inhabited this area and a number of smaller game animals as well, but this zone provided little else. Above this rose the barren rocky peaks of the *Arctic* zone above timber line. The plant life in this area is limited to some grasses, mosses, and lichens, and in the lower reaches, a few hardy trees. The mountain sheep roamed here and the often fat marmot, but in general the extremely high country offered little. Beyond the ridge of the Sierra the mountains fall away for nearly a hundred miles in ever-descending steps until in the foothills the pines give way to the oak-dotted grasslands typical of much of interior California. This zone was seldom a permanent home for the Washo, but it was often visited in order to collect acorns, which were exceedingly plentiful and exceedingly nutritious. Here too the deer population was high when compared to Nevada. In the summer and fall the weather is hot and dry, but the winters are comparatively mild and a few Washo families sometimes wintered there rather than risk being trapped by the snows in the mountains by attempting to return across the mountain too late in the fall.

Thus, the Washo were able to draw on the resources of three main types of country: the arid but botanically and zoologically varied land east of the mountains, the plentiful fish, game, and plant life of the high mountains; and finally the animal and plant life of the western slopes of the mountains. A list of all the plants used by the Washo for food and all the species of animals hunted would be far too long to publish here. An indication of the potential of this land can be found in the estimate made by one zoologist that on an average every square mile of Nevada contained a population of nearly 12,000 mammals of all species. Of course most of these animals were small—squirrels, gophers, and field mice—but even such small animals in the aggregate suggest a great potential for those willing to seek out and find them. The Washo country is the only part of Nevada in which a number of animals, including the bear and several other fur bearers, still exist.

In this section we have seen a very general picture of the stage on which the Washo worked out their way of life. It has been estimated that the tribe regularly occupied some 13,000 square miles of this country. This means that even if we accept the highest estimate of population, the human density in the area was only a fraction over four persons per square mile. This was among the higher density ratios for the Great Basin but not as high as some. It was, however, enormously higher than the ratio of two and a half square miles per person reported for Central Nevada.

4

Using the Land

THE FAMOUS ANTHROPOLOGIST A. L. Kroeber once listed the Washo as among the simplest cultures on the North American continent. Without agriculture or domestication and with an extremely simple technology such societies are heavily influenced by the quest for food. Although the Washo habitat was more benign than that of other Basin societies, it could provide adequate support for the tribe only if it was most carefully exploited. In large part, Washo society and Washo social behavior were shaped by the environment. One might say that the Washo, in the absence of a complex technology, used their social structure as a tool in exploiting their environment. In this section we will examine the actual business of making a living under these conditions and see how the institutions of Washo society served to most efficiently exploit the land.

The Washo obtained food by three means: gathering, fishing, and hunting. Each of these activities required knowledge and skills and could be most successfully carried out by groups composed in a certain way. No single means of livelihood could provide a year-round supply of food for these people. Their situation and that of the majority of people of the Great Basin was one in which the failure of any of the varied sources of sustenance could spell disaster. Far to the northwest an elaborate nonagricultural culture was developed by the coastal peoples who were able to depend almost solely on the endless supply of fish. On the Great Plains, the introduction of the horse and the great numbers of buffalo made possible the development of a vigorous and elaborate hunting culture. Over much of California the infinite supply of acorns served as a basis for large and relatively elaborate societies. But in the Basin, no matter how plentiful any given source of food might be, it would not support a population for an entire year. Therefore, the movements of the Washo people and even the organization of the family life were at least partially shaped by the exploitive possibilities of the environment. The Washo "calendar" might be said to be divided into three years: the fishing year, the gathering year, and the hunting year.

136

The Fishing Year

The year began for the Washo in hunger. The last of the seeds and meat taken in the fall were usually consumed by the end of the winter and the weeks before spring were a time of near starvation. Hunting was seldom good at this time and gathering even less so. Late winter was a time of death, for the very young and the very old. The early weeks of spring provided fresh food in the form of bulb plants and early grasses, and spring was a prelude to the season of plenty provided by the upland lakes. As soon as the snows began to leave the lower foothills young men and boys, often accompanied by young unmarried women, began to trek into the mountains. Before the snow had left its shores these young people arrived at Lake Tahoe. There they lived in caves and other natural shelters. Wearing only loin cloths and small aprons and protected from the still cold spring weather by rabbit skin blankets, they began to fish for whitefish. This early trek of the youths relieved the pressure on what little food remained available to the older people and children in the lowlands. In some cases, the young men would return to the winter camp with fish so that their families might have enough food to survive and to regain their strength for their own trek to the lake. Relieved of the continual threat of starvation that was part of the winter, on their own and away from their elders and free of the restrictions that winter placed on their movements, the young people treated these expeditions as adventures. Young men displayed their hardiness by entering the tributary streams with fish harpoons, although the water could have been only a few degrees above freezing. With plenty of food, there was time for social get-togethers between people from different parts of the Washo country. A form of field hockey was popular as were archery contests and races. Dancing was common and the presence of young women provided an opportunity for courtship and sexual relations. In addition to fishing, the woodchucks provided meat, albeit thin and not too nourishing after a winter's hibernation. Early spring plants provided much needed vegetable food. But the primary activity was taking the whitefish, which broiled on a stick was eaten while fresh in great quantity. The fish were also dried in the open air for future use.

As the weather improved, the people remaining in the lowlands began to move toward the lake. Each family decided for itself when to leave the winter camp and move. Families composed of younger and more vigorous people began earliest. Groups with old people and infants tended to wait until the weather was better before moving to the 6000 foot elevation of Lake Tahoe. By early June almost the entire Washo population was encamped on the shores of the lake. As we shall see later, the Washo tribe was rather vaguely divided into territorial groups. This division was adhered to in the spring migration, with the people from Sierra Valley and Honey Lake making camp on the north edge of the lake while the people from Carson Valley, Woodfords, and the southern portion of the Washo country camping to the south.

By early June, many species of fish began to swim out of the deep lake into the streams in order to spawn. The two most important species were native trout and a type of large sucker which came up the streams by the thousands, their bodies crowded from bank to bank. Informants recall that their older relatives told them of the times before the appearance of the white man when the spawning runs were accompanied with religious ritual, although its exact form has now been forgotten. A number of accounts suggest that certain men would dream that the run would start soon and would advise the people to be prepared. This waiting period was a time of dancing and singing when respected elders would exhort the people to obey the laws of the Washo and to live properly. There may have been some ritual attached to the taking of the first fish. The tribes to the west often had elaborate first fish ceremonies. Among the Washo, such ritual seems not to have been elaborate nor important and it was quickly abandoned as the whites appeared in the Lake Tahoe country. It may have been that only certain groups practiced such ritual at all inasmuch as it is most frequently mentioned in connection with the northern bands.

The actual spawning runs were time of intense activity. Men, women, and children from the oldest to the youngest assisted in gathering as many fish as possible from the hordes struggling up stream. Taking fish under these conditions required little skill. People waded into the streams armed with baskets, scooping up the fish and tossing them onto the bank. There the fish were taken up and boned, split down the back and the spine and ribs removed, leaving two meaty fillets. These were placed on racks to dry in the sun and air. Female fish were stripped of their roe which was eaten raw or spread out to dry to be stored against future need. And, of course, fresh fish was broiled and eaten regularly. Often, fishing at the height of the run continued through the night by torchlight, which reflected on the backs of the fish enough to allow the fishermen and women to work. The spawning runs lasted perhaps two weeks during which time enormous amounts of fish were prepared. The leading authority on the native fish of America reports that this area could produce, on a year-round basis, as much as 200 pounds of fish per square mile. However, Washo technology was not able to take full advantage of this resource. The Washo knew of no other way to preserve fish save to spread the fillets on a rack exposed to the sun and air. This method would keep the flesh edible for a long period in the high cool mountain country. However, the Washo had learned that if the dried fish were taken into the warm lowlands it would spoil. A knowledge of smoking, as was practiced on the northern coast, would perhaps have enabled the Washo to live nearly year-round on the resources of Lake Tahoe and its contributing streams. However, without this knowledge, the fish resources were useful only while the Washo remained in the high country.

As the summer progressed, the snow left the higher valleys which were the sites of many other smaller lakes. When the spawning runs began to decline, individual families began to leave their lakeside camps and head into the higher mountains. This was done with some reluctance because the spring fishing period was a time of much social interaction. Relatives and friends separated during the winters, renewed acquaintances. Leaders of the various groups met and conferred. Medicine men competed with each other in displays of their magical powers. Dances and games were held. Courtships were initiated or re-

newed and marriages consummated. News about the presence of game, the prospects for the gathering of seeds and other vegetable food, and the behavior of
the neighboring tribes was exchanged. Above all, it was a period when the
Washo, often scattered and isolated, were joined as a single people engaged in
the same activities. From Lake Tahoe, families and groups of families went to
Tallac and Blue Lake and dispersed throughout the mountain country where
they set up camps for the summer. The damp mountain meadows provided an
increasing amount of vegetable food. The animal life of the mountains became
more available for hunters. At Blue Lake every spring and summer great numbers of mountain quail, decoyed by the reflections on the water, were found
drowned. These were regularly gathered to add to the larder of the people who
camped there. The high mountain camps are still identifiable because of the
presence of granite boulders pock-marked with bedrock mortars, or *lam,* where
the Washo women sat during the day to grind seeds or berries or to pulverize
dried fish eggs. While the women gathered and prepared vegetable food, the
men fished the lakes and streams. In the absence of the spawning runs, fishing
was a business calling for a great deal of skill. The best fishermen often used a
two-pronged fish spear. The head was made separately of wood, sinew, and
bone, and fitted onto a pole. Fish could be taken with a spear by a man standing
on the bank or rock overlooking a river or stream. Frequently, fishermen stood
waist deep in the water, alert to the flash of a fish swimming nearby. Because of
the deflection caused by the water, skill with a harpoon was hard won, coming
only after long years of practice. Platforms were built over good fishing spots so
that the fisherman could take fish with a spear or with a net. Dip nets wielded
by a single man were woven of plant fibers. Larger nets were handled by several
men at once, working either from the banks or wading in the water. The Washo
also made rather elaborate bone hooks with which they caught fish from deep
pools or in the lakes. In addition to these active means of taking fish, the
Washo often diverted small streams so that they could gather the fish stranded
by the receding water or trapped in shallow pools. Sometimes, in rapid streams
where fish were difficult to see, dams were built to pond the water so that a man
with a net, spear or hook could see his quarry. In the absence of a net, a gathering basket might be wielded as a net and frequently willow wands were woven
into a fish trap. These traps, completely blocking a stream, were the property of
a single man or family. Fish wiers and dams were also constructed to enable
fishermen with specially made conical baskets to wade into the water after their
quarry. For bait, the Washo gathered angleworms, salmon eggs, and minnows.
As the summer went on, the Washo began to drift toward the lowlands. Some
families started the trip as soon as the fishing at Lake Tahoe dropped off, making their summer camps along the banks of the upper reaches of the Carson or
the Truckee rivers rather than at the high lakes. As the water level began to
drop in the heat of the summer, minnows would be taken from shallow pools in
flat-seed winnowing baskets. Hundreds of the tiny fish were taken at a time and
baked in an earth oven. This was a hole in the ground in which a fire had
burned for several hours. The fire was scraped out, the minnows put in the hole

and covered with earth, and another fire built on top of the hole. This method of cooking minnows disappeared soon after the Washo obtained frying pans from the whites.

The trek to the lowlands was not motivated by fish resources. In fact, by late summer, fishing was not good enough to supply all the food needed. The important issue, however, was the fact that the many different grasses of the valleys were ripening and the seed harvest was at hand. Interest in fishing waned as the gathering season approached. The fall was also the time of the most intense hunting of big game so that fishing became a secondary activity. However, it was never completely abandoned. Even in the depth of winter, when no other food was available, it was possible to fish. The ice on deep pools could be broken open and fish taken with hook and line or by spearing, or nets could be spread between two holes and the fish trapped in them. Minnows crowded into pockets in the frozen streams were also easy to catch. Thus, the fishing year lasted all year long with its peak in the early spring and its importance slowly tapering off until the following spring.

Fishing Technology, Society, and Culture

The fish resources of the Washo country were comparatively high. They were at their highest at a crucial time in the food gathering cycle. At the end of the winter when food was scarce, the spawning runs at Lake Tahoe provided an enormous amount of food for a relatively low expenditure of energy. From this high point, the return from fishing dropped until it became easier and more profitable to turn to other sources of food. However, throughout the entire year, fish provided the Washo with some and, at times, their only food. To obtain this important part of their diet, the Washo developed the most complex part of their technology. Compared to hunting and gathering, fishing required immeasurably more tools and devices and an exceedingly high degree of skill. The making of fishhooks and spears was a complex job, equal to the making of bows and arrows, and their use required as much practice. Fish weirs, dams, traps, and fishing platforms were all projects much more ambitious and complex than even the Washo winter house, or *galesdangl*. The Washo skill at basketry was employed in fishing as was the knowledge of string and rope making from vegetable fibers. We have seen, however, that technology failed them in the matter of preserving enough fish to last the year round. This failure profoundly affected the yearly cycle and the social organization of the Washo. Fishing was important socially because it tended to concentrate population. The most marked example is at Lake Tahoe where almost all the Washo people gathered in the spring. Perhaps at no other time of the year did all the Washo come together for so long a time. It is not surprising then that the lake plays an important role in Washo culture. It is the center of the Washo world, geographically and socially. Washo mythology and folklore centers around the lake. Even today, almost every bay, inlet, and stream mouth has a legendary or mythological association. On the shores of the lake grew the dangerous and semisacred wild parsnips. From the great rock where the shamans had a secret hiding place to the other end of the lake there is, according to Washo belief, a roadway of white sand on which a powerful shaman could walk without drowning. And, as we shall see, it was the lake and its environs which the Washo defended most vigorously against intruders.

However, fishing is an activity which does not require large-scale cooperation. One needs only to look at a modern trout stream or fishing pier to realize the truth of this statement. Each fisherman searches the same water, using the same methods, but each is lost in his own isolation. In a sense this was true of the Washo. Even during the spawning runs, each family fished for itself. The number of fish was so great that there was little competition. There was more than plenty for all. When fishing by other methods, a single man or, at the most, a few men could perform all the necessary tasks. A platform could be made by a man and his sons or brothers. A half dozen men, the males of a single big family or two average families, could build a fish trap or dam or divert a stream. A stream only a few yards wide could be swept by three or four men holding a net or pushing a bundle of willows to entrap the fish. There was no particular advantage to large-scale cooperation. If Washo technology had included the ability to build boats sturdy enough for long-line fishing on Lake Tahoe, perhaps institutions based on the necessary cooperation would have been developed. The Washo knew only of boats made of bundles of tule which were useful on shallow lakes. Fishing encouraged association, at Lake Tahoe and the lesser lakes of the mountains and along the banks of the streams and rivers, but it did not encourage organization. A man and his wife and children, with a few unmarried relatives, could catch all the fish they could use. Once again we can speculate about the development of more complex social institutions based on fishing had the Washo been able to maintain themselves year round on fish resources. But, as we have seen, this was not possible and we will see how the demands of gathering and hunting worked to prevent any further development of a more complex organization.

The Gathering Year

While fishing started at a high point, producing a large amount of food at a time when it was badly needed and tending to concentrate people after a period of winter isolation, gathering was quite the opposite. The amount and varieties of plant food available to the Washo in the several environmental zones they inhabited was almost infinite. But seldom was it available in large amounts in a single place. Moreover, it was available in the smallest amounts and in the most widely dispersed places in the spring. During the winter little vegetable food was available. Water cress grew all winter long in some streams and it was eaten by those who found it, but most winter vegetable food was limited to that which had been gathered and stored in the summer and fall. By spring, the Washo had been living on pine nut flour, grass seeds, and dried meat for several months with very little green food or fresh meat. Usually by spring the food stored against the winter was gone, or very nearly so. The gathering year began with the first appearance of early plants. Wild lettuce and wild spinach were gathered in the foothills as soon as the leaves appeared. These plants seldom occurred in large beds so that some people were lucky and others were not. For people camped in the foothills, particularly to the east near the piñon groves, there were crops of what are called wild potatoes and Indian sweet potatoes. But once again, these did not occur in large amounts or in heavy concentration. People who lived near such beds gathered and cooked the tubers but there was never enough to encourage people to gather and search for them. In the lower reaches of the valleys there were many small bulbous plants. These were an important source of food in the springtime, but they were usually dug up and eaten on the spot by whoever found them. There were never enough in one place to justify gathering them for the family to consume. Near the swamps and sinks, and particularly near the hot springs which dot the eastern edge of the Sierra, the new shoots of the tule were gathered and the roots were frequently pulled up and cooked. Gathering in the spring was a hand-to-mouth-activity, important because it supplied fresh food when it was badly needed in the Washo diet. Perhaps in bad years it staved off starvation. But it was only a temporary source of food for families headed toward Lake Tahoe or an adjunct to the spring diet of fish during the gathering at the lake.

As the summer progressed and the tribe began to disperse, the tempo of gathering picked up. While the men fished the lakes and streams, the women spent more and more of their days wandering in the mountain meadows or in the foothills gathering plant food. Their only tools were a digging stick and a burden basket. The plants gathered depended on the spot where the camp was located and the season. Some plant foods were available for only a few days or weeks. During the summer, the mountains produced a variety of plants but none of them in quantity sufficient to overshadow the importance of fishing. In the early summer, the high meadows produced a native sunflower from which the seeds could be stripped and ground into flour. Wherever there was a damp meadow or swamp, the common cattail offered roots, new shoots, and seeds. In the early part of the summer before the fluffy cattail was formed, the seeds were wrapped in leaves and placed in the fire. They cooked into a brown paste which was eaten like candy and considered a singular treat. The sap of the sugar pine was another confection. The sap balls were picked from the bark and chewed by children and adults. During July, the wild strawberry plants bloomed around Lake Tahoe. Later in the summer they appeared at the higher elevations and were picked wherever found to be eaten fresh or mashed into a juice to form a sweet drink. From the spring on through the summer wild onions grew in profusion throughout the high country and were eaten raw with meals. The gooseberry was gathered in the late summer, but the Washo had no way of preserving them so that they were eaten only while blooming. The damp places of the mountains also produced wild rhubarb which was eaten fresh and cooked and was often dried to be eaten later. In the brief period it was available, many people went into the mountains to gather as much as they could carry against the winter food shortages. A number of root plants and bulbs called by various names, turnips, potatoes, and so on were found in large amounts in the mountains and formed the greater part of the Washo diet during the summer, although once again they were not preserved.

As the summer lengthened and productivity of fishing began to drop, gathering became more and more important. Most of the people camped in the mountains began to trek into the valleys east of the Sierra. Usually a few families would head west toward the foothills overlooking the Sacramento Valley. There they would gather chokecherries and wild grass seeds and hunt deer while waiting for the ripening of the acorns. Some of these people would return before the snows, but every year a few Washo families would remain on the western side of the mountain wintering alone or moving into Miwok villages to wait for the spring when they would go east to join their fellow tribesmen at Lake Tahoe. For those who went east into Nevada, the late summer and fall were periods of much movement. The usefulness of plant foods depended on the ability of a family to take advantage of opportunities as they occurred. While some species of plants were widely distributed in the lowlands, they seldom were ripe at the same time. Grass seeds might be ready for harvest in one place while they were still green only a few miles away. Thus, to take advantage of the many plants, the Washo had to be almost continually on the move. A few days of picking in one area would exhaust the supply and then the family would have to move on to another spot.

The irregularity of summer harvest and the limited areas in which plants ready for collecting occurred led to a wide dispersal of population and frequent movements. During this period, the Washo lived without housing, often simply camping without shelter at a suitable location or throwing up a windbreak of brush called a *gadu*. The summer was also a period when especially desirable crops led families to undertake long journeys. The report of a plentiful supply of chokecherries would lead many families to travel 20 or 30 miles to gather them. Good harvests of buckberry were common around the present site of Topaz, on the California-Nevada line. These berries were gathered in great number and dried for the winter. The various plants, combined with the more than adequate number of fish available, made summer a time of plenty, although to take advantage of the food supply the Washo had to move often. A drought could, of course, reduce the supply of plant food, but seldom would a situation develop wherein none of the many dozens of varieties of berries, roots, grasses, and seeds were not available. A short supply, while it might not lead to summer starvation, boded ill for the winter. The summer was important for the amount of surplus food over daily needs that could be saved against the winter. Seeds— wild mustard—pigweed, saltbrush, rabbitbrush, sand grass, and many others were particularly prized because they stored so well. Fruit which could not be stored was eaten on the spot in great quantity in order to preserve the grass seeds for periods of scarcity. The large number of chokecherries consumed in the summer are credited by the Washo for the presence of clumps of this tree throughout their land. The discarded pits, they claim, grew into small groves of trees which mark the sites of old camp grounds. The tempo of gathering against winter famine increased in late summer. During this period, the seed plants matured and were ready for harvesting. When this occurred it was a race against time to collect as much as possible before the seeds were disgorged for natural reseeding. And, as we have seen, the harvesting period varied greatly from place to place. To gather an adequate supply of seeds, Washo families were almost constantly on the move at this time, racing to collect as many seeds as possible.

As the season progressed from late summer to early fall, the attention of the Washo shifted more and more toward the culmination of the gathering year, the piñon harvest. As provident as the valleys and foothills might be, the supplies of the summer would not have lasted through the early winter. The piñon pine was the answer not only for the Washo but for almost all the people of the Great Basin. By late fall the widely scattered Washo people were beginning to converge once again. This time the direction of the trek was to the east to the range of low mountains where the pinon pine grew. Unlike Lake Tahoe, the piñon groves were relatively widely disbursed and the piñon gathering period did not lead to the assembly of all the Washo. The northern bands tended to concentrate in the hills north and slightly west of Reno, Nevada. The southern bands converged on an area to the south and east of Minden and Gardnerville, Nevada. Unlike the spring trek to the lake, the Washo were not on the verge of starvation in the fall. Plant food was plentiful, game was available, the people were well fed and healthy. This was a time of celebration and ritual in preparation for the piñon harvest.

The piñon pine bears a big cone containing many dozens of extremely large meaty seeds commonly called pine nuts. Unlike the sticky cones on many other pines, the piñon cone gives up its seeds relatively easily. These seeds could be gathered in large amounts between the time of ripening and the time they were expelled onto the ground. It was this harvest which provided the staple food of Washo life. In two weeks or a month the Washo could collect enough seeds to provide a basic food through most of the winter. The piñon harvest was regular for the country as a whole, but sometimes the trees in a specific area would bear few, if any, nuts. Thus, even in this instance gathering required that the Washo be able to shift ground, seek a new gathering spot, or some other alternative. However, there were many groves and even the most industrious Washo seldom could gather all the nuts available. The unfortunate who found that his customary grove did not provide enough food for winter could usually find picking rights somewhere else. By early October thousands, perhaps tens of thousands, of pounds of piñon nuts had been gathered and prepared for winter storage. The gathering year was for all practical purposes finished. Save for those families which maintained winter camps near the piñon groves, the people began to drift west again. Along the foothills and in particularly desirable spots in the valleys they set up winter camps and began to collect firewood, making great piles, higher than their winter houses, against the deep snows and bitter weather.

We see that the gathering year was much shorter than the fishing year. It began slowly with the earliest appearance of plants in the spring and grew in importance as more and more plants became available. Toward the end of the summer, the Washo people were involved in an almost frenzied gathering round until the final culmination of the gathering year in the piñon nut harvest. If the summer was good and the piñon pines fruitful, starvation could be avoided.

Plants and the Pattern of Washo Life

Although the gathering year began slowly and lasted only through the growing months of the plant life of the region, gathering permeated every phase of Washo life. During this period from spring to fall, vegetable foods played an increasingly important role in supplying food. And, in the final phase of the gathering year, the piñon harvest spelled the difference between security and starvation in the winter. The technology of fishing is immeasurably more complex than that of gathering, requiring as it does the making of many fishing devices and the fishing skills to make use of those devices. The gatherer requires only a digging stick to probe for roots and bulbs and baskets in which to carry the harvest. And once learned, the skills of harvesting are relatively simple. But to be an efficient gatherer requires a vast fund of knowledge about the growth cycle of dozens of plant species, an understanding of the effect of weather on growth and knowledge of soils and growing conditions. These mental skills can be taught in part. Many of them required learning through experience, so it was the oldest of the Washo women who were the most expert gatherers. Except for the pine nut and those foods taken in small amount and eaten on the spot, all gathering was done by the women. Perhaps more than any other aspect of Washo economic life, gathering gave continuity to the Washo year. Fishing and, as we shall see, hunting tended to supply foods in large amount over relatively short periods. Gathering supplied food over a longer period. It also provided the link between the plenty of the summer and the following spring when plenty came again. Fishing could be done in specific areas or not at all. Animals tended to frequent the same zones or to be absent. However, plant life would flourish in one place in one year and somewhere else in the next. A knowledge of the hows and whys of plant growth and native understanding of the relationship between spring rains and fall harvests is an important element in the Washo understanding of his universe. It might be said that fishing and hunting were arts but gathering approached a primitive applied science.

The preparation of plants differed radically from either fish or game. The latter could be air dried and later ground to be boiled, or it could be broiled or roasted fresh to be eaten on the spot. One needed to know how to butcher but little else. Plants, however, required treatment before they were palatable or even digestible. Wild spinach had to be leached by being soaked in a rapidly moving stream, otherwise the cooked greens would be too bitter to eat. Most plant seeds had first to be husked and separated from their chaff, an operation for which special winnowing baskets were made. Most seed plants required cooking of some sort before they were digestible. Washo women knew how to parch seeds with coals in special baskets and then grind them into flour, which would keep for many months. The piñon nut, rich and oily, will not keep long in a freshly picked state. Several different methods of precooking the nuts were practiced in order to keep them for a long period. The acorn had to be hulled, ground into flour, and the tannic acid leached out of the meal. This was usually accomplished by placing the meal in a shallow pit in the sand and pouring warm water through it. The grinding was accomplished in a *lam*, or bedrock mortar, using an elongated stone pestle. Other seeds were ground on a *demge*, a flat stone similar to a Mexican *metate* save for the legs. These were carried from place to place when camp was moved.

The structure of Washo society reflects the influence of gathering. It has been demonstrated that in gathering operations of this nature cooperation is of no assistance in increasing the harvest. Ten women gathering wild mustard can collect no more per capita than one woman. In fact, the group distracted by gossip, may actually collect less per capita. Thus, there was little encouragement for large groups to form even in an area of luxuriant growth. Each family would gather for its own. At times, with crops which appeared in small plots, only small groups could take advantage of the plants. A large group would simply exhaust the supply but no one would get enough, whereas a single family or small group could exploit a small patch of seeds and completely support itself for a few days at least. Even during the piñon harvest, cooperation of groups any larger than the family was unnecessary. Therefore, while piñon harvest was sufficient to encourage larger gatherings for ritual and recreation, it did not support the development of larger institutionalized groups. Once the crop was exploited the families dispersed, each pursuing its own destiny. There was very little ritual connected with gathering. No one dreamed of plant harvests as men are said to have dreamed of spawning runs. No one had to observe taboos prior to gathering, as we shall see was so common in hunting. No women are reported to have had special magical powers to increase their gathering ability, as did all good hunters. There was a taboo against breaking the limbs of the piñon tree, but this was a practical conservation measure despite the semisacred nature of the taboo. A man could, if he feared that there would not be rain enough for a good harvest, soak an old piñon cone in water and leave it in a nearby grove. All in all, gathering was a much more mundane and rational activity than either hunting or fishing. However, the piñon harvest was an occasion of the largest ritual of the Washo people. These gatherings, mentioned earlier, were called *gumsaba*, usually translated by the Washo as "big time."

The Big Time

The early fall was a time when the three phases of Washo subsistence activity coincided and if the year had been good it was a time of plenty. Fishing had not dropped off in the lower streams and rivers, game animals were at their best at this time, the various grass seeds and berries were harvested and the piñon nut harvest was ready. And unlike the spring, when the people were suffering from a shortage of food if not outright starvation, the population was relatively well fed from a spring of fishing and a summer of gathering. This was a time when large numbers of Washo could come together with the assurance that there was food enough for all. A well fed population was ready physically and spiritually for ritual activities and games. Moreover, after a summer of constant movement and relative isolation they were anxious for a period of social interaction, of story telling, courtship, gossip, and good fellowship.

In the distant past it is probable that the Washo in various parts of the country held separate *gumsaba* near their gathering grounds. However, most Washo today remember the *gumsaba* which were held in the latter part of the nineteenth and early part of the twentieth centuries and these have come to be a model upon which modern descriptions are based. The most popular gathering place was a small valley amid the piñon groves known as Double Springs Flats. Toward the end of the summer families and bands began to gravitate toward this spot. As the piñon harvest neared, most of the tribe had set up camp in a large circle, the people from various sections of the Washo country camping together in specific segments of the circle. Some informants recall that an influential leader in the area would have a dream calling the meeting together and would send a messenger throughout the area with a rawhide string on which the number of knots indicated the number of days before the meeting. Each day the messenger untied a knot. As the people gathered, the men set out to hunt. Some informants reported that the hunting continued over a four-day period. Throughout the United States four was a mystic number in Indian life.

While the men hunted, the women began to gather piñon nuts and other vegetable food. Each day before they began gathering they took a ritual bath. During the four-day period the leader who had called the meeting fasted, drinking only cold water and eating small amounts of cooked pinon nuts. During his fast he prayed for the success of the piñon harvest and good luck for the hunters. Each night the people danced the shuffling and monotonous round dance, which served the Washo in all ritual and social occasions. Gambling games were staged between teams and in the daytime races were held with the winners receiving food and deerskins. Teams representing the various sections of Washo country played a form of hockey. At the end of four days, according to the accounts given by old people, the food gathered and hunted was pooled and a respected elder chosen to divide it equitably. Each family head received enough to feed his family. During the feast which followed, respected leaders prayed and exhorted the people to behave properly, to avoid marital strife and hostile actions toward other Washo, and to be hospitable and kind. At the end of the feast the people all took a ritual bath. At Double Springs Flats they used baskets to dip water from the springs. If the *gumsaba* was held near a river, the crowd of men, women, and children went there to bathe. After the ceremony, the Washo were free to disperse into the piñon groves for the real harvest. Most anthropologists who have worked with the Washo agree that the foregoing description is highly idealized. Washo culture appears singularly without rigid rules specifying time and place for group activities. Given the need to take advantage of whatever hunting, fishing, or gathering opportunity occurred, the

Washo could not adhere to a strict schedule of activities. Some informants remember the big times of the *gumsaba* lasting for as long as two weeks. The Washo felt that holding such gatherings were important in insuring an adequate harvest of piñon nuts, and many of the older Washo feel that abandoning the practice in modern times has caused poorer harvests.

Girl's Dance

Another important ceremony of Washo life was the "girl's dance" or puberty ceremony. This was intimately related to women's role as a gatherer. The ceremony, which is practiced in one form or another by Indians throughout the west and southwest, took place at the time of a girl's first menses. During this period a girl was urged to be active and not to be lazy. She was expected to move swiftly, running whenever possible, on her daily rounds of gathering. Whatever she gathered was made available to anyone who wanted it and of course was forbidden to her. Nor could she eat meat or salt, scratch herself, or comb her hair. In most cases she was expected to fast entirely during a four-day period, taking only cold water. At the end of the four days the girl's family would light a signal fire on a prominent peak as an invitation to all who saw it. When the neighboring families had assembled, a dance was held all during one night. During the dance the girl, often with a companion about her own age, carried a long straight wand of elderberry that was colored red with a special earth which had been collected and made into paint. Sometime during the night the girl, with a male companion, ran to the top of a nearby hill and lit several fires and then raced down to rejoin the crowd. At dawn a male relative would seize the elderberry wand and run away into the hills there to hide the wand in an upright position. It was believed that as long as the wand remained upright the girl would be straight and strong. If she had behaved properly during the dance and the four days preceding it, she would be hard working, energetic, self-effacing, able to withstand hunger, generous, and able to endure discomfort all of her life. As a final act of her ceremony, the girl was taken to a nearby stream, lake or spring. There she was dusted with ashes while her sponsors prayed that she would be healthy, strong, generous, and hard working. They emphasized that this was done early in the morning so that she would always be an early riser and not be lazy. The ashes were washed from her body with water carried in a basket woven for the occasion. The basket was then thrown into the assembled crowd as a prize. The girl was daubed with red paint on her chest and face. The girl was now a woman and her family distributed gifts of food and shell beads to the assembled guests as something of a payment for being witness to this important change in their daughter's social status. The view that at the time of her first menses a girl was malleable and that her entire life would be shaped by the way she behaved at this time was widespread. The goal which the ceremony tried to achieve was to develop a woman devoted to the business of collecting food energetically throughout her life.

The Technology of the Piñon

Unlike other gathering activities, the piñon harvest could provide more food if a certain degree of cooperation existed. Two or three persons working together could gather many more nuts than a single person and thus a family would divide itself into two or three such groups. The basic tool of the piñon gatherer was a long pole with a smaller and, sometimes, curved stick attached. This could be used to knock piñon cones from the very topmost limbs of the pine tree. This method was not dissimilar from that used by "almond knockers" today. The knockers' companions gathered the fallen cones in baskets. Cones which had fallen naturally were gathered. A man and his wife working all day could collect the equivalent of one and one half or two gunny sacks of pine nuts. The gunny-sack measure is, of course, a result of white contact.

The nuts had to be removed from the cone and prepared by various cooking methods to prevent their spoilage. During a month of intense activity the Washo collected and prepared literally tons of piñon nuts to be stored against the winter. With the end of the harvest the Washo once again dispersed, moving toward the camps they would occupy during the winter. From the spring to the fall the Washo had moved from the west to the east of their heartland. Expeditions outside this area had taken them into the mountains and well into the peripheral areas of Washo country, but fishing on the west and gathering piñon nuts on the east marked the shift from one side of the heartland to the other. The trek to the winter camps was slow. The large supply of pine nuts was difficult to move. Without horses and wagons, the supply was moved on human backs. Often a move of only a few miles required several days. The old people and children watched the nut supply while the able-bodied members of the family moved back and forth. Basket loads of nuts were carried by a trump line across the chest by the women and with head bands by men, a device which kept their hands free for weapons. A few families might remain in the pine nut hills, but there were only a few springs there and the area was subject to heavy snow fall. Most families lived along the eastern edge of the Sierra on high ground to avoid floods and yet near firewood and water. Baskets of nuts were stored in specially prepared holes or in caves, and the families began to settle in for the winter. During the late summer women had collected the twigs of the willow to be used to weave into the baskets which served so many purposes in Washo life. The winter would be a time for basket weaving for the women and the chipping of arrowheads and the manufacturing of hunting weapons by the men. Baskets ranged from large loosely woven carrying baskets to small woven jugs which could hold water. Cooking was done in baskets, so tightly woven that they would hold water brought to a boil by dropping in heated stones. Other baskets were used to winnow the chaff from seeds, and babies were carried on their mothers' backs in basketry cradles. With the coming of winter, the gathering year was all but finished. If the gathering had been good during the summer, there would be supplies enough to last until spring. If not, starvation would haunt the Washo. The taking of ice-trapped fish might help fill out an empty winter larder, but for the most part hunting offered the only source of food in the winter.

The Hunting Year

We have seen that hunting began as soon as animals appeared in the spring. Game was taken whenever and wherever it was encountered throughout the year, but in the main, hunting occupied a brief period beginning in the late summer and lasting until the first snows of the winter. Hunting was exclusively a man's activity and one for which boys began training in their earliest childhood. Until a man was too old to endure the hardships of hunting trips he sought game constantly. Even in his old age he would devote his efforts to the taking of small game that a younger, more able-bodied man would scorn. Often these small game expeditions to trap and shoot chipmunks and squirrels were made up of old men and young boys. The old men thus passed on to children their lifetime of experience in the ways of animals and the lore of the hunt. Unlike plants which, despite their diversity of species, required a generally similar technique for collection, each type of animal demanded special skills if it was to be taken.

The basic Washo hunting weapon was a short bow backed with animal sinew to increase its power. Arrows were tipped with flint or obsidian heads attached to a light shaft which was inserted into the larger arrowshaft. Although popular thought sees the primitive hunter as an expert archer, he was probably far less accurate than a modern bowman shooting for sport. The Washo hunter was successful not because of uncanny accuracy but because of his stalking ability. The purpose of the hunt was to get close enough to the game so that a miss was virtually impossible. To accomplish this required years of training. A knowledge of wind and scent and how these combined to warn the quarry was essential as was muscle control to allow a hunter to move without attracting attention. Above all, a complete understanding of the habits of animals was essential to a successful stalk. Even for the experienced hunter possessed of all these skills, chance played an important part in any hunt. This uncertainty of outcome appears to be the basis of the superstructure of ritual and magic which surrounded Washo hunting life. If plant species matured, there was no doubt that the seeds or roots could be gathered. If the fish appeared at the right time, the mass fishing party or fish trap was certain to yield results. The hunter, however, never knew whether his efforts would produce game or not and so turned to the supernatural for assistance. In addition to physical and weapon-using skills and a knowledge of animal lore, a hunter had to learn the ritual and magic which were part of hunting. It was a long apprenticeship and a demanding one that was not complete until a youth was a young man. Because each species of animal required different skills and knowledge and different social responses, we will examine the hunting year in terms of the major species taken.

Rabbit

Spread throughout the lowlands of the Washo country and extending into the foothills, the western jack rabbit was the most commonly hunted animal. In rabbit hunting, cooperation produced greater results than solitary hunting and we find one of the relatively rare occasions for large-scale cooperative activities among the Washo.

In the fall, just after the pine nut harvest, the jack rabbit was common on the flatlands just to the east of the Sierra Nevada. A number of people walking in a line across the flats could scare up and drive before them hundreds of rabbits, still fat from their summer feeding. A man who was a good shot with a bow could kill a great many rabbits simply by joining such a drive. But this was not the most productive method of taking rabbits. The rabbits, slowly contained by a curving line of people, could be driven very easily into a long net and killed there with ease. Almost every Washo family owned such a net, several yards long, made of sage fibers. When supported on sticks, the nets were perhaps three feet high. If several families combined their nets, a barrier over a hundred yards long could be put up. With part of the group waiting behind the nets and the rest driving toward the barrier, a mornings' hunt could collect hundreds of jack rabbits weighing several pounds apiece. Hunts like this were staged throughout the Washo country wherever the rabbit population was high. Camps resembling small villages would spring up and each day the nets would be set up and a drive conducted across a different area until the rabbit population had been killed or driven out. During these times, just before the onset of winter, the Washo gorged themselves on fresh broiled rabbit. Hundreds more were skinned and cleaned and hung on racks to dry. In the dry air of the high steppes the rabbit carcasses dried into an unappetizing appearing, almost completely dehydrated, mummy. During the winter these dried rabbits would be pounded into powder and added to soups or to pine nut and grass seed mushes. In extremely good years many more rabbits would be killed than could be consumed. Their skins were stripped off and the carcasses left. The skins provided the material for the most important and in many cases the only clothing of the Washo, the rabbit-skin blanket. The fresh skins were cut into strips and these woven on a frame into a blanket which served as both cloak and bedding. The soft rabbit fur made a warm covering which wore out quickly, requiring frequent replenishment.

Deer

The fall was not the only time for rabbit hunting. The large wily animals were stalked by hunters through the spring and summer. Washo hunting seasons were often determined by the condition of the animals, so that fewer animals were taken in the spring when they were thin than in the late summer when they were fat and toothsome. As important as the rabbit was to Washo subsistence, the hunting year, that is the portion of the year in which hunting rather than fishing or gathering directed Washo movement and organization, began before rabbit hunting was at its peak.

The late summer was a time when gathering, save for the pine nuts, was falling off and when the men began to prepare for large-scale hunts for the winter meat. The most important animal after the rabbit was the deer. The hunting parties often traveled well beyond Washo country into the lands of the Maidu and the Miwok in California where the deer were more numerous. Usually, however, hunts were conducted in the territory along the eastern edge of the Sierra. In a time of need, deer would be taken whenever encountered, but the Washo preferred to hunt them from late August until early winter, after the fawns of the spring were large enough to fend for themselves and before the rutting season when the flesh of the buck deer was rank tasting. As the winter progressed, the deer became thinner and less desirable and were taken only if the Washo faced starvation.

A single species of deer, the California mule deer, inhabited the Washo country. The Washo language contains a single word, *memdewe,* for deer although the people differentiate between deer which drifted west in the fall and those which moved east into the Basin. Washo men hunted deer in a number of ways. Most frequently a man, alone or with one or two companions, went out from his camp in the morning to stalk deer during the daylight hours. One might simply move cautiously through the forest hoping to come upon a deer before it was aware of human presence. Far more frequent was a stalk using a disguise. Wearing a stuffed deer head with the skin attached and draped over his shoulders, the hunter would locate a group of grazing deer and then begin to close in on his quarry. Remaining always to windward so that his odor would not reveal the deception, the hunter would approach the herd, expertly imitating the actions of a buck approaching a strange group of his fellows. An experienced hunter could imitate a deer so well that the herd would return to browsing after his presence was noted. In this manner the hunter could come to within a few feet of his quarry before throwing off his disguise, and drawing his arrow to the head and loosing it. At these close ranges he seldom missed. The ideal target spot was the area just behind the shoulder. An arrow point in this vital area would penetrate the lungs, and the convulsive movement of the shoulder blade, as the animal plunged away, usually broke off the shaft leaving the head and foreshaft in the deer's body. An arrow lacks the shocking power of a bullet and no matter how well placed seldom kills outright. A grievously wounded deer when pursued can run for many miles and often evade the hunter. The Washo hunter avoided this possibility through an exercise of patience. If his arrow struck home, he immediately sat down to wait. If the arrowshaft had been broken off he examined it for blood stains. If he found blood, he mixed it with saliva, started a fire and heated a stone and placed the mixture on the stone. The liquid boiled away. When this happened, the hunter extinguished his fire and began to track his quarry. A wounded deer that is not pursued will usually stop after running a short distance, loss of blood and shock and stiffening muscles often force him to lie down. A hunter who has been patient will find the deer a short distance away, dead or dying, usually exuding a bloody froth from his nose and mouth. The Washo argued that the ritual of the hot stone was a magic act which actually killed the deer. A more objective observer might argue that it simply gave the hunter something to do while he waited for his arrow to take effect.

Stalking with a disguise was the business of an expert. Any movement which might cause suspicion in the herd he was stalking, a misstep or abrupt movement caused by cramped muscles, or impatience could send the deer flying. Moreover, the disguise itself was a matter of concern. As we will see later, the Washo considered the remains, particularly the bones, of animals killed for food as sacred and dangerous if not handled with respect and consideration. Thus the disguise consisting of skull and antlers was not something to be handled casually. In fact, many hunters feared using a disguise made of real antlers and substituted branches of the manzanita bush. There also was an element of physical danger, particularly as the hunting season moved into the fall. A rutting buck deer is prepared to fight all comers and an expert imitation might invite a charge. A full-grown buck mule deer may weigh 200 pounds and his antlers and sharp hooves are exceedingly dangerous weapons, more so to a man encumbered by a deer head and skin. Having once been attacked by a young mule deer buck weighing far less than the writer, he agrees with his Washo informants that the possibility of attack was not one to be taken lightly. The less expert hunter had a number of alternative methods for taking the deer. The most common was to build a blind of brush near a spring or salt lick and lay in wait for his quarry. This was a good method except that it limited the time when hunting might be successful. Unless a hunter was in position before the deer came to the lick or spring, his wait would be in vain. The stalker, on the other hand, could search through an area and find the deer, rather than waiting for them. Hunting expeditions such as this supplied fresh meat for the immediate family of the hunters with each member of the small party getting his share. However, as the year progressed into the fall before the mountains were filled with snow and the passes closed, deer hunting became the major activity of all Washo men. In this period, the purpose was to accumulate dried deer meat for winter food. To this end, larger hunting parties set out, leaving their families, often going into California to hunt intensively. Usually a hunting party was composed of six to eight men. An older man usually accompanied the party to tend the camp and cook. Perhaps a boy or two would go along to learn the business of hunting. Once encamped in a good hunting area, the party might split up each morning with each man setting out on a stalk of his own. If there were many deer in the area, a drive might be organized. One or two of the best shots would be stationed along a deer trail while the rest of the party spread out below them and began to walk toward the bowmen, making enough noise to disturb the deer and cause them to move away from the drivers. There was no attempt to stampede the deer. It was more productive to disturb them only enough to force them to move past the ambush. In the course of a day several such drives could produce a number of deer. As the daily kill was gathered, the animals were skinned and butchered and the meat cut into strips. The meat was hung on drying racks to dry. Only the neck was dried intact and brought home with the bone left in. This was considered especially good feed for children and old people and was never eaten by the hunters. The rest of the skeleton, save perhaps the head and antlers, was taken with great care and submerged in a stream so that scavengers would not disturb it. The Washo believed, as did most American Indians, that game animals voluntarily allowed themselves to be killed for the benefit of man. If man did not appreciate this sacrifice and treated the remains of his benefactors callously, the animals would refuse to be killed.

If the hunting was good, a party would remain in the forest for two weeks, or even a month, hunting until they had collected all the meat they could carry. With the meat boned and dried, a single man could carry the meat of several deer quite easily. Eighty to one hundred pounds was not considered too heavy for an able-bodied Washo man. Thus a hunting party of eight could, if its luck was good, bring home between 800 and a 1000 pounds of dried deer meat and hides. Occasionally, larger groups of Washo collected for deer hunting. In the early fall when the foliage in the foothills was dry, a large area might be surrounded and set on fire to drive the deer into the open to be shot. The Washo also constructed a simple noose trap, suspended along a deer trail which could catch and choke a deer, although this method appears to have been rare.

Two other large game animals played a role, although not so important as that of the deer, in supplying meat for the Washo cooking baskets. To the north and south and farther to the east, pronghorned antelope appeared in great numbers but the Washo territory lay between the northern and southern ranges and in this area the pronghorn was not too plentiful. Nonetheless, when it could be taken it was, and the method is one of the most interesting links between the culture of the Washo and that of their neighbors in the Basin to the east.

Antelope

The antelope is an extremely fleet and sharp-eyed creature. Living on the flat steppes as it does, it is able to see danger at a great distance and flee from it. However, the antelope has two weaknesses which enabled the American Indian to develop successful techniques for hunting it. It is a herd animal, preferring to remain with its fellows even in the face of danger, and it is incurably curious. Early white hunters report that they were often able to lure antelope into gun range by simply waving a white cloth on a stick. Eventually, curiosity overcame caution and the pronghorns would come to investigate the strange sight. For the Indian without firearms the antelope had to be brought into even closer range than was necessary for the hunter armed with a rifle. An occasional skillful hunter could stalk an individual antelope and kill it with a bow. Or a group of hunters could occasionally form a drive similar to that employed in deer hunting. But the most common and most productive method was the surrounding or corralling method. When the presence of a herd of antelope was known, the people who had discovered it would send out the word to their neighbors to form a communal hunt. The first step in such an undertaking was to build a corral of brush or rope made of sagebrush bark. Occasionally brush would be piled at intervals to form a circle, the spaces to be filled by people at the time of the hunt. Frequently, wings would be built extending out from the opening of the corral. Once the corral had been finished, young men were sent to place themselves on the side of the herd away from the corral and slowly drive the antelope toward the trap. Moving slowly and keeping concealed in order not to stampede the herd, the drivers crept close, then one at a time, suddenly stood up and then just as suddenly hid themselves. These strange appearances made the herd nervous and generally forced it to move slowly toward the corral. As the herd approached closer, more and more people joined in the drive, appearing in every quarter save the direction of the trap. Soon the pressure of the human presence became more and more intense and active. Finally, at the entrance to the corral, the erstwhile quiet and cautious drive became noisy. The antelope were stampeded into the trap and the opening closed. Once the animals were contained there was usually ritual dancing and singing, often lasting all night. The trap and the sounds of the people surrounding them panicked the herd and drove the antelope around and around the corral until by dawn of the next morning they were exhausted. A specially selected archer killed the first antelope before the general slaughtering began. A herd of antelope could supply food for a relatively large number of people for several days, perhaps a week. The people would then disperse to continue their regular hunting and gathering rounds. One such hunt usually exhausted the antelope population in an area and would not be repeated there for several years.

Throughout most of the Great Basin the antelope hunt was a singularly important activity inasmuch as it brought together, for a short time at least, a large number of people cooperating and operating under a form of political authority absent in all other areas of their lives. Almost predictably, the entire process of the antelope drive was surrounded by an aura of sacredness and ritual. The discovery of a herd was always announced by a man with special power, an antelope shaman, who was believed to have the ability to locate a herd of antelope and charm them into the corral through the use of special magic. Most frequently, the shaman discovered the presence of the antelope in a dream and upon awakening made his announcement and sent messengers to inform the neighboring people. While the preparations were underway, he prayed and sang, weaving a spell of magic to charm the antelope to their deaths. The details of the hunt and its accompanying ritual varied greatly throughout the Basin, but it always had its supernatural element and the antelope shaman with his special power. Some groups believed that antelope power was so great that when used it invariably killed one of the members of the hunting group. This loss was considered as part of the cost of social survival for the group. For the few days of the hunt the shaman assumed political power inasmuch as he could direct the activities of the group. This phenomenon of the general pattern varying in detail from place to place has been called a "culture trait complex" and has been reported throughout the world in many areas of human activity. The Washo, living in the extreme west of the Great Basin and speaking a different language, displayed this "trait complex" in its least complicated form. There were, for instance, among the Washo no special antelope shaman. Any "dreamer," a person gifted with the power to receive prophetic dreams, might discover the presence of a herd. He would then become the leader of the drive. The use of magic by the leader was absent. What magic or ritual there was was conducted by the entire population engaged in the hunt. The entire hunting group observed a taboo against sexual intercourse during the hunting, and menstruating women could not take part in the hunt. The Washo considered the belief that a person would die as a result of an antelope hunt as a somewhat silly superstition. The antelope hunt as carried out by the Washo is an excellent example of another cultural phenomenon known as diffusion or borrowing of traits of behavior from neighboring people. Inasmuch as all such complexes are made up of a number of discrete traits, not all of which are necessary to the basic purpose of the complex, they may diffuse piecemeal from culture to culture. The Washo, alert to any environmental opportunity, would naturally want to hunt the antelope whenever possible. It is clear that they looked to the other cultures of the Basin for an example of how the antelope could be best taken. Thus we see the drive into a trap, but not the building of a corral. The Washo borrowed the practical aspects of the antelope hunt but rejected the ritual superstructure which had meaning to the neighboring Paiute and Shoshone. The Washo followed their own traditional patterns as to dreaming power and group magic and temporary leaders. We can also see that the Washo, who hunted antelope rather infrequently, were not as knowledgeable about this species as they were about the deer. Individual Washo hunters seldom, if ever, attempted to stalk antelope, apparently lacking the knowledge and skill to undertake this difficult job, although Paiute and Shoshone hunters frequently used this method.

Sheep and Bear

One other species of large game played a role in the pattern of Washo subsistence, although it was even less important than the antelope. In the Sierra to the west and in the dry desert mountains to the east there were populations of mountain sheep, a subspecies of the Rocky Mountain bighorn and a variety of desert bighorn. The Washo made no distinction between what we see as two different types of animals. Both were called *ogul*. The wild sheep was even more difficult to hunt than the antelope, living in the remote and rugged wildness of the high country, often above timberline. Keen eyed and agile, they were difficult to stalk. Nonetheless, occasional parties of expert hunters went into the mountains in the early fall when the first snows had driven the animals down from their summer haunts among the peaks. There, a careful hunter might stalk and surprise a sheep, which often weighed more than a man. The most frequent means of taking the mountain sheep was by applying a knowledge of animal habits. The sound of two rams fighting, their great curving horns smashing together in a headlong charge often attracted other rams and curious ewes. Indians throughout the sheep country took advantage of this and learned to imitate the sounds of fighting by striking sticks together. This usually drew the quarry close enough so that a hunter could shoot them from ambush.

The black bear was common in the Washo country and at least a few grizzlies are known to have inhabited the area, but the bear played a very minor role in Washo subsistence. In cases of extreme emergency, bear meat might be eaten but in general bear hunting was more of a ritual than an economic or subsistence activity. Like most primitive people living in the northern hemisphere, the Washo considered the bear a very special, if not sacred, animal possessed of enormous supernatural power. To kill a bear assured a man's reputation as a hero and possessor of great power. A bear hunt was not, properly speaking, a hunt at all. A number of men would band together and locate the winter lair of a hibernating bear. One of their number would enter the lair armed with a torch and an arrow or knife to prod the beast awake and then flee outside. As the bear, still groggy from months of sleep and blinded by the light, stepped out of his lair, the waiting companions fired arrows into the animal, aiming for the mouth in particular. The hide, a symbol of bravery and power, was taken by the man whose arrow first hit the animal and the meat might be eaten by the members of the party but it was not divided among the various families. A Washo legend tells of a time when a band of Paiutes bent on marauding were so cowed by seeing the Washo kill a bear that they decamped and fled as if they had been beaten in battle.

Birds

In addition to the mammals hunted regularly, many species of birds and wild fowl nested in the Washo country. The sinks and swamps in the eastern valleys provided nesting for a dozen or more species of water fowl and the sage flats and foothills were the home of quail, sage hens, prairie chickens, and doves. When great numbers of birds were present in the lowland lakes, many tribes, including the Washo, might camp on the shores and stage drives. Using a boat made of tule, the birds could be herded together and taken in large numbers. When the fowl were fat and found it difficult to fly, they could be taken by hand. In shallow bodies of water a rabbit net might be used and birds driven into it by hunters wading in the water. Small arrowheads were made for bird hunting and used by hunters stalking along the shores of a lake or sink. When the young were partially grown but still unable to fly, they were gathered up by parties of hunters, who always left enough to insure a crop in the following year. While the various Paiute bands might have a special chief to direct the waterfowl drive as they did for an antelope hunt, the Washo simply gathered together and cooperated in such an endeavor without formal leadership. Land birds were taken with bow and arrow, an easy task when pursuing large flocks of relatively large birds like the sage hen and prairie chicken. Some hunters made a special arrowhead with a guard of four crossed sticks to increase the chances of hitting a bird in flight. Snares and traps might also be used to take birds. The most productive period for bird hunting was once again in late summer and fall, although some species of water fowl nested throughout the winter in the Washo country and served as a source of food during periods of starvation. The limitation on the utility of fowl as food was technical. There is no evidence that any attempt was made to preserve birds by drying so that the take had to be consumed soon after the hunt to avoid spoilage. Fresh birds swelled the diet and reduced the pressure on stored food such as pine nut flour and dried deer meat. Birds appeared to be considered what in modern military language we would call a "target of opportunity." That is, very little general planning went into bird hunting. If they were present, they were taken, but seldom do Washo informants speak of shifting camp or making special long trips to hunt either waterfowl or upland game birds.

Other Animals

In times of starvation the Washo would eat any animal which could be taken, but, in general, they seemed to have weighed very carefully the effort against the return. Many fur-bearing animals were taken if they were encountered, their pelts being useful for clothing, blankets, or arrow quivers. Only the wild cat, muskrat, fox, and badger among the fur bearers are reported to have been eaten at all regularly. The porcupine, slow footed and slow witted and easily killed by even a child with a stick, was also a regular source of food. The woodchuck, common in the mountain country, was also a favorite target for hunters. There were many varieties of squirrels throughout the Washo territory and they were regularly taken. Adult hunters seldom set out specifically to hunt squirrel, but older men past their prime and young boys learning their trade hunted squirrel with both bow and traps.

The gopher and the ground squirrel were considered less than game and were frequently taken by women who smoked them out of their holes or flooded them out by diverting nearby streams. A split stick which would entangle in the hair of a rodent was poked into a hole and twisted until the gopher or squirrel was entrapped and could be pulled out. A number of lesser rodents, field mice and even moles, were occasionally eaten if they could be taken in large enough number to justify the effort. The unique kangaroo rat found in the flatlands of the valleys was also taken and eaten.

In general, once the fishing season was over, the taking of birds and mammals was a continuous activity, contributing substantially to the daily food supply. Hunting with the bow was an exclusive male function which often took men away from their families. Small animals and animals which could be taken in large number were the quarry of both men and women, often working together. In the last months of the summer and in the fall, hunting became a major activity as part of the preparations for winter. In the case of the rabbit and, less commonly, the antelope, the occurrence of these animals led to a movement of campsites.

Insects and Reptiles

The people of the Great Basin were always alert to any opportunity to gather food in quantity and so the insect life of the area was not overlooked. Periodically the locusts swarmed and migrated, covering an area with what was almost a blanket of voracious insect life. The Washo always rallied to gather as many of them as possible. Sometimes the insects would be gathered in baskets and roasted in the coals of a camp fire. At other times brush and grass was set on fire and the insects driven by the flames into a ditch where they could be gathered more easily. Dried and ground, they produced a nutritious and long lasting flour to be mixed with other foods.

At certain times of the year the common grasshopper appeared in great numbers. If a gatherer began early in the morning before the hoppers became active in the growing warmth of the day, he could pick them from the grass and bushes with ease. These were usually roasted in pits. The grasshopper could also be dried and ground into flour to be stored against the winter.

Bees' nests provided not only honey, which was consumed on the spot, but the "eggs," or larvae of the bee, were cooked and eaten. Although ants and ant eggs were eaten by all the neighboring people, the Washo stubbornly insist that they never used the ant as food. They did, however, eat caterpillars whenever they appeared in sufficient numbers to justify gathering them.

Long trips were often made south to Mono Lake, an awesome body of water so filled with minerals that no fish lived there. However, a small grub thrived in this water and often washed on the shore in great number. This grub, known as *matsibabesha* by the Washo, was gathered as food and as a powerful medicine or magic substance useful in bringing fishing luck.

Most reptiles and amphibians were avoided as food, but certain large lizards were considered to be worth taking and were killed and cooked whenever encountered.

The Culture of Hunting

Hunting and the more energetic forms of fishing were the domain of the Washo male and his training began in his early childhood. The ritual connected with hunting served to emphasize the importance of hunting and symbolize the division of labor between the sexes. All hunting and fishing equipment used by men was taboo to women, particularly menstruating women. If a woman handled a man's bow or his arrows or touched his fish harpoon, it was felt necessary to give the piece of equipment a ritual bath and say a number of prayers to restore its usefulness. To ignore this would certainly bring bad luck. Before a man set out to hunt, he bathed and sang prayerful songs. Usually he rubbed himself with the leaves of a certain plant to bring hunting luck. This may have helped obscure the human odor and made stalking easier.

As a boy grew into manhood, his hunting adventures became more and more demanding. Gradually he graduated from mice or wood rats to squirrels and then to woodchuck and game birds and the stalking of rabbits. During all this period he was never allowed to eat any animal he killed. Usually he gave this game away to neighbors or relatives, displaying at once the Washo virtue of generosity and learning the important lesson of mutual dependance and, incidentally, building up a number of small debts which he might some day call in if he needed food or assistance. Finally, as he became expert, a lad would attempt to kill a full-grown buck deer. If he was successful, the kill was of course, taboo to him but the event marked his transition to full manhood. He would be ritually bathed by his father or grandfather, who were also forbidden to eat the meat. The antlers of the deer would be set on their points and the naked boy would attempt to crawl through them. If he had killed a buck large enough to permit this, he was considered to have entered the status of adult hunter and incidentally to be a candidate for marriage.

So uncertain was the business of hunting that Washo men continually sought or at least hoped for assistance from the supernatural. Successful hunters were always considered to have special powers which allowed them to charm their quarry and make hunting easier. The Washo believed the neighboring California tribes had special medicine which put whole herds of deer to sleep. A hunter with medicine kept it secret and did not boast about it or pass the secret on to others. Hunting virtually dominated the Washo man's image of himself. Even today to suggest that a man had no taste for hunting and preferred to remain in camp with the women is an oblique way of attacking his entire character. The ritual of hunting, preserving the usefulness of his weapons, the respect shown to the hunted animal all combined in a pattern of behavior which influenced most of the day-to-day routine of a Washo man. We have seen earlier that the coming of age ceremonies of a young woman emphasized the womanly virtues of industry, generosity, and steady application to the business of collecting plant food. For the boy, the occasion was related to hunting which was the main occupation of men.

Trade

Hunting and gathering supplied virtually all the necessities of Washo life: food, what little clothing was worn, housing, and the tools and weapons needed to hunt and gather and prepare food. However, the Washo were not entirely self-contained. Areas outside the Washo country offered desirable goods which the Washo got through trade or by means of long gathering ventures far outside their home territory. The Washo country was inhabited by many more deer than was the region to the east, while further out in the Basin the antelope population was higher. Although they often fought each other, the Washo engaged in a lively trade with the Paiute, exchanging deer hides for those of the antelope. Occasionally, a buffalo hide obtained by the Paiute from peoples farther east would come into Washo hands to be traded west to California Indians. The need for salt and for mineral earths with which to make paints was often the excuse for the forming of expeditions to foreign territory to collect these materials. Obsidian for arrow points was sometimes gathered in this manner or obtained through trade.

The Washo, living between the rich country of California and the relatively impoverished Basin served as trade agents for many desirable goods from the west. Inasmuch as they had little that the California tribes could not obtain for themselves, the Washo frequently had to undertake long journeys to obtain trade articles. Tribal tradition recalls long trips during the summer which took families to the shores of the Pacific to gather shell fish. The mollusks were eaten on the spot but great packs of shells were carried back over the Sierra to be made into jewelry and ritual objects and to be traded to the people to the east. Bands of young men are said to have traveled as far south as San Diego to obtain particularly fine obsidian knives from the tribes in that region. The Yosemite Valley was well known to the Washo who viewed the area from the surrounding mountains. They were afraid to enter the valley because of a belief that the Indians who lived there were sorcerers. This wide network of travel made the Washo aware of the customs of many people and, as we shall see, served to spread some of these customs.

Summary

In this section we have examined Washo life in terms of the subsistence activities which supported the tribe. We see that hunting, gathering, and fishing each played an important role in supporting the Washo and in determining their annual movements. We have seen too that no single resource could be counted on to provide food and other necessities throughout the entire year. To take advantage of the varied opportunities of their homeland, the Washo developed an opportunistic culture able to change plans on a moment's notice and seize the main chance as it presented itself. Seldom actually starving, but equally seldom able to relax in the search for food, the Washo survived because of their ability to adjust to conditions. Few rules of Washo life were so rigid as to resist the demands of subsistence. Even the taboo of women hunting was broken by widows forced to fend for themselves and their families. Ceremonies were lengthened and shortened as resources permitted, campgrounds shifted around as food supplies appeared and disappeared.

With such a simple technology to use in exploitation, the Washo was unable to depend on tools and machines or manufactured goods to protect him from the vagaries of his environment. In place of technology, the Washo used his own social organization. Washo society can be viewed as a mechanism which exploited the environment while satisfying the basic social needs of all human beings. In the next section we will examine the various aspects of Washo social structure as a series of task forces, each designed to provide for human needs.

5

Society and Culture

VERY SOCIETY must function in such a way that its members are able to survive physically. If the society and its culture are to survive, social organization must provide a framework in which children can be conceived, born, and raised according to the traditions of their parents. Various societies meet these challenges in different ways, organizing themselves differently to meet different environmental and technical needs. The Washo environment was such that while it would provide a living for the energetic and alert, it provided very little margin for the elaboration of social institutions. Like many societies with a simple technology, the various social units had to perform multiple functions. For the Washo, social units had to be able to move quickly to take advantage of environmental opportunities and not exhaust the resources too quickly. The need for large-scale cooperation was minimal but not entirely absent. Hostile neighbors both to the east and west required that the Washo be able to muster enough fighting men to repell invaders. Social needs such as the change in status of a girl to that of young woman required the presence of as many people as possible. A number of subsistence activities, as we have seen, were more productive if a number of people could cooperate. The seemingly universal need of men to find identity in a group worked to encourage large gatherings of people whenever possible. However, the Washo could not live together for very long periods of time lest the food supply in any single area give out. Thus, we can examine the Washo social organization in terms of a series of groups of expanding size based on a single unit, the family.

The Family

The term family is best used to describe that social unit which has the responsibility of producing and training children, although even in everyday English the word has other connotations. Among the Washo the family unit

162

bore a heavy burden of responsibility besides caring for children. It was the basic economic unit, moving in search of food, without consideration for any other such group. Occasionally hunting trips might break up even this small unit, but in general it remained together, traveling, collecting food, and interacting with other families when the demands of nature or society called for or made cooperation possible. There are few households recorded with less than five members and even fewer with as many as a dozen. The relationships of the members were extremely varied and there seems to have been no set rule about who might join together to make a family.

In the eyes of the Washo, what we would call a family was identified with a single dwelling place, the winter house, or *galesdangl*. This was a crude home made of tree limbs leaning together to form a peak with a door in one end. Sometimes the *galesdangl* was covered with earth. In the valleys it might be made of brush or thatched with tule. This structure was used in the winter and unless a person died in the house, it was reused by the same people every winter. In the event of death, the house was torn or burned down and the spot abandoned in favor of a new winter location. The "family" they might be better referred to as the houshold, because the Washo tended to identify the group with the house. Usually, the basis of a *galesdangl* was a man and his wife and their children. A widow or widower, particularly if there were grown sons, might be the head of the household. In this case, the sons' wives might also join the group during the early part of their marriage or until the parent died. On other occasions brothers and sisters and their spouses occupied a single house and traveled together. Sometimes completely unrelated persons or "friends" joined a household. The Washo were occasionally polygynous, particularly if a first wife was barren. If a man married more than one woman, his wives might live in separate *galesdangl* quite close together or they might live in a single house. One man who married three sisters built two structures, one housing two wives and their children and the second serving as the home for the third wife and her children. This second home was soon filled by an unrelated man and later his wife and their children.

In many societies there are rather strict rules concerning where a newly married couple may live. In general, societies can be divided into matrilocal, those which require residence with the wife's parents; patrilocal, those requiring residence with the family of the husband; and neolocal, those requiring a newly married couple to set up housekeeping on their own. All three types of postmarital residence are reported in about equal number by the Washo. It is clear that the subsistence pattern of the Washo would not permit fixed adherence to any rule of residence. If one or another set of in-laws already had a large family, the addition of a son or daughter in-law might impose an insupportable burden on the ability of the entire group to survive. If, on the other hand, one of the parental families was shorthanded, the addition of an able-bodied hunter or an energetic gatherer might be welcomed.

Courtship, the first step in establishing another household, was relatively simple. Marriages were a matter of concern for the entire family. Occasions such as the girl's dance, or the *gumsaba,* were of course times for getting acquainted between eligible young men and women. If a son or daughter displayed interest in a particular person, his or her family would consider the person's working ability before encouraging the match. If both families agreed, there was often a prolonged exchange of small gifts before the mating became "official." Older Washo speak of a native ceremony of placing a blanket over the shoulders of a couple and having a respected elder lecture them on the responsibilities of marriage and parenthood.

A young man and wife constituted a partnership of skills: he a hunter and fisherman with many years of training; she a gatherer, cook, and basket weaver. By following their sexually determined activities, such a pair could easily provide for themselves. When a woman became pregnant and had a child, her ability to work was reduced until the child was weaned. Therefore, a household could easily use an older woman or a younger unmarried woman to assist with the gathering and home-making tasks. A successful hunter could provide for such a household with little trouble. Frequently the additional member of a household would be an aged parent no longer in his or her prime but able to contribute to the food supply by gathering or hunting small game. These oldsters were particularly helpful in caring for and instructing the children as they were weaned and forced to depend less and less on their mother. Anthropologists Stanley Freed and Ruth Freed have noted that even today an unusual warmth exists between relatives three generations apart, which seems to reflect this old relationship between the young and the old.

Not infrequently, a woman would urge that her husband seek another wife to assist her or to keep her company, or if she was barren, to provide children for the family to raise and care for. She often suggested a younger sister with whom she had been raised. The Washo felt this was a good solution inasmuch as women brought up together would be fond of each other and not fight. Moreover, a sister's children were closely related and could depend on loving care from their aunt should their mother die. Sometimes plural marriage was encouraged by a girl's parents. If a young man was particularly energetic in his hunting and fishing and had a reputation as a good provider, a girl's family would suggest that she attract his attention and become a second wife. A much rarer form of marriage, polyandry, in which a woman married more than one man was also practiced among the Washo. Such cases are infrequent and appear to have been temporary, that is, a woman married to one man also acted as wife to his younger brother. Her children were treated as offspring of the trio, but when the second brother married he left the children with his older brother and the woman. This arrangement seems to have developed as a result of the practice of the levirate. This is a widespread custom in which the widow of a man frequently marries one of his brothers. Inasmuch as a younger brother is a potential spouse and sexual partner, the exigencies of Washo life appear to have made it advantageous in some cases for the potential situation to become actualized until the younger brother found a wife of his own. It is possible that the marriage left the younger brother without a family unit and so he joined the new unit formed by the marriage of his brother. A woman with two adult men hunting for her was in a fortunate position and the extension of sexual privileges to the second brother may have symbolized her desire to maintain the situation. It is also probable that should her husband die she would have joined the household of the surviving brother as a second wife, thus transforming that which had begun as a relatively rare polyandrous marriage into the more common polygynous one. It was also a common practice for a man whose wife had died to marry one of her surviving sisters, a practice known as the sororate, which is also reflected in the frequency of polygynous marriages in which a man married two sisters.

As a family grew in size due to the birth of children, it might also grow through the addition of other relatives. Sisters or brothers left orphaned by the death of parents might join the household. Or, if the parental household was large, a younger sibling might find welcome in the household of his sister or brother where an extra hunter or gatherer would be useful. Widowed aunts or cousins might also join a household. The able were expected to do their share in the quest for food and the aged did what they could. Washo ethics demanded that the aged be cared for and supported by the group. Clearly, no household could successfully support too many ancients or too many small children.

It was the household group which moved in search of food, leaving the winter camp for Lake Tahoe and from there moving on the various rounds of the spring and summer and finally moving east to the pine nut hills. There the family would pick nuts from a plot marked off with stones. If a member of another group trespassed without permission, the owners of the plot could break his gathering pole and seize the nuts he had collected. A family inherited little else than the gathering plot inasmuch as a *galesdangl* was destroyed because of a death and all the dead person's personal property was destroyed or buried. Each spouse had the right to pick pine nuts on the plot used by his or her parents. A husband can gather on the wife's plot and she on his but with the death of a spouse, that right terminated. In addition to pine nut gathering rights, the family tended to have property rights in other areas. Fishing traps and platforms were generally considered the property of the family which built them and could be reclaimed from year to year and their use denied to others. The right to hunt eagles in a certain area was passed from father to son. The eagle was considered an exceedingly powerful bird, a messenger to the spirit world. His feathers were objects of great power and value and could be traded for almost anything an Indian found desirable. Taking eagles was a difficult and dangerous task requiring patience, courage, and skill. Young eaglets could be taken from the nest when discovered, risking, of course, the ire of the parents who might return during the robbery. The aeries were owned by an individual hunter who passed the right to take birds from that location on to his sons.

It is common today for Washo to claim leadership roles by referring to the fact that his father or some other paternal ancestor held such a position. He might even pick a maternal relative as a basis for his claim. This reflects a general tendency to bilateral descent and inheritance, but it is difficult to determine whether leadership roles were actually inherited in aboriginal times. There is

some doubt that aboriginal "chiefs" or "captains" were much more than respected men whose advice had been found wise and was heeded by his friends,
relatives, and neighbors.

Within the family the father appears to have had a great deal of authority, particularly in dealing with his sons. He and his brothers most frequently
taught a boy to hunt and told him tribal lore. A girl was the responsibility of
the women of the household, who taught her the skills of gathering, cooking,
and weaving, and sponsored her girl's dance. The family spent much of the year
alone or in the company of a few other such groups. It was the core of Washo
life. Training in the skills of adulthood and in Washo tradition and ethics were
learned in the family. It was at one time a biological unit, conceiving, producing, and nurturing children; an economic unit, gathering and hunting the food
needed by its members; and an educational institution wherein were learned all
the basic behavior patterns of Washo life. Inasmuch as there was little authority
in Washo life, the family might also be considered a minimal political unit as
well, allying to and cooperating with other such units but bound by no laws to
follow any desires other than its own.

The family was the unit wherein, not surprisingly, we find most of the
rituals of Washo life. This complex of rituals served to symbolize the limits of
this family group and re-emphasize its unity and the importance of the members one to the other. Not until adolesence are outsiders really needed for the
ceremonies of life.

Birth

In the popular mind, childbirth among primitive peoples is often viewed
as a casual almost animal-like event. All of us have heard stories of how women
disappear into the jungle and return with a child, ready to continue with their
chores as if nothing had happened. Although this may be true in some parts of
the world, it does not apply to the Washo or to any of their neighbors. The
birth of a child was an event of enormous importance surrounded by a complex
of ritual acts. Anthropologist Omer C. Stewart, who compiled trait lists for all
the northern Paiute groups as well as the Washo, lists over two pages of taboos
and ritual acts associated with birth. Of the over one hundred special birth customs mentioned, the Washo are reported to have practiced over fifty. In short,
in the matter of birth ceremonies the Washo were clearly part of a complex
common to all the tribes of northern Nevada.

During her pregnancy a woman observed no particular rituals or taboos
save that she was expected to work hard and remain active. The birth took place
in a regular dwelling house, *galesdangl* or *gadu,* and the mother was attended
by older female relatives, or friends if no older relative was available. Delivery
was achieved in a prone position. When the baby was born it was bathed,
wrapped in some soft material, and placed on a winnowing basket. When the
afterbirth appeared, it was wrapped in bark and buried. If a woman wished to
have no more children, the pack was buried upside down. If at a later date she

wished to have children, the spot where the afterbirth had been buried was turned over. A newly delivered woman was considered to be in extremely delicate condition and had to rest on a special bed until "her insides had healed." The special bed was a shallow pit filled with heated sand and covered with grass. Here the mother remained for an indefinite period, some informants insisting a month or six weeks, others stating that no specified time was required. During this post partum confinement, the mother was not allowed to eat meat or salt. Nor could she work or scratch herself with her fingers, being required instead to use a special scratching stick. Water was warmed before she was allowed to drink it and she was not permitted to bathe. When the father was notified of the birth, he went to the nearest stream and bathed. When he had finished, he left a deer skin or other valuable object on a bush near the edge of the water as a present for anyone who wished to take it. While his wife remained on her bed, the new father was required to remain extremely active, gathering fire wood and hunting every day. He was supposed to avoid gambling and smoking, and he could eat no meat, salt, or grease. At nights he remained awake as long as possible. His behavior was thought to insure that the child would be industrious and able to endure discomfort and hardship in its life. Sexual intercourse was forbidden to both parents and some informants say that this taboo was in effect for six months to a year.

When the infant's umbilical cord fell off, the mother announced it to the father who immediately went hunting and killed some animal which he brought home and distributed among the people of the household. On this day, anyone not related to the family could come and take whatever he wanted from among the father's possessions. It may be that this practice was thought to instill generosity in the infant or, perhaps, it created a debt which in future life the child could call in, making him not entirely dependant on his immediate family. The umbilical cord was tied to the right side of the baby's winnowing basket in the belief that this would make the baby right handed. About one month after the birth, a "baby feast," or *gumga.au*, was held by the family. The Washo word means literally hair cutting, and during the ceremony the mother bathed herself for the first time since the birth and had her own and her child's hair cut. The mother was assisted by another woman who dipped sagebrush in water and brushed it onto the mother and then ran her hands over the mother. The first haircut from the baby's head was wrapped in buckskin and attached to the hood of a basket cradle-board where the baby would rest from that time on. The winnowing basket which served as a bed for the infant was filled with various kinds of food and a few valuable items such as a bow, arrow, or eagle feather. The mother took some of the food, mixed it with sage leaves, chewed the mixture and then spat it out. After that the food and valuables were given away, the old being the chief beneficiaries, perhaps a ritual symbolism of the relation between the very young and the very old. After the ceremony, the taboos on meat, salt, grease, scratching, and, some say, sexual intercourse were removed and the parents could resume their normal lives.

Naming was not an important occasion among the Washo because an individual might have a great number of names in the course of his lifetime. A child was usually referred to by a baby name calling attention to some peculiarity of gait, appearance, behavior, or language. Later this name would be dropped in favor of an adult name reflecting some important event in his life or some idiosyncrasy of appearance or behavior. This name might change a number of times if events of hunting, war, or supernatural significance took place. When a person died his name was considered taboo and other persons with the same or similar names as the deceased usually dropped their names and chose another.

During childhood the loss of a milk tooth was an occasion of some minor ritual. The tooth was taken by an adult and thrown away. As he did this, the adult shouted to the small burrowing animals in the neighborhood, those with hard sharp teeth, that the milk tooth should be taken and exchanged for a strong tooth in the child's mouth.

The girl's dance was sponsored by her parents but required the presence of as many people as possible as participants. However, it was within the family group itself that a Washo child learned of a host of ritual activities and seemingly pointless acts which tied Washo society together and emphasized the Washo distinctness from all other people. Within the family one learned of the basic separation between men and women and of the important taboos associated with this. Girls learned of the need to protect the hunting weapons and fishing equipment of their men folk against defilement by menstruation. Boys learned to avoid this contaminating influence. Boys also began to learn hunting ritual and magic from their fathers while girls learned the role of women. Young girls and unmarried women were cautioned not to comb their hair at night lest they marry non-Washo strangers and become lost to their tribe. They learned that a woman in confinement would become wrinkled if she wiped perspiration from her face instead of dabbing it off. Taboos concerning dangerous foods were taught along with the skills needed to identify and gather desirable foods. Omens such as the hooting of an owl around camp, which presaged a death, were taught in the family circle. Girls were taught to avoid bats as creatures which would endanger their virtue. Boys were told of the power of various animals and how to overcome it. In short, the Washo family was a self-contained unit, composed of the right number of people to most efficiently exploit the environment and functioning to train children to become adult Washo with very little dependence on institutions outside its own limits. In reality, a Washo family was seldom totally alone. Winter camps were usually composed of from four to ten *galesdangle* within a short distance of each other and the various families tended to move together in an informal but recognized social unit called the "bunch." This unit seems to have been what we have come to call a band but we will retain the Washo-English term to distinguish it from the more rigidly defined group.

The Bunch

Despite the pressures of the past century, the dislocations and disorganization brought about by white intrusion, the Washo family remains a constant and with it much of the old ritual. The need for a social unit to produce, nurture, and train children is renewed each generation. The last "bunch" ceased to exist in Washo life sometime in the 1920s and with it much of the knowledge about its function. One is led to believe that as important as the unit was in aboriginal and early historical times, its existence was dependent on a set of environmental and social factors which are no longer present. The size and composition of the various "bunches" recorded by anthropologists over the past decades vary a great deal, and clearly the unit seemed to be in a constant state of formation, dissolution and re-formation in response to the environment and the accidents of the individual lives of its members. The winter camp or village of several households appears to be the basis of the bunch, although if several such villages were fairly close together and tended to move together they might be considered as part of a single bunch. Most frequently a bunch was identified with its leader and would be referred to as "so and so's bunch." The assumption of leadership of a bunch was an informal matter. A man with a reputation for wisdom, generosity, humility, and good humor would gradually assume the leadership role among his neighbors. His advice would be sought about hunting and gathering, and his directions, always given reluctantly and obliquely, would be followed in group activities such as a rabbit hunt or a dance. A man with special power was more likely to become a leader than was a man without power. A person noted for his power to dream the presence of rabbit or antelope or foretell the spawning run of fish was a useful man to have in one's group. In English these men were often called a "rabbit boss" or "antelope boss." They would notify their neighbors of the possibility or advisability of a hunt and then direct the group's activities. Although his powers were limited specifically to the single sphere, his importance to his neighbors tended to encourage their turning to him for counsel.

Usually men of the same "bunch" joined together to form hunting parties. The bunch might as a unit move to the west side of the Sierra to pick acorns or go to the ocean to gather shells for trading. In time of emergency the men of the bunch usually stood together in defense of attacks from raiders from the neighboring tribes. These groups might ally themselves with the men of other bunches to form large war parties or repel a large enemy party, although they appear to have been under no compulsion to do so. In general, we might say that the bunch consisted of a minimal number of families that could cooperate to do those things which an individual family could not do for itself—stage rabbit drives, form hunting parties, defend itself, and so on. The size of such a group might vary from year to year or even from week to week. Should a family decide to move to some area where they had heard that a good gathering crop was available, they were in no way compelled to remain with their erstwhile companions. Single families or groups of families might separate to hunt or gather in areas where the entire group could not find sustenance. Later they might rejoin the original group or, if they chose, ally themselves with some other bunch. Most often, the various families were related by blood or marriage, but there appears to have been no bar to unrelated families joining the group. In the course of events, as children grew to adulthood and married, they would become relatives.

We have seen that the Washo abandoned a house in which a person had died and moved away from the spot. Therefore, a family experiencing a death might of necessity have to seek a camp with another bunch for the winter. Young people might leave the bunch or join it as the situation dictated when they married. Personal animosities were often resolved by the removal of one of the parties to another area. Thus the bunch remained relatively the same size through the years, but its members, both families and individuals, changed frequently.

There was a tendency for the descendants of leaders to become leaders themselves, leading some to speak of inheritance. It is more probable that a boy grown to manhood in the company of a father or uncle who was a leader learned more about the business of leadership and as he became an adult gradually assumed the role. The Washo view that most successful human actions were the result of supernatural assistance and their feeling that power seemed to concentrate in certain families probably encouraged this succession of leadership. However, the Washo kinship system in which a person traced his descent in both the patrilineal and matrilineal lines allowed for a variety of claimants for leadership positions to appear.

The Washo, however, did not seek responsibility for the acts or decisions of others. Power, it was felt, was thrust on a person and was an uncomfortable and in some cases dangerous burden. As often as not, a man would seek to escape the responsibility of leadership which he seemed destined by descent to assume and some other person, more aggressive or willing, would take his place. A particularly forceful woman, especially an older woman, might assume the leadership and direction of a bunch if no man appeared to become leader. There is also a great deal of evidence that the limits of a particular bunch might expand or contract according to the activity in which it was engaged. Thus, a family was part of a bunch which regularly staged rabbit drives together, but this entire group was considered as part of some other leader's bunch in the event of a war party or antelope drive or girl's dance.

Although we have seen that kinship was not an all important factor in who lived with what bunch, or in fact who might become part of a household, the kinship system of the Washo was not unimportant in their lives. Indeed an understanding of the principles of Washo kinship helps shed some light on the dynamics of the family and the bunch.

Kinship

The basic principle of Washo kinship reckoning was bilaterality, that is, an individual Washo considered relatives of his mother and father as being related to him equally. This principle is similar to that observed in our own society but in distinct contrast with the practice in many societies. There are many examples of peoples who feel more closely related to one side of their descent than to the other. If the father's side is considered closest, the system is termed patrilineal. If the mother's side is felt to be closest, the society is called matrilineal. Societies of either type are called unilineal. Unilineal kinship systems often place rather specific strictures on the responsibilities and obligations of one relative to another. Such restrictions are clearly incompatible with the demands of Washo environment which requires a flexible and rather opportunistic pattern of human behavior if the human group is to survive. Thus we find the bilateral principle to be common throughout the Great Basin and indeed other parts of the world where human beings attempt to exploit a hostile environment with a simple technology.

Some fifty-four different kinship terms used by the Washo have been reported. An analysis of the entire system of terms is too complex an undertaking for this book. It is important to know, however, that the Washo distinguish their siblings by relative age so that there are separate terms for older brother and younger brother, older sister and younger sister. These terms are extended to cover the children of one's mother's and father's siblings as well, so there is no distinct term for cousin as there is in English. Words related to the sibling terms are used to refer to and address distinct relatives or friends whose closeness places them within a network of fictitious kinship relations and obligations. The largest number of terms is found in a class used by persons toward their grandparents and to their grandchildren. The children of the children of one's siblings are carefully distinguished. Special terms are used for father's mother's sisters and mother's mother's sisters who stand in the relation of a kind of extra grandparent. A number of terms occur to describe the relationship between a boy and his parent's brothers, the uncle-nephew relationship being particularly important. None are reported for the parent's sister, this being a rather unimportant relationship in Washo life. In addition to blood or consanguineal relationship terms, a number of special terms are used to describe relatives by marriage. Parents-in-law are recognized as are the spouse's siblings. The husbands and wives of one's parent's siblings are not considered relatives and no terms exist to describe this relationship. While the terms in one's own generation and that of his parents and grandparents carefully distinguish sex and often whether maternal or paternal, one term is used to cover all relatives of a third ascending generation or, as we would say, great grandparents. Similarly, there is only a single term for a great-grandparent to use toward a great-grandchild no matter which sex or in what manner descended.

All societies avoid as a moral imperative marriages between close relatives. In large complex societies such as our own, this presents very little problem inasmuch as the large population offers many opportunities to find unrelated persons to marry. In smaller societies living in fairly close proximity, the possibility of two persons being biologically related is greatly increased. Among many peoples, the Washo included, it is possible to trace the actual biological relationship of any two persons. This presents a problem in the avoidance of incest unless relationships are defined in such a way that the problem does not arise. Kinship systems are not then actual descriptions of biological relationships but rather systems used to describe socially approved and significant relationships. In unilineal societies a husband and wife must belong to different descent groups. Their children will belong to either the husband's group or the wife's group which will define the limits of incest. Thus marriage with a mother's brother's child would be approved in a matrilineal society because he or she would not be of the same descent group as your own mother or her brother. In unilineal systems large classes of people can be automatically excluded as possible partners and other large classes are automatically included simply by reference to the system of unilineal descent, without consideration of what the actual biological relationship may be. The problem is solved by the Washo by ignoring relationships past the third ascending or descending generation. All relatives three generations removed are called by the same term. In the next generation there is no term at all. Therefore, a boy and a girl with the same great-grandparent could not marry because they both called the same person *dipisew*. But, if they had the same great great-grandparent and no common relatives after that, they would be considered unrelated and thus able to marry.

Kinship does more than determine who may or may not marry. In Washo life where the vagaries of the environment may at any time force a person to seek assistance from his fellows, relationships are exceedingly important. We have seen that there are a great many people classed as siblings, that is, people of one's own generation whose life cycle will closely parallel your own. In times of emergency, siblings real or fictive can be expected to help one another, and if one person called brother or sister is unable to help, there are many others to whom a person can turn. Similarly, a grandparent must increasingly depend on his children's children for support in his old age. It is here that we see a large number of kinship terms defining the relationship between a person three generations removed from another and providing a great number of opportunities for an old person to seek assistance. Given the relatively brief life span of primitive peoples it is highly unlikely that a great-grandchild would be old enough to provide assistance to a great-grandparent, a situation which appears to be reflected by the single catch-all term for that relationship.

The individual Washo is embedded in a network of kinsmen and has at his disposal numerous terms of reference for each kind of relative. Along these lines of relationship he can seek assistance in hunting or war or courtship. He can refer to his relationship with some member of a household if he should seek to take up residence outside his own home or find a host should he be traveling. If he seeks to join another bunch, it is probable that among its members will be someone, perhaps several people, to whom he can refer as a close relative. Should this not be the case, he can call close friends by a sibling term or apply the sibling term to the most distant of relatives. Washo environment demanded a flexible system so that the individual and his family could survive and the Washo kinship system met those demands admirably. Even a complete stranger entering a group would, unless personal animosity developed to drive him out, soon become classed as a sibling or friend and thus become part of the network of kinsmen. As we examine other aspects of Washo social organization, we can see how kinship, subsistence activity, and the environment interacted to create social institutions significant beyond the level of the family and the local bunch.

Regional Groups or "Moieties"

An individual's identification with a bunch or even with a family household was impermanent and quite apt to change in the course of his life. There was, however, a broader level of organization with which a Washo individual was more permanently, but not irrevocably, connected. Some anthropologists have called this a moiety system, that is, a division of the Washo people into two parts. However, in most societies which display moiety organization, the divisions play a much more important role than they did among the Washo. Many anthropologists believe that larger divisions of Washo social organization cannot be properly considered as moieties but as a reflection on Washo "ethnogeography," that is, the way the Washo viewed and identified the land in which they lived.

Washo territory was divided into four major sections: the west, or *tangelelti;* the east, or *pauwalu;* the north, or *welmelti;* and the south, *hanelelti.* People were given an identification with a region based on the location of their winter camp, or *galesdangl.* Inasmuch as the west or *tangelelti* was in the mountains and subject to heavy snows, few, if any, people wintered there so there were no people identified with this area. Because the Washo could and did move frequently on their hunting and gathering rounds and often changed bunches, set up new homes and allied themselves with different households, it was possible for a person identified with one zone to establish a home in another. The tendency seems to have been for a person to remain in the general area in which he had been born. Most "southerners" then remained "southerners" all their lives, associating with the same people and interacting with their kinsmen. Such a situation makes these regional divisions appear more permanent and kin-based than they actually were. Persons designated by the same regional term were not considered kinsmen and there was no restriction on their marrying if they were not otherwise related. When marriages were contracted between persons from different regions, one of the spouses usually changed his or her designation to that of the marriage partner.

At large gatherings such as the spring fishing around Lake Tahoe and the *gumsaba,* people from the various regions camped together. In the spring, the northerners tended to camp along the northern shore of the lake, the southerners on the south, and the easterners on the eastern shore. This seems more of a convenience then an adherence to any rule, inasmuch as the various parts of the huge lake were simply closer to the winter camps in the various regions. At the *gumsaba* the large camp was formed in a circle with the various divisions each occupying part of the arc. There is some question as to whether any such large-scale gathering occurred in aboriginal times. In fact, the social usages surrounding these area designations may have been a result of the closer association of the Washo from various parts of the country after the white man's appearance had made great changes in Washo life. There is evidence of hostility between the "northerners" and the "southerners" which is displayed even today. Conflicting claims to the "chiefdomship" of all the Washo spring up in both areas and many traditional tales tend to suggest that northern Washo were considered as strangers by the southern groups.

When the tribe did come together, these regional divisions formed the basis for choosing sides in games and races, the northerners against the southerners with the easterners dividing themselves between the two. However, regional ties were so light that a man participating in the team gambling games that were so popular with the Washo would move to the other team in order to change his luck. One might ask why, if the regional divisions played such a small part in Washo life, they were important at all? Perhaps the reason that they are worth discussing is what they can teach us about social organization on such a simple technological level. And, despite their superficiality, these identifications were and are regularly used by the Washo themselves. They can probably be understood best if we examine the dynamics of a hunting and gathering culture in this kind of an environment.

The animal on which the Washo depended for a major source of their food, the deer, live in small herds and are particularly wary and difficult to hunt. Even with firearms, a successful hunter must know more than just how to use his weapon; he must have more than a general knowledge of forest lore. To be really successful, an intimate knowledge of a particular region is required. A hunter must understand the habits of his quarry, not in general, but in a highly specific way. Game trails, springs, and salt licks, favorite browsing areas and bedding places, the behavior of scent in certain areas and an understanding of the prevailing winds and the behavior of animals under certain microclimatic conditions are essential to a successful hunt, the more so if the hunter must approach his quarry within a few feet. To learn this requires many years of training, beginning in early childhood. Even the most successful hunter moving into a strange area would not be much better than the newest tyro until he knew the new area as well as he had known his previous hunting grounds. Thus, among most peoples who hunt game of this sort, there is a distinct economic advantage for a man to remain within the area where he has been raised. This is the area in which his grandfather, father, and uncles have taught him the business of hunting. In this way a bias toward the paternal side of one's family tends to develop. When a man marries, he sets up his own household in his home area. Inasmuch as people from a single region tend to see each other more frequently than people from different regions, there is a tendency for a young man to marry a woman of his home region. In this way, quite without reference to any over-all rules of kinship, several generations of a bilateral family may include only persons born and raised in a single region. This gives the appearance of kinship based units, although the basic factors involved have little to do with kinship reckoning. Nonetheless, these divisions did have meaning to the Washo and formed the conceptual basis for identifying groups of people within the totality of the Washo "tribe."

The Tribe

One of the most difficult terms to define precisely is the word "tribe." It has, in modern America, come to have a specific legal definition, but this helps us very little in attempting to understand the political organization of aboriginal populations. In some parts of pre-Columbian America, societies were organized in such a manner that Europeans could equate them with political units in the Old World. Leadership roles were clearly defined and the political rights and obligations were understood by all the members of the group or tribe. In the Great Basin, however, political institutions were weak, if not almost nonexistant, and nowhere were they less developed than among the Washo. Certainly there was no over-all chief or leader for all the Washo in aboriginal times. Even the distinction of language and culture, which served to delimit some many separate groups in aboriginal America, were vague. Along the edges of the Washo country, where there was a great deal of interaction between the Washo and their Paiute neighbors, bunches or bands existed in which intermarriage was so common as to cause them to be identified as "half Paiute" by the Washo. Leadership within the local bunches and in the loose alliances of a number of bunches was informal and transitory. A leader gave advice and counsel but there seems to have been no compulsion to obey. Temporary leaders of rabbit hunts, antelope drives, and deer hunting expeditions had authority to direct those activities but their power was limited and specific to the event. While a reputation as a successful antelope boss or rabbit boss might enhance a man's general reputation for leadership, it was no gaurantee that his wishes would prevail save perhaps among his immediate relatives.

Disputes between individuals or between families were not referred to any body of law but were settled according to an established code of conduct. Thus, if a man found a stranger trespassing on his pine nut plot, he seized his equipment, broke it, and confiscated the nuts. Inasmuch as this was in accordance with custom, public opinion sided with him and the matter was settled because the trespasser could not get support among his neighbors. Men might come to blows over the use of a fishing platform but here again custom established who had prior rights and if custom was followed, public opinion was not roused. Disputes over food were relatively rare as generosity and sharing were primary Washo virtues. A hunting party divided its take equally and assistance in any task automatically meant that a debt had been incurred which had to be repaid in goods, food, or services, either then or in the future. Failure to act generously brought down the disapproval of one's neighbors and threatened the miser with a withdrawal of assistance which was tantamount to a sentence of death or, at the least, pauperism. All of these things were carried out without formal courts or even public judgment of the "crime." In serious disputes between individuals there was always the possibility of a feud developing. Vengeance could be taken by killing one's antagonist. If this was done, the enemy was ambushed and killed. The act was kept secret by the killer and his family, because retaliatory killings could be expected if the killer's identity became known. Such feuds were relatively rare. Washo existence was too precariously perched on the foundation of a not always provident environment to permit the luxury of unrestrained feuding. The threat of schisms which would effect the cooperation of groups or even limit the mobility of groups in search of food was sufficient to inhibit murder and retaliation save under the most extreme circumstances.

While Washo custom worked to prevent hostilities and serious conflict within the tribe, it was necessary to contend with the aggressive acts of strangers and to protect the heartland of the Washo territory from unwanted intrusions. It is in this circumstance, action against foreigners, in which the Washo acted most like a single unit. The Paiute to the east and the Maidu and Miwok to the west were constant threats to the resources of the Washo country. People living near the boundaries of Washo territory were constantly on the alert for signs of raiding parties. If intruders were bent on peaceful activities, to trade or to gather vegetable food, the Washo did not interfere. Even hunting parties appear to have sometimes been allowed to hunt unmolested in what the Washo considered their own land.

The Washo were not a warlike people and their response to the presence of strangers was generally to withdraw and observe them until their intentions were clear. Washo bands inhabiting the border regions kept a constant vigil against encroachment. Washo tradition holds that certain lookout posts were always manned, although this seems unlikely. If the intruder's intentions seemed hostile, or it appeared that they intended to trespass on forbidden ground, the Washo would attack. The most common tactic was an ambush, preferably of the enemy camp at night. The weapon was usually the bow, using special large war arrows which are said by some to have been rubbed with a mixture of secret ingredients to effect instant death.

Occasionally, more formal battles appear to have been fought. Washo tales of using stone to build crude breastworks behind which they could stand and fire at their attackers are frequent. Older Washo informants, recalling the tales of their grandparents, stress the defensive nature of Washo warfare. They recite what is almost a litany of battlegrounds where the invasions of Paiute from the east and the California tribes from the west were resisted. The places mentioned form a definite boundary around the core of the Washo country. However, all Washo warfare was not purely defensive and there are traditions of aggressive raids particularly to the west against the Miwok or the Maidu or, as the Washo call them, "the Diggers." These raids appear to have been retaliatory in nature. The only goal was to inflict death and wounds on their enemies. When such an enterprise was planned, the leader of the bunch which originated the idea would send a messenger to leaders throughout the Washo country asking for assistance. The messenger carried with him the familiar deer hide thong with a knot to mark each day before the expedition was to march. Each day he untied a knot. The summons was not necessarily a command and no one was compelled to join the war party. In certain areas the Washo were famed for their "roughness," that is their willingness to enter into any kind of a fray. The people living in the area of Woodfords and Markleville, California, were always sought by other Washo because of their reputation for bravery, reckless courage, and some supernatural power in war. Other bands were equally famous for non-violence and seldom joined raiding parties.

Full-scale war parties of this type disappeared soon after the appearance of whites in the area and much of the ritual and ceremony surrounding war is now forgotten. There was a period of perhaps as long as a month during which warriors prepared for battle by dancing and praying but the exact nature of the ceremony is now lost. Warriors bedecked themselves in close-fitting hats covered with magpie feathers. A powerful and famous warrior might suspend an eagle feather from the top of his hat and, if he owned enough feathers, one from each of his upper arms. The Washo did not have any special war magic, but they did believe that the Maidu to the west were able to cast a spell over an enemy village and put everyone to sleep. The return from a successful raid was also the occasion for a ceremony but this too is all but forgotten. Old informants recall hearing descriptions of the dance honoring a returning war party and insist that the ritual included the use of a single scalp taken from the enemy. Another dance performed frequently during the 1890's in the Woodfords area and in the Sierra Valley area was called a "war dance" by both whites and Washo but appears to have nothing to do with warfare. The acquisition of the horse and firearms by the northern Paiute bands upset the military balance between them and the Washo. In response, the Washo abandoned attempts to resist Paiute intrusions and instead withdrew into the mountains and avoided contact wherever possible. The long-term consequences of this altered situation can never be determined because the new Paiute strength coincided with appearance of the white man and the diversion of Paiute efforts into unsuccessful attempts to resist the latter.

Hostilities were always a threat to Washo who moved outside of the center of Washo territory. Hunting parties traveling west and families coming into California to gather pine nuts usually camped without fires once they crossed the divide of the Sierra Nevada. After they had made overtures to the inhabitants of the area, they might be accepted into the village and remain there, eventually even intermarrying, but while they were traveling and until their intentions were clear they might be attacked. Hunting parties considered it an omen of a forthcoming attack if the meat drying rack fell to the ground. If this happened, they quickly decamped and went into hiding. This habit of caution while outside Washo territory was maintained well into this century, although intertribal war had disappeared and hostilities had been reduced to shouting insults and rock throwing. Although it is certain that on occasion Washo from various areas banded together to raid the enemy or defend themselves, it is doubtful that the entire population of warriors ever joined in a single expedition. People in the north tended to cooperate with each other, as did people in the south, but it was not until the appearance of the white man that the entire tribe ever joined in any united action.

The information on warfare illustrates the weak development of any political consciousness of a Washo tribe as a whole. While the Washo clearly differentiated between themselves and all other peoples, using various cultural criteria, it is clear that they felt no over-all obligations simply because of this relationship. War was one of the mechanisms for dealing with non-Washo people, but it was generally a local matter resorted to resolve local problems and not considered a "nation-wide" affair.

Peaceful Relations

As often as the Washo might fight with their neighbors, they had other contacts with the same tribes. We have described trade as one such relationship. Another was mentioned in the previous section. The Washo striking west to hunt or gather often chose to spend the winter in the villages of their hosts and erstwhile enemies. Many intermarriages are recorded and Washo men frequently brought back foreign brides. One of the reasons given for the fierceness of the men in the Woodfords area was the amount of Miwok blood in their veins. Reciprocal trips by the Californians to the east appeared to have been less frequent but not altogether lacking. With intermarriage relatively common, it was possible to extend the network of kinship relations beyond the tribe in finding "relatives" among foreigners. As was so common in Washo life, these "international" relations were a matter of family, bunch, or, at best, local band concern. The institutionalized social units of Washo society were few and thus had to serve many purposes.

In this section we have seen how the Washo organized themselves into groups to solve the problems of subsistence and interpersonal and intertribal relations. One other major aspect of Washo life deals with the way the Washo handled the problem of dealing with the supernatural.

6

Spirits, Power, and Man

WITHIN THE SCOPE of his limited technology, the Washo was a rational person, well aware of cause and effect and prepared to handle the exigencies of his position. However, the precarious balance of Washo society often made survival seemingly dependent on chance. Why should a well-trained hunter locate his quarry only to have it escape him at the last moment? How could a well-made and well-aimed arrow miss an easy shot? Why should one man on a raid be wounded or killed and another escape unscathed? Why should the pine nut tree be fruitful one year and not at all the next? How was it that sickness struck down one person and passed over another? Why indeed should a man, unwounded and unhurt, die at all? These questions plague all societies and in many, including our own, are more or less successfully resolved in sophisticated theologies. Among many primitives, the basis of religion is an explanation of both the how and the why of the vagaries of life. The ritual of many primitive peoples, including those of the Washo, are both expressions of the Washo view of cause and effect and an attempt to maintain an understandable order to life.

The Washo did not articulate a complete philosophy or theology. Their religious life dealt with the practical day-to-day events: hunting, war, love, birth, health, and death. Yet we can present an organized picture of Washo religious life. We must remember, however, that a systematic presentation of Washo religion is a device which helps us understand a foreign and confusing point of view. It does not reflect the minds of the Washo as they go about their daily tasks, scarcely separating the sacred and the profane.

Power

To many of the questions posed above the Washo's answer was "power." A successful hunter was more than skilled and careful, he was aided

179

by a special power. A man who dreamed of rabbits or antelope was more than simply lucky, he was a possessor of a special power. The nature of this power is not clearly defined in all cases. We can see how power works most clearly if we learn how a man becomes a "doctor," or shaman, among the Washo. The shaman was expected to carry his share of the burden of living, but his special powers set him apart from his fellows and contributed to his livelihood because his services were valuable and demanded payment. The shaman's special power was the ability to diagnose and cure illness.

Illness might come from three sources. A ghost, angry because some piece of his property was being used by the living, might make the user sick. A sorcerer might cause illness by using magic to "shoot" a foreign body into his victim. Or a person might become ill because he had violated some taboo such as mistreating pine nuts or piñon trees. To affect a cure, a shaman was called to perform a ceremony over the patient. The cure was felt to be brought about not by the shaman's skill but by his "power" which was felt to be apart from the person of the shaman himself. The shaman served as a medium through which the power could be used to the benefit of the sick person. A treatment required that the shaman work for four nights. In addition to the shaman, the patient's family and a number of friends gathered. On each of the nights the shaman prayed to his power to assist him, smoked tobacco, frequently a sacred or semi-sacred act among Indians; and sang special songs which were his alone. Accompanying his singing with a rattle made of dry cocoons, he passed into a trance and while in this state located the site of the illness and identified the cause. If a ghost was the cause, the shaman would identify the contaminating object and instruct the patient as to whether he should get rid of it or perhaps simply treat it differently. If, on the other hand, an enemy had "shot" a sickness into the patient, the shaman would remove it by sucking, employing an eagle feather and tobacco smoke to make the extraction easier. When the object was removed and shown to the patient and his guests, the shaman would lecture it and then throw it away into the night. He was able to produce an object by means of legerdemain. He did not, however, feel that this was in any way hypocritical. His ability to perform these slight-of-hand tricks was part of the exercise of his power. We might compare his use of slight-of-hand to instill confidence in his power to the bedside manner of a modern doctor attempting to instill confidence in his patients. For his services a shaman was paid in food and valuable objects. The process of becoming a doctor illustrates the nature of power as the Washo conceived it.

The power to become a shaman was not sought by the Washo, it came unsought and often unwelcomed. The first signs of receiving power were often a series of dreams. In these dreams an animal, a bear, an owl, a "ghost" or some other being would appear. The vision would offer him power and assistance in life. The Washo feared power; it was dangerous for one who had it and the greater and more clearly defined the power, the more dangerous it was. The trancelike state which was part of the curing ceremony seemed to many Washo to be akin to death, a loss of spirit. Because of this, a young man might ignore the offers of spiritual power. But a spirit being, or *wegaleyo*, frequently refused to be ignored. It would begin to inflict a series of ailments upon its chosen vehicle. Although it was not considered good social form to brag of having power or to openly seek it, some men did secretly hope for power. Men of this type today invariably complain of a long series of illnesses, seizures, and ailments. To the outsider such a person might appear to be simply a hypochondriac, but the Washo recognized this as a veiled claim to power. Under pressure from the *wegaleyo,* a man would usually succumb and accept his power. Once he had made this secret decision, his dreams would become instruction sessions. The *wegaleyo* would tell him where he could find a special spring or pool. This was "his water" to be used in ceremonies or for ritual bathing or to decontaminate sacred articles collected by the shaman in his career. The spirit also taught his pupil a special song which he would remember word for word when he awoke. In later years a shaman might learn many such songs from his spirit. He would also receive instructions as to what equipment to collect. This would always include a rattle and eagle feathers. Individuals might also possess special stones, shell jewelry, or animal skins. These objects were usually obtained under unusual or miraculous circumstances. One shaman, for instance, had a stone shaped like a human molar which attracted his attention by whistling until he located the stone. In addition to his instructions direct from his spirit, a prospective shaman would seek out an established practitioner and apprentice himself to the older man. The tutor would instruct his apprentice in the arts of legerdemain, ventriloquism, and such feats as smoking several pipefulls of tobacco without allowing the smoke to escape from his lungs. In time, after his powers were known through participation in ceremonies held by his mentor, a shaman would be asked to perform cures of his own.

Shamans were always considered to be potential sorcerers. Their power was neither good nor bad in itself and could be used for whatever ends the shaman sought. The ability to use power against others is illustrated in a traditional Washo tale, which also points out the basic suspicion held by southern Washo toward northern Washo. According to the story, a northern Washo appeared at a camp in Carson Valley and there asked for food. Because he was a stranger, he was refused by all but one old woman. She fed the stranger and allowed him to sleep in her camp. The man left the camp determined to work vengeance on the people who had been so miserly with him. Walking west from Carson Valley, the northerner rested at the hot springs near Markleville. There performing some unknown magic, he pointed his finger in the direction of the camp. The power he controlled killed all the members of the camp, save the old woman who had been generous to him. Modern Washo insist that one can see a barren line in the earth stretching from Markleville to Carson Valley. They also insist that the campsite is covered with skeletons and abandoned equipment. This winter camp may well have been struck by the plague or some other epidemic disease.

Tradition describes other uses of shamanistic power. In what might be described as advertising contests, shaman engaged in tests of power, particularly at gatherings such as the *gumsaba.* The most common demonstration of power was said to be setting a number of stakes in a line. The shaman would point at the sticks and the winner of the contest was the shaman who could knock down the most sticks. Shaman are reported to have engaged in casual displays of power by offering an unsuspecting victim a pipe, or in later times, a cigarette. The shaman's power would remain in the pipe or cigarette and the smoker would be knocked flat or perhaps unconscious. To possess such power was dangerous and inconvenient. A person who received his power from the deer, for instance, could no longer eat deer meat. If he did, he would become ill and perhaps die. The possession of power also made one subject to frightening and mysterious experiences. A well-known shaman in the early part of this century staged a curing ceremony during which he fell into the fire while in a trance. Burning his trousers off, he had to go home wearing his shirt as a loin cloth although he was not hurt. On his way the shaman stopped at a stream to bathe. As he bent over the water, he fell into a faint and was taken down into the water. There he was greeted by Water Baby, a spirit creature said to inhabit all bodies of water in the Washo country. The Water Baby took the shaman into a strange land to meet the king of the Water Babies who lived in a large stone house. There the shaman was entertained by five young girls who taught him a special song. The Water Baby guide then took the shaman back to the surface and left him where the frightened man awoke floating in the water.

If a shaman lost his sacred paraphernalia or it was destroyed, he would most certainly become seriously ill. Because of these dangers, many men tried to avoid power if it was thrust upon them and would employ a shaman to help them rid themselves of the persistent spirit. If this was successful they could resume the normal Washo life. If not, they had little choice but to quiet the spirit and accept its gift.

The nature of power is most clearly seen in the complex of Washo shamanism, but *wegelayo* often provided special powers of a less general nature. Some men with a water *wegelayo* were believed to be able to bring rain. Others who had been visited by the bear *wegelayo* might on accasion act like a bear and be particularly brave or notably short tempered. Others might have the power to handle rattlesnakes with impunity and cure rattlesnake bites. The Water Baby might act as a *wegelayo* and give a person the power to walk under water. There is said to be a broad road of white sand across the bottom of Lake Tahoe. This was the special route of men with Water Baby *wegelayo* who wished to visit the beds of wild poison parsnips on the north shore of the lake. These poison plants used to be eaten with impunity as a demonstration of power. Some specially powerful men received their power from a number of different sources all of which helped in curing or performing other miracles.

The most dangerous task for a shaman was to recover the soul of a person who had apparently died. It was believed that with the help of his *wegelayo* a shaman could go into a trance and, in spirit form, follow the soul of the dead person into the land of the dead. This was described as a place in the sky to the south of Washo country. Its approaches were guarded by a number of fierce warriors. Behind these sentries was a spring. If the shaman could overtake the soul before it had drunk from the spring he could return it to its earthly body and revive his patient. This land of the dead was said to be a happy place where people played games and gambled and danced unless they had committed a murder. Murderers were banned by the other shades and placed in a kind of heavenly coventry.

We have spoken of shaman as being males, but women could also become shaman and many did. Their experiences and training did not differ from those of men. Power was not exclusively a gift of the spirit beings to humans. In a general way, everything was viewed as having some power. Merely to live required some supernatural assistance. Successful survival was a sign of power and thus old people had demonstrated that they were powerful. There was a widespread belief that old people were dangerous and should not be offended or harmed lest they retaliate by using their power. This belief worked to assure that an ancient Washo in his final years would receive support from those who were obligated to him. Even though he might be unable to share the burdens of life, he could avenge himself on those who did not behave ethically. This general power was extended to all living things, animals, and plants and, as we have seen, was the basis of many of the behavior patterns associated with hunting, fishing, and gathering.

Ghosts

The spirits of the dead were to be greatly feared and avoided. No Washo ever thought of his ancestors as benign figures concerned with his happiness and welfare. Instead they were angry and vengeful. If their property was used or misused, is their burial was not properly conducted, or for any one of a dozen other sins of ommission or commission, the dead might return to plague the living. Therefore Washo funerals were not ceremonies designed to honor the dead or comfort the living. They were ways of making sure the dead person's spirit would not return. It was for this reason that his home was burned or abandoned. If he returned to familiar haunts, the house and family would be gone. For the same reason his clothing and personal property were burned or buried with him. A person using some possession of a dead man was always liable to a visit from the ghost who had located his property and found the user. The brief Washo burial prayers were really exhortations to the dead person to accept his death and leave the living alone. He was told that no one had killed him and that no one was angry at him. Association with the dead was slightly contaminating and upon returning from funerals people washed themselves before handling food or touching children lest the contamination spread and attract the ghost. The Washo argue that it is the nature of things that the dead should remain dead and not bother the living. For this reason they say a rain storm always occurs after a death to wipe out the footprints of the deceased and thus remove all traces of his existence. The taboo on using the name of the dead was another such precaution. Despite all these precautions, the dead did return. Sometimes they came on specific missions of vengeance and on other occasions to simply wander in the vicinity of human beings. The twirling dust devils so common in the summer in this region were thought to be ghosts, and a sudden puff of warm air on a still summer night was most certainly a shade. The belief in ghosts and personal power was an important factor in Washo child raising practices. Parents avoided striking or spanking or striking a child for fear of angering some dead relative. In this instance the ghost seemed to have some friendly concern for the living, but the manner of showing it was to cause the death of the child as a punishment to the parents. The fear of sorcery led the Washo to encourage their younger children to remain within their own family group. Associating with strangers, particularly old strangers, could be dangerous. This belief is obviously related to the development of deep ties of dependence on one's close relatives and the strengthening of the all important Washo family unit. The two major concepts of Washo religion are: ghosts, to be feared, avoided, and appeased; and power, to be used to accomplish the business of living. But, these were not all the facets of Washo religion. Like most people the Washo had explanations for the natural and human environment in which they found themselves. These explanations were preserved in a body of mythology. The corpus of myth was not an elaborate and involved body of scripture. Rather, it consisted of a number of rather simple tales, many of which seem confused and inconsistent to foreigners.

Creation

Two myths deal with creation and although they are quite different, the inconsistency seems not to trouble the Washo who use whichever set of tales seems most appropriate at the time. The world is described in one set of myths as having gone through a number of stages. In each stage there was a different set of inhabitants, the modern Indians representing the fifth inhabitation of the earth. The creation of the various cultural groups known to the Washo is attributed to "Creation Women" who made the Washo, the Paiutes, and the Diggers (a generic term for California Indians) out of the seeds of the cattail. Still another tale tells of how a different personage, "Creation Man," formed the three groups by separating his three sons so they would not quarrel. The natural features of the Washo country are usually explained by reference to a pair of weasels. These two, *Damalali* (short-tailed weasel) and *Pewetseli* (long-tailed weasel), traveled together. The wiser *Pewetseli* usually managing to save the day threatened by the impulsive behavior of the rascal *Damalali*. The general structure of these tales is reminiscent of a common theme of adventuresome twin brothers found throughout much of western North America. The many lakes in the mountain region are, for instance, said to be caused by one such misadventure of the weasels. *Damalali*, the story says, came upon a Water Baby and took it prisoner. The water creature at first begged for his freedom and finally threatened to flood the world. When neither pleading nor threats moved the weasel, the Water Baby made good his threat and caused a flood to come which covered the mountains to their tips. *Pewetseli,* furious at his companion's irresponsibility, forced him to release the water spirit and begged the creature to lower the waters. This the Water Baby did, but in every mountain valley a lake remained. The adventures of this pair are seemingly endless, many of the incidences are virtually meaningless to the outsider, and in many cases the modern Washo appear to have forgotten the real significance of the episode. In other cases they appear to be simply humorous or sometimes salacious stories told for amusement.

Other Figures

A number of other miraculous figures appear in Washo mythology, all of them threatening and dangerous at least in part. *Hanglwuiwui,* a great one-eyed, one-legged giant, is said to have hopped from hilltop to hilltop in search of his favorite food, Indians. Near Gardenerville, Nevada, there is a cave called by the Washo *Hanglwuiwuiangl,* the dwelling of Hanglwuiwui, which is still avoided or approached with caution, although most Washo say that the giant has been dead for a long time.

Another fearsome feature of Washo mythology was the *Ang,* a great bird which carried off human victims and terrorized the world. Birds such as this figure in many Indian myths. The *Ang* is said to have died and fallen into Lake Tahoe where its skeleton formed a reef, which the Washo insist can be seen by anyone flying over the lake. The failure of white airplane pilots to report the reef is felt to be a conspiracy to discredit Washo belief.

The coyote, a figure found almost universally in Indian mythology, was prominent in Washo legends. As is true in other tribes, the nature of coyote is exceedingly difficult to define. In some episodes he is a dangerous and threatening force, in others quite benevolent, and in yet others a rather stupid fellow given to jokes and tricks and generally finding himself the laughing stock. One such tale describes the coyote attempting to seduce a young woman who thwarts him by inserting a seed pot between her legs and injuring coyote in an embarrassing and painful manner. Most coyote tales still told emphasize his lecherous and rascally nature and are told as salacious stories rather than moral fables. Some persons were felt to be able to turn themselves into coyotes and threaten their fellow men. Stories of such occurences are not unknown today.

In addition to the one-legged giant, the Washo believed that the mountains were inhabited by another race, possibly human but possessed of much more power than ordinary people. These giants or wild men figure in many stories of disappearance or mysterious occurences while on hunting trips. Occasionally, they directly attacked humans, trying to steal food from them or otherwise bother them. In most cases in stories dealing with these direct confrontations, the wild man was bested by the cleverness or courage of the Washo. In 1911 an Indian appeared in Oroville, California, attempting to steal scraps from a local slaughterhouse. He was eventually identified as Ishi, the last survivor of a small band of southern Yana who had maintained a furtive and fearful freedom in the Sierra foothills. His appearance caused a minor sensation as the "last wild Indian" in the United States. Modern Washo believe that he was not an Indian but one of the wild men of their myths.

One Washo tale tells of a great battle between the Washo and the giants in which the giants, who had no bows, were defeated after building a fort and throwing stones at the Washo. It is possible that the wild men represent some previous culture inhabiting the region. References to them and to a great battle in which they were exterminated are found in the mythologies of many groups in the Great Basin. Many of the Washo myths have been forgotten or have become garbled as the Washo world changed and the conditions that they have described and explained disappeared. One figure has maintained its vitality and dominates the supernatural life of the modern Washo as it did that of the aboriginal tribe. This is the Water Baby mentioned previously. These little creatures are described as being two or three feet tall with long black hair that never touches the ground but instead floats behind the Water Baby when it walks. They are grey in color and soft and clammy to the touch and possess immense power. Every body of water, lake, river, stream, pond, sink, or modern irrigation ditch is occupied by Water Babies. There is, according to Washo tradition, a tunnel from Lake Tahoe to the Carson Valley used by the Water Babies when they travel. All Washo today have heard the high mewing call of the Water Baby luring them toward some body of water at night. When they hear such a summons they hide in their houses and resist the temptation to follow.

In aboriginal times certain springs and lakes were considered to be favorite haunts of the Water Babies. Persons seeking their assistance, in curing an illness for instance, made or purchased an especially fine basket and deposited it in the lake or pond as a gift. Water Baby was a frequent *wegelayo* for the most powerful shamans. As individuals, Water Babies visited human beings. Some Washo believed that simply to see a Water Baby brought illness or death. Others felt it was a good omen, a chance to obtain power. Some others argue that a Water Baby did not give power but instead exchanged it for a human life. A gift of Water Baby was repaid with the life of a relative.

While many of the figures of Washo mythology have grown vague, their stories half forgotten and their place in Washo life reduced, the Water Baby has demonstrated an amazing vitality. Stories of visitations, or hearing Water Baby calls from streams or ponds, of seeing Water Baby footprints are still told. In fact, the Water Baby has kept abreast of the times and one informant with whom I talked stubbornly insisted he could tell a female Water Baby's footprints because she wore high-heeled shoes! Almost all the Washo are somewhat fearful of the consequences of the ignorance of white men in the matter of Water Babies. Fishermen or hunters, they fear, might catch or kill a Water Baby by mistake. One such misadventure is said to have resulted in the San Francisco earthquake of 1906. A fisherman caught a Water Baby and gave it to the San Francisco aquarium. Despite the warnings of a famous Indian leader who went to San Francisco to talk to the mayor, the creature was kept in the aquarium. It remained there until the earth shook and the water came up over the city. When the water receded the Water Baby, of course, was gone.

A most important element of the Washo world was the view that animals were not really any different than human beings. That is, they had societies of their own and languages and a special place in nature and a supernatural power which in some cases was greater than man's. The large and ferocious animals like the bear were considered to be intrinsically more powerful than men and we have seen that to kill a bear was an act which conferred power. Other animals, like men, might or might not have power. But the old buck who successfully eluded the hunter and even a wily rabbit who would not be killed were considered to have special power and to be *mushege* or "wild animals." But the term was not limited to animals alone. A man of particular fierceness or power, one who hunted successfully or was a renowned fighter or who simply had an unpredictable temper, was also called *mushege*. This partial equation of men and animals and the behavior which it engendered, as we shall see, was particularly important in developing the contacts between the Washo and white invaders of their land.

Summary

In this chapter we have examined some of the basic concepts and figures of Washo religious life. Washo religion was not based on a well-developed theological scheme but instead must for the most part be analyzed from the behavior of people in day-to-day life. There were few, if any, purely religious acts. Instead, we see ritual reflecting a Washo view of the supernatural woven through nearly every act of the day. Hunting ritual, dreams of rabbits and fish and antelope, special power to obtain food, respectful treatment of the remains of animals, the minor ceremonies of childbirth and childhood were all viewed as essential parts of the activities with which they were associated. To go hunting without taking the proper ritual steps would be as foolish in Washo eyes as failing to take a bow or using a crooked arrow. To try and hunt with a weapon contaminated by a menstruating woman would be as hopeless as going into the field with a bow but no bowstring. Another feature of Washo religion was that its observance seldom required the participation of specialists or of special groups of people. The ritual of life was the ritual of individuals or individuals within the family group. Certain occasions when people could come together for extended periods were also times when religious rituals were performed. But they were also occasions for games and gambling and courtship and could not be considered purely religious occasions. Even in curing, when a specialist was needed, any shaman would do, if his power was great enough. There was no special caste of priests and any person, man or woman, might become a shaman. Shamans said to have Water Baby power were believed to have a secret cave which could be entered by sinking into Lake Tahoe and then rising inside a great rock. This is the nearest thing to an association or guild of specialists.

In short, Washo religion offered an explanation for the universe as it existed and for the accidents and misadventures of life. It also provided a system of ritual to be used in the business of life which probably allayed some of the fear and uncertainty of the hunting and gathering existence. Because each step in ritual was associated with practical matters, the sacred actions may have provided a framework within which the practical actions could be more easily learned and remembered. As simple as it might be, Washo religion played an important role in aboriginal life and has, as we shall see, a cornerstone of Washo cultural survival in the modern world.

7

California, the Washo, and the Great Basin

I N THE PRECEDING CHAPTERS we have seen how the Washo adjusted their lives to the environment in which they lived, how the one related to the other, and how they felt about and dealt with the supernatural world beyond man's understanding. The Washo world was on the border between two zones of life. To the west were the mountains; green, lake filled, laced with fish-filled streams, falling off into the verdant foothills and valleys of California with its warm summers and mild winters. To the east was the Great Basin; high, arid, covered with dry, quick blooming plants and inhabited by a wide variety of animals. These two life zones were the sites of contrasting systems of culture. The Washo shared in both traditions.

In the Great Basin, all peoples save the Washo spoke languages of the Uto-Aztecan family and practiced a way of life so uniform that it differed only in detail over hundreds of thousands of the arid, inhospitable square miles. In California, the people spoke languages related to every language stock in North America save that of the Eskimo. A wide variety of languages is matched by variations in cultural practices, although language and culture had little correlation. Northwestern California, with its fog-swept mountains plunging to the sea, cut by the Smith, Eel, and Trinity rivers and a hundred lesser streams, was in the zone of Northwest Coast culture which had its center far to the north in Washington, British Columbia, and Alaska. In this area we find speakers of Ritwan, Athapaskan, and Hokan sharing the same general social and cultural configurations. The nearest neighbors of the Washo on the west, southwest, and northwest all spoke dialects of California Penutian, a language stock which dominated an area from the divide of the Sierra west to the Pacific Ocean but was concentrated mainly in the foothills and plains of the great central valleys. These were the acorn Indians, supplied without stint by the millions of oak trees which dotted the area. Moreover, their territory was traced with watercourses. The Sacramento, American, and Feather rivers formed a northern network, the San Joaquin and its tributaries watered the southern zone. Throughout most of this area the salmon came to spawn, entering the inland rivers from the San Francisco Bay where the systems converged. In addition to fish, the foothills and lowlands were rich with game. Deer, antelope, and elk roamed the area in great number. The jack rabbits were plentiful as were other small game animals. The rivers, untapped by irrigation and uncontrolled by dams, flooded in the spring to form huge lakes and swamps which provided homes for dozens of species of waterfowl, geese, ducks, rails, mud hens, and coots. Two varieties of quail lived in the valleys and uplands. And, in addition to the staple acorn, a wide variety of plants provided seeds, roots, and berries. The coast provided fish, sea mammals, shellfish, and crustaceans. Perhaps no place on earth was as consistently provident and hospitable to nonagricultural man as was central California. In contrast to the Great Basin with its low population density, California was the most densely populated area in North America north of agricultural and civilized Mexico.

We know less of southern California in aboriginal times because the Spanish mission endeavors seriously disrupted the aboriginal life. The tribes of southern California have lost, even in their own tongue, identifying words for the aboriginal groups. Instead they are known, save for a few groups in the mountains, by the name of the nearest mission. While not blessed with the water sources found to the north, the southerners still enjoyed a provident environment. There was access to the sea. Some groups lived almost entirely by hunting and fishing on the coast and the coastal islands. The weather was always mild. Deer and jack rabbits were relatively plentiful. Acorns were widely distributed. With more than enough food California Indians were able to live in larger groups. Moreover, they could quite clearly define their territories because a finite zone could supply all the needs of the group. Winter villages were considerably larger than those in the Basin and houses more substantial. Some authorities feel communities of as many as 2000 people existed in ancient California. Houses were often commodious semisubterranean structures. In many areas each village boasted an extremely large house, partially underground, where the men could lounge, sweat in the heat of fires to purify themselves, and in which larger dance gatherings could be held. In the south substantial dwellings of thatch or woven mats replaced the earth houses. The summer was a time of limited wandering and the winter villages were abandoned as the tribe broke up to set up temporary summer camps. Aggressive warfare was almost unknown but the Californians were determined fighters in resisting trespass of their territories. The plentiful supply of food required hard work to collect, but as compared to the Basin, a minimal effort was needed to fill the larder. The Californians had leisure to devote to cultural elaboration. And because they had resources enough for larger groups they also had social problems unknown in the Basin. Larger groups required leaders and a more developed concept of authority. The leisure provided by the environment meant that time was available for the activities of leaders and councils and for ceremonials devoted to the welfare of the entire group. It also meant that within the limits of the technology the creative or ambitious or imaginative Indian had an opportunity to explore and experiment with his or her skills. There was time, for instance, to polish stone cylinders and then painstakingly pierce them from end to end using a sea-lion whisker twisted back and forth in a fine abrasive sand. There was time for women to weave beautiful baskets so small that the stitches can be seen only with a magnifying glass. These tiny baskets had no function save to display the skill of the maker. In the north men worked with obsidian to make huge dou-ble-ended blades, perhaps the finest example of flint knapping in the world, which served no purpose except to enhance the owner's prestige when they were displayed. On the coast and islands of the Santa Barbara area, beautiful bowls were hewn from blocks of soft steatite. The Chumash who inhabited that area made a seagoing plank canoe which has long intrigued ethnologists because the techniques employed are common in the Pacific islands. The dry mountains and desert passes east of the San Bernardino mountains had tribes that knew how to make pottery in which they stored their winter food supplies.

California religious life was varied and complex, far too varied and com-plex to be described in detail. Throughout the state elaborate large scale-ceremo-nies featuring costumed dancers were a part of community life. Puberty rites for boys and girls were more drawn out and complex than those found in the Basin. A form of sand painting was practiced in southern California. The restrictions placed on a young women at the time of her first menses were rigorous and in-volved. Only a society with enough food to allow young women to be totally nonproductive could permit such practices. Young men were initiated in large ceremonies requiring that they drink a concoction made of jimson weed which would produce a vision. Despite the many differences between the tribes and tribe-lets of California, there are certain basic similarities. Death was an obsession. Elaborate funeral ceremonies were held both at the time of death and in annual mourning ceremonies, held a year after the death. Images of the dead person were burned and in southern California the ashes may have been consumed in a drink taken by the mourners. Sweating in special houses to purify themselves before hunting and ceremonial participation was general also. The larger popu-lation and more complex communities of California evolved social structural ele-ments unknown or only vaguely present in the Basin. Many tribes were divided into moieties with clean-cut lines of patrilineal descent. These moieties func-tioned in many contexts, one of them, for instance, having the responsibility for disposing of the dead of the other. This disposal was frequently cremation.

The California tribes observed many of the day-to-day rituals of hunting and interpersonal relations that we have seen among the Washo. But California religion had room for elaboration and there was a tendency to develop special-ized cults. Animals and birds, particularly the eagle, were taken and kept for a time to be killed and ceremonially interred. An elaborate bird cult was de-veloped in the south-central portion of the state and burials of coyote, bear, bad-ger, and deer have been reported. As specialized cults evolved, so did special-ized shamanism. Among the Washo, we have seen a very weak development of special powers, the average shaman being a general practitioner. In California, shamans were given special power to deal with specific ailments or perform certain miracles. Some were said to be able to turn themselves into bears and they were the most feared. The Californians assumed the responsibility for the world's continuity and annual world renewal ceremonies, held to prevent the world from exploding, were common in many parts of the state. Perhaps this should be expected in an area of frequent earthquakes. This elaboration of religious activities and ceremonials and complexity of social order was reflected in an involved and well-developed body of mythology. The oral literature of the Californians was among the most beautiful and complex in the New World.

There was a tendency among early writers to disregard the achievements of California Indian cultures. Experienced with the farming cultures of the east and the warlike and aggressive tribes of the Great Plains or the well-ordered farming communities of the southwestern pueblos, they gave little notice to the Californians who fought little, seldom wore clothes and when they did, wore very little. This short-sighted view obscured the immense richness of California life. The lack of aggressive behavior is perhaps due to the environment which provided enough, in many cases more than enough, for everyone. Nor were there rich neighbors to tempt the Californians into aggressive actions. To the west was the sea and the east offered only the desert and the Great Basin. Neither external pressures nor internal demands created a need to organize on a larger political scale and form savage kingdoms or tribal alliances. Only along the lower Colorado River where Hokan-speaking tribes with a California culture had learned to farm and also probably had to defend the fertile river lands from envious intruders from the arid lands to the east was war an important activity. Elsewhere in California the defense of tribal territory was the only cause for war and often these disputes were settled by tribal champions while the warriors of the two groups cheered them on.

To some it has seemed odd that, in what is today one of the world's most productive agricultural regions, the Indians had not developed an agricultural tradition. To some it has indicated a lack of ambition and inventiveness among the native Californians. However, we must remember that the very areas of the central valleys which are so productive today were often under water and at the best were swampy. It is doubtful that any people using the techniques of farming known to natives of North America could have produced more food than nature already provided from these areas. Moreover, California is not well suited to the production of maize which requires summer rains and long hot growing periods. Even today maize is a minor feature in California agriculture. The modern productivity of the state is a testimony to advanced technology, irrigation, machine plowing and planting, and vast water control projects. No Indians of the native United States possessed such technical advantages or even knew of the crops which have been most successful in California. In the extreme south, and in the arid mountains lying between San Diego and deserts of the Colorado Basin, where the environment was least provident, some small-scale experimentation with farming was carried out but it was cut short by the changes wrought by white intrusion.

In general, California provided everything man needed for a comfortable life based on hunting and gathering, but it provided no incentive for social and political units larger than the relatively small tribe. Hunting and gathering still placed a premium on the subsistence activities of a family. There was perhaps less need for economic cooperation than in the Basin. Social cooperation was needed to order the life of larger groups but not to support it. This may have been the fatal weakness of the area. When confronted with the intrusion of white men, the California tribes were unprepared and unable to organize a defense. Before they learned the bitter lessons of disunion, it was far, far too late.

While California culture was a picture of primitive life painted in its greatest detail and in its brightest colors, the Basin was life reduced to its simplest elements. Nowhere in the Basin, not even the relatively provident Washo territory, was the land provident enough to support large groups or even semi-permanent settlements. All the factors which operated to keep Washo society divided into small independent and mobile units operated even more stringently as one moved east.

In contrast to the multilingual, multicultural nature of California, the Basin was a single entity. All the peoples found there, except the Washo, spoke either a dialect of Paiute or a dialect of Shoshone. The small bands moving regularly wherever food might be found could not defend any permanent territory because they might be forced to move on at any time preventing any attachment to a locality. Thus, there were no elaborate social forms, no moieties or clans or, of course, the ceremonials or ritual associated with such units. Leadership was transitory and informal. Leaders gave advice, not orders, and asked for cooperation instead of demanding it. Whenever an antelope, waterfowl or rabbit drive brought numbers of people together they, like the Washo, held religious and social dances and played group games.

Seldom did these Basin groups engage in warfare. Human life, so difficult to maintain, was not casually risked to defend a plot of pig weed or a grove of piñon trees. Better to move on if the matter could not be settled by argument or by a rock-throwing fight. Better yet, a place already occupied should simply be avoided because it obviously would not support a larger population. If it would, there was no reason for dispute and the two groups could exploit it together and then move on, going their separate ways.

While the Californians enjoyed a rich religious and ceremonial life, the Basin people had a very elementary one. There were shamans, generalists with curing power. Men with the power to dream about antelope and charm them existed and the antelope drive provided the nearest thing to a group ritual and, in many cases, the closest approach to a united political action under a secular leader who was, of course, the shaman. Basin mythology did not involve itself with abstract questions of origins. Simple tales, many of them obscene by our standards, described the adventures of coyote and his brother the wolf, another example of the mythological twins.

Unlike the California tribes, death was not the concern of the Basin tribes. The dead themselves were feared as contaminating and were quickly and fearfully disposed of. No ceremonies of mourning which might call back the ghosts were held.

Basin culture was not rich, Basin society was not involved, and Basin technology was exceedingly simple. Yet we must admire the ability to adjust and adapt which enabled the widely scattered people to live in this inhospitable land. A detailed knowledge of plants and animals and of water sources unknown to white men until recent years and of the cycle of growth in the region enabled the Basin peoples to survive probably far better than it seemed to the first white men who saw them, naked, subsisting on grubs and insects, unhoused and owning nothing more than they could carry. Yet the ability of these people to respond to environmental opportunities is found throughout the Basin. Many groups regularly burned off the brush in the fall and sowed the area with seeds to insure a crop in the spring. Others simply burned away the brush, knowing that it would encourage the growth of seed-producing grasses. In the Owens Valley south of the Washo at the base of the Sierra, groups cooperated in the digging of irrigation ditches to flood meadows where wild grasses grew. Although this practice might have been borrowed from the whites, it formed the basis of relatively permanent and stable communities with regular leaders exercising a degree of authority not known elsewhere in the Basin. In fact, the very simplicity of Basin culture and the need to adapt made it possible for the Paiute and Shoshone to adjust rather rapidly to new opportunities. The horse spread into northern Nevada in the second quarter of the nineteenth century, obtained from the Shoshone and Bannock of the plateau country to the north. The north Paiute quickly adopted the horse and formed Plains Indian-like bands with regular secular chiefs. However, the buffalo was long since gone from the Basin and the Great Plains were hundreds of miles away. The Basin itself provided no species which could be hunted successfully using the horse. Running down the antelope on horseback simply exhausted the supply of these animals that much sooner. The Paiute had little alternative save to turn their mounted war bands against the white newcomers. This raiding led to the wars of the 1850s in which the early successes of the Indians were followed by bloody defeats and a collapse of this short-lived phase of Basin culture.

Between California and the Basin the Washo, separated in language from their neighbors on either side, made their home. The influences of both traditions can be seen in Washo society and culture. A number of anthropologists have called the Washo a California tribe which was pushed over the Sierra and which developed a Basin-like culture.

The environment of Washo country is indeed more Basin-like, a fact clearly reflected in the subsistence cycle and the social organization of the Washo. But there is much of California in Washo culture. It might be likened to a crude water-color imitation, painted on a rough board, of a rich and detailed oil painting done on a well-prepared canvas. Many of the details are gone. The board would not accept the color and the details.

As compared to the Paiute and the Shoshone, Washo mythology was more elaborate. Elements of both the Basin and California can be found, sometimes not too well articulated. For the most part, as we have seen, Washo shamans were generalists but there was a tendency or perhaps a hope of special power. The practice and the opportunity for holding group ceremonials was more common. It is perhaps more important that such observances were expected. Whether or not they were ever really staged, the Washo believed that tribal gatherings were a proper part of life, that some ritual recognition should be given to pine nut harvest and the first fish.

While they did not divide themselves into the clearly demarcated groups which we find in California, there is a sense of permanency and proprietorship about the territorial divisions of the Washo. The traditions of sentries on the border and fights to preserve territorial integrity are more of the California than the Basin tradition. So too are the traditions of war dances and ceremonies before and after a raid. Washo attitudes about death and the dead are more of the Basin, although older informants recall an annual "cry," rather informal and unstructured, which commemorated the dead. If such an observance was made, it was probably borrowed from neighboring tribes and was quickly lost in the changes of the past hundred years. In general, the Washo seemed to look toward California, perhaps we should say back toward their abandoned homeland, for a model on which to base their behavior. Although modern Washo might refer to California tribes as "Diggers," it is clear that they viewed them as rich and powerful and worth imitating. Many of the things the Washo envied simply could not be brought into the Washo environment in aboriginal times. But, as we shall see, the appearance of the white man brought about changes which permitted the Washo to borrow from the Californians. The Washo provide an interesting vantage point from which to view the cultural and social picture of a vast area of the United States stretching from the Rocky Mountains to the Pacific Ocean. Because the history of the Washo since the appearance of the white man in many ways parallels events in both California and the Basin, the examination of this period is an introduction to what is often a sad but still an exceedingly important process, that of acculturation.

8

The White Man and New Alternatives

HE APPEARANCE of Europeans and Africans in the New World after Columbus' voyage set into motion forces which dramatically changed Indian societies and cultures. No matter how remote, no Indian culture survived unchanged when confronted with the pressures of the technically advanced, aggressive, and expanding new American culture. The precise nature of
these changes, exactly what elements of non-Indian culture the tribes accepted or
rejected, how they responded to new forms of political organizations and new
ideas about land ownership and commerce has long been a focus of anthropological interest. This process of borrowing, adapting, and reshaping cultures
in prolonged contact has been called acculturation. The term itself has been the
center of much scholarly debate and examination. For our purposes we will
define the term simply as the study of the changes caused by the intrusion of the
Euro-American culture. These changes began almost as soon as Columbus and
his men arrived and are continuing even today. Among the last to react to this
acculturative process were the scattered people of the Great Basin. The Washo
continued to follow their old established patterns well into the nineteenth century and carried them on, with a minimal change, until the twentieth century. In
this section we shall examine the past century of relations between the Washo
and the foreigners who entered their land and altered the conditions on which
Washo life has been based.

Before the First

Historians have carefully combed the records of western exploration in
order to establish the precise month and year when the first European entered

196

the Great Basin. It is possible that we will never know absolutely. The mountain men pushing west from the Rockies in search of new beaver country were not all given to writing journals and recording their trips. Nor have we as yet examined all the records of Spanish colonial exploration of the interior. Washo tradition stubbornly holds that Spaniards did cross the Sierra long before the Gold Rush. We do know that many of the earliest travelers in the area were semicriminals who did not leave records of their activities. The first whites to leave a definite record of travel in the Basin were forty trappers who were led by Jedediah S. Smith down the Humboldt River, then to the Walker River, and then following it to its source, crossed into California in 1826.

These early penetrations of the Washo country had no great effect on the Indian way of life. The Washo preferred to watch from a distance and determine what the strangers were up to. Captain John C. Fremont's party, in the 1840s, made contact with several small Washo groups who appeared to be quite frightened. Fremont was distressed by the nearly naked Indians enduring the cold and gave one man some red and blue clothes, the first recorded instance of the Washo receiving material goods from the new culture. Later Fremont employed a Washo as a guide and his presence attracted other Washo who followed the party on their curious round snowshoes. Traditions of the Washo themselves reveal the other side of these first encounters. The stories tell of watching the exploring parties and wagon trains. On one occasion, a cow or ox strayed from an emigrant train and was caught by the Washo. They had observed the travelers well. They packed the ox and led it for a time, then they experimented with riding the beast. Finally they tired of the novelty and butchered the ox and feasted on its flesh. Apparently very little occurred in the Washo country which escaped Indian eyes. During the travail of the Donner party in 1846, the Washo kept the emigrants under surveillance and from time to time left food for the marooned travelers to find. There is a story in the trans-Sierran country that the cannibalism practiced by the Donner party was the reason the Indians were afraid of the whites.

But long before the first sporadic appearance of whites from the east the Washo had been affected by the expansion of the Spanish into California, which made regular trips to the coast for shellfish hazardous. Washo trips into western California became less frequent and more furtive and perhaps stopped altogether. From the southwest, warlike tribes using horses raided into the Great Basin to collect slaves for the markets of Santa Fe and Taos. The first direct contacts between the Washo and white intruders were colored by these earlier experiences. The Washo could be tempted to approach the strangers and receive gifts but the entire relationship was marked with caution.

Before the Rush

The discovery of gold in California in 1848 set off the great migration into the area and many thousands of gold seekers crossed the Washo country enroute to the "diggings." Even before the Gold Rush the tempo of white activity in the Washo country was increasing. Emigrant travel was heavy enough to support a trading post on the Carson River in the vicinity of Woodfords, California. Criminals seeking to take advantage of the emigrants and to avoid even the feeble strength of Spanish law in California established camps on the eastern slope of the Sierra. Travelers usually arrived on the east slope of the mountains with their animals exhausted. The residents of the area would trade fresh animals for the exhausted ones. Usually the animals they traded were obtained from previous parties and grazed into good condition. In addition, there is evidence that they stole great numbers of horses and cattle from the Californians. We have little record of the Washo during this period. The character of the renegades living in the Washo country suggests that they were people with little concern for human life and suffering, and it would have been wise to avoid contact with them if at all possible. For the most part Washo life seems to have gone on unchanged. The cycle of movement was unaltered by the presence of this handful of white men. The Washo observed and learned something of these new people, watching for whatever new opportunity they might provide but unwilling to give up their own established and successful patterns. The fragments of European society lived among the Indians, not with them, and the Indians managed to avoid the strangers.

The Gold Rush

In 1848, a workman employed by John Sutter to build a lumber mill on the American River discovered gold. Sutter, an amazing and politically astute man with visions of empire, tried to keep the find a secret but the word leaked out and California's gold rush began. In the same year, the United States and Mexico signed the Treaty of Guadalupe Hidalgo, ending the Mexican War and bringing California under the American flag. With the war ended, a battalion of men raised in Utah to fight in California, the famous Mormon Battalion, began their march back to Salt Lake City. They constructed a wagon road over the Carson Pass and marched through the Washo country. Within the year, parties of settlers, colonizers from the Mormon state of Deseret, were moving into the Carson Valley. They intended to establish farms and a permanent settlement. They cannot have been completely insensitive to the commercial possibilities of raising food and animals on a direct route to the gold fields. The center of the Mormon colony was later to become known as Genoa. It was there, in the summer of 1849, that an enterprising man named Beatie set up a trading post for the season. It was also in the summer of that year that travelers crossing the Sierra set up many camps on the shore of Lake Tahoe, the heart of Washo life. At the same time, a party of 150 horse-riding Indians is reported to have appeared at the lake. These must have been Paiutes, newly possessed of the horse, beginning to expand and flex their military muscles. From this point on, Washo and white history became merged. Although the two cultures were separate and the two societies distinct, the behavior of one henceforth would have effects on the other. The Indian and white populations of the Washo country began to adjust to and depend upon one another.

By 1851 the Genoa trading post was being operated year-round. A number of gold seekers chose to seek the more mundane fortunes of agriculture and settled in the Carson Valley and near Honey Lake. Two years later, the trading post and scattered farms of the Carson Valley were officially organized into a town and settlements formed in Washo Valley and Eagle Valley. Mail and passengers were moving across the Sierra drawn by mule teams which left Sacramento three times a week headed for Salt Lake City.

The temporary camps on the shores of Lake Tahoe had become permanent trading posts in the mid-1850s. By 1858, a telegraph line connected western Nevada with Sacramento and the outside world. There were at this time not more than a thousand foreigners living within the Washo country. They were scattered over the best and most productive areas of the Indian land. Familiar with the aggressive Indians of the east and the Great Plains, the settlers expected to be attacked. That they were not is due to Washo caution and perhaps to the basic Mormon attitude, often violated in practice, of friendliness and consideration toward Indians. In 1858 the Comstock Lode, in the area of what is now Virginia City, Nevada, was discovered. The slow changes brought about by piecemeal and small-scale settlement ended abruptly and the course of Washo history took another direction.

The Comstock Lode

Silver was discovered in 1858 in the mountains east of the Washo country. In the following year, 20,000 fortune seekers swarmed over the Sierra Nevada. Great mines bored into the hills. Theaters, saloons, opera houses, hotels, bawdy houses, and elaborate churches were built with amazing speed. The silver barons erected mansions, their furnishings from Europe. Miners from the east and from Wales came to work in the mines. The famous entertainers played in Virginia City and hundreds of disreputable characters came to hover on the fringes of the great fortunes.

Within two years 5000 acres of land were under cultivation on the east fork of the Carson River. Ten thousand head of cattle, horses, and hogs were grazing on the most productive gathering land in the Washo country. The famous western explorer Major J. Dodge was appointed agent to exercise authority over the Indians of the region, including the Washo. From 1848 to 1860, the environment was changed dramatically and the Washo were forced to make adjustments to this new situation.

The New Environment

The small number of early settlers did not seriously discomfit the Washo, but they did presage the conflicts to come later. Each of the major white activities—farming, ranching, mining—had an effect on the environment which had to be reflected in Washo behavior.

RANCHING   In many parts of the United States, Indian tribes quickly adopted the practice of animal husbandry. The Washo, on the other hand, still look on cattle with some suspicion and hostility, and sheep are viewed with contempt and hatred. From the point of view of the gatherer and the hunter, livestock are competitors. Cattle and horses graze in the best collecting grounds, stamping and spoiling what they do not eat. Their grazing reduces not only the plant food available for man but drives off game animals such as the deer and antelope. Sheep, cropping ground cover to the roots, are even more destructive. The hog roots up valuable tubers, his sharp hooves cutting and killing the grass. Had the Washo been able to take advantage of the livestock by killing grazing cattle and using their meat, perhaps their response would have been different. But the Anglo farmers of western Nevada did not let their precious few animals graze widely and untended as did the Spanish grandees of the west and southwest. The Washo soon learned that to kill a cow or steer was to invite retaliation by bands of men with firearms and little concern with Indian lives. Thus, whole areas of Washo country were rendered less productive by grazing and there was no compensating factor involved. Ranching was a complete loss to the Washo.

FARMING   Farming had both pluses and minuses in the Washo ledger. Certain productive lands were taken away from them and planted to wheat, barley, or vegetables. But wheat and barley are useful foods and their seeds were scattered outside the farmer's fields to enrich the natural grasses. The edges of fields became good gathering grounds for a new type of sunflower. No white farmer was as careful a gleaner as a Washo woman and the harvested fields themselves were sources of seeds. The farmers also irrigated, and along the ditches a heavy growth of willow and cattail sprang up, providing habitat for cottontail rabbits, doves, waterfowl, and an important source of basket material. While farming took certain gathering lands away from the Washo, it provided compensating alternatives which permitted the Washo to continue living very much as they always had and still reap an advantage.

MINING   Mining required large numbers of workers. The mining cities soon drove away the larger game. Mine tailings blotted out good picking grounds and created ugly barren hillocks. Most importantly, the silver industry demanded lumber for mine shorings and charcoal for smelting. The groves of piñor. trees on the nearby hills provided both. Today the hills near Virginia City are nearly barren. Before the mines were sunk, both the Washo and the Paiute had picked pine nuts in this area. At first the white men cut the trees, but soon employed Indians to do the job and finally, because they could not depend on Indians, Chinese took over the task of cutting the trees and making charcoal. Washo prejudice against the Chinese is based on the fact that the orientals wiped out the sacred piñon groves. This may be a post-hoc rationalization and the real resentment may have arisen from the fact that the Chinese drove the Washo away from a profitable occupation. In general, mining was a total loss to the Washo hunting and gathering economy. On the other hand, it was in the

mining towns that the Washo began to learn a most important lesson about dealing with the white men. The whites were willing to pay money for labor and if
a man had enough money, he could buy any of the desirable things the white
man brought into the Washo country.

Two Sides of the Mirror

The impression one group forms of another will play an important role
in shaping the relations between the groups. The white impression of the
Washo can be found in old records. The Washo impression of the whites is a
more difficult matter to determine but well worth examining.

POOR, NAKED SAVAGES   Typical of early white response to the
Washo is the following quotation:

> They are more filthy than beasts and live in inhabitations which summer
> or winter are nothing more than circular enclosures, about five high without
> roof, made of artemisia or sagebrush, or branches of cedar thrown about the
> circumference of a circle and serve only to break the wind. (Ingalls 1913)

The same observer reporting on Washo clothing said:

> Their dress, summer and winter, is a rabbit skin tunic or cape, which
> comes down to just below the knee, and seldom have they leggings or
> moccasins. Children at the breast are perfectly naked, and this at a time
> when overcoats were required by Captain Simpson's party. Women frequently
> appeared naked down to the waist and seemed unconscious of any immodesty
> in thus exposing themselves.

To men experienced with the Indians of the plains or the plateau, who
were clothed in deer skin and wrapped in buffalo hides, riding horses and living
in warm tipis, the Washo must have appeared to be inferior persons indeed.
Moreover, a people so devoid of national pride as not to attack the whites,
which many of the settlers fully expected, attracted the contempt of the invaders. And, as soon as it seemed clear that the Washo were not going to make any
general resistance, their demands and welfare could be ignored. Many people
saw the suffering of the Indians in the winter, knew of deaths from starvation
and either consciously or unconsciously recognized their responsibility for having
ruined Washo hunting and gathering grounds. It was more comfortable to consider these unfortunates as inferior humans without the intelligence or ambition
to avoid their fate. The Washo were always seen as a very small tribe without
power, subservient to the more threatening Paiutes. This impression stems in
part from the fact that the Washo seldom assembled en masse. Settlers saw only
individual families or, at the most, local bunches and thus never considered the
Washo as a single people.

The Paiutes had, by the late 1850s, begun to form war bands and raid
white ranches and wagon trains as well as Washo encampments wherever they
were found. The Washo were in fact ground between the short-lived but violent
militancy of the Paiute and the relentless expansion of the whites.

THE POWERFUL BEAST   The Washo view of the white man is as much a reflection of his ignorance as is the white view of him. All things in the Washo world had a power of their own. Into this world came the white man who possessed more power than the most powerful and fearsome foreign Indian. His guns killed from great distances. He tore up the earth with plows and sent huge holes plunging into the hills. He controlled fearsome beasts, cattle, oxen, and horses, and he was quite unpredictable. As unpredictable, in fact, as a bear driven out of his cave or a man with bear power. All of these things were *mushege* or "wild." But the white man was the most fearsome *mushege* of them all. This suggestion of Washo attitudes toward the whites is found in their word for white man, *mushege*, which is the same word used for fierce animals or bad-tempered men. Today the word carries a connotation of insult and implications of madness or insanity. But then, to the Washo, much of what has happened in the past century must seem mad indeed. The Washo did not resist the white man for a number of reasons, not the least of which would seem to be the fact that he considered his own powers as insufficient to the task.

The New Alternatives

The Washo, unlike the Paiute, found himself virtually overwhelmed by the newcomers. The Paiute raider could flee into the vastness of Nevada and escape. The Washo had no place to hide. On all sides there were towns, ranches, farms, trading posts, stage stations, and railroads. The high mountains could not provide a refuge during an entire year. The Washo chose to adjust to the new world. Old resources were gone or reduced but the white man provided many opportunities for those who would take advantage. And the traditional life of the Washo had shaped a people ready to seize whatever advantage that came to hand.

The greatest new resource was the white man himself. Few in number, bent on success and fortune, there was more work than he could do. Much of it was the dirty drudgery of civilization which he did not want to do. The Washo were willing, even eager to supply his needs. In the fall, the Washo had always settled in their camps and collected great piles of firewood against the winter cold. Farmers were willing to pay to clear greasewood and sagebrush from fields. The Washo made new winter camps near a farm and, after the pine nut harvest, after the fall deer hunting, after the rabbit drives, he could work for pay. Sacks of potatoes or wheat flour, a side of beef, hams, and bacon made winter food more certain than in the past. The traditional cycle had to be altered only slightly in order to adjust to a new resource. In addition to earning food or money the Washo found the habitation of the whites a treasure trove. The whites soon accumulated refuse piles and garbage heaps. What was waste to the newcomers was a bonanza to the Indians. The slaughtering of a steer or hog left entrails, heads, hooves, and tails, all edible in Washo eyes. Although the white man might be contemptuous, the Washo was too overwhelmed by his new riches to notice. The castoff clothes of the white town, tattered and worn, mended and remended before being discarded as hopeless, were still better than nothing. Moreover, wearing clothes gave them more freedom of movement. Naked Indians were offensive to the Victorian eyes of the mid-nineteenth century. A pair of tattered trousers or a stained and much patched dress permitted a Washo to enter the town.

The willingness to beg food, clothes, or money was another mark against the Washo in the eyes of the white men. If we view it through Washo eyes, it is an understandable consequence of the situation. It was never against Washo ethics and manners to ask for food. It might not always be given, but generosity was a virtue aspired to by all Washo. It was not demeaning to ask for what one desired, particularly when the one you asked had such an immense store of riches and never seemed to suffer from hunger and cold. It was demeaning to refuse to give what one could spare easily. When the settlers were few, begging had taken the form of demands which were often met. Sometimes these gifts were conceived of as rents for Washo land, or so it was interpreted by the whites. The Washo came to feel the payments were their due, although they made no attempt to enforce payment by resort to violence. Many settlers appeared to find it was easier to make a few presents as a bribe to prevent stealing or, perhaps, to ward off violence which always seemed imminent to the whites. Begging, then, was only an extension of a relationship which began to take shape almost with the first white-Indian contacts in the area.

Stealing was also a source of income for the Washo. As early as the 1850's, a band of Washo had made off with horses tied outside a meeting house in Washo Valley. A posse formed to pursue them, routed them from around a fire only a few miles away busily eating one of the animals. Such lack of concern for pursuit suggests that the Washo did not expect it. A brief clash between whites and Washo near Millford, Caliornia, was known as the "Potato War" because a band of Washo had harvested three acres of potatoes without the permission of the owner. What set of misunderstood promises and conflicting expectations caused this "raid" will never be clearly understood.

The value of the white settlements was not limited to extensions of the old patterns of Washo gathering and gift giving. Ready to seize upon any opportunity provided, the Washo saw other possibilities in the presence of the whites. In the winter of 1857, an Indian leader called Captain Jim organized an entertainment for the whites in the Carson Valley area. The settlers were to come to a special Indian dance and bring a gift of a sack of flour. The value of a sack of flour in western Nevada was $8.00. The whites came, made their gifts, saw a number of Indian dances and games and were given a gift in return of a single deerskin apiece. The value of a deerskin at that time was $1.00. On a profit and loss basis, the Washo were singularly successful, but more important was the fact that they had obtained an important addition to their winter food supply.

In the first years, the Washo were successful in preventing the whites from fishing in Lake Tahoe. Threats of violence and occasional fist fights or clubbings discouraged white fishermen. By 1859, however, a commercial fishery had been established on the southeastern shore. There were already too many whites for the Washo to risk a battle. In 1862, white fishermen were using long seine nets, and by 1880, as many as 70,000 pounds of trout were being shipped from the settlement known as Tahoe City to be marketed in Reno, Carson City, Virginia City, and the other settlements. The Washo still made the annual migration to the lake, but some traditional fishing practices were discouraged. Fish traps were particularly distasteful to the whites. In 1868 an angry settler shot and killed a Washo he found building a trap. Oldsters still chuckle with merriment as they tell of white men who were beaten and thrown into a lake or stream when they tried to interfere with night fishing. Equipped with lake-worthy boats copied from models used by the whites, using long lines and steel hooks, the Washo themselves took to commercial fishing. Taking what they needed for food, they sold the surplus at Tallac on the shores of Lake Tahoe or hawked fish in the streets of Carson City and Genoa. A gunny sack full of average-sized fish sold for somewhere between one and two dollars. However, a large fish of four or five pounds or more was taken immediately to the hotel at Tallac and chances were sold at twenty-five cents apiece, the winner taking the fish and the Washo realizing several dollars.

Commercial fishing was practiced all during the fishing season on every stream and lake in the area. Tensions between white and Indian fishermen came to a head in 1880 when an attempt to prevent all trapping and spearing of fish in the streams leading into Lake Tahoe was made. The angry Indians banded together, prepared to resist in number, and restrictions were relaxed. Commercial fishing came to an end with the introduction of fish and game laws. These, in theory, also applied to the Washo. But a game warden was simply another white man to the Indians and an intercine war between the wardens and the Washo continued on all the fish-bearing waters of the region. Washo were arrested and jailed. Wardens were beaten or made fools of, and the Washo continued to sell fish to the white residents of the area who took none too kindly to fish and game laws themselves. This game of hide and seek over fish and game has not entirely disappeared, and it is a rare year that some Washo is not arrested for violating one or another of the game laws of two states.

The enormous amounts of fish taken from Lake Tahoe by commercial fishing greatly reduced the supply of fish in the entire area drained by the lake. Increased pressure of white sport fishing further reduced the fish supply. Fish and game laws made it increasingly difficult to fish. Land along the shore of the lake became more and more thickly settled. Clashes between whites and Indian fishing parties became more frequent. Gradually, fishing in Lake Tahoe became less and less important to the Washo. Well into the twentieth century, some bands still migrated there in the spring, but the great spawning runs were no more. When the energy expended was greater than the return, the Washo gave up. Today an occasional Washo, with fishing license or without, may spend an afternoon at the lake or in some tributary stream fishing, but fishing has not been a major source of either food or monetary income for the Washo for at least three decades.

A few Washo men in their late fifties and sixties know how to use a

pronged fish spear while standing waist deep in a mountain stream, but probably no fish have been taken by this method for twenty years. Today, the streams
and lakes are stocked artificially to supply the enormous demand of sport
fishing. White fishermen look on Indian spearing methods as an unfair advantage and are quick to complain. Some older Washo still carry a three-pronged
fish-spear head in their autos or keep one in their houses. Inasmuch as the ownership of such devices is against the law, this constitutes a final defiance of the
white man.

In summary, fishing has played an important role in the acculturation of
the Washo. The Indians were quick to learn white techniques of fishing to increase their catch and turned to commercial fishing very early, thus involving
themselves in the white economic system. In a time of reorganization of subsistence activities, fish continued to provide food but, more importantly, they provided money with which to buy food. Moreover, commercial fishing required
capital investment in boats, fishing line, and steel hooks so that some Washo
fishermen became entrepreneurs. Less certain is the role that defending their
fishing rights against the whites played in creating tribal unity.

Hunting

Firearms and the competition of cattle and horses soon killed off or
drove away the pronghorned antelope. Some of the oldest Washo remember stories told by aged relatives about hunts staged in their youth. This suggests that
the old style antelope drive disappeared among the Washo perhaps as early as
the 1860s. Men with power to dream of antelope and to charm them were, therefore, without opportunity to exercise their gifts. When they died, the entire
complex of practice and ritual of antelope hunting came to an end. Those social
bonds related to the antelope disappeared. Although the social consequences of
the communal hunt were important, the relative rarity of the antelope in the
area meant that it was not a major resource. The deer continued to be the main
quarry of Washo hunters.

A man with a rifle or even a shotgun was able to kill deer from a much
greater distance than was an archer. The old skills of disguise and imitation
were no longer necessary. Older men continued to use the bow and arrow until
the 1890s and, we can presume, continued to stalk game in the old manner. But
their sons quickly abandoned the bow in favor of firearms. An additional factor
was the presence of white hunters who might easily mistake an Indian in a deer-
head disguise for a real animal.

The knowledge and skills of bow making disappeared along with the use
of this weapon. By the turn of the century, some older men still knew how to
make bows but younger men saw no reason to learn. Firearms made hunting a
more certain occupation and may have reduced the felt need to insure success
through ritual. Women were, and to a large degree still are, forbidden to handle
rifles. Menstruating women in particular should avoid touching a gun. But on

the other hand, hunting power became much less clearly defined in the Washo mind. The bones of deer were still treated with some respect, but each generation observes these rituals less rigorously than the last.

Hunting continued to play an important role in Washo economic life. The practice of burning the forest to drive out deer was soon discontinued, in part because of white objections. Driving deer into an ambush continued to be a popular hunting method. In that way, men who did not possess guns could obtain meat by serving as beaters. Game laws began to restrict the freedom of the Washo hunters. A severe decline in deer population east of the mountains meant that nearly every hunt required a long trip to California. The long trip, problems created by white trespass laws, protests from California Indians, alternate sources of income, and the practical Washo point of view which carefully weighed effort against return, all combined to limit the role of deer hunting. For the first time, Washo men might grow to manhood without developing the skills of a hunter, preferring to work for wages, sell fish, beg or scavenge instead of undertaking arduous trips to the west. But in some families, at least, boys were required to undergo their initiation test until the late 1930s.

Conservation laws worked to restore the deer population and many Washo men hunt regularly today. One or two deer are still to be found hanging in Washo homes in the fall. Theoretically, the Washo are required to purchase a hunting license in the state in which they hunt and to observe open seasons, bag and sex limits, and other game laws. Most Washo hunters stubbornly refuse to obey these laws which they see as infringements of their right to hunt in their own territory. Arguing that inasmuch as they have no reservation and have never received compensation for their lands, they have the right to hunt on "Indian Land" as do any other Indians living on a reservation. Indian lands, in their minds, encompass all that once was Washo hunting territory. Federal and state authorities do not agree with this interpretation. Every fall, Washo men are arrested for violation of the game laws relating to deer hunting. Deer meat often is the margin between eating and starvation even today, and the Washo feel they are unfairly treated. There are no exact figures on how much deer hunting still contributes to Washo subsistence, but in many families the lack of deer meat would be a serious hardship. More importantly, surrendering to white law would be a final denial of Washo heritage and subjugation to white society which has already taken so much from them.

With the decline of deer hunting, rabbit hunting became even more important. Tales of simply stripping the skins from rabbits and leaving the carcasses recall a time before the childhood of most elder Washo. In their childhood, every rabbit was eaten or dried to be stored against the winter. The hunting net disappeared by the early 1900s. When in the 1890's a net drive was staged at the Stewart Indian School, a net had to be borrowed from Paiutes living near Walker Lake. None was available among the Washo in Eagle and Carson Valleys. Instead, an arc of men armed with shotguns would move across the drive area, flushing the rabbits before them. Unlucky hunters or poor shots usually could count on being given some of the take of their more fortunate fellows. In the 1900s, when old men who still used the bow were alive and many middle-aged men still used muzzle-loading weapons, three different drives might be staged in the same area at the same time.

Rabbit hunting is one of the few examples wherein the adoption of the horse played any significant role in Washo life. A man collecting rabbits on his belt soon found walking difficult and steadying himself for a shot almost impossible with as many as seventeen swaying rabbits hung around his waist. Seventeen is invariably given as the top limit for a day's hunt unless a man had a horse. If he did, his son, nephew, or younger brother would follow the gunner and pack the rabbits on the horse. A good hunter could kill upwards of forty or fifty jack rabbits in a morning's shooting. Rabbit hunting was encouraged by white farmers and ranchers who considered the big hares a pest. This resulted in the increased importance of the rabbit boss. Men who dreamed of rabbits and called their neighbors together for a drive became more and more like minor "chiefs."

Claims to leadership in the tribe today are occasionally made because of descent from some particularly well-known rabbit boss. Rabbits are still hunted, but the old practices have all but disappeared. As food, they are not important enough to justify leaving wage work to hunt. Almost invariably, a hunt takes place on a week-end and seems as much sport as necessity. The rabbit bosses have disappeared. Modern Washo life is such that the random inspirations of a dreamer are transcended by the demands of a white employer. There are men who always seem to attend rabbit hunts and who seem to always take charge. They may pray quietly to themselves away from the rest of the hunters before the drive starts. Today, rabbits are usually fried and eaten when they are killed. Dried rabbit is scarcely considered palatable food by any but the oldest Washo. One man keeps two dried rabbits hanging in a shed near his home. They are more desiccated symbols of his Indianness than potential meals. Some day, one of his daughters, her hair in curlers and perhaps wearing high-heeled plastic shoes, will take the rabbits down and throw them away. He will grumble a little but it is doubtful that he will ever bother to dry another rabbit.

The shotgun made it possible to kill birds, both upland game and waterfowl, much more easily than any of the older methods. The preponderance of small game in the late nineteenth and early twentieth centuries made the shotgun more prized than the rifle among the Washo. However, the great numbers of wild fowl soon disappeared under the terrible hunting pressure of market hunters and sportsmen. Today, few Washo would invest the effort in either quail hunting or waterfowling. The prairie chickens and sage hens which used "to cover them hills like snow" have long since been killed off.

The presence of the white man created new opportunities for hunters, as it had for fishermen. Venison could be sold to restaurants and hotels, as could wild fowl of all kinds. Washo hunters became professional market hunters and contributed to the decline in game. The wildcat, a relatively insignificant species in aboriginal times, became an important source of income. The Chinese formed a large minority population in most western towns. They believed that the wildcat meat was a restorative of sexual vigor. Washo hunters sold all the wildcats they caught at high prices. Some men trailed the animals during the winter in the mountains along with the aid of dogs. The use of dogs for tracking may have been aboriginal but this is not at all certain. Certainly traveling into the snowbound mountains in order to hunt wildcats was a new idea. One which once again reflected in the individual Washo's ability to seize new opportunities when they appeared.

In aboriginal times, the killing of a bear was a dangerous and relatively infrequent event. The possession of a bearskin robe was the sign of a man possessed of courage and great power. Armed with a gun, any man was able to kill a bear in relative safety. Soon the possession of a bearskin robe was common among most Washo men. One old white settler, born in the Carson River country in the 1870s, reports that almost every Indian man who died was buried in a bearskin robe. The ability to obtain the symbols of courage and power which had once been the possession of only a few respected men may have encouraged many men to claim the status which the symbol once designated.

Gathering

The appearance of the white intruders and their livestock upset but did not entirely destroy the aboriginal pattern of gathering. There is evidence of hardship in the early years, but we cannot discount the possibility that the attractions of living near white towns led many Washo to abandon their traditional gathering rounds. In this case, starvation or near starvation can be blamed not on an absolute lack of resources as much as to a change in social and economic patterns. However, as early as 1861, a United States Indian agent reported that the Washo's condition was due to the activities of the whites. Already, many of the tribe were reduced to accepting federal rations. The very willingness of the federal government to feed Indians may have contributed to the Washo failure to collect enough food in the traditional manner, preferring to take advantage of the new resource rather than search out unspoiled areas.

The pine nut was not too seriously affected save around the mining towns. In other areas, the nuts were regularly gathered and stored against winter. The groups which were left without a source of pine nuts had to move into the gathering areas of others, thus putting a greater strain on the supply. However, in aboriginal times, it seems clear that far more was gathered than could be consumed, and Washo storing methods were so primitive that as much as half the supply was allowed to rot or be eaten by small animals. If the following year was a good gathering year, the stored surplus was simply forgotten. Thus the abundance of nuts served as a resource even in the most dismal period of Washo history. In general, the new situation created few changes in pine nut gathering methods. The same knocking sticks were made and the nuts struck down in the same manner. In the fall, after a *gumsaba,* the families repaired to their gathering grounds, marked with rocks to show the boundary lines, and gathered pine nuts for from three weeks to a month. In the face of all the over-whelming technology of the newcomers, the gunny sack seems to have been seized upon earliest and with the most enthusiasm for collecting, carrying, and measuring pine nuts. Even today, the basic Washo measure of quantity is the gunny sack. Perhaps the adoption of the gunny sack for purely utilitarian pur-poses allowed the Washo basket weavers to devote their energies to the produc-tion of finer baskets for display and for sale to white people as souvenirs. In the years following the appearance of the white men, virtuosity in basket weaving increased. Some Washo women became locally famous as basket weavers. They experimented in size and design, often taking months to weave a single large and perfect basket. By the early 1900s, some Washo women had become almost full-time specialists in weaving. White collectors or traders supported these ar-tists, giving them food, clothing, and a little money against their basket produc-tion. Though any Washo woman could make baskets and of course some were better than others, aboriginal life had not permitted such a degree of specializa-tion.

Although the Washo were slow to adopt the horse and wagon, the grad-ual introduction of this means of transportation enlarged their gathering hori-zons. Trips with a wagon could be taken well into California to gather acorns and a single family could collect a wagon load rather than a few back-packs full. The old routes into California often did not provide grazing for animals. New trails and new camp grounds had to be found with an eye to the needs of the team.

The railroads also affected Washo gathering habits. The Indians were quick to learn that the land along the new rights-of-way produced exceedingly heavy crops of pig weed and soon the late summer saw many Washo families camped along the railroad tracks to take advantage of this new situation. It was also an early railroad practice to provide free transportation for groups of In-dians. This was a nineteenth century "public relations" gesture to insure coop-eration of the Indian tribes along the right-of-way who often warned friendly railroaders of washouts, fallen trees, and other dangers. During the late nine-teenth and early twentieth century, Indians camped near a railroad stop until enough were present for the agent to assign an empty railroad car to take them over the mountains to California. The Washo scattered into the hills to collect berries and then would wander the streets of Sacramento and other California towns selling the fresh fruit. When the crop was exhausted, the Indians would entrain once again for Nevada. The familiarity of the Washo with plant life and their willingness to work patiently in the collection of seeds suited them for the demands of early-day farming. Washo women were employed to pick weeds from farmer's fields. This tedious hand-work was usually payed for in food. Even today, weeding gardens in Minden and Gardnerville, Nevada, is a source of income for older Washo women. Harvesting potatoes was another task as-signed to the Indians who received their pay in kind. White men in the area de-veloped an elaborate and often curious folklore about the abilities of Indians. One such belief was that Indians, particularly the Washo, were more skillful in stacking hay than were white men. Whether there is any objective truth to this belief or not, for many decades harvest time was important to the Washo because of the wages to be earned in the hay fields.

In general, the white presence altered rather than destroyed Washo gathering resources. New plants appeared which were quickly incorporated into the Washo subsistence complex. New areas became productive and thus altered the patterns of movement. On the other hand, trespass laws and barbed wire sharply restricted the ability of the Washo to move freely. Agriculture provided many opportunities for gatherers to earn money or food. Thus, the Washo continued to gather but the pure aboriginal pattern of gathering could no longer support the entire population. Some families continued to follow the modified movement cycle, others became increasingly dependent on the new alternatives. However, as the white population in Nevada began to stabilize, the Washo either had to make over-all adjustments or disappear. The opportunistic Washo chose to make the adjustment. However, they were made in keeping with Washo tradition, piecemeal, family by family, often person by person. Some were able to maintain a modified form of the traditional life, others chose to live in houses and work in occupations provided by the new civilization.

Today, gathering is still very much a part of Washo life. Near every settlement, hidden under brush to keep it from the whites who might laugh, is a *lam,* regularly used to grind pine nuts and occasional acorns. If a wet summer produces a large crop of wild mustard or pig weed, many Washo will turn out to gather the seeds. The pine nut hills are still full of Washo in the fall. But a Washo family can no longer move through the country seizing whatever opportunity the floral life provides. Gathering today produces supplemental food or income or provides a touch of nostalgic Indian identity but it can no longer support a people. The plants have grown too few and the needs and demands of the people have changed to fit a new model of the good life.

Indian Culture and White Economics

The Washo were fortunate that the earliest permanent white residents of this country were traders. From them, the Indians quickly learned the utility of money and how money might be earned. The whites had a great many things which were desirable to the Washo. Clothing, guns, knives, hatchets, pots and pans, and gunny sacks. Many of these things retained their desirability in Washo eyes long after they had become useless to whites. Guns cost a great deal of money but money could be earned. Within a few years after the first white settlement, Washo men were making long trips on foot to Sacramento where they bought guns. The fact that the whites occupied almost all of Washo country, leaving the Indians no refuge area in which they could isolate themselves, is also important. The two cultures were almost forced to adjust and adapt to each other. This adjustment, gradual and piecemeal, not without conflict but never involving the drawing of clear-cut lines of hostility between the two peoples, was one which for many years was of benefit to both sides. The farmers of western Nevada needed the Indians to harvest the crops. Indians were also useful as general farm laborers. Moreover, Indian girls and women provided a sexual outlet for ranch hands, a distinct advantage to a rancher who otherwise might lose his crew to the carnal attractions of Virginia City. Also, the Washo soon learned that while the white community as a whole might be indifferent to the winter suffering in an Indian village a mile away from a town or hidden in some mountain cove, few white ranchers would let Indians starve if he knew them. Individual families and bunches began to develop close relationships with individual farmers. In the spring, the Indians drifted into the mountains to fish and hunt, but as the summer wore on, they came back into the valleys to gather what wild food was still available and to work in the harvests, hold a *gumsaba*, pick pine nuts, and then set up a winter camp near a ranch or farm. If their food ran short, they could depend on the farmer to contribute a few sacks of potatoes or flour or even a side of beef for their survival. During this period many Washo began to adopt the last names of their rancher benefactors. Because Indian girls often bore the children of early ranchers, the names were often deserved. These Indian-white relationships were the basis on which many Indian families recognized their kinship to a white family. The whites, more inhibited about the sexual adventures of their ancestors, are less willing to openly recognize the relationship. But nonetheless, there is a curious unspoken recognition even today between Indian and white decendants of the same pioneer forefathers.

The relationship between individual families and bunches and individual farms and ranches made a distinct change in Washo living patterns. The more remote Indian wintering places tended to be abandoned and distinct Indian communities began to form around individual ranches or on the outskirts of towns. Irrigation ditches provided a water source and the opportunity for winter hunting in the new willow groves. Each year, the same families tended to return to the vicinity of the same ranch and distinct "bunches" developed.

Particularly in the Lake Tahoe area, lumber camps sprang up. Some Washo men found employment in the woods. A few became teamsters hauling logs. Others became lumberjacks and yet others worked at odd jobs around the camps. The most important effect of lumbering, however, was that it provided a basis for Washo attempts to winter in the high mountains. The lumber companies left watchmen in the camps during the winter. These lonely men welcomed the company of any race. In the 1880s, some Washo families set up permanent camps near the lumbering operations. Old men who were boys during this period fondly recall the white watchmen cooking flapjacks in return for companionship in the snow-filled forests. As early as the 1880s, some Washo had become well enough versed in white law and customs to attempt to take advantage of the Homestead Laws and filed claims on desirable pieces of land. How many of these ambitious men ever succeeded in "proving up" and obtained full title is not known. As they were born and raised in a world with little or no concept of individal land ownership, their attempts are evidence of the Washo ability to adapt to new situations. Throughout the last quarter of the nineteenth century and until the end of World War I the Washo became increasingly involved in the economy of the white man. Several early-day newspapermen commented that the farming community of western Nevada could not operate without the assistance of the Indians. The importance of the Washo and their integration in a new social system is indicated by the fact that their activities were regularly reported by the newspapers of the day. The success of the pine nut harvest was reported as were Washo expeditions to catch wild horses in the pine nut hills. The deaths of prominent Indians were given attention. Accounts of their funerals were published in great detail. The tone of these stories was often patronizing, revealing a general attitude that the Indians were simple childlike people to be treated kindly if they behaved properly but to be punished severely if they transgressed. It was reported, for instance, how a marshal put a rope around an Indian man's neck and dragged him up and down the main street of Genoa until the Indian revealed where he had purchased a bottle of whiskey.

In the half century from 1850 until 1900, Washo life had undergone a number of gradual changes and by the latter date, a new balance had been achieved. No longer naked, the Washo had adopted clothing, and with clothing, they also became aware of shame. Nakedness was no longer acceptable even among the Indians. Washo innocence had been transformed into a prudishness equal to that of the whites from which it had been borrowed. Today, the single threat to the continuance of the girls' puberty ceremony is the modesty of the girls who object to being bathed in public even though they retain their underclothing.

The mountains still drew many Indians into the high country in the spring and gathering opportunities called them in the summer. The pine nut harvest was another occasion for moving, as was the opportunity to attend a girl's dance or some other gathering. However, the Indian towns around the white settlements became permanent. Individuals and families might leave and return but seldom were the towns abandoned.

Conflict, Cooperation, and Leadership

The change in Washo existence brought about changes in Washo social structure. The old institutions developed to exploit the aboriginal environment or to cope with foreign Indians were no longer functional. Indian wars were disruptive to white affairs and intertribal conflict was suppressed by federal troops. The Paiute Wars of the 1850s and 1860s ended in defeat for the Indians. For the Washo, this was a blessing. The new militancy of the Paiute had threatened Washo security and they were delighted to see the whites defeat and contain their old enemies. During the wars, many Washo served as guides and auxiliaries with white forces. Other bands divested themselves of their arms so they would not be confused with hostiles. The new situation made the "rough" Washo, the man who was careless of his safety and always ready to fight, a liability rather than an asset. Leaders of this type began to give way to men of a more conciliatory nature. When they had been more numerous than the whites, the Washo were willing to threaten violence to obtain concessions. As we have seen, when their vital interests were threatened, as they were at Lake Tahoe, the Washo were willing to fight or at least to bluff. But there never was a "Washo War" and conflicts which did develop were individual affairs. Hostilities of this nature were not infrequent. One band of Washo in Washo Valley north of Carson City were noted as horse theives and on several occasions a posse of angry whites was formed to punish the thieves. Other bands tended to ignore the event, certainly they felt no compunction to retaliate. Individual Washo, often drunk, attacked whites or attempted to obtain food by threats of violence. One young man in the 1880s caused a minor sensation by killing a number of dairy cattle and then fleeing into the mountains. Both the Washo and the whites with whom they fought over fishing seemed to view the hostilities as individual affairs to be settled man-to-man rather than by any collective action.

The Washo leaders during this period were for the most part peaceful men, manipulators, conciliators, very nearly confidence men, but seldom warriors.

In the early 1900s, a young man, Washo Jim, attempted a reconciliation with his wife who had left him to live with a white farmer. The young man, after first getting drunk, went to the farmer's house where he was met by his rival, beaten, and thrown off the property. The Washo all view the fact that he was beaten as inexcusable. His jealousy over the woman is not justification for a murder, or indeed even for disturbing the peace, however, they feel that a drunken man is not responsible for his actions. Washo Jim killed his wife's lover and fled into the Sierra. Posses and men of the law chased him, but he avoided capture. The local sheriff threatened to punish the entire Washo population unless the criminal was found. The surrender is illustrative of the intimate Indian-white relations of the region during this period. The murderer contacted a local white man and made arrangements to give himself up. The white man gave his personal assurance of fair treatment and trial, which he kept. The story of Washo Jim is still well known by all modern Washo, particularly in the area around Woodfords, California, and he is viewed as a kind of Indian Robin Hood.

Other Washo leaders are remembered as clever men who were useful in dealing with the whites. Unlike other tribes who often united behind a single man who acted as a link between the two peoples, the Washo developed many such leaders. In part, this was because the traditional Washo society was fragmented with many local leaders of limited influence. We cannot ignore the fact that Washo-white relations were themselves fragmented. Working on individual ranches, peddling berries, baskets, and other such activities brought the individual Washo in direct contact with the individual white. Knowledge of white ways and language was not the exclusive property of a single man who could use it to gain power among his own people. On the other hand, it was useful to the whites to deal with leaders who could, for instance, locate a law breaker. Out of these relations grew a uniquely Washo leadership type, which has come to be known as "the captain."

The Captains

It is difficult to determine the exact origin of the title captain among the Washo. Military rank was used as a form of address or title more freely in the nineteenth century than it is today. The leader of a wagon train or an Indian agent, was invariably called "major." Crew leaders on railroad and other construction projects were usually called captain, a fact testified to by the lyrics of many folk and work songs. It is probable that the Washo borrowed the term from railroad parlance. When employers needed workers, men of the law sought criminals, or if disputes sprang up, it was to the local captain that the white turned. There is little evidence that their power was any greater than that of the local leaders of earlier days. The Washo rallied around the man who could serve them the best. Some captains were felt to have supernatural power or to know prayers which were useful to the people. Others were simply wise men whose advice was frequently good. As in the past, the "jurisdiction" of the various captains appears to have overlapped and individual Washo could chose to follow a leader or not as their own interests seemed to dictate. Any working out of Washo "political history" is difficult because one of the earliest of these leaders chose the name Jim. This Captain Jim appears to have been quite successful in dealing with the white man and to have earned the respect of both peoples. His success led later ambitious men to adopt the name Jim. If such men were themselves successful leaders, their exploits were added to a growing legend of "Captain Jim." The first Captain Jim probably was already a leader at first contact. He negotiated with the whites for payment for a piece of land on which to build a stage station in Carson Valley. The Washo often speak of a "treaty" which they signed in the early days. No treaty was ever negotiated and the treaty of Washo memory may well be the agreement between Captain Jim and the stage company. Most certainly, it was this Captain Jim who traveled to Sacramento in 1851 to meet with the leaders of all the tribes of California and attempt to negotiate for payment for land seized by the whites. Such a treaty was negotiated and signed guaranteeing the Indians $1.25 an acre but it was never ratified by the Senate. The first Captain Jim's influence was confined largely to the southern portion of the Washo territory. His death in the year 1875 was reported in full by the local paper which referred to him as "King James I". A number of other captains led bunches of various size during this period and apparently contended for the role vacated by the first Captain Jim. Some of them are remembered today and their claims vigorously supported or, with equal vigor, denied by modern Washo.

By 1881, another leader named Jim had appeared, leading a band of about 375 Washo who lived in the northern part of Washo country. In the vicinity of Carson City, some 700 Washo looked to a man named Captain Joe for leadership and in the Genoa area Captain Dave was said to be the leader of nearly 2000 Washo. Two years later, a Captain Pete is reported to be the head of the Genoa Indians, suggesting how transient was power among the Indians. Typical of the confusion of names is the case of the second Captain Jim of the northern Washo. His Indian name was *Daokoye,* which means "big heels." This was mispronounced and he is sometimes referred to as Captain Hill and yet on other occasions as Washo Jim.

In the last years of the nineteenth century, another Captain Jim, whose Indian name was *Gumalanga,* appeared as leader of the Washo. Many modern Washo claim that his authority covered all of the Washo people. Others say he was only influential in the Carson Valley area. The last Jim appears to have been a man of supernatural power, a "prayer" as the modern Washo would say. He lived near Double Springs Flat south of Gardnerville, Nevada, and traveled little. He was devoted to the preservation of Washo identity and unity. He urged that the Washo give up white ways and return to the old practices. So completely had the Washo changed by the 1890s that the "old ways" were interpreted to mean wearing old cast-off white clothing rather than new clothes purchased in stores. It was he who announced the date and time of the *gumsaba* held during this period, and under his leadership these gatherings seem to have been more nearly tribal in nature than they were in the past. Many Washo claim that all the Washo gathered at Double Springs Flat, but it is doubtful that the northern Washo would travel all the way to the Carson Valley and then return to their own pine nut groves in the north. When older Washo describe the practices of the *gumsaba,* they usually refer to those held under the direction of the last Captain Jim. He is said to have been the last man to know all the prayers and songs. When he died, sometime in the early twentieth century, the annual *gumsaba* became more casual and informal. The leaders who stepped forward to replace him did not have his esoteric knowledge. An old woman who claims descent from this Captain Jim knows some of the proper songs and rituals of the *gumsaba* and has led attempts to revive the ceremony. The differences between the two Captains Jim are evidence of the changes which had taken place in the half century of white-Indian contact. The first great leader was an intermediary between Indian and white. The second man turned inward, emphasizing and attempting to preserve Washo separateness.

After the death of the last Captain Jim, no one appeared to take his place as even nominal leader of all the Washo. His daughter had married a man named Ed who assumed the title of Captain but his authority and influence were restricted to only a few families in the Carson Valley. Captain Ed's son Ed John has claimed to be chief of all the Washo since his father's death in the 1930s. His claim is ignored by all the other Washo save a few relatives and usually honored by them only when they are foced to live with him to share his old age pension checks. Ed John, now is in his eighties, volunteered to represent the Indians in a centennial celebration and was given a certificate naming him as chief of the Washo by the governor of Nevada. The certificate became the center of a three-sided comic opera episode as the Bureau of Indian Affairs and several other Washo claimants all contended with Ed John for the meaningless symbol of a nonexistent chiefdomship.

After the brief and partial unity under the last Captain Jim, Washo leadership became fragmented. Each band located near a white ranch seemed to produce its own captain and no single man was widely respected. In fact, the ancient position of rabbit boss, for a brief time, seemed to be more important than that of captain. Men who had the power to dream a rabbit hunt could, for this purpose at least, command the presence of Indians from throughout Carson Valley. Several modern Washo occasionally claim to be "chiefs" or captains because their father or grandfather was a rabbit boss. Today, a man who volunteers or is selected to carry out some group task, supervising the barbecue given by the sheriff, for instance, is called captain by those who help him.

Although from the point of view of the white man the Washo were dirty, underfed or eating refuse, dressed in rags, beset by idleness and strong drink, living in shacks or flimsy brush shelters, the Washo appear to recall the period around the turn of the century as sort of a golden age. Certainly all the ills seen by the whites existed and added to them were epidemics of smallpox, influenza, and measles. From the viewpoint of the Washo, they were in far better condition than in aboriginal times. Even ragged clothes are warm in the winter if one has ever experienced the snows with no clothes save a rabbit skin blanket. The garbage heaps of Genoa and Carson City contained many useful and palatable things. Their homes appeared flimsy, but, in fact, were probably more substantial than the *galesdangl* of aboriginal times. From the lumber mills they could obtain the slabs of bark taken from logs and of these construct a winter home far better than any they had built in the old days. A piece of discarded canvas thrown over some sagebrush was a better *gadu* than a windbreak using brush alone. As early as the 1890s, Indians around Woodfords had begun to build homes of board and bat construction. Although only a few families could support themselves entirely in the old manner, there were many new alternatives open to the Indians. It was during this period that we see an upswing of "big times," unassociated with the pine nut harvest or any other ritual occasion. As have so many other primitive people finding their way in a new world of surplus goods, the Washo devoted more time to leisure, to elaborate ceremonials or to recreational activity. In addition to the *gumsaba,* which became longer and more elaborate, local leaders began to hold gatherings called simply "big times" but carefully distinguished from the pine nut dances.

A Washo known as Doctor Bob who lived near Woodfords built a round, semisubterranean dance house after the manner of the California tribes and held dances and curing ceremonies. Gatherings devoted to gambling, dancing, and feasting were also held in the Woodfords area and are well remembered by many older Indians. A second dance house was built in the northern part of Washo territory. It is interesting that part of the change brought about by the white man was the borrowing of traits by the Washo from neighboring Indians, traits which had been known for a long time but which the Washo economy could not support in aboriginal times. Washo men, claiming to be chiefs or captains, adopted headdresses in the Great Plains style. These bonnets had been adopted by the Shoshone and Paiute during their short-lived attempt to develop a Plains style culture. The hand drum, absent in the aboriginal Washo culture, was borrowed as well as a number of gambling games and other traits. Gambling, always popular, became a major activity among the Washo. Newspapers often mention that the streets of the frontier towns were crowded with groups of Indians playing cards and Indian gambling games.

Perhaps the most significant evidence of the relative prosperity of the Washo in this period is the Washo response to the Ghost Dance and other nativistic movements among the Indians in the west.

Nativism

One of the expected responses of primitive peoples enduring the stress of rapid culture change is a turning to the supernatural world as a means of reducing the tensions which have no earthly solution. Usually such movements were initiated by a prophet, often a man who claimed to have died and returned to life or who had talked to God in a vision. The doctrine almost always included a rejection of many of the traits of white culture which had been borrowed. These nativistic movements occurred in the east among the Iroquois, sprang up in the Mississippi Valley in the early nineteenth century and reappeared in the west in the last half of the nineteenth century. Curiously enough, the two most famous movements called the Ghost Dances were initiated by men from the same family, both Paiutes from Nevada.

The first Ghost Dance was taken up by some Paiute groups but found its most eager converts among the dispossessed and dispirited tribes of California. The impact of the Gold Rush had all but destroyed the Indian cultures over much of that state. Indians were many times shot on sight. Posses, calling themselves militia, staged Indian "wars" which were simply sadistic massacres. To the embittered and bewildered Indians, the promise of the end of this terror was a last bright hope and the Ghost Dances swept throughout the state. When the promise was not fulfilled, the cult waned but some of the rituals continued to be used.

In the late 1880s, the grandson of the first Ghost Dance prophet "died" and returned to life. He told enraptured audiences of his journey to heaven and his discussion of Indian problems with God. His sacred instructions included a dance and some songs. If these were faithfully performed, promised the prophet Jack Wilson, the white man would go away, the game would return, and the Indians would once again reign over their own land. This time the response came from the east. The tribes of the Great Plains, defeated in the Indian Wars of the seventies and incarcerated on the reservations, heard of Jack Wilson's wonderful promise. Delegations went to Nevada to learn of his experience. The Ghost Shirt Dance, so called because Wilson promised the followers immunity from bullets if they wore a special sacred garment, reached a peak among the

Sioux in the Dakotas. A few Washo are reported to have joined the Paiute in the dances of 1890 but the earlier movement appears to have had no effect on the Washo. While the religious mania swept through the Basin and Plateau, over the Rockies and across the Great Plains, the Washo continued to work out their own destiny. There is a strong argument in this that the Washo did not view their situation as desperate or indeed, even uncomfortable. There are elements of nativism perhaps in the doctrine of Captain Jim but they appear to be more the advice of a wise old man to avoid excesses than the promise of an inspired prophet.

The Washo had experienced great changes in their lives since the white man first appeared. But the nature of these changes did not create the dislocations and disorganization so common in other tribes.

Tribe and Government

It is impossible to speak of the changes in Indian culture without discussing, however briefly, the role of the federal government and its policy toward Indians. In the earliest phases of white-Indian contact, the Washo country was so remote that there was some doubt as to jurisdiction. The political ambitions of the Mormon leader Brigham Young were to establish a theocratic hegemony over much of the intermontane and Great Basin region, independent of the United States or any other power. The first Mormon settlers in the Genoa area probably intended to expand the state of Deseret, as the Mormons called their territory. These ambitions were soon abandoned in the face of the power of the United States, and Utah became a territory which included the entire area of Nevada. Because of the importance of Nevada silver and the area's increasing population, a separate territory was established in 1861 and the state admitted to the Union in 1864. The boundary between California and Nevada bisected Washo territory, a fact which complicates Washo-federal relations even today.

The federal government has always assumed responsibility for dealing with Indian tribes. Until the 1870s, Indian tribes were considered to be separate and sovereign nations. In the east where the tribes were more sophisticated, this argument had some validity, but even there the treaties and agreements were more frequently broken than observed. In the west, where political structure was weak and often entirely lacking, the idea of Indian sovereignty led only to confusion, misunderstandings, half-understood promises being given and broken and treaties ignored until the legal fiction could no longer be maintained. During the administration of President Grant, the policy of treating Indian tribes as separate nations was abandoned and the Indians were ruled to be wards of the federal government. In 1859, Major James Dodge was appointed Indian agent for Nevada. He was responsible for dealing with all the Indians in the area, both Paiute and Washo. Dodge appears to have dealt principally with the first Captain Jim and the Washo in the Carson, Washo, and Eagle valleys and around Lake Tahoe. He did report two other bands, one under a man named

"Pos-Larke" and the other led by a Washo named Deer-Dick. Dodge recommended that a reservation be set aside for both the Washo and the Paiute but no action was taken on this suggestion. Dodge was struck by the suffering of the displaced Washo and wrote a poem inspired by the finding of two Washo who had died from starvation. (Price 1962)

> Many a weary day went by
> While, wretched and worn he begged for bread
> Tired of life, and lowing to lie
> Peacefully down with the silent dead,
> Hunger and cold, and scorn and pain
> Had wasted his form and seared his brain;
>
> At last on a bed of frozen ground,
> In the Sierra Nevada was the outcast found.
> No mourner lingered with tear or sighs,
> But the stars looked down with pitying eyes,
> And the chill winds passed with a wailing sound,
> O'er the foot of the mountain where the form was found,
> But where every human door
> Is closed to children accursed and poor
> Who opened the heavenly portals and wide
> Ah! God was near when the outcast died.

Neither official reports or flights of poetic inspiration moved the government and three years later Warren Wasson, a new Indian agent, made a report to the governor of the Nevada Territory, that some 500 Washo in his jurisdiction had requested assistance because much of their hunting, gathering, and fishing territory had been despoiled by mining and ranching. In 1887 the Daws Act authorized the government to make individual allotments of land set aside for Indians. The pine nut hills were set aside as tribal land and allotments made. The purpose of this division of allotments was to provide the Washo with land on which to live. However, there are few water sources in the pine nut hills and game was scarce. Moreover, the winters are severe and the Washo never wintered there. Unlike many other tribes, the Washo could not be induced to sell their allotments. The pine nut continued to be too important to Washo existence and the groves became more and more important as symbols of Washo identity as the ancient culture gave way under the pressure of the white presence.

In the 1890s, Captain Jim and another Washo leader, Dick Bender, were called to Washington to testify on the condition of the tribe. There is no exact record of what they said, but Washo imagination has it that the respected leader was given the privilege of the floor of the House. Accounts of his speech to Congress are examples of the oratorical imagination of the American Indian. Whatever really happened, little came of the trip. In 1917, a pioneer rancher donated forty acres to the Washo tribe. This land was held in trust for the

Washo and until the late 1930s constituted the only land actually owned by the Washo people as a whole. It is the site of the present "Sagetown" Washo community.

In the late nineteenth century, the government established an Indian School, operated by the Bureau of Indian Affairs at Stewart, Nevada. For years this school served the Washo and Paiute and played an important role in the adjustment of the Indians to white culture. Indians were taught trades and agricultural skills. The school was also headquarters for the Indian agent, responsible for the area. But even today, the scattered and mobile Washo continue to be an administrative problem. Exact numbers are lacking, many Washo have no contact with the agent: for the rest contact is infrequent. The situation is further complicated because of the Termination Act of 1953 which ended federal responsibility for all the tribes of California. Because these California Indians frequently live in Nevada for long periods, they move in and out of federal jurisdiction.

The Washo Tribe came into existence in 1937 after the passage of the Indian Reorganization Act of 1934 which authorized Indian tribes to elect their own governments and manage tribal affairs under the supervision of the Bureau of Indian Affairs. The Washo have not been very successful in the conduct of tribal government. In addition to the Sagetown plot, the tribe now owns 795 acres purchased by the government in 1938. After a few unsuccessful years of attempting tribal management, the lands were leased to white ranchers, the lease being supervised by the Indian agent at Stewart. Most of the pine nut area has also been leased to sheep grazers with the Bureau of Indian Affairs acting as agent in the arrangement. During the same period the government responded to the needs of the Indians in Nevada (and the demands of the whites who objected to the conditions of "Indian Towns" in the vicinity of white communities) and established a number of small communities or "colonies." As early as 1872 a reservation had been set aside to contain the warlike Paiute. Since that time no land had been set aside for the Nevada Indians. By the time redress was made there was no suitable large area available, so the colony system was begun as a compromise.

A detailed discussion of Washo-government relations would be out of place in this context. We can, however, see that the relation has always been tenuous and seldom has the government impinged on the individual Washo life. As compared with other tribes, many of whom experienced two generations of total control of every phase of life, the Washo were singularly free to work out their own destiny. This freedom has had both positive and negative consequences. Certainly the Washo are poorer for not having assigned to them a large tract of reservation land. Tribal unity certainly has suffered from having no common ground for all the Washo. On the other hand, the Washo have been free to make their own mistakes and to learn how to live in the modern world. Many individual Washo have been relatively successful in finding a place in American society. The condition of many Washo today is exceedingly poor, but it would be difficult to prove that this is due to the lack of government control and supervision. Nor can one argue that the successes of the Washo are due to government programs.

The End of the "Good Times"

Before World War I, the Washo had managed to make an adjustment to the changed situation brought about by the intrusion of the white man. Although their position was far from ideal, the Indians had become a part of the society of western Nevada and eastern California. Farms and many businesses owned by the whites depended on the Washo population in order to operate successfully. The general attitude, as reflected in newspaper and other accounts, was one of paternalism. Indian families and bands had developed dependence relationships with ranches. Indian towns were a source of casual labor and domestic help for white communities. Moreover, Indians were customers of the white storekeepers. Their needs and desires had forced the Indians to depend on manufactured goods which cost money. This is not to say that the Washo had completely integrated with white society. For the most part, they went to separate schools, if they went to school at all. The Washo still made regular trips to the pine nut hills for the fall gathering. Some families continued to make hunting and fishing trips into the mountains. In the winter most Washo lived in a *galesdangl* made of boards, canvas, and brush. When families went on gathering trips or traveled to work on farms, they lived in the crude *gadu*. The Washo did not vote, they could not openly buy liquor. Law enforcement was often informal and frequently brutal. Nonetheless, the two parts of Nevada society, white and Indian were dependent on each other. Were either to disappear, the life of the other would change drastically. Despite the hardships and the handicaps of the situation, the Washo remember this time with nostalgia. Under Captain Jim there was a degree of unity and independence as a people. Food shortages and starvation might occur but they were much less frequent. There was work available for those who wanted to work. The demands of agricultural work fitted neatly into the traditional cycle of Washo life, that is, it was short term and intense, permitting the mobility which was important to the Washo. However, the Washo had reached an adjustment with a style of life which itself was already passing from the scene. The style of agriculture began to change. The fields of wheat, potatoes, and truck crops grown on family farms began to disappear. In their places appeared herds of white-faced cattle. The sheep grazing industry, which had begun in the 1890s, became more and more important. The need for men to plough and harrow, to harvest field crops and stack hay and feed chickens began to decrease. The cattle and sheep industries required fewer workers and those with skills the Washo had not developed. The Washo had never completely adopted the horse. Although many families owned a wagon and team and riding horses were common, the Washo were notoriously unskilled horsemen. The job of cowboy which attracted so many western Indians was one which did not appeal to the Washo. A few Washo boys were given temporary riding jobs but none became full-time cowboys. The lonely job of sheep herding was never interesting to the Washo. Sheep ranchers preferred to import Basques from Spain. These men, used to the long periods of loneliness and familiar with sheep, formed a nucleus of a new ethnic group in the area.

As roads were improved, the string of little towns along the eastern slope of the Sierra began to lose population. Originally these settlements had been formed along the route of the stage lines, each one forming the center of a local area of farms and ranches. With the end of the stages and the improvement of roads, such local centers lost their function. The Indian towns associated with each town also disappeared and the population of the Indian settlements near the larger cities swelled. As the need for labor in agriculture decreased the local bands also moved into the cities. A few families attempted to establish homesteads in California. As the Indian became less important to the functioning of white society, the white became increasingly hostile to the Indian way of life. The Indian towns were an increasing source of friction as white complained of immorality, drunkenness, and threats to health. The decade of the 1920s was a dismal period in Washo history. Gradually the bands dispersed. The last mobile identifiable band dispersed and settled down in the late 1920s. Without opportunity to work, the Indians became increasingly poverty stricken and desperate, unable to support themselves in the way they had learned in the past three generations, and equally unable to return to the traditional practices.

9

The Sad New World

NEARLY NINETY YEARS had elapsed from the time of the first appearance of white trappers and explorers to the late 1920s. It had taken all this time for the Washo finally to abandon the last vestige of aboriginal life. As early as the 1850s some Washo were taking advantage of new alternatives presented by white culture. The old patterns of social organization had changed to fit new situations. The role of the antelope shaman disappeared, but the idea of a man with a special power involving communal hunting continued to be expressed in the person of the rabbit boss. Gradually, a more inclusive leadership developed under Captain Jim. Despite the fact that a few people were still attempting to survive in a more or less aboriginal manner, the first two decades of the twentieth century had seen the new balance achieved as the Washo became more and more a part of the economy of the region. This is a period of many "captains" and "chiefs." Each claimed recognition as the leader of all the Washo, although in fact their authority was local and sometimes limited to a few relatives. The old skills of the hunter and gatherer were replaced or supplemented by those of a suppressed caste engaged in the hard manual labor and low paying activities of an agricultural community. White law enforcement officers and officials were increasingly important to the Washo while native leaders lost their importance. Only one traditional role remained essentially unchanged, that of the shaman. These men still carried out curing rites among their fellows and were respected and feared because of the power they controlled. In the absence of secular leaders, the shaman became increasingly influential. Seldom did they exercise direct power over a particular bunch or band. Instead, they formed a distinct social type possessed of a kind of free-floating political power, undirected because there appeared to be no place for it to be applied. The Washo met the decade of the 1930s without formal leadership, without a distinct tribal structure, and with their place in Nevada society rapidly disappearing. The unsightly Indian towns on the outskirts of Reno, Carson City, Gardnerville, Minden, and other Nevada towns became increasingly irritating to the residents of these cities. In response to the demands to eliminate these communities the colony system was developed. Others moved into colonies near to (but not too near) Carson City and Reno. Permanent clusters of houses sprang up in the country near Woodfords and Markleville, California. Other families drifted west into California to live in isolation or join communities of other Indian tribes. The Washo genius for adapting and adjusting, for seizing new opportunities seemed exhausted. To add to the problem, the need for leaders was perhaps more acute than it had been since the beginning of the century. The isolation of the Indian population in colonies away from white communities created a more centralized Washo population. No longer could each Washo family go its own way, working out its own relationships with individual white men. The Washo had in some ways, become a "people." Because of their personal isolation, the Indians had become stereotyped. The conditions of the Washo communities were well known but the individual suffering which went with these conditions went unnoticed. Once again at least some Washo began to live in an almost entirely Washo world. The white world in which he had formerly moved, segregated and discriminated against, to be sure, but nonetheless a part of what went on around him, was now remote. The Indian town and the white town or city were now distinct places, one governed by city councilmen and protected by municipal or county law enforcement officers, the other vaguely controlled by the federal government. Socially, there was once again a field in which leaders might develop. Ideologically, there seemed no general agreement on what constituted a leader. The old patterns and beliefs which had joined the fragmented mobile groups of Washo speakers into a single people were no longer shared by all the people.

Some Washo had managed to avoid the economic deprivation experienced by most of the tribe. One of these was Tom George, one of three brothers who lived in the Woodfords area of California. Tom's father had been sometimes called the leader of the Washo after the death of Captain Jim, but this was disputed by most of the Washo. Chief or not, the elder George had been an ambitious and imaginative man who had begun to work as a guide for hunting parties and managed a mule pack train in the Lake Tahoe country as early as 1910. His eldest son Tom had taken over his father's business and continued to maintain the family fortunes as well as the respect of the white community earned by his father. Throughout the Washo country there were others like Tom George, men who had learned a trade or who had gone into business, one of them eventually becoming the owner of a saw mill and lumber business. Not a few of these men drifted away from their people, finding a place for themselves in the larger world. Some continued to think of themselves as Washo, although they publicly rejected many of the old practices of Washo culture which were so restrictive in the white world. Other families were able to maintain jobs working for white men and still live in Indian communities. The majority of Washo however, lacking education, their laboring skills less and less in demand, their English inadequate to life outside western Nevada, maintained a precarious existence in their colonies. The various claimants to captaincies or chiefdomships contended with each other, each with his own small group of supporters. The well-off frequently had no traditional basis for claiming leadership and the descendants of old-time leaders had no economic power. Nor was there agreement as to what aspect of power in the past constituted a valid claim to leadership in the present. Even those who did not claim to be leaders used their relationship to past leaders as a reason for not accepting the authority of some other person. Without reason for accepting the authority of one man whose advice was useful in meeting a specific situation, kinship and descent served only as a rationalization for claims to power. The only people who had real power were those who it was believed could cure illness or do harm to others. The shaman continued to perform curing rights, often for fees ranging from $20 to $60. But Washo life appears to have changed so dramatically that shamanism did not seem to be a means of finding security for the young men. The long period of training, the dangerous association with spirits, and the demands of one's power were restrictions that outweighed any benefits one might gain from becoming a shaman. Only a few young men attempted to learn the trade. At the same time, the fear of sorcery and witchcraft increased. With the old lines of society blurred and confused, everyone's hand seemed turned against everyone else. Accusations of witchcraft and campaigns of innuendo concerning certain people considered to be witches were common in every Washo community. The same beliefs in spiritual power which had shaped Washo aboriginal life now tended to disrupt it and create internal dissension. One reason for this may be the ending of the wandering way of life. The creation of increasing permanent settlements forced the Washo to live together in a way they had never experienced before. In the past, the hunting and gathering round and the cycle of agricultural work forced the Washo to move from time to time, meeting with other Washo, living with them for a time and then separating to move to some other area. In settlements like Sagetown, the tensions of communal living continued to build up, unbroken by the life of continual movement. It is probable that these tensions created the fears, anxieties, and hostilities which were expressed in terms of witchcraft accusations. Into this dismal situation two new factors intruded, a white man's law and an Indian religion.

The Legal Tribe

When Franklin D. Roosevelt was elected president in 1932, he appointed John Collier as Commissioner of Indian Affairs. Collier developed and saw the Indian Reorganization Act of 1934 passed into law. Indian tribes were authorized to elect councils, write constitutions, and begin to take over the business of governing themselves. The Washo took advantage of the law and set up a legal tribal government. This was the first time that anyone could speak of a political institution in which all the Washo, in theory at least, could participate and which could speak for all the Washo. Unfortunately, the Washo were unprepared for self-government as a separate people. A tribal council was elected and the form of self-government introduced. But the substance of self-government eluded the Washo people. Men who claimed to be chiefs continued to maintain their claims. The refused to accept the authority of the tribal council. Accusations of illegal acts and oblique accusations of witchcraft were made against council members and hurled back and forth between councilmen. Situations like this were common on many Indian reservations during the 1930s. Traditionally, Indian political ideology had not included the idea of majority rule. Indian groups preferred to delay decisions until persuasion, social pressure or exhaustion wore down the dissenter and resulted in unanimous decisions. American law, of course, has no real place for this kind of resolution. Therefore, Indian groups were forced to continue to operate within the new framework until they learned the methods of this new way of government. After nearly three decades of experience and education, many of them are becoming remarkably successful. For the Washo, the experience has not been sufficient. Without a reservation which would draw all the people together, forcing them, as it were, to learn a new way, the tribal form of government has had no real base from which it could operate.

Peyote, the New Way

As we have seen, Washo religion was centered around the concept of a personal experience with the supernatural, often in the form of a vision. This the Washo had in common with many other native religions in America. For the Washo the vision came unsought and unaided but among many other peoples the vision was actively pursued through fasting, self-torture, or the ingestion of hallucegenic substances; jimson weed, mushrooms, "red-bean," and the button of a small low-growing cactus known as peyote. Peyote was used in Mexico before the arrival of the Spanish. It appears to have been used aboriginally by some of the tribes in the southwestern part of the United States as well. In the 1880s a new cult based on the ritual ingestion of peyote developed in the Great Plains country and Oklahoma and began to spread in all directions among the reservation-bound Indians of the United States.

Some Washo may have known of the cult in the 1920s, but it was not until 1932 that peyotism found its way into the Washo country by a Ute shaman named Lone Bear. Lone Bear made a few Washo converts and held some curing meetings, but he was a notorious drunkard, often in trouble with the law, and the Washo avoided his peyote meetings.

Six years later, Franklin York, a half-breed Washo and a sometime bootlegger who had traveled widely over the United States in medicine shows returned to his home country to preach the peyote doctrine.

York was successful in spreading the peyote cult among the Washo and the neighboring Paiute. Soon his meetings were well attended and collections were often as high as $50. His first convert was a Washo shaman who combined traditional beliefs with peyote ceremonialism. Many of his other followers were the more acculturated and successful, people with steady jobs or even with businesses and bank accounts who had in large part abandoned their traditional past and, as the Washo put it, "gone the white man's way."

Very soon a schism developed between the more traditional peyotists and the more acculturated, some of whom were members of the tribal council. Before the dispute was over the matter had to be settled in a special hearing at the Stewart Indian reservation where accusations of marijuana use, witchcraft, and sexual orgies were made by the contending groups. Many of the Washo, in and out of the peyote movement, resented the fact that an Indian dispute had been taken to white authorities. Others feared the power of peyote as they had always feared supernatural power, pointing out that death, incest, and insanity were the consequences of partaking of the cactus. On the other hand, many others became devoted converts of the cult, traveling great distances to attend meetings and spending large sums to make the colorful feathered fans and beaded rattles which were part of peyote paraphanalia. Both traditional shamans and acculturated Washo, seeking a new basis for their claims to leadership of the tribe, experimented with the cult. Gradually, the old shamans died and none replaced them. Men who in the past would have become shamans became involved in the peyote cult seeking to become "chiefs," that is, people powerful enough to conduct meetings.

The peyote cult is a synthesis of native Indian beliefs and practices, incorporating the vision, drumming, singing, smoking, using the rattle, and Christianity. As such, it has a great appeal to Indians of all degrees of acculturation. Moreover, the benefits of peyote are open to all. Anyone may attend a meeting and eat the cactus and receive a vision. The dangers of power are not conceived of as being so great as were the dangers of power under the aboriginal system. They peyote cult takes many forms in various tribes, but the main outlines are the same wherever it is encountered. One of its primary commandments is a rejection of alcohol. Although there are many backsliders among the peyotists, the cult does give support to moderation in a facet of Indian life which was not present in aboriginal times when alcohol was unknown.

Peyote came into Washo life against the opposition of many whites. Although the cactus is not classed as a narcotic by the federal government, the Bureau of Indian Affairs was very much opposed to the cult. Perhaps because the cult gave Indians some organizational focus for their lives and made them more difficult to manage, perhaps because there was still a strong carryover in the Bureau from the days when Indians affairs were managed almost entirely by men appointed by the churches.

In the state of California the cactus was declared to be illegal, a law which is presently being challenged in the courts, and frequently county welfare agencies in Nevada refused to assist members of the cult. Some older Washo, grown used to the dependent relationship between Indian and white society, opposed the cult because it offended the missionaries who would then refuse to give Christmas presents and the like to the Indians.

In a sense peyote gave the Washo a sense of identity. In defying the white law and white disapproval and conducting peyote services, they were asserting themselves as Indians. Because peyote meetings were intertribal they were conducted in English and gave the Washo a sense of identity with other Indians. Most important was the fact that aboriginal religious practices, as meager and informal as they were, tended to disappear almost completely. The shaman no longer held sway in Washo life. The family rituals and ceremonials continued in many cases but almost as social conventions. Washo religious energy was devoted to the peyote cult. Even people who did not attend meetings became believers and peyote became the most powerful figure in Washo supernatural world.

The progress of the cult was not smooth. From time to time meetings would almost cease and only a few devoted adherents would remain. Then, inexplicably a new burst of enthusiasm would swell the meetings.

Today, because the Washo peyote meetings are the nearest ones to the urban centers of the San Francisco Bay area, the Washo country has become a center of peyote activity for Indians of many tribes. Indians living in the cities regularly make week-end trips to the Washo country to attend meetings. There they appear to renew their Indian self-image which enables them to return to the city and adjust to urban life for a time before they once again seek renewal.

To the Washo the changeover from the aboriginal religion to peyote is viewed as simply the addition of a new element of supernatural power provided to assist the Indian. The old patterns were not effective or needed in the new world. As one informant put it; "Them old doctors had to have a lot of power because the Indians didn't have (know) too much. But nowadays the white doctors have a lot of power and the Indian doesn't need his power anymore. But the peyote helps the white doctor take care of the Indians." It must be disheartening for the doctor in a modern hospital to realize that in the eyes of his Washo patients he is nothing more than a new and more powerful shaman assisted by peyote.

Sagetown

South of Gardnerville, off the highway and quite hidden from the traveler, is Sagetown. The forty acres of Sagetown sit dry and inhospitably on a bluff overlooking the Carson River. The road is paved part of the way to Sagetown, but until 1960 the road was unpaved and dusty and until 1941 there was no electricity. Even today, there is no sewage system and a single pump serves the entire population with water. The approach to the settlement is strewn with empty cans and wine bottles twinkling in the sun. Then a tangle of ruined automobiles purchased cheaply and abandoned when they quit running, stripped of spare parts to keep other cars running, appears. The houses are aged, unpainted board and batten structures. Between them is the litter of living: cans, bottles, old auto seats, and worn-out tires. And there are people. A young woman insensibly drunk; her child beside her on a cradleboard. An old man sleeping in the shade of a wrecked car, having abandoned his drunken trek home in favor of sleep. They both will wake sick on the cheap liquor and probably ashamed for having behaved like a "drunken Indian." They might even think about joining the peyotists in order to fight the temptation of the cheap barrooms of Gardnerville. From a ruin of a house a girl in her twenties emerges. "Hey white man," she shouts, "get this God damn white man outta my house." She is drunk and stumbles. From the house a white man, bleary eyed and unshaven, wearing dirty trousers and an undershirt, emerges. He curses the woman and she returns his obscenities with her own. They exchange ineffective blows and stagger together into the house shrieking with laughter. When she bears a child of this union she will probably not remember the man. The infant will be cared for by her mother and perhaps receive county welfare payments. Sagetown is sordid and if one sees no more than the surface of the community, fills the observer with hopelessness. Yet in the midst of Sagetown there are houses that are kept neat by Washo standards. Scrubbed children go off to the integrated schools of the white community. Young husbands and fathers go to work regularly, and their wives hang out wash and fight the relentless dust which sifts into the unsound houses. An old man spends his days painstakingly sewing beads onto baskets made by his wife in order to sell them to a tourist trading post. A middle-aged man and his wife walk along a nearby irrigation ditch selecting the best willow for basket weaving. She is an expert and her baskets sell to tourists in the California lake country. Sagetown is situated on the only ground actually owned and controlled by the Washo tribe. Its existence is an echo of a time long gone when the Washo were part of a social system including both whites and Indians. Although the Indians were viewed as inferior beings and certainly did not participate fully in white life, they were important to the economy of the area and the farmers and ranchers for whom they worked assumed some responsibility for the welfare of the Indians. Sagetown was given to the tribe by one such rancher for as long as the Washo continued to use it. Farm technology no longer needs a large local labor force to plant and weed and harvest. The Washo way of life, like that of many other minority peoples in the United States, is afflicted by marginality, a symptom of social and economic dislocation.

Economics

It is no longer possible to speak of a separate system of subsistence activities among the Washo. With very few exceptions, the economic alternatives open to the Washo are those open to any American. Wage labor is the only certain source of economic security. For most Washo this means work in the lowest levels of American economy. A few manage their own businesses. One operated a lumber company for many years and another continues to rent horses and operate a pack train for tourists. We have seen how changing agriculture virtually erased the special place the Washo held in the economy of the area. Today, Washo men compete with transient workers of all races for the agricultural work available. Some Washo are fortunate to have relatively regular but low paying jobs as gardeners in nearby white towns. Except for the few who have regular employment, wages usually are earned in seasonal activities. Construction work reaches a peak in the summer and Washo men, sometimes with their families, often without, scatter throughout the west to work where they can. Some few Washo, particularly the older people, manage to earn at least a few dollars by weaving and selling baskets to tourists.

A very few Washo have experimented with agriculture even as a subsistence activity. A very few today raise corn and a few vegetables for the table. The only attempt to farm commercially is being made by a young man near Woodfords, California. He grazes a few head of cattle on his allotment near the Carson River. In the fall, he helps his neighbors gather a winter wood supply and in exchange is permitted to cut the native grasses on their allotments and make a small hay crop. The only "native" activity which produces regular and important income for the Washo is gathering pine nuts. Many families go into pine nut groves and collect nuts, using very much the same methods as their ancestors used. Some of these nuts are kept as a part of the winter food supply. Some families sell the nuts locally, receiving from fifty to seventy-five cents a pound. However, nut gathering is hard work and the harvests are often uncertain. Measured in hourly earnings, the income is not great.

For many of the Washo, various types of pension and welfare payments constitute the only income. At times during the year, the only income in Sagetown consists of old age pensions, state and county welfare payments, and so on. In many cases, the only financial security afforded a Washo family is an elderly grandmother or grandfather who receives old age benefits. Many Washo have moved into California to live on family allotments in that state because the old age pensions are more liberal. Unlike many other Indian tribes, the Washo have no reservation which could provide a basis for economic development. In many cases, other tribes are involved in industrial activities, developing tourism, or exploiting the mineral, gas, oil, or timber resources. The Washo did not have these opportunities to develop their economic future on their own lands. Their future is linked inextricably with the society in which they live. For better or worse, the Washo are assimilated to American society albeit, for most of them, on the lowest and least profitable level.

Individuals have escaped the cycle of poverty completely. One such is a colonel in the United States Air Force, another holds an important and responsible position in the Bureau of Indian Affairs.

Residence

In the past, the cycle of subsistence determined the pattern of residence of the Washo. Gradually, residence patterns altered in order to take advantage of the new resources provided by white farms, ranches, and towns. Today, the Washo tend to cluster in settlements such as Sagetown or the various colonies in Nevada. Throughout the mountains on the eastern slope of the Sierra Nevada, individual families or small groups live on allotment properties in small communities. During the summer, many of the cabins and houses are abandoned as the family travels in search of work. The Washo are still extremely mobile and often travel to other Indian communities to visit relatives or attend ceremonies. Frequently, a family without income will spend weeks or even months sharing a cabin with some more fortunate relatives. Although the resources may be strained, this hospitality is seldom refused. When traveling, the Washo often camp, sometimes for weeks, wherever they find unoccupied lands. In the past few years, a few families have moved into permanent homes in the pine nut hills. The automobile, paved roads, and electric power lines into the area have made the region more habitable than in the past.

Society

The Washo are a society in the sense that they do constitute a distinct group of people with common heritage who interact with each other more than with any other group. However, there is little structure to Washo society. The old subsistence pattern has disappeared and with it the basis for the large units of Washo society. The old sectional "moieties" are vaguely remembered and some people still remember what group they were born into but the sections have little meaning. The bands based on antelope or rabbit hunting have all disappeared as have those which developed in relation to white farms or towns. Each Washo is in one sense at sea and on his own in a welter of individual social relationships which are without regular structure. The peyote cult may in the future provide a basis for new leadership and new social units. As yet, this has not completely developed. The legal basis of the tribe with the tribal council has not served to stabilize or reorganize Washo tribal structure. It seems unlikely that any future developments will lead to a self-contained tribal society for the Washo. Without a land base, there is little foundation for a tribal political system. Moreover, many of the functions of a tribal society have long since been taken over by white society, forcing the assimilation which exists today. White law enforcement and white laws govern Washo behavior. White government supervises the economic responsibilities carried out by the tribe in other situations. Welfare, charity, and old age security are functions of white government and it is doubtful that any Washo political body will ever have the vitality to take over these activities. In fact, the Washo are gradually becoming aware of their role in relationship to white society and government. In some areas, they constitute an important voting bloc and their favor is courted by local candidates.

The family still remains an essential and distinctly Washo social entity. The patterns of income have tended to develop a special family type based on the mother. The frequent absences of men working or looking for work and the fragile marriages which appear to be a result of the precarious economic situation tend to place the responsibility for raising children on the women of the family. Despite the pressures created by poverty, the Washo family today often follows a pattern not unlike the aboriginal family, that is, a married couple forming a core around which a number of lateral relatives and their children collect to live cooperatively. No longer is food gathered and shared but money is shared. Whichever member of the group works or receives a pension serves as the economic mainstay of the group.

Ceremonies and Recreation

The changes in economics and social structure have operated to erase from Washo life the ceremonial and recreational life which once set them apart. The *gumsaba* gradually disappeared in the 1920s and 1930s. An attempt to revive the gathering in 1953 was a failure. Only one person remembered the prayers and ritual, and she imperfectly. Moreover, she was feared as a witch. Only the older people attempted to recapitulate the traditional activities. The younger generations set up a phonograph in an empty house and held a white style dance. Neither group was happy. Oldsters say that in the event of poor pine nut harvests, the ceremony might be reinstated, but when the last people who know the ritual die there is little hope for the ceremony.

Shamanistic ceremonies have all but disappeared. One shaman is still alive but he has altered his ceremonies to conform to modern conditions. His curing sessions take only an hour or two. When he dies, another specialist in ceremony will disappear and the continuity of these skills will be impossible. Within the family the ceremonies, particularly those which did not require a specialist, persist in attenuated form. Women usually avoid eating meat for a time after they bear a child and sometimes observe the rituals related to bathing, hair cutting and the distribution of presents. As late as the 1930s, some young men went through the ritual of crawling through the antlers of a deer when they made their first kill. Some women avoid eating meat when they are menstruating if it was killed by someone they know. If the meat was purchased in a store, they do not observe the taboo.

The girl's dance is still held for every Washo girl when she first menstruates. Young girls today suffer some embarrassment in white schools, because the preparations and some of the taboos she must observe reveal her condition to her schoolmates, and insist on being bathed wearing a slip or brassier and panties. Perhaps the girls now in white schools will prefer their daughters to have puberty observances more in keeping with white style, but the ceremony seems still to have a great deal of vitality.

The games of field hockey, long distances races, archery contests, and the like which were important parts of any Washo gathering are no longer played. School-age children prefer basketball and baseball and dancing. Gambling in the Indian manner, which was part of every gathering, has also disappeared. People still play cards, but the motion pictures and gambling in the legal casinos serve as primary sources of recreation today.

The aboriginal ceremony related to death and burial was never complex. The casual and perhaps not universal annual mourning ceremonies have not been held for many years. White laws have forced the Washo to bury their dead in regular cemeteries. One such is a desolate and isolated patch of desert hillside known as the "Indian" cemetery. Another is a relatively well-tended plot near the Indian Agency headquarters at Stewart. Funerals are usually conducted by a white missionary. After the ceremony, however, an older Washo usually makes a short speech directed to the deceased asking him to leave the world and not bother the living. Frequently, the coffin is packed with the personal belongings of the dead. Larger belongings are taken into the mountains and thrown away or burned. Not infrequently a sick person is placed in a smaller shack, sometimes even a native style brush house outside the permanent home. This allows the deceased's family to burn down the secondary house without leaving the family without a home.

Food and Material Culture

A distinct Washo material culture no longer exists. A few people make rabbit skin blankets and nearly every family in the Carson Valley, at least, possesses one. Even these show the effects of change, with the strands being tied with cloth or string instead of sinew.

Basketry, the truly Washo art, is declining. Some few are made for gathering pine nuts and other baskets are woven for sale to tourists. Baskets are kept as nostalgic souvenirs of the past and one at least is found in every home. Near every Washo community a bedrock mortar or *lam* can be found. In many homes a *demge* is still kept. In the pine nut camps one can still see knocking poles, albeit bound with bailing wire, but still in the old tradition.

The Two Worlds

While the outward signs of Washo culture have disappeared and the Washo live in the world as it is, they have not abandoned their identity. The other world of the Washo is a world of the mind. The old tales are not forgotten, although they may be somewhat garbled and only half understood. The belief in the nature of power in the universe is still very real although its expression is most frequently found today in the peyote cult. Fear of the dead and concern about witches still sets the Washo apart from their neighbors. The patterns of leadership still rest on traditional attitudes toward human ability which are quite different from those of the white. Primarily, Washo identity is maintained by reference to the past. The features of the land on which they live have a different meaning to the Washo. Stories of old adventures, ancient miracles, and battles long past are told and retold and their locations pointed out. Stubbornly, the Washo view the land as being theirs. This relationship to the past was made real by the Washo claim against the federal government for the lands usurped without payment. The claim for 42 million dollars is before the courts and the possibility of a favorable decision helps provide a vague but real unity among the Washo people that is based on their past. This attachment to the land influences a retention of an attenuated version of the aboriginal annual cycle. In the spring and early summer, many Washo families travel to Lake Tahoe and the mountain lakes in the higher country. There they picnic and enjoy the scenery, the old members of the family telling traditional tales of the country around them. In a similar fashion, many families go into the pine nut hills in the fall, often for a single day, to picnic and gather a few pounds of nuts. These will be saved and eaten raw or cooked into the Washo favorite, a pine nut soup to be consumed in a single nostalgic meal. During the season, families will fish on some favorite stream and young men will go deer hunting. In short, the Washo has not changed his essential values in the face of a century of dramatic change. He has instead made whatever adjustments necessary to survive in a changing situation. The physical, economic, and social changes have been almost complete. The mental and ideological changes have been less extreme and constitute the core of Washo existence today. The conflict between the attitudes and ideologies and the realities of existence in the modern world is the basis of the Washo dilemma. Washo values often conflict with white values. Unfortunately, the Washo are, in the final analysis, dependent on the white world.

The Future

The nature of the Washo future will be determined by the processes of the Washo past. From the earliest contact between whites and Washo, the Washo have made adjustments to a changed situation. The whites in many cases were a new resource to be exploited to the benefit of the Washo. Many of the changes in Washo life were sought eagerly because they provided an easier and more profitable access to food and desirable materials. The pattern of wandering bands continued from the 1840s until the 1920s for some families. Hunting and gathering in the Washo environment required a flexible social structure and cultural patterns permitting the individual the widest latitude in seeking subsistence. The Washo response to the changes of the past century have been in keeping with this pattern. It has been opportunistic and flexible with the widest range of individual responses. The individual Washo and his family has made adjustments to the new situation as best suited him and served his purposes. Because of this pattern of change, the Washo have become increasingly involved with the white society and the future of the Washo people is linked to the future of America in general. Patterns of deprivation, racial discrimination, and education will determine the future of the Washo.

References Used

Direct citations are few in the text itself, but the author has frequently used information drawn from the following works:

ANGEL, MYRON (ed.), 1958. Reproduction of Thompson and West's *History of Nevada*, 1881. (Originally published by T. H. Thompson and Albert A. West, 1881, reproduced by Howell-North, Berkeley, 1958).

COOK, SHERBORNE, F., 1941, "The Mechanisms and Extent of Dietary Change among Certain Groups of California and Nevada Indians," *Ibero-Americana*, Vol. 18, pp. 1–59.

D'AZAVEDO, WARREN L. (ed.), 1963, "The Washo Indians of California and Nevada," University of Utah, Department of Anthropology, Anthropological Papers, No. 67, August. (Contains articles by S. A. Barrett, W. L. d'Azavedo, S. A. Freed, R. S. Freed, P. E. Leis, N. A. Scotch, F. L. Scotch, J. A. Price, and J. F. Downs).

DOWNS, JAMES F., 1961, "Washo Religion," University of California *Anthropological Record*, Vol. 14, No. 6, pp. 349–418.

INGALLS, G. W., 1913, "Indians of Nevada, 1825 to 1931," in Sam P. Davis, (ed.), *The History of Nevada*, pp. 239–69.

LOWIE, ROBERT H., 1939, "Ethnographic Notes on the Washo," University of California Publications in American Archaeology and Ethnology. Vol. 36, No. 5, pp. 301–52.

PRICE, JOHN A., 1962, "Washo Economy," Nevada State Museum Anthropological Papers, No. 6.

———, 1962, "Washo Economy," unpublished M.A. thesis, Department of Anthropology, University of Utah.

STEWART, OMER G., 1941, "Culture Element Distributions: XIV, Northern Paiute," University of California *Anthropological Record*, Vol. 4, No. 3, pp. 361–446.

———, 1944, "Washo-Northern Paiute Peyotism: A Study in Acculturation," University of California Publications in American Archaeology and Ethnology, Vol. 40, No. 3, pp. 63–142.

Recommended Reading

DRIVER, HAROLD E., 1961, *Indians of North America*. Chicago: University of Chicago Press.

A general reference work outlining the results of many years of research by many anthropologists in the collection of data on the distribution of culture traits. It includes information on many categories of culture for the several major culture areas of native North America.

KROEBER, ALFRED A., 1925, *Handbook of the Indians of California*. Bureau of American Ethnology Bulletin No. 78 (reprinted by the California Book Company, Berkeley, 1953).

A major compendium of information on the culture, language, social organization, and material culture of the tribes of California by the leading authority on the area.

————, 1948, "Cultural and Natural Areas of Native North America," University of California Publications in American Archaeology and Ethnology, Vol. 38, pp. 1–242.

An examination of the relationship between culture and environment among the Indian tribes of the United States and Canada.

LA BARRE, WESTON, 1938, *The Peyote Cult*. New Haven, Conn.: Yale University Publications in Anthropology.

A discussion of the history and dynamics of the peyote religion.

SPENCER, ROBERT F., AND JENNINGS, JESSE D., 1964, *The Native Americans*. New York: Harper & Row.

An excellent general treatment of the prehistory and ethnography of the American Indian prepared by a number of experts in the various culture areas of Mexico, the United States, and Canada, with ethnographic sketchs of representative tribes.

STEWART, JULIAN H. 1938, *Basin-Plateau Socio-Political Groups*, Washington, D.C.: Bureau of American Ethnology Bulletin 120.

A classic work describing the culture, social organization, and economic life of the peoples of the Great Basin.

TEPOZTLÁN: VILLAGE IN MEXICO

Oscar Lewis

formerly at University of Illinois

Oscar Lewis held the Ph.D. from Columbia University and was professor
of anthropology at the University of Illinois until his death. He was a consulting
anthropologist for the Ford Foundation and a Guggenheim Fellow. He did fieldwork
with Blackfoot Indians and Texas farmers, and in Spain, Cuba, and India, as well
as in Mexico, where he studied Mexican peasant culture intermittently since 1943.
Among his books are *Village Life in Northern India, Life in a Mexican Village:
Tepoztlán Restudied*, and *Five Families: Mexican Case Studies in the Culture of
Poverty*.

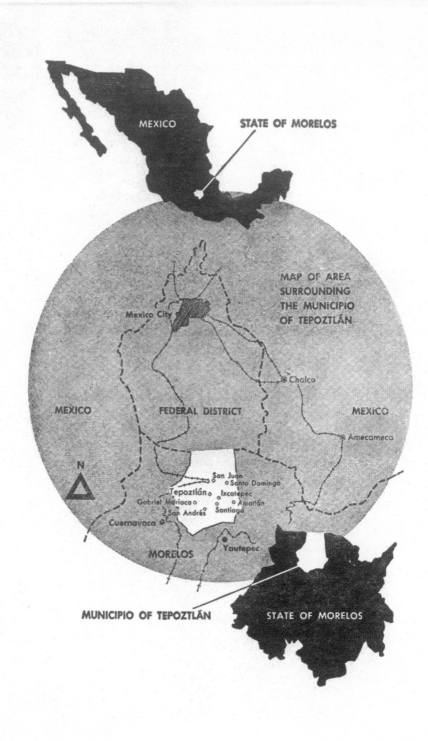

MEXICO STATE OF MORELOS

MAP OF AREA
SURROUNDING
THE MUNICIPIO
OF TEPOZTLÁN

Mexico City

Chalco

MEXICO FEDERAL DISTRICT MEXICO

Amecameca

N

San Juan
Santo Domingo
Tepoztlán Ixcatepec
Gobriel Mariaca Amatlán
San Andrés Santiago
Cuernavaca

MORELOS Yautepec

MUNICIPIO OF TEPOZTLÁN STATE OF MORELOS

Contents

Acknowledgments

I thank the University of Illinois Press for their kind permission to utilize materials published in my earlier volume *Life in a Mexican Village: Tepoztlán Restudied* (1951). To Alberto Beltrán I am grateful for the drawings of village scenes. I am also grateful to the Guggenheim Foundation for a Fellowship which made possible my second restudy of the village in 1956-57.

Introduction

ONE OF THE major trends in cultural anthropology during the last twenty years has been a shift from the study of isolated tribal peoples to the study of peasantry in the economically underdeveloped countries. The village of Tepoztlán, in Mexico, is especially interesting in this connection because it was one of the first peasant communities to be studied by an American anthropologist. Robert Redfield worked in the village in 1926-27 and in 1930 published *Tepoztlán—a Mexican Village*. Seventeen years later, in 1943, I restudied the village and in 1951 published *Life in a Mexican Village: Tepoztlán Restudied*. In 1956-57 I returned to Tepoztlán to learn what changes had taken place since my earlier work. In all, I have spent approximately three years of field work in the village since 1943. Few peasant communities have been studied more intensively by independent investigators. Moreover, the combination of archeological data, historical archive material dating from the sixteenth century, and three anthropological studies spread over a thirty-year period has given us an unusual time perspective for the study of culture change.

Tepoztlán may be designated as a peasant society in the sense that it has an old and stable population, the villagers have a great attachment to the land, agriculture is the major source of livelihood, the technology is relatively primitive (hoe and plow), and production is primarily for subsistence, with barter persisting, although the people also participate in a money economy. Moreover, the village is integrated into larger political units such as the state and the nation and is subject to their laws. The villagers pay taxes, send their children to school, and vote in national and state elections. Tepoztlán has also been exposed to urban influences and has borrowed from other rural areas as well as from urban centers, but it has managed to integrate the new traits into a relatively stable culture pattern. Finally, the community is poor, has a high incidence of illiteracy and a high birth and death rate, and has been under foreign domination for long periods of time. Thus it has developed that peculiar combination of dependence on and hostility toward government which is so characteristic of peasants and colonial peoples.

241

Since a peasant village is by definition part of a larger society, usually the nation, it becomes important to understand it within the national context and to determine how national institutions and national history affect it. On the other hand, a study of a single village in a predominantly· agricultural country can give us insight into many aspects of the nation as a whole. For example, Tepoztlán mirrors many national trends and brings into sharp focus some of the most pressing problems of Mexico. The changes which have occurred in Tepoztlán since the Revolution—the introduction of corn mills, the granting of *ejidos* to some of the landless (see p. 27), the building of a modern highway, the establishment of bus service, the expansion of educational facilities —are typical of changes which are taking place over wide areas in Mexico. Similarly, many of the problems which stand out in Tepoztlán can be seen in thousands of Mexican villages—for example, the poor agricultural resources, population pressure, the importance of forest and grazing lands in the agricultural economy, soil erosion, deforestation, the small size of land holdings, low yields, and the absence of adequate credit facilities. One advantage in studying these problems within the framework of a single village is that we can clearly see the interrelationship between geographic, historic, economic, social, political, and psychological factors.

Tepoztlán also reflects to a remarkable degree many of the characteristics of Mexico as a whole. Within the relatively limited area of the *municipio* (county) of Tepoztlán we find practically the entire range of the various climatic zones of Mexico—from the *tierra fría* (cold country) to the *tierra caliente* (hot tropical country)—and their accompanying variety of natural resources. Over 50 percent of the total land area of Mexico falls within the range of altitudes found within this single municipio—that is, from approximately 3,500 to 9,500 feet. The statistical indices of Tepoztlán also follow national figures for such items as the percentage of forest land to total land and the average size of landholding. In addition, the rate of population growth as well as the distribution of age groups closely parallels national figures for the rural population.

In Tepoztlán, as in Mexico as a whole, there are contrasting elements of the primitive and the modern, the Spanish colonial and the contemporary. Tepoztlán has a strong Indian heritage; many pre-Hispanic traits have persisted and are found in the village today. The system of communal landownership and the social organization of the municipio have remained practically intact for the past four hundred years. Many elements of pre-Hispanic agriculture are found; corn, beans, and squash remain the staple crops. Pre-Hispanic traits of material culture have also persisted, particularly in house construction, furnishings, cookery, and clothing. Among the more important of these items are adobe walls, the sweat house made of stone and mortar, clay-plastered granaries for corn, the hearth, the three-legged grinding stone, the clay griddle, the mortar and pestle, huaraches, chile, and *pulque*. In nonmaterial culture the survivals are found especially in curing and magic and in the customs pertaining to birth and other stages of the life cycle. The Nahuatl language has been retained. As late as 1927 Nahuatl was spoken by nearly all the villagers, although most of them also spoke Spanish.

The large number of Spanish colonial elements which still exist in the village culture were introduced early in the sixteenth century, soon after the Spanish conquest. The most important of these traits are the physical layout of the village with its barrios, streets, and central plaza; Catholicism and the churches; the Spanish language; a money economy; domestic animals; the plow and other agricultural tools; and the greater part of the beliefs and customs of the people.

Side by side with the pre-Hispanic and Spanish colonial elements are many significant items of modern industrial civilization. These include corn mills and sewing machines, a modern highway and buses, clocks, poolrooms, patent medicines, powdered milk, battery radios, and a few automobiles. The existence of both old and new traits and the varying degree in which they are combined from family to family creates cultural complexity and heterogeneity in Tepoztlán.

It is important also to consider how Tepoztlán is distinctive. If we compare it with other villages in Mexico rather than with the nation as a whole, we find that it is atypical in many ways. Tepoztlán is larger than 90 percent of the villages of Mexico and has a greater complexity of social organization. Unlike many other municipios, Tepoztlán has retained its communal lands, and specialized industries are absent or have disappeared. The proximity of the village to Mexico City and to Cuernavaca has exposed it to new ideas. It has a long tradition of literacy with a local intelligentsia which has existed since the 1850's. Moreover, at various times in the history of the village Tepoztecans have achieved positions of prominence in different fields and have had personal contacts with men in the highest political circles of the state of Morelos and of the nation. In the middle of the last century many young men of the well-to-do class left Tepoztlán to become doctors, lawyers, teachers, engineers, and priests. The village boasts of having produced within the last fifty years two governors of the state of Morelos, three justices in the state court, a senator, and more than half a dozen deputies to the state legislature. These men or their descendants have kept in touch with their relatives in the village and so have been a constant stimulus for culture change.

The first seven chapters of this book describe Tepoztlán as it appeared to me between 1943 and 1948 and are based upon my earlier study, *Life in a Mexican Village: Tepoztlán Restudied*. The reader may refer to the earlier volume for detailed references to source material and the methodology employed. Chapter 8 of this book describes the village as of 1956.

The Setting

TEPOZTLÁN is an ancient highland village in the state of Morelos, about sixty miles south of Mexico City. It has been continuously inhabited at least since the time of Christ. It is the administrative head of the municipio of Tepoztlán which embraces an area of 60,000 acres and consists of eight villages. The village of Tepoztlán is centrally located within the municipio and nestles in a broad alluvial valley surrounded by beautiful buttes or cliffs which rise to 1,200 feet above the house sites. The cliffs or *cerros* form a natural fortress and at various times have served as a refuge for the villagers. Each *cerro* is known to the villagers by its ancient Nahuatl name and each has a legend associated with it. One of the cliffs has been an important archeological site since 1895 when a stone temple of a Tepoztecan deity was unearthed. The temple and the great scenic beauty of the village have begun to attract tourists in recent years.

The location of Tepoztlán in an intermediate position between the *tierra fría* and the *tierra caliente* gives it an excellent temperate climate. The climate is one of the most healthful in the state of Morelos, and Tepoztlán has one of the lowest death rates in the state. Tepoztlán is just above the malaria area and although malaria occurs, it is generally contracted by villagers who have been working in the lowlands to the south.

The average annual rainfall in the village is about 60 inches, most of which comes during the rainy season beginning in May or early June and generally lasting until early September. The dry season begins in October or November and lasts for seven long months. Because of the dry season only one crop a year can be grown. Lack of water for irrigation is one of the most frequent complaints made by the villagers, who speak of the irrigated farming area of Yautepec, where several crops a year are grown, as an agricultural paradise.

There are twenty-six public fountains in the village to which water is piped from a spring in one of the *cerros*. Most of the fountains are made of clay and cement; some are semienclosed, protected by a roof, and topped by

244

a cross; others are merely open tanks. Although hauling water has been the traditional and common practice, it is now considered a hardship by more and more families.

A rich semitropical flora grows in the village. On almost any house site a great variety of plants and trees are found: papaya, coffee, hog plum (*ciruela*), *guaje,* avocado, *chayote,* mango, banana, maguey, and some prickly pear. Most families grow a variety of flowers and herbs which they use for cooking and as medicines.

Tepoztlán is located on a slope, the northern or upper part of the village being several hundred feet higher than the southern part. The upper part is steeper, rockier, and somewhat cooler, while the lower part is better watered and has a richer flora. The streets running north and south slope steeply and during the rainy season they often become cascading streams. To avoid erosion, many streets have been stone paved and terraced according to the Aztec system of terracing, which involves a series of alternating slopes and levels. Only the paved road and the plaza in the center are on a more or less level plane.

The village is large, sprawling, roughly rectangular in shape, and approximately a mile and a fourth in length and a mile in width. Although it contains 662 house sites, it does not have the compact or crowded appearance of some Mexican towns since for the most part the houses are separated from each other by gardens, corrals, or small *milpas.* The stone walls which enclose the house sites are low, do not block the view from the street, and permit overhanging trees to shade the street. Only a few houses in the center of the village are built contiguously in Spanish style and are enclosed by high, concealing walls.

Tepoztlán has a typical Mexican plaza complete with park, bandstand, shade trees, and benches. Around the plaza are grouped the chief buildings: courthouse, offices for the president, secretary, and other local officials, the schoolhouse, the main church, some stores, a grain mill, and a small marketing center. This central part of the village has the appearance and some of the hustle of a town, but it does not give the impression of a thriving community. The park, plaza, and public buildings show evidence of chronic neglect; only for the annual *carnaval* is the area well swept and the main fountain cleaned. The villagers seldom use the park, and it is usually abandoned except when there are tourists. The stores are small and dark with unattractive displays. On market days the few vendors and the small variety of goods for sale betray the lack of commercial activity.

The streets off the center are uniformly rustic and quiet and stamp Tepoztlán as a rural village. The names of only those streets nearest the plaza are indicated by placards. As is customary in Mexico, street names commemorate important historical events and outstanding local figures; some are in Nahuatl and refer to pre-Hispanic figures. Again, only the houses in the center are numbered, although not in any systematic order. Street names or house numbers are not used by the villagers in speaking or writing, nor do they appear on letters mailed in from the outside.

At night the village appears even more rustic because of the absence of public street lighting. When there is no moon it is difficult—even dangerous—to walk through the rough streets without a flashlight or candle, and usually only young men venture out at night. The only sounds are those of the animals, the serenades of romantic youths, and an occasional drunken peasant being taken home. Even during the day the village is not noisy, although many sounds may be heard: voices from within the houses, children crying or playing, housewives slapping tortillas into shape, people and animals walking over the stones, church bells, buses racing and honking along the main thoroughfare, and an occasional lone peddler crying his wares.

Population

The population of Tepoztlán, like that of Mexico as a whole, has shown a rapid increase in recent years. The village had a population of 3,230 according to the census of 1940; by 1947 it numbered well over 4,000. One of the causal factors for the rise was the sharp decline in mortality rates, especially for infants, during the period from 1930 to 1940. This decline, in turn, was caused by the increase and greater availability of medical services and the fairly intensive program of inoculation carried out by the Mexican Department of Health. Since 1930 there have been doctors in residence in the village for short periods, and some villagers visit private doctors and the free health clinic in Cuernavaca. Five mid-wives with some training in modern hygienic methods now live in the village. The longer life span of the villagers (15.5 percent of Tepoztecans are people over fifty as compared to 9.9 percent for all rural Mexico) is probably related to an increasingly higher standard of living in the village as well as to its healthful climate.

Language and Literacy

Two languages are spoken in Tepoztlán, Spanish and the indigenous Nahuatl. In 1920 nearly all the villagers spoke Nahuatl, but since that time there has been a marked decrease in its use, with a corresponding increase in the use of Spanish. About one-half of the villagers are still bilingual, but in 1944 there were only five persons who spoke Nahuatl alone. Nahuatl is still preferred at barrio meetings and for the ceremonial address at some fiestas. The bus companies have Nahuatl names, and in sports events the competitors will sometimes take Nahuatl names.

The younger generation has a distinctly negative attitude toward Nahuatl; people under thirty-five tend to be ashamed of speaking it in the presence of outsiders and frequently deny having any knowledge of it. Within most homes, members of the older generation customarily speak in Spanish but resort to Nahuatl to tell secrets and jokes and to express themselves more emphatically when they are quarreling. Thus many children have come to associate speaking Nahuatl with quarreling and scolding.

The greater use of Spanish in the village has not been accompanied by an equal increase in literacy. In 1940, 42 percent of the villagers could not read or write. In general there is a high correlation between membership in the middle economic group and literacy; many in the upper economic group are illiterate. The reading of newspapers has increased considerably in recent years. In 1920 no newspapers came regularly to the village, while in 1944 fifty-six people bought newspapers on an average of twice a week. These people have played an important role in determining village opinion on local, national, and international issues.

Means of Communication

With a modern highway, bus service, mail service, some telephones, telegraph, and a nearby railroad, Tepoztlán has relatively good means of communication. The railroad, built about 1900, encouraged the commercial exploitation of natural resources and is now used chiefly to transport wood and charcoal to Mexico City. Before the highway, communication between the village and surrounding regions was by burro and by foot, and most trading and social contacts were with the nearby town of Yautepec. With the coming of the road and the bus lines, Cuernavaca replaced Yautepec in importance. Because of the cultural sophistication of Cuernavaca, this shift accelerated the rate of change in Tepoztlán. The village has had mail service since 1926, and mail is delivered daily. It has had the telephone and telegraph since before the Revolution, but until recently they have been either out of order or used only infrequently.

Housing and House Furnishings

The houses of Tepoztlán consist essentially of three types: the flimsy *jacal,* the adobe house, and the more substantial dwellings found in the center of the village. The *jacal* and the adobe house are basically Indian, while the houses in the center show Spanish influence.

The *jacal,* the poorest type of house, and considered primitive and undesirable by the majority of the villagers, is constructed of cornstalks or Mexican bamboo (*otate*) and has a thatched roof and an earthen floor. Only 5 percent of the dwellings are of this type, and they are limited to the smaller, outlying areas, particularly the upper part of the village. According to the Mexican Housing Census of 1939, the *jacal* makes up 38.7 percent of all dwellings in the Central Mesa region in which Tepoztlán is located and the percentage for all Mexico is 44.9. These figures indicate a comparatively high standard of housing in Tepoztlán.

The great majority of Tepoztecan families (approximately 90 percent) are housed in the more solid adobe, tile-roofed houses. These sometimes have brick floors but more usually earthen ones, and consist of one or more rectangular rooms each of which generally has only one opening, a doorway. Some of the newer adobe houses have wooden-shuttered window openings as well. The door of each room opens directly onto the yard or porch rather than into other rooms in the interior of the house. Frequently, as families grow larger, additional sleeping rooms are built, and many families add a kitchen in the form of a bamboo lean-to with a tile roof.

In sharp contrast with the *jacal* and adobe houses, the few homes of the wealthier families of the center barrios show marked Spanish or modern urban influence, and several of them border on elegance. They are built of brick or stone, covered with plaster, and whitewashed inside and out. Large and imposing, they are surrounded by a high outer wall which is built flush with the street and in which glass-paned windows and small balconies of iron grillwork are set.

Although only the poorest live in *jacales*, it is by no means true that the wealthiest live in the finest houses. Families of every category of wealth live in simple adobe houses, and a few of the richest men who represent the conservative older generation continue to live in relatively unimproved houses. Newly rich families also tend to build homes with a simple exterior even though the interior may have a degree of elegance. The destruction wreaked against the homes of the *caciques* during the Revolution is well remembered, and there still exists some fear on the part of Tepoztecans of acquiring a reputation of being wealthy.

The great majority of the houses in Tepoztlán have no running water or sanitary facilities of any kind. A few families near the center have water piped directly into their patios or kitchens, a privilege for which they pay a small tax to the municipio. No attempt has been made to control this private use of the public water supply, however, and some persons with such a supply permit relatives, friends, or *compadres* to take as much water as they wish, even allow a neighbor to connect his pipe to theirs to avoid paying the tax. Invariably the few families with private water have flourishing orchards and gardens. Sometimes the uncontrolled private use greatly decreases the flow of water into the nearest public fountain, particularly during the dry season. Conflict has often been the result. Not infrequently, private water pipes are deliberately stuffed up or damaged by less fortunate neighbors, and sometimes groups of angry residents, headed by a political leader, break into houses to cut off the private water supply that is draining the public one.

The benefits of toilets are not generally recognized: only one private house and the two tourist homes have toilets that can be flushed. The new schoolhouse, however, has toilets and showers, and the younger generation is becoming accustomed to them. Bathing facilities for women and children consist of a small clay or tin basin used in the home, although many women bathe and wash their hair when they do their laundry in a stream or at the public washing place. The men and older boys bathe in the river.

No Tepoztecan house has any means of heating other than the kitchen fire. This gives little heat and, moreover, it is extinguished as soon as cooking is completed, in order to save fuel. In the winter the villagers generally retire early to keep warm, but since most families have few blankets they suffer from cold during winter nights. Of the various means of lighting the houses after dark, the most common and inexpensive is the candle. Some houses have kerosene lamps, and the stores and a few of the houses in the center have Coleman gasoline lamps. One house—that of a prosperous curer—has electricity which is supplied by his own generator.

Differences in house furnishings are even more striking than differences in house types. As an example of the unending variety of combinations of modern and primitive household items, it is not at all unusual to find a battery-operated radio, a pre-Hispanic hearth as the only means of cooking, a hand mill for grinding coffee, and the Indian stone *metate* for grinding corn, all under one roof. Some of the youth, the more educated, and the middle economic group, have a strong desire to live better and to invest in household comforts—in modern equipment for cooking, sleeping, and lighting. Most members of the older generation, however—even those with means—scorn innovations and prefer to live the way they have always lived, investing what surplus they have in land and cattle. Thus the use of modern household equipment correlates more with age and education than with wealth, and such equipment is found most frequently in the homes of families with a medium income. But the homes of the better-to-do almost always contain a greater quantity of household goods, whether primitive or modern.

Almost every house has a hearth, either on the floor or raised to almost table height by means of a cement platform. The *comal* (griddle) for toasting tortillas may be of clay or iron, but with the increasing consumption of bread the griddle is used less than formerly. The same is true of the *metate* (grinding stone), since almost all women now have their corn ground at the mill. Nevertheless, no Tepoztecan woman sets up housekeeping without her own *metate* for regrinding corn, for grinding coffee and large quantities of chile for fiestas, and for emergencies.

The remaining house furnishings are relatively few—mainly sleeping equipment, religious articles, and various containers for storage. The beds are of three kinds: the *petate* or straw mat placed on the floor; the *tepexco,* a raised bed of bamboo sticks tied together and placed on a wooden frame or on two sawhorses; and a brass or iron bedstead with metal springs over which a *petate,* rather than a mattress, generally is placed. The great majority of the villagers sleep either on the floor or on the *tepexco;* only about 20 percent sleep on a bed or cot. For Mexico as a whole, the proportion of those who sleep on a bed or cot is far greater (61 percent) and even for communities of 10,000 or fewer inhabitants it is 53 percent. Most Tepoztecans sleep on the floor because they cannot afford to buy beds, but the older people sleep on the floor by preference, feeling that it is safer, makes them less subject to *los aires* (evil winds), or is more comfortable. Pillows, mattresses, bed linen, and bedspreads are found in only a few Tepoztecan homes. A wool *serape* is all the bedding known to most.

Sleeping arrangements vary from family to family, but the most widespread custom is for children of from about two to six to sleep between their parents on the *petate* A nursing baby sleeps on the outside, next to his mother. Cradles are used only during the day. Older children sleep apart, the girls sharing one *petate* and the boys another. In homes with two rooms, the parents and small children sleep in one room and the older children in the other. Few homes have enough rooms to permit the separation of older brothers and sisters. Sometimes parents are embarrassed to lie down together in the presence of their children; the mother then sleeps with the daughters while the father sleeps with the sons.

Most homes have a makeshift altar in the main room of the house. This is usually a table, frequently covered with tissue paper, on which are placed candles, flowers, incense burners, and statues of the saints. Religious pictures are hung on the wall over the table.

Less than a dozen battery-operated radios and about forty-four spring-driven phonographs are owned by the villagers. In 1943 there were 215 sewing machines in Tepoztlán. These machines were owned by 25 percent of the families but they serviced many more than that number since it is customary to lend or rent them to relatives and neighbors. Most machines are in continuous use. Indeed it may be said that one of the secondary, although not unimportant, effects of the sewing machine has been to provide the women with an excuse for visiting each other, thereby extending their social life.

Diet

As in rural Mexico as a whole, the basic diet of the people of Tepoztlán consists of corn, beans, and chile, the proportion of the three staples to other foods varying sharply from family to family according to season, income, and food habits. In general, the poorer the family, the higher the consumption of the three staples as compared to meat, milk, bread, cheese, and other foods. Corn is the major food, ranging from 10 to as much as 70 percent of a family's diet.

Corn is most frequently eaten in the form of tortillas, occasionally as *atole* (gruel). At certain fiestas, tamales made of corn dough are eaten. A wide variety of beans is found in Tepoztlán, the most common being red kidney beans which are cooked with lard, chile, and sometimes tomato and onion. Green chile, ground with onion and tomato, is daily made into a sauce to be eaten with the tortillas and whatever other foods are served.

The basic diet is supplemented by other foods which are locally cultivated, gathered wild, or purchased in the stores and market place. Those locally produced include banana, orange, lemon, lime, grapefruit, hog plum, papaya, mango, prickly pear, avocado, squash, tomato, *zapote, chayote, manzanillos, pitos,* acacia seeds, sugar cane, *chirimoya, mameys,* peanuts, coffee, honey, spices, herbs, beef, pork, chicken, turkey, milk, eggs, cheese, and clotted cream. The fields, forests, and mountainsides provide several varieties of wild edible greens the year round. These are not considered a desirable food, but they are important because they provide food elements which the Tepoztecan diet would otherwise lack. During times of scarcity a large number of families eat wild greens in quantity several times a week; the chronically poor eat them regularly throughout the year.

Foods bought in the stores of Tepoztlán, Yautepec, Cuernavaca, or Mexico City are bread, sugar, salt, rice, certain types of chile and beans, noodles, and dried codfish. Chocolate is used but is considered a luxury. Evaporated and powdered milk, canned sardines, tomato herring, and other fish are used by a small minority but are slowly becoming more popular.

The eating of white bread made of wheat flour is of particular interest in Mexico since it is a relatively new trait and one which has been taken to indicate the degree of acculturation both of individuals and of groups. In Tepoztlán, bread is considered a very desirable food, and the social and economic status of a family is often judged in terms of the amount of bread it consumes. In 1940 over 31 percent of the villagers ate bread fairly regularly; three years later there was hardly a family that did not eat bread even though it may have been only once or twice a month. Bread is especially favored as a food for small children; even the poorest family tries to provide a piece of bread for its youngest child every day. There is no indication, however, that bread will eventually displace the tortilla, for even among the well-to-do families bread consumption represents at most about 10 percent of the total food expenditure.

There is, of course, much variation in the actual consumption of food. Except among the wealthier families, irregularity in diet is characteristic throughout the year; few families maintain a uniformly good diet from day to day even by local standards. The leanest season of the year is the three or four months preceding the harvest when many families are reduced to minimum quantities of tortilla, beans, and chile. Before fiestas, money is needed for new clothes, for the fiesta meal, and for other expenses. Many families pull in their belts at this time and eat less in order to sell their corn, beans, eggs, and chickens for cash. The best eating occurs just after harvest and on fiesta days when *mole,* made with chicken or turkey, and rice and beans are prepared. Other irregularities of consumption are caused by the seasonal availability of fruits and vegetables. If the family trees produce poor or little fruit, for example, the family goes without fruit.

Meat consumption rises during the dry winter months when pasture is scarce, for cattle are then slaughtered. Eggs are generally eaten only by the men, especially during the planting season when work is intense. Chicken and turkey are delicacies reserved for fiestas, weddings, baptisms, and birthdays. With the exception of the wedding feast, which is socially obligatory and served by rich and poor alike, many families must forego fiesta meals, sometimes for years on end, and partake of them only when invited by other families. Game is not eaten extensively; the few men who hunt do so only when, as in the dry season, there is no other work.

Differences in the diet of the rich and poor are principally differences in the amount of food eaten and in the relative frequency with which a family can afford to eat the more desirable of the locally known food types. There are no class differences in food quality, in food types, and in ways of preparing dishes. It is commonly said in Tepoztlán that the rich are too miserly to eat any better than the poor. Not wealth as such, but education or degree of acculturation is now beginning to create real differences in diet.

Tepoztecan families normally eat three meals a day, although many remember eating only twice a day before and during the Revolution. The entire family seldom eats together and often there are no fixed hours for meals. The father and older sons have breakfast together in the morning before they go to the fields; if the fields are at a great distance they carry their breakfast with them, to be warmed and eaten later. They may eat in the fields again at noon and have their dinner when they arrive home, at any time between 5 and 9 P.M. When they eat at home they usually are served first. The mother serves them, handing each person his food in a bowl or rolled in a tortilla.

The women and the children eat breakfast at 7 or 8 A.M., dinner at about 1 P.M., and supper at dusk. Usually the younger children are fed before the mother and the older daughters sit down to eat. In most homes the men sit on low chairs or stools and the women and children sit on the floor. Very few families use a table except for a fiesta meal and then only for the men and guests. Likewise, knives and forks, if used at all, are reserved for guests at fiesta time. Spoons are sometimes used, but usually food is eaten with the tortilla as a spoon.

Like most Mexicans, Tepoztecans believe that food can be classified as "hot" and "cold," a classification which has no relationship to the temperature or the flavor of the foods. (Ice cream, for example, is classified as "hot," while most meats are called "cold.") In general, "cold" foods are believed to cause diarrhea and to be less easily digested than "hot" foods. They are therefore not given to very small children or to women who have just given birth. During certain illnesses, only "hot" foods should be eaten; during others only "cold" foods. Foods may be neutralized—that is, made less dangerous—by mixing certain "hot" foods with certain "cold" foods. Tepoztecans are not meticulous about following the rules, however, nor do they always agree what the rules are or how a food, particularly a new food, should be classified.

Clothing

Both old and new styles of clothes are worn in Tepoztlán—age, occupation, and, to a limited degree, economic status being the factors which determine the style preferred. The old-type clothing is essentially Spanish in origin with some admixture and adaptation from pre-Hispanic times. For women it consists of a long dark-colored skirt, a white underskirt, a collarless undershirt, a high-necked blouse, a half-apron, a sash, and a *rebozo*. The old type clothing for men consists of white cloth pants (*calzones*), long white cotton underdrawers, white undershirt, a white collarless overshirt, a white cotton jacket, leather huaraches, and a straw sombrero. The *serape,* an important article of clothing, is used for warmth and for protection against rain.

The new type of dress was worn by the wealthier and more sophisticated Tepoztecans in the 1920's, but since that time members of all socioeconomic levels have adopted it. For women it includes a one-piece dress, a full-length slip, and a long apron. Unmarried girls wear underdrawers and a number of younger women have a pair of shoes and stockings for important occasions. The *rebozo* is still commonly worn, but sweaters and jackets are coming into use. Most of the changes are seen in the dress of women under forty; those over forty are more conservative and cling to the old styles.

Modern dress for men, worn mainly by the merchants, artisans, and teachers of the center, consists of dark, factory-made pants (*pantalones*), a shirt with collar and buttons, a jacket with collar, and shoes. The sombrero is sometimes replaced by a narrow-brimmed felt hat, but only the most "citified" men in Tepoztlán wear neckties. Modern dress for boys may be overalls or pants, a buttoned shirt, and a straw hat. The *serape* is now often replaced by a sweater or jacket, and many boys wear shoes. Peasants prefer the old-style dress which, they say, is cooler, cheaper, and better adapted to work in the fields.

Although clothing is becoming important as an indicator of social status, it is not necessarily an indicator of wealth. The middle economic group, rather than the upper group, tends to wear modern dress and shoes. The lowest percentage of those wearing shoes is in fact found among the wealthiest group because it is made up of the older generation.

Fiestas and Diversions

Fiestas, both religious and secular, are the major occasions for music (native drums, flageolets, and modern bands), dances, fireworks, the preparation of special dishes, rodeos, the burning of candles for a saint, flower decorations, prayer, processions, and the Mass. The fiestas serve to strengthen the *esprit de corps* of the villagers; some celebrations are joyous, others are occasions for sadness and mourning. The great majority of religious fiestas are in celebration of saints; relatively few are in celebration of Jesus or Mary.

The calendar of religious fiestas is a typical Catholic calendar which includes movable and fixed fiesta days and begins on the first of December with the opening of the season of Advent. The religious fiestas in which Tepoztecans participate are of four types: (1) the barrio fiestas in which each barrio celebrates its patron saint (see section on barrios p. 50); (2) the village-wide fiestas which celebrate the holy days in the central church; (3) the fiestas of other surrounding villages of the municipio (see municipio, p. 46); and (4) the fiestas of villages and towns outside of the municipio. Of the total of fifty-three named fiestas in which Tepoztecans participate, twenty-seven are village-wide fiestas, twelve are barrio fiestas, seven are fiestas of surrounding villages within the municipio, and seven are fiestas of villages outside of the municipio. Of the village-wide fiestas, the most important are the *carnaval,*

Ash Wednesday, the fiestas of Holy Week, the Day of *San Isidro,* the fiesta for El Tepozteco (the local culture hero) and María, the blessings of the *pericón* on September 28, the Days of the Dead, and the Days of the Posadas.

It is difficult to estimate the total number of days during a year which the villagers might devote to fiestas. Some of the fifty-three fiestas last three or four days, and a conservative estimate would be about one hundred days. It would be quite erroneous, however, to conclude that most Tepoztecans spend approximately a third of the year in fiestas, for most fiestas are attended by only a small portion of the population. Certainly less than 5 percent of the villagers attend the fourteen fiestas of the surrounding villages and other towns, and less than 10 percent attend the fiestas of barrios other than their own. There are probably less than a dozen village-wide fiestas during the year in which the village as a whole participates.

No one attends all the fiestas, but all attend some. Widows and older women are known to be great fiesta lovers and habitually attend as many as possible. The very poor tend to participate in the barrio fiestas of Tepoztlán and other villages, whereas the well-to-do are more careful to attend the religious services held in the central church. Children especially like to attend fiestas. The sharp drop in school attendance during certain fiesta times is a chronic complaint of the school. Tepoztecans also frequent the fairs of Chalma, Jiutepec, Tepalzingo, Tlayacapan, and Mazatepec. Some go to buy or sell, others go for religious devotion to a special saint, and still others go purely for diversion.

The establishment and the increasing popularity of many national holidays are encouraging a new type of sociability in the village. Unlike the traditional fiestas, these occasions are organized by the school staff and are carried out by the children. They consist of dances, plays, recitations, speeches, the singing of national songs, and parades. Occasional school dances and *kermeses,* where food and drinks are sold and games are played to raise money for various school needs, are enjoyed by the young people, but attendance is usually small because the older generation believes ballroom dancing is immoral.

Another common form of diversion is to go to Cuernavaca. On Sundays groups of young men go by bus and spend the day walking about, playing pool, drinking in the *cantinas,* and visiting prostitutes. It is the place for rendezvous, window shopping, marketing, and movie going. In short, a trip to Cuernavaca provides temporary personal freedom for Tepoztecans.

Sports as a form of recreation are limited. The traditional cockfights are all but gone and the rustic rodeos are disappearing because the young men now lack interest and skill. Hunting is seldom engaged in as a sport. Singing and serenading at night are still popular with the young men and are also a source of pleasure for most of the villagers. Organized sports or games were first introduced in Tepoztlán in 1922 during a national campaign by the Minister of Education. Baseball, soccer, volleyball, and basketball were taught by the school and had an immediate appeal. Soccer from the first was the most popular and at one time there were as many as fifteen teams. There are now five teams which play against each other and against teams from Cuernavaca and other nearby towns.

Further diversification of recreation came about with the establishment of two poolrooms in the village. Despite the pessimistic expectations of the older people, there is no evidence that the poolrooms have encouraged vice or helped to develop any new bad habits; rather they seem to have provided a harmless and much-needed diversion for the young men.

Tepoztecans have always been heavy drinkers but there are fewer habitual drunkards among them than in some of the surrounding villages. Within the last few years the price of alcohol has risen from forty centavos to five pesos a liter, a prohibitive cost which has been in part responsible for the return to the use of *pulque*. In 1942 a *pulquería* was opened in the plaza. Soft drinks such as Coca-Cola, lemonade, and other carbonated drinks are also sold in the village.

In 1939, movie equipment was installed in the school and moving pictures were shown in the village for the first time. After a month the entrepreneur moved out because of the small attendance. Two or three subsequent attempts have met with the same result, for to most Tepoztecans the admission charge of thirty or fifty centavos is prohibitive. From time to time a puppet show reaches Tepoztlán and runs for about a week. This, together with several school plays a year, makes up the theatrical entertainment.

In the past two years the church has attempted to take a more active part in providing leisure-time activities for Tepoztecans. These have included singing, presenting religious pageants and plays, celebrating saints' days, organizing religious pilgrimages, and money-making events. The new forms of entertainment have tended to make for greater differences among the various economic groups in the village, for invariably they involve an expenditure of money for dues, equipment, bus fare, clothing, or appropriate food. Thus the very poor cannot participate and continue to be limited to the fiestas and fairs.

A poor peasant's home.

2.

Village History

THE HISTORY OF culture change in Tepoztlán closely follows the major divisions of Mexican history—namely, (1) the Pre-Hispanic Period; (2) the Spanish Conquest and the Colonial Period (1521) to Independence in 1810; (3) 1810 through the Díaz Regime; (4) the Revolution of 1910-20; (5) the Post-Revolutionary Period, 1920 to the present.

Pre-Hispanic Period

Tepoztlán, like Mexico, has had a long and complicated history of mingling of peoples and cultures; it has never been a truly isolated village. Its marginal position between the high plateau area to the north and the lower valleys of the south, as well as its proximity to the major roads of travel, subjected it even in pre-Hispanic times to influences from many areas. The various ceramic levels unearthed in the village show Olmec, Toltec, and Aztec influences. The village had experienced a number of conquests and had long been under political domination and authoritarian systems even before the coming of the Spaniards.

According to the legendary history of Mexico, Mixcoatl, the founder of the Toltec Empire, invaded the valley of Morelos with a Nahua horde in the early tenth century and defeated the Tlahuicas, an earlier Nahuatl-speaking people who lived in Tepoztlán. Thereafter, the Tepoztecans worshiped the benign gods of the Toltecs with offerings of paper, quail, wild pigeons, and copal incense. The Mexican scholar Jimenez Moreno has identified the village god El Tepozteco as the deified figure of Topiltzin, the son of Mixcoatl and a woman of Tepoztlán. Because Mixcoatl was assassinated before the birth of his son and the mother died in childbirth, Topiltzin was reared in Tepoztlán. Later he went north to avenge the death of his father by killing his kinsman, Ihuitimal.

256

The Toltec Empire was destroyed in 1246 by the Aztecs, but Tepoztlán was not involved until 1437 when Moctezuma Ilhuicomina captured it. The village was under Aztec domination for about one hundred years, probably as a semiautonomous seignory like Cuernavaca and Yautepec. To its Aztec rulers Tepoztlán paid tribute in the form of cotton mantles, cloth, paper, pottery, shields, warrior costumes, and beans. Agricultural products made up a relatively small part of the tribute.

In this pre-Hispanic period Tepoztlán was a highly stratified society with a few lords and ruling families (*principales*) at the top of the social pyramid and the mass of commoners (*maceguales*) at the bottom. The commoners worked the lands of these rulers, built their houses, made their clothing, and gave them all they demanded. They could not deal directly with the higher lords who governed them, however, but only through the *principales* who had the position of judges. Class differences were important and pervasive and affected diet, clothing, marriage customs, and other aspects of life.

The pre-Hispanic economy was a varied one. In addition to corn production there were a number of important local industries and activities: cotton growing, weaving, paper making, lime production, and the extensive use of the maguey plant for a variety of purposes. This valuable plant provided fuel; fencing and thatching material; fibers for making sandals, rope, and cloth; gutters, files, nails, needles; and honey, sugar, vinegar, and *pulque*.

According to old legends, *pulque* was invented in or near Tepoztlán, and the villages of the municipio were famous for their celebrations and debauchery. Tepoztlán was the site of a special cult of Ometochtli (Two Rabbits), the god of *pulque*, whose fame extended throughout the Aztec Empire and made the village an important religious center. Foreigners from as far away as the kingdoms of Chiapas and Guatemala made pilgrimages there, and in certain seasons of the year the cult of Ometochtli had all the characteristics of a collective orgy. Under the Aztecs, Tepoztecans paid homage to Aztec gods and practiced the Aztec rites of human sacrifice, offering children to the rain god and the hearts of prisoners to the war god.

The Spanish Conquest and the Colonial Period to Independence, 1521-1810

Tepoztlán submitted to the conquering troops of Cortés in 1521 when they passed through the village on their way from Yautepec to Cuernavaca. Because some chieftains from Yautepec were hiding there, Cortés set fire to half the town during his one-day stay. His men reported that they found there "many pretty women and much loot." By decree of 1529 Tepoztlán was one of many villages granted to Cortés. When Cortés decided to make Cuernavaca the capital of his large estate, Tepoztlán became subject to the Corregidor of Cuernavaca and the complex administrative machinery set up by the Spanish.

Before the Conquest, the village was widely spread out. Numerous population clusters had settled along the valley near the *cerros* where there was an adequate water supply. To control the people and to facilitate taxation, the Spaniards brought together into Tepoztlán these population clusters from the outlying settlements. But in government as in other aspects of the culture, the village changed slowly, modifying rather than discarding its pre-Conquest institutions. The old hierarchal arrangements of the social structure persisted; the political and religious power was simply transferred to the new ruling group represented by the Spaniards. Moreover, many of the old *principales* were maintained in power by the Spanish conquerors. Sixteenth-century documents reveal the existence of a remarkably large government bureaucracy which included many church officials.

After the Conquest, some of the native industries, principally those concerned with the manufacture of paper and cotton cloth, expanded temporarily in response to the new market provided by the Spaniards. As late as 1575 the village was described as "swarming with workmen making paper." But in general the Conquest was a disruptive influence on local industries and caused Tepoztlán to be more and more dependent on its corn. One of the disruptive factors was the *repartimiento* system which made Tepoztlán subject to a yearly assignment of manpower for work on the haciendas, in the mines of Taxco, on construction projects in Cuernavaca and in Tepoztlán itself, and as domestic servants. In addition, Tepoztecans were required to furnish workers in emergencies. One such occasion required "400 common Indians" for the harvest of sugar cane when a hacienda ran short of Negro slaves. The villagers repeatedly complained against excessive demands for labor and begged for relief, but without success. The church and the hacienda owners worked together in exploiting Indian labor.

Tepoztlán was also subject to taxation. In the early years after the Conquest, Cortés followed the Aztec policy of collecting taxes in produce. By the latter part of the sixteenth century, however, Tepoztecans complained about making payments in kind and asked to be allowed to pay in currency. This was because the landless were forced to buy corn at exorbitant prices to pay their taxes. From 1567 on, taxes were collected both in corn and in money, an indication that the village was beginning to function as a money economy. Taxes were collected for three purposes: to provide payment to the Crown; to help support the local officials of the municipio; and to support the church and the village fiestas.

In terms of population, the Conquest and the ensuing Colonial period were drastically disruptive. The population of the municipio at the time of the Conquest was about 15,000, a figure considerably larger than at the present time or at any time after the Conquest. Sixteenth-century accounts indicate a rapid decline in the population; by 1579 the village population was 5,824 and that of the entire municipio 7,572. The major causes of the decline were epidemics, deaths in the mines of Taxco and Cuautla, and the fleeing of Tepoztecans from the municipio to avoid the high taxes. The decline continued through the colonial period; by 1807 the village population was 2,540, a drop of 56 percent in a 228 year period.

Christianity was brought to Tepoztlán with little difficulty, the polytheism of the ancient religion permitting a relatively easy shift from the old gods to the new. According to local legend, the king Tepoztecatl realized the superiority of the new belief, willingly became a Christian, received the new name of Natividad, and allied himself with the Dominican friars in converting the Indians peacefully. But although the growth of Catholicism and the church in Tepoztlán was rapid, many pre-Hispanic religious elements were carried over to the new religion. The figure of Tepoztecatl retained the name of El Tepozteco along with that of Natividad and thus permanently fused old Aztec concepts with those of the Catholic church. His figure is also confused with the god Ometochtli so that today he is known both as god of the wind and as son of the Virgin Mary.

After the Conquest, the Dominicans in Tepoztlán were mainly occupied in carrying out the administrative measures of the viceroy. They also attempted to extirpate all pre-Hispanic cults, and were especially vigorous in this activity during the sixteenth century when they attacked the native priests as witches and denounced the ancient idols as instruments of the devil. They slowly succeeded, as did other religious orders in Spanish America, in gathering the natives into religious associations, a move that facilitated the administrative and political functions of the colony. The church, united as it was with the state, became very strong. Church personnel were numerous and were paid from public funds, and high public officials were obliged to preside over all religious processions and ceremonies. Religious fiestas became numerous during the Colonial period, and greatly increased the church income and stimulated local trade.

Independence through the Díaz Regime, 1810-1910

The first years of Mexican independence passed almost unnoticed in Tepoztlán, where colonial forms of life continued. However, the population increased for the first time since the Conquest. By 1890 it had risen to 4,163 for the village and 8,589 for the municipio.

The first great change in Tepoztlán during this period came as a result of the Juarez Reforms of 1857, when the church and state were separated and church property was confiscated. The land belonging to the village church was distributed among a small portion of the population which became the new local aristocracy, the *caciques*. The *caciques* formed an elite who controlled the local government, naming the officials and prohibiting political parties and elections.

The *caciques* produced large crops on their lands, using oxen and hiring peons at eighteen centavos a day. They forbade the planting of *tlacolol* (communal lands) in order to assure a cheap labor supply for themselves. For the poor and landless it was a time of suffering and exploitation; food and goods were cheap but work was scarce and people went hungry. The poor often subsisted on herbs, mushrooms, and wild greens. Many were forced to pawn their sons as servants for from five to ten pesos a season. Debts were heavy and were passed down from father to son. When the haciendas began competing with the local *caciques* for laborers, wages rose, in some cases to as high as thirty-seven centavos a day. The recruiting agents and the overseers customarily beat peons who were unruly or who did not work quickly and those who protested were drafted into the army.

The church had reacted to the Reform laws by aggressively struggling against the liberal orientation of the Mexican government. But when Díaz came to power in 1877, the church recuperated much of its former glory. In Tepoztlán, the *caciques* supported the church as a strong conservative force and again united the church and the state. Once more, pompous religious fiestas were celebrated in the village and attendance at them was large.

A landmark in the history of Tepoztlán was the building of the railroad in 1897 through the upper part of the municipio. Although most Tepoztecans had opposed the coming of the railroad and had accused the *caciques* of selling out the communal land to the gringos, the whole population benefited from the railroad. Many villagers were hired as day laborers at three times the wages prevailing at the haciendas; trade increased, and several public works were carried out with money received by the village and municipio from the railroad company in exchange for permission to build on Tepoztecan lands. Among these were the building of the municipal building and park, the lighting of the main streets by oil lamps, and the piping of water into the village. With the railroad also came the first wire fencing and the first steel plows, and the appearance of freight trains encouraged commercial exploitation of the forests for charcoal making. The expansion of the economy at this time led to other changes. A small museum of Antiquities was founded, a public library was opened, and night classes for adults were instituted. This cultural florescence, though short-lived and limited to a small group of the well-to-do and intellectuals, earned for Tepoztlán the reputation as the Athens of Morelos.

The Revolution, 1910-20

Few villages in Mexico suffered more than Tepoztlán during the Revolution. In 1911, more than a year before Zapata's call for revolt in Morelos, Tepoztlán liberated itself by force from the rule of the local *caciques*. Later the village was the scene of repeated invasions, first by rebel troops and then by government forces, and it endured depredations at the hands of both. Cattle were killed, corn and other crops were requisitioned, women were raped or taken as hostages, and large areas of the village were burned. When the situation became even more dangerous, the villagers fled to the hills and lived there for as long as six months at a time, stealing back from time to time to pick some fruit or to bury their dead.

From the start, the villagers' sympathies were with the rebels, but only a handful understood the ideals of the Zapata movement and were motivated by them. The promise of land had great appeal, but most Tepoztecans tried to remain neutral and joined the conflict only when it became a matter of life or death. The lack of unity among the villagers became apparent in the early days of the revolt when the ablest Tepoztecan leaders killed one another in their fierce rivalry for power.

During these bitter years the religious life of the village came to a standstill. The priests and the *caciques* had fled for their lives, the church and chapels were abandoned and sacked, and the ancient monastery became troop headquarters and stables. Some functions of the absent priest were carried on by *rezanderos*, laymen who knew prayers from memory and who charged a fee for saying prayers for the dying, for difficult deliveries, and the like.

By late 1919 the state of Morelos again was peaceful and the village of Tepoztlán began its struggle back to normalcy. When the dispersed villagers returned from the hills and nearby villages they were without homes and in absolute poverty. Loss of life in battle and starvation and illness had again caused a rapid decline in the population; in 1921 there were only 2,156 persons in the village and 3,000 in the municipio.

Post-Revolutionary Period, 1920-40

The Revolution transformed the social structure of Tepoztlán. Some of the *caciques* or their sons returned to their battered or burned homes, but they had lost most of their wealth, particularly their cattle and their shops. It was necessary for all, rich and poor, to begin to build again. But the building took place in a new social framework. The participation by the villagers in the Zapatista forces had left its imprint on the psychology of the people and had acted as a distinct leveling influence. The revolutionary slogans of the Zapatistas had been "land and liberty" and "down with the *caciques*." Now the political dominance of the *caciques* was gone.

A fundamental economic change had also occurred, and it was one of the most important effects of the Revolution: the communal lands of the municipio (which constitute about 80 percent of all the lands) were again available to the villagers. And in 1929, under the National *Ejido* program, the village received additional lands from a nearby hacienda for distribution to landless families. This further broadened the landbase in the village and helped to increase production.

The political history of the village during the twenty-five years after the Revolution was intense, dramatic, and often tragic. It centered on the issue of the preservation of the forests and other commercial resources. Since the neighboring haciendas had been destroyed and work was scarce, the villagers began cutting down the forests for the commercial production of charcoal. Two groups then arose: one, chiefly ex-Zapatistas, wanted to conserve the forest resources; the other, led by sons of former *caciques*, favored their continued exploitation. These two factions, known as the Bolsheviki (later the Fraternales) and the Centrales, struggled for village control throughout the twenties and thirties, with assassinations, imprisonments, and even massacre marking their conflict. In 1930, a cooperative for producing charcoal was organized. At one time it numbered over five hundred members but by 1937, after many bitter political conflicts, it went into bankruptcy and was dissolved.

Because of its proximity to both state and national capitals, Tepoztlán is particularly subject to outside political influences, and almost every political current of national importance during this period had some repercussions in the village. In 1920, the Colonia Tepozteco, an organization of Tepoztecans living in Mexico City, was founded to eliminate illiteracy and preserve the Nahuatl language in the village. This organization became a major outside political force in the village and a permanent and active urbanizing influence.

The position of the church following the Revolution went through several changes in Tepoztlán. When peace was first restored, the priest returned to the village and religious life was resumed but without its former splendor. The new tranquility was shattered in 1926, however, when the Archbishop of Mexico ordered a policy of noncooperation with the government. All priests were to leave their churches and to cease public religious services. Tepoztlán's priest left the village and only clandestine services by the *rezanderos* were available for a time. Finally, in about 1929, regular church services were again resumed.

In the early thirties, Protestantism came to Tepoztlán when about fifteen families, most of them poor, became Seventh Day Adventists. These families were ostracized, their houses were stoned, and their children were the butt of jokes and abuses. In the face of such hostility their number dwindled. The Catholic church waged successful propaganda campaigns against other Protestant projects, and the villagers came to be suspicious of any strangers who might be non-Catholic.

Two technological innovations which reached Tepoztlán in the 1920's made great changes in the lives of the women. In 1925, the first commercial mill for grinding corn was built, but soon closed because of opposition from the men. In 1927, however, another mill met with financial success through "the revolution of the women against the authority of the men," and by 1942 there were four mills in the village which all the women regularly patronized. From the mills they gained from four to six hours of freedom daily from the grinding stone, and their new leisure enabled them to undertake commercial ventures such as the raising of fruit and animals for marketing. The sewing machine, which made its appearance in the village during this period, also lightened the women's work.

An event of great importance in the history of the village was the completion in 1936 of an asphalt road connecting Tepoztlán with the Mexico City—Cuernavaca highway. This road allowed more frequent and varied social contacts; it brought in the tourist trade; and it gave the village easy access to new markets for its fruits and other produce. Two bus lines were formed, both of them owned and operated as cooperatives by Tepoztecans. The bus lines not only improved means of communication but also became new economic and political factors in the village. The bitter competition between them divided the village into two factions. Their leaders took over political control from the peasants, and the employees constituted the first important group of non-farmers in Tepoztlán.

The school became another important agent of culture change in the village. Enrollment soared from less than 100 in 1926 to 611 in 1944. The school increased literacy, taught the children new standards of personal hygiene and cleanliness, and in effect became a symbol of the new in Tepoztlán.

In the twenty-year post-Revolutionary period, then, there were numerous primary influences for change in the village. The granting of *ejido* lands, the building of corn mills, the new road, and the expansion of school facilities were the most effective of these. The fact that they occurred at about the same time made them mutually reinforcing and the tempo of change was thereby accelerated. The cultural changes that resulted were far reaching: a rapid increase in population, an improvement in health services, a marked rise in the standard of living and the aspiration level of the people, the growth of a class of small landowners, the development of a greater variety and specialization in occupation, a decrease in the use of Nahuatl and a corresponding spread in the use of Spanish, a rise in literacy and the beginning of regular newspaper reading, and a greater incorporation of the village into the mainstream of national life.

Home of an old *cacique*.

3

Economics

THE ECONOMY of Tepoztlán is essentially a household economy of small producers, peasants, artisans, and merchants whose primary motive for production is subsistence. But it is not a self-sufficient economy and probably was not one even in pre-Conquest days. The village depends heavily upon trade with nearby regions for basic elements of diet such as salt, sugar, rice, and chile. From urban centers it obtains cloth, agricultural implements, sewing machines, Coleman lamps, kerosene, guns, patent medicines, water pipes, buses, and pool tables. It has few handicrafts, no pottery, no weaving, and no basketmaking.

From the point of view of agriculture, the basic means of livelihood, the resources of Tepoztlán are poor indeed. Only about 15 percent of the total land area is cultivable by plow and oxen and about 10 percent by the more primitive method of cutting and burning and hoe culture. Even if there were a perfectly equitable distribution of land there would be only 1.5 acres of cultivatable land per capita and about 8 acres of forest and grazing lands per capita. Furthermore, as has been noted, there is no irrigation and only one harvest a year. Since the village cannot support itself by farming alone, Tepoztecans seek other sources of income and are busy at a variety of jobs during different seasons of the year.

The Tepoztecan economy, though that of a peasant society, is neither simple nor primitive. It has many elements: well-developed concepts of private property, a high degree of individualism, a free market, a definition of wealth in terms of land and cattle and other forms of property, a relatively wide range in wealth differences, the use of money, a highly developed system of marketing and trade, interest on capital, work for wages, pawning of property, renting of land, the use of plow and oxen, and specialization in part-time occupations.

Despite this roster of familiar traits, the Tepoztecan economic system is quite distinctive and defies easy classification in terms of such traditional

264

categories as capitalistic or feudal. For side by side with the above traits are others—namely, communal land ownership, collective labor, hoe culture, production primarily for subsistence, barter, the absence of credit institutions, the lack of capital, the fear of displaying wealth except on ceremonial occasions, and the continued importance of religion and ritual in economic pursuits. A further complicating factor is that Tepoztecan economy and technology represent a fusion of elements from three distinct historical levels: the pre-Hispanic, the Spanish-colonial, and the modern western European.

Division of Labor

Division of labor by sex is clearly delineated. Men are expected to support their families by doing most of the work in the fields, by caring for the cattle, horses, oxen, and mules, by making charcoal and cutting wood, and by carrying on all the larger transactions of buying and selling. In addition, most of the specialized occupations—carpentry, masonry, and shoemaking—are filled by men. At home the men provide wood and water, make or repair furniture or work tools, repair the house, and help pick fruit. They also shell corn when the shelling is on a large scale. Politics and local government as well as the organization and management of religious and secular fiestas are also in the hands of the men.

Women's work centers about the care of the family and the house. Women cook, clean, wash, iron, do the daily marketing, shell corn for daily consumption, and care for the children. Mothers train their daughters in women's work and supervise them until their marriage. Many women raise chickens, turkeys, and pigs to supplement the family income; some grow fruit, vegetables, and flowers. Women also buy and sell on a small scale and control the family purse. Tepoztecan women are not expected to work in the fields and they look down on the women of neighboring villages who do so.

In general, women's work is less rigidly defined than men's. Many women, especially widows, engage in men's work without censure. In contrast, men almost never do women's work; the few who do are objects of ridicule. Only in the field, where there are no women, will men build a fire and warm their food without compunction. When a wife is ill or otherwise incapacitated the husband will seek out the assistance of a female relative or, even though poor, hire a servant. Occasionally one hears of a widower or bachelor who cooks and sweeps the house, but never of a man who washes or irons or grinds corn to make tortillas. For a man to be seen carrying corn to the mill is a great humiliation.

Women who have no one to support them may hire themselves out as domestic servants, laundresses, or seamstresses, or may become itinerant peddlers. The only profession an educated woman can practice in the village is that of school teacher. As a rule, women play only a minor part in public activities. The lack of rigidity in the definition of women's occupations, however, is reflected in the fact that on two occasions in the recent past, a woman has held the job of secretary of the local government, a post traditionally filled by men. Women are also members of religious organizations as well as of school committees.

Although 90 percent of the gainfully employed are agriculturists and the occupation of farming has high status, farming is not the sole occupation, as has been indicated, but is combined in various ways with other activities. Some Tepoztecans work on nearby plantations, others engage in trade or raise livestock. In 1948 there were about twenty-six nonagricultural occupations in which a total of 273 individuals took part. The occupations with the largest numbers include storekeepers (20), teachers (21), masons (25), bakers (23), *curanderos* and midwives (28), and rope makers (42). The next largest group consists of butchers (15), barbers (15), corn merchants (13), charcoal makers (13), tile and brickmakers (12), and employees of the bus line (17). In addition, there are shoemakers (5), carpenters (9), ironworkers (3), *chirimiteros*[1] (6), *huehuechiques*[2] (2), firework makers (6), mask makers (6), *mágicos* (1), silver workers (2), millers (3), druggists (2), chauffeurs (6), and plumbers (2). Fifty-three of the 273 individuals engaged in these occupations were women but they were found in only six of the twenty-six occupations, predominantly in teaching and curing.

The twenty-six occupations listed above represent a peculiar mixture of the old and the new. Some, like the *chirimiteros, huehuechiques, curanderos,* masons, mask makers, charcoal makers, and rope makers, probably had their counterpart in pre-Hispanic days. Others, such as storekeepers, shoemakers, and carpenters, have probably existed in the village since the colonial period. Still others—the teachers, bakers, millers, druggists, chauffeurs, and bus employees—are clearly more modern; most of the latter group date from the time of the construction of the road in 1936.

Land Tenure

Three kinds of land tenure are found in Tepoztlán: communal land holdings, *ejido* holdings, and private holdings. Communal lands comprise approximately 80 percent of the land of the municipio and include four of the five land types, *texcal* (see page 31), *monte, cerros,* and *terrenos cerriles.* The communal lands belong traditionally to the municipio and are under its control. They are not divided up into plots.

Ejido lands constitute somewhat less than 5 percent of the land within the municipio and consist primarily of arable land for plow agriculture. *Ejido* lands are communally owned by the municipio but are under the control of locally elected *ejido* authorities rather than the regular municipal authorities. *Ejido* holdings differ from communal holdings in that they are divided into small plots and assigned to individuals in accord with the rules of eligibility

---

[1] Men who play traditional music on the chapel roofs at fiestas in celebration of the saints. They play the *chirimia,* a native flute.

[2] Men who perform traditional ritual in Nahuatl at some of the fiestas.

established by the National *ejido* Program. Title to the *ejido* lands rests with the nation whereas title to the municipal land rests with the municipio.

Ejido and private holdings are practically identical except that while the latter can be bought and sold, the former may remain in the same family for many years and may be passed from father to son if the need for the land can be satisfactorily proved. Private holdings also consist mostly of land used for plow agriculture, and they constitute about 15 percent of the land in the municipio. Private holdings are in fee simple and ownership must be proved by legal title. It is important to remember that in Tepoztlán all three types of land holdings are worked individually rather than collectively.

The communal lands represent one of the oldest forms of landholding, and in Tepoztlán they have shown a remarkable stability down through the years. Actually, the system of communal landholding has remained practically intact through both the Aztec and Spanish conquests. Indeed, the similarity between the policy of the Spanish and of the Aztec conquerors of Tepoztlán toward the system of communal landholdings is noteworthy.

The titles for the communal landholdings of the municipio are precious possessions to the villagers and responsibility for their safekeeping is entrusted to one of the members of the local government in Tepoztlán. These titles are used principally in settling boundary disputes with neighboring municipios. The disputes have been going on for hundreds of years and loss and recovery of the land titles have occurred again and again in the history of the municipio.

In theory, any individual from any one of the eight villages of the municipio has the right to use any of the communal lands in the municipio provided he obtains permission from the municipal authorities or, as at the present time, from the forestry and *ejido* authorities. In practice, however, each of the eight villages has come to consider certain lands, generally those nearest the particular village, as its own. Thus moral boundaries have developed and are recognized by all concerned.

Although the municipio of Tepoztlán has managed to hold most of the communal lands intact against the encroachment of neighboring haciendas, before the Revolution of 1910-20 the *caciques* or ruling elite of the village prohibited the rest of the villagers from using the communal lands in order to assure a cheap labor supply for themselves. One of the most important results of the Revolution was that the communal lands were made available to all Tepoztecans.

The *ejido* lands are a relatively recent phenomenon, dating from after the Revolution. In 1929, Tepoztlán received 2,100 hectares of land in restitution from the Hacienda of Oacalco. Two hundred and sixty-seven (31 percent) Tepoztecan families now hold *ejido* parcels all of which are less than three hectares in size. Of these families, 109 also own private land; the remaining 158 have *ejidos* only.

Only 36 percent or 311 of the 853 families in the village own private land. Thus in a village where the family ideal is to own a plot of land, 64 percent own no land. Moreover, the landholdings are extremely small: over

90 percent of all holdings are less than nine hectares and 68 percent are less than four hectares. A villager with fifteen or more hectares is considered a large landowner, and only two holdings are between twenty-five and twenty-nine hectares. The size of cornfields, incidentally, is very small because many of the holdings are fragmented into parcels which are located in different places. The large number of landless people and the small size of holdings result primarily from the poverty of resources, however, rather than from the concentration of landownership in the hands of a few individuals.

The land problem in Tepoztlán is not a recent one. It was at least as severe in the twenties before the *ejido* grants and it was certainly more acute before the Revolution. Thirty years ago the 158 families who now have *ejido* parcels were landless. Thus the *ejido* program in Tepoztlán has had at least two beneficial effects. It has reduced the number of landless families and it has helped some families who had insufficient land to increase their holdings. But the *ejido* program has by no means solved the land problem, since 384 families still remain landless and have little prospect of becoming landowners. Nor has Tepoztlán benefited from the great advances in agriculture which have occurred in other parts of Mexico as a result of hydroelectric projects and of mechanization. There is still not a single tractor in the village and most families continue to work their tiny subsistence holdings by means of primitive methods.

Agricultural Systems

Two contrasting types of agriculture which represent different historical and technological levels exist side by side in Tepoztlán. One is the primitive pre-Hispanic cutting and burning system of hoe culture; the other is the more modern post-Hispanic agriculture which uses plow and oxen. The differences between hoe culture, locally known as *tlacolol,* and plow culture are not limited to the use of different tools; each system has far-reaching social and economic implications.

In Tepoztlán, both plow culture and hoe culture have been known since the Spanish Conquest. In hoe culture the land used is steep and rocky, while in plow culture it is less sloping, relatively treeless, and includes the broad valley bottom in the southern part of the municipio. Hoe culture is practiced on communally owned land and necessitates a great deal of time and labor but very little capital. Plow culture is practiced on privately owned land and requires relatively little time and labor but considerable capital. The former depends almost exclusively on family labor; the latter depends to a greater extent on hired labor. In hoe culture the yields are much larger than in plow culture, but the amount of corn planted by each family is relatively small and never reaches the amount planted by a few of the larger operators in plow culture. In hoe culture rotation of land is a necessity, for the fields cease to produce after the first few years; in plow culture the same fields may be planted year after year until the soil is completely exhausted.

Hoe culture is essentially geared to production for subsistence, while plow culture is better geared to production for the market. It is significant that most families who work *tlacolol* are landless and that *tlacolol* has traditionally been viewed as the last resort of the poor. Farmers who own small plots of land, however, may also work some *tlacolol* to supplement their meager income. Indeed, in the past few years inflation has brought a new trend to the village. Tepoztecans who own considerable land now rent it out or let it rest and work *tlacolol*. Twelve of twenty families who own private land and also hold an *ejido* grant now work *tlacolol;* these twelve are among the large landowners. This is resented by most *tlacololeros* who believe that the communal lands should serve the landless.

Other differences between hoe culture and plow culture include the cycles of work, the tools, the type of corn, the work techniques, and even the terminology. Generally speaking, the tools and techniques used in *tlacolol* are still known by their Nahuatl names, while in plow culture Spanish names prevail. Still another difference results from the location of the lands involved. With few exceptions the privately owned land used for plow culture is much closer to the village than the *tlacolol* lands. *Tlacololeros* usually rise at 4:00 A.M., walk for about two or three hours to reach their fields, and return home a few hours later than plow culture farmers.

The basic tools of production in plow culture are the plow, the machete, and the hoe and ax. Two types of plow are used: the *arado criollo* (wooden plow) and the *arado polco* (steel plow). The wooden plow was introduced by the Spaniards shortly after the Conquest. Before the Revolution of 1910-20 the steel plow was used only by a small number of families, and as late as 1926-27 Redfield reported only a few steel plows. By the early thirties, however, plows generally became more widely used, and in 1943 most farmers had steel plows as well as wooden plows, each kind being used for different operations. In 1943, approximately 213 families in the village (or 48 percent) owned plows.

Oxen have been used in the village since colonial times. In 1944, however, there were only 179 teams of oxen and only 57 percent of the landowners had oxen. There is little local buying and selling of oxen; most of them are bought in the neighboring state of Guerrero, although for many years the trip there was dangerous. The few villagers who traveled to Guerrero did so with considerable risk but also with considerable profit.

The work cycle of plow culture consists of four stages; preparing the land, planting, cultivating, and harvesting. The breaking of new land is known as the *barbecho;* the plowing of land formerly under cultivation is known as *los tres arados*. The system of plowing used in each case differs considerably. Most farmers prefer to break new land during the rainy season, generally in August, in preparation for planting the following year. The steel plow is used in the *barbecho* and the land is plowed in one continuous furrow to form a concentric rectangle. Tepoztecans pride themselves on having straight rows of corn and compete with one another to see who can plow the straightest.

One man with a single team of oxen can plow on an average of about two-fifths of an acre a day. If time permits, about two *barbechos* are made. In preparing a field that was under cultivation the previous year, the steel plow also is used and three plowings are made. The third plowing forms part of the process of planting.

Planting usually starts in early June after the rains have begun. The selection of seed for planting is generally made soon after the harvest in January; at that time the finest ears of corn are set aside to be shelled in May or June just before planting. Some Tepoztecans still hold to the tradition of having the seed blessed by the priest on May 15th, the day of San Isidro. The women select about ten of the finest ears of corn as well as some of the best beans and squash and take them to the church. They may also take along some copal and a censer. As they burn incense in the church the priest appears and blesses the seed with holy water. The corn that has been blessed is placed in the corn fields to rot; it must not be burned or the seed will not grow.

The ancient custom of addressing the seed in Nahuatl is no longer practiced but is still remembered by most men over fifty. The corn was spoken to in a short formal ritual just before it was planted in the fields, and often this ceremony was the occasion of great emotion and even of weeping. One of the speeches began, "My beloved body and strength go and bear the cold and the storm of the seasons; all is for us." A few Tepoztecans still follow a similar ritual today except that the recitations are in Spanish and the references are to the Christian God. "God bless you. I bury you and if you return while I live the satisfaction will be mine; if not then my descendants."

The corn fields usually are cultivated two or three times at twenty-day intervals. After the third cultivation, about mid-August, the corn plants in the first and last two rows of the *milpa* are hilled by hand with the *coa*. This hilling symbolizes the end of cultivation and it is looked upon as a decoration or an adornment of the work of cultivation. It also serves to strengthen the outside rows against the wind and Tepoztecans believe that it protects the inside of the corn field.

The termination of cultivation is celebrated by a fiesta both in the fields and at home. Immediately after the last hilling some of the villagers walk around the field and recite the following typical speech: "Now I have fulfilled my obligations of attending and cultivating you as you deserve. Now if you do not want to produce, that is your responsibility. For my part I now retire." A wooden cross is sometimes put in the center of the *milpa* after the last row is cultivated, and prayers and religious songs are intoned by the owner. Fireworks are set off, and bread and cheese, tequila and punch are served to the workers. The oxen are decorated with flowers and with pictures of San Isidro. The oxen are then driven home, more food and drink are consumed, and firecrackers are set off in the patio.

Toward the end of September when the first corn is ripe, the villagers go to the fields for another celebration during which they roast corn and drink punch. On September 28th, the day of San Miguel, they carry crosses made of *pericón* which have been blessed by the priest and place them on ach side of the *milpa* to protect it against strong winds. According to an old belief, if the corn is damaged by winds it is because the dancers who represent El Tepozteco at the fiesta of September 8th did not perform properly. Between ate September and early November there is little work in the fields. During this time the villagers pick the hog plums from the native *ciruela* trees, look after their animals, cut wood, and take care of various tasks around the house.

Harvesting consists of stripping the leaves in early November and of picking the corn in early December. Each family, sometimes with the aid of hired labor, harvests its own fields. By early January most fields are harvested and the corn is stored in storage bins, usually without being shelled so that it will better resist the corn worms which are a great problem to Tepoztecans. Many families leave the corn on the cob until April or May, the women shelling only what they need for daily use or for small-scale trade. Later the men do large-scale shelling, using as a sheller either the black volcanic rock or dry corncobs bound together in the form of a flat disc over which the corn is rubbed. The shelled corn is usually stored in sacks, although a few families still have the ancient clay storage bin or *cuescomatl*. Many families place a skeleton of a dog's head or a piece of pine wood and lime in the sacks to protect the corn against spoilage. According to an old belief, a death in a house will make the corn more subject to the ravages of insects.

Corn yields vary a great deal from field to field and from year to year on the same field. According to Tepoztcán classifications, first-class land will produce on an average of two *cargas* of corn on the cob for every *cuartillo* of corn seed planted; second-class land will produce an average of one *carga* for each *cuartillo* of seed; third-class land about half a *carga*. Thus the productivity of the best land is about four times that of the poorest. Most Tepoztecans do not use fertilizer; they are aware of its benefits but are unable to use it because of the shortage of manure and the cost of commercial fertilizer.

There is considerable variation in the number of man days of work necessary for clearing, planting, cultivating, and harvesting a corn field. The most important variables are the nature of the terrain, the quality of the soil, the speed of the oxen and the workers, and the type of seed used. The total number of man days of work needed for the production of one hectare of corn ranges from 35 to 65 with about 50 days as an overall average. This estimate, however, does not include the many days the peasant spends in guarding his field against cattle and trespassers. Of the 50 days, by far the most time is spent in cultivation and in harvesting. The preparation of the fields and the planting take relatively little time.

The land used for hoe culture is of two distinct types and located in different parts of the municipio. The first type is known as *texcal*, land covered with black volcanic rock and a semideciduous scrub forest where the leaves fall and rot during the dry season and make a rich but thin topsoil in little pockets among the rocks. The second type is known as *cerros*[3] and refers

---

[3] The term *cerros* here refers both to the spectacular buttelike rock outcroppings which surround the village and to the steep slopes covered with scrub forest.

to the steep slopes or mountainsides. Most of the *cerros* used for hoe culture are lime rockbeds with rock outcroppings. Both types of land are at some distance from the village.

In 1944, there were 189 families, or 21 percent of all families in the village, in which one or more members worked *tlacolol* land. Over 50 percent of these *tlacololeros* lived in the three larger barrios of Tepoztlán but they were only a very small percentage of the total number of families in these barrios. In the smaller and poorer barrios, on the other hand, *tlacololeros* constituted a much higher percentage of the families. About 96 families, or 50 percent, of all *tlacololeros* depended solely upon *tlacolol;* that is they had no private land or *ejido*. Thirty-nine *tlacololeros* owned small private parcels, 34 held *ejidos,* and 20 had both private land and *ejido*.

Most *tlacolol* clearings are small, requiring on the average between eight and twelve *cuartillos* of seed; the largest takes thirty-five. The great amount of labor necessary for clearing *tlacolol* land and the shortage of land are the two main factors responsible for the small size of *tlacolol* plots. Moreover, since *tlacolol* is definitely viewed as subsistence agriculture, any man who cleared inordinately large areas would incur the wrath of other villagers.

The use of plow and oxen for *tlacolol* is ruled out because of the steep and rocky terrain. Work in *tlacolol* begins in January, and a villager requires approximately 50 days to clear enough land to plant twelve *cuartillos* of corn seed. The trees are cut with an ax and the bush is cleared with a machete. Most *tlacolol* clearings are used two years in succession, however. The cut trees and brush dry out until April when they are burned and the ashes used as fertilizer. Enclosures of rocks and brush are built around the clearings to keep out stray animals. Planting begins in May before the rains. A small hole about four to six inches deep is made wherever there is enough soil, and the seeds are dropped in. There are no orderly rows and, unlike plow culture methods, there is no cultivation. There is usually only one weeding, after which the corn is left to grow, but occasional visits are made to the clearings to check the enclosures. Harvest procedures are very much the same as for plow culture.

One of the most striking differences between hoe and plow culture is the much greater amount of time necessary for the former. Approximately three times more man days are needed to produce one hectare of corn in *tlacolol* than in plow culture—that is, an average of 150 days as compared to 50. The single job of weeding by hand takes more time than all three cultivations with plow. There is also a great difference in the total time spent in preparation of the land, and a somewhat longer time period is spent for harvesting and transporting in *tlacolol* than in plow culture because the *tlacolol* fields are farther from the village. Fencing the *tlacolol* is time consuming and must be repeated each time a new *tlacolol* is opened; private *milpas* and *ejidos* in contrast have permanent stone fences.

In addition to the difference in actual time spent, there is also a difference in the nature of the work. Work in *tlacolol* is infinitely more exhausting than work in plow culture. Weeding by hand leaves welts on the hands of the toughest *tlacololero* that last for days and it is said that a *tlacololero* is known by his hands. But there is less time pressure in *tlacolol*. A man can clear his land any time between January and April. He can work for a few days at a clearing, spend a few days doing some other job, then return to the clearing. After planting there is considerable time leeway before the first and only weeding. This is not the case in plow culture, where once a field has been planted the cultivations must follow at regular intervals or the yield will be appreciably cut. The differences between the work cycles of the two systems are shown in the following chart:

Plow Culture	Month	Hoe Culture
	January	Clearing land with
	February	machete and ax
No work in fields	March	No work
	April	Burning brush,
	May	fencing, seeding
Clearing land, plowing, seeding	June	
First cultivation	July	Reseeding
Second cultivation		
Third cultivation	August	Weeding
Visits to field	September	
Weeding	October	Visits to field
Stripping corn stalks	November	
Harvesting and transporting corn	December	Harvesting and transporting corn

The average yield from hoe culture is about twice as high as that from plow culture. This would seem to make hoe culture very attractive, but there are a number of reasons why more villagers do not work *tlacolol*. The difficulty of the work discourages many, and the fact that *tlacolol* has traditionally been considered work for the poor and for the Indian is also a factor. Furthermore, many families who work as peons have no corn at harvest and must earn cash to support themselves. In other words, even in the case of *tlacolol* which takes so little capital, a man must have some corn (capital) to tide him over the long periods of time necessary for clearing the scrub forest. By far the most important reason, however, is the limited amount of *tlacolol* land, a shortage which has been felt more and more as the number of *tlacololeros* has increased. By its very nature the *tlacolol* system of cutting and burning demands large reserve areas, for it takes about ten years for cleared land to grow back into scrub forest and be worth clearing again. If all the villagers were to open *tlacolol* clearings in a single year, plantings in new clearings could not be made again for at least ten years.

At the base of this situation is one of the crucial problems in Tepoztlán —namely, the rapid increase of population with no accompanying increase in resources or improvement in the techniques of production. The increase in the number of *tlacololeros* represents rather a return to a more primitive type of production in an effort to escape the devastating effects of a money economy during a period of inflation. *Tlacolol* helps to resolve the immediate problem but it is by no means a satisfactory long-range solution. Were Tepoztlán a primitive culture with a small population, the system of *tlacolol*, although wasteful and inefficient, might be feasible. But in the face of an increasing population and of higher standards of living, the primitive *tlacolol* no longer is adequate. The necessity of clearing new plots of land every second or third year, the rapid depletion of the land and its forest resources, and the consequent danger of erosion are problems which will soon have to be reckoned with.

Livestock, Industry, and Trade

Tepoztlán has relatively little livestock and most of it is of poor quality. The Revolution of 1910-20 destroyed most of the herds and the present supply has been acquired slowly and with difficulty since that time. Cattle raising has never been an important industry in Tepoztlán and was never well integrated into the local economy. Climate and topographical conditions in the municipio are not conducive to large-scale stock raising, since the land is steep, rocky, and forested and the little level land is used for agriculture. Beginning in December, pasture becomes progressively scarcer and by March the cattle are excessively thin. During these months the herds are generally reduced by 15 to 20 percent.

The care given to animals is minimal and consists mostly of guarding them against being stolen or lost. Much time is devoted to this, irrespective of whether a family owns one or two animals or a herd of thirty or forty, for cattle stealing is one of the major hazards of cattle raising. Some families have lost over twenty-five head of cattle in a few years. It is said that cattle stealing increases markedly before important fiestas. Cattle owners often pay the priest to say a Mass for the protection of the cattle.

Animal ownership is on a small scale and is limited to a relatively small proportion of the villagers. Only 179, or 21 percent, of the families own cattle. Well over 50 percent of these families have between one and three cows and about 40 percent from four to ten cows. In 1943, the largest herd was over seventy head although estimates obtained in 1947 showed two herds of 150 head each. Cattle owners are expected to contribute generously to religious fiestas. When a villager sells a cow or an ox he usually lights a candle to El Señor de Ixcatepec. At rodeos and bullfights the larger herdowners contribute bulls and also money for *ponche* and fireworks. Most cattle owners have an image of San Antonio, the patron saint of cattle, in their homes. To keep cattle from wandering away it is customary to cut off hair from the ear of the cow or ox and bury it under the hearth.

The ownership of oxen is limited to 177, or 20 percent, of the families. This low percentage indicates the small extent to which Tepoztecan peasants own one of the basic means of production. The distribution of horses, donkeys, and mules as owned by families—28 percent, 11 percent, and 14 percent, respectively—reflects the local evaluation of work animals. Mules are more popular than donkeys, and horses are valued most highly. Riding horses in contrast to work horses are considered a luxury. The prestige associated with horse ownership probably goes back to the colonial period when only the leading men in the village were allowed to ride horses. Hogs are more generally owned by the villagers: about 40 percent of Tepoztecan families have at least one hog and many have two or three.

Most of the animals that are used for food are slaughtered in the village itself, for there is very little trade in cattle or hogs outside of the municipio. There is also relatively little buying and selling of cattle and oxen within the village since most of these animals are traditionally purchased in the state of Guerrero where prices are lower. The price of livestock, like that of most items, has increased sharply since the turn of the century, but the sharpest increase has occurred since 1940.

Milk is sold locally by about a dozen families, the local market consisting of a small but growing group of school teachers and Mexican tourists. Most of the milk produced, however, is converted into cheese which also is sold in the village. Milk products are used for medicinal purposes—whey, cheese, and butter for skin rashes and cheese as a poultice for snake bites. Some families use as a purgative milk in which a cow's tail has been soaked.

The production of charcoal is one of the most important sources of income for many families, especially for the poor. Generally it is carried on as a part-time activity by farmers during the slack season, but in the smaller barrios of San Sebastian, San Pedro, and Los Reyes it is a full-time occupation for many men. Until 1947, most of the charcoal was transported by burro to Yautepec, but since that time the bus line has agreed to transport it and now much of it goes to Cuernavaca.

Another important supplementary source of income for farmers is the sale of *ciruelas* or hog plums. Although they first became a cash crop when the railroad was built, it was not until the building of the highway in the thirties that trade in plums expanded. Merchants from Mexico City and Cuernavaca now send their trucks to Tepoztlán during the harvest to gather up the fruit which has been brought together by a few Tepoztecan middlemen.

Rope making is an important home industry among the poorer families in the barrio of San Sebastian. It is a family affair, requiring two or three persons for the major operation of twisting. The *ixtle* fiber is obtained from the maguey plants which grow on the communal lands. Only about a half of the persons who make rope gather their own *ixtle* fiber, however; the other half buy it.

Circulation and Distribution of Goods

Circulation of goods in the municipio is carried on by means of the local market, stores, itinerant merchants, intervillage trade, the sale and purchase of goods in Cuernavaca and other large towns, and the exchange and barter of goods between families in the village. Changes in the means of communication during the last twenty years have made some of these factors more important than others. In general, the effect of the highway has been to weaken the local market, to increase the importance of stores and trade relations with Cuernavaca, to decrease the extent of intervillage trade within the municipio, and to abolish completely earlier trade relations with other villages in the region.

The market days in Tepoztlán are Wednesdays and Sundays. As in Redfield's time, vendors from the satellite villages and from more distant localities gather in the central plaza where they offer their wares. Each of the seven villages of the municipio has its traditional place in the market, but it is only on a rare occasion that vendors from all the villages appear on the same day. In comparison with intervillage markets in a Oaxaca town of comparable size, the Tepoztecan market seems very poor indeed. Relatively little care is given to the display of food, and goods are limited in variety.

No organized credit facilities exist in Tepoztlán, nor is there any *ejido* credit. A few money lenders make loans at an interest rate of from 10 to 12 percent per month. Money loans are made by oral or written agreement but in many cases some property is necessary as security. The practice of pawning property as security for a loan is common. Usually the property is land, oxen, or *ciruela* trees, but smaller items such as an iron or even a woman's *rebozo* may be pawned for small loans from neighbors. Borrowing money is for the most part limited to emergency situations—for food, doctors, medicine, a funeral, or a wedding. There is little borrowing for investment in capital goods or for starting a business. Borrowing is considered more as an act of desperation than as a matter of everyday business. The idea of borrowing money from the bank in Cuernavaca is foreign to the thinking of all but a few sophisticated villagers.

Wealth Differences

The concepts of rich and of poor are frequently used by the villagers, but the terms are used in a relative way, are not easily defined, and are applied as a rule to individuls rather than to groups. All Tepoztecans tend to characterize themselves as poor, and there is little ostentatious display of wealth on the part of the rich. As noted earlier, the concealing of wealth is a deep-seated trait, the purpose of concealment being to avoid envy, the claims of friends, and taxes and contributions to the church and public affairs. Such an attitude tends to limit the function of wealth as a factor in social stratification. This is not to say, however, that there is a cult of poverty or that poverty is considered a desirable state.

In general, the rich are not readily distinguishable from the poor. Both work the land dressed in the same white *calzones* and huaraches; both hire day laborers when necessary. Men who own property, as well as those who do not, hire themselves out as day laborers when they need cash. Employees are frequently relatives, *compadres,* or friends with whom the employer has a reciprocal arrangement of aid or labor. There are no Tepoztecans who employ workers on a large scale; three or four peons are considered a good number, and they are hired for short periods during the busiest parts of the agricultural cycle. The relations between employer and employee are largely characterized by a spirit of mutual cooperation as well as by a recognition of equality of status. The employer works side by side with his workers, addressing them as *tu* if they are his own age and with the respectful *Usted* if they are older. In most cases a peon works for someone else only if he receives good treatment; frequently he feels that he is conferring a favor upon his employer by working for him. Full-time domestic servants in Tepoztlán are few, for women consider it humiliating to be servants. Orphans or daughters of the very poorest families seek such employment but they prefer to work in Cuernavaca or in Mexico City rather than in their own village.

The village does not have a leisure class nor is there any social stigma attached to physical labor. Many of the rich families were once poor and they cling to the habits of hard work and frugality. A rich man may explain the poverty of a neighbor in terms of his being backward, lazy, and ignorant, but he will treat him with due respect in most situations. There is sensitivity to differences in economic status but there are few barriers to social interaction. The villagers, however, tend to prefer the company of their equals or inferiors to that of people in a superior economic position.

Despite these leveling characteristics, the differences in wealth are striking. The rich have a somewhat higher standard of living than the poor: they eat better, dress better, and live in more comfortable homes. Twelve items were mentioned most frequently by informants as constituting wealth in the village. These were *ejido* plots, privately owned land, teams of oxen, plows, cattle, burros, mules, horses, hogs, sewing machines, plum trees, and urban property—that is, the ownership of more than one housesite. These items all have one characteristic in common: they are all means of production and a source of income.

To rank the families according to their wealth, we devised a point scale using one point for every hundred pesos of value. Points were assigned to each of the above twelve items in accordance with its approximate sale value, its approximate production value, or both. A score was obtained for a given family by adding the number of points accorded to each item. Families were then classified into different groups. It was found that 81 percent fell into the lowest group (point score 0-39); 13.9 percent fell into the middle group (40-99); and 4.4 percent in the upper group (100-407.4). The lowest group may be further broken down into three sub-groups: those with a 0 score, those from 1-19, and those from 20-39; these we shall call I-A, I-B, and I-C respectively. The middle group will be referred to as II, and the upper group as III-A (100-159) and III-B (160 and over).

The families with zero scores consist for the most part of young married men, most of whom live with parents who also have low scores; or they are widows or old men many of whom live alone. One-third of the group consists of women who manage to earn a living by small-scale trade and odd jobs. Groups I-A and I-B, in which there are 511 families with scores of 0-19, contain 97 percent of the landless people of the village and 354, or 70 percent, of the families in this group have zero scores for land. Approximately one-third of these people are *tlacololeros* but all of them depend upon a variety of activities which together with *tlacolol* provide a meager income. Many burn charcoal, sell wood, work as peons, are small traders, or have some other part-time occupation. They have some measure of security in that most of them own their own housesites or will inherit them. About one-third have hogs. Less than a third own a mule, horse, or donkey.

The 119 families in Group II include most of the artisans and merchants as well as the better-to-do farmers. The artisans and merchants are the most acculturated group in the village. They wear ready-made clothing, send their children out of the village to high school, and generally have a higher standard of living.

Group III consists of 38 families all of which have high scores on land, cattle, or both. About one-half of these families inherited their land from wealthy relatives who before the Revolution were *caciques* and dominated the village. The other half have worked their way up to their present position. It is the members of Group III who do not go in for modern dress or for ostentatious spending. They are a hard-working people and not a leisure class. One of their distinguishing characteristics is that they generally have hired men all year around, but they nevertheless work side by side with their peons.

Institutionalized barriers to vertical mobility do not exist in Tepoztlán. No single group has a monopoly of the means of production or of the sources of wealth. Nor does any group control sufficient capital or labor to achieve wealth by its use or exploitation. The rate of capital accumulation is very slow because of the limited natural resources, the poor technology, the low productivity, and also because of the spending patterns, particularly for fiestas. Nevertheless a trend toward the concentration of wealth is apparent, especially in land. The upper economic group, although constituting only 4 percent of all the families, owns approximately 25 percent of the land and this includes some of the best land. Cattle ownership shows a similar trend.

Two points should be emphasized here: first, that there are no younger men as heads of families in the upper economic group; and second, that the majority of the young men now in Group I and II have little prospect of ever achieving a top position. In this sense little upward mobility is possible in Tepoztlán. Most Tepoztecans are themselves convinced of the impossibility of becoming wealthy and accordingly do not organize their lives around the goal of wealth. It is mainly among the families of Group II that higher aspirations obtain and it is in this group that there is some upward mobility.

Despite the wealth differences in Tepoztlán, there are no clearly delineated class differences in the sense of broad social groupings differentiated from each other by distinctive modes of life and cultural expression. Sex, age, kinship, and occupation are the basic factors in social differentiation; differences in wealth, education, and living standards distinguish individuals but not cohesive social groups. As indicated earlier, the economic and social bases for class stratification were largely swept away by the Mexican Revolution of 1910-20. As of 1943, Tepoztlán might best be described as a community with incipient social stratification which will probably become intensified with the greater contacts with the outside, the increased wealth, and greater occupational specialization.

Tepoztlán does not show the full spectrum of the national Mexican class structure. There is no upper class of industrialists, bankers, factory owners, or even large landowners. Nor is there a rural proletariat, since the communal lands are available to the landless. Most of the people, then, are poor peasants and might be classified as a part of the rural lower class segment of Mexico. From a social and economic point of view, the contrast between the landholders and the landless among the peasants is not sharp because most holdings are tiny and Tepoztecans with an acre of land do not live much better than those without it, even though landownership of any size is considered highly desirable. The landless and the landowners certainly do not constitute distinct social classes. Moreover, there is a general similarity in the value systems between most of the people in the nonagricultural occupations and the peasants. In 1943, most of the carpenters, bakers, barbers, mask makers, and merchants were also part-time peasants and almost all of them came from families who were still peasants or of peasant origin.

Carrying corn to the mill.

4

Social Structure

THE SOCIAL STRUCTURE of Tepoztlán may perhaps be best understood in terms of various levels of organization: first, the village as an entity in itself with such village-wide institutions as the school, the church, the market, and so on; second, the village in relation to units smaller than itself and contained within it—namely, the barrio and the family; and third, the village in relation to units larger than itself and of which it is a part—namely, the municipio, the region and state, and the nation. These internal and external aspects of village life are closely interrelated and together constitute a continuum of socioeconomic organization. However, from the point of view of the villagers, the municipio is the crucial dividing line among the various levels. As the villager moves from the nuclear family to the barrio, to the village, and to the municipio, his relationships progressively become somewhat more distant and formal but he is still within a primary community where social, economic, political, and even personal bonds are quite strong. When he moves outside of the municipio of Tepoztlán, however, he moves into another kind of world. Here his knowledge of geography becomes vague, while the distinctions between villager and city person, between *paisano* and stranger, between *gente humilde* and *gente de cultura*, become sharp.

Throughout the levels of social organization certain basic themes or principles may be discerned. One is a strong in-group feeling among the members of a unit (family, barrio, and so forth) in relation to other units at the same level. Barrio members identify with their own barrio against other barrios, with their village against other villages, each jealously guarding its rights. This first principle may be called the isolating or boundary-establishing principle. A certain amount of pride and even of competitiveness is involved here. The in-group feeling should be conceived of as a gradient, however, which is strongest at the family level and becomes weaker as one moves out to the larger units. The occasions for acting out the sense of solidarity occur much less frequently in the larger than in the smaller units. For example, the sense of municipal solidarity will come into play during boundary disputes but a sense of family solidarity might be aroused daily.

A second principle, which runs in a somewhat different if not opposite direction to that of the first, is the principle of nucleation. A related principle is the dominance of the center over the periphery, the larger units over the smaller. The settlement pattern in highland Mexico is characterized by relatively self-contained nuclear groupings or pockets; the small number of villages which make up these pockets are centrally located so that the density of the population decreases almost to zero as one moves from the center to the periphery. Thus the village of Tepoztlán as a central village is dominant over the surrounding villages politically, economically, and socially. Tepoztecans feel superior to the people of the outlying villages and by and large have better means of communication, a higher standard of living, and better educational facilities. As one goes from Tepoztlán to the smaller surrounding villages one finds a greater persistence of older customs, less literacy, and more people who speak the Indian language. A similar relationship may be seen within the village itself between the larger central barrios and the smaller outlying barrios.

A third characteristic of the social organization of the village may be termed the principle of familism, by which is meant that an individual's primary loyalties are to his nuclear family. The bonds of kinship are those in which Tepoztecans place the greatest trust, and whatever social relations they have outside of the family are always fraught with caution if not suspicion. This great absorption within the nuclear family, combined with the weakness of the extended family, tends to make for narrow horizons, for self-interest, and for an atomistic quality in the social structure. It also helps to explain much of the quality of interpersonal relations, which will be discussed later. Although the discrete family units are organized into such larger units as the barrio, the village, and the municipio, these organizational forms are relatively impersonal; they do not impinge as directly upon the lives of the individual as does, for example, the extended family, the clan, or the caste, on the members of societies organized on these bases. In addition, the connection between the village and the state and federal government is in terms of elected officials who vote as members of their *demarcación,* an arbitrary political subdivision of the village that has little meaning for the villagers. In other words, in Tepoztlán, unlike more primitive societies, most of the organized relations outside of the immediate family are based upon social, religious, or political factors rather than upon kinship ties.

The nuclear familism of Tepoztlán must be understood from a historical point of view. It may be seen as a defensive reaction to the disorganizing effects of the Spanish Conquest which destroyed the ancient Indian *calpulli* or clan and transferred its landholding and other functions to the newly established village government. Because communal lands have persisted and because most Tepoztecans have not had private landholdings, the extended family has had little opportunity to develop as a corporate landholding group. This explains in part why Tepoztecans have a weak genealogical sense and why, in spite of the stability of the population and the great age of the village, most of them do not know who their great grandparents were. The present-time orientation of the villagers is due in large part to the cutting off of the extended family horizons.

The contemporary social structure of Tepoztlán may be seen as an interaction between two opposing elements, one the more collectivistic tradition of the Indian heritage with its communal lands and collective labor, the other the more individualistic and isolating familism. As we shall see, however, a major trend reveals that both the pre-Hispanic forms and the defensive familism are being superseded by new forms resulting from the increasing integration of the village in the modern Mexican nation.

The Village and the Nation

Three aspects of the relationship between the village and the nation may be distinguished—namely, the villagers' knowledge of the geography and history of the nation, the extent to which they perceive themselves as Mexicans, and the degree to which national institutions operate on the village level and affect the villagers' lives. The villagers think of themselves first and foremost as Tepoztecans but they readily identify themselves as Mexicans. Indeed, they refer to their ancient indigenous language not as Nahuatl but as Mexicano.

Despite this easy linguistic identification, however, their concepts of modern Mexico as a nation are quite limited. Most Tepoztecans know the names of some of the states even though, as of 1948, few had traveled beyond the state of Morelos and portions of the neighboring states of Mexico, Guerrero, and Puebla. But many villagers have had occasion to deal with people from other states. During the Revolution they came into contact with soldiers from various parts of the country; at one time norteños from Coahuila camped in Tepoztlán for months, and the villagers still speak of their strange customs. Tepoztecans also are familiar with many of the Mexican regional stereotypes. For example, they "know" that people from Monterrey are stingy and that Yucatecans are squareheads. The geographic horizons of younger people who have had some schooling are, of course, much broader.

The school has been one of the most important agencies in developing an awareness of and a sense of identification with the nation. With the federalization of the schools in the twenties, texts and teaching materials were standardized. The Mexican government eliminated most texts written by foreigners and substituted those written by Mexicans. The latter, seeking to arouse Mexican nationalism, used stories of Mexican Indians rather than of children of other lands and gave Mexican national heroes a prominent place. Moreover, the school personnel in Tepoztlán began to be recruited from various parts of the country rather than, as formerly, only from Morelos. Tepoztecans have had teachers from Yucatan, Oaxaca, Jalisco, and Nuevo Leon, and from them they have learned about the dances and customs of other regions.

The large new elementary school building, named *Escuadrón 201* after a squadron of Mexican aviators who were stationed in the Philippines in World War II, stands as a symbol of *Mexicanidad* to the villagers. The school was constructed in the early forties with national funds on the direct order of President Avila Comacho. Thanks to the school, the commemoration of such national holidays as September 15 (national independence) is assuming more importance in the village. At these times parents outfit their children in new uniforms, at a great sacrifice, and local officials prepare for the event months in advance.

Paralleling the work of the school is that of the traveling cultural mission, also a federal service, which has been visiting Tepoztlán for a number of years. The mission taught Tepoztecans how to make beds, chairs, and other furniture; it taught the girls sewing, knitting, and crocheting; it encouraged social dancing and sports like volleyball; it taught some women how to make inexpensive preserves; and it worked toward improving homes by persuading a few families to build privies (now in disuse) and to raise the hearth off the floor for more sanitary cooking. A mission doctor administered injections and gave advice on baby care.

Another federal service, the campaign against illiteracy, also reached Tepoztlán and helped somewhat to develop a greater awareness of the Mexican nation. Slogans used included "Mexico must be great because of its culture" and "The Fatherland must have citizens who can read." Publications which occasionally reach Tepoztlán are leaflets put out by the official party, presidential messages, and propaganda leaflets from some of the larger labor unions. The reading public in the village is still very small, however.

Other federal agencies which directly or indirectly influence the daily lives of Tepoztecans include the Department of Health, the Department of Agriculture, the Department of Indian Affairs, the Department of National Economy, *Gobernación,* and the Federal Supreme Court. All of these agencies have files on the village which date from the twenties and which reflect their increasing role in village life. Federal taxation, which touches most Tepoztecans directly, is a common subject of complaint even though the villagers pay relatively few taxes; these are mainly on the sale of charcoal, the slaughter of animals, and trade. The federal government has maintained a health clinic in Cuernavaca for years but the Tepoztecans still prefer *curanderos.* The Agrarian Department intervenes directly in the affairs of those Tepoztecans who hold land under the *ejido* program. The nationalization of some of the communal lands has lessened local control and has caused some resentment on the part of the villagers. National control of forest resources also has not gained the approval of Tepoztecans, especially when it conflicts with their local interests as in the case of charcoal production.

Perhaps the Tepoztecan peasant sees the power of the federal government most clearly in the form of federal troops. Tepoztecans are suspicious of and dislike soldiers, and when military conscription was first instituted in the forties they tried to resist it. Local feeling against conscription reached its climax when it was rumored by the Sinarquists (a right-wing political group that sympathized with the Nazis) that the young men were being prepared to fight against the Germans on orders given by the United States.

The Mexican Revolution was one of the most important factors in developing a sense of nationalism among Tepoztecans. Many of them joined the ranks of the Zapatistas and traveled widely with the guerrilla forces. Some of the *caudillos* of the Revolution, such as Zapata and Obregón, established the custom of visiting the peasants personally and discussing their problems. General Lázaro Cárdenas continued the practice, and the villagers remember his visit to Tepoztlán with pride. In 1935, Cárdenas arrived on foot without previous announcement or preparation. He set up a temporary office in the atrium of the church, where the Tepoztecans could come to see him. Their chief request was for help with the construction of the road to Cuernavaca. When their request was granted and the road was built with federal help, they began to think of the president not only as a representative of a powerful government but also as a popular figure and a friend of the peasants. It is now not uncommon for Tepoztecans to send requests or protests directly to the president. Indeed this has happened in almost every case of conflict between village factions or of boundary quarrels with neighboring municipios.

The national elections for president which occur every six years also give Tepoztecans contact with political affairs of nation-wide scope. Before the elections, delegates and politicians come to the village to organize local committees for the support of a particular group or candidate. During the campaigns the villagers begin to realize that they are acting not only as Tepoztecans but also as citizens of the Mexican nation.

Some indication of the Tepoztecan sense of belonging to the nation may be gathered from their reaction to the question of Mexico's participation in World War II. Most Tepoztecans were opposed to Mexican entrance into the war on the side of the democracies. Under the influence of Sinarquist propaganda, sympathy with the Axis powers first developed among a small but vocal sector of the population. Rumors began to circulate that Zapata was not really dead but was fighting with Hitler; this was why the Germans were winning so many victories. Latent anti-U.S. sentiment was fanned by further rumors that the Mexicans were being asked to fight to save the "gringos." The Tepoztecans accepted the Mexican declaration of war against the Axis as one of those decisions of an omnipotent federal government about which nothing could be done.

Just as Tepoztecans recognize an administrative hierarchy whose seat is in Mexico City so they recognize a religious hierarchy headed by the archbishop in Mexico City. The church in Tepoztlán has taken part in most of the recent campaigns of the national and international church organization to strengthen the church. For example, when the four hundredth anniversary of the Virgin of Guadalupe was celebrated throughout Mexico, church dignitaries came to the village to explain the great miracle of the apparition of the Virgin to Juan Diego shortly after the Conquest.

The Village and the State of Morelos

The average Tepoztecan has a more precise notion of the geography of the state of Morelos than of the nation. During the years of the Revolution many Tepoztecans traveled over large portions of the state, and many have taken trips for economic purposes or have made religious pilgrimages. Work in sugar plantations has given others some familiarity with the southern part of the state. The proximity of the state capital, Cuernavaca, also has played a part in developing a consciousness in Tepoztecans of being Morelenses. After the Revolution, the state of Morelos developed an intense political life and during the thirties a constitutional government was established. This meant that the governor and local officials were to be elected rather than imposed and that political campaigns and electioneering inevitably developed. State candidates devoted a great deal of attention to nearby Tepoztlán. In their attempts to obtain votes they appealed to a sense of state loyalty, sometimes using such slogans as "First the Morelenses and then the Mexicans."

The state of Morelos has its own civic fiestas which are celebrated with considerable flourish. Among the most important are the celebration of the birthday of Father Morelos, after whom the state was named, and celebrations of the birth and death of Emiliano Zapata, the most popular hero. As in the case of national holidays, the school is the organizing and driving force. The teachers and the school director, for example, give speeches reviewing the great achievements of Zapata and point out that five of his generals were Tepoztecans. Tepoztecans also send delegations to the official state celebration of Zapata's birthday. A few small newspapers published in Cuernavaca occasionally reach Tepoztlán but these are read chiefly by courthouse officials. Regional songs with lyrics about the state of Morelos are known to the villagers.

Tepoztecans fear and respect the power and authority of the state government. They fear the public jails and courts of Cuernavaca and the police officials who occasionally come to the village to make arrests or track down offenders. They have aversion for the state office of rents which collects the bulk of the village land taxes. Although the tax rate is very low, the state collected over sixty thousand pesos in the twelve years from 1931 to 1943, according to the official state tax records in Cuernavaca. During this same period the only state funds which were returned to the village was the salary of the state tax collector who was paid on a pro-rate basis. The *Procuradia* of the state handles property cases and summons Tepoztecans to appear in Cuernavaca for hearings. The villagers complain that this agency will summon them during the height of the agricultural season just as readily as at any other time. The governor is recognized as an important figure and is known by name to many villagers; indeed, some of them remember the names of the governors of the Díaz epoch. Tepoztecans tend to be more critical of the state than of the federal government and are less hesitant about sending a delegation to the governor than to the president.

The Village and the Municipio

The municipio is the functional resource unit for the villagers, an hence the relations of the village with the municipio are closer and more pe sonal than those with any of the larger units discussed so far. Tepoztecan know the municipio intimately; they know its geography, history, legend natural resources, people, and villages. Even small children can name th seven surrounding villages and know how to find their way to each one. Th limits of the municipio and the details of the many recurring boundary dispute with neighboring municipios are also well known. Village boundaries are vague essentially moral boundaries, but municipal boundaries are clearly demarcated It is within these bounds that the Tepoztecan has his everyday world. Here h works the communal lands, cuts and burns communal forests, grazes his cattle and hunts for medicinal herbs.

The municipio extends for about seventeen miles from the ragge mountains and heavily wooded country of the north down the slope of th Ajusco mountain range to the level, fertile lands of the sugar plantations nea Yautepec. From the northern limits to the southern limits the drop in altitud is from about 10,500 feet to about 3,700. Although most of the villages cluste near the center of the municipio, they are located at seven different levels The widest range is between San Juan in the north at about 7,000 feet and Sa Andrés in the south at about 4,300 feet. San Juan is 2,000 feet above Tepozt lán, although the villages are less than four miles apart.

The northern part of the municipio lies in *tierra fría,* or the cold zone the middle part in *tierra templada,* or the temperate zone; and the souther part in *tierra caliente,* or the hot zone. San Juan, the highest village, is at th lower limit of the *tierra fría,* while San Andrés, the lowest village, is a the upper limit of *tierra caliente.* Three of the villages, Tepoztlán proper Ixcatepec, and Amatlán, are at approximately the same level in the temperat zone. The villages each have a distinctive flora and some depend on charcoa production more than on agriculture. In San Juan, for example, there is littl crop land, no coffee trees, no hog plums, and no tropical or semitropical fruits But unlike the other villages, San Juan grows a little wheat and barley, an some potatoes, and produces a great deal of charcoal. It also has fruit or chards of peaches, pears, *capulin,* and *tejocote.* Each of the villages brings it products to the Tepoztlán market, thus making for interdependence withir the municipio.

The territorial unit which is today the municipio was already a socio political unit in pre-Hispanic times and is therefore much older than either th state of Morelos or the nation. According to legend, the surrounding village were originally defensive military outposts of the central village of Tepoztlár where political control rested.

The bonds between Tepoztlán and the surrounding villages of th municipio are numerous. The strongest bonds are the communal lands and th biweekly market at Tepoztlán. Administratively, Tepoztlán is the center ir which all municipal births, marriages, and deaths must be registered, taxe paid, and certificates of good conduct obtained. The other villages also are dependent on Tepoztlán for their religious services, baptisms, communions, Mass, and confession, for only Tepoztlán has a resident priest. On fiesta occasions a great deal of intervillage visiting occurs. Ties of marriage within the municipio, however, are relatively weak; only about a dozen persons from the other villages have married into Tepoztlán and cases of Tepoztecans going to live in the surrounding villages are practically unheard of. Ties of *compadrazgo* establish bonds between the villages of the municipio, but Tepoztlán's dominant position again is revealed by the fact that while other villagers seek out Tepoztecans to act as godparents for their children, Tepoztecans do not reciprocate.

That Tepoztecans feel superior is shown further by their characterizations of other villagers. The people of Ocotitlan are described as "dangerous," "violent," "assassins"; the people of Gabriel Mariaca as *tontos* or fools, wealthy but backward Indians. The women of Gabriel Mariaca are scorned because they work in the fields, wear straw hats, and carry heavy loads "like men." Some of the traditional Nahuatl nicknames for the surrounding villagers also are indicative of Tepoztecan attitudes: Gabriel Mariaca people are referred to as *cuatlateme* (dull heads) and those from La Calera as *cuatichtizatin* (white-headed people because they make lime).

The political dominance of Tepoztlán over the surrounding villages is clear. Although in theory, any male adult from any one of the eight villages of the municipio may become president of the municipal government, in practice he is almost always a Tepoztecan.

In recent years, conflicts over communal lands have set village against village and have seriously weakened municipal bonds. Competition which had not existed before arose when an increasing exploitation of communal resources for commercial rather than for subsistence purposes was encouraged by the coming of the railroad and the highway, and by a greater need for cash. The outlying villages finally demanded sole rights of control over the communal lands adjoining them. In effect they were insisting that moral boundaries be accepted as legal ones, in which case the communal municipal lands would be interpreted as village lands. The most serious quarrel flared up in the early twenties when the village of San Juan took advantage of the fact that the railroad ran through the village; since the railroad could transport charcoal, San Juan began to develop its charcoal industry on a commercial scale. The authorities of Tepoztlán at once challenged the right of San Juan to exploit municipal resources for the benefit of a single village. The dispute was bitter and led to violence. In the end, federal authorities had to intervene.

The Village

The physical aspects of the village, the population, language, housing, diet, clothing, and recreation have been described in earlier pages. Here we are concerned with Tepoztlán's social structure: the extent of village solidarity and identification, and the role of such village-wide organizations as the school, the market, the church, and the local government.

The village is a corporate body which enjoys legal status: it can sue and be sued in the courts. It is an administrative unit and most of the social, economic, and religious activities of the villagers take place within it. The stability of residence and the predominance of endogamous marriages (over 90 percent of all marriages are made within the village) encourage village identification, a trend which is further enhanced by the absence of well-developed class distinctions. Because each family, rich or poor, owns a house and housesite and has recognized status as a villager, each villager can proudly say "This is my village and the village of my ancestors." The sense of identification with the village is clearly apparent in those who have left it to live in Mexico City. Early in the twenties the emigrants formed a *Colonia Tepozteca* which still exists and which works in behalf of village interests. Further, many Tepoztecans in Mexico City maintain their ties with the village, visit regularly at the *Carnaval* or other fiestas, and express a wish to die and be buried in their home village. There is considerable verbalization about village community spirit. Political candidates always speak of *mi pueblo* and promise to improve the village. That once in office they may in fact do very little and are often accused by the villagers of stealing funds does not reduce the importance of village loyalty as an ideological factor that is potentially unifying.

The local government, located in the central plaza, is the most definitive expression of the village as an organized unit. The *ayuntamiento* or governing body consists of the president, the *síndico* or law enforcement officer, the *regidor* in charge of finances, and the secretary. In addition, there are the treasurer, the police chief, a sub-police chief, a judge, a secretary to the justice, and a porter. Eight *ayudantes* or delegates represent the eight *demarcaciones* into which the village is divided for governmental purposes. The president, *síndico, regidor,* and judge are elected for a two-year period. The other officials are appointed by the president in conjunction with the *síndico* and *regidor.*

The duties of the major officials are determined by state law. The president is the executive officer and the official representative of the village in its contacts with the outside. His signature is necessary for most correspondence and official acts, and he fixes the fines imposed for infractions of the law. Some of the villagers also bring their private difficulties to him—quarrels between neighbors and between husbands and wives, and litigations over property, and so forth. By far the greatest number of tasks, however, falls to the secretary of the local government who is generally the most literate of the officials. In the period from 1943 to 1948, the secretary was a competent typist, an unusual accomplishment in the village.

Salaries paid to government officials are very low even by Tepoztecan standards; the daily salary of the president is lower than the prevailing wage rate for a day laborer. Such low salaries encourage *la mordida* (the bite) or graft. The major sources of local government income are taxes from the slaughter of animals, payments in lieu of rendering public service, exemption of publication of acts in the public register, and taxes from the use of the communal lands. From 1940 to 1943, the average annual income of the government was about seven thousand pesos, a sum which covered salaries only and left nothing for public improvements. Lack of funds is one of the most demoralizing aspects of the local government, and Tepoztecans look to the federal government for help with the problem. It should be noted that the village and the municipio derive practically no income from land taxes, most of which accrue to the state government.

Public works such as improving roads and constructing public buildings are organized by the village authorities through the village *cuatequitl*, an ancient form of collective labor. Every able-bodied man between the ages of twenty-one and fifty-one is obliged to contribute twelve days a year in work. Failure to appear for service is punishable by fine or a jail sentence. A man may pay for a substitute, however, and a few of the better-to-do families prefer to do this because they consider some of the work below their dignity. The poor who cannot afford substitutes or fines are the main source of labor for the village *cuatequitl*. When the task is a relatively light one and more men are called up than are needed for the actual work, some may be asked to contribute food or drink instead of labor.

In recent years there have been relatively few *cuatequitls* of major importance but the tradition is always ready in case of an emergency. In 1925-27 the village washbasins were constructed during a socialistically oriented administration; in 1934 the village market place was improved. In the early thirties, a time when the village was split into two hostile political factions, an impressive demonstration of collective labor occurred in connection with the construction of the road to Cuernavaca. Led by two enterprising non-Tepoztecan school teachers and backed by the *Colonia Tepozteca,* the villagers decided to begin the road. The political factions known as the Bolsheviki and the Centrales refused to work side by side. Each then organized separate shifts, one beginning at Tepoztlán and working toward Cuernavaca and the other working from Cuernavaca to Tepoztlán.

The ability of the village authorities to organize the labor force of the village on crucial occasions is most impressive. In a recent boundary dispute with the municipio of Tejalpa, the authorities posted aides at all the roads and paths leading out of the village to intercept the men as they went out to their fields in the early morning. In this way six hundred men were recruited in one day to cut through the forest overgrowth and to re-establish a clear boundary between Tepoztlán and Tejalpa.

Although the village *cuatequitl* was intended as a means of benefiting the village as a whole, many obstacles have prevented its successful operation and it has been declining. The inherent individualism of Tepoztecans, their suspicious and critical attitude toward the local government, and the paucity of village funds all present difficulties. The villagers often criticize the *cuatequitl* as being a coercive rather than as a voluntary institution. Since the president and the *síndico* have the power to designate which citizens are to work in it, there is opportunity for favoritism and also for revenge against political opponents or personal enemies. It may be significant in this connection that when playing games, children will refer to the *cuatequitl* as a form of punishment. It should be noted also that historically this form of collective labor was a distinct aid to the Spanish conquerors in their organization and control of native labor.

The school, which was discussed earlier, is another important agency which helps create village-wide associations. Children from all the barrios meet at school and form friendships which tend to break down barrio localism; their parents sometimes serve on school committees. The stores, the corn mills, and the village market play a similar socializing function. Women from all parts of the village look forward to the exchange of news and gossip on their shopping trips.

Perhaps the most important single organizing and unifying factor on the village level is the central church. Catholicism with its village-wide festivals provides a common framework of symbols and ritual and brings the villagers together at the central church on all major holidays (see p. 13). The priest visits all the seven barrio chapels on special occasions. A number of religious associations are village-wide, among them the *Asociación Guadalupana,* the *Cofradia de la Virgen del Carmen,* the *Sagrado Corazón de Jesús,* and the *Acción Católica.* In 1948, the first three of these organizations each had a membership of about thirty women; the *Acción Católica* had a section of eighty boys and another section of thirty girls.

The Barrio

The village is divided into seven barrios or named locality groupings, each with its own chapel, patron saint, internal organization, and annual fiesta. The barrio is essentially a socioreligious organization with fixed boundaries and great stability; most of the present-day barrios were probably built up in the seventeenth and eighteenth centuries. The first mention of the contemporary barrios is found in a document of 1807 which is a census of the village by barrios and by the Nahuatl names of housesites within each barrio. It reveals that barrio boundaries have changed very little over the past hundred and fifty years. The names and the number of housesites of the present-day barrios are as follows: Santo Domingo, 174; San Miguel, 163; La Santísima, 139; Santa Cruz (large), 67; Los Reyes, 37; San Sebastian, 34; Santa Cruz (small), 29; and San Pedro, 19. With the omission of Santa Cruz (small) which, strictly speaking, is not yet an independent barrio, there are three large and four smaller barrios. The larger ones (Santo Domingo, San Miguel, and La Santísima) are grouped around the central plaza; the smaller ones are located above them on the mountain slope. Since the entire village is on a slope, the smaller barrios at the upper end are usually referred to as *los de arriba* and the larger ones at the bottom as *los de abajo.* Some Tepoztecans now refer to the paved road as the dividing line between the upper and lower halves of the village.

The barrios serve to break up the village into smaller communities which provide more opportunities for face-to-face relations. Kinship ties tend to be strongest within one's own barrio or with an adjoining one. As high as 42 percent of all marriages in a barrio occur among its own members; about 50 percent occur between persons of adjoining barrios. Most of the villagers in the smaller barrios of San Pedro, San Sebastian, and Los Reyes know each other by their first names and have considerable social interaction. The other barrios are much too large to be primary units. In all the barrios, however, most of the people have not visited the homes of any more than a dozen families in their barrio.

Barrio membership is determined mainly by ownership of a housesite in a barrio and by payment of a tax for the upkeep of the barrio chapel. In this fashion the barrio maintains its stability as a corporate unit despite any changes of residence that may occur. Since it is the housesite that traditionally belongs to one barrio or another, whoever lives on it, whether he obtains it by inheritance or by purchase, becomes a member of the barrio. Formerly, a housesite, especially in the smaller barrios, could not be sold without the agreement of the barrio members. A person usually belongs to the barrio in which he was born or raised, although a man who was born and raised in one barrio may purchase a housesite in another and establish his home there. If he pays the barrio tax and participates in the affairs of the barrio, he automatically becomes a member of the barrio where he now lives. He may for reasons of sentiment continue to support his barrio of origin and attend its fiestas, particularly if he still has relatives there, but this is voluntary.

A few persons own housesites in two or three barrios and pay taxes in each but consider themselves members of the barrio in which they live or where they were born and raised. Young couples sometimes buy a house in a barrio to which neither of them belongs and thereby acquire membership in a barrio new to both. Since patrilocal residence predominates, the men of any barrio are generally more closely related than the women. Upon marriage a woman becomes a member of her husband's barrio. Women more than men maintain dual barrio loyalties, however, and often return to their original home to help their parents prepare barrio fiesta meals.

Each barrio has a *mayordomo* who is responsible for the collection of funds for the upkeep of the chapel and for the organization of barrio members into collective work parties to clean the churchyard, repair the chapel or the streets, and help cultivate and harvest the corn on the plot of land belonging to the chapel. Preparing for the annual barrio fiesta is an extremely important job. The *mayordomo* decides how the fiesta is to be celebrated, whether to have a Mass or a sermon or both, and whether to invite a priest from Cuernavaca. He arranges for the band of musicians and for fireworks, and his family serves *mole, tamales,* and *ponche* to the guests, many of whom are from other barrios. Frequently he spends his own funds to assure a successful fiesta. Most of the expenses, however, are collected from barrio residents in the form of offerings or *limosnas;* these are considered a perpetual pledge to the saint of the barrio The *mayordomo* appoints assistants and committees for specific assignment. but he has no authority beyond his personal influence.

The selection of the *mayordomo* takes place in the barrio churchyard the evening before the Day of the Dead. Only the men participate. A bonfire is made, punch is served, likely candidates are discussed, and speeches in Na huatl are made by the older men. The *mayordomo* is usually chosen by mutual agreement; there is no tradition of formal voting. Yet the selection of the *mayordomo* comes closer to a true expression of the people's will than does the election of the village officials. The village priest does not control the choice of the *mayordomo* although he considers the barrios to be his parishes

To be eligible for the office of *mayordomo,* one must be a native of the village, a member of the barrio, and a married man, although there have been exceptions to the last requirement. A reputation for honesty and a willingness to serve the barrio are essential, for the position entails responsibility and expense. As a rule, the wealthier families do not seek the position but pressure is sometimes placed on them to accept. Formerly, the *mayordomo* was expected to serve for only one year, but in recent times a paucity of candidates especially in the smaller barrios has made it necessary for some *mayordomos* to hold office for as long as five years. Until recently, also, the position of *mayordomo* was considered a prerequisite for holding office in the local government, and a check of the members of the village council over the ten-year period from 1934 to 1943 showed that most of the presidents and *síndicos* of the local government had worked their way up through the job of *mayordomo.* This suggests an integration of secular and religious offices which is so characteristic of many Indian villages.

Important economic and social characteristics differentiate the barrios. On the whole, the smaller barrios are poorer and have a higher proportion of families that depend upon the communal lands, a higher incidence of illiteracy, and a reputation of being more Indian. San Sebastian is by far the poorest barrio, followed by San Pedro and Santa Cruz. Los Reyes is exceptional in that it has the highest proportion both of landholders and of large holdings. The larger barrios of the center, which show the widest extremes in poverty and wealth, have controlled the village politically: practically all the village presidents from 1922 to 1944 came from the three large barrios, and none from San Pedro or San Sebastian. Most of the *ejidal* authorities in the village have been selected from the central barrios, also, and the lion's share of the *ejido* land grants have gone to them.

Barrio *esprit de corps* is evidenced in interbarrio competition, especially at the annual *Carnaval,* and in the claims of superior miraculousness for some barrio saints over others. In the past, competitiveness was also evidenced in the traditional nicknames of the barrios which were believed to express an awareness of distinctive barrio personality. Thus Santo Domingo was called The Toads; La Santísima, The Ants; San Miguel, The Lizards; Santa Cruz and San Sebastian, *Cacomixtles;* Los Reyes, the Maguey Worms; and San Pedro, *Tlacuaches.* Nowadays these nicknames are rarely used and have little function in the community. *Esprit de corps* is at its height at the annual fiesta celebrated in honor of the barrio saint, which usually lasts from one to seven days. The chapel is decorated, candles are brought in ceremonially and burned, a *castillo* of fireworks is erected and burned, festal dishes are prepared, the ancient flute is played on the chapel roof, sacred dances and sometimes bullfights are held, and a Mass is said in the chapel.

During the Díaz regime, distinctions between the larger and the smaller barrios corresponded to class distinctions much more so than at present. Since the Revolution the general tendency has been toward a decrease in barrio differences. The various barrios now participate much more equally in village life. In contrast to 1926 when Redfield reported no letters arriving at the outlying barrios, by 1943 San Pedro and Los Reyes were receiving their share of the mail, and since that time this trend has been accentuated. Today contacts between the outlying barrios and the outside world are much less mediated through the center of the village.

Above, Mexican artist at his week-end village home.
Below, kitchen of a poor peasant's home.

5

The Family

TEPOZTLÁN is a family-centered community. The biological family, the predominant type, consists of parents and unmarried children and constitutes the basic production unit of the village. Families in Tepoztlán are strong and cohesive, held together by traditional bonds of loyalty, common economic strivings, mutual dependence, the prospect of inheritance, and, finally, the absence of any other social group to which the individual can turn. Cooperation within the immediate family is essential, for without a family the individual stands unprotected and isolated, a prey to every form of aggression, exploitation, and humiliation known in Tepoztlán. It is within the small biological family that Tepoztecans seek personal security.

The extended family provides some additional security, particularly in times of emergency. It is characterized by a limited reciprocity of cooperation which includes borrowing and labor exchange. No institutionalized day-to-day cooperative endeavors exist between families, related or unrelated, however, and as a rule little aid is given or received. Visiting among relatives is surprisingly infrequent; it is limited to such special occasions as the annual barrio fiesta, illnesses, births, weddings, and deaths.

Over 70 percent of the 662 village housesites are occupied by the simple biological family, only 16 percent by multiple families. Most of the latter consist of parents living with their unmarried children and also with a married son and his family. There are some cases of a married daughter living with her parents and of married siblings sharing a common housesite. The number of persons per housesite ranges from 1 (45 cases, mainly widows or widowers) to 17 (1 case), with smaller households more numerous than larger ones. Most housesites hold a single house, although some have two, three, or four.

Several factors reveal a patriarchal emphasis in family organization: a principle of male superiority (husband over wife, brothers over sisters), a strong preference for patrilocal residence, and patrilineal descent. Tepoztecans are deprecatory of matrilocal residence, saying that when a young man goes to live with his wife's family after marriage "He was given away like a dog" or "He went as a male daughter-in-law." Nevertheless, over 20 percent of all married couples showed matrilocal residence. Most of the husbands in these cases were poor young men, either orphans or men who had married much older women or women of higher social and economic status. Each person in the village is known by the surnames of both his father and mother, but the latter is always given last and with successive generations is eliminated.

The nature of interpersonal relations within the family may perhaps best be understood if we examine them as they occur between husbands and wives, parents and children, among siblings, with the extended family, and with *compadres.*

Husbands and Wives

According to the ideal culture pattern for husband-wife relations in Tepoztlán, the husband is authoritarian and patriarchal; he is master of the household and enjoys the highest status in it. He is responsible for the support of the family and for the behavior of its members, and he makes all major decisions. It is his prerogative to be given obedience, respect, and service by his wife and children. The wife is expected to be submissive, faithful, and devoted to her husband, and to ask for his advice and permission before venturing on any but the most minor enterprises. She should be industrious and manage to save money no matter how small her husband's income. She should not be critical or jealous of her husband's activities outside the home nor even show any curiosity about them.

In most homes there is outward compliance to the ideal pattern, but few husbands are the dominant figures they seek to be and few wives are completely submissive. Many marriages reveal conflict on the question of authority and the roles of the spouses. The most even-tempered marriages are those which follow a middle course: the wife does little to challenge the authority of her husband and the husband is not too overbearing toward his wife.

Conflicts of this kind between husbands and wives are fostered by a basic discrepancy between actual roles and ideal roles in the organization of the family. Even though the wife is subordinate to her husband, it is she who has the central role within the house. She is responsible for planning, organizing, and managing the household, and for the training and care of the children. The husband traditionally turns over all his earnings to her. She is thus in a position to do a great deal of spending, borrowing, and paying back in secret, particularly since in most cases the husband does not interfere with her handling of the money so long as she gives some to him whenever he asks for it. The "good" wife should not refuse her husband's requests for money; if she does she may receive a scolding or a beating. The wife is free to sell small quantities of the family corn or her own chickens and eggs. She is supposed to obtain her husband's permission before going to a doctor or a *curandero,* visiting, or buying or selling in quantity, but the husband's frequent absences permit her to do many of these things without his knowledge.

The husband's actual participation in family and household affairs is minimal. His work is outside the home. The division of labor is clear-cut; except for emergencies and for such jobs as hauling water and repairing the house, the husband does not concern himself with the house or the children. The men are gone a good part of the day, sometimes for several days at a time depending on their work and the season of the year. In the past, Tepoztecan men worked in distant mines or on haciendas, and were absent from the village for long periods; before the Revolution, large numbers of men worked on nearby haciendas and returned home only once every two weeks. At present, about 150 men work on haciendas for from four to six months during the dry season, making visits to their homes once a week. With the husband away, the wife not only is head of the family but sometimes also has to support herself and the children.

Even more important perhaps than a husband's absence from his home are his behavior and attitude when he is at home. He avoids intimacy with the members of his family with the purpose of gaining respect from them. He holds himself aloof from the petty details of the household and expects to be undisturbed by complaints, requests, or noise. Unless he is told otherwise, he assumes that the home situation is as he wants it. Since wives are held accountable for everything that happens in the home, they tend to withhold information which might bring them disapproval or punishment. Thus, the loftiness of the husband's position tends to separate him from the very persons he is trying to control and inadvertently to give his wife and children the freedom he does not wish them to have.

In many homes the husband's sense of security is a function of the extent to which he can control his wife and children or make them fear him. Wife beating, more common in the past than now but still widespread, is resorted to for offenses that range from not having a good meal ready on time to suspicion of adultery. A jealous wife or a wife who objects to her husband's activities or judgment may also receive a beating. Wives are not expected to offer any resistance to the punishment. Wife beating is a recognized legal offense in the village but few wives report their husbands to the local authorities.

Tepoztecan women readily express hostility toward men and often characterize all men as "bad." Self-pity and a sense of martyrdom are common among married women, many of whom break down and cry when telling their life stories. As they grow older they often become more self-assertive and oppose their husband's attempts to limit their freedom and their business ventures. They begin to show preference for work outside the home and to feel deprived when they are tied down by housework and children. The present trend in the village is for the younger women and even the unmarried girls to take on the more independent attitudes of the older women.

Women are more in conflict with traditional ways than are the men.

Their standards of behavior for themselves and their husbands are changing; they veer between the old ideal roles and new needs and experiences. They readily admit to the superiority of men and tend to admire a man who is *macho* or manly, yet they describe the "good" husband as one who is not dominating but relatively passive. They also tend to regard the very submissive wife more as a fool than as an ideal. Apparently the women do not feel inadequate when they do not achieve the ideal of feminine behavior; indeed, they seem to feel pride rather than guilt in self-assertion.

Husbands often find themselves in a defensive position. They must conserve the old order of things if they are to maintain their control in the home, but the changes within the village in the past twenty years or so make this objective difficult. Such technological advances as the corn mills, the road, and the bus service to Cuernavaca have affected the women more than the men. An increasing number of the more ambitious married women now raise animals, or grow fruit on a larger scale, or sell family produce at the Tepoztlán and Cuernavaca markets. The more capable women are able to help their husbands substantially, in fact, without exception, every man who has prospered since the Revolution has done so with the help of his wife. Most men balk at permitting their wives to sell at the Cuernavaca market, however, despite the fact that the extra money would be welcome. In the past, this type of work was carried on exclusively by widows or women who "had no man to control them," and many of them were promiscuous and had little status. The fear of giving his wife more freedom and the subsequent threat to his role as provider are factors which prevent most men from allowing their wives to earn as much as they might.

Most young husbands are equally unprepared to give their brides of one or two years the freedom and authority they need to assume the responsibility for running independent households. In the past, when young wives lived with their mothers-in-law often for many years, their husbands had little difficulty in controlling them and felt correspondingly more secure. The men are unanimous in believing that women must be kept under strict surveillance if their good behavior is to be assured. Wives are generally forbidden to have female friends, for their husbands see such friends as potential go-betweens for the wife and a lover. Most women discontinue all friendships when they marry, and men may drop their own friends after marriage for fear that an intimacy might develop between the wife and the friend. The majority of husbands are suspicious of any activities that take the wife out of the home. A young wife will often prefer to ask a neighbor or a relative to buy things for her rather than risk her husband's anger or village gossip by going to the market alone. Some young wives now do go out alone but they are considered suspect.

In sexual relations as in social relations, the Tepoztecan husband is expected to take the initiative and his wife to submit to his demands. It is believed that women have less *naturaleza*—that is, that they are sexually weaker than men. Husbands do not expect their wives to be sexually demanding or passionate, nor do they consider these traits desirable in a wife. Women who "need" men are referred to as *loca* (crazy) and are thought to be in an abnormal condition which may have been brought about by black magic. Respectable women properly express negative attitudes toward sex and do so forcefully. Some husbands deliberately refrain from arousing their wives sexually, as it is assumed that a passive or frigid wife will be more faithful. In general, sexual play is a technique men reserve for the seduction of other women.

The husbands' concern about the faithfulness of their wives generally lessens after several years of marriage. As the children get older and can help the mother and as the needs of the growing family increase, however, women frequently demand freedom for carrying on economic ventures. Since such activity necessitates their leaving the house more often, tension and suspicion are again awakened in the husband. Men feel most secure when their wives are pregnant or have an infant to care for; thus to have one child follow close upon another is a desirable state of affairs from the men's viewpoint.

Promiscuous sexual activity is a male prerogative in Tepoztlán, and the men feel under pressure to prove their manliness by having many "affairs." Usually they have extramarital relations with widows or unmarried women, less frequently with married women. Men now go to houses of prostitution in Cuernavaca, and venereal disease is becoming more common in the village. Although male adultery is considered undesirable behavior, it is nevertheless thought to be "natural" and a good wife is not supposed to be disturbed by it. Many women are resentful, however, especially if money is involved, and some openly quarrel with their husband and also withhold money from him. Interference by wives in such matters enrages the men and often results in wife beating.

Drunkenness is not as common in Tepoztlán as it is in surrounding villages or in other parts of Mexico, and it is more strongly disapproved of. Most men drink a small amount of alcohol regularly, but extensive drinking is limited to Sundays, fiestas, or formal occasions. Drinking is nevertheless an important emotional outlet for Tepoztecan men; they drink to get over *muina* or anger after a quarrel at home, to work up courage to punish a wife, to seduce a woman, or to fight with an enemy. Sometimes when the men come home drunk they are aggressive and beat their wives; at other times "because they lack judgment" they are affectionate and kiss and fondle the members of their family. Many wives resent their husband's drunken bouts both because of the probable violence and because of the money involved; only the most aggressive, however, try to break their husband of the habit.

Tepoztecans believe that wives who have suffered beatings or other harsh treatment may take revenge through sorcery, and Tepoztecan men are alert to this possibility. The most commonly feared type of sorcery is a potion made from a well-known herb called *toloache,* secretly dropped into a man's coffee or any other drink. This herb is said to contain a drug that will affect the brain if taken in large doses. In Tepoztlán it is also believed that it will make a man *tonto*—that is, stupid or foolish and easily managed—and that an extra large dose will make him an idiot. The most important symptom to Tepoztecans is that the drugged man can no longer control his wife but is dominated by her. The man's mother or sister may attempt to cure him by secretly putting a counter-potion into his coffee. It is interesting to note that there is not a single known case of *toloache* given by a man to a woman.

Parents and Children

Tepoztecan children are brought up to obey their elders and to submit to the will of their mother and father as long as they live under their parents' roof. From infancy on, they are encouraged to be passive and unobtrusive; older children are expected to be self-controlled and helpful. Great emphasis is placed on "good" behavior in children, for it is feared that a child improperly raised will not grow up to be a good worker and will get into trouble. Such a son or daughter is a cause for shame to his parents in the eyes of the community.

The mother is expected to teach the children good habits and to see to their religious training. As far as the children are concerned, family life revolves primarily around the mother. At an early age they learn not to expect to be held by their father or to have much physical contact with him. In many homes the father rules the children through the mother who then becomes the mediator between father and children, relaying requests, instructions, and warnings. The father expects the mother to help maintain his position of respect in the home, and in this most women comply. Children are repeatedly warned by relatives and other adults that the father must be respected Most children are subdued and inhibited in the presence of their father and remain so well into adulthood. They are less consistent in their behavior toward their mother, thus reflecting her own varying attitudes, for she is at the same time punishing and protective, authoritative and submissive, serving and demanding.

Popular stereotypes in the village depict fathers as "hard" by nature and the mother as "soft." It is thought natural that a mother feels closer to her children than does the father; a mother who abandons her children is considered abnormal or *machorra* (like a man). When a man deserts his children—a more common occurrence—it is disapproved of but not considered a sign of abnormality. Again, the death of a mother is recognized as more disruptive to the household than the death of a father.

According to village culture patterns a mother has more ways of showing affection to her children than a father. She may kiss, fondle, or carry a nursing child as much as she wishes, and if a child is the youngest she may continue this behavior until he is five. She may also express affection through giving food, sewing clothes, nursing illness, and other attentions. Mothers often protect their children by not telling the father of misdeeds or by attempting to stop the father from punishing a child. Such interventions and deceptions are infuriating to the father, but they are nevertheless thought to be "natural" in a mother. In contrast to the mother, a father is limited in his ability to be demonstratively affectionate with his children. Traditionally, a father expresses his affection by buying a child little gifts, giving him pennies, or taking him to the fields or to a fiesta. When a child is ill, the father shows his concern chiefly by agreeing to call in a *curandero*.

Our data show a wide variation in the form and severity of punishments meted out to children. This situation stems from the varying amount of help needed from children in the home and from the differential treatment given boys and girls, older and younger children, and a favorite child. A Tepoztecan child is always punished for flouting the authority of his parents and for unwillingness to work. Other types of misbehavior—grumbling or quarrelsomeness, for example—are not so consistently punished.

Most parents believe in early punishment and begin at about the time the child starts to walk. Infants may be slapped for crying too much, although this is uncommon. Some children receive their first severe beating at three or four years of age, but it is between five and twelve that children are most frequently and harshly punished. After twelve years, punishment is reserved for the most serious offenses. The father inflicts the most severe punishments but the mother punishes more often. Mothers tend to punish daughters more than sons; fathers punish sons more than daughters.

Severe punishment is traditional in Tepoztlán. Some adults in the village remember such punishments as hanging a child in a net over a smoky fire of chile seeds; partial asphyxiation and an illness that lasted for days was the result. (This practice is reminiscent of an ancient Aztec punishment which placed rebellious subjects in a room filled with the fumes of burning chile seeds.) Similarly, a child formerly was punished for breaking a dish by scraping his arms with a piece of the dish until blood was drawn. It is significant of changing attitudes in the village that some of the old practices which had a strong magical component and were not necessarily performed in a spirit of cruelty are today interpreted as cruel. Yet even today beatings with a stick or a rope are not uncommonly given by fathers. Mothers more often hit with their hands, pinch, kick, or throw small stones at offending youngsters. On the whole, Tepoztecans agree that punishment has become less severe and that there is greater toleration toward children's faults. This is particularly true among the more permissive and better-educated younger generation.

Fear is one of the most important means by which Tepoztecan parents control their children. Mothers threaten to desert their children, playing on their fear of being orphans or of having to live with a stepmother. In the days when few visitors or tourists came to the village, children were told that if they were naughty they would be carried off by a stranger who would make them into soap. In the more isolated villages children still run to hide when they see an unfamiliar person. Many mothers and grandmothers tell young children stories of owls and coyotes that come out at night to eat bad children, and of bats and opossums that drink blood. Children who lie or disobey are warned that they will turn into devils and burn in hell. When children cry they may be told the story of Cahuasohuantun who eats the intestines of such children.

Lying and deception play a large part in parent-child relationships. Parents and other adults use deception as another means of controlling children; Tepoztecans actually would be at a loss in raising their children if they were without it. The use of little lies is so common as to be taken for granted, and children early become accustomed to it. Mothers, particularly, tend to make and break promises easily and to trick their children into doing as they wish. The effort of parents to keep their children "innocent," or, as they say, "to keep their eyes from being opened," makes deception necessary. Children, in turn, lie to escape punishment and to assert their own wishes. Moreover, the many restrictions placed upon children encourage lying; there is, for example, much deception involved in courtship. Parents show little moral indignation about lying on the part of their children. They do not punish the lie so much as the misdeed the lie was meant to hide; likewise, a parent or child caught in a lie is ashamed rather of being caught than of having lied.

The frequent use of deception causes some mutual distrust between parents and children. The children seldom confide in their parents, and early stop going to them for help with their troubles or for information. The parents on their part do not encourage the asking of questions, particularly about sex. Absurd or teasing answers are often given to children's questions.

The father assumes an important role in the life of a son when the boy is old enough to go to the fields. Most boys enjoy working in the fields with their father and look forward to it with great pleasure. Fathers are proud to take their young sons to the fields for the first time and frequently show great patience in teaching them. But even when father and sons go to the fields together day after day, there is no weakening of the respect relationship. The father maintains the role of teacher and when he speaks it is to advise. Talk between them about intimate subjects, the telling of jokes, or discussion of women all are strictly taboo, even after the sons are married.

Regardless of age or marital status a son is subject to his father's authority as long as he lives with his father. He receives no recompense other than his support and care and whatever spending money he can manage to procure. Some fathers are generous with sons who do a man's work; others continue to treat them as children. In the past, comparatively few unmarried sons left home to seek work elsewhere; even young men who were acutely dissatisfied with their home situation were reluctant to strike out for themselves. A certain apprehension of the outside world still holds sons at home—fears of falling ill among strangers, of having to do menial work, of not having the family to support them in case of trouble, of not being properly respected by others. Moreover, many boys feel bound to their mothers. Still another factor that prevents sons from leaving home is their economic dependence on their parents and a desire for their share of the inheritance. The dependence is, of course, mutual. Fathers are eager to have their sons at home to help support the family, and in most homes grown sons who work enjoy much the same service and care that the father receives.

Although fathers say they prefer sons to daughters, they not uncommonly show a mild favoritism toward a daughter. Relations between a father and a grown daughter are formal and distant, however, and physical contact is avoided. Kissing and embracing have strong incestuous connotations for both

Even young girls are extremely shy in the presence of their fathers and some married women say they are embarrassed at being seen by their father when they are pregnant. Fathers expect their daughters to be virgins when they marry. Any violation of this moral law is a blot on the father's and on the family's honor and incurs severe punishment.

Mothers more than fathers tend to have favorites among their children; usually they favor boys over girls and small children over grown children. Many mothers try to protect their sons if they think the father works them too hard, but only an occasional mother will interfere in the boy's behalf. It is common for a mother to be indulgent with her youngest child; she may nurse him and sleep with him much longer than the usual period. The indulgence of the youngest child is often in sharp contrast with the treatment of the older children, but generally speaking mothers give partial treatment to all children under five. The small children are given more food and toys and are taken to fiestas and on trips. Although differential treatment of children according to sex and age is "accepted" as natural by Tepoztecan parents, there is evidence that habitual or gross displays of favoritism are resented by the other siblings. The resentment finds expression in surreptitious quarreling and fighting, in irritability, in unwillingness to share possessions, and in avoidance of one another.

From early childhood, boys are permitted more freedom of movement and of expression and more leisure for play than girls. The oldest son enjoys a particularly favored position. He receives more care and attention than subsequent sons, and his is often the only birthday other than the father's to be celebrated with a fiesta. But mothers sometimes have difficulty controlling the oldest son, for the boy may imitate his father in demanding service from the women of the family and in giving orders to the younger siblings. If the father dies, the oldest son is expected to take the father's place and to support his mother, brothers, and sisters. An extended struggle for authority as head of the family sometimes ensues between mother and son. Quarrels between mother and son about the inheritance also are apt to arise. Widows who inherit their husband's property have an advantage in the matter of maintaining authority and usually they keep the property until their death lest they lose all control over their sons.

Relations between mothers and daughters are usually very close. As the mother teaches the girl household skills and as they work side by side in the home, the daughter comes to identify with the mother and assume her role. A daughter's attitudes toward work, toward bearing children, and toward men and marriage are strongly influenced by her mother. The custom of having daughters work in the home is a deeply ingrained one, and a girl at home is at the complete disposal of her mother. With few exceptions mothers use their daughters very early for all types of errands and chores. Mothers tend to resent the fact that school takes the girls away from home for the major part of the day, and most parents remove their daughters from school as soon as they can. The majority of girls attend school only through the third grade or until they are eleven. Many mothers exploit their daughters, particularly the oldest, and some girls marry to escape the hard work at home. An occasional mother, however, identifies with her daughter and fulfills her own desire for schooling by allowing the girl to complete elementary school.

A mother is responsible for the chastity and reputation of her grown daughters. To many mothers this translates into a need to spy on them, to chaperone them, and to put pressure on them to conform. If a mother learns that a daughter has a *novio*, she may beat the girl herself rather than inform the father. If, however, a daughter becomes pregnant before marriage, the mother will usually be less harsh and more forgiving than the father. Respect relations between a mother and a daughter forbid them to speak of intimate subjects although not to the same extent as father-daughter relations. Mothers usually do not give their daughters information about menstruation nor discuss the body or any aspect of sexual relations with them. Nor do girls tell their mothers when they first menstruate or ask for information concerning pregnancy, birth, or marriage. When a mother learns that a daughter has begun to menstruate or is pregnant, however, she will offer advice. Mother-daughter relations are considerably weakened when a girl marries, particularly if the girl lives with her mother-in-law. If she leaves her mother-in-law to establish a home of her own, close relations with her mother are usually resumed. Women do not expect financial help from their married daughters but many do receive such help with or without the knowledge of their sons-in-law.

Siblings

Sibling solidarity is an ideal which parents hold before their children and to which lip-service is constantly given. In childhood, siblings are constant companions, sharing the same friends and the same games. The older children take care of the younger and are held responsible for their safety and well-being but they may not discipline them or exercise much authority over them. If a younger child cries or complains to the parents, the older child is scolded or punished. As a result, older children rarely run to their mothers with complaints or appeals for justice but younger children frequently do so. In the school, however, older children vent their aggression upon younger ones to such an extent that parents are reluctant to send small children to kindergarten.

The oldest sister in particular has the role of caring for the younger siblings and often shows maternal affection toward them; a newly-weaned child may sleep with her for several years. Some older daughters are now rejecting this role, however; they prefer to go to school and tend to be resentful if they cannot. The oldest brother has preferred status and can demand respect and obedience from younger siblings even though the parents try to frustrate his efforts in this direction unless or until he is an adult. The general pattern of male dominance, learned by boys from their fathers, is first put into practice in their relationships with their sisters. As soon as a girl is old enough to do housework, the brother begins to demand service from her just as his father does from his mother. A sister is expected to wash, iron, and mend her brother's clothes, prepare and serve his food, and so forth. Like their father, boys have a lively concern about their sister's "honor" and will beat her if they discover she has a *novio*.

Siblings of the same sex tend to associate with each other. Brothers work in the fields together, share confidences, and if there is no great age difference between them, share the same friends. This pattern is even stronger among sisters. Grown brothers and sisters, however, do not attend fiestas or other public affairs together, do not have mutual friends, and are reserved toward one another in public.

Many brothers and sisters, of course, have warm relationships throughout their lives, but in many families sibling relations are poor. Among infants and young children, sibling rivalry and jealousy are so common that parents think them natural and take them for granted. Children are not prepared for the arrival of a new sibling and the pregnancy and birth are kept a secret from them. An illness (called *chipilez*) that occurs in infancy is attributed to the child's jealousy of a new sibling. Even before the next baby is born, an illness in a nursing child or in a child being weaned is ascribed to jealousy. It is believed that infants "sense" when another child is expected and that the illness is caused by the fact that they are now "carrying the weight of the baby." Although death from *chipilez* is not infrequent, most children recover a few months after the new baby is born, since then, it is said, "the weight is lifted." If a child continues to cry for his mother and to show hostility to the new baby, he may be sent to live with his grandmother either temporarily or for as long as several years. Temper tantrums, common in the next-to-the-youngest child, also may be stopped in this way. Sometimes a youngest child is the butt of older siblings and for his own protection may be sent to live with his grandmother. The importance of the grandmother as a mother substitute is generally recognized in the village; the child who does not have a grandmother is considered unfortunate.

After marriage a number of factors weaken ties between siblings. Each brother or sister sets up an independent household, often widely separated, and in Tepoztlán practically no institutionalized forms of cooperation exist between married brothers and sisters. As we have seen earlier, only fourteen cases of married siblings living together on a single housesite were noted. Married sisters soon identify with their husband's interests. Moreover, since a married woman is under the authority of her husband, she is no longer free to visit her brothers at will. Brothers are more free to visit, but often there are strained relations between in-laws.

Again, favoritism on the part of the parents toward one or two married children may cause friction among adult siblings. For example, parents may show marked preference for a daughter's children or help a favored married daughter or son more than their other children. Division of inheritance also leads to quarrels among siblings; parents tend to leave more property to sons than to daughters, more to an older son, or to a favorite.

The Extended Family

During the time a married couple lives with the husband's parents, they have little contact with the wife's family. When they live alone, ties with the wife's family become closer and often supersede those with the husband's family. In any case, however, the closest kinship tie is with the grandmother, whether on the paternal or the maternal side. The importance of the grandmother, especially as a mother substitute, has already been pointed out.

Aunts, particularly maternal aunts, frequently have an affectionate relationship with nieces and nephews and in emergencies may act as mother substitutes. A boy who has eloped often brings his sweetheart to live with a favorite aunt. Uncles have a respect relationship with their nieces and nephews which may also be an affectionate one. Many children have a favorite uncle who singles them out for an occasional gift or favor. Work exchange between uncles and nephews occurs more often than between married siblings, but quarrels also are apt to occur, particularly over inheritance. After a man's death, a brother will sometimes claim a portion of the property from the widow, especially if her children are still small.

Cousins often have a relationship that resembles that of brother and sister. Parents encourage their children to play with their cousins, especially if they are neighbors; often a person's best and only friends turn out to be one or two favorite cousins. Cousin marriage is forbidden although some cases have occurred.

In-laws

Because of patrilocal residence, the mother-in-law and daughter-in-law relationship is the most important of all in-law relationships. When a young bride goes to live with her husband's family, she is expected to take the role of a grown daughter and give her parents-in-law the same respect and obedience she gave her own parents. The mother-in-law assigns her work to her; generally it consists of the most burdensome tasks—grinding corn, making tortillas, and washing and ironing clothes for the entire family. In the past, when girls married at twelve or thirteen, they were unskilled and the mother-in-law taught them housework. The mother-in-law for her part must look after her daughter-in-law when she gives birth and must chaperone the daughter-in-law and see to it that she remains a faithful wife. Many jokes depict the mother-in-law as a "policeman."

Although many mothers-in-law and daughters-in-law manage to get along fairly well, the relationship is a charged one and is recognized as such by Tepoztecans. Both women approach it with apprehension. Girls hear their mothers and other married women say that the daughter-in-law is the mother-in-law's "slave." They are afraid that they will not be able to please their mother-in-law and that they will feel like an outsider in a strange house. The mother-in-law fears that the girl her son brings home will be lazy, just another mouth to feed, or that she will be critical of the way the family lives.

Often the fears are justified and quarrels are the result. Perhaps this is even more true today than in the past because of the different standards of dress, cleanliness, and personal freedom held by younger and older women. Increasingly, the way out of an unpleasant situation for both is to separate the households. If the wife cannot persuade her husband to move and if her situation becomes intolerable, she returns to her parents' home. It is believed in the village that many marriages have been broken because the mother-in-law and daughter-in-law could not get on together. Father-in-law and daughter-in-law relations are similar to father-daughter relations but even more reserved.

Relations between the wife's parents and their son-in-law depend more on personal factors than on formal obligations, with the exception of the usual respect obligations. In the past, the son-in-law was required to provide his father-in-law with wood and water for two years as part of the bride price. Now any work done by the son-in-law is voluntary and usually is limited to times when the father-in-law is ill or in need. If the mother-in-law is widowed and has property, the son-in-law may help her farm; if she has no means of support, a good son-in-law may help support her or invite her to live in his home.

Tepoztecan men are wary of their mothers-in-law. They think of her as a meddlesome, trouble-making figure and prefer to keep the relationship a distant one. Actually, most mothers urge their married daughters to try to please their husbands and to bear up under domestic difficulties. Fathers are more apt than mothers to feel a personal affront if their daughter is ill-treated by a son-in-law.

Relations between sisters-in-law and brothers-in-law are not formalized and depend largely on personal factors. Sisters-in-law, whether the wives of two brothers or the husband's wife and sister, are thrown together more often than brothers-in-law. In some families the wives of brothers compete for the esteem of the mother-in-law and carry tales about each other to her. Quarrels over inheritance involve the sisters-in-law as much as the siblings.

Godparents, Godchildren, and Co-parents

The system of *compadrazgo* establishes two sets of formal relationships between nonrelatives: the one is between "spiritual" godparents (*padrinos*) and their godchildren (*ahijados*); the other a relationship known as *compadres* or co-parents, is between the parents and the godparents. The general purpose of godparents is to provide security for the godchild. The godparents are in effect an additional set of parents who will act as guardians and sponsors of the godchild, care for him in emergencies, and adopt him if he is orphaned. In Tepoztlán, however, the relationship between *compadres* is much more functional and important than that between the godparent and godchild.

Godparents address their godchildren in the familiar *tu* and are addressed by the respectful *Usted*. Traditionally the godchild kissed the godparent's hand at each meeting, but this is no longer common. The godparent usually gives the child a few centavos when they meet, but many children actually never receive anything from their *padrinos*. *Compadres* address each other with the respectful *Usted;* theirs is a reciprocal respect relationship and in this lies its strength, for such a relationship is highly desirable to Tepoztecans. By respect, Tepoztecans mean a recognition of high and equal status and the avoidance of intimacy or undue familiarity. The latter includes joking and discussing sex or any other subjects of a personal nature. Compadres also may not drink together. They do often exchange favors, and borrowing between them is probably more frequent than between kin. At the death of one *compadre* the other is supposed to contribute toward the funeral expenses. *Compadres* invite each other to barrio fiestas and treat each other with special deference. Tepoztecans prefer *compadres* who are neither neighbors nor relatives; most *compadres* come from other barrios.

The three most important types of godparents in Tepoztlán are those of baptism, confirmation, and marriage. Reliable persons are sought as godparents of baptism. The husband's parents usually select the godparents of baptism for the first child, but as the couple grows older the husband may make the selection and often friendship rather than higher economic status dictates his choice. The godparents of baptism are obliged to assist at the baptism, to buy the infant's clothing for the occasion, and to pay the priest's fee. They also accompany the mother and child to the *sacamisa,* or first Mass, forty days after the birth. If the child dies, the godparents arrange for the wake, dress the body for burial, and contribute to the funeral expenses. An important obligation of godparents is to urge their *compadres* to send the child to school when the time comes. If the child needs punishing, the parents may ask the godparents to scold him. The godparents of confirmation are usually selected by the godparents of baptism; occasionally the latter accept both roles. The godparents of marriage assist at the wedding and act as mediators if the couple later quarrels or separates.

One of the distinctive aspects of the *compadre* system in the village, and in fact in Mexico as a whole, is the way in which it has been extended far beyond the original Catholic forms. In most of Spain, only two or three types of godparents, popularly those of baptism, communion and confirmation, are known. In Tepoztlán, in addition to the three above, there are the following: godparents of *miscotón* (a Nahuatl term which refers to a small sweater which the godparent puts on the child to protect him from illness); of *medida* or *listón* (these terms refer to a small piece of ribbon, blessed by the priest, which is placed on a sick child as a charm); of *evangelio* (a woman of "bad" reputation is asked to become godmother to a sick child and to pray in the church for his recovery); of *scapulary;* of the Child Jesus; and so on. The godparent system has been extended to secular activities as well. At soccer and basketball games each team has its godmother who dresses in white, carries flowers, acts as the sponsor, and hands out prizes to the winners. At social dances godmothers act as chaperones.

Social, economic, and political factors may enter into the operation of the *compadre* system. Poor families look for better-to-do godparents for their children. Similarly it is thought desirable to have a *compadre* from the city, for it is assumed that a city family can be of greater help in time of need. The more godchildren a man has, the more *compadres* and the wider circle of persons who can be counted on for favors. For this reason anyone who aspires to a position of leadership in the village must have many godchildren. There is some feeling against using the *compadre* system in this fashion, however, and some villagers consider having many *compadres* as a burden. In this case they try to limit their *compadre* relations by asking one or two families to serve as godparents for several children.

6

The Life Cycle

Pregnancy

IN TEPOZTLÁN it is considered a sin for a married person not to want children or not to be grateful for all those sent by God. Children, it is emphasized, are economically useful and boys are preferred because they are economically more productive than girls. Women, however, tend to feel that having children is a burden to be endured and that bearing many children is a punishment from God. Not uncommonly they induce abortion and take medicines to cause sterility. The only approved method of avoiding conception in the village is abstinence. Tepoztecan men, however, prefer large families and frown on their wives' efforts to reduce the number of pregnancies.

Motherhood is not glorified. Girls grow up in a village atmosphere that indirectly encourages negative attitudes toward pregnancy, child bearing, and even marriage. There is prudery about pregnancy and women try to conceal it, especially from their children and from anyone in a respect relationship to them. The literal translation of the Spanish term used to describe pregnancy is "to become ill with child." When Tepoztecan girls married at an earlier age than they usually do at present, they were often ignorant of the signs of pregnancy for a sense of shame prohibited the giving of information by the mother to the daughter. Even today the young pregnant bride is dependent on her mother-in-law and a midwife for advice and care.

Sterility in women—which may be sufficient cause for abandonment by the husband—is believed to be caused by "cold" in the womb and is treated by massages with warm oil of rosemary and violet. It is also believed that if conception occurs during the full moon, the child will be strong, and married couples sometimes have intercourse during this time for this reason.

Care during pregnancy consists principally of abdominal massages given by a midwife. The patient lies down on her back with her knees slightly bent, and the midwife gently strokes the abdomen from right to left. No oils or unguents are used. It is thought that massage makes the birth easier and also allows the midwife to determine or even change the position of the fetus. Most women have great faith in the efficacy of massage and try to have it from two to four times a month. The midwife also advises the pregnant woman: she is not to lift heavy objects but she should continue to work, for too much sleep or rest would make the birth more difficult. She should not urinate where an animal has just urinated because the rising steam might cause inflammation of the womb. She should not bathe or wash clothes at the stream because *los aires* might endanger the child. Eclipses, rainbows, and earthquakes all are dangerous to an unborn child. No restrictions on sexual intercourse are made at any time during pregnancy. Miscarriages are generally blamed on the carelessness of the woman.

Birth

When the baby is expected, a curtain or *petate* is hung in front of the mother's bed. The woman lies on a *petate* on the floor and the midwife massages the abdomen, the back, and the hips with various heated oils. These are supposed to warm the infant, loosen it, and allow it to slip out more easily. Difficulty in giving birth is attributed to "cold" and is counteracted by heat. The woman is given a mixture of boiled herbs, chocolate, sherry, and egg to drink to hasten labor, or she is wrapped in a blanket to make her perspire. Sometimes leaves of *pericón,* rosemary, or laurel are burned in an old clay pot and the strong-smelling smoke is directed underneath the blanket to heat her lower body. The mother is discouraged from screaming during labor because, it is believed, this makes the child rise instead of descend. She is given something to bite on, usually her own braid, and is told to keep her mouth closed. It may be such practices which have led observers to describe Mexican Indian women as "stoical" during childbirth. Yet Tepoztecan women often pray and scream when they have severe pains.

After the child is born, a sash is wound around the upper part of the mother's abdomen to prevent the blood and the placenta from rising. The midwife may press a hot tortilla against the mother's right side or she may be given salt and onion to smell and mint to chew. When the afterbirth is expelled it is buried under the hearth. If it is carelessly disposed of or is eaten by a dog, the mother may die and the child's face may swell. The umbilical cord is cut with a scissors, tied with thread, and sealed with a few drops of tallow from a candle. The dried cord of a first-born son is believed to be an effective cure for certain eye diseases. A child born in a caul is destined to become rich and the caul is saved for good luck.

After the delivery, the mother is raised from the floor to a bed. The midwife binds her abdomen, tucking in a *muñeca* (literally, a doll), a piece of rolled up cloth, to add to the pressure and "fix the matrix." The mother's soiled clothing is removed and an old-fashioned Indian *huipil* made from a large square cloth is slipped over her head. A skirt made from another square is wrapped around her hips and legs. On the next day she is bathed and given her ordinary clothing.

The mother is kept on a restricted diet of corn gruel, cinnamon tea, and bread or tortilla until all flow of blood stops. The midwife massages and re-binds her every day for eight days to encourage the flow of blood and to "cleanse" her internally. The midwife also bathes the baby during her visits. If the mother's milk does not appear by the second day, several remedies are possible: the penis of an ox cut up and boiled, a gruel of sesame seed, chick peas, chocolate and cinnamon, or boiled *flor de pascua*. The first milk is considered harmful to the infant; it is expressed by hand and thrown on the ground or over the roof to prevent the mother's milk from drying up.

The care given to a new mother is striking. It consists of prolonged bed-rest (forty days is the ideal), freedom from household duties, sweatbaths, and abstention from sexual intercourse (for about one year). The prime motive is to delay another pregnancy as long as possible. Most women are glad to avoid intercourse, which they frequently call *abuso de hombre* (male abuse), and complain that their husbands do not wait long enough. The good husband and father owes it to both his wife and child to abstain. The husband is also supposed to hire a servant to help his wife for two or three months. Even among poor families, if the marriage has been consummated in church and approved by both families, women are well cared for after giving birth. This is not true for abandoned mothers, women without close relatives, or mothers of very large families.

The day after the birth close relatives come to the house with jars of food suitable for the mother. A week or two later more distant relatives come with food or perhaps with a gift of soap. Anyone who has recently attended a wake or a funeral should not come because he may expose the mother to a *mal humor* which causes "cancer" in menstruating women. Relatives who did not approve of the marriage usually stay away at this time.

For the first eight days the new mother remains behind the curtain. On the eighth day, if bleeding has stopped, she is carried by her husband or a hired man to the *temascal* for a sweatbath and then returned to her bed. After a minimum of fifteen days in bed, during which time she is urged to lie still without sitting up or turning from side to side, she is taken out for another sweatbath. Before each bath a special meal of *clemole* (chicken or beef cooked in a chile sauce) is eaten by the mother, the midwife, and any other women in the family. The new baby is briefly exposed also to the steam of the *temascal*. Almost every woman takes two steam baths; some take the traditional four. After the last bath, the mother may be given a boiled mixture of seventeen different herbs, and the same mixture is given to women who do not stop bleeding in good time. After leaving her bed, the mother is supposed to take precautions for two or three months—to sit quietly and to walk slowly with her thighs close together, and not to leave the house for at least forty days. Only the most unfortunate women do such heavy work as washing and ironing before three months have passed.

Many of the practices and beliefs pertaining to pregnancy and birth that are found in Tepoztlán are widespread in rural Mexico; they have been reported for Tarascan, Mayan, and Zapotecan groups. These similarities are due to contacts between these groups before the Conquest and to a common exposure to Spanish colonial influences.

Infancy and Early Childhood

No formal celebration is held at the birth of a child, for it is believed that during the first weeks of life the infant is particularly susceptible to "evil eye," "bad humors," and *los aires.* So that he can be protected from these dangers, the child sleeps behind a curtain, and *ruda,* chile, or a few drops of iodine are put in the cradle. Some families hang a gallstone, taken from the gall bladder of a bull, around the child's wrist to protect him from the "evil eye." After a month a centavo may be hung on a string around his neck to protect him from whooping cough. Babies in all families wear little caps for seven months to protect them from *los aires,* or, as more modern mothers say, from cold drafts, and they are generally kept indoors for the first four months.

Anyone coming in from the street must "cool" for awhile before seeing the baby because he may be "hot" and make the child ill. If the father has committed adultery and comes home "hot," his child may get infected eyes. Jealous wives sometimes accuse their husband of adultery if the child suffers any illness. Illness is also attributed to the fact that a child has weak *tonal* or *sombra;* this is something akin to a guardian spirit who protects him from disease. A very sick child may be treated by a *curandero* for spirit-loss.

Baptism usually occurs during the first week after birth. About forty days after the baptism the godparents present their godchild with a tray on which they have placed his baptismal clothes for the *sacamisa* or the first Mass attended by the mother and new baby. After the Mass the *compadres* visit the godparents with gifts of wine, cigarettes, turkey *mole,* and other festive foods. Later in the day the godparents may return the visit, bringing musicians and friends with them, and there will be dancing in the child's home. The *compadres* are obliged to serve food and drinks to all who come. The naming of children follows the Catholic custom of selecting one name from the list of saint's names on the day of birth and another, if desired, from the same list on the day of baptism.

Infants receive a good deal of attention and care and are generally kept fairly clean. Most babies under one year of age are bathed in warm water every three days, and most mothers handle them carefully and protect their eyes from soap. After the bath they are rubbed with alcohol, dusted with powder, and dressed in clean clothes. For the first three months the shirts and rag diapers are warmed at the hearth. Some mothers change soiled diapers often, others once a day or only after a bowel movement. Infants are traditionally swaddled, especially during nursing and sleeping, in a sheet or cotton blanket which binds their arms tightly down at their sides. This is done, it is said, to prevent the child from waking himself with a sudden movement of the hands which might cause *espanto* or illness of fright. It also prevents him from touching his genitals and from touching the mother's breast during nursing. Swaddling is considered an important part of child training, and its purpose is to make him more passive and quiet. It is believed that children who are bound in infancy will grow up to be less troublesome to the parents and not "turn out bad."

Infants are carried almost every waking moment up to the time they begin to walk; crawling on the ground is permitted only by "careless" mothers. Thus a well-brought-up child has little opportunity to explore. The baby is carried in the left arm, with one end of the *rebozo* or shawl tightly tucked around his body, and the other end brought around the mother's shoulders and also tucked under him. This makes him snug and also takes some of his weight off the mother's arm. Children are not slung in a *rebozo* on the mother's back as in some parts of Mexico, for Tepoztecans regard this method of carrying a child as primitive and as indicative of poverty—a poor woman needs both hands free to work. Most Tepoztecan women have someone to help them —an older child, a grandmother, some other relative, or a young girl hired for the purpose. The practice of entrusting an infant from the age of four months on to a child-nurse is general in the village.

During the day babies sleep in a shallow wooden cradle which hangs from the ceiling by a rope. The baby's face is covered with a cloth to protect him from *los aires* and to keep out light and flies. Cradles can be raised to safeguard the child from animals or lowered to prevent a high fall. Babies may be rocked to sleep in the cradle but most of the time they fall asleep in the mother's arms while nursing and are then placed in the cradle. At night babies sleep with their mothers on a *petate* on the floor or on a raised native bed or *tepexco*. If the mother sleeps on a modern bed, the child will be heavily wrapped at night to prevent wetting the mattress.

The baby is nursed whenever he cries. The breast is used as a pacifier and most babies are put to sleep in this way. Because nursing is considered good for the child and because it is believed to delay conception, mothers nurse as long as possible, usually until they are pregnant again. Tepoztecan women say they do not find nursing pleasurable, however, and consider it rather as part of a mother's sacrifice for the good of her child. Children who are nursed less than eighteen months are considered deprived.

Infants are not permitted to cry, for a crying child is thought to be hungry, neglected, or ill. If a crying baby is not consoled by the breast, the leaf of the *sapote blanco* or of the *dormidera,* a flower which closes when touched, is sometimes placed under the child's pillow. If the crying still does not stop, the child may be treated for *espanto.*

Children are not hurried in their development. If walking is seriously delayed, earth warmed by the sun may be rubbed on the legs to remove the "cold" in the bones. If a child cannot speak by the time he is three or four, a church key may be turned in his mouth to "unlock" it. It is believed that a child's fingernails should not be cut until he begins to speak because otherwise the palate will fall and he will be mute. It is also believed that a child's hair should not be cut before one year or he will become ill. When teeth come late, older people may advise bleeding the gums by rubbing them with a grass-hopper's leg, but few young people now follow this practice. Some mothers put mittens on babies' hands to prevent them from scratching themselves.

There is little preoccupation with toilet training, particularly during the first two years. As soon as a child is able to walk, he is taken to the *corral* by his mother and is shown the proper place to relieve himself. He may be scolded or spanked even before he is two for doing his "necessities" in the wrong place, but most mothers are not consistent in this. When he is able to tie and untie his pants, usually by four or five, he is able to go independently.

Infancy ends with weaning. This is accomplished by placing a bitter substance (*sávila*) on the nipple and by telling the child that he cannot nurse any longer. Some women bind their breasts to stop the flow of milk and do not permit the child to see the breast again. Others do it more gradually, letting the child nurse if he cries too much. Crying, even if prolonged as long as eight days, is considered a normal part of weaning, and few women consider weaning a difficult problem. The child does receive more attention during this period, however, sometimes going to live with the grandmother for a few days. Occasionally, if a child is inconsolable, he may be spanked or frightened into silence by being told that a coyote will come to eat him.

Illness and even death are frequent in children just after weaning. The change in diet may cause indigestion, diarrhea, or malnutrition. After weaning or the birth of another sibling, the close ties between the mother and the youngest child are broken. The child no longer sleeps with his mother, is not treated with the same indulgence and tenderness, is not kept as clean, and is given over to the care of older brothers and sisters.

Children between the ages of two and five are usually kept at home. They play with their brothers and sisters, cousins, or close neighbors in the patio and *corral* and are not permitted to go into the street unaccompanied by a grownup. They may join the games of the older children and learn many customs by playing house, school, *compadres,* fiesta, baptism, musician, funeral, and other games imitating adult behavior. Small children may receive rough treatment during play, either intentionally or unintentionally, and may be frightened or bribed into silence by the older ones. When young children are taken by their mother to the plaza or on a visit, they often show great timidity. Such nervous habits as chewing on clothing begin at this time. Enuresis is very common up to the age of five and is not infrequent in boys and girls of seven. It is not considered much of a problem, although children are scolded and shamed for it. Masturbation is not tolerated and is swiftly punished. Curiosity about the body and its functions is not encouraged. The questions we asked about the sex play of children received a blanket denial from parents, who maintained that their children were innocent and knew nothing of life. But from the life stories we gathered, it was clear that sex play does occur secretive-ly and in games.

As children grow older they are put under more pressure to be obedient in preparation for their future work. At about five they are given such small chores as carrying corn in a little can when going with the mother or older sister to the mill, borrowing things from a neighbor or a relative, feeding the chickens, or taking care of a younger sibling. Boys of five often have the regular daily chore of carrying a few small cans of water from the fountain and of bringing in firewood or charcoal from the patio. Girls are expected to settle down to regular work sooner than boys and are more apt to be punished for carelessness or laziness.

Children of School Age

Beginning school is the next important step in the life of a Tepoztecan child. Children of from four to six are accepted in kindergarten, but many parents are reluctant to send their children so early because they fear for their physical safety and because they believe that too early learning will "heat their heads." Most children therefore begin in the first grade between the ages of seven and nine. In any one year, school enrollment is highest in the first and second grades, lower in kindergarten, and successively lower in the third, fourth, fifth, and sixth grades. In 1941, approximately 49 percent of the children between the ages of six and fifteen were enrolled in school; throughout the six grades the enrollment of girls was consistently lower than that of boys.

According to the teaching staff of the central school, the most serious school problem is nonattendance. Absence from school is extremely high during all important fiestas and when work is heavy in the fields. Tardiness is also a problem because most parents are not time conscious and may keep a child home until he has completed his chores. Only a minority of the parents give school attendance priority over work. The ability to read and write on a simple level satisfies the standards of most mothers and fathers.

Fearfulness and crying among the children are problems in the kindergarten and the first grade. These children are sometimes too timid to ask to be taken to the toilet, and the results may be unfortunate. A first-grade teacher reported that children who had attended kindergarten showed much less fear than children who entered the first grade without previous schooling. Apparently the socializing role of the school in Tepoztlán is important. Second-grade children are more self-confident and mischievous; third- and fourth-grade children tend to be less respectful and more disobedient. Boys in these grades frequently play truant. Fifth- and sixth-grade pupils are the most serious and studious.

The influence of the school has been profound, not only for the children but for the village as a whole. Although schools have existed in Tepoztlán for about a century, they formerly affected only a small percentage of the better-to-do families. Now the school teaches most Tepoztecan children new ways of living as well as the usual academic skills. New standards of personal hygiene, diet, dress, social participation, public health, and family relationships are taught. The celebration of Mother's Day, Children's Day, and secular and patriotic national holidays is encouraged. New games learned in the school emphasize teamwork, competition, scoring, definite goals, loyalty, leadership, sportsmanship, and physical exercise. In contrast, the traditional games were characterized by quiet play, little or no physical skill or exertion, and little competition.

Going to school does not have the same significance for girls as for boys. To girls who were traditionally confined to the home, burdened with household chores, and permitted little leisure, school represents freedom and pleasurable activity. To be relieved of work and close surveillance for six hours a day and to be able to play with children of the same age and to form friendships with both girls and boys are the most valued advantages the school offers to girls. They tend to feel deprived if they have to leave school. On the other hand boys, who traditionally had more freedom than their sisters, associate school with confinement. Most boys prefer to tend animals, work in the fields, or play truant.

The school has not only helped reduce the amount of work done by children but for many it has also postponed the age at which they contribute to their own support. It has in fact disrupted the traditional division of labor and has thrown a heavier burden of work on the parents. Going to school has in addition awakened new desires in children by removing them from the limited sphere of parental influence. They are no longer content to stay within patio walls at the beck and call of their mother; they urgently want to be with friends and to play after school. Play always has been, and still is, considered a possible source of danger and a waste of time by parents. A constant tug of war now goes on between parents and children as to how much time should be given to play.

Rorschach tests given in 1943 to thirty-nine children of school age revealed that the strongest formative influences were still the traditional, familiar ones. For fourteen younger children (ages five to eight) little difference between the sexes was found. A few of the children were quite responsive and showed spontaneity and interest in the world around them. Apparently they were being allowed to enjoy themselves. Furthermore, they seemed to be accepted by adults in a matter-of-fact, detached manner. The tests of twenty-five older children (ages nine to twelve) showed clear-cut sex differences. The girls seemed to be expected to act like adults and were being pushed beyond their years, but they showed no signs of revolt or worry and were in control of their impulses. The boys had a somewhat broader interest in everyday events, exhibited more spontaneity, and did not seem to be forced to have interests beyond their years. Both boys and girls in the older group seemed to live in a less warm and accepting environment than the younger children. They also showed little creative fantasy and did not allow themselves freedom for enjoyment.

Adolescence and Courtship

The period between childhood and adulthood is ill-defined and un-marked by special occasion or ceremony in Tepoztlán. This period has been extended by several years in recent times and has begun to have the characteristics of adolescence as we know it. Not long ago girls were called *niñas* (children) until twelve and *señoritas* until fourteen. Often they went directly from *niña* to *señora* because of early marriage. Now girls are called *niñas* until fifteen and *señoritas* until marriage. Most parents still make twelve the transition point, however, and withdraw their daughters from school and expect them to conduct themselves not as children but as *señoritas*.

Boys have not been hurried into adulthood by early marriage but they have been expected to assume full-time adult work by fifteen. At one time this age was ten. As compared with girls, the changes in age status for boys occur later, more gradually, and with less strain. Boys are called *muchachos* from about seven to eighteen or until they marry. Youths older than eighteen may also be called *jovenes* until marriage. No fixed or recommended age for marriage has been established for boys. Unmarried youths, however, are not entrusted with positions of responsibility in the barrio nor may they hold public office.

Adolescents usually do not attend school but work for their parents. They thus become a decided economic asset to the family rather than a burden. The dependence of the parents on the children becomes clearer at this time and the young people tend to have a more secure position in the family. In contrast with our own society, there is a notable absence of open "revolt" against the authority and example of parents or of local tradition; the exceptions occur in connection with courtship and elopement. The authoritarian family and the lack of alternatives have tended to produce young people who are passive and dependent. A very small percentage are willing or able to strike out on their own, and no pattern of running away from home "to seek one's fortune" exists in the village. The only evidences of some break with tradition are shown by a very small group of boys and girls who have studied outside the village. As we shall see later, these patterns are rapidly changing.

In terms of behavior and experience, the period of adolescence has, however, a different—almost a contrasting—significance for boys and for girls. For girls it brings additional personal restrictions, chaperonage, a larger burden of not entirely desirable work, and few rewards. Between twelve and fifteen, girls are expected to give up their friends and play habits and to devote themselves to household chores. They are given almost the entire care of younger siblings, though they have little authority over them. On a girl's fifteenth birthday her parents prepare her for marriage by giving her a pair of shoes to wear on holidays, a bright-colored dress and apron, and perhaps silver or gold earrings. From then on she pays a great deal of attention to her appearance and is usually better groomed than either *niñas* or married women. She must now do almost everything that a married woman does—wash and iron the larger pieces of clothing, sew, grind corn and coffee, make different types of tortillas, cook all the food eaten by the family, and learn to prepare complicated fiesta dishes.

The appearance of the first menses is a traumatic experience for most girls, since they have usually been kept in ignorance of it. They associate it with something shameful, dirty, and even punishable, and keep it secret. Girls who remain in school longer generally learn about it sooner and feel less fear and guilt, but many girls express some shame and disgust about it. In the past, when girls married before puberty, it was widely believed that menstruation was caused by sexual intercourse. This belief has still not been entirely eradicated. The grandmother or the mother eventually gives the girl advice on proper behavior during menstruation. They warn that bathing or washing the feet or eating "cold" foods such as pork, avocado, beans, and lemon might stop the flow. Menstruation is expected to last three days and the flow is generally sparse.

The adjustment of an adolescent girl to her home situation varies considerably. In large part it depends upon her relations with her mother. The close relationship between adolescent girl and mother is recent in Tepoztlán, for child marriage and patrilocal residence effectively severed the mother-daughter tie in past years. The young daughter-in-law was considered a main source of help to the mother-in-law, and many of the attitudes of the mother-in-law—daughter-in-law relationship were later carried over to the mother-daughter relationship. Mothers of grown daughters tend to "retire" from most of the heavy household duties and to assume the role of director rather than that of partner. The life stories we have gathered show that at least in retrospect women resent their mothers for having overworked them. On the whole, however, adolescent girls seem satisfied with the more rewarding aspects of their life—nicer clothes, little luxuries that their parents see fit to buy for them, trips to the plaza or the mill, and attendance at church and fiestas. Courtship provides a good deal of excitement although it is also a source of worry and fear.

For boys, adolescence brings greater freedom than before and more respectful treatment at home. They begin to work seriously at farming, the most important and best-rewarded work in the village. Most boys and youths enjoy farming and are pleased at the prospect of becoming a peasant. When a boy is able to do a man's work, his status improves noticeably; he is given a larger share of food, clothing, and spending money, is served equally with his father, and has more authority over younger siblings. The work relations between father and son are generally smoother than those between mother and daughter. The authoritarian, reserved figure of the father usually inspires complete obedience from the son. Moreover, fathers tend to be patient in teaching their sons, and the work is done side by side, with the father usually taking the heavier burden.

Adolescent interest in modern sports is becoming a source of conflict. Parents object to the playing of soccer, volleyball, and pool—the three most popular sports among boys—as childish, wasteful, and dangerous. They believe that sports use up the precious energy needed in the *milpas;* they say the ax, *machete,* and team of oxen provide all the exercise a farmer can endure. Mothers complain that the boys get overheated and then are particularly susceptible to *los aires.* Older men dislike the new sports because they are replacing the older diversions such as rodeos and cockfights.

The most important diversion for youths and one that gives them a real sense of achievement is courtship—a relatively new phenomenon in Tepoztlán. Before the Revolution, most marriages were arranged by the parents with or without the consent of the children. The engaged couple were not permitted to be alone together and sometimes were not even acquainted before marriage. Only betrothed couples from the few better-to-do, literate families courted secretly by exchanging love letters. Today courtship and the sending of love letters are common in the village, and few girls over thirteen or boys over fifteen do not have a sweetheart. The local priest has recognized this situation and has stated publicly that having a *novio* is not a sin and need not be mentioned in confession. A great deal of secrecy still surrounds courtship, however, and the girl still fears punishment.

As a first step in courting the boy sends the girl a letter declaring his love. Some boys may send several anonymous letters before they have the courage to sign their name. Boys with more education and self-confidence may initiate courtship in person by trying to detain the girl on the street. If the girl consents to let him walk by her side, he will at once propose that they be *novios.* It is a common sight to see a young boy loitering around a street corner for hours, waiting to get a glimpse of his *novia* or to say a few words to her. This "cornering" of a girl is a regular courting practice in Tepoztlán. At night boys often gather at a corner to play the guitar and serenade a nearby *novia* of one of the group.

Because of the difficulty in meeting, sending letters is a necessity after a boy and girl become *novios.* Letters may be left in a secret place or delivered by a trusted friend or a child. Widows and girls may be hired for the purpose of delivering love messages, patching quarrels, or convincing a girl to become someone's *novia.* Known by the insulting terms of *alcahuetes* or *corre-ve-y-dile* (run-see-and-tell), such go-betweens are strongly disapproved of; they are also suspected of knowing how to use sorcery particularly appropriate for *novios.* Love magic may be resorted to if courting is difficult. Powdered bone from a human skull, placed in a girl's hand, in her hair, or in a sweet drink, will make her fall in love. The leg of a beetle placed in a girl's drink will make her desire sexual relations. The use of sorcery for revenge by a jilted *novia* is very much feared by young men. The *novia* is believed to be able to make her former lover ill by sticking pins through a picture of him. Chronic illness in young men is often attributed to some girl's black magic.

Novios do not necessarily marry and may or may not have sexual relations. They generally caress and embrace but rarely kiss. Kissing is a modern innovation of courtship which only the more sophisticated have adopted. It is common today to have several *novios* before marriage, but a girl who has many *novios,* or who has them simultaneously, is called *loca* or crazy and severely criticized. A boy who has many *novias* is credited with being *macho* or manly but is not considered a desirable marriage partner.

Rorschach responses of twenty-five girls and boys between the ages of thirteen and nineteen clearly reflect the different training and experience of the two sexes. The girls seem to be under more control; apparently they are expected to refrain from sexual activity and to carry out their duties. They have low energy drives, are less responsive than the boys and suppress their fantasies and impulses. They follow the pattern of older women; they are detached from childish interests and are most impressed by the concrete, everyday aspects of their life. Like the girls of from nine to twelve years, these girls seem to have been pushed into an adult female pattern, but they do not seem to be enjoying it.

In contrast, the boys are more expansive in their contacts with the world about them, have more varied experiences and interests, and exhibit less control over their fantasies and feelings. They are interested in the opposite sex and are trying hard to act like men; at the same time, they show some anxiety about their sexual fantasies and activities.

Marriage

Marriage is important in establishing adult status. Men who are married and are heads of families hold positions of leadership and are responsible for local government and politics. Women move to a higher status when they become mothers. There are three types of marriage in Tepoztlán: civil marriage, church marriage, and free union. In 1940, one-half of all the marriages in the village were both civil and church law, one-fourth were church only, 15 percent were free unions, and 10 percent were civil law alone. Civil marriage has been required by law since 1928; before that, most formal marriages were church law only. Church marriage still carries the greatest prestige, but the number of civil marriages is now steadily increasing although their status is almost as low status as that of free unions.

Most girls marry between the ages of fifteen and seventeen and most boys between nineteen and twenty. If a girl is not married by the time she is twenty, she is considered an old maid who will "dress saints" for the rest of her life. More and more girls are delaying marriage, however, to go through secondary school and become teachers. As noted earlier, the great majority of Tepoztecans marry within their own village. In 1944, only 10 percent of the marriages involved outsiders and even then the nonvillage partner came either from other villages of the municipio or from nearby regions. Almost one-half of the marriages are between members of the same *barrio* within the village. Patrilocal residence is the rule although a good number of matrilocal arrangements occur.

Romantic reasons—a girl's beauty or personality—are usually behind a boy's selection of a wife. Girls are more concerned with finding a husband who does not drink, chase women, or have the reputation of being aggressive.

Status factors are important for both sexes. Boys prefer a girl who is poorer than they and who has less education so that "the man can be the boss." They tend to "respect" and to avoid having affairs with the daughters of the more prosperous families for fear of incurring reprisals. Girls, on the other hand, try to improve their economic status with marriage, and it is rare for a girl to marry a man with less education. As a result, the daughters of the better-to-do families have difficulty finding husbands and tend to marry later or to marry men from outside the village.

In giving their blessing to a marriage, parents are chiefly concerned with the practical considerations of the prospective mate's health and his family's reputation. They are interested in the personal qualities of a daughter-in-law more than of a son-in-law, although laziness, drunkenness, disobedience, or rebelliousness in the latter would cause them to oppose the marriage. The traditional, most respectable form of arranging a marriage is the *petición de mano,* or asking for the girl's hand. This is done by the boy's father and by his godfather of baptism. The mother may act as a substitute or, if the boy is an orphan, an uncle, or the godfather alone. Formerly, the parents chose a wife for their son and asked for his approval. Now the procedure is reversed; usually the boy and girl have secretly become *novios* and agree to the marriage beforehand. When the *petición de mano* occurs, the girl's parents ask for a stay of a few weeks as a matter of form. A request for a stay of one year is tantamount to a refusal. When the decision is favorable, the girl's parents question the boy about his willingness to undertake the obligation of supporting a wife. They warn him of their daughter's faults to prevent him from being dissatisfied with her after marriage and blaming them. They also give advice to their daughter: she must try to please her husband and his parents, work hard, be obedient, avoid being jealous, and not leave the house without her husband's permission. If these conversations are satisfactory, a date for the wedding is set.

In the past, an underlying idea of marriage arrangements was to compensate the bride's family for the loss of a working member. A formal bride price, known as the *chichitomin,* which means payment for the mother's milk with which the girl was raised, was paid by the groom's family. It was paid in silver pesos and varied from a few pesos to twenty-five or thirty. In addition, the young man was expected to bring wood and water to his future in-laws for a period of one or two years, and the boy's mother brought flowers and candles in the name of the girl's saint every eight days for a month before the marriage. The boy's parents also brought gifts of chocolate, bread, and wine every Sunday from the time of the *petición de mano* until the wedding day. These practices are no longer followed. The boy's mother, however, is still expected to bring gifts during the marriage negotiations.

If there is opposition to the marriage from either set of parents, the couple usually elopes. Elopements in Tepoztlán do not have the same romantic connotations they have in the United States. Rather they result from the negativism of the parents, the fear and rebellion of the daughter, the assertion of the boy over his *novia,* the wish to escape wedding expenses, or, at worst, the absence of a sense of responsibility on the part of the youth. When an elopement or *rapto* occurs, the couple go to live as man and wife in the home of a well-disposed aunt or uncle or friend. If the boy intends to marry, his parents formally ask the girl's parents for her hand. If either set of parents remains intransigent, the couple may never marry or at least not in church. Most parents accept an elopement as a *fait accompli*, however, and marriage follows. The practice of elopement is old in Tepoztlán but it has increased considerably since the Revolution. In 1942-43, approximately 50 percent of all marriages began as elopements.

To be well married in Tepoztlán is to be married in church. In order to provide a fine church wedding, a boy's parents may sell their animals or pawn their house or, if they are unwilling to do this, the boy may work outside the home and save his money for the wedding. Church weddings are becoming increasingly expensive, the cost ranging from 300 to 1,000 pesos. A wedding in the church follows Catholic tradition with local variations. On the evening before the wedding, the boy's parents send a basket of bread, chocolate, wine, and turkey to the girl's home as well as the white wedding dress with its train and veil, shoes, stockings, and flowers. The girl and the clothes are taken to the home of the godparents of marriage, where the girl spends the night. The godparents give her marital advice, emphasizing the fact that she must obey her husband. In the early morning the godmother helps her wash and dress and the godfather delivers the bride to the groom at the church door. The marriage vows, the placing of the ring, and the giving of the thirteen coins (*arrastomines*) take place at the church door, after which the couple enter the church for the Mass.

After the ceremony the wedding party returns to the godparents' home where refreshments are served and where the couple again receive marital advice. At noon the couple and their guests go to the groom's house. Some couples still carry burning incense over the threshold, but this custom is disappearing. A festive dinner of *mole poblano* follows. From then on for a year or two the couple live in the groom's house, in many cases sleeping in the same room with the rest of the family.

Civil marriage is much simpler and less expensive, and partly for this reason it is increasing. If a couple decide to live in free union, there is no celebration or announcement of any kind. The more acculturated Tepoztecans no longer regard free union as a form of marriage, no matter how many years a couple live together nor how many children they have. Most villagers, however, regard such a couple as man and wife and their children as having equal rights with other children. About a half of the free unions involve young people, although for most of them it is a second marriage.

Rorschach tests given to twenty-one adults between the ages of twenty and thirty-nine show that the young married Tepoztecan woman has learned to conform and to accept her role in life without asking for sympathy or understanding. She is a controlled, efficient individual who takes care of the material needs of everyday living with less tension than the adolescent girl. But she shows few signs of liveliness or warmth, expresses no emotional needs, and does not offer love and affection. She seems to receive little satisfaction from sex, is passive and adaptive, timid and cautious, and accepting of male domination.

On the basis of the test protocols, the young adult male seems to be fairly secure in his role as master of the house and capable of making decisions and maintaining authority. There are evidences of a carry-over of the anxiety concerning sex that was seen in the adolescent boy, however; probably the adult male is able to function well only when he feels secure in his sexual role. Indications of impulsivity, depression, and bodily preoccupation are apparent also, but these are under control.

Old Age and Death

Traditionally, old age is the time when a Tepoztecan receives the greatest respect and consideration; the consensus, however, is that less and less respect is now being shown to old people. Children have begun to address their grandparents in the familiar *tu* and some of the old customs of respect— kissing the hand of older people, for example—are falling into disuse. Old men no longer take part in politics and do not generally have positions of leadership. Because the culture is changing rapidly, the *ancianos* find themselves out of step with the times. Their values conflict with those of the younger generation, and, moreover, some of them speak Spanish poorly. They are treated with relative respect, however, and the grandparent-grandchild relationship is often a very affectionate one.

It is not old age as such that is feared by Tepoztecans, but dependence on others, or the inability to be self-supporting. Most old people work until they can no longer stand. The situation of the aged varies considerably from family to family. Ownership of property, particularly the kind that brings in a cash income from rental, is the best assurance for a secure old age, and for this reason parents usually do not divide their property among the children before their death. But most of the people in the village are poor, owning only their house and site and perhaps a few fruit trees and a pig; they can be self-supporting only by working. Many old women, especially widows, take in washing and ironing, raise pigs and chickens, sell tortillas, fruit, and produce, or earn money as midwives and *curanderas*. There are few nonstrenuous jobs for old men who can no longer farm. The lack of handicraft skills or other means of support is a real handicap to these men.

The Rorschach records of twenty-one men and women between the ages of forty-seven and seventy-four show a marked contrast with the records of young adults. The control and discipline learned by women in their younger years become their strength in old age. Undisturbed by daydreams, sexual urges, and emotional needs, the older woman takes over the household and becomes its dominant member. She still functions in a concrete, realistic way, but she is rigid, pedantic, and fussy. She is also efficient and determined. She still does not show warmth toward people, however, or the desire to cooperate in a friendly way. Older men, in contrast, have moved from a conventional, everyday way of life to a more uncontrolled and explosively emotional one. They seem to be unreflective, given to impulsive outbursts, thoughts, and ideas. They show some preoccupation with sexual functioning and have feelings of impotence. It is as though they are overwhelmed by circumstances they cannot handle and react with impulsivity, anxiety, depression, and helplessness. Apparently they have lost the mastery of their world and are traumatized and conflicted by it.

Death apparently inspires no undue fear or preoccupation. Old people freely speak of death, using the expressions, "when I am dead," or "when I am underground." Perhaps because from childhood Tepoztecans have not been protected from the facts of death, they see it as a natural occurrence. Display of grief is restrained at a death, although it varies according to the age and status of the deceased. Suicide is uncommon, and in no case has anyone killed himself because of the death of a loved one. When a Tepoztecan dies soon after the death of someone close to him, however, it is often said that he died of *sentimiento* or grief. The death of an old person or of an infant causes relatively little emotional disturbance.

Tepoztecans are concerned with the release of the soul from the body at death and with its journey to heaven. They say that those who have led wicked lives have difficulty giving up their souls and take a long time to die. They say also that often children "cannot die until they receive a benediction from their parents or godparents" and that a father or a mother "cannot die if their children cry too much." In such cases the children are taken away to hasten the death. When death comes, the soul leaves the body and may be seen as a white, foamlike figure which resembles the deceased and which walks without touching the ground but disappears after leaving the house.

When a person is at the point of death, he is taken from his bed and placed on a *petate* on the floor. With death the body is dressed with clean clothes, covered with a sheet, and placed on a table. A newspaper is spread on the *petate* and a cross of sand and lime is fashioned on the paper. Flowers are placed above the cross, and a candle, kept burning day and night for nine days, is placed at the head of the *petate*. If the deceased is a man, his sombrero and huaraches are laid next to the candle; if a woman, her *rebozo*. All the clothes of the dead person are washed and ironed and also laid on the *petate*. A *rezandero* is hired by the bereaved family to come to the house to pray twice a day for nine days. The women of the house are required to be present on these occasions and to kneel in prayer. A wake is held day and night, and coffee, alcohol, bread, and cigarettes are provided for those who come to keep vigil. Close relatives may help with the expenses. At the death of a young godchild, most godparents fulfill their obligations to provide a coffin, burial clothing, and perhaps music.

The next day a few men go to the cemetery to dig the grave. The deceased is placed in a coffin and, accompanied by the mourners, is carried to the cemetery. If the deceased is a prominent person or a member of the *Acción Católica*, the funeral procession may enter the church for a benediction before proceeding to the burial place. The church bells will be rung if a special fee is paid. On the ninth day or *novena* the ceremony of the raising of the cross of lime and sand takes place at a night wake similar to the one held on the day of the death. This time, however, an offering of tamales, *mole verde,* oranges, chocolate, and bread is left for twelve hours on the altar in the home in order to provide the deceased with food for each month of the year.

For the raising of the cross, a boy and girl who are not relatives are selected to act as *padrinos.* Accompanied by the *rezandero* and carrying flowers, the two children walk toward the *petate* which holds the cross of lime and sand. Prayers are first recited and the children are then given new brooms with which they sweep the sand and lime onto a tray that is later carried to the grave. The clothes of the deceased are also raised. As each article is picked up, the *padrinos* recite a prayer. The ceremony closes with the singing of hymns in honor of the dead. A year after the death another wake may be held, a special Mass arranged and the grave revisited.

A child's funeral is somewhat different. Because the child's soul goes directly to heaven, it is supposed to be a joyous occasion, and gay music is played. The child is dressed like San Jose if a boy, like the Virgin of Guadalupe if a girl. A crown of paper flowers is placed on the head, the face covered with a veil, and the feet fitted into socks and sandals lined with gold paper. When the body is laid out, the hands and feet are tied together with ribbons, which are untied at the grave. A small painted gourd, placed beside the body, is believed to provide the soul with water during its journey to heaven. The litter is carried by children of the same sex as the deceased and, as the body is taken out of the house, the barrio chapel bell is rung.

7

Ethos

THE TRADITIONAL world-view of Tepoztecans has been conditioned by the limitations of their physical environment, technology, and economy, by their turbulent history, by their three-hundred years of colonial status, by their poverty and high death rate, and finally by the haphazard nature of social changes caused by urban influences. To Tepoztecans, the world and nature present a constant threat of calamity and danger. A strong fear of natural forces and a high anxiety about the imminence of misfortune, disaster, and death were revealed in Thematic Apperception Test stories and in dreams collected from a sample of the villagers. The sample included members of the younger generation who had been under the influence of the school.

The world in which Tepoztecans live is filled with hostile forces and punishing figures which must be propitiated if their good will and protection are to be secured. El Tepozteco withholds rain if he is neglected; *los aires,* the spirits who live in the water, send illness to those who offend them; and *naguales,* humans in pact with the devil, can turn themselves into a pig or dog to do harm at night. Catholic figures, too, are seen as threatening. God is a punishing figure rather than one of love, and most misfortunes are ascribed to Him. He brings good fortune only rarely.

The saints are seen as intermediaries between God and man, and Tepoztecans devote themselves to cultivating their favor. The saints with the greater punishing power—for example, Saint Peter of the barrio of San Pedro—are the most assiduously worshiped. If not enough dancers turn out for Saint Peter's feast day, he brings illness and bad luck to those who did not participate. He is also said to use the lion, whose image accompanies his, to frighten children into dancing for him. The lion will also be sent to frighten a villager who does not accept the office of *mayordomo* of the barrio of San Pedro.

Most Tepoztecans do not distinguish clearly between the punishments of God and the work of *el pingo,* the devil. The powers of the devil are relatively few, however, and may be mitigated by reciting a prayer to Saint Michael

326

or to Saint Gabriel. (To avoid angering the devil, a small candle is lighted to him at the same time.) Nor do Tepoztecans have a clear conception of the Catholic heaven and hell. The Aztec religion depicted heaven as a pleasant place reserved for dead warriors and women who died in childbirth. The equivalent of hell was only a region of the dead, *Mictlan,* where souls continued to live the same life as they had on earth. Hell as a place for expiating sins committed in life was totally unknown, and many Tepoztecans still have no notion of eternal punishment. Hell is thought, rather, to be a purgatory which punishes only the greatest sinners. Ordinary people do not fear hell and usually have no concern with sin, with confession, or with life after death.

The profoundly practical nature of Tepoztecans precludes religious fantasy, mysticism, or any preoccupation with metaphysics. They seek from religion concrete solutions to the problems of daily life. They can understand punishment for things done or not done and the need for protection. They bow to superior powers by doing what is expected of them or by giving or doing something that should please a particular being: lighting a candle, offering a few coins or flowers, burning incense, reciting a special prayer, or performing a certain dance. They believe these offerings incur an obligation on the part of the recipient to favor or protect the donor.

To traditional Catholic symbols Tepoztecans impart magical powers which give them additional protection. They receive the Ash on Ash Wednesday in the belief that the cross, the formal Catholic symbol of penance and sorrow, will guard them against sorcery and enemies. Old holy images are burned to make more efficacious ashes. The palm blessed on Palm Sunday is used for protection against lightning; its ashes are used to cure headaches. Peasants trim their plants on Holy Saturday so that they will produce more, mothers cut their daughters' hair to make it grow longer, and children are struck on the legs to make them taller. On September 28, crosses of *pericón* that have been pressed are placed on doorways and *milpas* to ward off demons and evil winds.

Tepoztecans view people, too, as potentially hostile and dangerous, and their typical reaction is a defensive one. Security in the threatening world is sought first and foremost through the economic independence of the biological family. To be able to provide one's wife and children with food, clothing, and shelter is the only real assurance against want and interference. Work, industry, and thrift, for the purpose of accumulating property in land and animals, are the highest, most enduring values in Tepoztlán. So long as a man devotes himself to work, he feels secure and blameless, regardless of how little he produces. Material success is not openly admitted as an important personal goal and is not admired in others. With faith in his own power and with the help of God, the Tepoztecan lives as an individualist, withdrawn, self-reliant, reluctant to seek or give economic aid, or to borrow or lend. Despite the tradition of collective labor, there is a general unwillingness to cooperate with others in public and private enterprises.

The Tepoztecan's individualism and independence are tempered, however, by his loyalty to and cooperation with his immediate family. The dependence of families on the communal lands and the occasional need for group effort to defend these lands and to maintain public property also modify Tepoztecan individualism. This individualism, however, is not competitive as in the United States. In the village, the individual does not try to win security and recognition through development of his personal talents or through self-aggrandizement but rather through conformity and submission to the needs of his family. It is an enclosing, inward-turning individualism which permits families to live side by side in privacy and with no power over one another. This is what gives the village its segmentalized character.

Tepoztecans also seek security through respect and the extension of the respect relationship, which they value highly as a safe one. In such a relationship each party is guaranteed friendly, respectful behavior and the fulfillment of formal obligations. Respect status may stem from a superior social, economic, or political position, from advanced age, from education, or from a specific, formal relationship established between two individuals or families— for example, in-laws or *compadres*. Among young people who have studied outside the village there is now a tendency toward the urban usage of *tu* and *Usted;* this means the practice of using *tu* only for relatives and intimate friends and using *Usted* for all others. This results in fewer *tu* and more *Usted* relationships.

Tepoztecans are not an easy people to get to know, for they are not outgoing or expressive. Most interpersonal relationships are characterized by reserve and carefully guarded behavior. The man who speaks little, minds his own business, and maintains some distance between himself and others is considered prudent and wise. The people are sombre and quiet, especially in the street. Boisterousness and noise coming from a house soon earns the family an unpleasant reputation. Women and girls are expected to walk with eyes modestly downcast; those who smile freely may be thought flirtatious or flippant. To smile very much at other peoples' babies is to be suspected of the evil eye. Most children do not learn to smile at strangers or visitors until they attend school. Tepoztecan men, particularly, tend to be undemonstrative and limited in their ability to express warmth and affection and the more tender emotions. One informant succinctly described himself and his fellow villagers by saying, "*Somos muy secos*"—that is, "We are very dry."

Creativity and artistic expression are limited to the point of constriction. As noted earlier, there are practically no handicrafts, no pottery, woodcarving, weaving, or basketmaking. Music and dancing are not well developed. Religious artistic expression consists only of decorating the church at fiestas and of making costumes and masks for a few annual religious dances. Clay utensils and household articles are for the most part undecorated. The clothes of the village women are traditionally drab, although young girls are now beginning to wear brighter colored dresses. Bright colors, particularly in clothing, have not been in accord with Tepoztecan ideas of propriety and in the past were actually believed to be dangerous because they might attract the rainbow. Most of the color in Tepoztlán comes from the beautiful flowers that grow in the gardens.

Constriction is also evidenced in Tepoztecans' gestures and in their avoidance of bodily contact with others. Perhaps the only major exception occurs in the mother-child relationship during the nursing period; after a child is five, he experiences little physical contact of a tender nature. Kissing, except of infants, is not customary even in courtship, as we have seen. From the Spanish, Tepoztecans learned the gesture of kissing the hand of the priest, parents, grandparents, and godparents but this custom is now disappearing. Shaking hands and the typical Mexican double embrace are not generally practiced in Tepoztlán. It is when Tepoztecans drink that their restraint relaxes; male companions may then walk arm-in-arm and, as we mentioned earlier, drunken men sometimes try to hug and even kiss their children or wives.

Normally, the Tepoztecan shows his affection for another by fulfilling reciprocal obligations: the father expresses love for his wife and children by providing them with the necessities of life; the child shows affection by obedience, respect, and diligence; *compadres* and members of the extended family demonstrate their friendship and goodwill by carrying out their formal duties. When these obligations are carried out, Tepoztecans consider that they have a satisfactory relationship with each other and demand little more. Some of the younger people, it is true, are no longer content with formal reciprocity and seek out friends on the basis of personal interest. Younger parents are beginning to express affection for their children through gift giving and through greater indulgence and concern with their children's aspirations.

Tepoztecans place value on sexual restraint not because they are puritanical or guilt ridden but because of practical considerations of safety and self-preservation. They believe in conserving themselves for work. They also fear too strong attachments, unwanted pregnancies, and jealousy and sorcery. From childhood on, sexuality is discouraged and discussion of sex is taboo in the home; infant sexuality, masturbation, and sex play among children are strictly forbidden. For women, there is little inconsistency between childhood training and acceptable adult behavior. Girls grow up with negative, prudish attitudes toward sex, marriage, and childbearing; they are expected to be sexually restrained both before and after marriage. For males, however, a discontinuity exists in connection with sex. Although sexuality is inhibited all through childhood, young men are subjected to pressure from members of their age group to be sexually active; they are expected to prove their manliness through sexual conquests both before and after marriage. In practice, however, the attitudes toward sex and the slow development of boys create an aura of anxiety about sexual activity and boys are often timid in courtship. The prevailing attitude is, nevertheless, that sexual activity in men is an expression of manliness, while in women it is a form of delinquency.

Tepoztecans are an indirect people who rely on formality and intermediaries to facilitate interpersonal relations. Any direct expression of aggression is discouraged and competition between individuals is rare. Underlying the smooth surface, however, is a feeling of oppression, particularly for those individuals who are trying to improve themselves or who, for one reason or another, deviate from strict conformity. A good deal of suppressed hostility finds indirect release in malicious gossip, stealing, secret destruction of other's property, envy, deprecation, and sorcery. The *indirecta* or indirect criticism is a common, accepted form of aggression. Assault in the form of surprise attack and murder occurs from time to time. Men in positions of wealth, power, or authority often carry a gun for protection and prefer not to venture out at night. The most feared, although perhaps the least common, form of indirect aggression is sorcery.

The sanctions against any overt expression of aggression sometimes give rise to an interesting type of illness known as *muina* or anger, in which the aggression is apparently turned inward against the self. The symptoms of *muina* are loss of appetite, inability to keep down food, loss of weight, and very often death. *Muina* is a fairly common condition and occurs among members of both sexes; it is mainly an adult illness but children sometimes have it. It may be caused by insults, humiliation, bad luck, or any frustration that arouses anger.

In Tepoztlán the motives of everyone are suspect, from the highest public officials of the nation to the local priest and even close relatives. It is assumed that anyone who has power will use it to his own advantage. Honest government or leadership is considered an impossibility; altruism is not understood. The frank, direct person, if he exists anywhere in the village, is thought to be naive or the greatest rogue of all, so powerful or so shameless as to have no need to conceal his actions or thoughts. Friendships are few. To have friendships outside the extended family is not a Tepoztecan ideal, nor is there a long tradition of a "best friend." Adults consider friends a source of trouble and a waste of time. Traditionally, women and girls are not supposed to have any friends whatsoever. While men may be friendly with many individuals, these relations tend to be based on a definite, limited purpose—that is, for work exchange, or for borrowing, or for drinking together.

There is a relative lack of concern for the future, and no "saving for a rainy day." Only a minority who recognize education as an important source of security save for an advanced education for a son or daughter. And it is only among these families that one encounters the familiar urban middle-class pattern of self-denial in the present in order to gain a future reward. The rest of the villagers exercise a general thrift, but they spend when they have money and pull in their belts when they have none. Young people planning to be married do not save in anticipation of future needs but marry at short notice. As we have noted, the boy's parents supply the money for the wedding by selling an animal or by borrowing, and the boy sometimes goes to work for two or three months to raise the money.

The majority of Tepoztecans seem to lack strong drive or ambition for self-improvement. They tend to be satisfied if they have enough food and clothing from harvest to harvest. Among the young people, too, there is a general acceptance of the way of life. Young men wish to be peasants like their fathers and most young girls continue to work at home and to serve their elders. The rewards they seek are not impossible to achieve: occasional new clothes, shoes, a sweetheart, permission to attend the fiestas, and ultimately marriage, with some parental help.

Of particular interest for the understanding of the relative absence of frustration, anxiety, guilt, and self-blame is the tendency to shift personal responsibility onto others or onto impersonal forces and to explain nonconformity in terms of magical or other supernatural forces. The individual cannot help what he does, for these forces control him. Such traits as fatalism, stoicism in the face of misfortune, passivity, acceptance of things as they are, and a general readiness to expect the worst tend to free the individual from the burden of being in control of his personal fate. Even in the face of gross injustice, in which a villager could be protected by law, there may be little or no self-defense.

The patterns of child training, which we have discussed earlier, reflect many adult attitudes and value systems. One of the underlying principles in child rearing is to develop children who are easy to control. The great amount of attention given an infant is primarily for the purpose of limiting and protecting him rather than of stimulating him. Activity, aggression, self-gratification, curiosity, and independence are all discouraged from infancy through young adulthood. Although the young child, especially if he is a boy, is indulged in some ways and permitted a degree of ego development, so long as a son or daughter lives under the parental roof, he is dependent on the parents and subject to their authority—and this situation may continue through marriage.

Although, by and large, the training the child receives adequately prepares him for adult life in the village, nevertheless there are some points of conflict and inconsistency between theory and practice. Perhaps the primary area of conflict is found in the roles of men and women and in the relations between the sexes. On the whole, men are under greater pressure than women, experience more discontinuity in the transition from childhood to adulthood, and face greater contradictions between their ideal and actual social roles. Although boys are favored more than girls, their early training is not conducive to the development of independence or a real ability to dominate, qualities required by the ideals of a patriarchal society. We have seen that husbands frequently rely on fear to maintain authority. As the men grow older and as their sexual powers and their ability to work decline, they find it more difficult to keep their position of dominance; older men in the community receive little social recognition and have little power. It is interesting to note that the life cycles of men and women take an opposite course: in early life men are in a comparatively favored position but as they grow older they are weighed down by life situations. Women begin with less freedom, lower aspiration levels, and earlier responsibilities, but as they mature after marriage they slowly gain more freedom and often take a dominant position in the household.

Discrepancy between theory and practice in Tepoztecan society is also

found in the different degree of socialization of men and women. The men
have greater freedom and higher social status, but it is the women who seem
to be better socialized. This greater socialization begins early in life. While
girls are taking care of their brothers and sisters under the watchful eye of
their mother, their brothers are out in the fields, often alone, guarding the
animals. Women are seldom alone. At home they are surrounded by members
of the family and have opportunities to chat with neighbors and relatives.
Their daily trips to the plaza offer occasions for gossip and news. They attend
church more often and prepare festive meals with the aid of other women.
Men continue to spend most of their days alone at work in the fields. Occasions
for communal work are few and even these seem to have to be accompanied
by drinking. In fact, the men do not seem to be at ease in groups unless they
are fortified by alcohol.

A highly respected native curer.

8

The Changing Village

THE DESCRIPTION of Tepoztlán given in the preceding pages is based largely on my study of the village in 1943. Since that time many changes have occurred both in the village and in Mexico as a whole. Here I will sketch briefly some of the major changes on the national level and then examine those in the village as revealed by my restudy in 1956. In this way the reader can see to what extent Tepoztlán has participated in national trends.

The Nation

Mexico has undergone great changes since 1940. The population has increased by over ten million to reach a high of about thirty million in 1956. This increase has been accompanied by a surge of urbanization, with millions of peasants and villagers moving into the cities. The population growth of Mexico City has been phenomenal—from one and a half million in 1940 to four million in 1956. The economy has been expanding and the country has become acutely production conscious. A boom spirit has been created reminiscent of the great expansion in the United States at the turn of the century. Many Mexicans believe that their country has found a formula which will soon take it out of the ranks of the underdeveloped nations and will serve as a model to other countries.

Achievements in agriculture and industry have been record breaking; in view of the arid nature of the country, those in agriculture are even more impressive than those in industry. Since 1940, about a million and a half hectares have been brought under irrigation; the total harvested area has been increased by about 70 percent; and the number of tractors has increased from 4,600 to over 55,000.

Increased national wealth has led to some improvement in the standard of living of the general population. More and more rural people sleep on beds instead of on the ground, wear shoes instead of huaraches or instead of going barefoot, use store-made pants instead of the home-made white *calzones*, eat bread in addition to tortillas, grind their corn in the mill instead of by hand, drink beer instead of pulque, use doctors instead of *curanderos*, and travel by bus or train instead of on foot and on burro. In the towns and cities the trend has been from adobe to cement, from clay pots to aluminum, from charcoal to gas cooking, from tortillas as eating "implements" to tableware, from the *metate* to the electric blender, from phonographs to radios and television, from cotton to nylon, and from cognac to whiskey.

Another significant trend since 1940 has been the increasing influence of United States culture. The major television programs are sponsored by foreign controlled companies and only the use of the Spanish language and Mexican artists distinguish some of the commercials from those in the United States. Such American department store retail practices as self-service, attractive open displays of goods, standardized and guaranteed articles, and fixed prices have been made more popular in the past ten years by stores like Woolworths and Sears and Roebuck. Self-service supermarkets, complete with packaged foods and many with American brands, are opening in the better-to-do neighborhoods of Mexico City and in some of the smaller towns. American-made clothing and shoes are sold in the higher priced shops.

Increased employment in factories and office buildings has led to the spread of the quick lunch, eliminating the midday meal at home as well as the traditional siesta. The American-style breakfast—juice, cereal, ham and eggs, and coffee—has become popular, displacing the traditional beans, chili sauce, and tortillas. The practice of eating roast turkey on Christmas eve has been adopted by some urban middle-class families. The same trend is seen in the substitution of the Christmas tree for the customary Nativity scene and in the giving of gifts on December 25 instead of on January 6, the Day of the Three Kings. The spread of English is also noteworthy. English has replaced French as a second language in the schools.

Despite the increased production and the apparent prosperity, Mexico has many problems to face. Although the national wealth has increased greatly, its uneven distribution has made the disparity between the incomes of the rich and poor more striking than ever before. And despite some rise in the general standard of living, over 60 percent of the population were still ill-fed, ill-housed, and ill-clothed in 1956, 40 percent were illiterate, and 46 percent of the nation's children were not going to school. A chronic inflation since 1940 has squeezed the real income of the poor, and the cost of living for workers in Mexico City has risen five times since 1939. According to the census of 1950 (published in 1955), 89 percent of all Mexican families reporting income earned less than 600 pesos a month or $69 dollars at the 1950 rate of exchange.

The great increase in agricultural production in the past twenty years has been concentrated in only two regions of the country, the north and northwest, where a new commercial agriculture based upon large private holdings, irrigation, and mechanization has developed. The great mass of the peasantry, including those in Tepoztlán, continue to work their tiny subsistence holdings with traditional backward methods. And the contrast between the old and the new agriculture in Mexico is becoming sharper: less than 1 percent of the cultivated land is worked with the aid of the country's 55,000 tractors; about 20 percent of the land is still worked by the pre-Hispanic method of cutting and burning without benefit of plow and oxen. The production of Mexico's two basic food crops, corn and beans, has managed to keep up with the rapid population growth in the past twenty years but the margin of security has been slight. In drought years Mexico has been forced to spend its precious dollars to import huge quantities of corn to feed its people.

That the Mexican economy cannot give jobs to all of its people is indicated in the fact that from 1942 to 1955 about a million and a half Mexicans came to the United States as *braceros* or temporary agricultural laborers, and this figure does not include the "wet backs" and other illegal immigration. Mexico has also become increasingly dependent on the United States tourist trade for stabilizing its economy. In 1957, over 700,000 tourists from the United States spent almost 600 million dollars in Mexico, making tourism the single largest industry in the country. The income from the tourist trade is about equal to the total Mexican federal budget.

One aspect of the standard of living which has improved very little since 1940 is housing. With a rapidly rising population and with urbanization, crowding and slum conditions in the larger cities and towns are actually getting worse. Of the 5.2 million dwellings reported in the Mexican census of 1950, 60 percent had only one room and 25 percent two rooms; 70 percent of all houses were made of adobe, wood, poles and rods, or rubble, and only 18 percent of brick and masonry. Only 17 percent had private, piped water.

The Village

How has Tepoztlán changed in the light of these national trends? In 1956 the village did not look much different from the way it looked in 1943. The plaza and market still seemed rather desolate and unprosperous; no additional buildings had been built in the center. There were no new streets or paved roads except for two long cement treads which led up a steep street to the *Posada del Tepozteco*, the new tourist resort run by an American family. More automobile and bus traffic entered the village, and trucks came in with such new items as purified water and tanks of cooking gas for the homes of the foreign colony.

Village men still carried water to their homes from the nearest fountain; women still queued up to have their corn ground at the mills. The older people looked much the same, but the clothes of the younger people were more varied, colorful, and citified. More young women had short hair and permanent waves, and one young girl wore blue jeans. The young men wore modern trousers, shirts, and jackets, and more children had shoes, sweaters, and store-bought clothes. The small shops sold more canned goods and packaged foods, mostly to the employed people who live in the center. Old women sold ready-made tortillas in the plaza. There was still no restaurant but there were more saloons. A blare of radios came from the houses and inside some homes one saw a new kerosene or Coleman stove, aluminum pots, kerosene or gasoline lamps, forks, and hand presses for shaping tortillas. At least one home had overstuffed furniture.

But many more changes have occurred than meet the eye. As a result of the population increase—from 3,500 in 1940 to approximately 4,800 in 1957—there is a shortage of housesites and housing, and Tepoztecans petitioned the local government to make available some of the nearby communal lands for new housesites. Several homes have been built on the outskirts of the village and in the surrounding *cerros*. Formerly it was not customary to rent a house; if a Tepoztecan had an extra house he would allow another villager to use it simply for the care of it. Now rental has become quite usual.

Since the late forties Tepoztlán has had a resident doctor and since 1952 a doctor from Cuernavaca who formerly practiced in the village has come once a week to see his patients. The clientele of both doctors has been increasing. In 1950, the resident doctor had an average of 75 patients a month; by 1956 the average was 160. Tepoztecans now complain about the expense of medicines and the delay caused by having prescriptions filled in Cuernavaca; the local "druggist" cannot fill prescriptions and carries few patent medicines. The village has a free federal government health clinic which cares for children and pregnant women and administers injections. About ten patients, most of them expectant mothers, come there every day. In 1955 approximately two thousand vaccinations and revaccinations were given.

The clinic and the doctor have by no means replaced the *curanderos*, however. Tepoztecans believe that doctors can cure only certain diseases, and still frequent *curanderos* for those illnesses which they attribute to *los aires*, anger, hot or cold foods, evil eye, and sorcery. Most births are still attended by the native midwives. If the doctor happens to cure an illness thought to be caused by *los aires*, this is taken as proof that the *aires* were not truly the cause. Although the villagers have substituted new terms for old concepts—for example, *los aires* are now sometimes described as tiny animals or microbes and injections are called "cleansings"—it is questionable whether this represents much of a departure from the earlier magical thinking about the causes of disease.

Like many villages in the densely populated central plateau area, Tepoztlán has not had the benefit of the great new hydroelectric and irrigation projects. Its agricultural base has remained very much the same; there has been no mechanization and no new important cash crops have been introduced. The peasants continue to work their land as before, although a few are now using some commercial fertilizer. Because the lack of change in agriculture combined with the rapidly increasing population has forced Tepoztecans to seek work in nonfarm occupations, a much lower proportion of the gainfully occupied are now peasants. The federal campaign for the preservation of the forest resources sharply reduced charcoal production in the village and many families have thereby lost a traditional source of income. Some found work as agricultural laborers on the two or three gladiola farms that have been established in Tepoztlán; others have been employed by the nearby Y.M.C.A. Many more found work in Cuernavaca or as day laborers on road construction.

The changes in the occupational structure of the village have accentuated earlier trends. The number of nonagricultural occupations increased from 26 in 1944 to 33 in 1956 and the number of people engaged in these occupations rose from 273 to 565. This increase has been accompanied by greater specialization and a decline in the role of agriculture in the total economy. In 1944, approximately 70 percent of those engaged in nonagricultural occupations also farmed; in 1956, the comparable figure was only 25 percent! Today there is a much greater participation of women in the nonagricultural occupations than formerly. Women still predominate as teachers, *curanderos*, and corn merchants, but they now are also full-time tortilla makers, dressmakers, and hairdressers. Other new occupations in the village are those of tailor, *ciruela* merchant, and milk merchant. The increase in the number of teachers has been striking—from 21 in 1944 to 101 in 1956, an indication of the growth of a middle class in the village. Whereas formerly there was a shortage of teachers in the village, there is now a shortage of teaching jobs, and 70 Tepoztecans teach in rural schools outside of the village. Other occupations that have shown a large increase in numbers are: bus line employees, from 22 to 35; barbers, from 15 to 22; butchers, from 15 to 32; and storekeepers, from 20 to 64.

The distribution of people engaged in nonagricultural occupations by barrio shows an intensification of the older pattern of concentration in the larger central barrios: La Santísima, 27 percent; Santo Domingo, 25 percent; San Miguel, 23 percent; Santa Cruz, 11 percent; San Sebastian, 8 percent; Los Reyes, 5 percent; and San Pedro, 1 percent. Similarly, 85 percent of those engaged in the new occupations come from the three central barrios. The trend toward barrio differentiation of occupations, however, has been offset by a spread of services from the central plaza to the barrios. Each barrio now has its own corn mill and at least one store. Another interesting and symptomatic change has been the rise in the number of money lenders—from about 6 in 1944 to 18 in 1956. This reflects a much greater need for cash as well as an influx of wealth.

The only occupations that have shown a decline in the number of members since 1944 are those of carpenter, *curandero, chirimitero* (flute player), maguey fiber collector, and charcoal maker. The *huehuechiques* (ceremonial barrio officers) have completely disappeared, as I predicted in my earlier study. The *chirimiteros* are being replaced by modern secular musicians. As noted earlier, the decline in charcoal making was forced on the village by the federal authorities.

The most dramatic occupational change and one which has become a major new source of income to the village is the *bracero* movement. In 1948, fewer than thirty Tepoztecans were *braceros*—that is, temporary agricultural workers in the United States; by 1957, over six hundred men had been *braceros* for periods that varied from forty-five days to over a year. This occupational change has made for other great changes in the village. In 1943, Tepoztlán suffered from an acute land shortage. Now, because in many cases the *braceros* return to the village only to rest a few months before setting out for another period in the United States, it suffers from a shortage of manpower, and many *milpas* go uncultivated. The *braceros* earn more in some months in the United States than they could earn in almost two years in the village, and many of them have invested their savings in improvements for their houses and in land and cattle. Many have brought home portable radios, mechanical toys, clothing, and cloth—the village now has four full-time tailors who are kept busy providing tailor-made pants for the villagers. Although the *bracero* movement has broadened the perspective of some Tepoztecans, who now greet American visitors with a few words of English, most of the *braceros* are isolated in work camps or on farms, speak no English, live on a Mexican diet, and on the whole learn little about the United States and its way of life. Very few learn agricultural skills that can be applied in the village.

Most of the *braceros* from Tepoztlán are young men between the ages of twenty and thirty. They come predominantly from the upper segments of the lower economic group (Group I) but also from the middle group II (see p. 37). Few come from the poorest families and fewer from the wealthier families of Group III. This is an interesting change from the pattern in the early forties when only individuals with political connections and with experience outside of the village became *braceros*. At that time most Tepoztecans feared to leave the village for a distant country or even to go to the government recruiting stations for *braceros* in Mexico City. With more education, the younger generation developed a greater readiness to explore the outside world and to dare the hazards of a long journey. The sudden spurt in *bracerismo* did not occur, however, until a school teacher in one of the outlying villages became a *bracero* recruiter (locally called *coyote*). He had been a *bracero* himself and knew how to make the necessary legal arrangements. Tepoztecan men paid him a fee in the hope that he would get them longer contracts and also jobs in California rather than in Texas or Arkansas. The fees, which the *coyote* purportedly shared with government authorities, ranged from 200 to 400 pesos depending on the length of time of work specified in the contract. Most of the villagers who signed up had to borrow from local money lenders at the usual high rate of interest but they had avoided having to deal directly with the authorities and so had found the courage to take the initial step.

The *bracero* movement has served as a partial though temporary solution of the agrarian problem in the village. Tepoztlán has become dependent on the United States economy. Were the United States suddenly to close its borders to Mexican *braceros*, there would probably be a crisis both in the village and in the nation.

Another important change in Tepoztecans is their greater readiness to sell their land. In 1943, it was difficult to find anyone in the village who would consider selling a house-site or an agricultural plot. For example, in 1942 a leading Mexican banker who wanted to build a home in the village negotiated for over a year before he succeeded in buying a modest-sized idle plot of land whose owner was living in Mexico City. By 1956, Tepoztecans had sold almost forty plots to as many outsiders for building homes in the village and in the lovely valley below. Tepoztecan middlemen are now speculating in land because of the steadily rising prices. A village site valued at about 50 centavos per square meter in 1943 sold in 1957 for as much as 12 pesos a meter (100 centavos to the peso).

Tepoztlán has become an international tourist colony. The non-Tepoztecan home owners now include native Mexicans, naturalized Mexican citizens of Spanish, French, German, Dutch, Japanese, and Italian ancestry, and a few Americans. Few of these people live in the village the year around but spend their holidays and vacations there. The construction of thirty-five new homes for the foreign colony has given employment to some Tepoztecan masons and day laborers. Some of the building materials—stone, sand, and tiles—also have been purchased locally. A number of the families have taken Tepoztecan girls as domestic servants both in the village and in their Mexico City or United States homes, and about a dozen Tepoztecans have jobs as caretakers. The colony also provides some additional income to local meat and milk dealers and other merchants. On the whole, the "foreigners" form few friendships in the village and except for the *Carnaval* participate very little in village affairs. It is said that most of the outsiders opposed the campaign to bring electricity to Tepoztlán for fear that it might spoil the primitive rustic quality of the village. It should be noted that among the non-Tepoztecans who have lived in the village are some of Mexico's leading intellectuals and artists and a few doctors. Some of these men have taken a great interest in the villagers and have helped them in their efforts to build a new high school, to obtain city water, and most recently (June 1958) to procure electricity.

Other forms of tourism have also grown rapidly and tourist facilities have improved. Most important has been the conversion of the banker's private home into one of the most charming resorts in Mexico, the *Posada del Tepozteco*. Since the late forties, Mexican and Hollywood movie producers have used Tepoztlán as the setting for a number of movies.

Since 1943, educational facilities have been expanded in the village. Two new schools built in the larger barrios gave the village a total of four elementary schools. Attendance rose from about 750 in 1950 to over 900 in 1956. In 1950, a high school was completed, and attendance rose from 54 in the first year to 110 in 1956. Boys still predominate over girls in both elementary and high schools. The surrounding villages have begun to reach out for higher education and now send their children to the central high school in Tepoztlán. Each year a number of Tepoztecan high-school graduates go on to the university in Mexico City.

In the past ten years bus travel to Cuernavaca has almost doubled and travel to Mexico City also has increased. On an average week day approximately 500 Tepoztecans take the bus to Cuernavaca to work, shop, study, sell produce, and to find recreation. Some of the peasants now think it worthwhile to take the bus to their *milpas*, a distance of two or three kilometers, rather than spend the time and energy in walking. A count made on a Wednesday in July 1956 showed that 84 vehicles entered the village and 94 left it between 5 A.M. and 9 P.M. Thirty-six percent were buses which ran about two times an hour in both directions (to and from Cuernavaca), 41 percent were passenger cars, and 23 percent were trucks. The trucks carried various products—corn, pigs, plants, beer, gravel, groceries, soft drinks, and petroleum. A similar count made on a Sunday gave a total of 373 vehicles entering and leaving. The buses carried approximately 800 passengers during the day.

In 1943, the number of radios in the village was only three or four; by 1956 it had risen to eighty, battery operated, for electricity had not yet come to the village. The owners were mainly under forty; older people showed little interest in radios. Most of them had been bought in Cuernavaca since 1950 at prices ranging from 400 to 3,500 pesos. They were intended chiefly for family use but their presence has increased visiting and sociability among the younger people. The listeners are usually not program conscious. Whenever they want to listen to something, they turn the dials to whatever sounds good. *Ranchero* music is the most popular attraction, news a secondary item. Major obstacles to the further use of radios have been lack of money and the absence of electricity, which meant trouble and expense in keeping the batteries charged. About 15 percent of the sets were not working in July 1956 because the batteries had run down. Tepoztecans who had relatives or *compadres* among bus drivers could have their batteries installed in a bus for a day and so have them charged without cost.

In 1956, as part of a federal government project to improve communications, a telephone exchange was installed in a small grocery store in Tepoztlán. Six phones were listed for the village in the Cuernavaca directory, almost all of them for local businesses. Storekeepers can now make orders, politicians can arrange meetings, and in emergencies ambulances and doctors can be reached by phone. During the day, calls are sent and received through the central office; at night, when the central office is closed, calls go to the *Posada*. The grocer charges 50 centavos to call someone to the phone, provided they live near the center of the village. During my stay in the village in 1956 a few calls from Hollywood were received by the village government—arrangements for the filming of another movie in Tepoztlán were in process!

Tepoztlán now has a movie, operated by a villager who had been a *bracero*. The movies are shown on week-ends from October to May in one of the large rooms of the municipal building which seats about 300 people. The movie business is an insecure one in Tepoztlán, however; it cannot always successfully compete with the fiestas. Most of the films are Mexican cowboy and war pictures which appeal to young people. Adults over forty do not frequent the movies and most of the peasants do not permit their daughters to attend.

Despite the higher educational level, greater travel, and the increase in radios, our data suggest that there has been no increase in the number of people who read newspapers. On the contrary, there seems to have been some decline since 1943. In 1956, only about twenty-five individuals read a newspaper with some regularity and none of them were peasants. Magazine reading has increased, however. In 1956, about fifty villagers had magazine subscriptions. About half of these were for *Selecciones,* the Spanish version of the *Readers Digest;* others were for such publications as *Life, La Granja, La Tierra, La Sevilla.* Over a third of the subscriptions were held by teachers and most of the others by persons in nonagricultural occupations. The majority of the subscribers were under fifty, and reading was predominantly done by the men. Except for school teachers and some officials, few people owned books, but many children read comics.

Related to the developments noted above are changes in every stage of the life cycle, particularly the rearing of children. Again, most of the changes are found in the middle economic group, and the following discussion of the direction of change applies mainly to this group. Changes are occurring among the tradition-oriented members of the lower groups also, but at a much slower rate.

Women still prefer to give birth on a *petate* with the help of a midwife, but a doctor is often called in for difficult cases. Many young women are rejecting some of the "Indian" customs and cures of the midwives—the food taboos, for example, the use of smoke to help labor, and the wearing of the *huipil.* Magical practices like burying the first milk or throwing it over the roof are being discarded. Because more babies are being bottle-fed, the druggist now keeps a supply of baby bottles and nipples, as well as of formula mixtures. Young women feel less need to follow such customs as sweatbaths or the forty-day postpartum seclusion before the *sacamisa.*

A definite trend toward greater child-orientedness on the part of both parents is evident. Parents tend to be more permissive and more demonstratively affectionate with their young children. More fathers can be seen on the street carrying small children and a few help a little with the children at home. The swaddling of infants has been completely abandoned as "cruel" by some mothers. Parents indulge their children more, especially the first-born, and openly show their pride in their infants by buying them toys, shoes, and attractive clothing. This is in sharp contrast with the older attitude of guarding children from the attention of others through fear of the "evil eye." Younger and more educated parents punish more lightly, permit more play, and send their children to school for as long as possible. The period of adolescence is becoming longer and more clearcut, and the time when youths are expected to contribute to the support of the family is often delayed by years of study.

Arranged marriages have completely disappeared and more couples are marrying for love. Church weddings have become more elaborate and expensive and are patterned after those of the urban middle class. Newlyweds try to set up independent households immediately after marriage or as soon as it is economically feasible to avoid the problems of living with mothers-in-law. Some young wives work as school teachers or shopkeepers, but this is still unusual. More couples are resorting to legal divorce rather than mere separation or abandonment.

A noticeable change has occurred also among the educated middle group in attitudes and values and in the quality of interpersonal relations. It is too early to tell how deeply these changes have affected the ethos and character of the villagers, but all signs point in the direction of more profound changes to follow. In 1956, Tepoztecans seemed on the whole more outgoing and friendly and less bothered by the presence of outsiders. Children were noisier and smiled more; they were as apt to run toward as away from a stranger. Indeed, they begged tourists for centavos. Small groups of unchaperoned adolescent girls laughing and talking together were not unusual sights, and occasionally a village girl might be seen walking side by side with a boy in broad daylight. In general, the villagers were more accepting of their sophisticated members and provincialism seemed to be on the wane. There was more competition for jobs and scholarships and in general display.

That Tepoztecans have more drive and ambition for self-improvement is obvious. The young people are restless and have found the courage to leave the village to look for better opportunities. They are making greater demands on their parents for education, and they have more confidence in and more ability to cooperate with people outside the family over longer periods of time. Friendship not based on formal reciprocal relationships has become increasingly important; *compadrazgo* has assumed a new significance in providing connections and social advantages. Material success and a higher standard of living are consciously admired and worked for and the motivation to hide wealth is weaker. Respect has come to be based more and more on wealth and social status. Education imparts higher status; a young man or woman who has a teacher's certificate expects to be treated more respectfully by his or her elders. The middle class, especially, feel that status is also gained by discarding folk beliefs and practices and becoming more Catholic.

It is apparent, then, that Tepoztlán has made great strides ahead in the past fifteen years. The changes have been uneven, however, and not all the sectors of the population have equally benefited. Faced with limited agricultural resources, low yields, an absence of irrigation, and little prospect of solving their agricultural problems through mechanization, the villagers have by-passed their agrarian problem and have instead become dependent on new occupations and on jobs outside the village.

Most of the changes in the village are enjoyed by the middle economic group which even in 1943 had shown the most initiative and interest in raising its level of living. This group has doubled in size and now constitutes about 25 percent of the total population. Moreover, it is no longer merely an economic group; it is emerging rather as a true middle class, consisting of professionals, white-collar employees, and self-employed artisans and shopkeepers whose values and goals have come to differ substantially from those of the peasantry. The sharpening cleavage between the middle and lower economic groups, between peasant and nonpeasant, is perhaps the most far-reaching and significant change in the village.

Although the lower economic group is proportionately smaller than it was in 1943, it still constitutes the great majority of the villagers—approximately 65 percent. Our data suggest that this group has become even poorer, both because of inflation and because its members have been deprived of a traditional source of income by the prohibiting of charcoal production. Members of the lower segments of this group have gained least from the processes set in motion by the Mexican Revolution. They have been unable or unwilling to leave the village for jobs in the cities or to work as *braceros*. They have taken least advantage of the greater educational opportunities. They continue to farm for subsistence and cling to the old ways of life largely because these are cheaper.

As Tepoztlán moves further into the modern world, it is leaving behind its Indian language, many of its Indian customs, its local autonomy and the collective forms of pre-Hispanic times. Even the communal lands—the bulwark of the traditional order and formerly one of the most important bases for the corporate life of the community—seem destined to be divided up into *ejido* plots, and perhaps later into private holdings. With improved means of communication, greater faith in technology, greater dependence on a money economy and outside jobs, increasing occupational specialization, and a desire for a higher level of living, a change has come about also in the character of the people. As we have seen, Tepoztecans are now less suspicious, less withdrawn, and more concerned with personal development.

Tepoztlán today poses many questions which can be answered only with time. Will the growing individualism bring greater anxiety and frustration? Will it bring greater participation and trust in government? Will the traditional patterns of village life be able successfully to incorporate and reinterpret the present new elements—as has often been done with new elements in the past—or will the old and stable village culture soon be unrecognizable? Will Tepoztecans continue to sell their ancient lands and thereby convert Tepoztlán into a miniature Cuernavaca? Will the recent arrival of electricity be followed by the establishment of factories and the growth of a landless proletariat? Or will the village culture absorb the industrialism that seems to be on its way as some other villages have done?

Changes in village culture are exemplified in changing styles.

Recommended Reading

BEALS, RALPH, 1946, *Cherán: A Sierra Tarascan Village.* Washington, D. C.: U.S. Government Printing Office.
An ethnographic account of a Tarascan town of 5,000 inhabitants in the state of Michoacan.

FOSTER, GEORGE M., 1948, *Empire's Children, The People of Tzintzuntzan.* Mexico: Imprenta Nuevo Mundo, S.A.
A modern ethnography of a contemporary Tarascan village in the state of Michoacan near Lake Patzuaro.

GRUENING, ERNEST, 1928, *Mexico and Its Heritage.* New York: Century Company.
An excellent overall history of Mexico tracing the major social, economic, and political events since pre-Hispanic times.

LEWIS, OSCAR, 1951, *Life in a Mexican Village: Tepoztlán Restudied.* Urbana, Ill.: University of Illinois Press.
A comprehensive description of village life with an analysis of the changes which have occurred since Robert Redfield's earlier study of 1926-27.

PARSONS, ELSIE CLEWS, 1936, *Mitla, Town of the Souls.* Chicago: University of Chicago Press.
A good description of a Zapotecan Indian village of 2,500 people in the state of Oaxaca. Especially interesting for its chapter on town gossip and the discussion of what is Indian and what is Spanish.

REDFIELD, ROBERT, 1930, *Tepoztlán: A Mexican Village.* Chicago: University of Chicago Press.
A pioneer study of a Mexican village especially good for the detailed description of the fiesta cycle.

———, 1950, *A Village That Chose Progress, Chan Kom Revisited.* Chicago: University of Chicago Press.
A study in culture change by an outstanding anthropologist who returned for a second look to the site of one of his earlier studies.

TANNENBAUM, FRANK, 1950, *Mexico, the Struggle for Peace and Bread.* New York: Knopf.
A concise survey of Mexico's sociology, politics, economics, and psychology by a leading historian who has had almost three decades of familiarity with the country.

WHETTEN, NATHAN L., 1948, *Rural Mexico.* Chicago: University of Chicago Press.
A comprehensive description and analysis of rural Mexico which provides an excellent background and frame of reference for the understanding of a particular village like Tepoztlán.

BUNYORO:
AN AFRICAN KINGDOM

John Beattie
Oxford University

John Beattie received his D.Phil. in social anthropology from Oxford University, where he has taught since 1953, excepting for a brief interlude at the University of Amsterdam. Previous to that he had taught philosophy at Trinity College, Dublin, for two years and then served as a district officer in Tanganyika for eight years before deciding to become a professional anthropologist. He is interested in philosophy, the methodology of the social sciences, and the ethnography of East Africa. He has published a number of theoretical papers as well as articles on aspects of Nyoro social life. Of particular interest to readers of this case study is his methods study, *Understanding an African Kingdom: Bunyoro*, annotated under *Fieldwork in Anthropology* at the end of this volume.

345

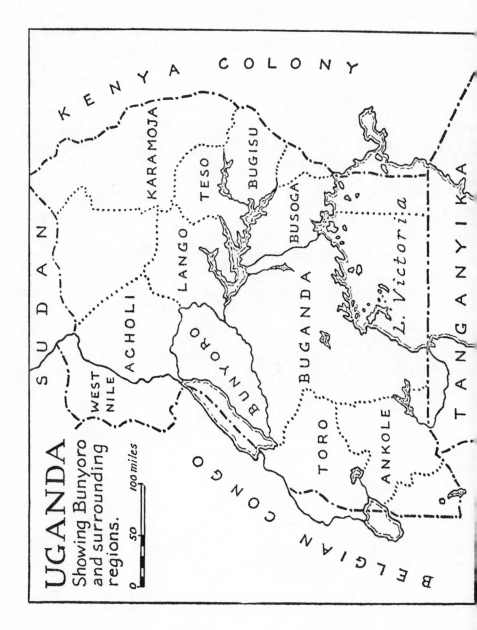

UGANDA

Showing Bunyoro and surrounding regions.

0   50   100 miles

KENYA COLONY

SUDAN

KARAMOJA

TESO

BUGISU

BUSOGA

LANGO

ACHOLI

WEST NILE

BUNYORO

BUGANDA

L. Victoria

TANGANYIKA

TORO

ANKOLE

BELGIAN CONGO

Foreword

THE FIELDWORK on which this book is based was carried out under the auspices of the Treasury Committee for Studentships in Foreign Languages and Cultures, London, and I owe much to their generosity and to the freedom they allowed me in planning my research. I spent altogether about twenty-two months in Bunyoro, spread over the years 1951 to 1955, living with the people and, after the first six months or so, working through the Nyoro language. For most of the time I employed one or two Nyoro research assistants, who were particularly helpful in assisting me to carry out detailed household and genealogical surveys in the four villages which I studied intensively. In obtaining information about the career histories of chiefs and about types of land holding I made use of a stenciled questionnaire form, and I had household survey forms printed, for use as a comprehensive *aide-mémoire* rather than as a formal instrument of research. I also invited literate Nyoro to write essays on topics selected by me, and awarded cash prizes for the best. I am greatly indebted to the many people who submitted long and interesting essays, and also to the eminent Nyoro who helped me to judge them.

In carrying out fieldwork one incurs obligations to a great many people. I cannot acknowledge more than a few of these here, but I must record the willing help of the Mukama of Bunyoro, Sir Tito Winyi Gafabusa IV, C.B.E., and of many members, past and present, of his Native Government. I and my family also received much assistance and kindness from officers of the Protectorate Administration and their wives, also (and especially) from the representatives of the Church Missionary Society at Hoima. From the Director and members of the East African Institute of Social Research at Makerere College, Kampala, I received both hospitality and intellectual stimulus in generous measure. But my greatest field obligation is to my Nyoro assistants, and above all to the very many individual Nyoro of all classes who were my friends, companions, and teachers. If any of them should read this book, I should like them to know that I am well aware that no foreigner can hope in the brief period of something less than two years to acquire a full understanding of the whole culture of another people, especially one as rich and complex as that of Bunyoro. I am not so arrogant as to claim to have done so. If I have learned something of a few of Bunyoro's most important social institutions and values, and if in the following pages I have succeeded in communicating some of this limited understanding to others, I have done all that I could have hoped to do.

Dr. John Peristiany, Professor I. Schapera, Dr. H. Meinhard, and Dr. Audrey Richards have commented helpfully on earlier drafts of various parts of this book. For valuable criticism of the present draft I am particularly indebted to my teacher, Professor Evans-Pritchard, and to Dr. R. G. Lienhardt and Dr. Rodney Needham.

J. B.

Oxford, England
December 1959

Contents

*King (Mukama) of Bunyoro in front of one of his "palace" buildings.
(Photo: Department of Information, Uganda Protectorate.)*

*Banana beer being trodden out in
banana grove.*

Family with traditional beehive-shaped house.

*Family with modern mud-plastered and iron-
roofed house.*

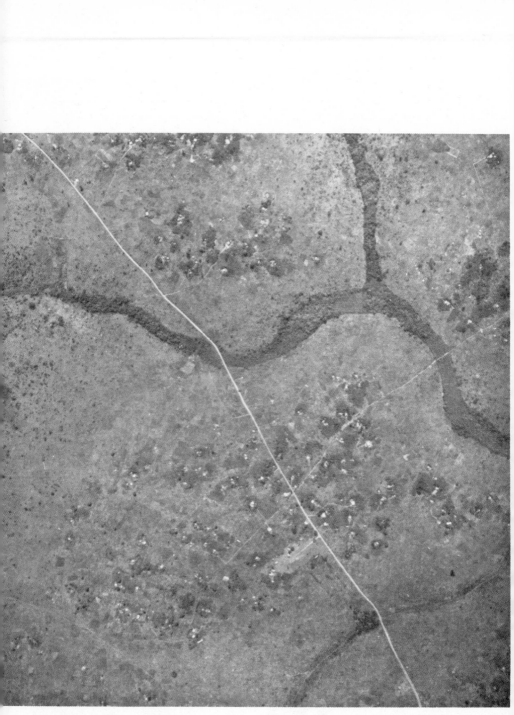

Air photograph of comparatively densely settled area a few miles from district head-quarters, intersected by motor road. Note especially disposition of homesteads and gardens on raised areas separated by swampy streams. Scale approximately 3½ inches to one mile. (Photo: Hunting Aerosurveys Ltd.)

I

Introductory

THIS BOOK is intended to provide a brief general introduction to the
social life of the Nyoro, a Bantu-speaking people who live in a fertile
country of small hills and swampy valleys in the uplands of western
Uganda, in east central Africa.[1] They number about 110,000, and occupy a region of about 4,700 square miles, so their country is not densely populated, less
so in fact than the neighboring kingdoms of Buganda, Toro, and Ankole. But
Nyoro are not evenly distributed over their territory; most of them live in
fairly closely settled areas, separated by wide stretches of uninhabited bush.
Though they do not live in compact villages, as some African peoples do, their
homesteads, which typically consist of one or two mud-and-wattle houses
round a central courtyard, surrounded by banana groves and food gardens,
are rarely more than shouting distance from at least one neighbor. Every
Nyoro belongs to one of a number of exogamous, totemic clans, membership
of which is acquired in the paternal line.[2] But as these do not form distinct
local groups, a man's neighbors generally include unrelated persons, as well
as kinsmen and relatives-in-law.

Long ago Nyoro had great herds of cattle. But these have been practically wiped out by war and disease, and there are now only a few thousand

---

[1] Nyoro speak of themselves as *Banyoro* (singular Munyoro), their language as
Lunyoro, and their country as *Bunyoro.* I omit the prefix, except in the last case, in the
interest of simplicity.

[2] *Exogamous* (substantive *exogamy*) means "marrying outside," and implies that
marriage is forbidden within a specified group, usually though not necessarily a *clan.*
Totemism (adjective *totemic*) usually refers to a ritual association between specific social
groups in a society (usually *clans*) and specific animate or inanimate objects, which are
called *totems.* Where (as in Bunyoro and elsewhere in Africa) members of totemic
groups are required to respect and to avoid injuring the totemic species, we may speak
of *totemic avoidances.* A *clan* is usually a named group of people who believe themselves to be descended in one line (that is, either through males only or females only)
from a common ancestor in the remote past. Members of the same clan usually
have special obligations toward one another.

head, mostly in a favored corner of the country which is free from tsetse fly carrier of the fatal cattle disease trypanosomiasis. At the present time th typical Nyoro is a small farmer, who cultivates from four to eight acres o land, and owns some goats and chickens and perhaps a few sheep. For fooc he grows millet (the traditional staple), sweet potatoes, cassava, and differen kinds of peas and beans. Bananas he uses mainly for beer making. He grow cotton and tobacco as cash crops, and in a good year these may bring him tw hundred shillings or more.[3] Some Nyoro are itinerant traders and shopkeep ers, but most trade is still in the hands of the immigrant Indian community, a in other parts of East Africa.

Though Nyoro are not wealthy, they are not badly off by East Africa standards: most people have some good clothes, many have bicycles, and som own cars and lorries. In 1953 Nyoro men paid annual local and governmen taxes amounting to about 26 shillings. There are good main-road communica tions in the kingdom, and innumerable cycle paths and tracks. The main town of Hoima (the capital) and Masindi have hospitals, and there are dispensarie at various points in the district. Education is almost wholly in the hands o the two main Christian missions, the Native Anglican Church (associated witl the Church Missionary Society) and the Roman Catholic White Fathers. Liter acy in Bunyoro is estimated as between 30 and 40 percent over the age o ten, but as yet only a minority of school children read beyond primary level

Bunyoro is almost wholly "African." There are about 800 Indians mostly engaged in retail trade. Only a few square miles are alienated to non natives, mostly Indians. The hundred and forty or so Europeans are mostl employees of the Railways and Harbors administration, which handles th considerable traffic which passes between Uganda and the Sudan, via Lak Albert and the Nile. The British government, which administers the whol of the Uganda Protectorate, is represented in Bunyoro by a district commis sioner stationed at Hoima, and two or three assistants. There are also a fev departmental officers, responsible for agriculture, veterinary matters, polic work, fisheries, and so on. But the indigenous Nyoro people form the mas of the population.

The Bunyoro native government operates under the general supervisio and control of the British administration. At its head is the hereditary rule of Bunyoro, the king or Mukama. Nowadays he is advised by a central secre tariat, consisting of a prime minister, a chief justice, and a treasurer. He i the head of a graded hierarchy of territorial chiefs, of whom the most impor tant are the four county chiefs, each responsible for one of the four district into which the country is divided. Beneath them are the subcounty chiefs, anc below them again are the "parish" chiefs and the village headmen. So Bunyorc is, as it is said always to have been, a centralized, hierarchically organizec state, with the Mukama at the apex of the pyramid of traditional authority and the hundred and fifty or so village headmen at its base. In pre-Europea

---

[3] The shilling, made up of a hundred cents, is the standard coin in East Africa Twenty of them make a pound. Approximately seven shillings equal one Americar dollar.

imes the Mukama was thought of as the ultimate source of all political
authority; nowadays everybody knows that he is subject to the superior au-
hority of the European administration. This of course has important effects
on traditional attitudes toward the Mukama and his chiefs.

Not much can be said of Nyoro origins. The orthodox view is that the
original inhabitants of the country were negroid agriculturalists, and it is
supposed that the impact on these of successive waves of immigrants, some
at least of whom were pastoral, has resulted both in the wide range of
physical type and in the strongly marked distinction between rulers and ruled
which are now characteristic of the peoples of this part of Africa. Throughout
this region the pastoral Hima invaders (called Huma in Bunyoro) assumed
the role of overlords, dominating the indigenous Iru, or peasant peoples, who
form the governed majority. But for Bunyoro this is an oversimplification.
Although the cattle-herding Huma have always regarded themselves as superior
to Iru, in Bunyoro the matter was complicated many generations ago by the
arrival from the north of the Nile of a third element, the Bito, whose affinities
are with the non-Bantu Acholi and Alur of present-day Uganda. These darker-
skinned Nilotic invaders took over the Nyoro kingship from an earlier dynasty, and the present Mukama claims to be the twenty-sixth Bito king. Much
of the prestige and authority associated in the more southerly kingdoms of the
region (which the Bito did not reach) with the Hima attaches in Bunyoro
to the Bito, especially to members of its royal lineage.[4] But although status
distinctions are strongly marked in Bunyoro, we do not find there the rigid,
castelike discrimination described for some neighboring peoples such as the
Ankole, and it has always been at least theoretically possible for able Nyoro
commoners to rise to positions of high authority in the state.

Nyoro believe that their kingdom was once much greater than it is now,
and that their Mukama is the direct descendant in the male line of the ancient
rulers of an empire which extended over most of present-day Uganda and
perhaps beyond it. We cannot now say much about this ancient state, or even
be quite sure that it ever existed, but we may be certain that if it did it was
not a compact political unit, but rather a loose association of semi-independent
states connected with the central kingdom through the sporadic payment of
tribute. It is certain, however, that in historical times Nyoro territory has been
much reduced both by the British and by the neighboring Ganda. Nyoro are
very conscious of their former greatness, and we shall find that present-day
Bunyoro cannot be understood unless we know something about its traditional political system and about the historical events that have befallen it.
For the past determines the present, and attitudes and values which were
appropriate to the traditional system still survive in the radically altered
social and political scene of today.

---

[4] A *lineage* consists of all the descendants in one line (that is, either through
males only or through females only) of a particular person through a specified number
of generations. It differs from a *clan* in that while usually all the members of a lineage
know exactly how they are related to all the other members of it, and together they
often form a corporate group, clan members may not be able to trace genealogical
links with other clan members, and often clansfolk are widely dispersed.

These are some of the elementary and essential facts concerning the people whom this book is about; it may still be asked "What are Nyoro really like?" We shall be better able to answer this question, if it is the kind of question that can be answered at all, at the end of our study of their social institutions. But a good many Europeans, from the time of the first contact just a century ago until the present, have passed judgment on Nyoro character, and it is a fact of considerable anthropological interest that almost all of these judgments have been unfavorable. Thus a nineteenth-century writer described the Nyoro (whom he had never seen) as "mean, grasping and selfish"; a lady missionary reported that work was repugnant to them and that nothing attracted them irresistibly save indolence and ease; and official and missionaries have referred from time to time to their "apathy," "decadence," "habits of intemperance," and "evident sense of inferiority." Usually assertions like these tell one more about the persons who make them than about the people they are made about. In any case it is the existence and origin of such opinions, rather than their truth or falsehood, that interest anthropologists. I must say here, however, that I found Nyoro to be very courteous, hospitable, and generous people. Most of them are quick witted, thoughtful and humorous, and many have in recent years achieved high distinction by European standards.

But there is still in Bunyoro a widespread underlying fear and distrust of Europeans. This is rarely explicit, and certainly there is no overt hostility relations between individual Europeans and Nyoro are usually good and often excellent. But it is widely believed among the less educated majority that Europeans dislike Nyoro and are hostile to their interests, and this is bound to lead to some mutual distrust and suspicion. Some of the grounds for this belief are considered in Chapter 2. Though I lived in close social contact with Nyoro, and have many Nyoro friends, very few trusted me completely (why should they?), and those who did were mostly younger men. Right up to the end of my stay in the country many of my best friends continued to deny firmly that such things as sorcery and divination could possibly occur nowadays, despite ample and continuous evidence to the contrary. They knew, of course, that I knew about these things, but it was better not to talk about them. We shall see why when we come to Chapter 7.

There are many good reasons why the kingdom of Bunyoro is worth studying, but four of them are especially relevant here. The first applies to all studies of peoples remote from ourselves. It is that we have here a community of real people, who have, so far as we can tell, pretty much the same innate constitution and capacities as any other people, and yet who have developed their own distinctive social system and way of life. As members of the same human family, we are bound to be interested in the very different ways of life which other peoples have worked out for themselves. And in the case of preliterate or only recently literate societies, our interest must be an urgent one, for rapid industrial and technological advance are quickly destroying or altering many of them, so that soon perhaps there will be none of them left to study.

Turning from general considerations to more particular ones, a second

...ason why Bunyoro is worth studying is just because it is the kind of kingdom
t is. Although it is changing rapidly, it still preserves many of the characters
of a centralized, "feudal" state, oddly reminiscent in many ways of the feudal
kingdoms which existed centuries ago in Europe and elsewhere. I use the
word "feudal" here in its simplest sense, to refer to the kind of political
system which is based on the relation between a superior and his inferior or
vassal, where the latter holds lands, and authority over the people living on
these lands, "in feud" from the former. This means that the vassal must
render homage and services of various kinds (the onus of which will chiefly
fall on his peasant dependants) to the superior lord from whom he holds his
lands and authority. Traditional Bunyoro has many features in common with
such a system, and we shall find that many attitudes and values appropriate
to it still survive in present-day Bunyoro, though not always very harmoniously.
Thus a second reason for studying Bunyoro is that it has, or had until quite
recently, a type of social structure having many points of resemblance with
kinds of societies known to us in history. Perhaps we may acquire a clearer
understanding of certain features of our own historical past by studying such
present-day "feudal" states as Bunyoro.

But Bunyoro, like other recently preliterate societies, is undergoing
radical change as a result of contact with a powerful and complex Western
culture, and this is a third reason why it should be studied. A living culture
is always something more than "a thing of shreds and patches"; in at least
some respects it is a systematic whole, as we indicate by giving it a name.
This does not mean that its parts all fit neatly together like the pieces of a
jigsaw puzzle, as certain "functionalist" anthropologists seem sometimes to
have supposed. In times of change it often happens that incompatible beliefs
and institutions come to coexist, and when this happens various kinds of conflicts may arise. This has occurred in Bunyoro as it has in other societies;
perhaps more acutely than in most. So here we can write an actual case history
of social change; we can record what happens when a coherent social system
is subjected to the often disruptive impact of European civilization.

The fourth important reason for studying Bunyoro is its ethnographic
representativeness. Almost the whole of the vast region between the great
lakes of Victoria, Albert, and Tanganyika is occupied by centralized native
states; these vary greatly in size but have very similar constitutions. They are
all hereditary monarchies; they all have strongly marked, sometimes extreme,
distinctions of class and status; and they are all hierarchically organized. All
these peoples speak related Bantu languages, and it has become usual in
ethnographic literature to refer to them collectively (and also to a few other
peoples in the area who traditionally lack centralized government) as the
interlacustrine Bantu. Although Bunyoro differs from some of these states in
important respects, it resembles them in many more, and may even be said
to be typical. So in studying Bunyoro we are not simply studying a unique
culture, though one with historical analogues: in analyzing it we are informing
ourselves of many of the essential characters of the type of native states which
have for centuries occupied this vast and populous region of Africa.

These are some reasons why it is worthwhile to learn about Bunyoro; it remains to make clear what kind of study is proposed for this book. Since anthropology means different things to different people, it is important that the author make clear what he is attempting. The first thing that must be said is that since this book is written by a social anthropologist, it will be mostly about social relations; that is, about the ways in which Nyoro generally behave towards and think about one another. The word "generally" is important: the social anthropologist is not interested in every social relationship that he can discover, only in those which are "institutionalized," standardized, and hence characteristic of the people being studied. In Bunyoro, as in every other society, there are special patterns of behavior and special attitudes and ways of thinking which are held to be appropriate in dealings between people who belong to certain categories (such as chiefs, diviners, clansmen, strangers, fathers, sons, neighbors, and so on). If this were not the case, ordered social life would be impossible, for people's behavior would be unpredictable. We may say that in our study we are primarily concerned with the statuses and roles which are characteristic of Bunyoro. We are interested in the kinds of people there are and the kinds of things they are expected to do, rather than in the particular individuals who happen to occupy particular statuses at a particular time. Of course we are interested in real people (these are the raw material of our study), but our concern is with what these real people share with other real people—that is, with their common culture, rather than with what is unique and peculiar to them as individuals. And this common culture includes their shared framework of social relations, and their beliefs and values. It is because this book is centered on social relations that its four central chapters are concerned respectively with the king, the chiefs, relatives, and neighbors. For relationships centering on some or all of these four categories of persons comprise for most Nyoro practically the whole ambit of their social life.

A concern with social relations does not, however, imply neglect of "culture." No adequate description of a social relationship can omit reference to the ideas and beliefs which the parties to it have about themselves and about one another; this kind of mental content is a large part of what culture means. The main focus of our interest will be in social relationships, but we shall be concerned with other aspects of Nyoro culture insofar as they help us to understand these relationships. Thus Chapter 2 deals with the past and with Nyoro ideas about it, rather than with contemporary social relationships, for we cannot fully understand the latter unless we know something about Nyoro history and their ideas about it. In the same way, Nyoro beliefs about the supernatural, discussed in Chapter 7, are cultural data, but we shall see that many of them play a very important part in interpersonal relations. Though a good deal has been said and written about the difference between culture and society, it is really very much a question of relevance; to give a coherent account of anything it is necessary to deal with it from one point of view at a time, and in this book we study the kingdom of Bunyoro primarily in its aspect as a working system of interpersonal relations.

I have said that our study is of present-day Bunyoro; strictly speaking it is of Bunyoro as it was during the years from 1952 to 1955, when I was there. This book does not attempt to reconstruct a traditional past which no longer exists. But we can understand the present situation better if we know something of how it came to be as it is. This is one reason why social anthropologists should not, and usually do not, neglect history. They are not historians; they do not seek to understand the past for its own sake. They are concerned with it only when it can be shown to be directly relevant to the understanding of the present. In some simpler preliterate societies there *is* no history to be studied prior to the very recent impact of Western civilization; there are no written records, and the past is seen as differing from the present only in respect of the individuals who occupy the different roles in the society, which themselves continue unchanged. And where there is no history, of course it cannot be studied. But Bunyoro has a history of contact with Western culture now almost a hundred years old, as well as its own traditional dynastic history which stretches back through the centuries. We cannot afford to neglect it.

But there is another sense in which history may be important, and this is in its aspect not as a record of past events leading up to the present, but rather as a body of contemporary ideas about these past events. This is what the English philosopher Collingwood aptly called "incapsulated history," because these ideas are contained in and so form a part of contemporary social attitudes and relationships. We shall find that Nyoro ideas about the history of their relations with Europeans differ in some important respects from European ideas about the same history. It might even be said that there are two histories of these events, and if we are to understand how present-day Nyoro think about themselves and about Europeans we shall have to know something about them both.

Two more introductory themes must be considered briefly before we go on to the detailed story. The first of these relates to the problem, which faces every modern anthropologist, of translating the essentials of one culture into terms of another culture, his own. The earlier anthropologists (with some notable exceptions) were hardly aware of this problem; they were mostly content to record their findings in their own cultural terms, for their knowledge of the people they wrote about was rarely deep enough for them to see that often this approach involved gross misrepresentation. Nowadays the position is very different. Advances in field techniques, and in the depth and extent of the knowledge so gained of hitherto little-known peoples, have highlighted this communication problem. It has become increasingly plain that although there is a great deal that is common to all cultures everywhere (if this were not so, no understanding would ever be possible at all), there are also very many significant and subtle differences in the ways in which different peoples "factor out" their universe. This means, of course, that in every culture there are concepts which do not have any exact equivalent in another culture, so that any translation is bound to be to some extent a mistranslation. We shall see in Chapter 5, for example, that since many of the categories of Nyoro kinship terminology have no exact equivalents in English, to translate them by familiar English kinship terms may lead to serious misunderstanding. There is no easy solution to this problem; I have to write my book in English and not in Nyoro. But it is important to be alert to the possibility of misunderstanding arising from this fact. I shall try to avoid misrepresentation as much as I can by presenting Nyoro categories of thought and behavior as far as possible as they conceive them, even if this sometimes involves circumlocution. Only thus may we hope to gain some idea of what their own social and cultural system means to Nyoro.

This leads to my last introductory point, which is an attempt to answer the question: What are the basic values of Nyoro society, in terms of which their social and cultural life makes sense? It might be thought that this question rightly belongs at the end of our inquiry, not at the beginning. But the wholeness of Nyoro social life will emerge more clearly if we know from the beginning what its most striking features are. We must remember that a book is not itself a social study; it is only a report on one. For me the salient features of Nyoro culture emerged only after many months of fieldwork, but the reader is not required to retrace with me this long and sometimes tedious process; my responsibility to him is to present my findings as clearly and accurately as possible. There are two associated concepts which I believe to afford the key to Nyoro culture, and in presenting my material in the following pages I shall be particularly concerned with them. The first of these is the distinction between the superimposed, centralized, pyramidal state on the one hand and the relatively homogeneous, closely knit community on the other; the second is the pervasive concept of superordination and subordination— the notion that some people are always above others, and some people always below.

The first of these notions, the distinction between state and community, has long been familiar to sociologists. It is a distinction which Nyoro themselves often make quite explicitly. For them, social relationships fall broadly into two categories. First there is the system of political relations (concerned with territorially based power and authority) which centers on the kingship and the hierarchical system of chiefs. This is the realm of the state, which sociologists regard as a particular kind of association, concerned with the maintenance of public order through an organized system of authority. It is not at all the same kind of thing as a community, which comprises a great number of different kinds of associations, directed toward different ends. The state is a political entity, and it is defined in terms both of the end to which its activities are directed (the maintenance of order in a certain region) and of the means which it uses for this purpose (which usually include the use or threat of force by an accepted authority, such as a king or chief). Nyoro often speak about the state, in contradistinction to the local community of neighbors and kinsmen, and when they do so they are referring to their relations with the chiefs, of whatever ranks, or with the Mukama himself. The words they use for this political or "statal" dimension of their social life are *bukama* and *bulemi,* which we may translate respectively as "kingship" and "government." But at once we are faced with the difficulty of translation which we have just discussed. For *bukama* means more than we mean by "kingship"; it also has strong implications of proprietorship and even personal ownership. And *bulemi* means a good deal more than merely "government." It is associated with the verb *kulema,* one of the commonest verbs in the language, and its primary meaning is "to rule," but it has the further strong implication of a thing's being difficult and burdensome. Thus Nyoro say "the king rules his people," "a master rules his servants," and so on, but they also say of a task or problem—or even of a person—which has proved intractable, "it has ruled me" (*kindemere*), meaning that it has been too difficult to cope with. The idea of being overcome, subordinated to something more powerful than oneself, is an essential part of the meaning of the term. In Chapters 3 and 4 we shall be concerned with the political side of Nyoro social life.

To this field of sometimes oppressive political activity Nyoro oppose the sphere of the community—the intimate, face-to-face relationships which subsist between fellow villagers, neighbors, and kinsmen who see each other constantly and who share the same kind of social background, interests, and values. At this community level, everybody knows everybody else, and there is a kind of corporateness which makes the community conscious of itself as against other communities and, especially, as against the superimposed governmental system. The Nyoro term *kyaro* ("a place where people stay") refers to the territorial aspect of the community; the rights and obligations which it entails are implied in the terms for clanship, consanguinity, and, in particular, neighborhood. In Chapters 5 and 6, and in the greater part of Chapter 7, we shall be dealing with relationships characteristic of the local community. We shall find that Nyoro themselves are well aware of the conflicts which may arise between community values and those of the state, with its implication of subjection and subordination to a superior authority.

This leads to the second and associated notion—in fact an aspect of the notion just discussed—which I found to be most strikingly characteristic of Nyoro culture: the idea of superordination and subordination. It is remarkable that in Bunyoro this idea of "ruling" is not restricted to the political sphere (though of course it is especially characteristic of this sphere); it pervades the whole field of social relations. Almost all institutionalized social relationships in Bunyoro have an inegalitarian, hierarchical aspect; the notion that people occupy different categories, and that these are almost always unequal, is ubiquitous. Thus Nyoro often speak of fathers as being superior to and ruling their children, fathers-in-law as ruling their daughters' husbands, husbands their wives, "sisters' sons" their "mothers' brothers," and so on. Through the whole field of social relations, those of community as well as those of the state, we find this notion of ruling, of exercising authority over someone. In some African societies the homely idiom of kinship is extended even into the field of political relations; in Bunyoro the tendency is in the reverse direction: here the idiom of government, of ruling, is extended from the political into the community and even into the domestic sphere. Such a state of affairs is consistent with the centralized, "feudal" structure of Bunyoro, in which all authority, right down to the base of the pyramid, is thought of as being at least ideally derived from and validated by the Mukama.

2.

Myth and History

Myth

WHAT INTERESTS US most about myths is the way in which they may express attitudes and beliefs current at the present time. Mythologies always embody systems of values, judgments about what is considered good and proper by the people who have the myth. Especially, myth tends to sustain some system of authority, and the distinctions of power and status which this implies. Thus Nyoro myths tend to validate the kinds of social and political stratification which I have said are characteristic of the culture, and to support the kingship around which the traditional political system revolved. In Malinowski's phrase, Nyoro legend provides a "mythical charter" for the social and political order.

For Nyoro, human history begins with a first family, whose head is sometimes called Kintu, "the created thing." There are three children in this family, all boys. At first these are not distinguished from one another by name; all are called "Kana," which means "little child." This is of course confusing, and Kintu asks God if they may be given separate names. God agrees, and the boys are submitted to two tests. First, six things are placed on a path by which the boys will pass. These are an ox's head, a cowhide thong, a bundle of cooked millet and potatoes, a grass head-ring (for carrying loads on the head), an axe, and a knife. When the boys come upon these things, the eldest at once picks up the bundle of food and starts to eat. What he cannot eat he carries away, using the head-ring for this purpose. He also takes the axe and the knife. The second son takes the leather thong, and the youngest takes the ox's head, which is all that is left. In the next test the boys have to sit on the ground in the evening, with their legs stretched out, each holding on his lap a wooden milk-pot full of milk. They are told that they must hold their pots safely until morning. At midnight the youngest boy begins to nod, and he spills a little of his milk. He wakes up with a start, and begs his brothers

361

for some of theirs. Each gives him a little, so that his pot is full again. Just before dawn the eldest brother suddenly spills all his milk. He, too, asks his brothers to help fill his pot from theirs, but they refuse, saying that it would take too much of their milk to fill his empty pot. In the morning their father finds the youngest son's pot full, the second son's nearly full, and the eldest's quite empty.

He gives his decision, and names the three boys. The eldest, and his descendants after him, is always to be a servant and a cultivator, and to carry loads for his younger brothers, and their descendants. For he chose the millet and potatoes, peasants' food, and he lost all the milk entrusted to him, so showing himself unfit to have anything to do with cattle. Thus he was named "Kairu," which means little Iru or peasant. The second son and his descendants would have the respected status of cattlemen. For he had chosen the leather thong for tying cattle, and he had spilt none of his milk, only providing some for his younger brother. So he was called "Kahuma," little cowherd or Huma, and ever since the cattle-herding people of this part of the interlacustrine region have been called Huma or Hima. But the third and youngest son would be his father's heir, for he had taken the ox's head, a sign that he would be at the head of all men, and he alone had a full bowl of milk when morning came, because of the help given him by his brothers. So he was named "Kakama," little Mukama or ruler. He and his descendants became the kings of Bunyoro, or Kitara, as the country was then called. When the three brothers had been named, their father told the two elder that they should never leave their young brother, but should stay with him and serve him always. And he told Kakama to rule wisely and well.

This myth explains and justifies the traditional division of Nyoro society into distinct social categories based on descent. At the beginning, people were undifferentiated—this is symbolized by the three boys having no separate names or identities—but this was confusing, and the only orderly solution was to grade them in three hierarchically ordered categories. It is true that in Bunyoro the distinction between Hima and Iru is of decreasing social importance, but the distinctions of status implied by the myth and especially the differential allocation of authority are still strongly marked in social life. What is validated is basically the "givenness" of differences of status and authority based on birth and, in general, the preeminence of ascribed status over personal achievement. Subordinates may find subordination less irksome, and superordinates may rule more calmly and confidently, when everyone acknowledges the difference between them and the divine origin of that difference.

Many stories, all of which point a moral, are told of the very first kings, Kakama's earliest descendants. The following is one of the best known. King Isaza came to the throne as a very young man; he was disrespectful toward the elders whom his father had left to advise him, and he drove them away from the palace, replacing them by gay youngsters with whom he used to go hunting, which was his favorite pastime. One day he killed a zebra, and he was so pleased with its gaily striped hide that he determined to dress himself in it at once. So his young companions sewed the skin on him. But as the day wore on, the hot sun dried the skin, and it quickly shrank and began to squeeze Isaza until he was nearly dead. He begged his friends for help, but they just laughed at him and did nothing. When he had driven the old men away, two had stayed nearby, and now Isaza sent to them for help. First they refused, but after a while they relented, and told Isaza's young men to throw the king into a pond. They did so, and the moisture loosened the hide so that it could be removed. Isaza was so grateful to the old men that he called them all back to the palace, gave them a feast and reinstated them. At the same time he reprimanded his young associates, telling them that they should always respect the old.

This Nyoro "cautionary tale" points the familiar moral that a person in authority neglects at his peril the advice of those older and wiser than he, and that old men are likely to be better informed than callow youths. But it also stresses another important feature of Nyoro ideas about authority—namely, that it is not inappropriate for young persons to have power. It will be remembered that in the previous myth it was the youngest son, not the eldest, who succeeded to his father's authority; in fact, succession by the youngest, or a younger, son is a characteristic feature of Nyoro inheritance. The role of the older brother is to act as guardian until the heir is old enough to assume full authority. Nvoro say that a first son should not inherit; we shall see that the Mukama may not be succeeded by his eldest son. But the Isaza myth also stresses the wisdom of the old, and the respect due to them. Age is a qualification for advisory, not executive, authority; it is right that the aged should be spared the arduousness of decision making, but right that they should guide and advise those in power. The legend of Isaza and the zebra skin is a popular one, for it expresses values important to Nyoro and which we shall meet again.

It is important also to examine the cycle of dynastic myths which merge into traditional history and link up (if the series be regarded chronologically) with the "real" history which we shall go on to consider. Nyoro believe that there have been three royal dynasties; first, the shadowy Tembuzi, of whom Kakama was the first and Isaza the last; second, the Chwezi, part-legendary hero-gods whose marvelous exploits are still spoken of; and third, the Bito, the line to which the present king belongs. We shall see that part of the significance of the myths which we now discuss lies in the way in which they link these three dynasties together into a single line of descent, so creating an unbroken chain between the present ruler and the very first king of Bunyoro.

The story is rich in descriptive detail, but here we can only give an outline account. It begins by telling how the king of the world of ghosts, called Nyamiyonga, sent a message to king Isaza (whose hunting exploit has just been recounted) asking him to enter into a blood pact with him. Isaza's councilors advised against this, so Isaza had the pact made on Nyamiyonga's behalf with his chief minister, a commoner called Bukuku. When Nyamiyonga discovered that he had been united in the blood pact with an Iru or commoner, he was angry, and he determined to get Isaza into his power. So he sent his beautiful daughter Nyamata to Isaza's court, where she so attracted the king that he married her, not knowing who she was. But he resisted all her efforts to persuade him to visit her home, for he could not bear to be parted from his cattle, which he loved more than anything else. So Nyamiyonga thought of another plan. He caused two of his most handsome cattle to be discovered near Isaza's kraal, and these were taken to the king, who soon loved them most of all his herd. One day they disappeared, and the distracted Mukama went in search of them, leaving Bukuku to rule the kingdom in his absence. After much wandering, Isaza arrived in the country of ghosts, where he found his two cattle and also his wife Nyamata, who had gone home some time previously to bear him a child. Nyamiyonga welcomed the Nyoro king, but he had not forgiven him, and he never allowed him to return to the world of men.

In due course Nyamata's child was born and was named Isimbwa. When Isimbwa grew up he married in the world of ghosts and had a son called Kyomya, of whom we shall hear more later. Isimbwa, unlike his father, could visit the world of living men, and on a hunting expedition he came to the capital where Bukuku still reigned in Isaza's place. Bukuku was unpopular because he was a commoner and had no real right to rule, but there was no one else to do so. He had a daughter called Nyinamwiru, and at Nyinamwiru's birth diviners had told Bukuku that he would have reason to fear any child that she might bear. So he kept her in a special enclosure which could only be entered through his own well-guarded palace. When Isimbwa reached Bukuku's capital he was intrigued by this state of affairs, and after making clandestine advances to Nyinamwiru through her maid, he managed to climb into her enclosure and, unknown to Bukuku, he stayed there for three months. He then left the kingdom and was not seen again for many years.

After a time Nyinamwiru bore a son, to the consternation of Bukuku, who gave orders for the child to be drowned. So the baby was thrown in a river, but by chance its umbilical cord caught in a bush, and the child was discovered by a potter, Rubumbi, who took it home and brought it up as a member of his family. He knew that it was Nyinamwiru's child, and he told her that it was safe. Bukuku, of course, believed it to be dead. The boy grew up strong and spirited, and was constantly in trouble with Bukuku's herdsmen, for when the king's cattle were being watered he would drive them away, so that he could water Rubumbi's cattle first. This angered Bukuku, who one day came to the drinking trough himself to punish the unruly potter's son. But before Bukuku's men could carry out his orders to seize and beat him, he rushed round to the back of Bukuku's royal stool and stabbed him mortally with his spear. He then sat down on the king's stool. The herdsmen were aghast, and ran at once to tell Nyinamwiru what had happened. The story tells that she was both glad and sorry; glad because her son had taken the throne, sorry because of her father's death. So Ndahura, which is what the young man was called, came to his grandfather Isaza's throne, and he is reckoned as the first of the Chwezi kings.

There were only three—some say two—Chwezi kings; Ndahura, his half-brother Mulindwa, and his son Wamara. Many wonderful things are told of their wisdom and achievements, but during Wamara's reign things began to go badly for them. So they called their diviners and an ox was cut open so that its entrails could be examined. The diviners were astonished to find no trace of the intestines, and they did not know what to say. At that moment a stranger from north of the Nile appeared, and said that he was a diviner and would solve the riddle for them. But first he insisted (wisely, as it turned out) on making a blood pact with one of the Chwezi, so that he could be safe from their anger if his findings were unfavorable. Then he took an axe and cut open the head and hooves of the ox. At once the missing intestines fell out of these members, and as they did so a black smut from the fire settled on them, and could not be removed.

The Nilotic diviner then said that the absence of the intestines from their proper place meant that the rule of the Chwezi in Bunyoro was over. Their presence in the hoofs meant that they would wander far away; in the head, that they would, nonetheless, continue to rule over men (a reference to the possession cult, centered on the Chwezi spirits, which will be discussed in Chapter 7). And the black smut meant that the kingdom would be taken over by dark-skinned strangers from the north. So the Chwezi departed from Bunyoro, no one knows whither.

Meantime the diviner went back to his own country in the north, and there he met the sons of Kyomya, who was, it will be remembered, Isimbwa's son by his first wife. Kyomya had married in the country to the north of the Nile, and had settled down there. The diviner told Kyomya's sons that they should go south and take over the abandoned Nyoro kingdom of their Tembuzi grandfathers. There were four brothers altogether: Nyarwa, the eldest; the twins Rukidi Mpuga and Kato Kimera; and Kiiza, the youngest. They were the first Bito. Nyarwa (as we might expect) did not become a ruler, though some say that he remained as adviser to his second brother Rukidi, who became the first Bito king of Bunyoro. Kato was allotted Buganda, then a dependency of the great Nyoro empire (Ganda, of course, have a rather different version of these events), and Kiiza was given a part of what is now Busoga, a country many miles to the east of present-day Bunyoro.

When the Bito first arrived in Bunyoro, they seemed strange and uncouth to the inhabitants. It is said that half of Rukidi's body was black and half white, a reference to his mixed descent. They had to be instructed in the manners appropriate to rulers; at first, they were ignorant of such important matters as cattle keeping and milk drinking. But gradually Rukidi assumed the values and manners proper to the heir of the pastoral rulers of the earlier dynasties. So began the reign of the powerful Bito dynasty, which has lasted up to the present.

This series of myths establishes a genealogical link between the three recognized dynasties of Nyoro rulers. Having noted the importance in Bunyoro of hereditarily determined status, we can see that a major function is served by the genealogical linking of the present ruling line with the wonderful Chwezi, whose exploits are still talked of throughout the region, and, through them, with the even more remote Tembuzi and so with the very beginnings of human existence. The connection enables the present ruling line to claim descent of an honor and antiquity not exceeded even by that of the pastoral Huma (who are said in some contexts to look down upon the Bito as "commoners"). The marking off of the ruling Bito from all other Nyoro contributes to their unity and exclusiveness, and so lends validity to their claims to special respect, prestige, and authority. And not only the rulers, but all Nyoro, share in the glory of their ruling line and the wonderful feats of its progenitors. The exploits and conquests of Isaza and the Chwezi rulers are known to every Nyoro. When people think of themselves, as Nyoro sometimes do (for reasons which will become plain later), as being in decline, there may be compensation in the thought of past in default of present greatness. And we may suppose that historically the genealogical link was important for the immigrant Bito, who lacked the prestige of the already existing Huma aristocracy, and needed the enhancement of status which this "genealogical charter" provided. So the main social function of Nyoro mythical history is the establishment of Bito credentials to govern, by emphasizing the distinction and antiquity of their genealogical antecedents.

According to the myth, the present Mukama is descended in an unbroken patrilineal line[1] from the very beginning of things, and it may well be asked (as indeed it has been) why in this case there are said to have been three dynasties in Nyoro history, and not only one. But the question implies a too literal interpretation of the myth. The fact is that for Nyoro there *are* three dynasties, and whatever the truth about their real relationship to one another, if any (or even, in the case of the earlier ones, their very existence), Nyoro believe them to have been three quite different kinds of people. In other contexts the Chwezi are spoken of as a strange and wonderful people who came from far away, took over the kingdom from the Tembuzi, remained in the country for a generation or two, and then mysteriously disappeared. There is linguistic and other evidence to support the view that the Bito are of quite different racial and cultural stock from the people whose country and kingship they took over. The myth is not to be understood as an attempt to reconstruct a history that has been lost forever; it is rather to be seen as providing a genealogical charter for a structure of authority whose existence is contemporaneous with the myth itself.

History

The story of the Bito dynasty, from the time of its first king, Rukidi, until the arrival of the Europeans in the middle of the nineteenth century, spans perhaps eighteen generations. Many stories are told of its kings, and they become more detailed and circumstantial as we approach historical times. Myth, chronologically regarded, begins to merge into history. Here we can only indicate general trends. The traditional history of the Bito dynasty falls

---

[1] *Patrilineal* descent is reckoned exclusively through males—that is, through the father, the father's father, and so on.

into two parts. During the first period, up to the time of the seventeenth Bito king, the great empire believed to have been inherited from the Chwezi was maintained in much of its former greatness. The fourth Bito Mukama fought with the Ganda, who had by now asserted their independence, and killed their king. Other Bito kings are said to have fought successful wars as far away as the borders of Zande country in the Congo, and in Ruanda and Ankole, the latter of which is said to have been a part of the Nyoro empire until about the end of this period. There were constant wars against the small but aggressive Ganda kingdom. At all periods there were numerous revolts, but these were usually successfully quelled. The second period, from the reign of the seventeenth Mukama until historical times, is marked by a gradual decline in Nyoro fortunes, brought about both by successful revolts in outlying areas and by annexations by the Ganda, whose expanding state now began to acquire the wider political dominance which it holds at the present time. The decline was not continuous, for strong kings sometimes temporarily reversed it; but losses tended to exceed gains, and when the historical period begins, Bunyoro, though still a substantial and powerful kingdom, was no longer comparable in size or importance to the ancient Kitara empire. Thus by the reign of the present king's great-great-grandfather, the one-time province of Toro had asserted its independence (though it needed European support to maintain it), Ankole had long since become a separate kingdom, Buganda had gained much Nyoro territory in the east, and we hear no more of successful campaigns in far-away regions like Ruanda and the Zande country. But Bunyoro was still very much a power to be reckoned with; the final blow to its former greatness was struck not by the Ganda, or at least not by them alone, but by the Europeans.

The history of Bunyoro since the 1860's is essentially a history of European-Nyoro relations. There might indeed be said to be two different histories of these relations—a European one and a Nyoro one—and it would be possible and perhaps instructive to give these as two separate accounts. For they exemplify a situation, only too familiar in relations between peoples of different cultures (especially when one is subordinated to the other), in which the same events are so differently regarded by different people that misunderstanding is added to misunderstanding, and in the end serious conflict arises. This is a practical aspect of the problem of communication which was considered in the last chapter. But such a dual treatment of our material would be tedious and repetitious, so for reasons of space and for simplicity of presentation I give a single account, indicating important points of difference or misunderstanding as they occur. The story could fill a book by itself, so here I can record only the most important events.

The first Europeans to visit Bunyoro were the explorers Speke and Grant. When they arrived, in 1862, Mukama Kamurasi (the present king's grandfather) was at the head of a kingdom which was very much larger than present-day Bunyoro. It included much of what is now Buganda, parts of the present Toro and Ankole districts, and it extended some distance north and east of the Nile and west of Lake Albert. But although it seems that all these regions acknowledged the suzerainty of the Nyoro king, it would be a mistake to picture the whole as an orderly and well-administered political unit. There were frequent revolts, sometimes led by dissident "princes," members of the royal Bito clan (the first establishment of Toro as a separate kingdom was the result of such a successful rebellion), and there were constant wars with Buganda, then rapidly increasing in size and power.

Speke and Grant came straight from the Ganda court to Kamurasi's capital, and they stayed there for two months before going north to the Sudan. They described the Mukama as "not unkindly," and as "of a mild disposition compared with Mutesa" (the Ganda king). But they found him suspicious, and they were irritated by his constant demands for gifts and for armed help against his cousin Ruyonga, who was in revolt in the north of the kingdom. Nevertheless they left the country safely, hoping that they had succeeded in laying the foundations of future good relations between Europeans and the Nyoro kingdom. Unfortunately their confidence was misplaced; certainly it was not shared by Nyoro. The Europeans had come straight from the hostile Ganda king, accompanied by a Ganda escort, and furthermore they did not come together but separately, like enemies preparing an attack. And the Ganda, then (as later) anxious to foment trouble between Nyoro and Europeans, in order both to discomfit their traditional enemies and to keep European favor and its concomitant advantages for themselves, spread stories among the Nyoro that the Europeans were cannibals, and given to the most terrible deeds. Ridiculous though these tales seemed to Speke and Grant, they naturally seemed less so to Kamurasi and his advisers, who had never seen Europeans before. Nevertheless the visitors were treated hospitably, and given ample food and beer. And if Kamurasi was sometimes exigent in his demands for gifts and assistance, this was natural enough when these alarming but ostensibly well-disposed strangers were so rich in powerful firearms and other unfamiliar and desirable things.

A little over a year later the explorer Samuel Baker and his intrepid wife arrived from the north, having met Speke and Grant on their way. They spent an uncomfortable year in the country, in the course of which they discovered and named Lake Albert (of course it already had a name, "Mwitanzige," or "the killer of locusts," but such considerations as this rarely inhibited the nomenclatural proclivities of Victorian explorers). Baker and his wife possessed amazing hardihood and courage, but he was a blunt and tactless man, and his relations with Kamurasi were continuously strained. He wrote bitterly about him in his book about this expedition, and accused him of treachery, cowardice, and greed. He and his wife left the country safely, however, and when we consider the circumstances of their arrival this may be thought remarkable enough.

These circumstances included the fact that shortly after Speke's and Grant's departure in the previous year a party of Sudanese had arrived from the north claiming to be these Europeans' greatest friends. After they had been hospitably received on this account they suddenly turned on their hosts and, in collusion with Kamurasi's enemy Ruyonga, killed about three hundred of them. Of course this was not the Europeans' fault, but it is not surprising that Kamurasi and his people were subsequently more than a little suspicious of strangers, especially white ones. Another factor which determined Nyoro reactions to the Bakers' visit was the latters' close association with one of the several Sudanese slaving gangs which were at this time operating, with quite appalling savagery, in what is now the southern Sudan and northern Uganda. These large armed gangs, whose guns gave them the advantage over any local tribe, used to ally themselves with one tribal ruler against another, taking as reward for their aid a rich booty of slaves, ivory, and cattle from the defeated side. Often they would then turn on their allies and add their women and cattle to their spoil. These raiders caused vast destruction and misery; whole regions were depopulated, for many of those who were not carried off or killed died from famine or disease consequent to the destruction of their homes, crops, and cattle. A man is known by the company he keeps, and even though Baker did his best to avoid participation in his companions' raids and intrigues, it was hardly surprising that the Mukama and his people regarded him with deep suspicion.

Unfortunately he did little to counteract this inevitable impression. He even went so far as to threaten Kamurasi with severe reprisals from these very raiders if he did not do what he wanted. Kamurasi once complained to Baker about the bad behavior of one of the latter's Sudanese associates, who had insulted him publicly and threatened him with a gun. Kamurasi told Baker that had the Sudanese not been one of Baker's companions he would have had him and his men killed. Baker, instead of apologizing for his associate's offensive behavior, or even undertaking to look into the matter, advised Kamurasi "not to talk too big, as . . . he might imagine the results that would occur should he even hint at hostility, as the large parties of Ibrahim and the men of Mohamed Wat-el-Mek [two of Baker's Sudanese associates] would immediately unite and destroy both him and his country." Baker reports that "the gallant Kamurasi turned almost green at the bare suggestion of this possibility." (See Baker 1867.) This incident provides a good example of Baker's manner of dealing with the Nyoro king, and helps to explain the suspicion with which Kamurasi and his chiefs regarded him.

The Bakers left Bunyoro in 1864, and returned eight years later, Sir Samuel Baker (as he now was) having been appointed governor-general of the Egyptian province of Equatoria, in which Bunyoro was supposed to be included. He found that Kamurasi had died two years earlier, and had been succeeded by his son Kabarega. During this visit, which only lasted for a few months, there was constant friction between Baker and Kabarega, ending in open conflict shortly after Baker had formally proclaimed the annexation of Bunyoro to Egypt, in the presence of the Mukama and his chiefs. Baker claims that he had first obtained Kabarega's consent to the annexation, but Nyoro deny this. A few days later there was a fight, after the king had (according to Baker) sent poisoned beer to the European and his men, from the fatal effects of which they were only saved by the prompt administration of emetics. Shortly after, Baker states, he and his men were treacherously attacked, and after an affray in which he had to defend himself with a machine gun, he was forced to retreat northwards to the Nile. Here he proclaimed the now aging rebel Ruyonga as the official representative of the Egyptian government in Bunyoro, authorizing him to rule, on Egypt's behalf, in Kabarega's place. This coup had little effect on the existing political situation and of course none at all on Kabarega's authority, though no doubt it relieved Baker's feelings. Unfortunately it did have some historical repercussions.

Naturally the Nyoro version of these events differs considerably from Baker's. I have spoken of the ravages of the slave trade, and in the interval since Baker's first visit these had extended into northern Bunyoro. The slavers were known to come from Khartoum, which most Nyoro did not clearly distinguish from Egypt, so Baker could not have expected to be received with open arms when he returned as a representative of that country. Further, Baker's Sudanese followers inflicted revolting cruelties and abuses on the people everywhere they went. Nor was Baker's hurried annexation of the country just before he fled from it calculated to increase Nyoro confidence in European intentions. Nyoro say that Kabarega and his chiefs were surprised and indignant at Baker's action. They also say that the beer sent to Baker and his men was not poisoned but just particularly strong, and that they drank too much of it. In the fracas which followed these events, they say, Baker mowed down large numbers of Nyoro with a Maxim gun, set fire to the king's enclosure and all the neighboring villages, and departed.

We cannot now know the truth about these events, nor is it our present concern to conjecture about it, still less to allocate praise or blame to either party. My present point is that, whatever actually happened, there subsequently existed two quite different histories of it, one held by Nyoro, the other incorporated into the European record. Certainly some efforts were afterwards made to modify the latter; Emin Pasha, writing five years later, reported that he received in Bunyoro an account of Baker's visit very different from that given by Baker, and many years afterwards the missionary-anthropologist Roscoe, who visited Bunyoro in 1920, also heard the Nyoro version, and noted the serious effects of the affair on Kabarega's attitude to Europeans. But by this time the damage had long since been done; already in the 1870's two different and conflicting versions of Bunyoro's first relations with Europeans had, in Collingwood's phrase, "incapsulated" themselves in the unfolding series of events, and the basis had been laid for further misunderstanding and hostility.

Baker was succeeded as governor of Equatoria by the famous soldier Colonel Gordon, whose attitude to Kabarega and the Nyoro was naturally influenced by Baker's reports. He completely ignored the Nyoro king, dealing instead with Baker's puppet Ruyonga. Gordon's main concern was to stamp out the slave trade, and to do this he established fortified posts in northern Bunyoro and elsewhere, which he staffed with Sudanese and Egyptian soldiers, without, of course, consulting Kabarega first. The Nyoro king and his people were bound to consider this provocative, especially as the occupying garrisons were scarcely less of a menace to the local populations than the slavers themselves. Nevertheless, Nyoro say, Kabarega did not attack these forts, for he did not wish to start fighting the Europeans. Gordon was succeeded in 1878 by the curious and complex German doctor known as Emin Pasha, who unlike his predecessors (and most of his successors) was a trained scientist and scholar as well as an administrator and an explorer. Alone among these early Europeans Emin got on well with Kabarega, and spoke highly, even warmly, of his character and intelligence. Emin's administration lasted much longer than either of his predecessors', and seems to have been successful until the repercussions of the Mahdi revolt in the Sudan in 1884 led to his isolation and to the final breakdown of his administration. Even though Emin realized that Kabarega never really trusted him or any European, his tact and good sense enabled relations to be maintained on a friendly enough basis for several years. But with Emin's reluctant departure with Stanley in 1889 this relatively satisfactory state of affairs came to an end; Kabarega began a new series of raids into Buganda and Toro, and from this time onwards relations between Europeans and the Nyoro king were hostile.

In 1890 Captain Lugard arrived in Uganda as a representative of the British East Africa Company, within whose sphere of influence Buganda and the surrounding regions, including Bunyoro, now fell. Unlike Baker, Gordon, and Emin, he approached Bunyoro from the east, through Buganda, and not from the north, and there is evidence that the Kabaka of Buganda and his advisers made the most of their opportunity to prejudice Lugard against the western kingdom. Lugard relied on Baker's account of Kabarega's character, and it is plain from his own writings that he never even considered the possibility of negotiating with the Nyoro king. Shortly after his arrival in Uganda he decided to collect and reenlist the Sudanese soldiers who were supposed to have remained in the region of Lake Albert after Emin's departure, and to use them to maintain order in Buganda, which was then in a very disturbed condition. On his way there he confirmed a young man called Kasagama, whom he had found as a fugitive in Buganda, as king of Toro, a region which had formerly been part of Bunyoro, but which had revolted a generation or two earlier, and which Kabarega had recently been attempting to regain. This inevitably involved some brushes with Kabarega's warriors. Lugard eventually collected from the neighborhood of Lake Albert about six hundred Sudanese troops, together with their now numerous camp followers and dependants, and he used some of these to garrison a chain of forts which he established across northern Toro, with the object of protecting the new king and his people from Kabarega's attacks. These undisciplined troops soon started to lay waste the country around the forts, which in turn led to more reprisals by Kabarega's men. These forays intensified Lugard's conviction that there could be no peaceful settlement with Kabarega. He acknowledges that envoys came to him from Bunyoro to sue for peace, but he refused to negotiate with them, on the ground that Kabarega was so implacably opposed to Europeans that there would be little point in doing so. He was determined to conquer Bunyoro by force of arms, and serious preparations were now made for a campaign.

So in 1893, after an ultimatum had been issued to Kabarega calling for guarantees for his future good conduct and a substantial indemnity for his past misdeeds, to which apparently no reply was received, a force of nearly 15,000 men, over 14,000 of whom were Ganda, invaded Bunyoro under European leadership. They quickly overran the country, but Kabarega, though constantly harried by the invaders, carried on in retreat a protracted guerrilla warfare, sometimes north and sometimes south of the Nile. In the following year Kabarega's forces sustained some major defeats, but he was still in the field, and in 1895 an even more enormous army was sent against him, consisting of six companies of Sudanese with two Hotchkiss and three Maxim guns, and twenty thousand Ganda. In 1896 the commander of these forces reported that Kabarega had been driven from his country and many hundreds of cattle captured. But although the traditional Nyoro state had been reduced to chaos and the population was undergoing great hardships, the elusive Kabarega still held out with a few followers north of the Nile. Not until 1899 was he finally captured, after being severely wounded in the final engagement. He was exiled to the Seychelles islands, but was allowed to return in 1923, by which time he was an old man. He died on the way, without seeing Bunyoro again.

Nyoro think that the long military campaign against Kabarega was unjustified, and that their Mukama was a good deal less intransigent than he was said to be. They believe that Lugard was misled by the Ganda, and that Kabarega would have been willing to come to terms if he had been allowed to do so. They point out that his overtures were always repulsed, or else huge indemnities were asked, as though he were doing wrong in occupying and defending his own country. Throughout the campaign, Nyoro say, the king carefully avoided directly attacking the Europeans. He did what a king should do; he fought a defensive war, in the face of huge odds, against invasion. Nyoro believe that the British attitude toward their country was due largely to Ganda misrepresentation, and indeed the Ganda did profit handsomely by the downfall of their old enemy.

At the end of the nineteenth century, Bunyoro was thus in very poor shape. The country was largely depopulated by war, famine, and disease. It was regarded as conquered territory, and its administration was for the most part in the hands of Ganda chiefs, who were sent there to teach the Nyoro how to govern themselves. With their king captured and exiled, their country devastated, disease and famine on all sides, and their hereditary enemies the Ganda lording it over them, Bunyoro's downfall was complete. In 1900 Sir Harry Johnston concluded the famous Uganda Agreement with the three regents of Buganda. As well as laying down the principles which should govern political relations between Buganda and the Protectorate government, this agreement defined the territorial boundaries of the Ganda kingdom. Within these it included some large and populous areas which were, as everybody (including Johnston) knew, part of Bunyoro. Thus at a stroke the Nyoro were punished for their resistance and the Ganda rewarded for their assistance to the British campaign. As a result almost 40 percent of the Nyoro people have lived in Ganda territory and been subject to Ganda chiefs for the past half-century, a state of affairs which the Mukama of Bunyoro and his people still deeply resent, especially as the graves of almost all of the former kings of Bunyoro, which are national monuments of great importance, lie in this alienated area. The Uganda Agreement also provided that many chiefs and other important people in Buganda should receive what amounted to freehold rights over large areas of land. It was afterwards recognized that this provision was based on a misconception. But by then the Agreement had been made and it was too late to alter things; the notion of private ownership in land had been irrevocably introduced. The Government was determined not to repeat what it believed to have been an error, and despite repeated claims by the king of Bunyoro and his chiefs (who regarded this as another instance of discrimination) no similar grants of land were made in Bunyoro.

A settled civil administration began to be established in Bunyoro soon after 1900, and the past half-century has shown steady political and economic advance. By the end of World War I almost all the Ganda chiefs had been replaced by Nyoro, and in 1933 the Bunyoro Agreement provided the kingdom with a political status analagous to, though not quite as favorable as, that enjoyed by Buganda. But Nyoro think that even during the past fifty years they have suffered from disabilities not shared by the neighboring kingdoms. The tenure of most of Bunyoro's important chiefships by Ganda in the early years of the century rankled, and in 1906 a number of Nyoro chiefs and people demonstrated in protest. Some chiefs were sentenced to terms of imprisonment or exile in consequence. During the first decade of this century, also, famine continued to afflict Bunyoro. It is said that in the 1920's the remnants of Bunyoro's herds of cattle, already decimated by war and disease, succumbed in large numbers to anti-rinderpest inoculations carried out by the Government. The Government's intention, of course, was to help, not to injure, the Nyoro, but many people still believe that these deaths were the result of a policy designed to keep Nyoro in a properly humble and submissive state.

Even European missionary activity has been regarded as being directed to the same end, and some pagan Nyoro still so regard it. The old religious cult, centering on spirit possession, is still strong, and one of its most important aims is the ensuring of fertility. Many other magical rites are directed to the same purpose, and to the health and prosperity of their practitioners. All these practices have been rigorously suppressed both by missions and by the Government, and Nyoro have told me that this is because the Europeans do not really want Nyoro to increase in numbers, health, or prosperity. Such beliefs are by no means absurd to semiliterate Africans with no first-hand knowledge of Europeans. Certainly the rigor with which indigenous Nyoro religious and magical cults have been suppressed is unusual in an African dependency; even the missionary anthropologist Roscoe criticized this repressive policy, the chief effect of which has been to drive these practices underground.

To bring this history quite up to date, reference would have to be made to Bunyoro's increased economic prosperity, and to the several constitutional advances which have been made in recent years, providing for the increased devolution of authority on to the Mukama and his chiefs and, latterly, on the people themselves, through popular representation on the chiefs' councils.

Some of these matters have already been touched on; others will be considered when we discuss the contemporary political system in the next two chapters. Thus far I have attempted to bring to life Nyoro ideas about their own past, and to do this I have had to review the history of European-Nyoro relations. It should, perhaps, be reaffirmed that it is no part of the social anthropologist's task to say what should or should not be, or have been, done: he knows that people are bound to act within the broad lines that their culture prescribes, and that, for example, the ideas and standards of a Victorian soldier or explorer are bound to differ vastly from those of a tribal African king, and even very considerably from our own. So he will not make the elementary mistake of condemning either party for failing to act in accordance with contemporary standards of practical morality and psychological "know-how." But there is no doubt that Bunyoro has been unlucky in some of her relationships with Europeans, and that some of her grievances are real ones. Only when we have understood this can we understand how contemporary Nyoro think about themselves and about Europeans, and how Europeans think about Nyoro. It is because Nyoro are historians, not because we are, that this historical section has had to be included; a book about Bunyoro which neglected its history would be like *Hamlet*, if not without the Prince of Denmark, at least without his father's ghost.

3

The King

Rituals of Kingship

SOMETHING has already been said of the kingship, and in the last chapter
we followed the fortunes of the most famous of Nyoro kings, the re-
doubtable Kabarega. We now examine the Nyoro monarchy first as the
symbol of Nyoro nationhood, the focus of Nyoro ideas about political
authority, and second, as the center of the network of social relations which
is what we mean when we talk about the political system. Therefore in the
first part of this chapter I consider the ways in which the kingship is traditionally regarded; this will entail a discussion of its ritual character. In the
second part I discuss the king's actual relationships with the different kinds
of people who make up Nyoro society; this will enable us to determine his
position in the social structure. Throughout, our main interest is in the present-
day situation. But we cannot understand this unless we understand the traditional elements which still persist. What I describe is still in important respects
a traditional African monarchy, but it has been much modified by European
influence, and in the course of my account I shall take note of these modifications. This will reflect the manner in which these modifications present themselves to the field anthropologist, indeed to thoughtful Nyoro themselves; that
is, as impacting at various points and in various ways on a traditional political
organization.

We have seen how myth and traditional history validate the Mukama's
claim to special distinction. He and his Bito kinsmen are thought of (and
think of themselves) as quite different from ordinary people. Unlike some
African rulers, Nyoro kings are not thought of as kin with the people they
rule; they are not "fathers" of their people, but rulers of their people. Where
the distinction between those born to rule and those born to be ruled is as
sharply made as it is in Bunyoro, the intimacy of a blood tie (which in fact
always exists through the female line, since kings' mothers come from non-Bito

375

clans) between these two quite different kinds of people is unlikely to be asserted, even in metaphor. The Mukama is the traditional ruler of all Nyoro, and in pre-European times all political authority in the state was seen as deriving from him. Nowadays, of course, outside political power is injected into the system at all levels by government officials, missionaries, and others, and nearly everybody knows this. But the Nyoro kingship is still essentially authoritarian. There are African kingdoms in which the king's importance is traditionally ritual rather than political; in Bunyoro this is not so. Though his power was not absolute, the Mukama was essentially a ruler. He is, indeed, surrounded by ritual, but this ritual makes sense only when it is seen as a symbolic expression of the king's political preeminence and power. A look at some of this ritual will make this point clear.

Broadly, Nyoro royal ritual falls into three categories. First, there are rites which express the ways in which Nyoro think about the kingship itself. Second, there is the ritual associated with the king's accession to and retention of authority, and his relinquishing of it at death. And third, there are those rites which are concerned with the ways in which the king may delegate his authority.

The rituals in the first category are mostly concerned with the Mukama in his aspect as "divine king," which means, for Nyoro, that he is mystically identified with the whole country of which he is the head. This means that the king must keep physically healthy; if he does not, the country and people as a whole will suffer. Formerly, a person, or even an ox, who was sick had to be removed at once from the royal enclosure, in case the king's health should be affected. The king had to avoid all contact with death; when I asked why the present Mukama did not attend his mother's funeral in 1953, I was told that it was because of this rule. In pre-European times, if the Mukama himself fell sick the matter was kept strictly secret. It is said that if his illness were serious, if he suffered any physical incapacity or mutilation, or if he grew too old and feeble to carry out his duties properly, he would either kill himself by taking poison or be killed by one of his wives. This was, of course, because any imperfection or weakness in the king was thought to involve a corresponding danger to the kingdom. We do not know for sure whether any kings ever were killed in this way, but the important thing is that it is thought that they were. This shows us how Nyoro traditionally thought about their country and their kingship.

As well as maintaining physical health, the Mukama had to keep himself in a good ritual or spiritual condition. This imposed on him certain ceremonial acts and avoidances. He was not allowed to eat certain kinds of food which were said to be of low status, such as sweet potatoes, cassava, and certain other vegetables. His numerous attendants also had to keep themselves ritually pure; for instance, his cooks had to abstain from sexual intercourse during and for some days before their periods of service in the palace, which were only for a few days at a time. On ceremonial occasions his special dairy-maids, who had to be virgins, smeared themselves with white clay. This symbolized purity and goodness (for Nyoro, as for many other peoples, whiteness and purity are closely associated—indeed, one word is used for both). The king had to carry out certain rites associated with the royal herd of cattle "for the good of the country." These entailed his presence in the byre at milking time, and his ceremonial drinking of some of the new milk. Other usages also stress the Mukama's difference from and superiority to ordinary people. He has to be spoken to and greeted with special words (he is always addressed, and replies, in the third person singular), and he has a large number of distinctive names and titles. These refer to him as exceeding all men, ruling justly, relieving distress, and so on. Even today the most important officers of his own government kneel to hand him anything or to make a request of him in his own house. There is a special vocabulary referring to the king's person and activities, not used in regard to anyone else. He has extensive regalia, consisting of ancient crowns, drums, spears, stools, and other objects, and all of these have special names and their own custodians. In addition to these regalia keepers there are also a great many palace retainers and household officials of various kinds, most of whom have special names and titles.

The effect of these rituals and ceremonial usages, many of which are still observed, is to stress the Mukama's importance as the head of the state and the source of all political authority within it. By symbolically identifying him with the whole country, they justify his being treated as unique, and show why his physical and spiritual well-being must be sustained, while at the same time they enhance tribal unity by providing a set of symbols acceptable to everybody. But though ritual attaches to the kingship, it would be a mistake to think of the Mukama as a kind of priest, in the sense that he intercedes with a god or gods on behalf of his people. Such intercession is the work of the spirit mediums, initiates into the possession cult which is Bunyoro's traditional religion. The Mukama is not a priest, though he has his priests, just as he is not a rain maker, though he has his rain makers—magical experts who are subject to his discipline and control. In some African countries the real importance of chiefs lies in their magical or religious powers, and if they are secular rulers they are so only in a secondary capacity. In Bunyoro it is otherwise. The Mukama is first and foremost a ruler, and that is how everybody thinks of him.

The second of the broad categories of ritual which I distinguished was that concerned with the acquisition, retention, and relinquishing of kingly power. Nyoro accession ceremonies are lengthy and complex. This is what we should expect. In Bunyoro it is not known who is to be the new king until after the old king is dead. Traditionally the heir to the throne was supposed to be the prince who succeeded in killing whichever of his brothers (and he might have a good many) was his rival for the throne. Thus the successful prince undergoes a great change of status on his accession: formerly he was one of a considerable number of equally eligible princes; now he is king. Nyoro accession ritual marks this assumption of new status in the strongest and most emphatic terms. Both its ritual and political aspects are stressed. The accession ceremonies include washing, shaving, and nail-paring rites, anointment with a special oil and smearing with white chalk, ceremonial milk drinking, and animal sacrifice. In pre-European times, it is said, they included the placing on the throne and the subsequent killing of a "mock king," who would, it was believed, attract to himself the magical dangers which attended the transition to kingship, so protecting the real king. The king's accession to political office is equally stressed. He is handed various objects symbolizing political and military power, such as spears, a bow and arrows, a dagger, and a stick, and he is formally admonished and instructed to rule wisely, to kill his enemies, and to protect his people. His territorial authority is also symbolized in a ceremony in which a man who represents neighboring regions formerly subject to Bunyoro presents him with ivory and some copper bracelets as "tribute." Another rite is the ceremonial acting-out of the settlement of a lawsuit in which one man sues another for debt. This is not really a judicial hearing; it is a symbolic way of impressing on both king and people the important part he is to play as lawgiver and judge. Finally, there is a ceremony in which the king shoots arrows with the bow he has been given toward the four points of the compass, saying as he does so: "Thus I shoot the countries to overcome them." Several of these rites are repeated at "refresher" ceremonies, which used to be held annually.

Accession and "refresher" rites stress the king's attainment to supreme political power equally with his accession to the high ritual status associated with this authority. These themes are also evident in the ritual connected with the Mukama's death. Here what is principally expressed is the continuity of the kingship, even though the king is dead. Traditionally there was an interregnum of several months during which two or more of the sons of the dead Mukama might fight for the succession, while civil disorder and confusion prevailed. For some days the king's death was concealed; then a man climbed to the top of one of the houses in the king's enclosure carrying a milk-pot, and hurled this to the ground, shouting "The milk is spilt; the king has been taken away!" As this man descended, he was killed, for such things may not be said. In pre-European times the royal corpse was preserved by disemboweling it and drying it over a slow fire. When a prince had succeeded in winning the kingdom he came and took the late king's jawbone, which had been separated from the corpse and carefully guarded, and had to bury this at a selected place, where a house was built and certain of tne late king's regalia preserved under the supervision of a chosen member of the royal Bito clan. The rest of the corpse was buried separately and the grave forgotten; the tombs which are remembered and venerated today are those where the royal jawbones are buried.

The third kind of royal ritual which I distinguished related to the delegation of the Mukama's authority. A ruler—at least in the conditions of a tribal African kingdom—cannot keep all his power to himself, but must give some of it away; this is one of the major limitations on political authority. Thus, like other kings, the Mukama of Bunyoro traditionally had to confer quite a high degree of independent authority on his great chiefs; hence the loose, "feudal" type of organization (involving close interpersonal bonds between king and chiefs) characteristic of traditional Bunyoro.

To delegate political authority to his chiefs was at the same time to confer ritual status upon them. There is a Nyoro word, *Mahano,* denoting a special kind of spiritual power, which is applied to many objects and situations which are strange and awe inspiring. This mysterious potency may be dangerous, calling for the performance of special ritual to preserve or restore normality. It is especially associated with the Mukama; therefore, when he delegates political authority upon his chiefs, he also imparts to them something of his own ritual power. Thus the delegation of political authority is not just an administrative act, it is also a ritual act. The ritual involves, in particular, a ceremony known as "drinking milk" with the Mukama, and it is said that (in the case of important chiefs, at least) the milk formerly was taken from the cows of his special herd. Nowadays, it seems, milk is not used, but roasted coffee berries are handed by the Mukama to the person upon whom he is bestowing authority. The recipient of this favor is then supposed to kiss the Mukama's hand, a ceremony strikingly reminiscent of the kiss of fealty in medieval and later Europe. This expresses the chief's obligation and personal devotion to his sovereign, who has confirmed him in authority over a specific territory and its inhabitants. Theoretically, at least, all territorial authority in Bunyoro was held from the king and by his grace, and its grant implied enhancement of the recipient's ritual status as well as of his political status. Nyoro royal ritual is best understood as the symbolic expression of royal authority, and one of its effects is to sustain and validate this authority.

The King and His People

We now consider the king's relations, both in traditional times and at the present day, with the more important of the various categories of persons who make up Nyoro society. These are the members of the royal Bito line and their two heads, the Okwiri and the Kalyota, the king's mother, his regalia keepers, domestic officials, and advisers, his territorial chiefs of various grades and, finally, his people at large.

The word "Bito" denotes one of Bunyoro's hundred or more clans; it also denotes the present ruling dynasty. These are not quite the same thing. Though all Bito have the same avoidance object or "totem" (the bushbuck), only those who can establish a real genealogical link with the Mukama are accorded special prestige, and the closer the relationship the greater the prestige claimed and acknowledged. It is these close kinsmen of the king who are generally meant when the Bito are referred to; members of the Bito clan who can show no such explicit connection are not distinguished socially from members of commoner clans. Those who can demonstrate patrilineal descent from a Mukama of a few generations back (rarely more than four) regard themselves as a distinctive hereditary aristocracy, among whom the most distinguished are the "Bito of the drum," the actual sons of a Mukama. There are still a good many of these important Bito; former kings had many wives, and some were notably prolific: Kabarega had over a hundred children, some of whom are still living.

In the past, most important Bito received large estates from the Mukama, together with the political rights which such grants implied. They were thus important territorial chiefs. Nowadays, as we shall see in Chapter 4, European influence has broken down the traditional association between rights over land and political authority, and it has at the same time radically altered the basis on which land is held. A consequence of this is that Bito are no longer, as a class, the wealthy and powerful group which they formerly were. But they still claim special privileges and prestige; and they still preserve, under the nominal authority of their head, the Okwiri, the ability in certain contexts to act as a group.

The Okwiri, the Mukama's "official brother," is traditionally the eldest son of the late king, and he is formally appointed by the new Mukama after his accession. He is said to "rule" the Bito as the king rules the country as a whole. Structurally his office is interesting in that it provides a way of "detaching" the king from the exclusive Bito group to which he belongs by birth, so making possible his identification with the whole kingdom, non-Bito as well as Bito. For the King is not directly concerned with Bito interests, which often conflicted (and still do) with those of the people as a whole; these are the business of the Okwiri. This official nowadays represents the Bito on the central council of the native government, and resolutions (which are rarely if ever adopted) claiming for them special rights and privileges are still occasionally tabled through him. Even today, Bito claim special deference from commoners and are usually accorded it; many of them still hold large private estates which they administer autocratically; and they are sometimes said, not always without justification, to be arrogant and demanding, and heedless of others' rights. Like aristocracies elsewhere which have survived the political conditions in which they played an effective part, Bito still cling to the outward signs of an authority which they no longer have, and lord it over a peasant population which still shows little resentment. It might be thought that Bito, anxious for the reality of power, would have found places for themselves in the modern chiefly service. But very few have done so. This is consistent with traditional Bito values; service in the modern Nyoro government would involve official subordination to non-Bito, and to some of the more old-fashioned, this would be intolerable.

Corresponding to the Okwiri's position as the head of the Bito "princes" is that of the king's "official sister," the Kalyota. She is a chosen half-sister of the king (she has a different mother), whom he appoints to be the head of the Bito women or "princesses." These royal ladies enjoy a prestige similar to their brothers'. They were, indeed, said to be "like men," for like the princes they ruled as chiefs over the areas allotted to them. Formerly they were not allowed to marry or bear children; this helped to preserve the unity and exclusiveness of the king's lineage, for it prevented the growth of lines of sisters' sons to the royal house. To old-fashioned Nyoro, it would have been unthinkable for persons of such high status to assume the markedly subordinate status of wives. Today, however, the king's daughters, like other

Bito women, may marry and have children, but they usually marry men of high social standing who can afford to keep servants, for Bito princesses do not dig or carry water like ordinary women. Bridewealth is not paid in such marriages, for that would imply some degree of social equality. "How," an informant asked, "could a Bito and a commoner haggle about bridewealth? A Bito's word should be an order."

Like the Okwiri, then, the king's official sister was really a kind of chief; her appointment to office included the handing over to her of certain regalia, and like other persons succeeding to political authority she underwent the ceremony of "drinking milk" with the Mukama. She held and administered estates, from which she derived revenue and services, like other chiefs. She settled disputes, determined inheritance cases, and decided matters of precedence among the Bito women. She was not, as she is sometimes thought to have been, the queen, if by queen we mean the king's consort. It is said that in former times the Mukama could sleep with her if he wanted to, but he could do this with any of his royal sisters, so long as she was born of a different mother from his own. We may best regard her, then, as a kind of female counterpart of the king—the head of the Bito women, and so the chief lady in the land. We may see her office, like that of her brother the Okwiri, as one of the means whereby the royal authority was distributed. Though there is little place for her in the modern system, she still holds official rank, and her status is constitutionally recognized (as is the Okwiri's) by the payment to her of a small salary under the Bunyoro Agreement. Nowadays she is socially overshadowed by the king's true consort, the Omugo, whom he married in Christian marriage and who has borne him several children. It was she, not the Kalyota, who accompanied the Mukama on his visit to England for Queen Elizabeth's coronation in 1953, and she sits at his side at ceremonies and entertainments at which Europeans are present.

As in some other African monarchies, the king's mother also traditionally had considerable power, and kept her own court and ruled her own estates. She no longer has such authority today, but she is still much honored, and like the Okwiri and the Kalyota she receives a small official salary.

I referred above to the numerous regalia keepers and other palace officials who traditionally surrounded the king. Even today there are a great many such persons. Some are salaried officials; others, whose services are required only occasionally, receive gifts from the Mukama from time to time. These officials include the custodian of the royal graves, men responsible for the more important of the royal drums, caretakers, and "putters-on" of the royal crowns, custodians of spears, stools, and other regalia, cooks, bath attendants, herdsmen, potters, barkcloth makers, musicians, and many others. The more important of them have several assistants, and their duties are not onerous, for the care of a particular spear or attendance on the Mukama on ceremonial occasions occupies only a small part of a man's working life. This complex establishment is therefore not to be understood simply as an overcumbersome attempt to run a large household; neither in ancient times nor now can it be regarded as an economical or even as a particularly efficient way of doing this.

Sociologically, the point of it is that it provided a means of involving a great many different groups and kinds of people in a common interest in the royal establishment and so in the maintenance of the kingship itself. It did this both through the clan system (for different offices were often hereditarily vested in particular clans, all of whose members shared in the honor of representation at the palace) and through occupational specialization (since it meant that all of Bunyoro's crafts were represented at the capital). In these ways the huge royal establishment served to integrate the Nyoro people around their center, and so to sustain the political system itself. Even in modern times prestige still attaches to these occupations, even where they are part time and unpaid, and I know of young men who have refused to take up profitable employment elsewhere in order to retain them. Moreover, a man who had served for some years in the palace might hope, if he gained the Mukama's personal favor, to be rewarded with a gift of an estate somewhere in the kingdom, thus becoming a kind of minor chief over its peasant inhabitants. Grants of this kind have been made even in recent times, though they have latterly rather taken the form of appointment to minor official chiefships. Such grants are not appropriate to a modern "civil service" type of administration; we shall return to this point.

In addition to this large body of palace and domestic officials, there was a loosely defined category of informal advisers and retainers. As well as certain officials in the last category, these included diviners and other persons who had attached themselves to the Mukama's household as dependants. These informal and private advisers had no official standing and they did not receive salaries. Some of them have, in the past, exerted considerable influence, and they have sometimes been said to be "nearer to the king" than the official chiefs. They acted at times as intermediaries between the chiefs and the king. They might expect to receive informal rewards from time to time, and they, too, might have received estates or minor chiefships for their services.

A much more important category of persons in traditional Bunyoro were the "crown wearers." To men whom the king wished specially to distinguish he gave elaborate beaded headdresses, with fringes or "beards" of colobus monkey skins. The award of a crown implied the grant of very high dignity and ritual status (recipients had to observe the same food restrictions as the king himself and were said to have a great deal of *mahano*). At the same time it involved accession to high political authority over considerable territories. Like other important chiefs the crown wearers had to take an oath of loyalty to the king, and to undergo the milk-drinking rite referred to above. In the past, crowns were awarded to persons who had performed some considerable service for the Mukama, such as winning a major victory in war; a crown was also traditionally awarded to the head of the king's mother's clan. Crowns, once awarded, were hereditary in the male line. The Bunyoro Agreement still provides for the grant of this award, which it describes as "an old-established order of distinction," but the institution is now falling into disuse, and no crown has been awarded for many years. The high ritual value that formerly attached to the Mukama's political authority no longer does so to the same extent, for such authority is seen nowadays to derive from other and more potent outside sources.

The system of territorial chiefship is discussed in the next chapter; here we need only note that traditionally all political authority was seen as deriving from the person of the king himself; as in feudal Europe, chiefs held their territories as gifts from the king, and this implied a close bond of personal dependence and attachment between him and them. Chiefship was essentially territorial; a chief was a person to whom the Mukama had granted rights over a particular territory and its inhabitants. These rights, even where they tended to become hereditary, were held only by the Mukama's favor: they could be withdrawn by him at any time, and sometimes they were. Though it does not seem that in pre-European times there was any such formal political hierarchy as there is now, there were different ranks of chiefs, from the great rulers of areas which roughly correspond with present-day counties, to minor chiefs with only a handful of peasant dependants.

This personal way of looking at the relationship between a ruler and his subordinates was quite appropriate to the relatively simple, "feudal" organization of pre-European times. Where political office is thought of as the sovereign's gift, it is important to seek and retain his personal favor, and it is natural that a return should be made for such a gift. If, even in modern times, chiefships should sometimes have been given, and promotion awarded, to persons who have rendered gifts or personal service to the king, and persons who have incurred his personal dislike should have been passed over, this would be wholly consistent with the values implicit in traditional Nyoro political structure, where personal attachment and loyalty were the supreme political values. It would be a serious mistake to regard such transactions, even now, as constituting breaches of tribal morality, although in terms of the impersonal standards of modern Western administration they are both wrong and politically harmful. It is natural, in such a system, that personal attachment should count for more than conformity to bureaucratic standards of efficiency and incorruptibility. And we must remember further that the exercise of political authority in pre-European times needed far less special training and knowledge than are demanded now. In Bunyoro, at all events, it is said that the expression of personal loyalty to the Mukama was until recent times hardly less necessary a qualification for political appointment than administrative experience or a high educational standard.

Appropriate though these attitudes were to the traditional system, they are plainly less so to modern times. Like other Western administrations, the British authorities are committed to encouraging the development of more modern and democratic political institutions, better adapted to the contemporary world of which Bunyoro is now a part. Traditional attitudes to chiefship are incompatible with these institutions. Many educated Nyoro realize this, and I have heard such people complain that faithful service in the Mukama's bathroom or kitchen is hardly an adequate qualification for even minor political office, and that the king's personal favor is not in itself an obvious qualification for the highest administrative posts. The situation, too, is greatly altered by the introduction of a cash economy, for when gifts formerly of kind are commuted to cash, they at once assume a different and more mercenary character But it is an important part of the anthropologist's task to point out that such transactions are not properly understood when they are simply condemned as misdemeanors; rather, they have to be seen as usages surviving from a context in which they were proper and appropriate into one where they are no longer so. When values and patterns of behavior which are mutually incompatible come to coexist in the same rapidly changing political system, strains and conflict develop. We shall see in other contexts also that feudal values and bureaucratic ones do not always mesh smoothly.

Another example of uneasy coexistence of new and old values is found in the economic aspect of the relationship between the Mukama and his people at large. In the traditional system the king was seen both as the supreme receiver of goods and services, and as the supreme giver. Typically in systems of the Nyoro type, goods and services have to be rendered to the "lord," the person who stands next above one in the political hierarchy. Thus in Bunyoro the great chiefs, who themselves received tribute from their dependants, were required to hand over to the Mukama a part of the produce of their estates, in the form of crops, cattle, beer, or women. But everybody must give to the king, not only the chiefs. Even today the ordinary people make presents to him on certain ceremonial occasions. When he pays state visits to different parts of his country, as he often does, gifts of produce, for which there is a special Nyoro word, should be brought to him by peasants as well as chiefs. And larger gifts, in cash or kind, might be made to him from time to time by people who wish to obtain and retain his favor. All these various kinds of gifts express in traditional terms a kind of attachment between ruler and ruled which is important in a relatively small-scale feudal society. In addition, they formerly provided a sort of social insurance, for those who fell on hard times would naturally look for help to their chiefs and, ultimately, to the king.

The Mukama's role as giver was, accordingly, no less stressed. Many of his special names emphasize his magnanimity, and he was traditionally expected to give extensively in the form both of feasts and of gifts to individuals. But here, too, attitudes and values have survived the social conditions to which they were appropriate. People nowadays complain that the king no longer gives the great feasts which their grandfathers enjoyed. Their offerings of foodstuffs, they say, are taken away in a truck, and no feast, or at best a very inadequate one, is provided. They think that nowadays only the Mukama's circle of personal friends receives help from him. They do not see that the political changes of the past half-century, and in particular the advent of a cash economy, have made their attitudes and expectations anachronistic. For the truth is that the Mukama himself does not receive produce in the same quantities as his predecessors did, since the cultivators can now sell their surpluses for cash with which to satisfy their new needs. And to provide meat for huge feasts now, when cattle are virtually nonexistent and meat is prohibitively expensive, is economically impracticable. Also, as we have noted, many of the gifts which the Mukama now receives are in cash, not kind. And cash, unlike food and beer, does not have to be consumed quickly and communally in the form of gifts and feasts; it can be converted into many other desirable objects not formerly available. This state of affairs is not, of course, peculiar to Bunyoro; on the contrary, it is one of the most characteristic features of African kingdoms at the same stage of change. But in Bunyoro the economic aspect of political authority is particularly strongly institutionalized. It is thus inevitable that the incompatibility beween the traditional idea of rulers as centers for the collection and redistribution of goods, and the new pattern of bureaucratic authority which is now developing, should lead to bewilderment and strain. Nor should we be surprised that the nature of these conflicts is not always fully understood by those most closely involved in them.

4

The Chiefs

The Traditional System

IN THE TRADITIONAL Nyoro state all political authority stemmed from the king. Advised by his formal and informal counsellors, he appointed his territorial chiefs to office, and their authority, down to the lowest level, had to be confirmed by him personally. Traditionally, political office was not thought of as hereditary, though it often tended to become so. A chiefship could be taken away by the king at any time, but often it would be passed on to the original chief's heir. Chiefship, then, was not just a formal administrative office; rather, it was a private and personal (though conditional) possession, which like any other private property was thought of as hereditable.

The great chiefs had to maintain residences at the king's capital and to attend there constantly. This served as a check (though not always a very effective one) on rebellion. It also strengthened the group of advisers upon whom the king could rely; in political systems of this "feudal" type there was no need for a central secretariat, for the same people could serve both as royal councillors and as territorial administrators. When a chief was away from the court he had to leave behind him a representative or deputy, who assumed all his titles and took his place on ceremonial occasions. This use of deputies is characteristic of Bunyoro, as it is of the interlacustrine kingdoms generally; it may be said to express the dual quality of delegated political authority. For a territorial chief is essentially a "king's man," and so must be in constant attendance on him. But he is also a territorial ruler, personally responsible for the good administration of his area. To have a formal deputy to "double" for him provides a means of reconciling his two roles. Chiefs also had to provide the king from time to time with grain, beer, and cattle, as well as with ivory and other goods, and to supply men for work at the capital in peace time and for fighting in time of war. These exactions, of course, fell on the peasant population, and in return for them the peasants looked to their rulers for security and protection.

386

In the old days the chiefs did not occupy clearly distinguished grades, as modern chiefs do. They nevertheless fell into two broad categories. First there were the great chiefs who ruled over large areas and were answerable only to the Mukama; these probably included several crown wearers. Next there was a great number of lesser chiefs, having authority over very much smaller areas. These authorities could hold their areas directly from the king, just as the larger chiefs did, or they might be assistants or dependants of the major chiefs, to whom, rather than to the Mukama, they owed direct allegiance. But in either case their authority, like that of all persons wielding political power in the kingdom, would have to be formally validated by the Mukama. Below the dozen or so great *saza* or provincial chiefs, who ruled over definite regions of which the names and boundaries are still well known, chiefs seem not to have been thought of as occupying separate grades, but rather in terms of a gradual scale of power and importance. The status of any chief on this scale depended both on the number of subjects he governed and on the closeness of his relationship with the Mukama.

It does not seem that subordinate political authority in Bunyoro was ever a prerogative of members of the ruling Bito aristocracy. Some Bito did govern large chiefdoms, but most chiefs were either members of the respected Huma cattle-owning class, or people of commoner origin (though usually members of families with a tradition of chiefship). Usually a man was made a chief because he or one of his patrilineal forebears had earned the Mukama's gratitude either by service or by gift. The king often gave chiefships to his maternal or affinal relatives. In addition, palace officials and servants were often granted minor chiefdoms; as in the feudal states of medieval Europe, personal service to the king might bring a rich reward. Typically feudal, also, was the relationship of personal loyalty and dependence that existed between the king and his chiefs. In the language of modern sociology, the relationship between a political superior and his subordinate was "diffuse" rather than "specific"; that is, the chief's dealings with his subordinates were not restricted to a narrow official sphere, but extended over the whole of the subordinate's personal life. Even today many Nyoro feel that chiefs should be interested in them as persons, and not simply in their tax-paying or working capacity; we shall note later that the impersonal character of modern administration is a common ground for complaint.

One other aspect of the traditional Nyoro system must be discussed, and that is the connection between political authority and the possession of rights over land. The grant of a chiefship by the Mukama was essentially the bestowal of rights over a particular territory and the people in it. Nyoro did not think of these two things as being different; to be granted political authority was to be allotted an area in which to exercise it and of which to enjoy the profits, and to be given an "estate" was to be granted political authority over it. When, therefore, an ordered administration through chiefs was reintroduced early in the present century, it was natural that the persons appointed to chiefships should think of their areas as official "estates," from whose inhabitants they could exact goods and services for their support. With the introduction of money, the tribute paid by the peasant cultivators came to be commuted to an annual cash payment. This payment, which was seven shillings per adult male, was the chiefs' main source of revenue until the Bunyoro Agreement of 1933 provided that they should receive salaries instead. But in addition to the official chiefships, during the early 1900's the Mukama began to give plots of populated land to retired official chiefs as their private property, in reward for their services: chiefship was not then a pensionable office as it is now (at least in the higher grades). Similar gifts then began to be made increasingly to chiefs who were still in office, and also to members of the royal household, to palace officials, to Bito "princes" and "princesses," and to various other people whom the Mukama wished for one reason or another to favor. These gifts conformed with the traditional usage whereby the grant of minor chiefdoms provided a way for the Mukama to discharge his obligations toward persons to whom he was indebted. The estates or "fiefs" so granted were regarded as the private property of their owners, who enjoyed tribute and services from their occupants just as the chiefs did on their official estates. At about this time the quite new idea of unalienable, "freehold" tenure of land was gaining currency in Uganda, mainly owing to the terms of the Uganda Agreement of 1900, which—through a misunderstanding of the nature of the land rights involved—provided a large number of chiefs and other important people in Buganda with what amounted to freehold rights over considerable areas of land in that country. A consequence of this was that Nyoro fief holders came to think of their land rights not only as personal, but also as permanent and hereditable.

By 1931 a very large part of populated Bunyoro had been taken up in these private estates, the occupants of which found themselves subject not only to the official chief of the area, but also to the proprietor of the estate they lived in. Indeed these proprietors were regarded by their tenants no less as "chiefs" than the persons officially so designated. And the proprietors so regarded themselves, demanding from their peasant tenants the respect due their superior status. To a large extent they in fact fulfilled the role of chiefs; they settled disputes between their peasant tenants and often acted as intermediaries between their people and the official chiefs. The peasants themselves on the whole found nothing to resent in this arrangement. Indeed in some ways these landed proprietors have conformed more closely (they still do) to traditional Nyoro notions of what a chief should be than have the official chiefs themselves. For they are not, like the chiefs, liable to transfer, and their personal stake in the land gives them a closer interest in and knowledge of their "tenants" than is possible for a county or subcounty chief, much of whose time is taken up by court or office work, and whose stay in the area may be limited to a few years or less. Thus even today these proprietors may be said to fill a role not wholly filled by the lower grades of the official chiefs; they may even in fact find themselves in opposition to these officials, for village headmen sometimes resent the assured status and social prestige of the larger estate owners. Conversely, it is still popularly considered that the proper persons to hold authority in these estates are their proprietors, and these proprietors some-times resent interference in the internal affairs of their holdings by the govern-ment chiefs, whom they regard as "outsiders."

This widespread grant of private estates during the first quarter of the century and afterwards was not, then, a proliferation only of estates and "land-lords"; it was at the same time a proliferation of minor chiefs. In 1933 the Protectorate Government tried, by legislation, to do away with these populated estates, but the system of proprietary estates and the "feudal" way of thinking which they implied were too deeply ingrained to be eradicated. Although the official chiefs were now provided with salaries and were much reduced in number, and although the exaction of tribute was now forbidden, large popu-lated estates, even though no longer a source of profit, continued to be attrac-tive. Their attraction was not, and never had been, mainly economic; it lay rather in the enhancement of authority and status which their possession implied. Hence the result of the 1933 reforms was not, as had been hoped, the gradual disappearance of populated estates; it was, rather, the creation in the popular mind of two kinds of chiefs, the salaried official ones and the proprie-tors of these estates.

From the point of view of the official chiefs, this dualism could only be resolved by establishing themselves as authorities in both categories, and this is exactly what they tried to do. Even today most official chiefs consider that as well as administering their official chiefdoms they should also possess private estates of their own. One of the first things a chief does on appointment is to acquire a tenanted estate (if he does not already possess one) in some popu-lated area not already claimed by somebody else. Almost all of the official chiefs do possess such estates, mostly obtained, or their extent increased, after their appointment or promotion. And the higher the chief's rank, the larger the estate he is likely to possess; a county chief's estate may have up to fifty occupying households, subchiefs average a little over a dozen, lower chiefs may have five or six. The official chiefs are the largest single category of recipients of populated estates, and they tend, also, to receive the largest areas.

Thus the traditional identity between political authority and the pos-session of personal and private rights over particular territories and the people on them is still viable in Bunyoro. It has survived to a significant extent into the increasingly "bureaucratic," impersonal kind of chiefship which is de-veloping today. For Nyoro, a chief is still much more than an impersonal civil servant, just as the proprietor of a populated estate is much more than a kind of landlord. The nature of present-day chiefship, and the kinds of attitudes toward it which exist, cannot be understood unless this is recognized.

I have applied the adjective "feudal" to Bunyoro's traditional political organization. Let me conclude and summarize this section by comparing some features of traditional Bunyoro with those characteristic of a typically "feudal" state of medieval Europe. The term "feudalism" is usually applied to a medieval European polity that is based on the relations of vassal and superior arising from the holding of lands in feud—that is, in consideration of service and homage from the vassal to his lord. England after the Norman conquest was just such a state, and there is a striking resemblance between some of its political institutions and those of traditional Bunyoro.[1] We have seen that, in Bunyoro, lands were held and authority over them exercised very much on this feudal pattern. Even the beginnings of Norman feudalism in England are paralleled in Nyoro tradition. The Norman invasion of England was not a wholesale immigration; it was rather a conquest whose aristocratic leader won a kingdom for himself and distributed estates among his followers. Almost the same words could be used of the coming of the Bito to Bunyoro. Rukidi and his companions seem to have been a small group of Nilotic adventurers who took over the old Chwezi kingdom and divided it among themselves. There was no mass invasion of Nilotes; the Bito formed merely the "top layer" of a community which remained basically unchanged. In Bunyoro, too, the idea was fostered that all land belonged by right to the king, and could be held by others only as a gift from him, in reward for specified services. Personal loyalty to the king was all-important in both policies; in both, failure to render service when called upon was considered as rebellion and dealt with accordingly.

In twelfth-century England, feudal holdings were scattered about the country, so that a tendency on the part of any one of them to expand excessively would be checked by the others. In Bunyoro, the traditional allocation of territorial rights, and even the wide distribution of private estates during the first half of the present century, may be said to represent a similar policy. Further, the holders of European fiefs had to attend their lord's court when summoned; so also the great chiefs in Bunyoro had to be constantly present at the Mukama's headquarters, and even had to maintain permanent houses there. William I constantly traveled about the land with his entourage so as to secure the obedience of the more remote parts of the country. Likewise, in traditional times the court of the Mukama of Bunyoro moved often; it is only since the imposition of European rule in the present century that the king has had permanent headquarters. And he still makes lengthy tours of his kingdom, spending a week or more in certain places where an extensive though temporary replica of his palace is erected, complete with audience hall and living accommodation for himself and his entourage, at considerable local expense in time and labor. On these visits, too, he and his court are supposed to subsist on the gifts of food brought to him by his subjects.

We are told that William the Conqueror used to hold three great feasts yearly, at which he wore his crown and entertained in state. Great numbers of his lords and subjects would attend, thus both showing their loyalty and forming a body of advisers and assessors to the royal court. The Mukama of Bunyoro held one great feast yearly, attended by all the chiefs and many people, at which full regalia were worn and feasts provided.

---

[1] For the comparison which follows I have made particular use of D. Stenton's *English Society in the Early Middle Ages,* The Pelican History of England, Volume 3, 1955, which gives a short and readable account of English political institutions at and after the Norman conquest.

Like the English king, the Mukama of Bunyoro maintained a large body of palace and household officials, and these people were specially honored, as their counterparts were in medieval England. William often rewarded such dependants with an estate in land; we have seen that this, also, was the practice in Bunyoro. The English king, we are told, prohibited private war; the same thing was done in Bunyoro (as of course it must be where centralized political authority is enforced): it is said that in pre-European times blood vengeance could only be undertaken with the Mukama's consent, which might be withheld. We read that the English king tended to gather about him able men of commoner origin whom he sometimes ennobled for their services; similarly in Bunyoro any person could attach himself to the court and might achieve high office regardless of his hereditary standing. Finally, it was a tradition in Bunyoro, as it was in medieval Europe, for young men and boys to enter the households of people more eminent than themselves for their education. Even the Mukama's own sons were supposed to be brought up in the original home of some of the earlier Nyoro kings (now a part of the neighboring Toro kingdom), an area in which the aristocratic Huma clans were well represented.

Analogies are notoriously dangerous, the more so when they are drawn between peoples so remote from one another in space and time as the English of the Middle Ages and pre-twentieth-century Nyoro. But the resemblances between the two systems are sufficiently numerous and striking to make the feudal analogy an illuminating one, so long as it is critically used, and provided that the institutions which are compared are first of all analyzed and understood in their own proper contexts. After all, in a country with poor communications and a relatively low level of technological advancement there are certain natural limits to the possible ways in which a central authority can maintain any kind of orderly government. And perhaps the Bito rulers of Bunyoro faced problems of political organization and control not so very different from those which faced William and his Norman knights just nine hundred years ago.

The Modern Chief

Today, a Nyoro chief, whatever his rank, is a salaried official with specified duties. There are four grades of official chiefs; the county chiefs, the subcounty chiefs, the "parish" chiefs, and the village headmen. Each of the four county chiefs is responsible for an area of several hundreds of square miles, with an average population of around 25,000 people. Under each county chief there are four or more subcounty chiefs, each responsible for his division of the county. Every subcounty has two or three "parishes," each in the charge of a parish chief. At the lowest level are the village headmen, who are responsible for areas of perhaps two or three square miles, each containing a hundred or so people living in from forty to sixty or more households.

What men become official chiefs and how are they appointed? Though chiefship in Bunyoro is not hereditary, nonetheless a man who belongs to a family whose members have been chiefs has an advantage, for he knows something about the job and, also, he may be personally known to senior chiefs and perhaps even to the Mukama himself. Many chiefs are, in fact, sons or other relatives of former chiefs. Membership of the royal Bito clan is not by itself a qualification for appointment, and Bito are not particularly strongly represented in the ranks of the official chiefs. Traditionally, chiefs were simply men whom the Mukama had decided to make so. Essentially, they had to be people who had "made themselves known" to the Mukama, either through personal service or by being introduced to him by an existing chief or favorite. In recent times, although a candidate for chiefship must be acceptable to the Mukama, "achieved" as well as "ascribed" qualities are required. Thus for many years some degree of literacy has been an essential qualification, even for the lower grades. But there is a marked difference in educational level between the lower and the higher grades. In 1953 all except one of the county chiefs had been educated up to secondary standard, and so had just half of the subcounty chiefs; all had received primary education. On the other hand, less than a sixth of the parish chiefs had had secondary education, and no village headman had advanced beyond primary school. Nobody with secondary school education would take so humble a job as a village headmanship. In 1953 nearly half of the subcounty chiefs had been appointed from outside the service—that is, otherwise than by promotion from parish chiefships—and all except one of these had had secondary schooling. This new requirement of literacy in candidates for political appointment is obviously a major departure from traditional standards.

After the British conquest, chiefs were appointed by the European administration without much regard for the traditional system. But in 1933 the Bunyoro Agreement, which restored a limited degree of autonomy to the kingdom, gave the king authority to appoint and dismiss his own chiefs, subject only (in the case of the higher ranks) to the district commissioner's approval, and without consultation with his official Nyoro advisers. Though in fact the Mukama would usually take account of his chiefs' opinions and recommendations, an unintended effect of the Agreement was to personalize rather than to depersonalize the Mukama's relations with his territorial chiefs. Certainly when I was in Bunyoro, appointment and promotion in the chiefly service were said to depend hardly less upon the Mukama's personal favor than on such qualifications as experience and efficiency. It must be added here, however, that a new Agreement was concluded in 1955 (after my departure from Bunyoro), and this provides, *inter alia,* that chiefs shall be appointed and promoted only on the recommendation of special appointments committees, upon which nonofficials as well as chiefs are represented. Thus the Mukama no longer possesses the powers in this respect which he previously had.

Before 1933 the main remuneration of chiefs came from money and goods paid to them as "tribute" by their peasant occupiers. In the case of the higher chiefs, this was supplemented by a rebate on the tax collected by them for the Government. The idea that chiefs should receive regular official salaries is thus a comparatively recent one. In 1953 the county chiefs had salaries of about £400 to £500 per annum, the subcounty chiefs from about £120 to £200, the parish chiefs from £30 to £40, and the village headmen less than £20 a year. For the lower grades of chiefs especially, these emoluments were quite inadequate to maintain the standards of living and hospitality appropriate to their positions. Salaries have been much increased since 1953, but village headmen and parish chiefs are still among the lowest paid employees in Bunyoro, and this is bound to affect adversely the esteem in which they are held by their people. County and subcounty chiefs may be given pensions on retirement; the two lower grades are not pensionable, though cash gratuities may be awarded after long service. The upper grades have free quarters provided for them by the Native Government, usually well-built permanent or semipermanent houses. Parish chiefs are also entitled to free houses, but these are usually ordinary mud-and-wattle houses like those of other villagers. Village headmen do not have free housing; they are usually local people, and it is assumed that they can continue to live in their own homes.

A chief's chances of promotion, especially from the lower ranks, are not great. A large proportion of the subcounty chiefs (about 40 percent of the total in 1953) are direct appointees who have never served as parish chiefs, and an even larger proportion of the parish chiefs have never been village headmen. The main reason for this incursion of "outsiders" at the middle levels is, of course, the need for the higher chiefs to be educated to a higher standard than formerly; almost all of the subcounty chiefs appointed from outside the service (and nearly half the total were so appointed) had had secondary education, unlike most of their colleagues who had risen from the ranks. An effect of this system is to keep most village headmen at the same level throughout their service, and also to diminish very much a parish chief's chance of becoming a subcounty chief.

Another important consequence of this dual mode of recruitment, especially at the subcounty level, is that some men who become chiefs in the higher ranks have little first-hand knowledge of or contact with the people. A county or subcounty chief lives in a small official world, with an office and courthouse, and a staff of clerks and messengers. These subordinates, together with the local parish chiefs and village headmen, inevitably tend to form a barrier between the higher chiefs and the peasant population, with whom they have relatively little direct contact at an everyday level. Unless such a chief has already had experience as a lower chief, he is bound to lack the intimate acquaintance with the details of day-to-day administration which his subordinates have. Of course subcounty chiefs do meet and tour among the people of their areas, but they do not live among them like parish chiefs and village headmen, who have neither offices, clerks, nor police, and who share the same kind of life as their peasant neighbors. Contact between county and subcounty chiefs and their people is also restricted by frequent transfer. Unlike men in the two lower grades, county and (especially) subcounty chiefs rarely remain in the same area for more than a year or two. It is hard for a chief to acquire an intimate knowledge of his district in so short a time, or to get to know more than a very few of its thousands of inhabitants. In contrast, parish chiefs often stay in the same parish for six years or more; ordinarily they are only moved on promotion to a subcounty chiefship, and such promotions are infrequent. Village headman are scarcely transferred at all except, rarely, on promotion; and they are almost always natives of the areas in which they are appointed.

What kind of work do chiefs do? There is a marked difference between the work of the two upper and the two lower grades. County and subcounty chiefs have to spend a lot of time on paper work; returns relating to tax collections, court cases, beer-brewing permits, food crops, vermin destruction, and many other matters have to be prepared and submitted monthly, and an extensive correspondence with superiors and subordinates has to be carried on. The formal hearing of criminal and civil cases in court may take one full day or more every week. All the chiefs are responsible for keeping order in their territories, for apprehending tax defaulters and other offenders, and for seeing that adequate food reserves are maintained. The collection of the annual tax is an urgent preoccupation, and it is common to see a subcounty or parish chief, with table, clerk, and policeman, established wherever money is being paid out—for example at cotton markets or tobacco-buying posts. All chiefs, but especially parish chiefs, spend a good deal of time in the informal settlement of village disputes "out of court."

The two lower grades of chiefs have much closer contact with the people than do the higher grades. Parish chiefs and village headmen have no office or clerical work to keep them at home, so they are constantly moving around among their people. They inspect growing crops, issue permits to brew the popular banana beer, supervise work on the roads and paths, organize and take part in communal hunts of such pests as wild pig and baboon, which do great damage to crops, tell cultivators where and what they should plant, summon people to court, and carry out innumerable other small day-to-day tasks. They are among and "of" the people in a way in which the higher chiefs cannot be, and it is through them that the force of Government is transmitted to the peasant population. One cannot fail to notice the informal way in which a village headman or even a parish chief drops in for a drink or a meal wherever he is visiting; when a subcounty chief is on tour, a very much more formal and constrained atmosphere prevails.

A formal system of advisory chiefs' councils was introduced some years ago. Under this system each chief, down to the parish level, has a panel of advisers who include, as well as the subordinate chiefs of the area, some popularly elected representatives of the people. These councils are supposed to meet at regular intervals, though they do not always do so. They all keep written records of their deliberations, and submit recommendations to the authority next above them. It was my impression in 1953 that the councils did not as yet have very much effect on the chiefs' decisions; this was no doubt partly because the principle of popular representation is likely to evoke only mild enthusiasm—to begin with, at any rate—where hierarchical and "feudal" values are as strongly entrenched as they are in Bunyoro.

The ways in which chiefs regard one another are in many respects more characteristic of the quasi-feudal traditional system than they are appropriate to a modern civil service. Internal differences in status are strongly emphasized. When a county or subcounty chief pays a formal visit to one of his subordinates, especially when he does so for the first time after appointment, the lower chief should give his superior a present of meat or cash, the amount depending on his rank. When a subcounty chief officially visits one of his parish chiefs or village headmen, there is usually a good deal of excitement. The premises are cleaned, everyone wears his best clothes, and food is specially prepared; the atmosphere is tense and formal. When a parish chief visits his village headmen, on the other hand, as of course he does constantly, there is no such formality. For these authorities live in the villages and are in daily contact with the people and with one another. Here again the cleavage between the remoter and more transient subcounty and county chiefs and the two lower grades is marked.

But all official chiefs, whatever their ranks, show a solid front to outsiders, who may include people of higher social and economic standing than (at least) the lower chiefs. Such are the proprietors of large populated estates, schoolteachers, clergy, members of the medical and other Government services, shopkeepers, and others. Political power, however, still rests mainly in the official hierarchy of chiefs, and this power has been used to suppress or at least to discourage adverse criticism or comment. Thus laymen are not encouraged to bring complaints—of bribery or oppression, for example—against chiefs. In one court case a mission teacher accused a local village headman of accepting a bribe. The headman was acquitted, but the complainant was charged with slandering the village headman and was himself convicted. The judgment was not based on the truth or falsehood of the allegation of bribery; it was concerned with teaching the defendant that it was none of his business to criticize the village headman. Such criticism is only tolerable from an official superior. The insecurity of the lower chiefs' status vis à vis some of their wealthier and more distinguished subjects occasionally makes them sensitive about their official dignity and importance. It should not be inferred from this, however, that relations between the lower chiefs and the people are unsatisfactory; the case is very much otherwise. The point has been mentioned because friction does sometimes occur, and hence its underlying causes should be sought.

What do present-day Europeans and Nyoro expect of chiefs? As elsewhere in Africa, the European officials tend to look for efficiency in tax collection, expeditious handling of court work, quick despatch of correspondence and other business. Irregularities in the handling of cash are especially condemned, as are drunkenness and idleness. A bright and willing manner with Europeans is expected. The qualities that most Nyoro peasants look for are quite different. The traditional basis for their respect is the fact that the chiefs are the king's nominees, "the Mukama's spears." There must be chiefs, they say, for how otherwise could the country be ruled? Chiefs should be calm, dignified, and polite; they should not shout at their people or abuse them angrily. They should know their subjects and visit them often; people do not like a chief who sits in his office all day. Chiefs should be strong but not "fierce," and they should be generous and give frequent feasts and beer drinks.

Thus the qualities which European administrators and the mass of the Nyoro people look for in chiefs do not always coincide. A subchief whom I knew well was reported by touring European officers as being "a good chief with lots of drive and character," and "full of energy," but he was cordially disliked by his people for his jumpiness, lack of dignity, and abusive manners to his subordinates. The words "indolent" and "drinks too heavily" were applied to an older chief of good family and great Nyoro popularity who was less efficient by European standards. Since chiefs are expected to conform to two different and not always compatible standards, it is inevitable that they should be criticized by both Europeans and Nyoro. European criticism is mainly concerned with lapses from Western standards of good administration. Nyoro criticism is twofold, and itself reflects these dual standards. Older, less educated Nyoro criticize the chiefs for failing to conform to the traditional norms; younger men with European-inspired educations and ideals condemn them for failing to achieve what they think of as modern standards of democratic leadership. Thus older men often say that modern chiefs lack good family background, but are simply upstart commoners, who happen by some means or other to have won the Mukama's favor. Modern critics, too, have objected to the personal factor in the appointment of chiefs. Older men sometimes refer to the present-day chiefs as mere "hired laborers," implying that they are simply paid servants of the Government, concerned only with their salaries and prospects of promotion, and not interested, as chiefs traditionally were, in knowing and caring for their people as individuals.

It is commonly said that chiefs no longer provide feasts and beer parties for their people as they formerly did. The people who make this criticism do not always realize that a chief cannot do this unless his people bring him food and beer, for he certainly cannot do it on his salary. And such gifts are no longer brought as they used to be; when a man has paid his tax he considers that he has no further obligations toward his rulers, for tax is supposed to have replaced the old tribute payments, not to have been added to them. One old man shrewdly commented: "In the old days chiefs trusted and depended upon their subjects, for their living came directly from them. Now they do not care about their people, nor their people about them, for their money comes not from the people but from the Government." Nyoro are quite well aware of the degree to which the constant exchange of goods and services between people who know one another personally promotes social cohesion. Unlike such exchange, the annual payment of tax is a purely formal obligation; it involves no intensifying of personal relations. To the ordinary peasant it is simply a payment which he has to make to the Government and for which he receives no tangible return. Inevitably, then, chiefs are no longer bound to one another and to their people by the old ties of mutual and personal interdependence; they are more and more becoming impersonal civil servants—though, as we have seen, they are as yet by no means quite this. Everybody knows that times have changed, and the older and more traditionally minded regret it.

In summary, what is happening in Bunyoro is that the personal basis of political relations characteristic of the traditional system is being destroyed, and its place is being taken by the impersonal, bureaucratic organization which the efficient running of a complex modern society demands. But the changeover does not proceed evenly on all fronts, and we should not be surprised that attitudes and values appropriate to the older system still survive into, and may even modify, the new. Nor should we be surprised if the nature of these changes and the difficulties they give rise to are not always clearly understood by the people whom they most concern. Their most important practical consequence is that Nyoro chiefs, like chiefs in other emergent African societies, are expected to conform simultaneously to two separate and often incompatible sets of standards. Expectations regarding them are sometimes those appropriate to the "feudal" state which long ago ceased to exist in its traditional form; sometimes they express modern Western ideals by no means all of which have yet been fully assimilated. The Nyoro political system is no longer the traditional one, but neither is it the impersonal civil service which it is sometimes thought to be; it contains elements of both, together with features which are inconsistent with either. Chiefs are on the one hand respected because they are "the Mukama's spears"; on the other hand, they are despised because they are sometimes poorer and less educated than some who are not chiefs. They are praised by their European superiors and by the educated minority when they show efficiency and enterprise in carrying out their official duties; yet they are criticized by their subjects for failing to mix with them and to provide feasts for them as their predecessors did. They are expected, often, to be two different and incompatible things at the same time, and the remarkable fact is that they succeed so well.

5

Relatives

Kin

IN THE LAST TWO CHAPTERS we have been concerned with the Nyoro state, the system of political relations which centers on the king and the hierarchy of territorial chiefs subordinate to him. This system, as we saw, not only is an instrument of political control, but also, in its traditional "feudal" form, implies a pervasive way of thinking about social relations. Central to this way of thinking is the notion of superordination and subordination, the idea that some kinds of people are naturally above or below other kinds of people. But although these ways of thinking are characteristic of political or "state" relations, they are not confined to the strictly political sphere. They also pervade the community relationships which are to be our concern in this and the following chapters. By community relationships we mean those day-to-day relationships characteristic of village life, which subsist between near neighbors and kinsfolk who not only live in the same place, but share common interests and values and a common way of life.

In some of the simpler societies nearly everybody in a particular community is related by kinship to nearly everybody else. It is not quite like this in Bunyoro. Though in any settled area a good many people do have relationships either of kinship or through marriage with a good many other people, a man always has many neighbors who are neither kin nor related to him by marriage. Thus Nyoro think of relationships of kinship and affinity,[1] and relationships of neighborhood, as different, though of course they know quite well that they may and often do coincide. We shall follow Nyoro themselves in keeping the two topics separate. In the first part of the present chapter I consider kinship, and in its second section I discuss marriage and the affinal

---

[1] *Affinal* relationships (substantive *affine;* abstract *affinity*) are what we call relationships "in law"—that is, by marriage.

relationships to which it gives rise. I leave till Chapter 6 the consideration of those relationships which neighbors have and should have with one another even when they are not kinsfolk or affines.

Kinship is usually of great significance in the simpler societies which most anthropologists study, and hence social anthropologists attach much importance to it. Where a person lives; his group and community membership; who his friends are and who his enemies; whom he may and may not marry; from whom he may inherit and to whom pass on his property and status—all these considerations may depend upon kinship ties and be thought of in terms of them. Kin relationships are less important for Nyoro than they are for some peoples (though it is likely that they were more important in the past), but they are still significant in very many social situations.

The kinship basis of group membership is particularly important. A Nyoro inherits his clan name and associated totemic avoidance, his membership of a particular group of kinsmen, and, usually, his status and property, from his father. Nyoro say that in former times patrilineal descent determined membership of the actual groups of men who lived in particular territories, so that almost all the men in any particular settlement (which might be from one to three or more square miles in extent) would be related by descent in the male line from a common ancestor. Nyoro clans are exogamous, meaning that men must marry outside their clans, and wives come to live at their husbands' homes. Thus the married women in such localized descent groups or lineages would be of different clans from those to which their husbands belonged. Where residential and cooperating groups are formed in this way, loyalty to the other members of one's group is a most important social value.

However things may have been in the remote past, in Bunyoro nowadays the principle of unilineal descent[2] is no longer the most important factor which determines membership of territorial groups. But membership of a group of patrilaterally related kinsmen, or agnates,[3] is still very important in connection with personal loyalties, marriage and inheritance, and in various other contexts. Nyoro still attach high value to mutual devotion and support between agnates. Thus it is still thought proper for sons of the same father to build their houses near to one another and to maintain close and friendly relations, and many still do so. It is only by understanding the profound importance of this kind of *group* membership, and the wide range of social relations in which membership of such a group is important, that we can make sense of Nyoro ways of thinking about kinsfolk and affines, and in particular of their kinship terminology.

Nyoro kinship terminology is classificatory, like that of many simpler peoples for whom affiliation with a particular group of kin is important. This means, usually, that terms which one applies to relatives in one's own line of descent are also applied to certain other relatives who are in collateral lines

---

[2] *Unilineal* descent is descent reckoned through one line only—that is, either exclusively through males or exclusively through females.

[3] *Patrilateral* kinsfolk, also called *agnates* (adjective *agnatic*), are persons to whom one is related through males only.

of descent. Thus one's father's brother may be called "father," his son may be called "brother," and so on. Even a father's sister (who is a member of one's father's group and generation) may be called "father," and the Nyoro term for this relative can be translated "female father." As far as one's patrilateral relatives are concerned, this classificatory usage means that all of them, however distant the connection, are "brothers," "sisters," "fathers" (both male and female), "grandfathers," "children," or "grandchildren." And to call them by these terms means that one should behave toward them, to some extent at least, as one would toward one's nearest agnatic kinsfolk in these various categories. In Bunyoro this usage even extends to people with whom no genealogical relationship at all can be traced, for any member of one's own clan (and clans are widely dispersed and often no real genealogical relationship can be traced between clansmen) is regarded as an agnatic relative, and placed in the appropriate generation. One of the effects of this classificatory usage is to enhance and stress the unity of groups of agnates, for it implies that the same kind of cooperation and mutual support should be extended to and expected from all its members, whatever the degree of relationship. Indeed it would be unseemly to inquire about the exact relationship; Nyoro say that where clansmen are concerned the important thing is friendship, not the degree of relationship.

But the classificatory system is not restricted to one's agnates. A man's mother's sister (who of course is not his agnate, since her link with him is not through his father but through his mother) is regarded as a kind of mother, and is so referred to. His mother's sister's children, like his own mother's children, are called "brother" and "sister." Even his mother's brother is a kind of "mother" (even though he is a man), and he is called "male mother." This is not so strange as it sounds, when it is remembered that the most important thing about your mother's brother is that he is a member of the same agnatic group or lineage to which your mother belongs. In quite a real sense *all* the members of your mother's agnatic group are "mothers": your attitude toward them is quite different from your attitude toward your "own" people, the group of agnates of which you yourself are a member. In systems like the Nyoro one, where one's father's people (and so one's own) and one's mother's people belong to quite separate and distinct social groups and are quite differently regarded, it would evidently be most misleading to translate the words for both father's and mother's siblings (that is, brothers and sisters) as "uncles" and "aunts," as we do in our system. We use, for instance, the same term, "uncle," for both father's brother and mother's brother, because we think of them both as the same kind of relative. To Nyoro, on the other hand, they are as different as can be, for one's father's brother is a member of one's own group, while a mother's brother is a member of an entirely different group. And a Nyoro's expectations and obligations in regard to members of these two distinct groups are quite different.

These ways of classifying kin provide a means of placing in a few simple categories a great many of the people whom a Nyoro peasant is likely to have dealings with in his everyday life. Everybody he meets is either a member of his own clan or he is not. If he is, he must be treated as a father, a brother, or a son, depending on their relative ages. If he is not, he may be a member of a clan with which the speaker is related through either kinship or marriage. Thus he may be a member of his mother's clan and so a kind of mother, or of a grandmother's clan and so a kind of grandmother, or of his wife's or his brother's wife's clan and so a kind of brother-in-law. Or he may belong to a clan in which there is another member with whom the speaker or one of his clansmen has made a blood pact, in which case friendliness and mutual help are prescribed. In all these cases there is a ready-made set of behavioral categories, labeled with kinship or affinal or "blood-partnership" terms, through which amiable personal relations may, and should, be established and maintained. In these ways the Nyoro clan system, combined with the classificatory mode of designating relatives, provides for the extension of a few quite simple relationship categories over a very wide social field.

In considering kinship, it is particularly important to bear in mind that one is dealing not simply with a set of abstract concepts, but with real people and the ways in which they act toward and think about one another. Hence before discussing the different kinds of social behavior which are prescribed between different kinds of kin, I must say a few words about Nyoro territorial and domestic organization. A Nyoro homestead usually consists nowadays of a rectangular four-room house, with mud-and-wattle walls and a thatched roof. Some wealthier people have brick houses roofed with iron. In remoter areas the old-fashioned "beehive" type of house is still common. The homestead faces on a central courtyard of beaten earth, around which there are usually one or two subsidiary buildings: a kitchen, a smaller house or two for second or other wives if the household is polygynous, and nowadays a small latrine. The home is usually surrounded by food gardens interspersed with fallow land, and often a shady banana grove adjoins the house. There are probably other similar households not very many yards away. A number of such scattered homesteads make up a settlement area or "village." Such villages may occupy a square mile or more, and they are often separated from other similar, settled areas by narrow winding streams or by swamps or by unoccupied bush. Three or four such settlements may make up the area administered by the lowest grade of territorial chief, the village headman.

The average homestead nowadays contains four or five people, though some households are considerably larger. The basic domestic unit is generally the elementary family of a man, his wife, and their children, though this pattern is modified when a man has more than one wife and so is the head of two elementary families, or when an adult son continues to live in his father's household after he is married; though this last is still the ideal Nyoro pattern it is not now very common. Other relatives, such as an unmarried brother or sister of the household head, or one of his wife's kinsfolk, may also stay in the homestead for longer or shorter periods.

The family head, or (as Nyoro call him) the "master of the household," is much respected. This is what we should expect in socially stratified Bunyoro. People say that he "rules" the household just as the Mukama rules the whole country. He is the master and ultimate owner of everything the household contains; even property which is apparently at the disposal of his adult sons is, strictly speaking, his. Though nowadays the traditional authoritarian pattern is tending to break down, and sons, like wives, are becoming increasingly independent owing to the opportunities which they now have to grow cash crops and take paid employment, the very high status of the household head is still an important Nyoro value. This is made especially clear when we consider the relationship between fathers and sons.

Though there may be genuine affection between them, Nyoro culture stresses the authority of the father and the dependence and subordination of the son. A son should always be polite and deferential, and he should address his father as "sir" or "my master"—the very same terms that he would use to a chief. A man should not sit on a chair or stool in his father's presence; he should sit or squat on the floor. He should not marry a girl whom his father has not selected for him, or at least approved. He should never wear any of his father's clothes or use his spear. And he may not begin to shave or smoke until he has made a small token payment to his father. Thus the relationship is essentially an unequal one, and it may even be said to express a latent hostility between fathers and sons. Such hostility is to be expected in a strongly patrilineal society, where the father's very considerable authority and status pass on his death to his son. It is as though the son's growing up were a kind of challenge to the father, whose authority the son will soon take over; and the father seems accordingly almost to resent his son's developing adulthood as a threat to his own preeminence.

The pattern of Nyoro inheritance is consistent with the existence of such attitudes as these. The heir (who should not be the oldest son) is ceremonially installed in the presence of his agnates. The ceremony stresses the transfer of authority rather than the transfer of property, and the heir is even said to "become" his father. Indeed after he has been installed his sisters' husbands should address him as "father-in-law," not as "brother-in-law" as they formerly did, and they should treat him with great respect. It is also of significance that in Bunyoro there can be only one heir; the household and the patrimonial land are never divided up (though movables may be), for they are indivisible, like the parental authority which they symbolize.

The relations between fathers and daughters express the same theme of superordination and subordination; a father "rules" his daughters just as he rules everyone else in his household. Indeed a daughter is doubly subordinate, for as well as being a child she is also a woman, and women should always be subservient and respectful to men. She will marry elsewhere, and the bridewealth which is obtained for her may be used to obtain a wife for her brother, perhaps even another wife for her father himself. Her children will not increase her father's posterity; they will belong to another clan, her husband's. In traditional times, at least, her feelings were not much considered in marriage. Even today fathers sometimes try to compel their daughters to stay with uncongenial husbands, so that they will not be called upon to return the bridewealth which they have received for her. The relationship between fathers and their children, then, is one of marked inequality: fathers "rule" their children and children "fear" their fathers. It follows from what was said earlier that the relationship with father's brothers, or "little" fathers, is similar; even father's sisters, or "female fathers," are thought of as being rather severe, like fathers, and quite different from one's mother and her sisters, with whom the relationship is much more friendly and intimate.

We have noted that the term which we translate "mother" is applied to one's mother's sisters as well as to one's mother, and even (with a masculine suffix) to one's mother's brother. It is even applied to one's mother's brother's children, whom we should call our matrilateral cross-cousins,[4] and to one's mother's brother's sons' children. The explanation of this peculiar usage is that all these relatives are members of the same agnatic descent group as one's mother, and so are all thought of as "mothers." The child of one's mother's sister is not a "mother," for she belongs to a different lineage and clan from one's mother, since clans are exogamous. The child of a mother's brother's daughter is not a "mother" for the same reason. A Nyoro thinks of himself as the child of the *whole agnatic group* of which his mother is a member, and he therefore thinks of all its members, even men and persons younger than himself, as being in a sense his "mothers." From all the relatives whom he calls "mother," and especially from the women, he looks for love and indulgence. Nyoro often contrast the friendly intimacy of the mother-child link with the comparatively strict and authoritarian relationship between children and their "fathers." Men have a very keen affection for their mothers, and aged women often live with their adult sons. This friendly intimacy also characterizes the relationship between men and their real or classificatory "male mothers"; a sister's child may make much freer with his mother's brother's property than he can with his father's; for example, he may help himself to food or borrow clothes or other property without formality in his "male mother's" house. Nyoro often say how happy they were when they visited their mothers' people as children. There is, nonetheless, an undercurrent of hostility in the relations between men and their mothers' brothers; we shall see why this should be so when we discuss affinal relationships in the next section.

A Nyoro thinks of his father's brother's children, and of his mother's sister's children, as relatives of the same kind as his own father's and mother's children respectively—that is, as his own brothers and sisters—and he so refers to them. When he wishes to distinguish between his real or classificatory siblings on his father's side and those on his mother's side, he does so by calling them "children of my father" and "children of my mother" respectively. Between sons of the same "father" the stress is, as we might expect, on mutual solidarity and support. Brothers should help one another in quarrels, they should build near to one another, and they should help to take care of one another's children. There are terms for distinguishing older and younger siblings, but a

---

[4] *Matrilateral* kinsfolk are persons to whom one is related through females only. *Cross-cousins* are the children of a brother and a sister. (Children of two brothers or two sisters are called *parallel cousins*.)

brother is not especially respected because he is older. When, however, one brother becomes his father's heir (which he may do while still quite young), the other brothers must treat him with the deference due a household head. But despite the stress on solidarity, Nyoro are realists, and they recognize that brothers sometimes hate and are jealous of one another. There is a Nyoro saying to the effect that when a man becomes rich he treats his brother as an inferior, and it is true that a wealthy man may resent the claims made upon him by less fortunate fellow clansmen. Nyoro are well aware that social relationships may be ambivalent; they realize that inconsistent attitudes and patterns of behavior very often coexist in the same relationship.

It is natural that Nyoro should attach great importance to good brotherly relations, for the idea that agnates should stick together and support one another is central to the traditional pattern of local territorial grouping. Sisters, of course, do not form groups in this way, for when they grow up they marry into other families and separate. It is significant that although Nyoro often use the word for "brotherhood," one never hears a corresponding word for "sisterhood." In the context of group relations there is no occasion for such a concept, for although sisters often maintain friendly relations throughout their lives, the nature of the Nyoro social system makes it impossible for them to form corporate groups as their brothers do.

Brothers and sisters usually maintain close and friendly relations throughout life. They grow up in close contact, and there is not the competition for authority that there is among brothers. They may talk freely to one another about their affairs, including sexual ones. A boy may jokingly address his sister as "wife," for he perhaps will marry with the bridewealth which is received for her. But he must not sleep with her; that would be incest and would bring about a condition of grave ritual danger.

We noted above that Nyoro think of their fathers' brother's children and their mothers' sister's children (relatives whom we think of as cousins) as brothers and sisters. But they think quite differently about the children of their fathers' sisters and the children of their mothers' brothers (relatives whom we think of as cousins too), and they have quite different terms for them. They are not thought of as siblings at all. One calls one's mother's brother's son and daughter "male mother" and "little mother" respectively, just as one calls one's mother's brother and sister, and one calls one's father's sister's children "children"—though one distinguishes them terminologically from "children" in one's own clan. This odd usage, which seems to put one's matrilateral cross-cousins in the generation above and one's patrilateral cross-cousins in the generation below one's own respectively, is sometimes called the Omaha system of cross-cousin terminology, after an American Indian tribe among whom it was long ago recorded. Though puzzling at first sight, it is really quite simple when it is realized how important membership of a particular descent group is for many peoples throughout the world. When grouping is based on agnatic descent, one's mother, her brother, and her brother's children are all in the same descent group, and this is one of the most important things about them. Thus, as we noted above, a man thinks of himself as a child not only of his mother, but also, in a sense, of his mother's group as a whole. All the members of that group are therefore "mothers," either male or female. If you look at the relationship from the other end—that is, from the point of view of a member of the agnatic group of "mothers"—your father's sister's children, no less than your sister's children, are your "children." What is happening here is that you are identifying yourself with your own agnatic lineage as a whole, so the child of any woman of that lineage (whether of your sister or your father's sister or even of your father's father's sister) is also your own "child," and you are its "mother." Of course such "children" are not the same as one's own children, for they belong to another clan. Hence Nyoro have a separate term to distinguish them.

A word should be said about the relationship between grandparents and grandchildren. In accordance with the classificatory usage which I have described, a grandfather's siblings are called "grandfather," regardless of sex, and a grandmother's siblings are called "grandmother," regardless of sex. Indeed all the members of both parents' mothers' lineages (who are all "mothers" —either male or female—to each of the parents) are called "grandmothers." Thus the odd fact that Nyoro may have male "grandmothers" and female "grandfathers" makes sense when the essentially "group" reference of Nyoro kinship terms is understood. Further, the assertion that Nyoro can marry their grandmothers seems less bizarre when we realize that what is meant is that it is permissible for a man to marry into his father's mother's clan.

The relations between grandparents and grandchildren are friendly and intimate, contrasting strongly with those between fathers and sons. A boy may joke and play with his grandfather in a way which would not be permissible with his father, and Nyoro grandparents, like their Western counterparts, are often said to "spoil" their grandchildren. We spoke earlier of the incipient hostility between fathers and sons; grandfathers have already been replaced by their sons, and so are, as it were, out of the battle. Nyoro sometimes say that grandfathers are "like brothers," thus stressing the equality and friendliness of the relationship.

Marriage and Affinity

Nyoro think of marriage as a more or less permanent union between a man and a woman, the offspring of whom have recognized status as their children. Ideally marriage should involve the payment of brideweath (formerly in cattle, now in cash) and the establishment of enduring relations between the husband and his wife's people. Even where no bridewealth is paid, the children still belong to the father's clan and lineage, but the husband's status, especially in regard to his in-laws, is then much lower. Bridewealth nowadays averages about ten pounds, which is quite a lot of money in a community where most peasants' cash incomes during a year hardly exceed this amount. Most marriages are monogamous, but Nyoro still like to have two or more wives if they can afford it, and even Christians sometimes have another wife besides their "church" or "ring" wife. A Nyoro may not marry into his own, his mother's, or his mother's mother's clan; he may marry into his father's mother's clan, provided that the relationship is not too close. Nyoro approve of marriage with neighbors; they say that it is a good thing to know something about one's prospective wife and her family before one becomes engaged. Most marriages are still between families who live within a day's walk of each other; this means that most people have affines within easy reach and see them often.

In pre-European times most marriages were arranged by the parents. Nowadays many still are, although young people often choose their own mates. Marriages could be arranged while the intended partners were still children, or even before they were born. In this latter case, a man might say to a close friend: "My wife is pregnant; I give her child to you!" He would mean by this that if his child were a girl his friend could have her as a wife for his son, provided of course that he paid bridewealth for her. If the child turned out to be a boy there would be no marriage, though the boy might become a kind of dependant in his father's friend's household. For a man may give away women and slaves, but he cannot give away husbands. This traditional antenatal betrothal illustrates two important points. First, it shows that traditionally the woman is not one of the two contracting parties in marriage; she is rather the subject of a transaction between two men and the groups of kin they belong to. Secondly, it stresses the fact that for Nyoro the woman's group is always the giver and the husband the receiver. And the giver always has superior status, while the receiver is subordinate and must be humble and respectful to his prospective in-laws. This is still so today, even when bridewealth has been paid. Nyoro theory is that however large the bridewealth, it can never balance the inestimable gift of a woman, who will bring to her husband's group both her labor and, most important of all, her capacity to bear him children to continue his line.

In traditional Nyoro marriage (to which even today most marriages conform) a number of formalities have to be carried out which extend over many weeks and even months. First, the prospective bridegroom, accompanied by a few kinsmen, pays a formal visit to the bride's father's home, bringing a gift of a large goat and some jars of banana beer. Everyone is dressed in his good clothes and is on his best behavior. The bridewealth to be paid is discussed. The suitor and the girl's father do not engage in direct negotiations; all discussion is carried out through intermediaries, for it would be unseemly for the prospective father-in-law to stoop to what might become acrimonious wrangling about the amount of bridewealth to be paid. Often a pretext is found for "fining" the bridegroom or a member of his party for some real or imagined impropriety in the past; the aim is to show that they are uncouth, worthless people, unfit to receive a woman from the host group. Other pretexts may be found for mulcting the bridegroom's party of a few more shillings. Throughout, the bride's group assumes an air of haughty superiority, and the bridegroom's party accepts a humble and deferential role.

Some weeks or months later a representative of the bride's family formally visits the bridegroom's father's home to collect the bridewealth. He is courteously received and given beer to drink. After collecting the money (for which he nowadays writes a receipt) he demands other small traditional payments, including some cents to repay him for the energy he expends in beating the bridewealth cattle along the road home (there are really no cattle, but there might have been long ago!). After another interval the main "giving away" ceremony is held. The bride is brought to her new husband's home after dark, accompanied by a group of her own and of her future husband's kinsfolk. Her head is veiled in barkcloth, and the procession moves slowly, taking an hour or more for the short journey. There is singing on the way, and many of the songs extol the great value of the gift that is being brought. When the husband's homestead is reached, the bride and bridegroom are ceremonially seated on the bridegroom's parents' laps, there is a ritual washing of the bride and groom, and the family's Chwezi spirits are invoked. That night the marriage may be consummated, and there is a feast which should continue for several days and nights.

On the next morning the relatives of both parties assemble, and a letter from the bride's father (who is not himself present) is read out by his representative. The letter is in conventional form and instructs the bridegroom's father (not the bridegroom himself) to treat the girl well, not to punish her with undue severity, to permit her to visit her relatives, and so on. It is read out in a threatening and passionate manner, and the bridegroom's father replies humbly. Others of the bride's family may add their own admonitions to what has been said. Some days later the bride returns to her father's house, where she spends several days before going back to her husband with gifts of food from her family.

To an observer of the complex series of rites involved in traditional Nyoro marriage, what is most striking is the strong emphasis on the different statuses of the two groups involved. This status difference is strongly marked in the relations between the husband (and his close agnates) and all his wife's agnates, but before we consider these relationships a word must be said of the husband-wife relationship. We have already noted the high status of the household head; this is particularly marked in his relations with his wife or wives, for men are always superior to women. Most of the domestic and farm work falls to women; a wife is required always to be submissive and deferential to her husband; she should kneel to hand him anything, and should address him as "sir." But she is by no means a slave; she has definite rights, and between many spouses there are very close bonds of affection. Her husband must provide her with a house, clothes, and a hoe to dig with; if he fails in his obligations, or constantly neglects or abuses her, she may complain to her own people and in the last resort she may leave him, provided that her people are able and willing to return the bridewealth paid for her. Nyoro men are nowadays much concerned about the increased economic independence which a woman can gain through growing and selling cash crops, because it means that she can, if she wishes, repay her own bridewealth and leave her husband on what he may consider an inadequate pretext, or indeed on no pretext at all.

A man feels constraint in the presence of his wife's people; he must always be polite and formal in his dealings with them (as they should be with him), and he should, in particular, avoid seeing or talking to his wife's mother. He and his brothers refer to his wife's people as "those who make us feel ashamed"; they mean that they would feel ashamed if they behaved overfamiliarly or discourteously to them. Nyoro themselves explain this restraint by pointing out that a man and his wife's agnates belong to different descent groups. In his own group a man feels an easy assurance and a sense of security, but his wife's group are "strangers," and if they are offended they may break off relations with him, which is something that his own agnates cannot so easily do, however greatly he offends them. Hence his attitude to his in-laws is ambivalent: on the one hand he feels gratitude and respect toward them, for they have given him a wife; on the other hand he is conscious of fear and even hostility toward them, for they are not his own people, but outsiders. He stands to his father-in-law, and so to his father-in-law's whole lineage, as a "child"; "the one who has taken our daughter." Hence from their point of view, also, the relationship is ambivalent: on the one hand a son-in-law is a "child," and children are to be not only loved but ruled, and they owe respect and obedience to their parents; on the other hand he is an outsider, who must be treated formally and politely.

A man has many obligations to his wife's father. He should visit him often, and bring him presents. He should help him in bush clearing, building, and other work, and he must always behave respectfully to him. If he fails in any of his obligations, his father-in-law may "fine" him (I have known of such cases). Nyoro often say, in the pervasive idiom of subordination and superordination, that men "rule" their daughters' husbands, and husbands often complain of the heavy demands their wives' fathers make upon them.

A man feels something of the same constraint even with his wife's brothers, one of whom is his father-in-law's heir and so will become his father-in-law when the father dies. But here the constraint seems to be mitigated by the fact that brothers-in-law are likely to be generational equals, and there is a friendly, give-and-take quality about the relationship which is not found in affinal relations between members of successive generations. But a formal element still exists there, at least when the different group membership of the parties to the relationship is relevant, as it is, for example, when formal visits are exchanged. And brothers-in-law should always be polite to one another, and give one another gifts. In a man's relations with his wife's sister, however, this formality is conspicuously lacking, for he feels toward her something of the intimacy and familiarity that characterize his relationship with his own wife. She may even jokingly be called "wife," and a man can marry two sisters if he likes; I know of several polygynous unions of this kind. The fundamental inequality which exists between the wife-giving and the wife-taking groups thus is modified in the relationship between a man and his wife's siblings, especially his wife's sisters. Here the status difference between the two parties seems to be submerged beneath the closer affective ties which the husband-wife bond implies.

It remains to consider the relationship between men and their sisters' children. I said above that this topic would be more suitably considered in an affinal context, and perhaps it is already plain why this should be so. Nyoro themselves often compare the mother's brother—sister's son relationship with the affinal one. They point out that a sister's son, like a daughter's husband, is "a man from outside," for of course he derives his clan and lineage membership from his father, who is "son-in-law" to his mother's lineage. We noted that there was constraint in the relationship between men and their daughters' husbands, and Nyoro see something of the same constraint as being carried on (on both sides) into the following generation—that is, into the relationship between men and their sisters' children. But as well as being an outsider, a sister's child is also a "child" to his mother's group in quite a literal sense; unlike a son-in-law he is a blood relation and, as we saw, all the members of his mother's lineage are "mothers" to him. So the relationship is ambiguous; in English we should have to say that the sister's son is thought cf both as a kinsman and as an affine at the same time. The relationship thus implies both familiarity and constraint, and these two attitudes are not entirely compatible with one another. Let us see how Nyoro culture deals with this potentially difficult relationship.

First of all, friendly intimacy between men and their mothers' brothers is much stressed. A man may make himself quite at home in his mother's brother's house. He may borrow almost anything he wants without asking, and he may help himself to food uninvited. His mother's brother's wife must always prepare a meal for him if he asks for one; if she fails to do so he may stamp on the three hearthstones where she cooks, and if he does this, it is believed that food will never cook properly on that hearth again. The sister's son has a right to the head of any animal killed by his mother's brother, and he can also claim a payment when any girl of his mother's brother's lineage marries, for he is being deprived of a "mother." We noted above that Nyoro often speak of the happy time they spent at their mothers' brother's homes when they were children. But as well as this friendly intimacy there is an undercurrent of antagonism, and this is expressed in certain ritual prohibitions to which the sister's son is subject. Thus he must not sit on or kick the cooking stones in his mother's brother's house, on pain of the consequences we have just noted. He may not sit on the grinding stone; if he does, his uncle's teeth may fall out. He may not climb on to his mother's brother's roof, nor walk through his growing crops, nor should he take hold of anything new in his mother's brother's house. And he may not climb on to his mother's brother's bed, or sleep with his wife. It is interesting to note that if the sister's son commits any breach of these prohibitions it is not he but his uncle who will suffer for it: in the idiom of superordination and subordination, Nyoro say that a man "rules" his mother's brother. It is significant that a sister's son's ghost is much feared, and so is his curse. It appears that political and social inferiority may sometimes be compensated for by the attribution of ritual power to the occupant of the inferior status; if this is so, then in Bunyoro the ritual power which a man has over his mother's brother may be regarded as a compensation for the inferiority of status thrust upon his father by his wife's people.

Thus a man loves, yet fears, his sister's son. The latter "rules," but acknowledges ritual restrictions in regard to his mother's brother. One's sister's son, like one's daughter's husband, is an outsider, since he belongs to a different clan and lineage from one's own. But at the same time, unlike a daughter's husband, he is your "child," for you are a member of his mother's agnatic group, and so his "mother." Children are loved, outsiders are feared; therefore one who is both is both loved and feared. That is why the mother's brother –sister's son relationship in Bunyoro is an ambivalent one. The symbolic restrictions which surround it provide a way of expressing and controlling this ambivalence.

6

Neighbors

Good Neighborliness

I TURN NOW to consider the ways in which Nyoro should, and do, behave toward one another simply as neighbors, whether or not they are kin to one another as well. Nyoro attach a high value to neighborliness. They like their neighbors to take an interest in them, and they tell the following story to illustrate this.

Once a man moved into a new village. He wanted to find out what his neighbors were like, so in the middle of the night he pretended to beat his wife very severely, to see if the neighbors would come and remonstrate with him. But he did not really beat her; instead he beat a goat-skin, while his wife screamed and cried out that he was killing her. Nobody came, and the very next day that man and his wife packed up and left that village and went to find some other place to live.

Nyoro like to live near one another, and on the whole neighbors get on well. But inevitably they sometimes do not. In the first part of this chapter I consider the kinds of rights and obligations which are involved in "neighborliness," and the ways in which village solidarity is expressed. In the second part I discuss some of the types of interpersonal conflict which arise in the Nyoro village community, and the kind of action which may be taken to resolve these conflicts.

Neighbors should help and support one another in their everyday occupations. A man who cuts himself off from his fellows and lives far away from other people in the bush is distrusted and may be suspected of being a sorcerer. When a man builds a house he expects help from his neighbors, and he should recompense them with a meal at the end of the day. Neighbors should help one another in agricultural work, especially in bush clearing and harvesting. Nowadays a group of neighbors (who may not be kin to one another at all) often combine for tobacco growing. They jointly cultivate and care for a common seedling nursery, and sometimes they plant out the seedlings in a large communal field which they have together cleared of virgin bush. The obligation of neighbors to give help in time of trouble is especially stressed. If a man's house burns down, as houses sometimes do, his neighbors should hurry to help to rescue his family and goods, and they should assist him to build a new house. The Nyoro alarm call is a loud ululation, the sound of which carries a long way, and all able-bodied men should respond to it. Failure to do so would be unneighborly; today it is an offense punishable in the chiefs' courts. It is good that neighbors should meet together often and talk about village affairs, and mutual visiting is common. A guest is always politely received, and he should be offered food and drink if the householders themselves are at a meal. It is bad manners to refuse such an invitation, for it suggests that you suspect your host of being a sorcerer, who wishes to poison you.

Eating and drinking together express the friendly relations which should subsist between neighbors. It is thought to be a bad thing for a man to eat alone; Nyoro say that in the old days a man could be "fined" by an informal court of neighbors if he persisted in eating by himself. Communal beer drinking, especially, is a means of emphasizing and affirming village solidarity, and beer parties are common. People come together to feast and drink beer on various occasions, some of which are explicitly concerned with the maintenance of social solidarity or its restoration when it has been disrupted. Nyoro also drink beer for no other reason than that it is available and that it is agreeable to drink. Formerly, anybody would have joined in a beer party without payment; nowadays a small profit may be made by the retail sale of a part of the brew to anyone who wants and can afford it. But even today, where the brew is a small one and the guests are a few close friends and neighbors, no charge is made.

The beer now usually drunk is made from a special variety of banana. The fruit is cooked for some hours in an underground earth oven, then peeled, mixed with a sweet-smelling species of grass, some water added, and the mixture trodden out in a prepared hollow in the ground which is lined with segments of banana stems. The treading out of the beer is itself a social occasion; neighbors sit around talking in the shade of the banana trees while the beer is being prepared, sometimes drinking a glass of the sweet unfermented juice. This liquid is then decanted into a large wooden trough which may hold up to twenty gallons, some grain is put in to hasten fermentation, and the brew is covered over and left for three days. On the fourth day it is ready for drinking. Quite a lot of beer has to be brewed at once (it would not be worth the trouble involved to prepare only a small amount), and the beer will not keep for more than a day or so. This means that beer drinking is bound to be a social occasion, since one man and his family cannot consume a whole brew, and it also means that all the beer brewed must be drunk at one sitting. Thus beer parties usually start early in the morning, and they continue for as long as the beer lasts, rarely later than the early afternoon. They usually take place in the open, often in the shady banana grove where the beer was brewed. Most guests sit on the ground, or on handy logs or wisps of dry grass, but senior or especially respected men are sometimes given European-style chairs or stools to sit on. In former times women did not attend beer parties; now they often do, but a married man would be angry if his wife went to a beer party otherwise than in his company or with his permission, and domestic quarrels sometimes arise from this cause. Women usually sit in a group by themselves a few yards apart from the men, though even this degree of segregation is now breaking down, and especially in the beer shops near the town the sexes mingle promiscuously.

At every beer party there is a formal "host." He selects another man, usually a member of his own household but perhaps a friend of lower status than himself, to dispense the beer, which is brought in to the center of the party in a large earthenware pot containing several gallons. From this it is ladled into the gourd drinking vessels (or nowadays often the enamel mugs or glasses) of the guests. There is a strict order of priority; after the host has tasted the beer, it is first given to the more important people present, and lesser guests may have to wait a long time for their turn. If the host (or, where the beer is for sale, any person who can afford it) wishes to compliment somebody, he may present him with a gourd containing up to a gallon or more, or even a whole pot. Such a gesture is greeted with clapping and shouts of satisfaction by all present, even by those least likely to profit by it. The recipient is under no obligation to drink all or even any of his gift himself; it is now his, and he should in any case give a good deal of it away to his own intimates.

If there is only a little beer, the drinkers may sit around in groups and talk about the topics of the moment for as long as the beer lasts. But if there is enough beer, before long somebody is certain to fetch a drum, and dancing and singing begin in a cleared space in the middle of the group of drinkers, who sing and clap their hands in rhythm with the dancing. One or at most two individuals dance at a time, and the dancing and songs often have an implicitly or explicitly sexual reference. The movements of the dancers' hips are often emphasized by a cloth or even a folded jacket tied around the waist. Nowadays women sometimes join in the dance, which they perform in the same manner as the men. After each dance everybody cheers and thanks the performer, and shakes his hand. The party continues for as long as the beer lasts; people then gradually drift away. It is unusual in rural Bunyoro for serious quarrels or fights to break out at beer parties where all the drinkers are near neighbors, though sometimes they do. Communal beer drinking is traditionally regarded as a good thing (though constant drunkenness is not), and although a man who spends all his time at beer parties is despised, one who never drinks beer with his neighbors is regarded as an eccentric or worse.

Most of the occasions on which people come together to drink beer conform to this general pattern. But as well as the informal beer drinks which take place simply because the beer is there, there are also more formal occasions when neighbors and kinsmen should drink beer together and, sometimes, eat together as well. We go on to note some of these occasions, bearing in mind the traditional part that drinking plays in bringing people together in close and friendly relationship.

In addition to the informal kind of drinking party which has just been described, there is in Bunyoro a traditional custom of bringing a gift of food and drink to a friend's house as a gesture of friendship and regard. This is usually rather more than simply a transaction between two individuals. On the day appointed, the bringer of the gifts (if he is a man) comes accompanied by his wife and members of his household, together with a number of his friends and neighbors. The person who is to receive the gifts has also assembled a number of his kinsmen and neighbors in his house, and has laid in a stock of food and drink. They have a party, and the combined stocks of food and beer are consumed amid great singing, dancing, and rejoicing. Anybody may "feast" another in this way, except that a man may not "feast" a woman, since it is for women to serve and make food for men, not vice versa. But it is particularly appropriate between men who are associated by a blood pact, between a girl and a young man whom she hopes to marry, between a family and a man who stands in the relation of "son-in-law" to it, and between a group of neighbors and one of their number who has returned from a long journey. A young girl may also take a feast to the homestead where her older sister is married, partly in the hope of receiving a return present of money or clothes. For reciprocity is involved; the person or household which is feasted must itself contribute to the feast by providing food, beer, and perhaps a goat, and should also, nowadays, make a money present to the person who has brought the gifts. This money is divided among the gift-bringing party. Nyoro have a special word for this making of a return present, and such a return should be made by anyone who receives a gift. The return gift should bear some proportion to the gift given, but the correspondence should not be exact; a return gift of identical value with that given would offend, for it would suggest that this transaction was a purchase and not a friendly interchange of gifts, and it would imply that the receiver did not wish to continue the friendly relationship initiated by the first gift. Though the institution of "feasting" another person or family is now declining, Nyoro still value it highly. It expresses vividly the kind of relations which, Nyoro feel, ought to subsist between neighbors: it is a good thing for people who live near to one another to make feasts for one another from time to time.

Beer drinking and feasting in Bunyoro are also associated, as they are in other cultures, with what have been called "rites of passage"—ceremonial occasions when members of the community undergo important changes of status. The most obvious and important of these are birth, marriage, and death, and feasts are associated with each of these three events in Bunyoro. Some time after a child is born there is a small ceremony called "taking out the child," in which the infant is taken out of the house for the first time and placed on a mat where everybody can see it. The child is then named, usually though not necessarily by a patrilineal relative, a father or grandfather. There follows a small feast, which is usually attended by members of the household and a few relatives and neighbors. A goat may be killed, beer is drunk, and some small presents, nowadays usually a few cents, are given for the child. This is not a major occasion for feasting, and the party is mostly a family one. It lasts only for one day.

We have spoken already of the marriage feast, which is held when the bride ceremonially enters her husband's home. For Nyoro this is the greatest feast of all; it is attended by crowds of people, enormous quantities of beer, meat, and other food are consumed, and the party should continue for three or four days. At the same time a smaller but still considerable party is taking place at the home of the bride's parents (who are not allowed to attend the main feast). There beer specially provided for them by the bridegroom's family, called "the beer that comforts," is being drunk. Meat is also being eaten; the bridal party, then at the bridegroom's home, are expected to send home to the bride's parents at least one hind leg of a large goat which has been given to them by the bridegroom's father. Some months after the marriage the wife's mother, and a party from her home, should pay a formal visit to the newly married couple's house. This occasion is also marked by a feast, to which both groups contribute. Meat and beer are consumed, and there is much singing and dancing, though of course the wife's mother and her son-in-law may not meet face to face or address one another directly. In the old days, it is said, this feast used to continue for two or three days; nowadays the custom has almost died out.

Feasting is also associated with mortuary ceremonies. When a person dies, the members of the deceased's household may not prepare food or indeed do any kind of work for some days after the death. The interval is four days for a man's death, three for a woman's; four is associated with masculinity, three with femininity, in many cultural contexts in Bunyoro. Food is provided by neighbors for the bereaved. They may not wash, shave, or put on clean clothes during this period. On the third or fourth day relatives, friends, and neighbors gather at the deceased's house to eat and drink the food and beer that have been brought to "comfort" the bereaved. Burial takes place as soon as possible after death, except in the case of a household head, whose body should lie in his house for one night. At the mortuary feast for the head of a family a date is decided upon for the inheritance ceremony, which also entails a feast. This ceremony involves the formal installation of the heir in his father's place, the presentation to him of his father's spear and stick, and a good deal of speech making in the course of which the heir's new duties and responsibilities as head of the family are impressed upon him. After this, food and beer are consumed by the members of the household together with the relatives, friends, and neighbors present.

Feasting in Bunyoro is also associated with traditional religious ceremonies, of which the most important are concerned with the spirit possession cult and with sacrifice to the ancestral ghosts. These topics are considered in the next chapter; here I record merely that they, too, were occasions on which communal or group solidarity was manifested in ceremonial eating and drinking. Although the spirit possession cult is now largely an individual affair, it was formerly concerned with the well-being of extended family or lineage groups. Membership in the cult involves a lengthy process of initiation, at the end of which a feast is held. This feast is attended not only by all the local members of the cult group, but also by uninitiated friends, relatives, and neighbors of the new initiate. Though such feasts are now rarely held, Nyoro speak of them as having been among the most important of communal feasts, ranking with marriage feasts, with which they are often compared. The essentially religious nature of the spirit-cult feasts is stressed. Only certain kinds of food can be eaten at them; there should be meat, beer, and millet porridge, but "low status" vegetables such as beans, sweet potatoes, and cassava are not used. Included in the meal is a species of white fungus: the color white is important because the occasion is essentially one of "purifying" the house and its inhabitants, and in Nyoro culture (as in many others) the notions of whiteness and of purity are associated. The other ritual occasion for feasting is less important; traditionally, groups of closely related patrilineal kinsmen would meet together from time to time to sacrifice and to pay respect to the ghosts of the dead fathers of their lineage, and the accompanying ceremonies would include a shared meal. Strictly speaking, only kinsmen were concerned, but as with almost all Nyoro feasts and ceremonies any neighbor who happened to be present could attend.

There are other, lesser occasions upon which feasts may be held, such as the birth of twins, the successful conclusion of a hunt, or the occupation of a new house. But one major occasion for communal drinking and eating remains to be discussed, and that is when a dispute between villagers has been settled by an informal tribunal of local people. This is one of Bunyoro's most important communal institutions, and I discuss it in the context of the interindividual frictions and disputes in the settlement of which it traditionally played (and still plays) an essential part.

Disputes and Their Settlement

Although social relations in a Nyoro village community are on the whole strikingly easy and friendly, rules are bound to be broken sometimes and interests to conflict, and disputes and disagreements inevitably occur. Often trouble arises over property; petty thefts take place; debts remain unpaid; brothers sometimes quarrel after their father's death about the disposal of goods or livestock. Men sometimes quarrel about, and with, women; accusations of adultery are made; husbands and wives accuse one another of cruelty or neglect, and one or other wishes for divorce. There may be arguments about the custody or the paternity of children. People sometimes abuse or slander one another, and perhaps even accuse one another of sorcery; young men may be disrespectful to their fathers or to other senior people toward whom they should behave with propriety. Men may quarrel over cultivation rights, or trespass by stock. All these issues, and many more, may lead to disputes which are too serious to be settled simply by the parties themselves.

Nyoro culture provides various means of expressing the antagonisms which arise in these several ways. Sometimes people resort to violence, but this is on the whole unusual in Bunyoro. Hostility is more likely to be expressed in mutual recrimination and personal abuse, in which threats of sorcery may play a part. More seriously, it may express itself in the imputation and perhaps the actual practice of sorcery (I leave this for discussion in the next chapter). It may also find expression in the destruction of property, typically in arson. The old-fashioned type of house—roofed, and sometimes walled as well, with dried grass—is highly inflammable, and it is easy for a man to thrust a lighted brand into an enemy's thatch and get safely away before the alarm is raised.

Certain grave criminal offenses such as homicide, rape, or robbery are nowadays the concern of the Uganda Protectorate police force, which is responsible for the apprehension and prosecution of criminals. But in rural areas the police count on the help of the local authorities. Such serious cases are tried in the first instance in the district commissioners' or the resident magistrates' courts. Cases involving Europeans, or civil cases between Africans where the property in dispute is valued above a certain limit, are also heard in the European courts. But lesser disputes or offenses involving neighbors may be dealt with in one of two ways. The case may be taken to the nearest official native court of first instance for hearing; these are the subchiefs' courts, established by Protectorate legislation and having powers to fine, imprison, and award compensation. A litigant dissatisfied with the decision of such a court may appeal to the court next above (the county chief's court), and thence, through the district court, to the High Court of the Protectorate. But, as in other African societies, disputes within a Nyoro community may, if they are not very serious, be dealt with by an informal local tribunal or "court" of neighbors, which I call a "neighborhood court." They *should* in fact be so dealt with in the first place, and when a minor dispute is brought before a chief he may ask whether an attempt has been made to settle it at the neighborhood level. If no such attempt has been made, he is quite likely to send the intending litigants away. In the remainder of this chapter we shall be concerned with these local tribunals, which strikingly express the social values basic in Nyoro community life.

A neighborhood court consists simply of a group of neighbors gathered together quite informally to adjudicate upon a matter in dispute. It only comes into being when somebody makes it known that he has a complaint against somebody else and wishes to have the matter dealt with in this way. In such a case a few neighbors experienced in arbitration, or with particular knowledge of the matter in issue, may be invited to attend, but any neighbor may drop in without invitation, provided that he is a householder in good standing and a reputable person. These courts are not clan or lineage tribunals: there are some kinds of disputes which are mainly the concern of kin, such as quarrels about inheritance, but as a rule the basis of representation is neighborhood as much as, sometimes more than, any kind of kinship link. Whether the dispute is between kin or unrelated persons the basic pattern is always the same, though the proportional representation may vary; in either case kinsmen of the parties may be present, and so also may neighbors who are kinsmen of neither.

After the parties to the dispute have stated their cases and the witnesses, if there are any, have been heard, the assembled neighbors discuss the issues raised and usually reach a unanimous decision. They then direct the person who has been found to be at fault to bring beer and meat to the injured party's house on a specified day and time. If the person charged accepts the tribunal's decision, he does this in due course, and there follows a feast, in which both the parties, and the neighbors who adjudicated on the case, take part. After this the dispute is supposed to be finished, and it should not be referred to again. The following is an example of a case settled in this manner:

At a beer party a middle-aged man, Yonasani, was drunk and insulted a youth called Tomasi. Tomasi wanted to fight with Yonasani, but was prevented from doing so by his companions. However, he left the party early, and lay in wait for Yonasani on the path to the latter's house. As Yonasani passed he hit him on the head with a stick, knocking him down, and fled. But Yonasani suspected who had attacked him, and the next day he complained to Tomasi's father. When Tomasi was accused, he denied all knowledge of the affair, but on Yonasani's threatening to take the case to the chief's court Tomasi's father said that he and his son would agree to have the case settled in a neighborhood court. About half-a-dozen neighbors were accordingly summoned to adjudicate on the matter, and they met at Tomasi's house. After everybody had spoken, the neighbors discussed the case briefly, and they all agreed that Tomasi had hit Yonasani, and that he had been wrong to do so, for if he had a complaint against Yonasani he should have taken it before a neighborhood court. The court accordingly ordered Tomasi to bring four large jars of beer and five shillings worth of meat to Yonasani's house about a week later. He agreed to do this, and on the appointed day all the people who had attended the hearing were present, as well as Tomasi and Yonasani and the members of their households. Tomasi was told to serve the beer, and to choose a friend to roast the meat. Then, in the words of an informant who was at the party, "We began to eat and drink, and everyone started to joke and laugh, as they do at a wedding feast. Soon some people began dancing, and we accompanied them by singing and clapping our hands. By now Tomasi and Yonasani had become quite friendly with each other as they used to be before they quarrelled. And from that day to this the quarrel between them has been finished."

The case of Yonasani and Tomasi exhibits the characteristic features of this kind of settlement. The initial action is taken by the complainant, not by the court, which of course does not exist until it is summoned. A penalty is always imposed, and this penalty is always the same, a payment of beer and meat which are to be consumed in a joint feast by all the parties to the case. Although Yonasani's case might have been taken directly to the chief's court for settlement, it was not, since the complainant had expressed himself willing to have it heard in the village. This last point is important; Nyoro villagers consider it unneighborly to take a minor case to the chief's court, or, as they would put it, "to the Government" (opposing in this as in other contexts the superimposed state to the local community), and it shows kindness and for-bearance on the part of a complainant not to do so. To permit the case to be heard among neighbors and friends implies that the offender is still accepted as a member of the community; to send the case for hearing by "strangers" in the chief's court, where heavier penalties such as imprisonment may be im-posed, would suggest that his own community rejected him.

The neighborhood court aims if possible to reconcile the parties to the dispute—at any rate to reach a compromise which they will accept. The insti-tution expresses the high value which Nyoro attach to good relations between neighbors, and its most important function is to restore village harmony when this has been breached, by reintegrating the delinquent into his community. Of course neighborhood courts do not always succeed in achieving complete, or indeed any, agreement between the parties; it would be astonishing if they did. Sometimes no solution is reached, and sometimes one party is dissatisfied and refuses to accept the court's decision, preferring to have recourse to the more powerful sanctions of the chiefs' courts. But in the great majority of cases a satisfactory settlement is reached at village level.

It is plain that the primary aim of these village tribunals is the restora-tion of good relations, not the punishment of an offender. It is true that meat and beer cost money, but the order to provide them is not imposed simply to inflict hardship on the delinquent. If one suggests that the culprit suffers by being penalized in this way, Nyoro point out that he enjoys—or should enjoy —the feast just as much as the other people present do. Indeed he is the formal host, and the position of host is an honorable one. Thus he is really being paid a compliment, and the community is reasserting its confidence in him. The beer and meat are not a "fine", for their purpose is to rehabilitate rather than to punish. If it ever should happen that the traditional payment in kind is commuted to a payment in cash (there is luckily no sign of this happening as yet), it is obvious that the neighborhood courts will completely change their character. First of all, a money payment would inevitably sooner or later find its way into the pockets of the powerful or less scrupulous; secondly, hard cash cannot be eaten or drunk, and it is the communal feasts that are their proper conclusion that give these informal courts their great social im-portance. We have seen that feasting together is the most important way of manifesting and reasserting social solidarity and good-neighborly relations. It is by this means, too, that breaches of such good relations are traditionally repaired, errant individuals reintegrated into village society, and the most vital community values themselves reaffirmed.

7

The Supernatural

IN THE CONDITIONS of most simple societies everyone has frequent and direct experience of illness and death, but there is still little or no understanding of the physical causes of these events. Thus in rural Bunyoro illness is common and often fatal, the rate of infant mortality is high, and hospital facilities, though they exist, are few and far between. One has to live for a period in the primitive conditions to which many of the less advanced peoples are accustomed, far from Western medical aid, in order to realize how powerless one can feel when illness attacks or threatens. A Westerner in such circumstances feels that there is nothing much he can do: he probably inclines to fatalism and hopes for the best. But for a member of the simpler culture there is much that he can do; his culture provides ways of dealing with such situations which are socially and psychologically, if not clinically, satisfying. Thus Nyoro, like other people, have beliefs in what we would call supernatural agents, and it is believed that these may be propitiated by sacrifice and prayer, or made use of by certain magical techniques. The slow decline of witchcraft beliefs in Western countries shows how tenacious such systems of thought and the patterns of behavior based on them may be. Often they survive, perhaps adapting themselves in the process, into times very different from those with which they were traditionally associated. We shall see that this has happened in Bunyoro.

Supernatural beliefs and practices, then, may be in some degree understood as providing acceptable explanations for events which would otherwise be inexplicable, and so relieving ignorance and doubt. But they are more than just a body of beliefs; most important of all, they provide a means of coping with events. To act is better than to remain inert in the face of actual or threatened misfortune, and where the victim cannot refer to a body of empirical knowledge for help, then magical and ritual procedures, which are not ordinarily subject to empirical testing in the same way as practical techniques, may provide a socially acceptable recipe for action. Even though these activities do

420

not (we suppose) bring about the ends they aim at, at least they make the performer feel that he is dealing effectively with the situation, and so relieve his anxiety. And there is always some kind of internal consistency about such systems of magical beliefs, so that failure, when it occurs, is generally explicable in terms of the system itself.

Education is advancing in Bunyoro, but most peasants still cling to the traditional magical practices, even though administrators and missionaries have actively discouraged them for over fifty years, and some of them have been made into criminal offenses punishable in the courts. We shall see that in certain cases Nyoro have even adapted their ancient ritual, without altering its essential character, to the changed circumstances of today.

People usually seek magical help in situations of misfortune; if everything were for the best in the best of all possible worlds, there would be no need for magic. The commonest kind of misfortune is, of course, illness, either one's own or that of a person for whom one is responsible, such as a child or another member of the family. The first thing to be done is to discover the cause of the illness, and to do this it is necessary to consult a diviner. Diviners may be consulted, however, for other reasons besides illness. A man may hate another, and wish to injure him, and he may want to know the best kind of magic medicine or technique to employ. Women may be childless, and wish to discover what it is that is preventing them from having children. A woman may believe that her husband has lost interest in her, especially if he has just procured a second wife or is talking of obtaining one, and she may wish to know how to recover his affection. A man may want to discover the identity of a thief or an incendiarist, or at least to bring down punishment on such a person even though he remain unknown. In Bunyoro, problems of these and many other kinds are brought to the diviners, and the diviners provide what are on the whole acceptable answers.

In Bunyoro most diviners work part time; they are usually subsistence farmers like everyone else, and they are not held in any particular regard except when they are actually divining. But a few people have made big reputations as doctors and diviners, and these often travel long distances to practice, and may make large profits. Most diviners are "doctors" as well; in addition to diagnosing the cause of the trouble they may also provide a cure. In other cases a diviner may pass a patient on to another doctor who specializes in the treatment of the particular kind of affliction which has been diagnosed. Simple divination by an ordinary part-time diviner is not very expensive; the cost varies from about fifty cents to a few shillings. The treatment of some kinds of ailments, however (for example, those requiring initiation into one of the several spirit-possession cults), or the procuring of medicine to kill an enemy, may cost several pounds. The fee depends both on the kind of treatment needed and on the fame of the practitioner who is consulted.

There are many different ways of divining, but by far the commonest nowadays is by the use of cowry shells. These small seashells, which were formerly used as currency in many parts of Africa, have their convex sides leveled off, so that when they are thrown on the ground there are equal chances of their falling with their natural cleft or their leveled side up. Nine are used for divination (nine is a ritually auspicious number in many contexts). When a man goes to consult a diviner, they both sit on the ground facing each other, with a goat skin spread out on the ground between them. The client describes the symptoms to the diviner and puts some money "for the shells" in the small bowl placed on the mat for the purpose. The diviner then holds his handful of cowries to his mouth and says "thus my forefathers divined before me; this is true divination and not deception." He also entreats the shells to divine well. He then scatters the handful of shells on the mat several times, and in due course, partly according to the way the shells fall and partly according to his own independent interpretation, he identifies his client's trouble, and says whether he can do anything to help him. It is difficult to know how far the diagnosis is conventionally conditioned by the way the shells fall at each throw, and how far the diviner is free to diagnose as he thinks fit. There are certain patterns which everyone knows how to interpret: if the shells fall with the cut-off side down the prognosis is bad, if the other way up it is good; if one shell comes to rest on top of another a death is imminent; if the shells scatter widely a journey is prognosticated; three or more in a straight line mean a safe return; and so on. But my impression is that although there are some conventions of this kind, in this and other divining techniques it is preeminently up to the diviner to make his own interpretation, which he ordinarily does in the light of his local knowledge of the case, and of his client's unintended revelations of the circumstances.

If the diviner diagnoses sorcery, as he is quite likely to do, he hands the cowries to his client to throw. Before the client throws them he whispers to them inaudibly the name of a suspect. After seeing how the shells have fallen, the diviner says whether or not the person named is the culprit. The throw may be repeated several times before a positive decision is reached (it may not be reached at all), and often a client tests the diviner by naming people whom he is quite sure are innocent before naming people he really suspects. To accuse anyone of sorcery is a serious matter, and most diviners are careful never themselves to name a particular person as a sorcerer or even to indicate him in unambiguous terms. The diviner simply says that his shells confirm what the client has himself suggested, or else he indicates the sorcerer in vague terms ("a tall dark man living to the north") which the client himself applies to the person he suspects. If the consultation reveals the identity of the guilty person, the client may, if he wishes to make quite sure, go to one or more other diviners to confirm or correct a first opinion. If he is satisfied, he may ask the diviner what he should do. The diviner may then sell him an antidote to the medicine which has been used against him, or provide him with the recipe for medicine to kill the sorcerer, or, sometimes, send him to another practitioner who is more skilled in dealing with the kind of sorcery diagnosed.

But other troubles besides sorcery may be diagnosed (though this is probably the commonest), and there are other techniques besides the throwing of cowry shells (though this is the most usual). Other oracular techniques are the throwing on a mat of nine small squares of leather, the ensuing patterns being studied as in the case of the cowry oracle, and the sprinkling on water of the ashes of the burnt leaves of certain species of plants, the forms the ash assumes being interpreted by the diviner. There is also a rubbing oracle, a short stick which the diviner smears with the blood of a slaughtered goat and rubs up and down with his fingers; this oracle gives its decisions by causing the manipulator's fingers to stick at certain points. Like the ancient Greeks, Nyoro also practice divination by examining the entrails of animals and birds, especially fowl; from certain signs in the internal organs a diviner can determine whether his client will recover. It is said that in ancient times cattle were sometimes used for this purpose; such a case occurs in the Nyoro myth recounted in Chapter 2. Of considerable importance even today is divination by means of spirit possession; it is believed that through their living mediums certain powerful spirits may answer questions put to them by clients.

I have said that, in Bunyoro, illness or other misfortune is often attributed to sorcery. It may, also, be thought to be due to ancestral or other ghosts, or to the activity of certain other powerful nonhuman spirits. We now consider in more detail the content and contexts of these three different kinds of responses.

The Nyoro word which I translate "sorcery" means to injure another person by the secret use of harmful medicines or techniques. These usually (though not essentially) involve what we should call a magical or non-empirical element. They generally have a symbolic or "expressive" quality, and they are not usually tested and varied experimentally as practical techniques are. Thus for Nyoro it is sorcery to make a medicine out of bits of hair, nail parings, and other parts of a certain person's body, to put this medicine in an animal horn, and to place the horn in the roof of that person's house with intent to injure him. But it is also sorcery to obtain a deadly medicine from an expert and to place it in an enemy's food or drink. Even to set a man's house on fire at dead of night in the hope of destroying him and his family is a kind of sorcery. These illustrations afford another example of the danger of uncritically applying the vocabulary of Western culture to other people's ways of thought: for Nyoro, sorcery implies secret and harmful activity, usually carried out under cover of darkness, and although it usually implies what we should call magical procedure it need not do so. An informant put the matter clearly when he said,

A sorcerer is a person who wants to kill people. He may do it by blowing medicine toward them, or by putting it in the victim's food or water, or by hiding it in the path where he must pass. People practice sorcery against those whom they hate. They practice it against those who steal from them, and also against people who are richer than they are. Sorcery is brought about by envy, hatred, and quarreling.

We saw in Chapter 6 that sorcery and imputations of it provide one of the commonest ways in which interpersonal conflicts, when they do occur, express themselves in Bunyoro. If a man becomes ill, or if one of his children sickens and dies, and it is known that he was on bad terms with somebody, that person is likely to be suspected, especially if they have recently quarreled. There are certain phrases, such as "you'll see me!," which are often, *post hoc*, construed as threats of sorcery, and which may even be used as such.

Since sorcery expresses interpersonal antagonisms, it is not usually thought of as acting at a distance; if there is no personal contact then there can be no occasion for its use. As we should expect, it occurs and is suspected most often in those social relationships where there is social strain. Thus women often accuse their co-wives of sorcery, and husbands their wives. Men sometimes accuse their brothers of sorcery; we noted in Chapter 5 that jealousy between brothers is not unusual. Unrelated persons may also engage in sorcery because of some dispute, or because one of them resents the wealth or eminence of the other; thus rich people are supposed to be especially susceptible. There are men and women who are likely suspects because of their surly or unsociable dispositions; such people may in the course of time build up reputations as sorcerers. The following is an example of a sorcery situation:

> Yowana bought a piece of timber to make a door with, but it was stolen before he could use it. After searching the village he found it in the house of a neighbor, Isoke. He accused Isoke of stealing it, but since Isoke denied the theft and there were no witnesses, the charge failed. A few days later Yowana's house was burned down and he lost all his property. He did not know who had done this (though he suspected Isoke), so, informants afterwards said, he obtained from a vendor of powerful medicines a substance which if smeared on those of the posts of the burned house which remained standing would cause the incendiarist to suffer from dysentery and burning pains in his chest. Yowana is said to have applied the medicine as directed, and four days later Isoke became ill. His brothers consulted the local diviners, who said that Yowana's medicine was the cause of the illness. Isoke then summoned Yowana, confessed to him that he had burned his house and also that he had stolen the timber, and promised to make restitution. Isoke's brothers begged Yowana to get an antidote from the vendor of the original medicine, so that Isoke might be cured. Yowana promised to do so, but unfortunately Isoke died. In this case complaints were made to the Protectorate police and Yowana was arrested for suspected murder, but an autopsy on Isoke's body showed no signs of poisoning, and Yowana was released. Nonetheless, nobody doubted that Yowana had killed Isoke by sorcery, least of all Yowana, who was heard to boast at beer parties of his prowess.

Many other cases could be quoted to show how easily interpersonal disputes of all kinds can turn into sorcery accusations. If one man hates another he will wish to injure him, and it may be supposed that if he has the knowledge or can afford to pay for it he will use one or another of the numerous techniques of sorcery to achieve his end. He may in any case be tempted, when his feelings are aroused, to utter threats which may give him the best of the argument by terrifying his opponent, but which may afterwards be interpreted as threats of sorcery.

There are several alternatives open to a victim when sorcery has been diagnosed and the sorcerer identified. Where the sufferer knows that he has wronged the sorcerer (as in the case just quoted) he may acknowledge his fault and beg him for an antidote. He may, if the illness is not grave, be treated for it by the diviner-practitioner. He may turn the same weapon on his attacker, using a more powerful medicine to injure him. Or he may, if all else fails, retaliate with physical violence; a considerable proportion of Bunyoro's few homicides arise in this way. He may, finally, bring an accusation of sorcery before the local chief; this would usually happen in the case of persons believed to be habitual sorcerers, who have become a serious public menace. In pre-European times such persons, if convicted, were tied up in dried banana leaves (which are very inflammable) and burnt; nowadays they are tried in the chiefs' courts and if found guilty may be sentenced to a term of imprisonment. On their release, public opinion may force them to move to another village where they are not known.

The modern courts are not authorized to convict people of being sorcerers or witches, for these crimes are not recognized by the European government. But it is a statutory offense to "hold oneself out to be" a sorcerer or a witch, and the distinction between this and actually being one is less clear to Nyoro than it is to European legislators. And it is plain from the evidence given in court cases that there are people who do practice sorcery. Men have been caught in the act of placing magic medicines in the thatch of people's houses, and when the homes of accused persons are searched, as they usually are, recognized implements of sorcery such as animal horns, bones, and various medicines are very often found. Accused persons often admit their guilt: to do so may incur conviction, but it may also greatly enhance the respect and fear in which an otherwise inconsiderable person is held.

Like other African peoples, Nyoro say that sorcery is more common now than it was in the past, and they attribute this to the very much milder penalties now imposed. But we may suppose that the increase, so far as it exists, rather reflects the increase in interpersonal tensions and the growth of individualism which are involved in the breakdown of many of the traditional standards and sanctions. Certainly sorcery beliefs and the associated techniques are still widespread in Bunyoro. And, anachronistic though they are in the "modern" African society into which Bunyoro is slowly developing, there is no doubt that they are still effective sanctions for conformity to approved norms. Nyoro villagers know that unneighborly behavior may arouse the enmity of others, and they believe that such enmity may be expressed through sorcery, probably with serious consequences. Equally, the unsociable or bad-tempered person may bring down on himself accusations of sorcery, and although the penalties for this are less severe than the traditional ones, they may still serve to discourage (though not to eliminate) certain kinds of socially disapproved behavior.

For Nyoro, misfortune may be due to the action of ghosts and of other kinds of spirits, as well as to sorcery. A ghost is the disembodied spirit of a dead person. When a person is alive this vital principle has another name, which we may translate "soul," and it is thought of as inhabiting the breast.

Ghosts are never seen, though they may manifest themselves in dreams; they are thought of rather as immaterial forces diffused through space. They are associated with the underworld, and with the color black. On the whole they are maleficent, and Nyoro say that when people die they cease to think of their living relatives as "theirs." By this they mean that ghosts no longer acknowledge the ties of affection and obligation which they felt when they were alive. It is natural that ghosts should be thought of as on the whole ill-disposed toward the living, for it is only when illness or some other misfortune takes one to the diviner that ghosts, like sorcerers, become socially relevant.

If ghostly activity is diagnosed as the cause of misfortune, the agent is most likely to be the ghost of somebody who has been wronged or neglected by the "victim" and who has died with a grudge against him. Most ghosts are therefore those of deceased relatives, for, as we have seen, every Nyoro is bound to many different kinds of relatives and affines in a network of mutual obligations which should not be neglected. Where particular obligations are stressed, as between sons and fathers, sisters' sons and their mothers' brothers (a sister's son's ghost is specially feared), and brothers, so that a breach of these obligations is particularly serious, ghostly activity is often diagnosed. Few people can be sure that they have not at some time neglected or offended some relative who has since died. Even the ghosts of distant relatives, or of unrelated persons, may be responsible for illness. In former times the ghosts of war captives or domestic slaves were particularly feared—another example of the way in which a culture sometimes invests with ritual power people who occupy positions of social subordination. So, like sorcery beliefs, fear of ghostly vengeance may be a sanction for good interpersonal relations; bad behavior may lead not only to reprisals by the living through sorcery, it may lead also to reprisals by the dead through ghostly activity.

Here is a typical case in which illness was explained by reference to the activity of ghosts:

> Yozefu's small daughter became ill, and shortly afterwards the son of Yozefu's full brother Yowana became sick too. The diviners were consulted, and it was found that the cause of these illnesses was Yowana's ill treatment of his father, who had died some months previously. Just before his death, Yowana had forcibly dissuaded his (Yowana's) wife from preparing food for him, on the ground that he had his own wife to take care of him. This had angered the old man; he had died without being reconciled to his son, and it was his ghost which was causing the children's illness. When this was discovered the ghost was enabled to say what it wanted through a possession ceremony, a shrine was built and a sacrifice was made, and eventually the sick children recovered.

The above example of Yozefu and Yowana shows that ghostly vengeance often attacks not the offender himself, but his (or even his brother's) children. A man is most vulnerable through his children, for not only will posterity remember him through them, but also after his death they will provide his ghost with the attentions it needs. Nyoro can hardly be described as ancestor worshippers, but the ghosts of the father and the father's father are nonetheless regarded as important, and sacrifices and other attentions should be given to them from time to time. Such sacrifices provide one of the occasions for feasting which was referred to in Chapter 6.

When ghostly affliction is diagnosed, two kinds of action can be taken. If the ghost is an important one, such as that of a near relative, it must be induced to "possess" the victim or someone who represents him, and through him or her to say what has offended it and what it wishes to be done. Nobody can be posssesed by the ghost of a dead person until he has undergone a lengthy initiation into the spirit possession cult, some account of which is given below. The directions given by a ghost usually include an instruction to build a small spirit hut or shrine for it; it may also demand the sacrifice of a goat. Ghosts conventionally express their resentment at neglect in terms of food; they say that they are hungry and want meat. Alternatively, the ghost may demand that a black goat be consecrated to it; such a goat may not be sold or slaughtered for secular purposes, but must be reserved in the homestead as the property of the ghost. Ghost shrines are small untidily made replicas of huts, cone shaped, and usually about eighteen inches high; in them are put the skull and some of the other bones of the sacrificed animal, together with certain other small ritually significant objects, such as a piece of a special kind of termite hill. If the ghost is an unimportant one, however—that of a stranger or a slave or a very remote relative, for instance—there is no need to enter in this way into an enduring relationship with it. It may be "caught" and destroyed by an expert who is skilled in such matters. When the offending ghost has possessed the victim or his representative, it may be induced to "leave the head" of its victim and to enter an ordinary earthenware pot. The pot is then quickly closed and, together with the enclosed ghost, it is disposed of either by burning it or by throwing it in an unfrequented part of the bush. I have been told that some practitioners place dried banana leaves in the pot and also imprison a small lizard in it: the rustling of the lizard in the leaves is then represented as being the ghost's struggles to escape.

I turn now to the third major class of "nonnatural" agents which may be held to be responsible for particular illnesses and other misfortunes: spirits or "powers." The cult of certain of these spirits is the traditional Nyoro religion. I spoke in Chapter 2 of the Chwezi, a wonderful race of people who are supposed to have come to Bunyoro many centuries ago, ruled the country for a brief period, and then vanished mysteriously. These people are said to have possessed amazing wisdom and skills, and to have left behind them a technique of spirit possession of which they themselves were the objects. We cannot now say whether there ever were such people, or whether, like the earliest Greek gods, they are partly or even wholly personifications of certain elemental natural forces. Certainly different Chwezi spirits are traditionally associated with particular natural features, such as thunder, rain, and so on. Also, they are thought and spoken of rather as things than as persons, and Nyoro clearly distinguish them from ghosts. There are said to be nineteen important Chwezi spirits, and in the traditional cult each one of the various localized agnatic groups into which Bunyoro is said to have been divided stood in a special relationship to one or other of these powers. Every such group had its initiated shaman or medium, who might be either a man or a woman, and on ceremonial occasions this medium would become possessed by the Chwezi spirit associated with his or her group; in this way the spirit would express its needs and wishes. These "tutelary" spirits were supposed to take care of the health, prosperity, and, especially, the fertility of all the members of the group, and these group possession ceremonies were occasions of great feasting and rejoicing. Even today, sterility and other afflictions are sometimes diagnosed by diviners as being due to the neglect of a household or group Chwezi spirit.

In recent times, however, the cult of spirit possession has become increasingly individualized. Even in traditional times the power responsible for a particular illness or misfortune could be a Chwezi spirit other than the one associated with the sufferer through his group membership. It could even be an alien, non-Chwezi power; some of these, immigrants from neighboring countries, have been known for a long time in Bunyoro. Nyoro distinguish between "white" and "black" spirits. The white ones are the group Chwezi whose influence on the local community, so long as they are not neglected, is supposed to be wholly beneficial; the black ones are all the non-Chwezi spirits. In recent years there has been an enormous increase in the variety of "black" spirits, and all informed Nyoro agree that the traditional group cult is declining at the expense of the more individualistic "black" cults. Among powers currently the objects of individualistic cults are various spirits supposed to have come from the Nilotic regions to the north of Bunyoro, as well as from other regions. Those powers which are directly or indirectly associated with Europeans are especially striking. These include such spirits as "Europeanness" (not, it should be noted, individual Europeans), "aeroplanes," and—peculiar perhaps to Bunyoro—a remarkable spirit called "Empolandi," or "Polishness." This last grew from the fact that during the last world war several hundred expatriate Poles spent some years in a large camp in northern Bunyoro. So large a number of white persons all in one place was something new, and more than a little ominous, to Nyoro, and the phenomenon was readily enough assimilated to the traditional mediumistic cult.

What is common to all the spirits or powers which we have discussed is that they express, or may originally have expressed, new, formidable, and potentially dangerous kinds of power. The spirit cult appears to afford an acceptable way of coming to terms with such phenomena, with which, at Bunyoro's present stage of cultural development, there is no other obvious way of dealing. Thus, for example, through the possession cult, a Nyoro peasant may come to some sort of terms with "European-ness" (as he conceives this abstraction), whereas it is less easy for him to make any sort of real contact with actual Europeans, important though he knows these remarkable people to be.

I spoke in Chapter 6 of the feasting traditionally associated with initiation into the possession cult. Initiations nowadays are smaller and necessarily clandestine affairs, for participation in the cult is now regarded as a criminal offense. But even today, whatever the spirit or power whose activity is diagnosed, the only way of dealing with it is by the formal initiation of the sufferer (or of an appropriate representative). Until this has been done the spirit cannot enter properly into the sufferer's head (though it may continue to afflict him in various ways), so that it can, through him, say what is needed to achieve a cure. Initiation is a long process. It involves the participation of a number of previously initiated mediums, and it may require the payment of a substantial fee, nowadays up to twenty pounds or more. In addition, the initiate and his family must provide large quantities of food and beer for the feast. I cannot here describe the complex rites involved in initiation, which culminate in the manifestation of symptoms of possession by the initiate and others, after a state of actual or simulated dissociation has been achieved through the rhythmic use of drums, gourd rattles, and singing. The ritual seems to express four main themes. First, it stresses the initiate's change of status; he ceases to be an ordinary person, as he was before. This change is dramatized in the ritual acting out of death and rebirth, in the bestowal on the initiate of certain cult objects, in certain food restrictions, and in the learning of a new Chwezi vocabulary. Second, there is a strong emphasis on secrecy; cult secrets may not be disclosed to noninitiates, and this is impressed on the novice by threats of physical violence and by formal cursing. Third, the initiate's new responsibilities to and his solidarity with his fellow mediums are emphasized, typically by the use between them of kinship and affinal terms. Finally, it is believed that initiation, like certain other major crises such as childbirth and death, puts the initiate into a state of grave ritual danger, which can only be relieved by the performance of specific ritual acts; in this case they include an act of ritual intercourse with a senior member of the cult.

Here I note only that spirit possession is the traditional Nyoro method of coping with dangerous spirits and powers, as well as with ghosts. As in the case of the beliefs and practices associated with sorcery, there is little reason to suppose that the incidence of the cult is declining; the chief effect of half a century's rigorous repression by both missionaries and Government has been to drive it underground. Indeed, the cult has shown a remarkable capacity to adapt to changed conditions. I suggested earlier in this chapter that where practical, "common-sense" techniques are lacking, or are inadequate to cope with the dangers and difficulties with which people are faced, magical and ritual remedies are usually resorted to. And we have seen that traditional Nyoro modes of religious thought have shown themselves well able to adapt to the new and unfamiliar forms of power associated with the coming of the Europeans. Nyoro have interpreted these manifestations of power as implying a proliferation of new kinds of spiritual entities, with which the preexisting possession cult is quite fitted to cope. It is a sign of the times that these new spirits are associated with the fortunes and misfortunes of individuals rather than of groups, with divination (for some "black" spirits can profit their mediums by divining), and sometimes even with sorcery, rather than with the traditional group cult.

8

Conclusion

IN CHAPTER 1 the point was raised whether it is reasonable to ask what Nyoro are really like. We can now try to answer that question, but we must first be clear as to what we are asking. The answer does not lie in merely assessing Nyoro temperament or character, which in any case I am not professionally qualified to do. As in most human populations, there are wide ranges in psychological type, and I have neither been particularly struck by nor attempted to establish the statistical preponderance of any one of them. As I said at the beginning of this book, by and large Nyoro are good-tempered, cooperative, intelligent, and tolerant; if there is some reserve and a touch of melancholy in their make-up this should not surprise anyone who is acquainted with Nyoro history. For the social anthropologist it is enough for all practical purposes to say that psychologically Nyoro are much the same as any other people, which is just what we should expect.

From the social point of view, on the other hand, it is possible to characterize Nyoro culture in individual terms, and to distinguish it from other cultures. This book has been written about the most important kinds of social relationships in which Nyoro participate, and we know that an essential part of any institutionalized social relationship is the way in which it is regarded by the people who participate in it. No social relationship can be made intelligible unless account is taken of the expectations, duties, and rights that it involves, and of the concepts and symbols by means of which the people who have it represent it to themselves. It is this ideological dimension of Nyoro social life that constitutes the sphere of Nyoro social values, and it is only by comprehending these (as far as we can) that we can hope to gain any real understanding of how Nyoro regard the world they live in. As Aristotle pointed out more than two thousand years ago, to be human is essentially to be social, and the world which Nyoro, like all other people, occupy is essentially a social world. In this book I have not only attempted to describe what Nyoro do (it would in any case be impossible to do this intelligibly without reference to what

430

they think they do); I have also tried to show how they regard the various categories of persons who together make up their whole social environment. For almost all Nyoro the most important of these categories are the king and his relatives, the chiefs, the various kinds of kinsfolk and affines, the neighbors, and—not the least important—the Europeans who have in the past century so radically affected the social system, both directly and indirectly. I have said a good deal in the foregoing pages about Nyoro attitudes to all of these categories of persons, and in describing these attitudes I have at the same time been describing Nyoro social values.

I have remarked, also, in many contexts the degree to which, in recent years, many of these social values have been in conflict with one another. But this conflict is not new; it would be an illusion to suppose that in pre-European times Nyoro inhabited a sort of Golden Age, in which all values were in perfect harmony. We have seen that traditional Nyoro social structure exhibited a radical dichotomy between the "feudal," hierarchical state on the one hand, and the closely knit village community on the other. All Nyoro men had obligations in both contexts, and there is no doubt that these sometimes conflicted. But we may suppose that on the whole these conflicts were readily resoluble in terms of values which all Nyoro shared. Everybody acknowledged and accepted the hierarchical ordering of society, and (as we noted in an earlier chapter) throughout the social system roles were allocated on an ascriptive basis rather than on grounds of achievement. Whether a man was a chief or a peasant, it may be supposed that he found security and satisfaction in having a proper and recognized place both in the social hierarchy in which he enjoyed a definite status, and in the social groupings of family, kin, and neighborhood in each of which he was an accepted member. Even though state and community made different demands, these could on the whole be reconciled, for fundamentally similar attitudes to society and to the individual's place in it were implicit in both.

Western influence on the traditional organization has, on the other hand, been radical. We saw in Chapter 2 that its initial impact was violently disruptive of the old order, and over the years it has profoundly affected Nyoro attitudes and values at all levels. In the chapters which followed I indicated some of the main points of change. I stressed, too, that social change does not proceed evenly upon all fronts; traditional values and patterns of behavior sometimes coexist oddly—and uncomfortably—with modern ones in the same social situation. Thus many Nyoro still think of their Mukama as the traditional ritual and political head of the Nyoro kingdom, from whose personal favor all political authority should flow; yet at the same time most people recognize that for more than half a century he has been not the source but merely the instrument of political power. It is still sometimes thought that the chiefs, like the king, should be bound to their dependents by ties of personal acquaintanceship and mutual dependence; but it is increasingly being recognized that salaried, transferable chiefs cannot in the nature of the case maintain the old "feudal" relationships with the people they serve, and quite new kinds of expectations are growing up in regard to them. People still strongly feel that the king and his chiefs should provide constant feasts of meat and beer; at the same time the introduction of a cash economy has provided the peasant cultivators with new values and incentives which divert the products of their labor away from the chiefs into new and private channels. People still claim support and hospitality from their relatives and these claims are in principle admitted, but where a man's surplus energy goes into the growing of cash crops, or even into paid employment, and not into the production of food in excess of his immediate requirements, he cannot meet these claims. Clan and village solidarity are still highly valued, and Nyoro know that in the old days no man could live for himself alone; but they realize, too, that present-day conditions enable men to pursue their individual self-interest regardless of traditional obligations. Men still think that women should be subordinate, modest, and obedient, but they are forced to recognize that with increased economic independence they are increasingly claiming the same social independence as men, and are no longer as meek and obedient as they used to be. Nyoro say that money has made available many new and desirable things, but it has also brought new anxieties, for it has to be earned by the performance of new and not always congenial tasks if taxes, school fees, and other expenses are to be met.

There is, indeed, scarcely any aspect of Nyoro social life in which traditional and contemporary values are not, to some extent at least, at odds with one another. Nyoro are well aware that the economic and social conditions which Western contact has brought about have made many changes in the old pattern of political and community life, and the more traditionally minded disapprove of these changes. They say that their effect has been to lower the standards of morals and social behavior which prevailed in pre-European times. Old customs are dying out and old obligations are being neglected; the stress nowadays is no longer always on the group, but increasingly on the individual. When to these considerations are added Nyoro memories of military defeat and consequent subjection which, though fading, still survive, and their awareness of the rise of Ganda fortunes concomitantly with the decline of their own, it is understandable that old-fashioned Nyoro sometimes say (and they say it with resignation, not bitterness) that the Europeans have "spoiled" the country. It is understandable, too, that in this century Nyoro should have taken more pride in their past than in their present state, and that the charges of "apathy" and lack of enterprise sometimes leveled against them should have come, to some extent, to be reflected in Nyoro opinions of themselves.

But human cultures are, fortunately, tough and resilient, and though Bunyoro's private history is no doubt unique, the strains to which it has been subjected have been suffered in some degree by many other cultures. It has been part of the aim of this book to show that Nyoro culture is still a vital one, and there are no real grounds for supposing that it will cease to be so. It is, all the time, both changing and adapting itself to change: even during the short span of my fieldwork progressive change was taking place, and no doubt Bunyoro today is not quite the same as it was when I last saw it a few years ago. And this persisting process of adaptation, disruptive and painful though it often is, implies the continuous creation of a new social synthesis whose character is not resoluble to a mere sum of preexisting cultural elements hitherto uncombined. Any culture, any society, is a unique phenomenon at any point in time, and a great part of the fascination of anthropology lies in this fact. And just as it has been one of the themes of this book that Bunyoro's past is contained in its present, so, it may be presumed, its present will be incapsulated in its future. If the researches of social anthropologists today can help future inquirers into social institutions to understand them better, their work will not have been wasted. Social anthropology is no less valuable when it changes into social history.

Recommended Reading

General Reading on Culture Area

FALLERS, L. A., 1956, *Bantu Bureaucracy*. Cambridge, Eng.: Heffer & Sons.

An account of the social and political organization of the Soga, an important Bantu people in Uganda, some of whose territory is said formerly to have been subject to Bunyoro. The book shows the effects of a European administration on a traditional political system, and describes, in particular, the changed role of the chiefs.

FORTES, M., and E. E. EVANS-PRITCHARD (Eds.), 1940, *African Political Systems*. London: Oxford University Press.

Describes the political organization of eight African tribal societies, of which five are Bantu, and two, Ankole and the Bantu of Kavirondo, are members of the Interlacustrine group, to which Bunyoro belongs.

KUPER, H., 1947, *An African Aristocracy*. London: Oxford University Press.

A graphic account of the Bantu kingdom of the Swazi of South Africa. Though a long way from Uganda, the state described shows interesting parallels and contrasts with Bunyoro.

MAIR, L. P., 1934, *An African People in the Twentieth Century*. London: Routledge & Sons.

An account of the social and political organization of the Ganda, Bunyoro's powerful neighbors to the southeast.

ROSCOE, REV. J., 1911, *The Baganda*. London: Macmillan.

The earliest full account of the neighboring kingdom. The author spent many years in Buganda as an Anglican missionary, and his account of its traditional culture contains much of comparative interest for the student of Bunyoro.

RICHARDS, A. I. (Ed.), 1954, *Economic Development and Tribal Change.* Cambridge, Eng.: Heffer & Sons.

An interesting account, by various authors, of the social effects of the development of a cash economy and consequent labor immigration on the traditional way of life of the Ganda and some neighboring peoples.

SELIGMAN, C. G., 1957, *Races of Africa.* London: Oxford University Press.

A useful introductory account of the various peoples of the African continent. There are two chapters about the Bantu-speaking peoples, and some account of the Interlacustrine group, of which the Nyoro are members.

RICHARDS, A. I. (Ed.), 1960, *East African Chiefs.* London: Faber and Faber.

Descriptions by social anthropologists of a number of contemporary East African political systems, including some in Uganda. The chapter on Bunyoro, by the present author, provides a more detailed account of modern Nyoro chiefs than could be given in this book.

MAIR, L., 1962, *Primitive Government.* Penguin Books.

A detailed discussion of the various institutional means through which social and political order were traditionally maintained among various East African peoples, including the Nyoro.

Specific References to Bunyoro

There are references to Bunyoro in a great many books and articles by explorers, missionaries, administrators, and others. Only a few of the more important are listed here.

BAKER, SIR S., 1867, *Albert Nyanza, Great Basin of the Nile.* London: Macmillan.

Describes Baker's first visit to Bunyoro, and his relations with the Nyoro king, Kamurasi.

BEATTIE, J. H. M., 1958, *Nyoro Kinship, Marriage and Affinity.* London: Oxford University Press. (International African Institute Memorandum)

A detailed account of the terminology of Nyoro kinship and affinity, and of the social relationships which these terms imply.

FISHER, (MRS.) A. B., 1911, *Twilight Tales of the Black Baganda.* London: Marshall Brothers.

Contains a very full account in English of Nyoro myth and traditional history.

JOHNSTON, SIR H., 1902, *The Uganda Protectorate* (2 vols.). London: Hutchinson & Company.

An early description of Uganda and its peoples. Volume II contains a brief account of the Nyoro.

LUGARD, SIR F. D., 1893, *The Rise of Our East African Empire.* London: Blackwood & Sons.

————, 1900, *The Story of the Uganda Protectorate.* London: Marshall.

Both of these books contain references to Nyoro-European relations during the last years of the nineteenth century.

ROSCOE, REV. J., 1915, *The Northern Bantu.* Cambridge, Eng.: Cambridge University Press.

————, 1922, *The Soul of Central Africa.* London: Cassell & Company.

These two books contain chapters on the Nyoro.

————, 1923, *The Bakitara or Banyoro.* Cambridge, Eng.: Cambridge University Press.

The first full-length study of the Nyoro. It contains interesting if not wholly accurate chapters on the kingship, customs connected with cattle, and other matters.

SPEKE, J. H., 1863, *Journal of the Discovery of the Source of the Nile.* London: Blackwood & Sons.

Describes the first European contact with Bunyoro.

Further Reading*

GEOGRAPHIC AND CULTURE AREAS REPRESENTED

Paperbacks from the following series published by Holt, Rinehart and Winston: Case Studies in Cultural Anthropology (CSCA), Case Studies in Education and Culture (CSEC), and Studies in Anthropological Method (SAM).

Africa

BASCOM, WILLIAM, 1969, *The Yoruba of Southwestern Nigeria.* 118 pp. CSCA.

BEIDELMAN, THOMAS O., 1971, *The Kaguru: A Matrilineal People of East Africa.* 134 pp. CSCA.

COHEN, RONALD, 1967, *The Kanuri of Bornu,* 115 pp. CSCA.

DENG, SIR FRANCIS MADING, 1972, *The Dinka of the Sudan.* 174 pp. CSCA.

GAMST, FREDERICK C., 1969, *The Qemant: A Pagan-Hebraic Peasantry of Ethiopia.* 128 pp. CSCA.

GAY, JOHN, AND MICHAEL COLE, 1967, *The New Mathematics and an Old Culture: A Study of Learning Among the Kpelle of Liberia.* 100 pp. CSEC.

GRINDAL, BRUCE T., 1972, *Growing up in Two Worlds: Education and Transition among the Sisala of Northern Ghana.* 114 pp. CSEC.

KLIMA, GEORGE J., 1970, *The Barabaig: East African Cattle Herders.* 114 pp. CSCA.

KUPER, HILDA, 1963, *The Swazi: A South African Kingdom.* 87 pp. CSCA.

LEIS, PHILIP, 1972, *Enculturation and Socialization in an Ijaw Village.* 112 pp. CSEC.

MIDDLETON, JOHN, 1965, *The Lugbara of Uganda.* 96 pp. CSCA.

MIDDLETON, JOHN, 1970, *The Study of the Lugbara: Expectations and Paradox in Anthropological Research.* 78 pp. SAM.

PESHKIN, ALAN, 1972, *Kanuri Schoolchildren: Education and Social Mobilization in Nigeria.* 156 pp. CSEC.

READ, MARGARET, 1968, *Children of Their Fathers: Growing Up Among the Ngoni of Malawi.* 97 pp. CSEC.

UCHENDU, VICTOR C., 1965, *The Igbo of Southeast Nigeria.* 111 pp. CSCA.

Pacific Oceania

BARNETT, HOMER G., 1960, *Being a Palaun.* 87 pp. CSCA.

DOZIER, EDWARD P., 1967, *The Kalinga of Northern Luzon, Philippines.* 102 pp. CSCA.

HART, C. W. M., AND ARNOLD PILLING, 1960, *The Tiwi of North Australia.* 118 pp. CSCA.

HOGBIN, IAN, 1964, *A Guadacanal Society: The Kaoka Speakers.* 103 pp. CSCA.

HOLMES, LOWELL D., 1974, *Samoan Village.* 111 pp. CSCA.

JOCANO, F. LANDA, 1969, *Growing Up in A Philippine Barrio.* 112 pp. CSEC.

KIEFER, THOMAS M., 1972, *The Tausug: Violence and Law in a Philippine Moslem Society.* 145 pp. CSCA.

LESSA, WILLIAM A., 1966, *Ulithi: A Micronesian Design for Living.* 86 pp. CSCA.

POSPISIL, LEOPOLD J., 1978, *The Kapauku Papuans of West New Guinea,* 2nd edition. 132 pp. CSCA.

Mexico

CHINAS, BEVERLY L., 1973, *The Isthmus Zapotecs: Women's Roles in Cultural Context.* 122 pp. CSCA.

KEARNEY, MICHAEL, 1972, *The Winds of Ixtepeji: World View and Society in a Zapotec Town.* 140 pp. CSCA.

MODIANO, NANCY, 1973, *Indian Education in the Chiapas Highlands.* 150 pp. CSEC.

PI-SUNYER, ORIOL, 1973, *Samora: Change and Continuity in a Mexican Town.* 116 pp. CSCA.

TURNER, PAUL R., 1972, *The Highland Chontal.* 96 pp. CSCA.

Native North America (American Indians)

BASSO, KEITH H., 1970, *The Cibecue Apache.* 106 pp. CSCA.

DOWNS, JAMES F., 1971, *The Navajo.* 136 pp. CSCA.

---

* See also Recommended Readings at the end of each case study.

DOZIER, EDWARD P., 1965, *Hano: A Tewa Indian Community in Arizona*. 104 pp. CSCA.
DOZIER, EDWARD P., 1970, *The Pueblo Indians of North America*. 224 pp. CSCA.
GARBARINO, MERWYN C., 1972, *Big Cypress: A Changing Seminole Community*. 137 pp. CSCA.
HICKERSON, HAROLD, 1970, *The Chippewa and Their Neighbors: A Study in Ethnhistory*. 113 pp. SAM.
HOEBEL, ADAMSON E., 1978, *The Cheyennes*, 2nd edition. 156 pp. CSCA.
JONES, DAVID E., 1972, *Sanapia: Comanche Medicine Woman*. 107 pp. CSCA.
KING, RICHARD A., 1967, *The School at Mopass: A Problem of Identity*. 91 pp. CSEC.
MCFEE, MALCOLM, 1972, *Modern Blackfeet: Montanans on a Reservation*. 134 pp. CSCA.
OPLER, MORRIS E., 1969, *Apache Odyessey: A Journey between Two Worlds*. 301 pp. CSCA.
ROHNER, RONALD, AND EVELYN ROHNER, 1970, *The Kwakiutl: Indians of British Columbia*. 111 pp. CSCA.
SPINDLER, GEORGE, AND LOUISE SPINDLER, 1971, *Dreamers Without Power: The Menomini Indians*. 208 pp. CSCA.
TRIGGER, BRUCE G., 1969, *The Huron: Farmers of the North*. 130 pp. CSCA.
WOLCOTT, HARRY F., 1967, *A Kwakiutl Village and School*. 132 pp. CSEC.

RECOMMENDED TEXTBOOKS

BEALS, ALAN R., WITH GEORGE AND LOUISE SPINDLER, 1973, *Culture in Process*, 2nd edition. New York: Holt, Rinehart and Winston. 394 pp.
KEESING, ROGER M., 1976, *Cultural Anthropology: A Contemporary Perspective*. New York: Holt, Rinehart and Winston. 512 pp.
OTTERBEIN, KEITH F., 1977, *Comparative Cultural Analysis: An Introduction to Anthropology*. 2nd edition. New York: Holt, Rinehart and Winston. 230 pp.
SCHUSKY, ERNEST, 1975, *The Study of Cultural Anthropology*. New York: Holt, Rinehart Winston. 352 pp.
SPINDLER, GEORGE D., ed., 1970, *Being an Anthropologist: Fieldwork in Eleven Cultures*. New York: Holt, Rinehart and Winston. 304 pp.

BASIC ANTHROPOLOGY UNITS

This series consists of relatively short paperbacks designed to replace or accompany larger texts. Each deals with a particular subject that is acknowledged to be significant in an anthropological framework. Many relate quite closely to materials in the Case Studies in Cultural Anthropology and Case Studies in Education and Culture, but all draw from the whole range of anthropological writing on their particular topic.

FRIEDL, ERNESTINE, 1975, *Women and Men: An Anthropologist's View*. 192 pp.
Sex roles in hunting, gathering, and horticultural societies.
GAMST, FREDERICK C., 1974, *Peasants in Complex Society*. 82 pp.
Economics and production, exchange, the family, relations to the larger society, the future.
GARBARINO, MERWYN, 1977, *Sociocultural Theory in Anthropology: A Short History*. 103 pp.
A very useful unit that provides a surprisingly comprehensive overview of anthropological theory written for beginners.
HOSTETLER, JOHN A., 1974, *Communitarian Societies*. 65 pp.
Succinct, sharp analyses of three communitarian societies and their relevance to anthropology.
LANCASTER, JANE B., 1975, *Primate Behavior and the Emergence of Human Culture*. 112 pp.
The social behavior and ecological adaptations of monkeys and apes, their communication patterns and social life.
LUSTIG-ARRECCO, VERA, 1975, *Technology: Strategies for Survival*, 96 pp.
Presents a systematic scheme for analysis of technology and applies it to selected examples representing a wide range of technology and social complexity.
NORBECK, EDWARD, 1974, *Religion in Human Life*. 74 pp.
One of the most succinct treatments of religion from an anthropological point of view ever written.

SCHUSKY, ERNEST L., 1974, *Variation in Kinship.* 72 pp.
One of the easiest routes to a minimal understanding of the complexities of this important topic suitable for beginning students.

SPINDLER, LOUISE S., 1977, *Culture Change and Modernization: Mini-Models and Case Studies.* 177 pp.
The first relatively brief text to deal with a broad range of culture change, modernization, and urbanization in a systematic manner.

FIELDWORK IN ANTHROPOLOGY AND OTHER BOOKS ON METHOD

BEATTIE, JOHN, 1965, *Understanding an African Kingdom.* New York: Holt, Rinehart and Winston. 61 pp. SAM.

BERREMAN, GERALD D., 1962, *Behind Many Masks: Ethnography and Impression Management in a Himalayan Village.* Ithaca, N.Y.: Society for Applied Anthropology, Monograph No. 4.

BOWEN, ELENORE SMITH, 1964, *Return to Laughter: An Anthropological Novel.* New York: Anchor Books, Doubleday.

BRIM, JOHN AND DAVID SPAIN, 1974, *Research Design in Anthropology: Paradigms and Pragmatics in the Testing of Hypotheses.* New York: Holt, Rinehart and Winston. 118 pp. SAM.

CHAGNON, NAPOLEON A., 1974, *Studying the Yanomamö.* New York: Holt, Rinehart and Winston. 270 pp. SAM.

COLLIER, JOHN, JR., 1967, *Visual Anthropology: Photography as a Research Method.* New York: Holt, Rinehart and Winston. 138 pp. SAM.

GOLDE, PEGGY, ed., 1970, *Women in the Field.* Chicago: Aldine.

HENRY, FRANCES, AND SATISH SABERWAL, eds., 1969, *Stress and Response in Fieldwork.* New York: Holt, Rinehart and Winston. 79 pp. SAM.

LANGNESS, L. L., 1965, *The Life History in Anthropological Science.* New York: Holt, Rinehart and Winston. 82 pp. SAM.

MIDDLETON, JOHN, 1970, *The Study of the Lugbara: Expectation and Paradox in Anthropological Research.* New York: Holt, Rinehart and Winston. 78 pp. SAM.

PITT, DAVID C., 1972, *Using Historical Sources in Anthropology and Sociology.* New York: Holt, Rinehart and Winston. 88 pp. SAM.

POWDERMAKER, HORTENSE, 1966, *Stranger and Friend: The Way of the Anthropologist.* New York: Norton.

WILLIAMS, THOMAS RHYS, 1967, *Field Methods in the Study of Culture.* New York: Holt, Rinehart and Winston. 67 pp. SAM.

Index

Letters before page numbers indicate the case study for which pages are given: *G* (Gururumba), *W* (Washo), *T* (Tepoztlán), *B* (Bunyoro).

439

GN
378
.C 84

CULTURES AROUND THE WORLD

Many students of anthropology have learned about diversities and commonalities in human culture from the Case Studies in Cultural Anthropology Series, edited by George and Louise Spindler. For the convenience of students and teachers of anthropology, as well as the general reader, five individual case studies have been brought together in one volume:

CULTURES AROUND THE WORLD: FIVE CASES
edited by George and Louise Spindler
The Tiwi of North Australia by C. W. M. Hart and Arnold R. Pilling
Ulithi: A Micronesian Design for Living by William A. Lessa
The Swazi: A South African Kingdom by Hilda Kuper
The Navajo by James P. Downs
The Vice Lords: Warriors of the Streets by R. Lincoln Keiser

The enthusiastic reception of the first volume has resulted in another—*Cultures around the World II.* The culture cases included have been carefully selected to represent major culture areas. They also represent major subsistence types and different levels of sociopolitical complexity. And they have been selected for their readability. These are time-tested case studies and are among the most widely used in the series.

CULTURES AROUND THE WORLD II: FOUR CASES
edited by George and Louise Spindler
Knowing the Gururumba by Philip L. Newman
The Two Worlds of the Washo by James F. Downs
Tepoztlán by Oscar Lewis
Bunyoro: An African Kingdom by John Beattie

Also available:
NATIVE NORTH AMERICAN CULTURES: FOUR CASES
URBAN ANTHROPOLOGY IN THE UNITED STATES: FOUR CASES

HOLT, RINEHART AND WINSTON
383 MADISON AVENUE
NEW YORK, N.Y. 10017

0-03-039726-X

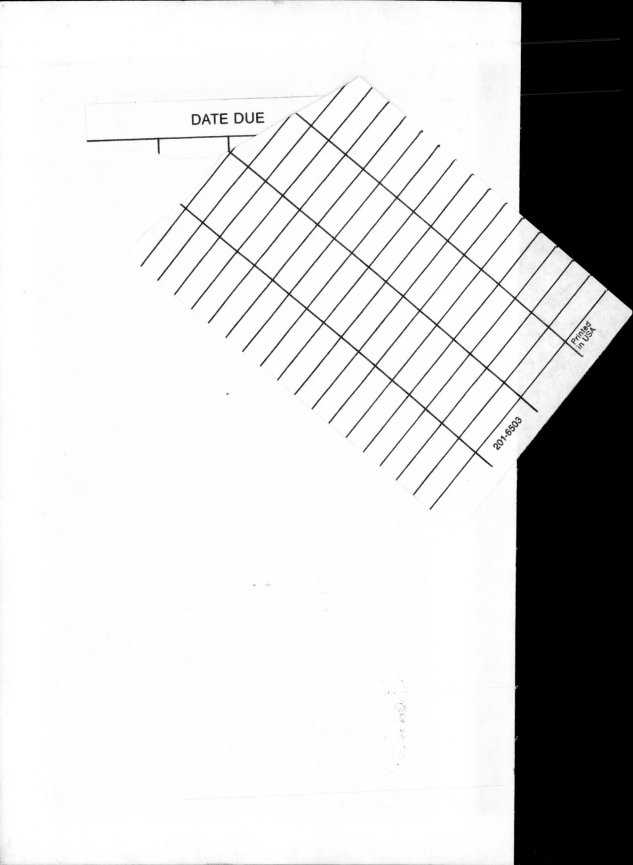

DATE DUE

201-6503

Printed
in USA